Luminos is the Open Access monograph publishing program
from UC Press. Luminos provides a framework for preserving and
reinvigorating monograph publishing for the future and increases
the reach and visibility of important scholarly work. Titles published
in the UC Press Luminos model are published with the same high
standards for selection, peer review, production, and marketing as
those in our traditional program. www.luminosoa.org

Nakba and Survival

Nakba and Survival

The Story of Palestinians Who Remained in Haifa and the Galilee, 1948–1956

Adel Manna

UNIVERSITY OF CALIFORNIA PRESS

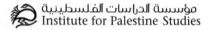

مؤسسة الدراسات الفلسطينية
Institute for Palestine Studies

The Institute for Palestine Studies is the oldest institute in the world devoted exclusively to documentation, research, analysis, and publication on Palestinian affairs and the Arab-Israeli conflict. It was established in 1963 as an independent, nonprofit Arab institute unaffiliated with any political organization or government.

This work expresses its author's opinions, which do not necessarily reflect the views or positions of the Institute.

University of California Press
Oakland, California

Suggested citation: Manna, A. *Nakba and Survival: The Story of Palestinians Who Remained in Haifa and the Galilee, 1948–1956.* Oakland: University of California Press, 2022. DOI: https://doi.org/10.1525/luminos.129

Library of Congress Cataloging-in-Publication Data

Names: Mannā', ʿĀdil, author.
Title: Nakba and survival : the story of Palestinians who remained in Haifa and the Galilee, 1948-1956 / Adel Manna.
Other titles: Nakbah wa-baqā'. English
Description: Oakland, California: University of California Press, 2022. | Includes bibliographical references and index.
Identifiers: LCCN 2021053073 (print) | LCCN 2021053074 (ebook) | ISBN 9780520389366 (paperback) | ISBN 9780520389373 (ebook)
Subjects: LCSH: Palestinian Arabs—Israel—Haifa—20th century. | Palestinian Arabs—Israel—Galilee—20th century. | Israel-Arab War, 1948–1949—Personal narratives. | Israel—Ethnic relations.
Classification: LCC DS113.7. M26813 2022 (print) | LCC DS113.7 (ebook) | DDC 305.80095694—dc23/eng/20220314
LC record available at https://lccn.loc.gov/2021053073
LC ebook record available at https://lccn.loc.gov/2021053074

31 30 29 28 27 26 25 24 23 22
10 9 8 7 6 5 4 3 2 1

CONTENTS

FOREWORD

From the Series Editor

Nakba and Survival constitutes an engaging, accessible, and innovative departure in Palestinian historiography. It focuses on how 120,000 Palestinians were able to remain in the Galilee during and after the 1948 war, when most other Palestinians were driven out or forced to flee in a series of events Palestinians call the *Nakba*, or catastrophe. Through intimate and well-researched stories of people and events, Adel Manna crafts an absorbing read full of new historical detail and insight.

Narrating an understudied aspect of Palestinian and Israeli history, based on family documents, oral history, and hitherto unstudied archives in Hebrew, Arabic, and English, *Nakba and Survival* also tells the intimate story of Manna's own family. It contributes as well to the controversial debate about the role of Palestinian leaders of the Israeli Communist Party and others during and after the 1948 war. Its combination of boldness and intimacy constitutes a striking departure in our understanding of the seminal events of 1948 in Palestine.

Reviewers of the Arabic and Hebrew editions of *Nakba and Survival* offered extensive praise for its groundbreaking contributions. For decades, Israeli narratives dominated Western understandings of the 1948 War. English-language historiography of the *Nakba*, especially as told from the Palestinian perspective, remains seriously underrepresented. Here the story is told from the point of view of a segment of the Palestinian people who would become second-class minoritized citizens in their own country, where they today constitute 20 percent of the population. The shock and trauma they experienced in 1948 and afterwards as a result are at the heart of this remarkable book, which one reviewer described as "a rich, powerful and paradigm-breaking contribution to the history of the *Nakba*, and to Palestinian historiography more generally."

Nakba and Survival provides the Anglophone reader with access to an important historical narrative that was previously available only in Arabic or Hebrew. It also offers a wealth of detail culled from a wide variety of sources regarding a seminal event in Palestinian history, as refracted through the experiences of the 120,000 Palestinians who managed to remain in Israel after over 750,000 of their compatriots were forced to leave their homes. Focusing not on the latter, but on those who remained and survived in the Galilee, it provides a unique insight into how, by managing to stay in their homes and on their land, they resisted the wave of ethnic cleansing that transformed Palestine in 1948 and that persists to this day.

IN THE BEGINNING WAS THE STORY

Since my childhood, I have been hearing the story of what happened in Majd al-Krum in 1948—first from my father, then from my mother and our relatives. The broad lines of the story were consistent, starting with the occupation of the village by Jews and the peaceful entry of a number of their soldiers from the western side of the village. But things turned upside down in a week, when other soldiers came from the east who tore down houses and killed young men in al-'Ayn Square. Despite the huge shock caused by the massacre, most residents stayed in their homes and their village. But the events of the Nakba (catastrophe) in our village did not end there. The Israeli soldiers came back two months after the massacre, and this time they evicted hundreds of residents, including myself and my parents.

Each time I heard this story I tried to put together new details of what happened, including the alienation of displacement, and then the return to our house after more than two years as refugees living in 'Ayn al-Hilwa camp in Lebanon. For a child, these tales ranked first after *A Thousand and One Nights*. But the tale of the calamity that befell Majd al-Krum remained a secret that had to be kept to oneself, so I spoke to no one outside our house about this, as my father had recommended.

In June 1984, I gathered the courage to publish an article in *Haaretz* which included a paragraph about my personal history and another on the events in Majd al-Krum during 1948.[1] The reaction was swift: aggressive attacks came from ordinary and "specialized" Jewish readers—effectively silencing my interest in researching the subject. This experience taught me that I was approaching the flame whenever I tried to tell the general story of Palestinians and especially of those who stayed in Israel.

I had learned my lesson, and stayed away from these incendiary topics relating to the Nakba and its impact on Palestinians for several years, returning to the safe area of research on the history of Palestine under the Ottomans. During those years I completed my doctoral dissertation at Hebrew University and devoted the bulk of my activities and my time to family concerns and academic work. Thus, like most people, particularly those waging a struggle of survival, my priority was immediate daily life and other important issues were deferred.

What I had said about the massacre and the subsequent expulsion of the inhabitants of Majd al-Krum during the war had provoked readers' reactions and aroused their anger. Since my account of what had occurred in our village had relied on the stories told by my father and the eyewitness accounts of my relatives, the reaction was to deny emphatically the veracity of everything I had written. I had pointed out at the time that the article's scope did not permit relating the story of our village at any length—but I promised "the day will come when I will write it down in detail, in Hebrew no less!" That was not just a passing remark but a commitment made out of a sense of responsibility, and a decision that I have borne the consequences of for many long years and decades. I therefore feel a great sense of satisfaction that my book will now be available in English translation, in addition to the earlier versions that I wrote both in Arabic (2016) and Hebrew (2017).

It had been my conscious decision as a historian to keep away from the story of the Nakba and concentrate on the history of Palestine under the Ottomans. But I had been haunted since I first heard about the painful saga of 1948 a decade later, and was eventually encouraged to take on the responsibility of writing about that period. In the spring of 1958 I participated with childish glee along with my fourth grade classmates (and students of my elementary school in general) in the week-long festivities of the tenth anniversary of Independence Day.[2] I remember that I was proud to play two roles on the festival stage which the parents and guardians of the children were invited to watch. In the first role, accompanied by a band, I sang the festival anthem "My Country's Independence Day," most of the words of which I still remember. I also had a role in a drama presentation that the students staged for the parents. Until that day I did not doubt what we had been told in school about the history of Zionism and its success in establishing the state of Israel, whose tenth anniversary we were celebrating. Israel, according to that narrative, had succeeded in repelling "aggression" on the part of seven Arab states which attacked it in the hope of destroying it. We also learned that Israel, after its success in that war, grew stronger and continued to flourish every year.

I remember that the schoolchildren worked energetically and happily on the preparations for the week of festivities, which captured our interest in contrast to the boring educational material most of our teachers taught us. Following the main festival day, I expected to hear tender words of praise from my father for the two roles I had played. When I broached the subject of the school festivities with him, I heard him say for the first time things that were unknown to me. I heard a narrative that contradicted what we had learned at school about "Independence Day" and its causes. At first hesitating to answer my question, my father said: "'Independence Day' is not a day for rejoicing, it is a disaster and a tragedy for Arabs in general and particularly for the people of our village. It is not a day of *istiqlal* (independence). What happened to us in 1948 was *istihlal* (occupation)."[3]

Presenting the story so that a child like myself could understand, my father told me what happened in our village in 1948. The story I heard was a sad and painful one, involving occupation and the killing and expulsion of villagers from their homes, quite the contrary of the Zionist narrative of victories and liberation. My father's story lit my child's imagination, and I strained to picture the sequence of events: the expulsion from the village, travel to places of refuge, and then our return to the village in the summer of 1951. The story of the return from 'Ayn al-Hilwa camp in a fisherman's boat to Shavei Tzion north of 'Akka sounded like it had been taken from a Zionist drama.[4] Out of all places in the country, the boat discharged its Arab refugee passengers in a Jewish village, the name of which ("Returnees of Zion") bore great symbolic significance in the history of Israel.

The story of our village in 1948, especially the details of the deportation of our family and our living in the diaspora, lodged itself in my memory. Suddenly new information about our village and my family were added to my memory, things which had not registered before in my memory and I did not know—children's early memories being transient. However, after my father told the story again and again, the events took root in my memory and became part of my personal and familial identity. Images of our life in the camp, the return by sea, and other events ran through my imagination. I then heard the story several times from my siblings, who were increasing in number and whose interest in the details grew with each retelling. At the same time, celebrations of "Independence Day" continued at school with no mention of the calamitous events of 1948. In this way, I grew up in the late 1950s with two narratives of the events of 1948—the creation of the state of Israel, and the Nakba which befell the Palestinian people.

I understood from the stories of my father and my relatives that the soldiers who had occupied our village were not on the defensive in a confrontation with "powerful enemies." The army unit that entered Majd al-Krum from the direction of the village of al-Birwa (subsequently Ahyahud) respected the terms of the surrender agreement and did no harm to the inhabitants. However, other soldiers came from the east one week after the surrender and they perpetrated acts of cold-blooded murder in al-'Ayn Square. I also learned from my father and relatives that the massacre in the village was not the only one of its kind; it was not unique, as similar massacres took place in 'Ilabun and other villages in the Galilee. When the soldiers returned two months or so after the massacre, they told the men of the village to assemble so that a "search and identify" operation could be carried out. During this operation, the soldiers did not kill any of the inhabitants, but they expelled hundreds of them in trucks to Wadi 'Ara.[5] From there, those of us who were being deported had to continue the way on foot to Nablus and Jenin where they joined tens of thousands of refugees.

We remained for a few months in the vicinity of Nablus, where many of the refugees coming from the Galilee passed, before continuing on our way to southern Lebanon. We went with them from Nablus to Transjordan, and from there to Syria and then Lebanon. The roads were difficult but the journey ended safely when refugees from the village reached 'Ayn al-Hilwa camp near Sidon. My uncle and other inhabitants of the Galilee had arrived there before us. We remained in the camp until my father took a firm decision to return to our village. During the two years of exile my father "infiltrated" into Israel alone to visit his mother, making the difficult journey on foot. My grandmother and aunts kept him hidden during his visits and gave him some money which they had saved. When we made our way back by sea in the summer of 1951, my mother was pregnant with my brother Muhammad, which was a factor in the decision to return by night and by sea from the port of Sidon, rather than overland, which was the route most returnees took.

I learned from the stories told by my relatives about the 1948 war and its aftermath that the first person to be executed in our village by the army was Abu Ma'yuf, the husband of my grandmother, whom the villagers called "al-Ja'uniyya" after her village, al-Ja'una, which later became Rosh Pina. My grandmother did not live in our house, but in a room which we called *al-khushe* next to my uncle Ahmad's house. In contrast to the willingness of my father to talk time and again about the massacre and the story of our expulsion from the village, all of my attempts to get my grandmother to talk about what happened were unsuccessful. It appears that she preferred not to delve into those memories, which were an open wound she tried to conceal and forget. On the few occasions when I asked her directly about the events of 1948 and her experiences that year, she tried to distract me by offering me sweets or biscuits. On other occasions she encouraged me to climb a fig tree and eat its fruit. From conversations with my family and relatives, however, I was able to piece together the details which my grandmother kept hidden.

For example, I heard from one of my aunts that a Jewish family had taken up residence in the area of my grandmother's family, and that their son, Mano Friedman, had been treated like a member of my grandmother's family. I also learned that my grandmother, Zahra, had moved from al-Ja'una to Majd al-Krum at the end of the First World War after she married my grandfather, Salim al-Hajj Krayyim.[6] My grandmother had lived with him for only ten years when he died, leaving her with three small children. The life of a young widow bringing up young children with no support from her family was not easy, nor was it customary in village life. So one year after the death of Salim al-Hajj Krayyim, "al-Ja'uniyya" married one of his relatives, Abu Ma'yuf. In 1948 Zahra was in her early fifties. She felt the presence of a new threat to her family and her home. My aunt says that Zahra sought out her old neighbor, Mano Friedman, whom she considered to be her milk-brother, and asked him for a letter that would protect her household from the "Jewish army."

When Israeli soldiers came to my grandmother's house, she gave them Mano Friedman's letter. This did not prevent a new tragedy, as Abu Ma'yuf was the first to be executed in al-'Ayn Square, after they blew up his house in front of his own eyes. My grandmother and her children were not harmed on that day on which some villagers were killed and a number of houses in the village were torn down. There were many opinions as to what Mano Friedman's letter may have contained. Some accused him of complicity in the disaster that befell the family, whereas others thought that the letter might have prevented a bigger potential tragedy, such as expulsion along with the hundreds who were exiled. At any rate, Mano Friedman's name became an item of information that stayed in my memory about the 1948 war. These bits of information somewhat softened the image of Jews: there were those who carried out the massacre and then expelled many villagers, but alongside them were "good Jews" who had helped the people and saved some of them from certain death or expulsion.

The tragedies that befell my grandmother Zahra did not begin or end with the killing of her husband and the demolition of her family home in front of her children. Her youngest son Samih, the dearest to her heart, had been killed in a bomb explosion earlier in 1948. Then Zahra al-Ja'uniyya had prevailed on her entire family to leave al-Ja'una—and most went to Syria. Finally, in January 1949, more than two months after the massacre in al-'Ayn Square, the expulsion of the Majd al-Krum population began, and our family was included. My father and uncle and some of my aunts became refugees in Lebanon. By 1949 my grandmother had lost many members of her family and her loved ones. Although she was able to remain in the village, disaster had befallen her from all sides.

The historical literature on the Nakba usually focuses on the death of men and their sacrifices and sufferings in the diaspora. That literature has far too little to say about the tragedies of women, especially their sacrifices as mothers and wives who lived with loss and bore the responsibility of supporting their families. The case of my grandmother Zahra is an example of a woman who lost her husband and her home, and who emerged from the ruins to take responsibility for those of her family who had survived.

US AND THE JEWS

Until 1958, as I recall, I thought of Jews as a tribe whose members I did not encounter in my daily life. Children growing up in a Galilee village did not meet Jews in their towns and cities until the age of ten. Even Jews who worked for the military government at the police station of the British Mandate east of the village were far removed from the daily activities of people of my generation. None of that hindered my ability to imagine a picture of the Jewish soldiers carrying out the massacre in our village in 1948, and then chasing away hundreds of villagers to the other side of the border. I understood from the stories I heard at that time that Jews did not like Arabs and that was why they expelled them from the country and tried to prevent them from returning to Palestine. Despite the fact that these stories portrayed us as victims of acts of savagery, the other side did not always consist of evildoers who grasped every opportunity to hurt Arabs. The stories included the names of "good Jews" who played a role in helping the villagers and preventing their continued killing and expulsion.

One of those "good" Jews was Haim Orbach, who arrived at the village at the time of the massacre at al-'Ayn Square. He intervened to stop the killing. I heard that Orbach was a friend of Abu Sa'id, one of our relatives, because both had worked at the British army camp near 'Akka. When he arrived in Majd al-Krum, he intervened immediately and stopped the killing of innocent residents.[7] Orbach's arrival coincided with that of Shafiq Abu 'Abdu, who had come to visit some of his relatives who had sought refuge in Majd al-Krum. I learned that this Abu 'Abdu had crossed over to the other camp and fought alongside the Jews in the 1948 war. He too played a role in stopping the massacre. Abu 'Abdu's personality and his role in the war muddled the division into two warring camps, with Arabs and Jews on opposite sides in the conflict. I had heard that Abu 'Abdu was married to a Jew, so some of his children became Jews and fought in the Israeli army.[8] In spite of that, I did not sense in the conversations of the grownups that they felt hatred towards him; rather, they seemed to be grateful for his role in stopping the massacre.

The first Jews that I met in my childhood years were from Kiryat Motzkin and Kiryat Bialik near Haifa. At the end of the 1950s and the beginning of the 1960s, I accompanied my father on his trips there to sell figs. After a season or two of helping my father, I started to go by myself, carrying a basket or two. Selling figs in the months of summer vacation opened my eyes to a new and different world. I learned many things in those months that were not part of our school curriculum. I found out, for instance, that most Jews lived in apartments in shared buildings, and that the streets in their towns were wide and clean and shaded by trees. Most of the customers for my figs were housewives. I was happy not to have to deal with Jewish men and youth who, in my eyes, represented the "evil Jews." I can still remember an incident or two when I was taken aback seeing a young man in military uniform come out of a building or onto a street, the blood freezing in my veins until he put some distance between us.

Interacting directly and closely with the women who bought my figs reinforced what I had learned from the stories of 1948: that not all Jews were evil. Most of the women's interest was confined to the quality and price of the figs, but some of them expressed interest in my age and education, which elevated them in my opinion. Those whom I appreciated the most were those who offered me a cold glass of juice. This simple human gesture made me shower them with compliments, such as "generous" and "merciful mothers." The experience of selling figs led to the blurring of a polarized view of us and them. I learned to differentiate between the "evil Jews" who killed Arabs and expelled them from their country and "good Jews" who did not hate Arabs and did not dream of harming them.

While my familiarity with Jews increased in those days, I had no occasion to meet Palestinian refugees who had been expelled from their homeland. I tried to imagine the life of a refugee such as my uncle and his family, who were living in 'Ayn al-Hilwa refugee camp. Many a time I tried to imagine my family continuing to live in that camp, had my father not taken us back to Majd al-Krum. I formed a strong conviction that despite the hardships of life in our village, we were lucky to have escaped the humiliation of life as refugees and to have returned to live in our home and on our soil. I did not need to meet my uncle's family and refugees like them in south Lebanon to appreciate the difficulties of life in the diaspora. Many refugees from Sha'b, al-Birwa, al-Damun, and other villages in the Galilee took up residence in Majd al-Krum itself. Some of those refugees were our neighbors, and their sons, our classmates. It was no secret that their material circumstances and their social status were lower than the people of the village, because they did not own houses or land like the others.

BETWEEN MEMORY AND HISTORY

The story of Majd al-Krum is a good example of the suffering of the Palestinians who fell victim to the policies of killing and expulsion, some of whom managed to return to their homes. The stories of these people and others like them in the Galilee are not recorded in Israeli historical literature. Even those who stayed feared to tell their stories for various reasons. The Palestinians in Israel did not have universities or research institutions that could tackle these and other important issues. The few who attended Israeli universities and tried to study the events of the Nakba usually did so with great caution. I myself returned to study and write about these issues only in 1998 when I told the story of our expulsion, life in refugee camps, and return to the village for an article on the fiftieth anniversary of the Nakba. I credit the great poet, the late Mahmoud Darwish, for encouraging me to write and publish it in al-Karmel magazine after hearing me tell the story.[9]

I have to admit that I approached this research with a mixture of joy, fear, and trepidation. It is not easy to write about this complicated and painful subject and then publish it for all to see. In this case, the chronicler has the responsibility to search for the truth in a tragic, complex, and very highly sensitive story. The history of the 1948 war and its ramifications is still an open wound. But this wound is very familiar to the author, since it concerns not only his people but his close relatives as well. Opening old wounds may hurt the victims, and will disturb those Jews who will see the telling of the stories as an unfair accusation.

The burden of personal and familial memories poses a danger also to the work of the historian who intends to search for the pure truth. Nevertheless, the professional researcher who is aware of the shortcomings of memory relies on it with the required caution, turning it into a real asset. Intimate personal memories (as the great historian Eric Hobsbawm has taught us) permit us to present a distinctive picture based on sources and knowledge which are difficult for other researchers to depict.

The stories of Palestinians who remained in Israel after the Nakba occupy a grey area between the private and the personal, and between the public and the historical. I therefore decided to share my personal and family history with the reader, in the form of memories that are an important source for making heard the voices and the point of view of those who have been silenced. Traumatic and tragic events persist in the memory for decades, as is well known. They constitute a rich and important source for describing the past in detail and accurately. On many occasions the victims of those tragic experiences choose not to speak and not to share their buried secrets with others. However, those who do choose to speak add personal and human perspectives which are missing from collective nationalist narratives, archival documents, and the memoirs of victors.

Following the war of 1948, Israel succeeded in marketing its narrative of the war's events to its citizens and to the outside world, including the circumstances of the "flight" of the Palestinian refugees. Israel's leaders had their own important reasons for propagating that story, and many Jewish researchers and their supporters collaborated in it. Those who perpetrated atrocities and war crimes themselves participated in weaving that tale even though they knew the truth. Those who had committed disgraceful acts against innocent civilians or had given orders to carry them out pretended to forget their role. As for the victims, they were in no position to forget what had happened to them, even if they were obliged to suppress their memories and not to divulge them for a period of time. When they did speak out, they were able to recall those events accurately, including intimate and painful details.

One of the eyewitnesses to the events of the Majd al-Krum massacre of 1948 was prepared, in our last meeting, to divulge a detail that others had been ashamed to talk about. In response to a question about the feelings of fear and shock that spread when the men were executed in al-'Ayn Square, he asked:

> What do you think? Many men did it in their pants, and the bad smell began to spread. All we wanted was for the horror show we were seeing to end as quickly as possible. The slow pace of the executions, one every half hour, doubled the fear that it would be our turn next. Furthermore, the stench that was becoming pervasive undermined our morale. Men who had been squatting for hours did not dare move or speak out of fear of the soldiers' rifles. So we sat like that for hours at al-'Ayn Square until Haim Orbach and Shafiq Abu 'Abdu came. They seemed to us like angels who had descended from heaven to end the torment.

Some details of the atrocities perpetrated in the Galilee, the killing, expulsion, and maltreatment of the population, will not be easy for readers to absorb or digest.

I chose to present the personal and very human accounts of some eyewitnesses without revealing their names or identities for reasons that are not difficult to understand. Eyewitnesses with whom I spoke more than once sometimes felt comfortable in sharing with me details and secrets which distressed them and which they had not had an opportunity to reveal to anyone. One woman, who had been barely a teenager, not much more than ten years of age in 1948, said that seeing her family's home demolished before her eyes caused her to wet her bed at night like little children do. At the end of the war she was nearing the age of twelve and she was terrified that this condition might endure. The family was occupied with this new problem, which went on for more than a year. The mother's greatest worry was: what if a would-be bridegroom were to ask for her daughter's hand in marriage while she still suffered from this problem? This is just one example of how the trauma of killings, the demolition of houses, expulsions, and maltreatment affected the population, young and old. These aftereffects are an open wound and reading the statements of some eyewitnesses is very difficult and unforgettable.

We know that the myths of origin and birth are hard to dismantle. It is not easy to convince ardent believers to rethink their convictions by putting new facts before them. However, most readers today are not ardent believers in the myths of 1948. Now that Arab and Israeli researchers have discredited some of these myths, perhaps the task of the researcher will be easier. This author hopes that the discomfort that this book causes to Zionist and pro-Zionist readers will drive them to seek out the truth in a quest for knowledge. The stories of the Nakba of the Palestinians, particularly those who remained in Israel, are "present but absent," like the situation of the refugees who were displaced within Israel. Without the stories of the Palestinians, particularly the stories of those who remained in what became Israel in 1948, dialogue between the two sides of the conflict will remain a dialogue of the deaf.

This book is first and foremost a history of a generation of Palestinians who remained in their estranged homeland after the Nakba and who bore the brunt of some of the events that took place: women like my grandmother Zahra who had to surmount the trauma and mourning and only one year later went to work washing the clothes and cleaning the houses of Jews in Haifa. My research tells the stories of many "ordinary" people who remained in their homes despite the massacres and the expulsions. Some of them initially became refugees, but returned to their homes with their families despite the many difficulties and dangers they encountered on the rough roads of return. They came back in order to bring up their children in their homeland after they had tasted the insults and the shame of displacement and dispersal. This generation of mothers and fathers was not defeatist.[10] Rather, they experienced the struggle for survival, and used the wisdom and spirit from having feet planted firmly on the ground; they could bend with the wind during the storm, let it pass, and then rise from the ruins and build a new life for themselves, their children, and their grandchildren.

The authors of *The Stand-Tall Generation* were accurate when they said that the capacity of the Palestinians who remained after the Nakba to conduct "effective political action was limited."[11] In the years following the stupefying shock and while living under military rule, it was difficult to expect much from the remnants of a fate-stricken people. In the struggle for survival, people give up on other struggles that are likely doomed to fail in favor of what is possible and necessary: life, the home, and the family. Once these are guaranteed, it is the turn of earning a living, the children's education, and their upbringing. The generation of those who stayed after the Nakba fought to be able to continue to live in their homes and their homeland, having witnessed with their own eyes the national and human disaster that had overtaken them. Those who stayed in Israel after 1948 were not a submissive generation who bowed their heads, nor were they a generation of great heroes. For the most part, they were a generation who succeeded in the struggle for survival.

When I promised myself in June 1984 to write the story of the Nakba, I knew that my father would not live to read it. Indeed, cancer did not allow him much time; he died two years later. During the last seven years that I have worked on this research project, my mother became the repository of the family's memory of alienation. I set aside time during my frequent visits to the village to talk to her of events that took her back in her imagination to the days of her youth. I could see the positive effect of our "historical" discussions; they would take her mind off illness and weakness of the body, and she would relive beautiful moments in her memory which she would relate to her children and grandchildren. She and others like her among the generation of the Nakba and its consequences for the Palestinian people feel happy when they find ears to listen to their stories. This book chronicles the tale of the sons and daughters of the generation who stayed, who were contemporaries of the Nakba and its consequences, who endured and provided a better life for the generations to come. I dedicate this book to my mother and the members of her generation, those who died and those who are still alive.[12]

ACKNOWLEDGMENTS

I am grateful to the more than one hundred people whom I met in Haifa, Nazareth, and many Galilee villages, who opened their homes and their hearts to me. The importance of their testimonies for enriching the narrative as told by written and published documents and references cannot be overstated. I would also like to thank my wife 'Aziza who became my companion throughout the development of the idea and the preparation of the study. I came to know her and then met her parents, 'Ali and Fatima (Shrayda) Hulayhel, in the village of 'Akbara near Safad. From them, I learned the details of those suffering as "present absentees," the label for persons who had been expelled from their villages—Qadditha in this case—in 1948 and have not been allowed to return to their houses and their lands. When the research was at the point of implementation, my dear wife became the first to listen to my ideas and my "discoveries." She did not hesitate to give her advice and support, and provided a home atmosphere that was encouraging for the research and analysis.

I am thankful to the many individuals who provided support, encouragement, advice, and valuable information as well as some documents and publications during my seven years of research and writing. In particular I would like to mention Hanna Abu Hanna, Zahi Karkabi, and 'Awda al-'Ashhab (Abu-'Adnan) from Haifa, and Anis Srouji, Wadi' 'Awawde, and Ahmad Mruwwat from Nazareth. A number of colleagues and researchers read chapters or the entire manuscript, and contributed helpful written or oral comments and advice which were instrumental in improving the quality of the study. In particular, I would like to mention Yehuda Shinhav, Nur al-Din Masalha, Ahmad Sa'di, Mustafa 'Abbasi, Bashir Bashir, Hillel Cohen, Hassan Jabareen, and Amos Goldberg.

I would also like to extend my thanks and appreciation to the Institute for Palestine Studies and the team of trustees and employees who encouraged me to write this study and contributed to its publication, as with my previous books. I would like to mention in particular Salim Tamari, Khalil al-Hindi, and Khaled Farraj in Ramallah. For this English edition (2022), I would like to thank Rashid Khalidi and Beshara Doumani for encouraging and supporting the idea of translation and publication of the book. I would like to extend my thanks also to those who contributed to the process of shaping the English edition, to the translator Muhammad Jenab Tutunji, and particularly to the editor, Anita Vitullo. Should the attentive reader find any errors which remain (not many I hope), the author is solely responsible.

Note on transliteration: The book follows the standard rules of Arabic transliteration used by the Institute for Palestine Studies, with the exception of names of personalities, organizations or locations where another spelling has been adopted by the person or organization, has entered the common lexicon, or is preferred by the author to reflect local usage.

Introduction

A Story of Catastrophe and Survival

NEW APPROACHES IN THIS BOOK

This book introduces a number of new elements related to theory, methodology, sources, and references for examining the 1948 war and its aftermath for the defeated, whose voice has not been heard before in the recounting of the events of the Nakba—the Palestinians inside Israel. These Palestinians, who became "citizens" in Israel, have long suffered from double marginalization by the two sides to the conflict. Hearing their voice allows us to construct a more complex picture of the consequences of the Nakba from the inside, through their testimonies as Palestinians inside the occupied homeland where the Jewish state was established. The experiences of those who remained during the war and its aftermath are different and distinct from those of other groups of fragmented Palestinians; their particular experiences led them to develop a critical awareness of, and evolving positions toward, nationalist points of view and narratives which excluded them and marginalized their history, at least for a while.

This research proposes critical reading and complex analysis rather than generalized and polarized narratives. Instead of dismissing the previous stereotypical positions about past events, this book will gradually weave a history from the base to the top. This history is not restricted to the viewpoints of the elites; it also takes into account the testimonies and even the sayings of popular groups. As is well known, peasants formed the vast majority of those who remained in northern and central Palestine. Their reasons for and their opinions on remaining in Palestine after the 1948 occupation have been absent or clouded over by a fog and rarely illuminated by historians. Adding these voices to the narratives of the struggle brings color and shading to the stark black and white image that characterizes accounts by the elite, giving the picture new and complex dimensions.

This book also renews the investigation of issues which are disputed by research-ers, and not confined solely to the history of Palestinians in Israel. One such issue is the dispute about whether indeed there was a plan to expel the Palestinians during the 1948 war or if they were forced out by the events and conditions of war. Even if we were to accept the assumption that there was no comprehensive and all-embracing plan to drive the Palestinians out, their dispersal and the refusal to allow them to return became an official objective and actual policy after the estab-lishment of the Jewish state. This study focuses on the issue of "non-expulsion"—the other side of this controversial issue—and adds a new angle to the analysis and discussion by posing questions and breaking down prevailing narratives into two fledgling fields of research connected to the Nakba and its consequences.

Firstly, instead of undertaking research once again into the question of the expulsion of the Palestinians who became refugees, this book focuses on those who were not expelled or who returned to their homes and towns. These "remain-ers" are those whose valuable stories this research will try to uncover, stories that are absent in most studies relating to the Nakba. The reasons and circumstances which led Palestinians to remain in Haifa and the Galilee were numerous and diverse. Their unexamined history in 1948 is the other face of the refugee problem which has occupied the prime focus of researchers.

Secondly, instead of forging anew into the question of the existence or non-existence of a general Israeli plan and policy to expel Palestinians in the year of the Nakba, the focus will be on cases of "non-expulsion." This research will try to answer questions concerning the circumstances and reasons for remaining and the extent to which there was a pattern indicating high-level policy and direction on this point. The two fields of research are interconnected, and related to the question of ethnic cleansing. The novelty in the angles of research concerning the circumstances for remaining could enrich our knowledge about the policy of expulsion through close examination of cases of "non-expulsion." It is clear that "non-expulsion" in northern Palestine was not arbitrary, but was the result of high-level orders and policy on the part of the Israeli leadership. Saying this does not contradict the principal objective of the Zionist leadership to keep as few Arabs as possible in the Jewish state, since the exception due to special reasons and circumstances proves the rule.

Thirdly, this study documents the role of those who remained in their towns. In addition to cases of being allowed to remain due to orders from above, many Palestinians successfully resisted the policy of expulsion despite orders and plans to disperse them. Did they succeed because of geography and the topography of their mountainous region? Did their sectarian makeup (as Druze, Christians, or Muslims) play an important role? Did the timing of the occupation have an influ-ence on some remaining in the Galilee? What about local leadership and the deci-sions taken at critical moments in the war? Are accounts of resisting the policy of expulsion—particularly on the part of communist activists—true, or did surrender and readiness to collaborate with the Israeli side play the more significant role? The answers to these questions could uncover remarkable aspects of the history of this Palestinian minority during the year of the Nakba and its aftermath.

Events show that there were several cases of "non-expulsion" in the Galilee that came to light in the "Battles of the Ten Days" (the so-called Operation Palm Tree, between the first and second truce, 8 July–18 July 1948), first in the Druze villages, then in the city of Nazareth and the villages in its district. On 15 July 1948, the villages of Abu Snan, Kufr Yasif, and Yarka surrendered without a battle.[1] This was followed by the surrender and occupation of many villages in lower Galilee between Shafa 'Amr and Nazareth, without the army expelling the major- ity of the population. It became quite clear from these examples that there was a policy and orders from the top echelon which we will discuss later. Furthermore, the policy of "non-expulsion" continued in the Galilee until its occupation was completed through Operation Hiram. The Druze in upper Galilee also were not targeted by the policy of expulsion which uprooted the inhabitants of dozens of neighboring villages.

Even the agreement by David Ben-Gurion and his advisors on the return of thousands of Palestinian refugees after the war was an attempt to serve regional and international political interests. One example of this was the permission granted to dozens of communists and their families to return to Haifa and the Galilee in the summer of 1948. After the parliamentary elections in early 1949, a number of communist rivals were also allowed to return, most prominently Melkite (Catholic) Bishop George Hakim and hundreds of his community, and the attor- ney Muhammad Nimr al-Hawwari and his extended family. The ruling Mapai (Workers Party) turned family reunification into an instrument that served its interests, particularly during electoral battles. At the same time that some Palestin- ians were being permitted to return to the occupied homeland, the policy to expel thousands of others continued to be implemented.

The sword of expulsion was a constant threat over the heads of Palestinians in the Galilee and in other areas even after the end of the war when Israeli security forces conducted a fierce campaign against attempts by refugees to return to their own villages. Israel criminalized those returnees by labeling them as "infiltrators" in order to justify its iron fist policy, which included firing indiscriminately on any refugee seen trying to return to their home or village.[2] This Israeli war on attempts to return has been examined previously as an aspect of the struggle with neigh- boring Arab countries. But little has been written concerning the actions of Israeli authorities in the early 1950s against many of the Palestinians who remained and whom it tried to expel as infiltrators. Like most published studies on the 1948 war that ignored the fate of the "remainers," studies on the "border wars" also ignored the consequences for the Arabs in Israel from 1949 to 1956.

The policy of ethnic cleansing during the 1948 war was more complex and expansive than a specific plan such as Plan Dalet. The leaders of the Zionist project to establish a Jewish state in Palestine imagined it as empty of its Arab population, which is the cornerstone of the subsequent ethnic cleansing policy. Using the same model as all European settlers, the Zionists had convinced themselves from the end of the Ottoman era that the indigenous population would benefit from their project, and would not oppose it. But the Palestinian Arabs declared that they would resist, and then resorted to arms in the 1936–39 revolt against that settlement project and its cradle in British Mandate policy. It was then, following the Peel Commission plan of 1937, that the expulsion of the Arabs from the Jewish state—or "transporting" them to neighboring Arab countries—became a declared policy.

The leaders of the Zionist movement formed the habit of posing practical questions, such as "What can be done?," at each stage of their settlement plan, rather than talking about the final objectives. That is what also happened in the 1948 war, when it became clear that the objective that enjoyed the unanimous support of Zionists of all inclinations was to establish a Jewish state with the smallest possible number of Palestinians. The important question at that stage, from their perspective, was what could be done through means that would not hurt their own interests. Plan Dalet was important during a certain phase in the war; however, the Zionists employed the same policies and instruments both before that plan and after it as well. The prohibition of return, the expulsion of thousands of those who had remained in the Galilee and elsewhere, and the destruction of villages and eviction of their population under military rule, particularly from 1948 to 1956, represented other links in the chain of the ethnic cleansing policy.

As we shall see later, the history of the Palestinians who remained in the Galilee both attests to the existence of a high-level policy of ethnic cleansing at times and refutes that policy at other times. Those cases which are not consistent with the general policy are due to causes connected to geography and the differential treatment of non-Muslims. The Druze were treated in a different way from the general Arab population. Christians were generally treated more leniently and with some sensitivity, out of fear of the reaction of Western states and churches. This unequal treatment of Palestinians in Haifa and the Galilee emerged during the months of war and several years after. These and other examples demonstrate that cases of "non-expulsion" were not spontaneous but rather the result of a high-level policy of Israeli leaders based on their political interests and also connected to the positions adopted by the leaders of those religious and political sects.

This study offers a new and different reading of the history of Arabs in Israel from their own perspective, based on Arabic sources to which researchers have rarely paid attention. This reading allows us to be acquainted with personal and human stories that may be at odds with the narratives of the national elite which largely ignored local history. The emerging panorama studded with local events is similar to a mosaic in which the interconnected stones demonstrate a new multifaceted form of the historic tale. The interlacing of the local and the personal alongside the general narrative of events which this historical study offers allows us to examine the abstract mega or meta-narratives and to deconstruct them. Those who stayed in Haifa and the Galilee were not merely the victims of acts of murder and expulsion but also people who initiated actions and adopted positions which often saved them from the tragedies that befell other Palestinians.

Historiographies are the counterpart of theories in the social sciences, which always require events and facts encountered in the field to support the general theoretical-analytic framework. It goes without saying that facts alone are not enough to construct a general framework for events. In turn, the historiography or the theory are in dire need of facts to validate them and affirm their veracity. This study is based on local historical events (microhistory) without attempting to impose a historiography or comprehensive theory. It is not content, however, with simply chronicling detailed facts; rather it places them within a general context (macrohistory). In this way the reader is able to see the "forest" and also closely examine the various "trees." These trees are the stories of the people and towns, which form the basic raw materials for the historical narrative.

This work tells the story of the Palestinians who remained in Galilee and other areas in several contexts. The first context is their adaptation to their new reality as an undesired minority. Family reunification and the building of their lives under military rule are two basic aspects of the struggle for survival. Just as the issue of Palestinian refugees arose during the war, then crystalized into the policy of forcibly preventing their return during the 1950s, so too arose the story of those who remained. Those who were not expelled, and those who managed to return, carried on the struggle to remain in the face of policies to isolate them and expel them until 1956, at least. At the beginning they had to foil the attempts to expel as many as possible of those who remained. Subsequently, the struggle to remain evolved into devising modes of conduct and tools that would enable their adaptation to the policies of eviction, repression, and permanent surveillance.

The second context for the history of Palestinians in Israel is the Arab world. Until 1948, the Palestinians who remained in Israel were considered an organic part of the Palestinian people and the Arab world in general, but the Nakba isolated them from their people and the neighboring Arab states. The new borders between Israel and its neighbors turned into enclosures that prohibited communication and contact, and this added a new element to the painful reality of those who remained in northern Palestine. During the first years after the Nakba, a not insignificant number of Palestinians continued to cross the border despite the considerable danger involved; the gradual sealing of the gaps in the enclosure had an enormous effect on the lives of those who remained in what became the "Israeli prison." The isolation of those who remained—from the Jews in Israel and from the Arabs in neighboring countries—was one of the main givens of their existence, particularly in the first decade after the Nakba.

The particular context for this study is the international arena. It is true that the world has not heard of and knows little about the Arabs who remained in Haifa and the Galilee. The enclosures which locked them in after the Nakba also closed what small windows there had been to the larger outside world. A number of Western churches retained some interest in the Christians in Nazareth and its environs and their conditions. The communist bloc was concerned about the comrades in Maki (Israeli Communist Party) who resisted the policies of discrimination and repression. This connection with the communist countries strengthened the political opposition to military rule and contributed to the development of cultural institutions in Haifa and Galilee. The policies of Maki were devised in Moscow to a large extent, which made it necessary to take into account the Cold War links between the capitalist and socialist camps for understanding the local policies of communist parties.

The Arabs who remained sometimes found themselves facing two bitter choices: either to become refugees and go into exile, or to stay and cooperate in some way with the victors. In order to remain in the Jewish state, some of them were forced to pay a price which would have been unacceptable in a normal crisis: they were obliged to bow to and cooperate with the occupation and its policies so that it would consent to their remaining in their homeland. The Palestinian communists who joined Maki appeared ideologically convinced that their choice to cooperate with Zionism formed part of the international proletarian struggle; their class analysis of the struggle was dominant over the national dimension, so most accepted Moscow's positions. However, the majority of the Arabs who remained in Haifa and the Galilee were neither collaborators nor communists, but steadfast people who preferred living under occupation in their homeland to exile in refugee camps. Not long after the Nakba it became apparent that whatever the ideological choices of those who remained, they were all subject to the same military government and to the repression of the colonialist emergency regulations.

This research study is based on the argument that the war period was the real beginning of the history of the Palestinian minority in the Jewish state, the details of which are absent from most of the historical literature about the circumstances of Palestinians in Israel. The root of the problem is the existence of a division or total breach between those specializing in the study of the 1948 war and those specializing in the study of the circumstances of the Palestinian minority in the Jewish state after the Nakba. The first group pays no attention to the question of those who remained and then centers on relations with the Arab countries after the war.[3] The second group begins with the history of the Palestinian minority, usually following the end of the war, without devoting much attention to the Nakba and its consequences for that minority. This study will bridge that methodological and epistemological division which imposes an imagined split on history and reality that obscures knowledge and clouds vision.

Although the Arabs who remained experienced the full trauma of the Nakba, they rose from the ashes and tried to rebuild their lives anew despite their subjugation under the occupation. They did this under unusual circumstances that isolated them from the Arab world and even from the rest of their people from whom they had been inseparable until 1948. So, we pose the following question once again: why and how did a relatively large number of residents of the Galilee manage to remain, compared to other regions which were totally emptied of their Palestinian population? What does the Nakba mean to this Palestinian minority which lived under the dominance of a Jewish majority? What are the consequences and repercussions of forced demographic change and of living as a marginalized minority whose presence in Israel was undesirable? How did those who remained adjust to the new reality and how did they live with the social and cultural outcomes and consequences of the Nakba? However, before we begin to answer these questions, let us draw in broad strokes some preliminary characteristics of the subject of our study: those who remained.

WHO ARE THE PALESTINIANS WHO REMAINED?

During the 1948 war Israel was born and the Palestinian refugee issue was created. A minority of the stricken population stayed in their country, particularly in Haifa and the Galilee. The Nakba was like an earthquake that severed connections among the Palestinian people and caused the loss of a homeland where Palestinians had lived for centuries. The refugees lost their homes and lands, and lived as strangers far from their destroyed cities and villages. Those who remained stayed in their towns and communities, subject to the rule of their enemy who was responsible for the catastrophe, the Nakba. The consensus among studies that trace the history of this Arab minority in the Jewish state is that those who remained totaled 156,000. This estimate, made in the summer of 1949, relied on Israeli statistics following the conclusion of the armistice agreements and the drawing of borders. However, these numbers of the new demographic reality minimize the details of the tragic events that continued for nearly one and a half years.

The Arabs who remained suffered from the trauma of the Nakba and its consequences for a long time. They were overcome by a sense of loss, confusion, and incapacitating anger, as well as a sense of betrayal and humiliation in the wake of the defeat. The vast majority were peasants (*fellahin*) who lost the Palestinian city and so, like flocks without shepherds, had to adapt on their own to the new tragic reality and to the language and laws of their new rulers. These laws and policies aimed to further restrict them and to grab their remaining lands and property. However, the leaders of Israel were still unsatisfied, and continued to look for the means and the appropriate time to rid themselves of the remaining minority. Thus, the remaining Palestinians spent their first years in their estranged homeland tormented by the fear of being uprooted and displaced.

The initial nucleus of the society of "remainers" in Haifa and the Galilee consisted of 69,000 people who were registered in the first census in November 1948. The residents of Nazareth and twenty villages in its district were the largest and strongest demographic bloc after their occupation in July 1948. Also, a not insignificant number of residents of 'Akka and western Galilee remained in their homes and villages. Those who remained in Haifa and the Galilee represented the largest segment of Palestinians whom the census proved had not been expelled. Most of these Palestinians took part in the first parliamentary elections at the beginning of 1949, which consolidated their status as citizens and the fact that they remained under Israeli rule but, at the same time, lent legitimacy to the "democratic" nature of the Jewish state. Those elections constituted an important turning point in the struggle to remain, based on a complex mechanism of give-and-take between the vanquished and the victors who had established their state on the ruins of the Palestinian home.[4]

Israel had completed the occupation of the Galilee through Operation Hiram when the census took place. However, the Palestinians who had remained in the recently occupied territory were not included in the census although they were included in subsequent months. The continuation of the movement of people between the Galilee and Lebanon made it a possibility to also live under the occupation without being registered. In the last month of 1948 and the beginning of the following year, Israel expelled thousands of those who had remained in the Galilee to neighboring Arab countries. This act of uprooting, especially those cases that occurred after the census, was illegal even by the Israeli understanding of the matter. Some of those expelled returned on their own, and then resorted to the courts, which ordered that they be given identity cards and citizenship. However, the legal process was limited and came late in most cases. Prior to that, most returnees managed to stay due to mechanisms and loopholes they found and exploited to defeat the policy of ethnic cleansing.

The interim government that oversaw the war effort after May 1948 under the leadership of Ben-Gurion included twelve members, among them Bechor Shitrit, the minister of police and minority affairs. The Palestinians, who had been the vast majority of the population of the country, were classified as a minority in the Jewish state at its creation. As for the claims Israel has made about equal treatment of its Arab citizens, events and policies in practice were the exact opposite. Since the beginning of the implementation of Plan Dalet up to May 1948, a very small number of Palestinians managed to stay in their homes in the cities or villages which had been occupied. In that month, the new state of Israel expanded its borders beyond that demarcated as the Jewish zone in the partition plan, and Shitrit was put in charge of minorities in a letter of appointment which was clear regarding the desired demographic objective for the expanded borders.

July 1948 represented a turning point in the history of the war and the Palestinian Nakba. After the ten-day battles ended and a cease-fire was declared for the second time without a time limit, the defeat of the Arab armies and the events of the Nakba were obvious for everyone to see. From a practical standpoint, the war between Israel and its neighbors—Syria, Lebanon, and Jordan individually—had ended. The Egyptian front, where fighting continued, was very far from the Galilee, and the Egyptian army there changed its position from offense to defense. Clearly, the defeat of the Arab armies opened the door for Israel to expand its territory without regard for the partition plan borders. It was then that many Palestinians began to absorb the lesson of the catastrophe that had befallen them and saw with their own eyes how Israel acted to prevent the return of the refugees through all means available. The historian Constantine Zurayk monitored these events and the results of the war, and then wrote and published his well-known book *Ma'na al-Nakba* [Meaning of the Catastrophe].[5]

The Nakba was an earthquake that shook Palestinians everywhere, but its particulars and consequences differed from place to place. Even within the Galilee, some villages were subjected to acts of terrorism (massacres and mass expulsion), while other villages in their locale escaped. All of the residents of some villages were expelled and became refugees either outside their homeland or within it. In some cases, such as 'Ilabun and 'Illut, internal migrants were allowed to live in the Galilee, or even to return to their villages and homes. However, in eastern Galilee (in the vicinity of Safad, Tiberias, and Bisan) only a few villages escaped the uprooting and dispersal of their residents. The fact that those few towns or villages, despite being isolated from their Arab milieu, had survived had a huge psychological, social, and cultural impact on the lives of their inhabitants. But in areas where there were adjacent population clusters, as in the area of Nazareth, al-Battuf, and al-Shaghur valley, the inhabitants were less vulnerable to feelings of isolation and estrangement.

In general, the Nakba had diverse consequences in the Galilee as compared to the Triangle (around Kufr Qari', 'Ar'ara, Baqa al-Gharbiyya and Umm al-Fahm) and the Naqab (Negev). The history of Arabs who remained in the Naqab remained unknown for several decades after the 1948 war; even today our knowledge of this subject continues to be meager. This study does not attempt to cover the history of this region in southern Palestine, which requires a special study. But some important events in the villages of the Triangle in the central area will be referred to and will be compared to events in the Galilee region. While villages in the central area did not suffer massacres and mass expulsion, they did experience the same policy of repression and discrimination following their annexation after being transferred from Jordanian to Israeli control at Rhodes in the spring of 1949.

Aside from the geographic factor, Israel's separate policies towards the adherents of the three faiths—Muslim, Christian, and Jew—should be noted. At the end of the war, it became apparent that the Druze had not suffered from killings, uprooting, and evictions. All of the villages they inhabited remained intact and their inhabitants were not subjected to collective punishment. Even the village of Yanuh, where there was a heated battle in which a large number of Israeli soldiers were killed (most of them Druze), suffered no serious punishment. This was largely due to the decision by Israeli leaders to conclude a cooperation agreement with some leaders of this sect on the eve of the creation of the state. Thus, in addition to the case of Nazareth, the treatment that the Druze received is another paradigm of the policy of "non-expulsion" due to orders from above: to guarantee the survival of all Druze villages and their inhabitants due to their cooperation with the victors at an early point in 1948.

It was well known that dozens of Druze youth fought for Israel in 1948. Their Christian and Muslim neighbors saw how Israel and its army gave differential treatment to the Druze. At the other end of the spectrum were Muslims who suffered from the iron-fist implementation of the policy of ethnic cleansing that included massacres, demolition of houses, and expulsion of the population of the Galilee and other areas. The treatment meted out to Christians fell somewhere in-between: in some places (such as Nazareth) strict orders were given to the soldiers not to attack the Christian holy places and residents of the city, while residents of some Christian villages were killed and expelled, as happened in 'Ilabun. In addition, a number of Christian border villages were destroyed and their residents evicted, as happened in the case of Kafr Bir'im, Iqrit and others.

Despite the fact that Christian villages were subjected to collective punishment, Israel's treatment of the adherents of the Christian faith was in general lenient compared to its treatment of Muslims. In the case of 'Ilabun, the residents had been subjected to killings and forced expulsion, yet those expelled were allowed to return to their homes and village shortly after their expulsion—a permitted return that has become well known as a unique case in the history of the Nakba. As for the inhabitants of Kafr Bir'im and Iqrit Israel allowed the inhabitants of the two villages to live elsewhere in the country instead of expelling them to Lebanon, contrary to what happened to the inhabitants of Muslim villages along the border strip with Lebanon. The villages that remained and were not uprooted under the military plan were inhabited by either Christian or Druze (Fassuta, Mi'lya, Tarshiha, Hurfaysh, and Jish). This discriminatory policy was the result of the international and regional calculations of the leaders of the Jewish state.

During the 1950s Israel consented to the return of thousands of refugees under the family reunification program. We do not know the exact number of those who benefited from this mechanism, but the official figures put the number at twenty thousand. Permission continued to be granted in a limited number of cases for the purpose of family reunification until the mid-1950s; still, the policy of expelling Arabs from Israel continued at least until 1956. The expulsion of several thousand residents of the city of al-Majdal-Asqalan at the end of 1950 is well known. However, any mention of the expulsion of thousands of residents after that time is largely missing from the historical literature, including the expulsion of several thousand residents who had remained in villages of the al-Hula plain. Some residents of Krad al-Baqqara and Krad al-Ghannama had been expelled across the border to Syria, while others were sent to the village of Sha'b in 1953. In 1956, Yitzhak Rabin, commander of the northern region at the time, took advantage of the outbreak of the Sinai war and ordered the soldiers under his command to expel about two thousand residents who had remained in their villages to Jordan and Syria.[6] In the Naqab, the expulsion of thousands of Arab residents continued until 1959.

Rabin and other army officers who led the 1948 war considered the presence of Arab residents near Israel's borders with its neighbors a problem in need of a solution.[7] On the Jordanian front, which remained quiet during the Sinai War, Border Guard troops carried out a massacre in Kafr Qasim on the evening of 29 October 1956. The killing by Israeli troops of forty-nine Arab citizens in cold blood, eight years after the Nakba, signals clearly how they were viewed by the ruling majority and its representatives in the security agencies. There was some speculation that keeping the eastern front open and unguarded on the day of the massacre hints that there was a plot to terrorize the inhabitants and force them to leave. This massacre in the Triangle on the first day of the 1956 war reminded Palestinians of the trauma of killing and expulsion in 1948.[8] The massacre and the expulsion of the remnants of al-Hula's Arab population were clear indicators of the still-present danger faced by those who remained in their homeland.

The objective of remaining in one's homeland after the Nakba continued to guide Palestinians not just through the months of war but also for many years after. When it became apparent after the guns had fallen silent that a large number of Palestinians remained in the Galilee, the leaders of Israel were relentless in attempting to remove a large number through a policy of repression and direct expulsion. Even after the decline of expulsion operations after 1952, plans were drawn up and action taken to encourage Palestinians to leave the country and to immigrate to Arab and foreign countries far from Palestine, such as Libya and Argentina.[9]

The Suez war of 1956 was tantamount to the "second round" in the Arab-Israeli conflict, but it did not constitute for Israel the wished-for opportunity to rid the country of those who remained. In the early 1950s, many statements by the leaders of the Jewish state were published to the effect that the fate of Arabs in Israel was not yet decided. Although it is difficult to remove tens of thousands of people under normal circumstances, war had its own rules. However, the residents of the Triangle villages all stuck resolutely to their homes and lands, and refrained from any actions that could have justified their expulsion by the army despite the horrific massacre. Since the 1956 war was far from the Jordanian and northern (Lebanese and Syrian) fronts, it became difficult to justify collective expulsion. The remaining residents of two villages in the Hula region were exceptions to this rule. In general, the 1956 events showed that Palestinians in Israel had learned the lesson of the Nakba, and became a resilient and permanent part of the population.

Still the fear among those who remained of being expelled was ever-present for at least another decade.

WEAK INTEREST IN THE CONDITIONS
OF PALESTINIANS IN ISRAEL

Most of what has been written since the Nakba has revolved around the "Palestine Question," and little of it has dealt with the fate of the Palestinians. Arabs openly told themselves and the world at large that what had happened was a grave injustice, and that establishing the state of Israel on the ruins of Palestine was morally illegitimate, unfair, and unjust. This legalistic defensive discourse contributed to the neglect of the fate of the disaster's victims. Generally speaking, the Arab elite adopted the "Palestinian cause" but paid much less attention to the Palestinians themselves. As for the Palestinians in Israel, the Arab boycott of the Zionist entity was a barrier that disrupted the possibility of attending to what had befallen them. The Arab world went through a somewhat protracted phase of instability after the defeat in 1948, punctuated by military coups, revolts, and assassinations of the leaders who had been accused of betraying the cause. For these and other reasons the Arabs who had remained in the "lost Paradise" were forgotten.

It may be surprising that Arab academics who were themselves among the Palestinians who remained paid scarce attention to the history of the Nakba and its consequences for them. However, that surprise dissipates once we realize that this remnant of the Palestinian people produced only a few historians, most of whom stayed far away from chronicling the Nakba and its results. Furthermore, the Arabs in Israel are without a university or research institution with a strong interest in history. Consequently, this double marginalization and fear of unearthing sensitive and complicated matters relating to the 1948 war led them to distance themselves from the subject. The communities in which a few historians resided who did poke into the events of the Nakba and its consequences considered this to be a form of indulgence that was harmful to present-day struggles, which led researchers to avoid these painful subjects.[10] Gradually, however, the sense of fear and embarrassment waned and led to important studies, some of which have been published.

In the last year of military rule (1966), two pioneering studies were written by sons of "remainers." Subhi Abu-Ghosh wrote a doctoral dissertation at Princeton University, and Sabri Jiryis, a lawyer and political activist at the time, authored the first book on *The Arabs in Israel* in Hebrew. Abu-Ghosh based his dissertation on field research in an Arab village, and its conclusions are similar to those by Israeli Orientalists about the same village. For instance, he claimed that modernization and development of Arab villages was thwarted by the traditional social structure governed by the heads of families and clans. He argued that state institutions and other external parties were the agents of progress and change, and that the obstacles were internal and Arab, that is, unconnected to the military government and the policies of repression and expulsion. This dissertation, which earned Abu-Ghosh a PhD, has not been translated from English and has not been published in Israel.[11]

Even Sabri Jiryis's book, although originally published in Hebrew, did not attract much attention initially.[12] The author, a courageous radical and daring critic of the military and its policies, was a graduate of Hebrew University law school (1963) and a nationalist activist. His book avoided generalities, and provided ample details about Israel's methods of repression and their instruments: military rule, the defense (emergency) regulations of 1945, the intelligence services and the police, and others. Jiryis argued that these institutions were responsible for repressing the Arab population and preventing the development of their independent economy. He also claimed that they obstructed every attempt at independent political organization, and attempted to strangle any initiative for infrastructural development and education. Jiryis's book and its conclusions are the antithesis of Abu-Ghosh's, and constituted a model for a new generation of youth who broke the fear barrier and issued a challenge to repression.

Following the establishment of a number of Palestinian institutions for study and research in Beirut, some researchers began to devote attention to the Palestinians in Israel, drawn first to the poetry of resistance and the maintaining of the Arab identity of the population of the Galilee. In the mid-1960s, resistance poets such as Mahmoud Darwish, Samih al-Qasim, and others became popularized and expressions of admiration came from Beirut and Cairo and other Arab capitals; some raised their voices in praise of the steadfastness of the Arabs in Israel and their adherence to their Arab identity. Darwish's uncomfortable reply to this sudden embrace after long years of neglect came in his famous article "Save Us from This Cruel Love."[13] The encounter with resistance poetry resulted in an increase in interest in this remaining minority and in the publication of studies exploring it. Jiryis's book was translated into Arabic and published in Cairo and Beirut, and an updated edition was later issued in English.

Some leaders of the generation of those who remained in Haifa and the Galilee chose literature as the mechanism to express their position. The most prominent among them was Emile Habibi (1921–1996), who in 1974 published his enduring masterpiece *Al-Mutasha'il* [The Pessoptimist].[14] This satiric novel exposes some of what had been concealed about the story of Palestinians remaining in Haifa and the Galilee under Israeli military rule. Dalia Karpel's documentary film *Emile Habibi: A Remainer in Haifa* was a response to Ghassan Kanafani's (1936–1972) famous novel *Returning to Haifa*.[15] Habibi and Kanafani represented two distinct generations of fathers and sons who gave expression to the Nakba of the Palestinians through the form of the novel. As is well known, writers and poets do not need archives and documents to record the experiences of the defeated and to tell their stories. Consequently, they were the first to tell the story of the fate-stricken Palestinians on both sides of the border which emerged in 1948–49.

The author of *The Pessoptimist* used to say that he carried two watermelons (politics and literature) in his arms for most of his life. Since 1974 he had been denying that his novel contained any autobiographical elements, but two decades later, on the eve of his passing away, he admitted that parts were in fact autobiographical. In the film, he reads aloud one section after another of *The Pessoptimist*, particularly concerning the road of his return from Lebanon to Haifa. This admission in Karpel's documentary film was reaffirmed by Habibi in a final interview published in *Masharif* magazine.[16] In reality the novel is not just the story of one person divorced from his political and social milieu; it also gives voice to the Palestinian generation who lived through the Nakba. He chose a way to remain in Haifa with the leaders of the National Liberation League, which united in October 1948 with the Israeli Communist Party (Maki).

The Pessoptimist demonstrates total loyalty (to Israel), and full readiness to carry out all the tasks assigned to him, as part of his adjustment and submission to the rules of "Israeli democracy." The fate of Saʻid Abi al-Nahs (Happy, the Ill-Fated—the name of the Pessoptimist) is not as bad, relatively speaking, as that of others among his fate-stricken people, as he receives several payments and rewards for his cooperation. In spite of that, he does not rise to the same level as the average Israeli citizen, but suffers as a result of the iron grip of military rule and the actions of its representatives in Arab towns. The author of *The Pessoptimist* allows himself, behind his satiric mask, to acknowledge his weaknesses in the year of the Nakba and beyond. In contrast to Habibi the politician, the novelist admits that he and many of those who remained in Israel were searching for a way to stay at any price. We shall return to this treatise, which guided Habibi and many of his comrades, in a later chapter concerning the role of the communists in 1948 and afterwards in Israel.

In contrast to such Palestinian writing, the Israeli side did not produce anything new in the 1970s on Palestine and the Palestinians in the Nakba or its aftermath. The treatment of the history of the country by Israeli academia is relegated to sections and departments with little to connect them. The departments dealing with the history of "the land of Israel" and the history of the people of Israel do not deal with the history of the Palestinians. Usually the professors and students in those departments do not have a command of Arabic, so they do not attempt to make use of Arabic-language sources and references in their studies and research. Most studies on the Palestinians are conducted by Orientalists and security experts who serve in the Israeli occupation agencies. On the other side, we find many Palestinian researchers who wrote on the Nakba and its consequences and on many aspects of the Arab-Israeli conflict, but who do not have familiarity with Hebrew. In their writings, most researchers into these topics on both sides of the conflict take their point of departure from the maxim "know thine enemy," and this approach has produced many studies with biased views and propaganda for the sake of mobilization, instead of searching for the truth, which often contradicts what is known and familiar.

Interest in the conditions of Arabs in Israel increased considerably in the 1980s. For example, Ian Lustick's *Arabs in the Jewish State* focuses on describing and analyzing the mechanisms which enabled the continuation of Israeli control and its suppression of Arab opposition even after the end of military rule.[17] His book contributed a great deal to the understanding of the regime of Jewish control and its mechanisms in dealing with the Arab minority. In *1949: The First Israelis* Tom Segev, contrary to the practice in much of this literature, allocates an appropriate place to the Arabs who remained in Israel,[18] not just in terms of the number of pages dedicated to the conditions of Arabs in Israel during 1948–49, but in exposing the policy of systematic repression and harassment of this minority. The journalists Uzi Benziman and ʿAtallah Mansour followed in his footsteps in their book, *Agents of a Third Party*, which expands its account of policy towards the Arabs in Israel in several areas, from the creation of the state to the 1980s.[19]

Research by Benny Morris, Ilan Pappé, Avi Shlaim, and others who were classified as revisionist historians offered new information and a new perspective on the Palestinian disaster. Following these, Arab and Jewish researchers published studies on the Arabs in Israel and the treatment doled out to them since 1948. These research works caused some to believe that there was not much to add or to update on these topics. This incorrect impression was due in the first place to the divorce, even in the most critical studies, between the Nakba and the origins of the history of the Palestinian minority in Israel. Unless this gap is addressed, the mistaken impression will prevail that there is no connection between them, and that the 1948 war and its outcome are not a founding event in the history of that minority. But the young generation of Arabs and Jews who were the students of the critical non-Zionist school began to participate in critiquing the Israeli narrative, even as the older generation of researchers continued to make their own contribution.

Pappé is considered one of the most daring and productive researchers to challenge the historical Zionist narrative. In the last decade, he became famous for his book *The Ethnic Cleansing of Palestine*, which describes a policy that Israel carried out systematically in the 1948 war.[20] The book created a sharp controversy which demonstrates that the Nakba is still a burning issue in need of further research and investigation. There is now a general consensus among the parties to the historical discussion that there were dozens of massacres and acts of expulsion of Palestinians from their country prior to and after May 1948. The debate revolves essentially around the extent to which the top Israeli leadership was responsible for these acts and gave the orders to carry them out. Pappé, Walid Khalidi, and others believe that Plan Dalet was a methodical blueprint for ethnic cleansing—the expulsion of the Palestinians from their homeland—in the year of the Nakba. However, Zionist historians, including Morris, still insist that the massacres and the acts of expulsion carried out by the Israeli army were not the result of deliberate top-level planning or policy.[21]

The era of the revisionist historians in Israel ended during the first decade of the twenty-first century. While Pappé adopted the Palestinian historical narrative, Morris returned to the Zionist narrative in which Israel wraps itself in the robes of the victim, claiming it was acting in self-defense. He allowed himself free rein in a 2004 interview with Ari Shavit of *Haaretz*, declaring his support for the expulsion policy which Ben-Gurion led, and now blaming him for not having expelled all Palestinians from Israel.[22] Morris retracted the claim that there was no planning or execution of a plan by the top leadership, and added that the field commanders had absorbed what the top leader wanted them to in terms of expelling the Palestinians after occupying their towns and villages. Even more provoking is that he justified the policy of murder and expulsion, adding that he did not think it far-fetched that Israel might expel the Palestinians in the future, including those who had remained in 1948, which he said he did not oppose.[23]

In addition to Jewish researchers, in the last decade of the twentieth century there emerged a new generation of researchers from among the Arab "remainers." Two of these, Ahmad Sa'di and Nur Masalha, specialize in the Palestinian Nakba and its effects on the lives of Arabs in Israel during the 1950s and have contributed, separately, a number of important studies on this subject.[24] Mustafa Abbasi authored a number of important articles and books on the cities of the Galilee pre- and post-Nakba.[25] Mustafa Kabha also published studies, some of which concern the fate of the Triangle area while others deal with general Palestinian problems. He is also supervising an oral history project at the Umm al-Fahm museum. Both Abbasi and Kabha succeeded in combining documents and other written sources with the use of oral history as an important resource for their research. Their studies are excellent models for documenting and chronicling forgotten aspects of the history of Palestinians in Israel.

Hillel Cohen is a prolific Israeli researcher who has published a significant number of books and articles on the Arabs in Israel. He devoted his master's thesis to the study of "The Present Absentees."[26] This study, subsequently published in Hebrew and Arabic, deals with Palestinian refugees since 1948 who were expelled and then prevented from returning to their homes and lands and became internal refugees in the Galilee. Later, Cohen published a book on Arab agents who collaborated with the institutions of the Jewish state during the period of military rule (1948–67).[27] This book also covers the activities of the communists and other Arab opponents of the policy of military rule, based largely on police, intelligence, and military government records.

Another recent study based on diverse sources attempted to highlight the role of Arabs in shaping their own history. Shira Robinson's dissertation, later published, is based on Israeli archives and various Arab sources.[28] The author does not restrict herself to published documents and sources, but augments these with

interviews with dozens of eyewitnesses in the Galilee and the Triangle. This combination of a range of sources from both sides of the conflict is very important, as
is the author's selection of theories of Zionist settlement and colonialism which
makes it possible to see the larger picture of the circumstances of the Palestinian
minority remaining in Israel after 1948. The studies by Cohen and Robinson are
perhaps closer to the topic of my own study on the Palestinians who remained,
particularly in Haifa and Galilee in the 1948–56 period.

THE STRUCTURE AND CONTENT OF THE BOOK

The occupation of Nazareth, and the subsequent declaration of the second cease-
fire in mid-July 1948, constitute the real beginning of the story of the Arabs who
remained. By that time, it was clear to Israel's leaders that it had scored a victory in
its military war. The Arabs and most of their leaders also became aware of this fact.
The ten-day battles ended with a relatively large Arab minority remaining in lower
Galilee, and it became necessary for Israel to formulate a policy regarding those who
remained. A military governor of Nazareth was appointed immediately after it was
occupied to run the affairs of the city and offer services to its residents in cooperation with the city's institutions and leaders. Business and education were at the top
of the list of priorities. During this period Radio Israel launched a broadcast in Arabic, and a daily Arabic-language newspaper began to publish in order to transmit
the government's views and policies to the Arab citizens in their own language.[29]

The first chapter of this book sheds light on the various meanings of the Nakba
in northern Palestine until the months of the second cease-fire in the summer of
1948. In that period the term "al-Nakba" was coined to describe the Arab defeat
in the Palestine war, as it had become known that the Arab armies had not halted
the expansion of the borders of the Jewish state and the expulsion of the Palestinians from the territories it occupied. The chapter reviews those events and focuses
on those who remained under occupation until September 1948. The Palestinian
cities of Haifa, Jaffa, Safad, and Tiberias were depopulated, but the fate of the
hundreds of thousands of refugees from those cities and villages of the area is
mentioned only as background, in order to focus attention on the fate of the tens
of thousands who remained and to expose the circumstances and reasons which
contributed to their staying and not being expelled.

The second chapter relates what occurred in the Galilee on the eve of the renewal
of the fighting, and then reviews the events of the occupation of northern Palestine
in what was called Operation Hiram. In mid-October 1948, war broke out again
on the Egyptian front and the likelihood of battles erupting in the Galilee increased.
The residents were aware of the limited capabilities of the Jaysh al-Inqadh, the
Arab Rescue Army,[30] in any confrontation with the Israeli army. Consequently,
most of the residents of the area chose to support their local leaders who tried to
ensure that the inhabitants would remain in the event of a renewed outbreak of

the war. The Arab communists in Haifa and the Galilee were some of those local leaders who played an important role in the struggle to stay and to rebuild the lives of the Arab minority in Israel. This chapter, which monitors the events of the war during the Israeli effort to complete the occupation of the Galilee, closely follows the role played by the residents and the conditions which allowed them to foil the Israeli army's policies of uprooting the population in the region.

The third chapter sheds light on two groups among those who remained in northern Palestine: the Druze and the communists. Both groups, acting separately, altered their positions toward the Jewish state for different reasons during the months of war, and their leaders' actions contributed to thousands of residents remaining in the Galilee. In Haifa and Galilee, the majority of the leaders of the National Liberation League chose to cooperate with Israel and opposed the entry of Arab armies into the Palestine war. This position became particularly apparent in July 1948 when League leaders chose to cooperate with the Israeli occupation in their regions and completed a 180-degree turn when they joined Maki before the war had ended. These important aspects of the history of Maki and the role played by its leaders is still unknown to many readers who embraced the party's narrative about its struggle against military rule with no awareness of its activities during the war.

The fourth chapter completes the task of monitoring of the circumstances of the Palestinians remaining in northern Palestine after the end of the war in early 1949. Israel had formulated criteria for classifying the status of those who remained in the territories it had occupied, noting that some had become citizens while others (suspected of leaving their homes and then returning) were considered temporary residents of the Jewish state. The thousands who had been evicted from the area along the Lebanese border were considered "the present absentees." The first plebiscite did not include all the villages of upper and central Galilee, where some of the residents were considered "infiltrators" and were under relentless threat of expulsion for a long time. There was a persistent internal migration of the population of upper Galilee and border crossings in both directions for several years. While several thousand managed to return and secure a place in their homeland, thousands of other Palestinians were expelled from their homes and lands and became refugees.

Chapter 5 deals with new areas that were not explored in the earlier chapters. Residents of the Triangle, which was annexed to Israel in the spring of 1949, began to adapt to Israeli rule in that later period, as those villages on the border with Jordan, from Kafr Qasim in the south to Umm al-Fahm and its villages in the north, were arbitrarily and suddenly separated from the towns and villages of the West Bank; their population, numbering over thirty thousand, became citizens of Israel even though Israel had not stopped trying to rid itself of, or at least reduce, the Arab minority. This chapter also presents the stories of individuals, families, and villages whose experiences in the struggle to remain have not yet been told. Despite the general policy of expulsion and preventing return, Israel allowed the residents of three villages ('Ilabun, 'Illut, and Kufr Qari') to return.[31] Shedding light on the stories of the inhabitants of these villages and the fate of members of certain families gives a vital human dimension and overturns the black and white stereotypes drawn by a number of studies.

Chapter 6 follows the progression of the struggle to remain by identifying the tools and adaptation behaviors employed for adjustment to Israeli military rule. Those who remained in Palestine realized that receiving citizenship and blue identity cards had removed the sword of expulsion hanging over their heads, and they quickly began to learn new ways to thwart the continued attempts to uproot them. One way, for example, was to resort to the Israeli Supreme Court. In Jaffa, the first such case was filed towards the end of 1948, and involved Hajj Ahmad Abu-Laban, followed by many other cases in the following years. These cases and their judgments constitute important topics for research. Most petitions were against the appropriation of land and the expulsion of residents and their arrest, as well as appeals to prevent the authorities from expelling some of those who had succeeded in returning to their homes for a second time.

The seventh and last chapter deals with the political mobilization of Arabs in Israel and their voting patterns in the Israeli Knesset elections. Like citizenship and the blue identity card, voting became a mechanism and avenue for Arabs to arrange to stay and avoid expulsion from the country. This helps explain why the communists on the one hand, and the collaborators on the other, hurried to urge their supporters to vote in the first general elections in January 1949. When the security forces resorted to the pretext of proximity to the country's borders to uproot Arab villages, some expressed readiness to defend those borders themselves. The leaders of Maki and others demanded that Arabs be recruited in the Israel army as a demonstration of their loyalty and an attempt to ensure they could remain and enjoy equal rights. In its analysis of political conduct, this chapter will reveal many daring and unusual positions adopted in those crucial years.

The conclusion to the book completes the cycle of events from the Nakba to the war that Israel started against Egypt in 1956. This war and its aftermath served as a reminder of the 1948 war in the Galilee. The villages of the Triangle escaped the massacres and the expulsion of residents which befell Palestinians in the Galilee and other locations, but the 1956 war reopened that danger when the army declared a curfew on the villages of the Triangle hours before the war began on 29 October 1956—and announced it only after villagers had left to tend their fields. This sudden movement restriction resulted in the killing of forty-nine people from the village of Kafr Qasim by Border Guards as they returned from their fields that evening, unaware of the curfew. Yet the aftermath of that massacre was contrary to the expectations of those who planned and executed it, as it reinforced the solidarity of those who had remained and added determination to their struggle.

RESEARCH METHODOLOGY AND SOURCES

Gaps offer an inviting opportunity for researchers in general, including historians. This thought kept returning to me at the beginning of my study of the history of Arabs in Israel after the Nakba. However, as the research progressed, it was apparent that the situation was complex and required explanation and clarification. Despite the obvious gap, few had approached the topic to try to study it seriously and deeply. When I entered the stage of conducting interviews and collecting oral testimonies from those who experienced the period under study, I found some of them reluctant to discuss it. I became preoccupied with trying to explain why researchers had kept their distance from the subject, as did some storytellers. The reason why many refrained from entering into the details and depths of the subject provides an important basis for understanding the history of the Palestinian minority in Israel. Why did those who lived through this period not write memoirs concerning their roles and activities during and after the 1948 war?

Most Palestinians, particularly the peasants, could not read or write at the time, and therefore did not keep diaries or write memoirs. The oral testimonies of Palestinians who were contemporaries of the events of the Nakba became the primary source for presenting the point of view of the defeated in that war. Memory is a problematic source for writing history if we rely on it without close examination. However, the categorical rejection of oral documentation due to the problematic nature of memory is an obstacle that has been surmounted by historical research. Some Arab literary figures and researchers have collected the testimonies of the "Nakba generation" in order to tell certain aspects of the disaster that transformed Palestinians from home owners and people with a homeland into destitute refugees.

The reactions of most Israelis to the stories told by Palestinians range from total rejection to casting doubt on the testimonies and those who rely on them. An example can be found in some of the Israeli reactions to the novel by Elias Khoury titled *Gate of the Sun*, which was translated and published in Hebrew.[32] The historian and journalist Tom Segev issued a strongly worded indictment of the book after it was published in Israel. In his review, titled "An Arab Story," he writes: "A Lebanese author accuses the Israeli army of committing war crimes. Where is the proof? A literary fact opposed to an historical fact."[33] Segev recoils from the tales of killing and repression and the eviction of the population of Sha'b in the Galilee, the main theater of the protagonist's memories. He notes that "what Benny Morris wrote about the rise of the 'Palestinian problem' does not even approach those atrocities." From his point of view, Morris and his archival documents constitute the proof that the discussion revolves around made-up stories to which the author gave literary form. Then Segev pronounces categorically that "the burden of proof rests with the teller of the story," even in a literary work and not just in researched studies. He concludes: "Khoury does not provide any kind of proof of what he alleges. He is not a well-known author in Israel, and there is no reason for us to believe him."[34]

Segev's last sentence is of the essence: what if he had he been "a well-known author in Israel"! Segev assumes, if that had been the case, that people would have believed him. In this way many believed the tales of *Khirbet Khiz'eh* (Ruins of Khiz'ah) by S. Yizhar,[35] without asking him for proof or documentation. Similarly, they believe the statements of victims of the Holocaust, Europeans and other Jews, when they tell their stories to the world. Elias Khoury is a prolific writer and is quite famous in the Arab world, but not in Israel. Why should Jewish readers of Hebrew believe him? But the more important question that arises from Segev's assertions is: What constitutes proof from the perspective of the historian? Endowing archival documents with sanctity, as is apparent from Segev's absolute reliance on Benny Morris, is a problematic issue which requires ample discussion, for which we do not have space here.

Many Jews and Arabs have only heard the narrative of the winners in the events of 1948. Few of them, particularly in Israel, have heard the human story of the losers. The year 1948 witnessed the creation of the state of Israel and the Nakba, with the tragic consequences that Palestinians are living to this day. The world that they knew and inhabited has been demolished since that tragedy, which was man-made and not the work of fate or nature. Despite the writings of the revisionist historians, there are many documents still shrouded in secrecy in Israeli archives. Tom Segev alluded to the fact that most of these secret documents concern massacres and the expulsion and repression of the population at the hands of Israeli soldiers. Segev adds: "A state that conceals printed war crimes concerning its history is retroactively complicit in those crimes."[36]

As is well-known, the output of historians is not absolute; their research findings are time bound and not comprehensively precise, as they do not constitute the whole truth about the period under study. At the time that Tom Segev permitted himself to fiercely attack Elias Khoury, relying on Morris's *The Birth of the Palestinian Refugee Problem*, Morris had published a new book, *Correcting a Mistake*, in which he cast doubt on some of his previous findings.[37] In an article on Operation Hiram in the Galilee, Morris affirmed the large number of massacres, expulsions, and acts of terrorizing the population carried out by the Israeli army to expel Palestinians from the Galilee outside Israel's borders. He went on: "Our information about these massacres is very limited because of the secrecy imposed by Israeli army archives on the relevant documents."[38] We will just have to wait to see—if these secret documents are declassified—what they will add to our knowledge. Until that happens, are the victims supposed to go to their graves without being given a chance to tell their stories because they do not possess written documents to support what they have to say?

In the absence of Palestinian archives, this study will depend on the testimony of eyewitnesses, some of whom have kept diaries while others have given testimonies before the author and other researchers. Only a limited number of Palestinians had written autobiographies until the 1970s, but in the last two decades there has been an increase in the use of this literary form, which also constitutes a historical document. Because of the limited abilities of some authors some memoirs had to be published locally at the expense of the authors and distribution was limited. These locally published memoirs and autobiographies constitute an important source for hearing the voices of the defeated and the forgotten in national historiographies. A strong point of these memoirs is that they retrace lives of Palestinians before the Nakba, and then show how those lives were shattered during the war and in the postwar years.

Since there are few memoirs of those who remained in Israel from the Nakba generation, most of whom could not read or write, listening to oral testimonies has become an urgent necessity in the last few years. Those among this generation who are still alive and in good health do not number more than a few hundred. Therefore, listening to the testimonies of 120 people who lived through the Nakba and the subsequent years in Haifa and the Galilee is a way of rescuing the personal and human experiences which would otherwise be lost with the passing of their owners. I am saddened that a fair number of those whom I met once or more than once are no longer alive. However, their testimonies remain as important building blocks of a personal and human dimension to be added to published documents and sources. These testimonies which I have collected in the field are a treasure and a precious addition, the importance of which cannot be overestimated, to the other available sources.

Historians and other researchers have concluded that oral testimonies are important as living documents to which attention must be paid; they should not be neglected because they present some problems. As in the case of any source on which historians rely in their research, one should be cautious and compare them with other written and published sources to create a fuller picture. Military documents which some Israeli researchers treat as sacred are not free of the intrusion of self-interest, politics, and the self-image of those who wrote and classified them. The author of this book, who has read a not inconsiderable number of Israeli archival documents, has discovered on more than one occasion that some were fake, and that attempts to hide things and mislead were made to conceal some war crimes, whereas eyewitnesses have offered detailed descriptions of those events, albeit decades later. That is why oral testimonies constitute an essential and indispensable addition here, in order to give voice to the victims and the defeated in the war of 1948.

The perpetrators of war crimes have always tried to silence the voice of their victims, to erase them from the historical record, and to transfer responsibility for crimes to the victims. Usurpers fear memories, as our poet Mahmoud Darwish has said. The Palestinian-Israeli case is no exception, particularly when talking about the events of the Nakba and the years following. Most of the Zionist accounts of those events vary between denying they ever happened to placing the blame on the Palestinians and their leaders for what happened, rather than being open and frank with themselves and with others. Escaping historical accountability and its political liabilities is today's version of burying one's head in the sand.

The Palestinians, who cannot forget the Nakba and its consequences for their present and future, transmit the memories of events from one generation to the other so that they will not be forgotten and will not be extinguished by the logic of power. Research on memory has demonstrated that the victims of acts of extreme violence store details of what they witnessed and what made their bodies tremble for decades. The significance given to those painful events that imprinted their lives may differ, but the essence of the story and its details remain constant even as time passes. The testimonies by those who survived concerning the events of the Nakba and its direct consequences are distinctive documents to be added to other available sources. They should be relied on using caution and in a professional manner in order to contribute to making the voices heard, especially since many sides have tried to silence them in order to conceal war crimes and their consequences for the Palestinians who remained in Haifa and the Galilee after 1948.

The oral testimonies which have been collected for this study, and on which it relies, are personal memories, distinct from the public or collective memory that states and their institutions promote. The eyewitnesses whom I interviewed were mostly victims of acts of ethnic cleansing carried out by the Israeli army in the Galilee during the war. The memories and identities of those witnesses were forged by the extreme violence they experienced that had been intended to terrorize the population. Contrary to those responsible for those acts, who did all they could to forget them and keep them concealed, the victims stored the details in their memories where they remained resistant to forgetfulness. A number of other researchers and activists have preceded me in conducting similar interviews. In this respect, noteworthy is important work that is being carried out by Zochrot, an Israeli nonprofit organization.[39] Oral testimonies have also been published in local history books about dozens of villages in the Galilee and other regions over the last two decades, thus rescuing them from loss since many of the contributors have since passed away.

This study relies on oral narratives and local written history, supported by a large number of primary and secondary sources and references, to try to present a macro-picture of events that is interspersed with the stories of local individuals and groups. The aim is to offer a comprehensive and integrated interpretation of its scope, by uncovering the events of what happened to those who remained, particularly in northern Palestine. The oral narratives have been subjected to the methodology of critical reading and comparison, the same tools on which the historian relies when dealing with written texts and documents.

The study relies first and foremost on primary and secondary written sources from both sides of the conflict. Communists, their documents and press (both in Arabic and Hebrew), and the memoirs of some of their activists make up the major share of the list of sources and references for this study. Dozens of members of the party and others whom I met have added important testimonies about the events of their time, which provide vital documentation of the local history, and are not represented either in archives or in the contemporary press. *Al-Ittihad* weekly newspaper provided the other side of the coin to *al-Yawm*, the organ that presented governmental policy and propaganda to Arab readers. Furthermore, the Mapam party and other Arab and Jewish groups have left us their documents and newspapers, which monitored the events after the Nakba with a critical and penetrating eye.[40]

Finally, we should remember court rulings, particularly those of the Supreme Court, from which many victims of military rule sought help and protection. In many cases, the plaintiffs and their witnesses came to the court and gave testimony concerning events in their villages in 1948 and after. Those testimonies, on which the court relied in passing judgment, were made by witnesses who swore to tell the truth, and at a time when the events they related were still fresh in their minds, having occurred only a short time earlier. In this way, some plaintiffs from Galilee villages succeeded in obtaining judgments that forced the interior ministry to give them identity cards and prevented the military authorities from expelling them again. A quick comparison of those testimonies with later ones confirms that oral histories are an important and vital source for relating the stories of the victims and their points of view regarding the events they lived through and which were imprinted on their identities and their memories.

Al-Nakba and Its Many Meanings in 1948

In *Ma'na al-Nakba* (The Meaning of the Catastrophe), written and published in late summer of 1948, Constantine Zurayk defines the conceptual parameters of the Palestinian tragedy.[1] This book, modest in size, is not a comprehensive study of the Arab defeat and its long-term significance, but rather a report on the event itself whose full details and scope were unknown at the time. Nevertheless, Zurayk draws a clear and bold picture of the event's meanings. He introduces the term "al-Nakba" to describe the defeat, and explains the broad lines of its meanings. In successfully reading the reality of the Arab situation at the time, he warns that al-Nakba could turn into a greater disaster if its causes were not addressed quickly.[2] The book contains many important observations about the meaning of al-Nakba and its causes which required courage to point out in those difficult days. Fortunately, the American University of Beirut allowed intellectual freedom of expression, and the Lebanese capital was a safe place to publish critical and penetrating works without fear or trepidation.

Zurayk mentions five other terms in the beginning of his book to describe what had befallen Palestine before selecting "al-Nakba" for the title.[3] It became in time the dominant definition for the Arab defeat in Palestine in 1948—leading to the tragedy of Palestine contributing a new concept to the international discourse on Palestinian struggle and destiny. In the decades that followed the terms "fedayeen," "intifada," *al-naksa* (setback), and others were added to the international language, enriching it with new concepts connected to the continuation of the Nakba and attempts by Palestinians to regain their "lost paradise." Before expanding on the meaning of al-Nakba, however, we would do well to get acquainted with the author.

Constantine Zurayk (1909–2000) is considered one of the most prominent Arab thinkers of the twentieth century. He was a professor of history at
the American University of Beirut from the early 1930s, and became one of the
most influential and appreciated lecturers by the students, many of whom were
Palestinian. He became vice-president of the university in the 1940s.[4] Zurayk's
personal background helps explain his decision to take upon himself the role of
a critical thinker who went beyond simply casting blame on others and labeling
them as traitors; he was committed to keeping hope alive in the hearts of youth
and students, while also diagnosing the factors of internal weakness. And so we
find him, despite the cruelty of events and time, trying to chart a path out of the
ruins to build a better future.

Under the title "The Oppressiveness of al-Nakba" on the book's first page,
Zurayk writes the following: "Seven states take on the task of invalidating the partition and suppressing Zionism, and lo and behold, they emerge from the battle
having lost a considerable portion of the land of Palestine." The historian adds:
"History has no record of a more just and righteous cause: a country is usurped
from its inhabitants to be turned into a homeland for small groups of human
beings who descend upon it from the four corners of the earth and establish a state
there in defiance of its people and the millions of their brethren in the neighboring
countries." He then completes the picture with numbers: "Four hundred thousand
or more Arabs are expelled from their homes, they are stripped of their property
and possessions, and they wander listlessly in what remains of Palestine and other
Arab countries."[5]

After Zurayk draws the broad outline of the meaning of the Nakba and its consequences, he moves on to a discussion of the causes of the defeat and the way
out of the calamity. He points to the responsibility of Arabs, first of all, and their
ill-preparedness for the battle of destiny, their disunity, and their underestimation
of the strength of the enemy who was well prepared for the war. Consequently,
he points to the need to accept responsibility for the defeat and learn from the
mistakes made, and warns against doing nothing other than passing the blame
to others. The Arabs should not be satisfied with cursing the Jews, he argues, and
disparaging "the British, the Americans, the Russians, and the Security Council . . .
and everyone who stands against us in this struggle."[6]

The August 1948 first print run of Maʿna al-Nakba sold out quickly and the
book was reprinted again in October. At the time, the second cease-fire was in
effect, but Zurayk did not update his book or add anything to the first edition.
Although fighting did not resume in the summer months, circumstances in the
Arab world went from bad to worse. Instead of closing ranks, disunity increased
and the contending Arab parties heaped accusations on one another, particularly
between some Arab regimes and the Palestinian leadership under Mufti Hajj
Amin al-Husayni.[7] The military defeat which followed on the heels of the political
catastrophe after the partition resolution caused the conflicting interests of some

Arab parties to become prominent so that differences prevailed both inside and outside the Arab League.[8]

Following Zurayk, George Hanna (1893–1969) published a book on the Palestinian tragedy in November 1948.[9] Hanna, a graduate of the American University of Beirut, was a socialist and became the head of the Soviet-Lebanese Friendship Society. In 1947 he visited Moscow and then wrote the book *I Have Returned from Moscow*. Hanna's political affiliation was with the Soviet side, as was his perspective on international politics, which gives his book special importance in understanding and analyzing the causes and roots of the Nakba.[10]

Hanna goes beyond blaming the enemies of the Palestinians—the Americans, British, and Russians[11]—for their calamity, and stresses that none bears the real responsibility. He argues that the foremost and genuine responsibility lies with the defeated Arabs who were then searching for excuses for their failure by blaming others, instead of facing up to their responsibility and making the necessary reforms in order to transcend the catastrophe. But he not only blames Arab regimes and leaders, he also blames the people, writing: "We are attracted to the banalities of civilization, but not to the substance. . . . We lack a collective spirit. . . . We have no sense of responsibility, because we are the enemies of duty. . . . "[12] He therefore does not expect an exit from the calamity or salvation from the crisis without social and political reforms, and the crystallization of an awareness of the importance of those reforms. In this context, he does not ignore the issue of the status of Arab women as evidence of the ignorance and underdevelopment prevalent in society that are hindrances to development and reform.[13]

It should be emphasized that George Hanna mentions the Russians alongside the British and the Americans as external factors in the Palestinian Nakba. He points to this role briefly, then expands on it: "And Russia, the third major power, is also responsible. Despite its hostility to Anglo-American policy, and its constant quarrel with it, Russia endorsed partition, and the establishment of a Zionist state next to the Arab state, in the hope that one of them would allow it a foothold into the Middle East."[14] These statements in November 1948 have very important historical significance. This straight thinking on the part of this socialist doctor was unique, because he does not couch his statements in justifications such as concern for peace, or choosing "the lesser of two evils," or assertions of that sort which the communists adopted later. Instead, he said frankly that the imperialistic interests of Russia were the main factor in its positions and policies which contributed to the Palestinian Nakba.

The third author who analyzed the factors responsible for the Nakba in order to extract lessons from it was Musa al-'Alami (1897–1984). Like his predecessors, al-'Alami chose Beirut as the venue for publishing his book, released under the title *'Ibirat Filastin* (The Lesson of Palestine) after the 1948 war had ended.[15] Consequently, he could expand on its results and its several stages up to the cease-fire and the signing of the armistice agreements between Israel and the neighboring

Arab countries. Al-'Alami shares the opinions of his predecessors in his analysis of the factors responsible for the Nakba; however, this attorney, who knew the British well and spent most of his life in Jerusalem close to the British mandatory government, points to the fact that the primary responsibility for the Palestinian Nakba belonged to Britain.[16] At the same time, he did not neglect the role of the Americans and the Russians in issuing the United Nations Partition Plan for Palestine and in the Palestinian tragedy in 1948.[17]

Al-'Alami divides the war into two stages. The first began from the announcement of the partition plan until the declaration of the establishment of the state of Israel in mid-May, a period of about six months when the principal burden of the war fell on the Palestinians who tried to defend their country and homeland. The second stage was from mid-May 1948 until early the following year, when the responsibility for fighting Israel was transferred to the Arab states and their armies. Those states were defeated, and one armistice agreement after the other was signed with Israel. This division of the Palestine war, which al-'Alami first sketched, became prevalent and was accepted by observers, then by the historians who chronicled the Nakba and the war of 1948.[18]

Many books and studies on the Palestinian Nakba were published in the 1950s, and there is no need to mention them all. The common denominator of most is that they were written by members of the Arab political and cultural elite and published in Beirut. Muhammad Nimr al-Hawwari's book is an exception to this rule in that it was published in Nazareth after his return there.[19] Al-Hawwari was born in 1908 and became a prominent lawyer and a leader of the Palestinian national movement up to 1948. He joined the ranks of the opposition to the mufti and founded the al-Najjada (Helpers) movement in Jaffa, leading it until he left the movement during the early events of the war. He eventually returned to Nazareth with Israel's consent after living in exile for almost two years, during which time he represented the cause of the refugees at the Lausanne Conference in 1949. Given this background, it is possible to understand the stinging criticism he directs at the Palestinian leadership, from the mufti to the communists, who saw him as a political opponent following his return. In later chapters we shall review the political role that al-Hawwari tried to play.

Al-Hawwari's book is an elegant indictment of the mufti, the Arab countries, and their leaders in general. The author rains accusations and insults on the Jaysh al-Inqadh (Arab Rescue Army, also called the Arab Salvation Army) under the leadership of Fawzi al-Qawuqji.[20] After reviewing the events of the war, the book concludes by saying that the Palestinian people, particularly the refugees among them, paid a dear price in the Nakba. He poses the controversial question: why did the refugees leave their homes and their country? In his answer he mentions ten reasons at least, and directs his arrows at several Arab parties. However, the fact that he blames Arabs does not make him neglect Israel's role entirely; he mentions, for example, that following the first cease-fire, the Israeli army carried out killings, plundered property, and attacked the residents of villages and cities in many parts of the country, such as Lydda, Ramla, Bisan, Majdal, al-Tira, Ijzim, 'Ayn Ghazal, Lubya, Saffuriyya, and al-Mujaydil.[21]

We conclude this brief review of the literature on the Nakba published directly after the calamity by mentioning one of the most important detailed works on the subject, *Al-Nakba: Nakbat Bayt al-Maqdis wal-firdaws al-mafqud 1947–49* (The Disaster: The Disaster of Jerusalem and the Lost Paradise).[22] Jerusalemite 'Arif al-'Arif published many works on Jerusalem, the Bedouins in southern Palestine, and other topics prior to the Nakba. During the Mandate, he was among the prominent Palestinian leaders known for nationalist activities.[23] His six-volume work expresses the Palestinian point of view on their calamity shortly after it occurred. Since the author depended heavily on his diaries, he chose to present events chronologically, beginning with the partition decision of November 1947.

There are several common denominators among the early publications on the Nakba. Despite some differences in reading and analysis, the authors agree on Britain's principal role in the Nakba of Palestine, and that other states, such as the United States and the Soviet Union, contributed to the Palestinian calamity. They also agree that there was an imbalance of forces favoring the Jewish side compared to the weakness and disparity of the motives among the Arabs. In the rest of this chapter we shall present a new reading of the point of view of the Palestinians who remained in their country and were not expelled in 1948. This brief review does not constitute an alternative to the ample literature on the history of the cause, but simply provides the groundwork for analyzing and understanding the opinions of those who remained.

THE BEGINNING OF THE NAKBA

Palestinians saw in British policy, exemplified in the Balfour Declaration, support for the beginning of a Zionist colonial aggression. The British promise to the leaders of the Zionist movement that "His Majesty's government view with favour the establishment of a national home for the Jewish people . . ." was a strong blow to the national rights of the Palestinian majority. Issuing such a pledge while disregarding the right of the Arabs in Palestine to self-determination, and making this the basis of British mandatory policy, laid the cornerstone for the Nakba. The Palestinians—overwhelmed by the ramifications of the geopolitical changes affecting the Arab region at the beginning of the Mandate—had not yet crystalized an organized national movement. This left them unable to thwart that policy, endorsed later by the League of Nations,[24] which enabled Jewish settlers to establish the institutions of their future state while preventing Palestinians from undertaking their own state-building process.

The history of the Palestinian cause during the British Mandate does not need to be reviewed here, except to point out the second event along the road to the Palestinian calamity, the years of revolution, 1936–39.[25] In addition to the disastrous results of that revolt for Palestinian society and its economy, we must highlight the partition proposal of 1937, which was the first proposal for a part of Palestine to be sliced off to create a Zionist state. The worst aspect of that proposal was that the rest of Palestine would be placed under Jordanian Hashemite rule rather than become an independent Palestinian state. The disdain for Palestinian demands, as seen in proposing Prince Abdullah as the ruler of that area, was a harbinger of plans by Britain and other colonialist powers. Consequently, the revolt was renewed after the Peel Commission partition proposal, causing Britain to retreat partially, and issue the MacDonald White Paper of May 1939. In the end, the lessons of the results of the 1936 revolt were not adequately absorbed by the Palestinian leadership.[26]

The Palestinians and their leaders had an absolute conviction about the righteousness of their cause, as they were the indigenous population of the country and the absolute majority of its population up to 1947. However, the discourse concerning justice and rights blinded them to seeing international and Arab political interests. The results of World War II and the onset of the Cold War between the United States and the Soviet Union altered the contours of the international scene. The defeat of the Arabs in the corridors of the United Nations, which took it upon itself to determine the future of Palestine following the end of the British Mandate, had already begun and the 1947 partition plan was worse than its predecessor of a decade earlier.[27] When that resolution won a two-thirds majority in the United Nations General Assembly, the calamity that was to befall the Palestinians had already begun. General Assembly Resolution 181 of 29 November 1947 constituted a decisive defeat of the right of the Palestinian people to self-determination on the entirety of its national soil. It was expected that the Palestinians would not accept this unjust resolution, which gave 54 percent of their homeland to the Jews and gave them, who constituted two-thirds of the population, only 45 percent.[28]

Political defeat after the issuance of the UN partition resolution did not alter the convictions of Arab and Palestinian leaders, who continued to make threats. This position failed to lead to a close examination of the consequences of the rejection of the UN resolution or to present an alternative that was acceptable to the world community of states. Some Palestinian leaders became active in Arab capitals mobilizing support for the Palestinian cause. The Jewish side, on the other hand, understood all too well the meaning of the resolution, which gave it a green light to establish a state in Palestine at the end of 1947 with the support of the Western and socialist camps. Britain began to prepare for its withdrawal from Palestine at the end of 1947 and to guarantee its interests in the region through its relations with Jordan and its king. With that, the drums of war began to beat while the Palestinians lacked a united leadership or the preparedness for the decisive war.

The Arab advantage over the Jews in Palestine was purely demographic. The Jewish community in Palestine (Yishuv) had superiority over the Palestinians in all fields that decide the outcome of any struggle, including the military battle. However, the Palestinian leadership, which was aware of the unfavorable balance of power, could not accept the unjust partition resolution. Being content to say "no" without presenting acceptable alternatives put it in the position of the aggressor, and the Jewish side appeared to be the victim who was threatened with annihilation at the hands of neighboring Arab states. Despite their resounding utterances, these states were not prepared for a military battle in Palestine, nor were they united in their opinions as to what needed to be done. The Palestinians found themselves being propelled into battle without preparation and with neither a unified command nor sufficient awareness of what was happening in the corridors of the Arab League.

The Jewish side and its leaders were well aware of the fact that the Palestinians were not prepared for war. In a meeting between Ben-Gurion and experts on Arab affairs, Eliyahu Sasson estimated that the mufti had mobilized "between two and three hundred fighters, and this figure has doubled or tripled today."[29] There was a consensus among experts about Sasson's figures, and they confirmed the unpreparedness of the Palestinians for war, and that they faced an arms shortage. The Jewish side was also aware of internal Palestinian differences between the mufti and his rivals. The gathering estimated that, in addition to King Abdullah, it was possible to benefit from the rivals of the mufti in Nablus and Jenin and other places to weaken Palestinian ranks. It is glaringly obvious from Sasson's remarks that the Jewish side had connections with some leaders of Jaffa as well, and by way of example he mentioned Nimr al-Hawwari, the leader of al-Najjada, who kept the town quiet until he was obliged to leave in December 1947, adding that "disturbances started" after the latter's departure.[30]

The Palestinian leadership directed the decisive war for the future of Palestine from outside the country, despite the criticism that this decision elicited,[31] which fell on deaf ears. The events of that decisive war rolled on without a united leadership or a clear plan. Dr. Husayn al-Khalidi and Ahmad Hilmi 'Abd al-Baqi, who were in Jerusalem, tried to convince the rest of the Higher Arab Committee members to return to the country, but to no avail. The Palestinian leadership declared a general strike for three days (2–4 December 1947) in protest against the partition plan, which was unjust to the indigenous population of the country. This strike and the skirmishes that accompanied it reminded people of the events of the 1936 revolt.[32]

The categorization of the early skirmishes between Arabs and Jews as a revolt rather than a war had disastrous consequences for the Palestinians. This image was shared by leading social cadres who understood the bloody events as another link in the chain of previous revolts. Al-Sakakini himself, who saw with his own eyes the events in al-Qatamun and neighboring quarters in western Jerusalem, was pessimistic, and even despaired of Palestinian military capabilities compared to the Jewish side. He writes: "By God, I do not know if we can endure in the face of the aggression of the Jews, considering that they are trained and organized and united and equipped with the most modern arms, while we are none of those things. It is high time that we learned that unity wins over division, that organization overcomes chaos. . . ."[33] These words, penned by al-Sakakini in the early days of 1948, were a truthful expression of the large disparity in the capabilities of the two sides to the Palestinian-Israeli conflict.[34]

The eventful year of 1948 is one of the most frequent topics studied on both sides of the Palestinian-Israeli divide. This book is not attempting to rewrite the history of the 1948 war in Palestine, but to draw the broad outlines of the events in the north of the country. These events may be divided into three stages, which differ according to the policies pursued towards the Palestinians and their conduct in the months of war and afterwards. This chapter and the next will tell the story of those who managed to stay in the Galilee. The Zionist leadership had been planning to expel the Arabs of Palestine from the land of the Jewish state since the late 1930s at least. What then is the explanation for why a relatively large number of Palestinians remained in the Galilee compared to the center and the south of the country? To answer this question in depth, we shall closely examine the differences in geography, the periods of occupation, and Israeli policies, as well as the reactions of the Arab population and their conduct during the various stages of the war.

The three active stages of the war in Palestine, and the Galilee in particular, were:

—from early December 1947 to late March 1948
—from early April to late July 1948
—the completion of the occupation of the Galilee (Operation Hiram) from late
   October to December 1948

In the first stage of the war the gap in preparedness between Palestinians and Jews was not apparent due to the defensive policy adopted by the Haganah. The presence of British forces in parts of the country during that period played a role in the adoption of that tactic, as did the desire not to provoke a comprehensive reaction on the part of the Arabs. Despite that, when the Haganah chose to mount military operations, it became apparent that the Palestinian citizens were exposed and had no effective protection. One of the first operations was directed at the village of Khisas, north of Hula Lake, and was conducted by the Palmach on 18 December 1947. A dozen residents of the village were killed, including some children. The blowing up of houses and the killings caused panic to spread among the villagers and the inhabitants of neighboring villages as well, so that hundreds took flight and went about searching for a refuge for their families in Syria. This operation provoked some protests and even criticism among Jewish security institutions, but the clear effect of the operation on the panic-stricken Arab residents of the Hula region was considered to be an important achievement.[35]

The Khisas village operation was neither alone nor unique among Haganah and Palmach operations against peaceful Arab residents in their homes, but it continued to concern Israeli public opinion for several years because of the friendly relations between some villagers and neighboring Jewish settlements.[36] Dozens of residents of the village, under the leadership of Shaykh 'Atiyeh Juwayyid and his sons, did not leave their village in the hope that the Jews would not forget the services they had rendered to Jewish settlers in the region. Some members of 'Atiyeh Juwayyid's family along with their neighbors, the 'Arab al-Hayb, had in early 1948 fought on the side of the Jews against their Arab brethren. But even that did not spare them from expulsion at the end of that same year. Contrary to what happened to the majority of residents on the Lebanese border strip, members of that family were moved to the interior of Israel, and all political and legal attempts to permit their return to their homes and their lands failed, as we shall see below.[37]

To spur Palestinians to leave their cities and villages was an objective that the Jewish side implemented as part of the Zionist operation to uproot and occupy. The Zionists had two cherished objectives: fewer Arabs in the country and more land in the hands of the settlers. The argument between so-called extremists and moderates was not about fundamental differences, but rather a question of the timing and evaluation of the negative consequences of some terrorist activities carried out by Jewish organizations. Indeed, at the end of December 1947 there were several attacks on Arab villages in the middle of the country, particularly in the vicinity of major cities where there were concentrations of Jews. This happened in the Haifa district in the zone allocated to the Jewish state according to the partition plan, and the Arab residents of the city and neighboring villages suffered from the terror of those attacks.

In Haifa and its vicinity Arabs and Jews lived in relative peace and worked together in factories and government institutions. The city was also known for the rise of labor organizations which engaged in common class struggles. However, these good relations between the two sides were gradually undermined after the issuance of the partition plan and the start of skirmishes and acts of violence. Indeed, good neighborly relations and peaceful coexistence turned into bloody clashes at the end of 1947, most significantly in the events at the oil refinery, then the attack by the Palmach on the village of Balad al-Shaykh and the Hawwasa quarter in the first week of 1948. Palmach operations in these two areas once again demonstrated the superiority of the organized Jewish forces to the Palestinian side, by mobilizing their organized forces, taking the initiative and catching the Arabs by surprise, attacking Arab villages and quarters, and then withdrawing without suffering major casualties.

On 30 December 1947, the oil refinery in Haifa was the scene of bloody clashes with dozens of dead and injured workers. The events began with the Irgun organization (Irgun Zva'I Leumi [IZL or Etzel]) throwing one or more bombs at Arab workers who were gathering at the gate of the refinery before work, and rumors spread quickly that there were dozens of dead and wounded.[38] Arab workers inside the refinery retaliated with a fierce and bloody attack on Jewish workers, using their tools and iron bars and whatever else was at hand, killing a large number of Jewish workers, greater than the number of Arabs who had been killed that morning. A number of Arab employees at the refinery lived in the village of Balad al-Shaykh and a shanty town called Hawwasa to the northeast of the city of Haifa. The Haganah quickly decided to mount a revenge operation, and a Palmach (strike force) unit was chosen to carry it out in the village of Balad al-Shaykh.

After midnight of the new year, the Palmach unit carried out an attack on the village from the east, using firearms and grenades, which resulted in dozens of dead and wounded among the residents who were asleep in their homes. This attack and others on Hawwasa and neighboring Arab quarters caused a wave of panic and confusion among the Arab residents of Haifa, some of whom were laborers who had come from villages in the Galilee to work in the city and had taken up residence in those quarters. In the wake of these bloody attacks in the first week of 1948, many workers decided to return to their homes and villages in the Galilee.[39] Some well-to-do families moved to Nazareth and Shafa ʿAmr, and even to Beirut and other Arab cities outside Palestine.

These bloody attacks on unarmed Arab citizens completely contradict the image which Israel succeeded in marketing at the beginning of the war. The two operations in the village of Khisas in eastern Galilee and in the village of Balad al-Shaykh near Haifa were part of a blueprint to terrorize Palestinians in the areas allocated to the Jewish state in order to drive them to leave.[40] In fact, Palestinian migration from the areas in which those acts took place increased rapidly. It later became apparent by the end of the 1948 war that the vast majority of Palestinians living in the areas allocated for the Jewish state, according to the partition resolution, had become refugees, and only a small percentage remained.[41] That was the situation in eastern Galilee and along the coast from Haifa in the north to Tel Aviv in the south, and in the Marj ibn ʿAmir area and other places. This topic relating to the geography of who became refugees and who remained in 1948 is very important, and one to which we shall return later.

The National Committee for the Arab residents of Haifa, under the leadership of Rashid al-Hajj Ibrahim, attempted to stem the departure of Palestinian residents from their quarters, and to bolster their ability to defend themselves, to no avail. This committee went so far at times as to opt for the departure of women and children from the city, moving them to safe areas in the country or even outside, particularly in Lebanon. In this stage of the war (the first quarter of 1948), the Arab population of large mixed cities paid an exorbitant price, with hundreds killed and thousands wounded. Despite the fact that the Jewish side lost similar numbers of dead and wounded, the morale among Palestinians was worse due to the weak organization and the absence of effective leadership on their side. It was therefore natural that the families of some of the elite and members of the upper middle class, who had the means and financial resources, should distance themselves from the areas of combat and leave the country. Since their understanding of war at the time was in terms of rebellions and revolutions, the idea of distancing oneself from dangerous areas and then returning sometime later was usual and acceptable to most people.

Zionist leaders used various ways to encourage Palestinians to migrate, by propagating rumors on the one hand and by passing on "advice" to mayors, mukhtars, and local leaders to leave the country temporarily, on the other. When Palestinian migrants began to realize what was happening, Israeli state institutions prevented the return of those people to their homes and lands using various ways and means. The Zionist forces and, after 15 May, the leaders of the Jewish state, did not make much distinction between residents of villages and cities, nor between areas allocated to the Jewish state and those outside the limits of that state that fell under their occupation. In this way entire Arab quarters in Jerusalem, Haifa, and Jaffa were emptied, as were many neighboring villages in the first quarter of 1948. Migration increased in the spring when the superiority of Jewish forces became glaringly obvious as well as their success in severing transportation links between Arab Haifa and the cities and villages of the Galilee. Tens of thousands of the residents of Haifa migrated before the fall of the city and its occupation on 22 April 1948.

Among those who migrated from Haifa before it fell: the brothers Nadim and Jamal Musa, who reached 'Akka by sea and went on from there to the village of al-Bi'na in mid-Galilee;[42] the brothers Kamal and Jamil Ghattas, who went to the village of al-Rama; and the brothers Anton and Jibra'il Bishara, who returned to their village of Tarshiha in upper Galilee.[43] The stories of these and other members of the National Liberation League, and details of what happened to their villages, will be told in the next chapter. Importantly, the events and fate of Haifa had a strong impact on the residents of the Galilee, particularly those who worked and lived there, even if not for very long. The events of the village of Balad al-Shaykh and the Hawwasa quarter as well as other Arab quarters, which were subjected to repeated bombardment and attacks, caused thousands of families to lose the sources of their livelihood in that city.

As of January 1948, groups of Arab volunteers were organized in what became known as the Arab Rescue Army (ARA), and served as an addition to the Palestinian fighting force.[44] The entry of hundreds of fighters into Palestine was a morale booster for the Palestinians in the areas where clashes took place. The Arab side was successful in paralyzing traffic in the streets, and took a heavy toll on Jewish caravans in the Galilee and the Jerusalem districts. The Palestinians were able to cut transportation lines between Jerusalem and the coastal plain; Haganah forces tried to reopen them but several initial attacks mounted on Bab al-Wad failed. For a brief period, it looked like the Palestinians had achieved some success and had undermined Jewish confidence in their military superiority. This military situation in the field caused the U.S. State Department to rethink the capability of the Yishuv to establish a state and defend it. Consequently, some states considered the possibility of ignoring the partition resolution and establishing a UN trusteeship in February 1948. This proposal was a political blow to the Jewish side, and an achievement for Palestinians who wanted the world to reverse the resolution to divide their homeland.[45]

At this critical juncture, the Soviet Union chose to declare its firm position in favor of the partition resolution and the immediate establishment of a Jewish state. It did not just provide political support for the Zionist side, but made sure that Czechoslovakia would conclude and expedite an arms deal. Ben-Gurion, who quickly grasped the consequences of backtracking on partition, decided to change the rules of combat in the field before the United Nations could agree to a trusteeship regime. He called an emergency meeting of military commanders and ordered that Operation Nachshon be launched in the mountains of Jerusalem. That same evening, 31 March 1948, a Czech plane landed in Bayt Daras airport containing the first batch of arms: machine guns, rifles, and ammunition.[46] These modern arms reinforced the capabilities of the attacking Jewish forces. What had appeared as a weakness in the capabilities of the Haganah relative to the Palestinians was a miscalculation based on the tactics of defense employed by the Jewish leadership. When it became apparent that delaying the assault would be very costly, orders were issued for the implementation of Plan Dalet and for the offensive to begin.

PLAN DALET AND THE ONSET OF THE ARAB DEFEAT IN APRIL 1948

For some historians Plan Dalet was clear proof of an Israeli policy to occupy the country and expel the population, that is, ethnic cleansing.[47] This study, which revolves around the Palestinians remaining in Israel after the war, will not contest the meaning of that plan and its significance for the policy of ethnic cleansing. The action of killing Palestinians in their homes by the dozen and spreading terror to push them to emigrate from the country began at the end of 1947, while the policy of expulsion itself continued even after hostilities ceased in early 1949. There is a consensus among virtually all researchers that the Zionist community was trying to bring about a Jewish majority in the state as a top priority. The war which began as local skirmishes in late 1947 provided an opportunity to expel the population of the Palestinian areas who had no military protection against Jewish attacks; this led to Palestinian migration beginning several months before Plan Dalet had crystalized in March 1948.

The implementation of the plan in the field, begun in early April, represented a new phase in the Palestine war with disastrous consequences for the occupation of Arab cities and villages, such as Tiberias and Haifa and their vicinities. Up until early April the number of those killed on each side was less than one thousand, and a few thousand wounded; it had been akin to a civil war with lim-ited damages and destruction until Plan Dalet was implemented. The occupation of Tiberias and the expulsion of its entire population in mid-April, followed by the fall of Haifa and the forcing of tens of thousands of panicked Palestinians to flee the city was a major shock and brought a dawning awareness of the defeat. The uprooting of the Arab residents of Haifa (and Tiberias before that) in full view of the British was an important juncture in the war in northern Palestine. In the following pages we shall review some details of these important events and their consequences for the Palestinians in Haifa and the Galilee.

Not far from the events in Tiberias, a famous battle took place between the two parties to the conflict in the villages of Husha and al-Kasayir southwest of the town of Shafa 'Amr, in which dozens of fighters from both sides were killed. But the more significant result of this battle was the decision of the Arab battalion, which was made up of Druze fighters under the leadership of Shakib Wahhab, to stop fighting the Jews and withdraw from the battlefield in agreement with the Zionist side; this constituted an important juncture in the events of the war in the Galilee. The Jerusalemite historian 'Arif al-'Arif makes a distinction in his history between Arab and Druze fighters,[48] which clearly reflects the tense relations between the Druze minority and the other sects in Palestinian society. Al-'Arif set aside several pages of his book *The Catastrophe of Jerusalem and the Lost Paradise 1947–49* for a discussion of this significant battle. We shall return later to this topic and to the decision by Shakib Wahhab and the rest of the Druze elders to withdraw from the battles against the Jews.[49]

From the beginning of the implementation of Plan Dalet, the superiority of Jewish military forces over the Palestinian fighters was crystal clear. Offensive military operations began in the mountains around Jerusalem. Two events that occurred within a short time had a huge impact on the Palestinians, and revealed the weakness of their organization: the first was the martyrdom of 'Abd al-Qadir al-Husayni in al-Qastal on 8 April 1948.[50] The killing of this prominent commander at that stage of the war exposed the weakness of the military political leadership and how little organization there was, as well as the scarcity of arms in the hands of the Palestinians. The occupation of al-Qastal also crowned the operation to open the road to Bab al-Wad (Operation Nachshon) and the breaking of the siege on Jewish quarters in west Jerusalem.

Before the Arabs could recover from the killing of al-Husayni, the second pain-ful blow came the next day. Not far from al-Qastal, the Irgun (Etzel) and terrorist Lohame Herut Yisrael (LHI/Lehi or Stern) gangs carried out a treacherous attack on the peaceful village of Dayr Yasin, killing and wounding hundreds of men, women, and children.[51] When news carried the details of the massacre, including the mutilation and burning of corpses and the humiliation and torture of hun-dreds of prisoners, panic and a sense of insecurity spread through Palestinian ranks. These two events in the region of Jerusalem represented the beginning of the Palestinian defeat, which ended with the destruction of the country and the dislocation of its population. They acquired symbolic significance in the history of Palestine: the first referring to sacrifice and martyrdom, and the second referring to the barbarism of the Zionist side and the victimization of the Palestinians. These events in the mountains of Jerusalem had a huge impact on Palestinian morale throughout the entire country; the martyrdom of 'Abd al-Qadir al-Husayni, a relative of the mufti and his nominee for the leadership of the war effort, had a very deep impact, as did the exaggeration of the news of the massacre in Dayr Yasin and its wide circulation.

Less than one week after these painful events in the Jerusalem mountains, the Jewish assault moved to the north of the country. In the same month, the Galilee witnessed military events which had a decisive impact on the course of the battles. The Arab Rescue Army's attempt to occupy kibbutz Mishmar Ha'emek failed and was followed by a counterattack by the Haganah which demonstrated the weakness of Arab fighting capabilities. In this attack several villages in Marj ibn 'Amir were occupied and their residents all expelled. At the same time, the Jewish side began operations in Tiberias to occupy the city and the villages in its district, having prior to that attacked the village of Nasir al-Din to the southwest (on the Nazareth-Tiberias road) and killed dozens of its defenders and civilians. The news of that massacre, carried by the survivors who reached Tiberias, had a heavy effect on the morale of the Arab residents of the city.

Most of the six thousand Palestinians from Tiberias reached Syria and Lebanon; only a few hundred residents were allowed to head west and seek refuge in Nazareth. One week after the fall of Tiberias, it was Haifa's turn. This blow was worse than the one before, because most of the seventy thousand residents of the city, along with the residents of nearby villages, were forced to leave. The fact that this occurred under the eyes of the British forces played an important role in the uprooting of the population of one of the most important Palestinian cities. By the end of April, Palestinian determination and morale had crumbled, and they were waiting impatiently for the armies of Arab states to arrive by mid-May to save them from their mounting tragedy. But Jaffa fell before the Arab armies arrived and most of its population was uprooted, as happened in Haifa. These events in important Palestinian cities and their environs demonstrated to all parties concerned the power superiority of the Jewish side, and the ease with which Arab cities and municipalities could be occupied and their residents expelled in the absence of a deterrent.

The fall of Haifa made Palestinians in the Galilee profoundly aware. The occupation of a city of that size and the expulsion of its population in one week within sight of the British troops stationed there made the residents aware of the enormity of the disaster which was befalling the Palestinian people. Ben-Gurion received a report of what was happening in Haifa after its occupation and recorded some of it in his diary,[52] which reflected the Zionist narrative of events. Historical research in recent decades has brought to light new facts which show the complex and diverse aspects of the events in Haifa. Nevertheless, we shall make use of what is recorded in Ben-Gurion's diary on 1 May: "There are now less than ten thousand [Palestinians] in Haifa, perhaps six thousand."[53] He added: "There is an Arab committee in the city: Farid al-Sa'd [manager of the Arab Bank]; George Tawil, a municipal officer; George Mu'ammar; Jiryis Khoury (municipal employee); the lawyer Kusa (who is a deputy public prosecutor); Farid Nasr (a Christian); and Victor Khayat— a very rich man."[54]

Elias Kusa was a member of the Arab delegation that went to see British General Hugh Stockwell on 22 April 1948 to try to secure a cease-fire and save the Arab residents of Haifa. He himself saw the departure of tens of thousands of panic-stricken Palestinians from the city. He recorded in a letter that the mayor of Haifa had distributed a circular to the population calling on them not to leave the city, but he stressed that this circular had no effect because Haganah fighters were at that time raining bullets and grenades on the Arab quarters and using force to push families to the port where ships were waiting to take them away. In the case of Haifa, as in other cases in 1948, the great gap between the statements and the actions of the Zionist leadership were blatant, even as those leaders succeeded in marketing their telling of events. What happened in Haifa under the command of Abba Hushi and other leaders of Zionist parties and labor organizations is an example of cunning and conspiracy with Britain to expel the Palestinians from their country.

In Tiberias and Haifa districts, and later in Jaffa and elsewhere, Plan Dalet was operationalized to break the back of Palestinian society, to render it incapable of resisting the occupation, and to expel the population. The operation to kick out tens of thousands and later hundreds of thousands of Palestinians from their homes was an important strategic objective of the Zionist movement, leading to establishing its state on the ruins of Palestine. The seemingly uncertain defensive policy in the first quarter of 1948 was only a preparation while waiting for the suitable time to unleash the offensive plan. In Tiberias and its villages, for example, they lost no time tearing down Palestinian houses so that the Arabs would have nothing to go back to. When some did try to return, they were forcibly prevented from doing so. This policy was applied weeks prior to the entry of armies from the Arab states, and became the official government policy after the establishment of the state of Israel in mid-May; it was designed to prevent the return of the refugees and calculated to facilitate the expropriation of their lands and property. (The Hebrew press recently, on 26 May 2015, published news of the auction of a letter from Ben-Gurion to Abba Hushi in which he urged the latter to prevent the return of Arabs to Haifa.)

Palestinians migrated by land and by sea from Haifa to 'Akka and from there to Lebanon and Syria, but a few thousand came to Nazareth, Shafa 'Amr and other villages in the Galilee. Bulus Farah, one of the most prominent leaders of the National Liberation League during the British Mandate, relates in his memoirs the difficult circumstances in Haifa after its fall, and how he left the city to go to Nazareth. During his stay in Nazareth, he heard from Tawfiq Tubi "that the Jews were forcing stores open and pillaging their contents . . . and that in two or three days they would come to my bookstore and empty it of its contents."[55] Farah describes how he went back to Haifa to save his bookstore, and how he managed to reopen it with the help of some Jewish friends. However, he was not able to return to his home on al-Anbiya' Street, recounting that the invaders who had taken it over chased him away with shouts and curses. Bulus Farah, then, became a member of the Palestinian minority which stayed in Haifa but were pushed into the Wadi al-Nisnas quarter which soon became known as the ghetto.[56]

Days after the fall of Haifa and the migration of most of its Arab residents, the Jewish side began its assault on a second important coastal city, Jaffa. Unlike Haifa, the vast majority of the residents of Jaffa were Arabs. However, Tel Aviv, which was established nearby, had eclipsed the Arab city for some time. Despite the presence of Palestinian villages in its vicinity whose residents helped the people of Jaffa, the city and its villages became a pocket surrounded by Jewish settlements. The Jaffa district was allocated to the Palestinian state, according to the partition resolution. When the Irgun began to attack it, the British feared being accused once again of colluding with the Haganah to empty Arab cities of their residents. They intervened militarily in a conspicuous way to prevent its fall to the Jews a week after the fall of Haifa. On 28 April, British forces made a military parade of their intervention against the belligerent forces, and indeed the Irgun was forced out of al-Manshiyya quarter in the north of Jaffa. This intervention did not save the "Bride of the Sea"—Jaffa—from its fate, but it did allow the British to save face, until they withdrew from the district shortly thereafter.

The majority of Palestinians were convinced that their city would not endure for long in the face of encroaching Zionist forces, so they continued to migrate by land and sea to flee the killing and destruction. At the beginning the British did not try to stem the tide of migration or to calm the fright of innocent citizens;[57] all they wanted was not to be accused anew of collaborating with the Jewish side. The fact is that the small Irgun gang (and not the Haganah) was the group that had attacked Jaffa, which made it easy for the British to put on a military show. After relative calm returned to the city, the British encouraged the remaining Arab leadership in the city to sign a surrender agreement with the Haganah on 13 May. And so Jaffa fell, and the Jewish state was established on the evening of the following day in Tel Aviv in a section of Palestine that spilled over the borders of the state according to the partition resolution. In the middle of that month, Israel stood on two steady legs astride the developed coastal cities, with its back open to the sea and the West that supported it. As for Palestinian society, it had reached almost total collapse and fragmentation, and was awaiting the entry of the regular armies of Arab states to protect what was left of Palestine.

When the establishment of Israel was declared on the evening of 15 May 1948 as a state for the Jews, only a small number of the Palestinians who had previously lived in the areas taken over by the Jews were left. From eastern Galilee to the Syrian-Lebanese border, passing through Tiberias and Bisan and Marj ibn 'Amir, then Haifa and the coastal area to Jaffa, only a small number of villages inhabited by a few thousand Palestinians were left, in addition to a similar number in Haifa and in Jaffa. Most of the four hundred thousand Palestinians who lived in those areas had become refugees before the intervention of the Arab armies began. The rest who remained in their homes and villages until the end of the war were the 'Arab al-Hayb in Tuba al-Zanghariyya in eastern Galilee, as well as the residents of the small al-Zu'biyya villages east of 'Afula due to the collaboration of their leader with the Haganah. In Jabal al-Karmil, there remained most of the residents of the Druze villages of 'Isfiya and Daliyyat al-Karmil. Thus, the vast majority of Palestinians were expelled, leaving a small number who had demonstrated their loyalty to the Jewish side during the war, or even before.

The Arab armies reached the battlefronts in the middle and the south of the country in May 1948, but not in the Galilee. The attempted attacks by the Syrian army in the early months of the war in Palestine were repulsed. The small Lebanese army did not try to cross the international border to participate in the war. The Arab Rescue Army, which had demonstrated its ineffectuality in April, became the butt of jokes by the population because of its unpreparedness and its showy maneuvers which could not withstand any attack by the Haganah. In other words, the Galilee's situation was different from the situation in the center and south of the country because of the absence of regular armies which could be relied on. The residents, then, had an important role to play in their districts in defending their cities alongside Arab volunteers. This special situation of the residents of the Galilee was well known to the inhabitants, and had a considerable influence on their conduct and performance in the second half of 1948.

Indeed, as of May, the concern of many residents of the Galilee was how to stay in their homes and on their land. The fall of Tiberias, Haifa, 'Akka, and many villages in their districts as well as the expulsion of the populations of those villages increased people's fear about their future and their trust in the abilities of the Arab Rescue Army declined.[58] Under these circumstances, when defenseless citizens found themselves facing an escalating tragedy, it became a question of practical survival for the residents of the Galilee, rather than a war to save Palestine and prevent the establishment of a Jewish state. This awareness of the dimension of the tragedy and the responsibility that had to be borne by defenseless citizens created a new orientation which amounted to the need to hold onto home and land far from the slogans of the national elite, who had not prepared their people for a war of destiny.

THE NAKBA AS SEEN AND EXPERIENCED
BY THE RESIDENTS OF THE GALILEE

At the beginning of the summer of 1948, the experience of the disaster differed from one district to the other. Not all Palestinians, particularly the refugees among them, whose number was estimated at the time at 400,000 or more, experienced events in the same way. The meaning of the Nakba for the urban elite in Haifa, Jaffa, and Jerusalem differed from the meaning for the *fellahin* whose lives were completely destroyed by the loss of their homes, lands, and means of living. Whereas the well-to-do classes from the cities had social and cultural ties with the residents of the cities where they migrated, *fellahin* were forced to live in tents and shanties. The loss of their homeland had a different dimension for them, economically and socially, than it did for the elite. They were transformed overnight from owners of homes and lands which supported them into refugees comparable to indigents, who lived on Arab and international charity.

In July, the differences between what residents of different areas of Palestine experienced became apparent. In the center and south of the country, Lydda and Ramla and villages in their district were occupied and emptied of all their inhabitants during the very hot days of the month of Ramadan. Israel did not spare a single village in occupying this area and expelled tens of thousands of the inhabitants. The picture was different in western Galilee, and even more so in lower Galilee; apart from the tens of thousands of Palestinians who were expelled from ʿAkka and neighboring coastal villages, a few thousand managed to remain in place. But what is more important is the survival of dozens of villages to the east of ʿAkka in western Galilee, as well as Nazareth and its environs. Who were those survivors, and how were they able to escape being uprooted after the occupation?

Some Israeli historians have used the fact that many Palestinians in the Galilee managed to remain to support their claim of there being no comprehensive Israeli plan of expulsion.[59] On the other side, those historians who affirmed that Plan Dalet was the basis for the comprehensive policy of ethnic cleansing did not try to explain why tens of thousands remained in northern Palestine. Researchers from both sides, as we said, focused on Israeli policy to explain the fate of the refugees. This study, however, chooses to stress the story of those who stayed behind and to focus on their conduct, and the crystallization of their awareness that they had to remain in their homes regardless of Israeli attempts to uproot them.[60] The story of endurance, particularly in Haifa and the Galilee, is complex and varied and one should not try to flatten it. All of the points of light and shadow need to be studied.

An examination of the literature on the Nakba and the 1948 Palestine war shows that most researchers assumed that the two sides to the conflict adhered to nationalist positions which guided their actions. Whereas this may be largely true in the case of the Jewish settler society, which was fully mobilized to participate in the war effort, it does not apply to all of the Palestinian people. Alongside the growing nationalist consciousness among the urban elite and the revolutionary villagers who participated in the events of the 1930s, pre-nationalist (ethnic, sectarian, tribal, and other) identities were still strongly rooted among Palestinians. While Zurayk was searching for the meaning and causes of the Nakba from a comprehensive nationalist perspective, thousands of Palestinians were busy trying to ensure that they could remain and to halt the migration and expulsion drive that was encroaching on their towns. Those who faced the calamity unarmed did what they could to ensure they could stay and save their families and their homes from destruction. Their understanding of the Nakba in the early summer of 1948 was pragmatic, rather than intellectual or philosophical. These multiple interpretations, even if they did share in describing the enormity of the catastrophe, led to disparate practical conclusions.[61]

The task of protecting the Galilee fell on the shoulders of the volunteers in the Arab Rescue Army and the local residents. The interpretation by the people of the Galilee of the Palestinian tragedy and the possibility of stopping it was different than the reading by the residents of Jerusalem and Gaza. The Arab volunteers and the people of the Galilee who were defending their towns lacked the most basic military preparedness to face the organized Israeli army, who had been equipped with the latest weapons which poured in from Czechoslovakia and other countries. As we mentioned earlier, units of the Israeli army experienced no difficulty in mounting offensive operations against Arab positions when it was ordered to occupy the north of the country. As for the citizens, they found themselves without any reliable defensive capabilities and facing an army. The different situation compared to the situation in the center and south of the country was no secret to the residents of the Galilee and formed part of their consciousness concerning the calamity they faced.[62]

One term for the occupation of Arab cities and villages that became widespread was "the fall." In describing events, people said, "when the country fell," as though it were a ripe fruit on a branch that only needed the tree trunk to be shaken to fall to the ground. Most people did not speak of "war" because the majority took no part in real battles, nor were they prepared to do so in the first place. The author of *Bab al-Shams* (*Gate of the Sun*) expressed the sentiments of the people of the Galilee best through the characters of his novel. Yunis says from his hospital bed, "By God, it was no war, it was like a dream." He then adds: "Son, don't believe that the Jews won the war of '48. We did not fight in '48, we didn't know how. They won because we did not fight. They too did not fight: they just won, and it was like a dream."[63] Alongside the collapse and the destruction, there was a loss of confidence in leaders who asked the *fellahin* and simple folk to fight and be steadfast without preparing them to face this unexpected catastrophe.

Many residents of the Galilee began to comprehend the true balance of power between the two sides to the conflict after the fall of Haifa near the end of April, followed by the entry of the armies of Arab states and then their agreement to a ceasefire after just a short period of fighting. The Druze in Jabal al-Karmil and along the coast, the communists in the National Liberation League, and other local leaders in the Galilee decided to end their participation in the "theater of war." They declared they were withdrawing from the fight against the Jews to prevent the establishment of a Jewish state in Palestine, and the stand they took had a huge impact on the conduct of the Israeli army in Shafa 'Amr, then in Nazareth and the surrounding villages in the ten-day battles of July. The withdrawal of the Arab Rescue Army from Nazareth, for example, left the city and its district defenseless in the confrontation with the Israeli army. We shall return later in this chapter to the subject of the fall of Nazareth and the circumstances of the surrender of the leaders of the city.

The Palestinian national leadership under the mufti lost what remained of its reputation and stature after the entry of the regular Arab armies to fight in Palestine. Hajj Amin al-Husayni and many of his aides and others close to him were far from the helm of the sinking Palestinian ship. From their positions far from the battlefield they asked the Palestinians to stand fast before the enemy, but when it became apparent that the Arab states and their armies were unable to save Palestine, the Palestinians realized the magnitude of the catastrophe. Consequently, naïve faith in the triumph of Palestinian rights began to shrink in the face of the expanding tragedy, and was replaced by a sense of frustration, disarray, and failed trust in the national leaderships. Against the background of this change in consciousness, some Palestinians decided to join the victors to ensure their survival. Thus, while many Palestinians sided with King Abdullah in the mountains of central Palestine, some in the mountains of the Galilee decided to accept Israeli rule, and even collaborated with Israel to ensure they could remain in the country.[64]

As history tells us, in times of catastrophes the dominant pre-catastrophe nationalist values recede in the face of the need for survival. As the value of social solidarity weakens other factional and tribal values come to the fore among groups trying to save themselves. In the Galilee, which the regular Arab armies never reached, and which was far from the hotbeds of the nationalist movement in Jerusalem and other cities, alternative local sectarian, tribal, and political leaderships consolidated their positions in the theater of events and took control to safeguard the survival of their collectivities. At the beginning, before the war, these groups had not been active in the Palestinian national movement, and did not participate in nationalist action or discourse. Prominent among those groups in the Galilee were the Druze, the communists, and some Bedouin tribes and rural clans.

We referred earlier to some 'Arab al-Hayb from Tuba al-Zanghariyya joining forces with the Haganah and fighting alongside the Jews against their Arab neighbors. Yitzhak Hankin mobilized and trained them to fight. In May 1948, for example, Bedouin recruits from this clan took part in the attacks on Syrian army camps, blew up bridges and engaged in other acts of sabotage in the Arab areas. They participated in attacks on their neighbors, the residents of the village of Fir'im, who had left their village after the Israeli army occupied it and were trying to return to it. Army reports mentioned that some 'Arab al-Hayb attacked the village, burned down its houses, and seized some farm animals and property.[65] A section of that clan continued to serve alongside the Israeli army in upper Galilee in information gathering and intelligence operations. Its members became active in the war that Israel launched against the refugees who were trying to return from Lebanon to their country; they set ambushes, attacked them, and stole their belongings, then expelled them for a second time beyond the borders.[66]

During July, Shafa 'Amr and its neighboring villages were occupied in the ten-day battles (8 to 18 July); those villages remained standing and their residents were not expelled. The same thing then happened in Nazareth and its neighboring villages. The Druze of Shafa 'Amr played an important role in the fall of their town; they were implementing a secret agreement which had been concluded earlier between officers of the Israeli army and some Druze leaders. On the basis of this agreement, which required the withdrawal of the Druze from the fight against the Jews, most of the fighters in the Arab battalion returned to their homes in Syria and Lebanon, while dozens joined the Israeli side in the war.[67] In return, the Israeli side guaranteed the Druze that their villages would not be subject to the maltreatment, killing, or destruction that Palestinian villages in the Galilee and other areas had suffered. In this way, Druze leaders guaranteed that their sect members could stay in the homes and on their lands, and they were also able to use their close ties with the Israeli side at times to help their Muslim and Christian neighbors.

Before the fall of Shafa 'Amr, members of the Ma'di family in Yarka played a role in helping the residents of neighboring villages to conclude surrender agreements. One, for example, was Kufr Yasif, which was inhabited by Christians, Muslims, and some Druze. Whereas the majority of the villages along the coast of 'Akka had their residents evicted after their occupation in May, the nearby Druze villages and some neighboring villages remained as they were. When fighting renewed after the end of the cease-fire, Yani Yani, head of the Kufr Yasif municipal council, took advantage of the relations of his Druze neighbors with the Jews to save residents of his village from being uprooted and expelled, and signed an agreement to that effect mediated by Haim Orbach from Nahariyya on 10 July. When the Israeli army entered the village, they commandeered one of the houses as a barracks for some of their soldiers. They expelled the refugees who had found refuge in Kufr Yasif, and dozens of young men of conscription age were arrested and placed in prisoner of war detention centers, despite the fact that the village had surrendered without resistance. Nevertheless, the residents of Kufr Yasif and neighboring villages, such as al-Makr, al-Jdayda, and Abu Snan, felt relief because their fate was better than that of coastal villages which had been totally evacuated.

The occupation of Nazareth on 16 July, and the fact that the city and its residents remained due to an agreement between the mayor and city notables, and the Israeli army, had special significance amidst the chain of events of the war and their destructive outcomes. Contrary to the disastrous and painful results just a week earlier in Lydda and Ramla, Ben-Gurion issued a clear order on the eve of the occupation of the city prohibiting the soldiers from attacking the residents of Nazareth and its holy places.[68] This military order by the prime minister and minister of defense was obeyed, so the residents of the city and most of its refugees remained in their homes and did not suffer theft, murder, and plunder. The activists in the Mapam party and its newspaper 'Al Hamishmar quickly noticed the different situation in Nazareth compared to other cities; they wrote much about the "occupation of hearts,"[69] contrary to what happened in Lydda, Ramla, Jaffa, Haifa, and other Arab cities.

The population of the Galilee were not under the influence of the mufti, and many of them supported his opponents. Most areas in the Galilee had been allocated to the Arab state according to the partition resolution, yet Israel began occupying more and more of the Galilee after the fall of 'Akka. The residents benefited from the fact that most areas of the Galilee were occupied in a late stage of the war, after they had learned about the Nakba events, which included the expulsion of hundreds of thousands of Palestinians by the summer of 1948, and the prevention of their return. They therefore searched for opportunities and the means to guarantee their continued existence in their homes and on their lands. The Palestinians had seen what happened in Lydda and Ramla prior to the occupation of Nazareth in terms of killing, destruction, and the forced expulsion of tens of thousands. Against this background of tragic events, the survival of Nazareth and its villages was a surprise and represented a distinctive event. The question we pose here is: how did the city escape the fate that befell other Palestinian cities, and why?

THE SECRET OF NAZARETH'S SURVIVAL AND ESCAPE FROM DESTRUCTION

Nazareth, as opposed to Tiberias, Safad, and Haifa, was an Arab city that was distant from the borders of the designated Jewish state. The Jews did not build settlements in its vicinity. Its position in the middle of the Galilee, far from the coastal plain and the strategic border areas, led to the postponement of its occupation and the Jewish domination of its district. Ben-Gurion and other leaders of the Jewish state were well aware of the religious significance of Nazareth for the Christian world in general and the Vatican in particular, which led to the decision to treat the inhabitants and the holy places with care and delicacy. As mentioned earlier, Nazareth had absorbed hundreds of Palestinian refugees from Tiberias, then Safad and Bisan. Perhaps the fact that the Jewish forces allowed those hundreds (the majority of whom were Christians) to go to Nazareth instead of Syria or Lebanon was an indication that the city of the Annunciation would probably have a different fate. The city was spared as a result of the convergence of factors of time and place as well as a top-level policy decision and the positions taken by various local leaders in the field.

Ben-Gurion's caution and sensitivity to the reactions of the Western world to the actions of the Jewish state are well known. A group of Jewish leaders shared his position, and indicated some time before the outbreak of war that it was important to behave with sensitivity towards three holy cities, namely Jerusalem, Bethlehem, and Nazareth. Jerusalem and Bethlehem were supposed to be part of the designated international zone. At any rate, Israel did not occupy either Arab Jerusalem or Bethlehem because the Jordanian army entered both districts and prevented their fall. However, Nazareth's situation was different, as it became a unique test of the conduct of the Israeli army regarding its residents and its holy places. When Israel began its military operations to occupy lower Galilee, it was clear that the Arab Rescue Army in Nazareth would be unable to protect the city and its district. Both the decision of the leader of the ARA unit to withdraw and the decision of Israel to behave differently in the case of this city that was sacred to Christians played an important role in sparing Nazareth from the fate of other Palestinian cities.

A number of Palestinian communist leaders who accepted the partition resolution in February 1948 lived and worked in Nazareth, and renewed their old relationships with their Jewish communist comrades and with activists in the Mapam party.[70] Furthermore, a number of opponents of the mufti, who had established cooperative relations with the Jews from the 1930s, lived in the city and its district. Prominent among them was Sayf al-Din al-Zu'bi, whom Israel set up as a leader of the Arabs in Israel after its establishment, as a reward for his services. The presence of many opponents of the mufti and his men in Nazareth, and their relationships with influential Jewish parties, were two other factors which contributed to protecting the city from destruction and its inhabitants from expulsion. Another contributing factor was the presence of priests, clergy, journalists, and employees of charitable institutions. Finally, the inhabitants of Nazareth escaped maltreatment and expulsion due to the actions of Israeli army officers, with Ben Dunkelman (who had Canadian citizenship) at their head, and due to the role played by city leaders who chose to act wisely and signed a surrender agreement.

Nazareth was occupied during the ten-day battles, according to the Zionist account of events. The Arab Rescue Army in the area was made up of a mixture of volunteers, and included a not insignificant number of Palestinians; one of its units was led by Mahmud al-Saffuri. Prior to the occupation of lower Galilee, the Israeli side had concluded an agreement with Shakib Wahhab and some local Druze leaders, according to which the Druze withdrew from the battle against the Jews, and in return Israel guaranteed that all their villages would be protected from harm.[71] The first practical test of this secret agreement was in the village of Shafa 'Amr, whose inhabitants did not suffer from maltreatment and expulsion.

This relatively benign approach to occupation indicated a different policy compared to the conduct of the Israel army days before in Lydda, Ramla, and all the villages of their district.[72]

The murder of dozens in the Dahmash mosque massacre in Lydda, and the subsequent expulsion of tens of thousands of the inhabitants of the city and of neighboring Ramla on a blistering hot Ramadan day (11–12 July), in addition to the pictures of refugees wending their way across valleys and mountains on their way to Ramallah and Jerusalem, inflamed sentiments.[73] Sharp criticisms were levelled at King Abdullah and his army, which had British officers, for their recalcitrance in providing assistance to the inhabitants of Lydda and Ramla despite their being stationed in nearby Latrun. The photos and articles published by the Arab and foreign press about the refugees and the forcibly expelled, and about the murder of dozens in the streets and in the Dahmash mosque, had a considerable impact on the political atmosphere.[74] Did that atmosphere, and the Jordanian and British reactions, play a role in the exercise of greater caution when Nazareth was occupied? Perhaps. In this respect, we know that some, particularly members of the Mapam party which was represented in the Israeli provisional government, went to see Ben-Gurion, and referred to the serious damage done to the Jewish state as a result of the promulgation of the news about Lydda and Ramla. This atmosphere may explain the adoption of the clear position that such events should not be replicated when Nazareth was occupied.

After the fall of Shafa ʿAmr and nearby villages, the Israeli army quickly advanced eastwards. Saffuriyya, a large village known for its fighters, became the focus of attention because units of volunteers from its residents and from neighboring villages were stationed there. Those fighters did not surrender easily, but the superiority in numbers and equipment that the Israeli army enjoyed made it impossible for them to stand up to the heavy bombing, so the survivors withdrew and the villagers ran towards nearby Nazareth, seeking refuge. Saffuriyya fell quickly, and Madlul ʿAbbas, the commander of the Arab Rescue Army unit stationed in Nazareth, realized he had to withdraw before the city was totally cut off from the north. But before withdrawing, that commander asked the residents to stay in their homes and not to migrate. Soldiers serving in the unit stopped briefly in al-Khannuq region to make sure that the residents were not following them. ʿAbbas thus performed a valuable service to those who had been thinking of leaving.

After the withdrawal of the Arab Rescue Army from Nazareth, Mayor Yusif al-Fahum consulted with the heads of Christian sects and notables in the city on Friday morning, 16 July, on how to cope with the situation and save the city.[75] It was evident to everyone that the residents of Nazareth could not confront the Israeli army or prevent the fall of the city. In the afternoon, Ben Dunkelman had entered from the north (al-Khannuq) to the city of Nazareth after shelling the remnants of the retreating ARA. The Israeli forces did not advance to the center of the city; instead, that officer had sent someone to look for the mayor and the heads of Christian sects so that they could sign a surrender agreement that would protect the city and its holy places, according to the orders of the top echelons of the army. Indeed, it was only a few hours later that officers of the Israeli army were signing an agreement for the surrender of Nazareth in the house of Shafiq al-Jisr.[76] The agreement had eleven articles, which collectively constitute a rare document of its kind for the events of the 1948 war, and it is worth pausing to examine its contents and significance.

At the top of the list of (Arab) signatories were the mayor, Yusif al-Fahum, and the head of the National Committee, Ibrahim al-Fahum. The agreement included two clauses guaranteeing that the activities of the municipal council and the civil affairs administration would continue in coordination with the military governor. Among the signatories were police officer Samu'il Khamis, and Nakhle Bishara, representing the Arab Orthodox sect. From the Israeli side the agreement was signed by army officers acting in the name of the Israeli government, with Ben Dunkelman at the head of the list. This agreement strived to give a civilized face to the Israeli side, who wrote the text in advance and signed it with leaders of the city. The ninth clause, for example, refers to the commitment of the government, represented by the army officers, to its recognition of "the civil rights in which all the residents of Nazareth are equal with the citizens of Israel without discrimination on the basis of ethnicity or language." It seemed likely that these words had been copied from the independence document of the state of Israel, and that the document for the surrender of the city had been prepared in advance under the directions of the prime minister and defense minister of Israel, Ben-Gurion.[77]

After the events in Lydda and Ramla, and one week before the fall of Nazareth, Israel tried to whitewash its image in local and international public opinion. In a telegram that Ben-Gurion sent Moshe Carmel, commander of the northern front, the prime minister and defense minister ordered the setting up of a special administrative team to conduct the affairs of Nazareth without unnecessary contact with the population. The military directive to Carmel was that he had to issue very strict instructions prohibiting the desecration of monasteries and churches, and prohibiting looting and theft.[78] These strict orders from Ben-Gurion concerning Nazareth prior to its occupation are noteworthy for revealing the aggressive tactics that had become expected during the Palestine war in other cities and regions where Ben-Gurion had not issued specific orders prohibiting attacks, looting and expulsions of the population. Contrary to what happened to Palestinian residents of Haifa and Jaffa and other Palestinian cities, the case of Nazareth clearly showed a population that remained in their homeland and in their homes because they were not terrorized and forced to emigrate.

Ben-Gurion's clear and decisive written orders on the eve of the fall of Nazareth, and the Israeli army command compliance, prevented the mistreatment of the population and attacks on the holy places. This demonstrates the importance of top-level policy formulated by the prime minister and defense minister during the war. In Nazareth, the Israeli army behaved differently, not with the longtime inhabitants of the city only, but also with the new refugees. Contrary to the usual policy, the Israeli government allowed thousands of refugees who had flocked to Nazareth to return to their cities and villages after a short while.[79] The clear exceptions to this rule were the refugees from Tiberias and Bisan which Israel decided to turn into Jewish cities denuded of their Arab population. But those refugees from Haifa, 'Akka, Shafa 'Amr, and some villages in the vicinity did gradually return to their homes. This unusual policy toward refugees, like that toward the residents of Nazaeth, demonstrates the importance of the policy decisions taken by the government under Ben-Gurion.[80]

There were other factors, besides Ben-Gurion's orders to the Israeli army command, which helped residents to stay in Nazareth. Officers of the ARA who withdrew from Nazareth one day before it fell prevented dozens of families who wanted to migrate from the village from doing so, sometimes by force. Despite that, about one thousand people left Nazareth, and joined hundreds of thousands of Palestinian refugees in Jordan, Syria, and Lebanon. Most migrants from the city were Muslims, particularly the families of notables and merchants, like the al-Fahum family and others.[81] But this minority who migrated is proof that the vast majority chose to stay. In addition to Nazareth, most villages of the district also escaped destruction and forced expulsion; the residents of twenty villages in the region of the city escaped, but four villages were destroyed and depopulated— Ma'lul, al-Mujaydil, Saffuriyya, and 'Illut. The first three of these villages remained deserted, but the residents of 'Illut alone were allowed to return to their village, which we shall discuss later.

One day after the fall of Nazareth, Ben-Gurion recorded in his diary that Moshe Carmel issued an order on 17 July to expel the entire population of Nazareth. This concise sentence indicates that there was a tense drama in which the northern region command tried to undo what had been agreed a day earlier. According to Ben-Gurion's memoirs, Ben Dunkelman, commander of the seventh battalion, "hesitated" to carry out the expulsion order, so Haim Laskov contacted the defense minister to inquire what should be done in this case. Ben-Gurion (lightly) records that he intervened and prohibited the expulsion of the population of Nazareth. Dunkelman confirms this incident in his memoirs, which he prepared for publication in the 1970s.[82] He mentions that Laskov issued an order to expel the population of Nazareth, but that he refused to execute that order, and consequently there was an attempt to withdraw Dunkelman's troops from the city and replace them with another battalion led by Elie Yafeh. The mere attempt by Carmel and Laskov, who were in charge of military operations in the northern region to expel the population of Nazareth after they had signed an agreement with the leaders of the city to protect their safety and their rights indicates that they were not thinking anyone would punish them for that act.

More than one historian and researcher into the history of the 1948 war have indicated that Ben-Gurion never issued written orders for the expulsion of the Palestinians from their villages and cities. There have been many interpretations of Ben-Gurion's famous "waving his hand," which Yitzhak Rabin understood to be a sign that the residents of Lydda and Ramla should be expelled. This still troubles some Israeli historians. In the same days in which tens of thousands of Palestinians were expelled from Lydda and Ramla, the command of the Israeli army general staff asked for the consent of Ben-Gurion for the expulsion of about four thousand Palestinians from 'Akka, either across the border or to the city of Jaffa.[83] Minister Bechor Shitrit strongly objected to this based on his responsibility for the Arab residents. In this case too, Ben-Gurion reversed his initial approval of the expulsion of the remainder of the population of 'Akka after one official insisted on the need for a written order from the minister of defense. In this way the remaining residents of 'Akka were saved from expulsion, as were the residents of Nazareth, out of fear of the reaction to written orders of expulsion.

The attempt to expel the residents of Nazareth after its surrender under an agreement signed in the name of the Israeli government did not elicit sufficient attention on the part of historians on both sides of the conflict. Is it credible that Moshe Carmel or Laskov would issue expulsion orders without the knowledge and approval of Ben-Gurion? Was it the "hesitation" or opposition of Dunkelman to the expulsion orders that saved the people of Nazareth from being uprooted? Was Ben-Gurion's decision when Laskov approached him the result of a genuine opposition to the expulsion or was it due to a fear of the political and media scandal that might ensue if it was uncovered? These are important questions worthy of close examination and study on the part of defenders of Ben-Gurion and his policies during the war. The residents of Nazareth were unaware of the drama surrounding their fate on 17 July, for ultimately they remained in their homes and the army did not evict them. An important factor leading to this result was the second cease-fire which came into force the following day, 18 July.

The attempt to expel the people of Nazareth remained unknown to them, even if some had heard rumors. But nothing was written about it either in their memoirs or as part of the history of the war.[84] Apart from Dunkelman, who relates this account in his memoirs, the other officers on the northern front remained silent, nor has any document concerning the situation been released from the Israeli archives, either because there is no such document to begin with, or because no one has taken the decision to release it so far. Nazareth was better off than other places where agreements were signed and subsequently violated only a few days later, as was the case in Haifa and its surrender agreement with the leaders of the Haganah, as well as other agreements in the Galilee concluded but not adhered to.

The answer to the question posed earlier concerning the secret of the escape and survival of Nazareth along with the majority of villages in its district is that several causes contributed to that outcome: the fact that it is a holy city for the Christian world, as well as the behavior of the inhabitants and their leaders who chose to remain in their homes. No doubt, Ben-Gurion's strict orders to the army command was what finally allowed the Palestinians to remain in their city. Activists in the Mapam party who had ties to the Liberation League in Nazareth noticed this behavior differed from what happened in Lydda, Ramla, Jaffa, and other places. Eliezer Bray, one of the leaders of the party and the editor of 'Al Hamishmar, refers to this in a penetrating article he published in the paper in November 1948, in which he counters the narrative that had begun to make the rounds in Israel concerning "the flight of the Arabs," and places the blame for the rise of the refugee problem on Britain and the Arab states. He also points the finger of blame at Israel and its government, saying: "In Nazareth and Majdal 'Asqalan the Arabs stayed because we wanted them to stay there. If they did not remain in other places, the authors of the 'transfer' policy had a share in that."[85]

The editor of 'Al Hamishmar was certain of what he said. Following the occupation of Nazareth, the same paper published several articles commending the good treatment that the inhabitants received. One week after the surrender of Nazareth, as one article recounts: "In Nazareth there was an occupation of the hearts."[86] The paper's special correspondent reveals several matters worth quoting at length: "The example of Nazareth proves that looting and the maltreatment of people and property which were a feature of the Israeli occupation of Arab places were not inevitable." He adds to his explanation of the different way in which Israel behaved in Nazareth: "There was awareness that the eyes of the world were on our behavior in this city. Had the actions and manifestations seen elsewhere (Lydda and al-Ramla) been repeated in Nazareth, it would have led to severe reactions."[87] The correspondent concludes by expressing the hope that the example of Nazareth would not be unique.

Indeed, it seemed at first glance that Israel had decided to turn a page in its dealings with the occupied places. Following the occupation of Nazareth, the government did what it could to return to normal life in the city. The city was fortunate to receive visits from four cabinet ministers, one after the other, within a single week. First came the Mapam minister in the provisional government, the minister of agriculture, followed by the minister of labor and housing the next day. Then came the minister of minorities, Bechor Shitrit, then the minister of religious affairs, Rabbi Yehuda Leib Fishman. Minister Shitrit, who came from Tiberias and was fluent in Arabic, met with the mayor, a judge, and a delegation representing the National Liberation League. The atmosphere in those meetings was cordial, and the minister promised his hosts to look into their demands and deal with them. The military governor Elisha Soltz worked to return life in the city to its normal routines, and asked, for example, the municipality and the local police to resume work as usual under the auspices of Israeli rule.[88]

Minister Shitrit, who visited Nazareth on 19 July and met with the mayor and a number of city leaders, was well aware of the importance of treating the inhabitants well and preserving the Christian holy places. One day before his arrival, Elisha Soltz (who had earlier served in the office of the minister of minorities) was appointed military governor. The minister advised him to be sensitive and just in his dealings with the people of Nazareth. When Shitrit returned to Tel Aviv, he asked for the appointment of a judge for the city, and for the renewal of the activities of the municipality so that it could provide services to the population. Shitrit told the members of the provisional cabinet that the state of Israel "had to issue strict instructions to the army to treat the population of the city justly and in a suitable manner, due of its special importance in the eyes of the world."[89] In that moment, all the ministers agreed with what he said, without any objections.

Elisha Soltz met with cooperation not just from the municipality and the mayor but from local leaders as well, including the communists as well as a well-known figure, Sayf al-Din al-Zu'bi, whose family was on good terms with the opponents of Mufti Hajj Amin al-Husayni. Sayf al-Din himself was a real estate broker who had worked with HaKeren HaKayemet (the Jewish National Fund), and for that reason had been the subject of an assassination attempt in 1947 which he survived.[90] During the 1948 war, the villages of the Zu'bi clan in Marj ibn 'Amir concluded a peace and good neighborliness agreement with Jewish settlements in the area. Intelligence services belonging to the ARA accused Sayf al-Din al-Zu'bi of collaboration with the Jewish forces, and an attempt was made to arrest him and put him on trial.[91] After the occupation of Nazareth, al-Zu'bi came to the city and became one of the prominent local leaders who openly collaborated with Israel in general and with the military government in particular. Thus, Elisha Soltz found cooperation from various parties which helped him to return normal life to the city quickly.

The history of Arabs in Israel begins with the "gentle manner" in which Nazareth was occupied, and the cooperation of its city leaders with the military governor and the Israeli government. It is true that prior to that, thousands of Palestinians escaped expulsion from Haifa, 'Akka, and many cities and villages in the Galilee; however, the continued existence of Nazareth and the escape of its population from uprooting constitute a unique precedent, where an entire city with its institutions and its political and cultural elite remained intact. Therefore, it is possible to consider the conduct of the Israeli government and its head in this case as a clear indication of the willingness of the Jewish state to accept an Arab minority, albeit in limited numbers. On the other side, the conduct of the people of Nazareth and its political leaders across the political spectrum was an indication by those who remained of a new awareness of the defeat and their acceptance of the new reality, so that they could continue to live in their homes and their country. The convergence of the conduct of the government and the army on the one hand, and the readiness of city leaders to cooperate with the new rulers on the other, laid the foundations for a new phase in the history of the Palestinians who remained under Israeli rule.

Did the occupation of Nazareth and the villages in its district set a precedent to be emulated in how Israel was to spread its control over the rest of the Galilee in Operation Hiram? The answer to this question will come in the next chapter. We close this chapter by addressing the question of the situation of the Palestinians during the second cease-fire which lasted three months or more, in which no military battles were fought on the official fronts, but struggles of a different kind occupied the Palestinians and the Arab states. In this period Constantine Zurayk finished his book, *The Meaning of al-Nakba*, and the residents of the Galilee became busy trying to comprehend what was happening around them, and what the future held in store for them, in the event that fighting resumed and Israel undertook to occupy all of central and upper Galilee.

CONDITIONS IN THE GALILEE DURING
THE CEASE-FIRE (SUMMER–FALL, 1948)

By the end of July, the war between Israel and Syria, Lebanon, and even Jordan had ended from an operational point of view, while battles with the Egyptian army, which shifted to the position of defense, continued. Contrary to the first cease-fire, which was set in advance to last a month, the second cease-fire was not of a limited duration. The military defeat of the Arab armies was clear, and that is why they agreed to the cease-fire despite the fact that Israel had not agreed to their demands concerning refugees and other matters. At this stage (early summer 1948) the Nakba grew worse, and it was clear that the Arab armies were unable to stop the calamity that was befalling the Palestinians. Zurayk, the historian and penetrating thinker, absorbed the meaning of that historical moment and published his book about the Nakba and its meaning. The Palestinians also absorbed the magnitude of the national catastrophe, each from the position in which they found themselves, and tried each in their own way to save what they could from the rubble.

At the international political level, Count Folke Bernadotte, since his appointment as a mediator and United Nations envoy, had tried to arrive at a cease-fire and unlimited armistice agreements between Israel and the Arab states. Following the cease-fire in July, he sought an agreement that was acceptable to Israel, Britain, and the Arab countries. In his negotiations with the parties concerned, he tried to take into account the situation in the field, so he proposed that Israel either annex the entire Galilee, or the western and southern portions of it which it had occupied. After Israel, Jordan was the second beneficiary from Bernadotte's proposals, while the Palestinians were the main losers. The Arab states, which were competing with each other even after their defeat, were unable to arrive at a common agreement or position concerning Bernadotte's proposals. These facts were no secret to the Palestinians, who followed the news and realized that there was no Arab force capable of preventing Israel from occupying the rest of the Galilee.[92]

The inhabitants of the Galilee felt in the summer of 1948 that their region would fall under Israeli rule, either by agreement or by force and occupation. This awareness of the facts contributed to their adoption of pragmatic positions in their dealings with the Israeli army and government. Bernadotte's assassination by the terrorist Lehi organization (Stern gang) cut short his attempts to reach an agreement. His successor, Ralph Bunche, accused the Israeli leadership of responsibility for the hostile atmosphere which led to the assassination. Indeed, the Israeli government opposed the proposals of the UN envoy and criticized them severely, and leftist labor parties, including the Mapam party and even the Israeli Communist Party, refused any compromise or agreement with King Abdullah and "his British masters."

The issue of Palestinian refugees kept UN institutions busy, and Israel feared that it could be subjected to pressure to allow some to return to their homes and country. The Israeli government had taken an official decision in mid-June prohibiting their return; however, as the number of those forced to become refugees increased so did pressures on Israel to permit the return of some refugees at least. But the Jewish state, which had begun to absorb Jewish immigrants from Europe, refused to bow to the pressures and became steadfast in its refusal. Nevertheless, Israel grew more concerned following the assassination of Bernadotte that pressures might increase in a way that could harm its global political relations. But these concerns dissipated quickly due to international developments in the neighboring Arab region, and due to the renewal of fighting on the Egyptian front.

It is clear from developments during the cease-fire months that they coincided with military developments in the field which were not in the interest of the Palestinians. In the Arab context, divisions and internal conflicts drowned out discourse stressing common interests and the need for unity. The principal dispute concerned the fate of the Palestinian territories that Israel had not occupied, and which were under the control of Arab armies, particularly those of Egypt and Jordan. Would those states allow the Palestinians to establish their own state according to the UN partition resolution? If such a state was not established, what would be the fate of the territories and their inhabitants? These and related questions resulted in the exacerbation of disputes among Arab states, and between some of them and the Palestinian leadership under the mufti.

According to the UN resolution to partition Palestine into two states, one Arab and other Jewish, this had to be done by 1 October 1948. Consequently, September witnessed moves by several Arab states, headed by Egypt, Syria, and Saudi Arabia, in favor of establishing a Palestinian government under the leadership of the mufti, Hajj Amin al-Husayni, which was to administer the territories under the control of Arab armies. Egypt (contrary to Jordan) supported this move and encouraged convening a Palestinian National Conference in Gaza toward the end of September, during which the establishment of an "All-Palestine Government" headed by Ahmad Hilmi 'Abd al-Baqi[93] was declared. The mufti and his supporters had an overwhelming majority among the members of this government, which elicited strong opposition from Jordan. King Abdullah adopted political measures and took steps on the ground to annex the West Bank to his kingdom with the help of the opposition to, and those Palestinians competing with, the mufti.

Despite the Jordanian opposition, the mufti tried, as of September, to prove that he was the sole leader of the Palestinian people, and that the All-Palestine Government in Gaza enjoyed the support of all Palestinians. But this government had many enemies from its birth: Britain, Israel, Jordan, the mufti's own opponents, and others. It was also formed very late, and was not fated to live long. The king of Jordan was the most hostile to the All-Palestine Government; he convened a conference in which he gathered all his supporters in the capital, Amman, where the conferees presented him with a petition to protect the West Bank and annex it to his kingdom. Britain, which had supported the king's steps, encouraged him to conclude an agreement with Israel so that he could annex the West Bank according to an understanding between the two sides. Egypt was not in a position to compete with King Abdullah and to continue to support the All-Palestine Government unconditionally. This became apparent after the renewal of the fighting, Israel's attack on the Egyptian army, and its bombardment of Gaza City itself at the end of October.

Israel controlled most parts of Galilee except for the pocket of villages in upper and central Galilee during the months after the cease-fire. Life returned to normal in Nazareth: schools opened their doors with the beginning of the new school year, and the mayor, along with local leaders, including the communists, conducted the business of the people in cooperation with the military governor.[94] This cooperation with the Israeli authorities has been branded as treasonous and attacked with adjectives that are not indicative of understanding that historic phase. Decades later the critics changed their minds and admitted the error of their previous hasty position. Some declared that they consider the Palestinians who remained in Nazareth and other parts of the Galilee to be sensible people who behaved with wisdom and steadfastness in their homes and homeland.[95] Indeed, the seventy thousand Palestinians who were counted in the survey of Israel at that time were the nucleus or the beating heart of the Arabs in Israel.

The pocket in upper and central Galilee which had not yet been occupied by Israel was still populated by thousands of *fellahin* who lived in sixty Arab villages. This region—called the Galilee pocket—appeared slated to be occupied by Israel, and the residents were trying to glimpse their future: would they become like those who were uprooted and expelled or like the villages of western Galilee and the city of Nazareth and its villages? There were also thousands of refugees living in the area who had not completed the process of migration beyond the borders of historic Palestine, in addition to the original inhabitants of the villages in the Galilee pocket. There was a prevalent conviction among the inhabitants of that region that the ARA units would be unable to defend them should Israel decide to occupy it.

The ARA's performance during the previous months and its unpreparedness were apparent to them, which contributed to the spread of negative attitudes towards those volunteers.[96] A number of people whom I interviewed in the Galilee said they used to rely on radio broadcasts and newspapers to understand what was happening around them, adding that some officers of the ARA admitted that they would not be able to protect the area if Israel decided to occupy it.

Prevalent in the collective memory of those who remained in the Galilee after the Nakba is the fact that volunteers in the ARA were accused of mistreating the residents of the area; however, an in-depth examination of relations between the residents and most units in the ARA points to a complex situation which differs from the attitude that was developed retroactively. It is true that the residents of some Druze and Christian villages refused to cooperate with the Arab volunteers, which contributed to tensions and friction between the two sides, but in other cases there was cooperation and solidarity for the protection of villages close to the lines of contact with the Jewish side. The residents of these villages were asked to contribute to the defense of their villages, by bearing arms, building fortifications, and providing food supplies to the volunteers. In some villages, local committees were established to run the affairs of the residents in cooperation with officers of ARA units. Israel was in control of the eastern, southern, and western sides of the Galilee pocket. However, the open borders with Lebanon guaranteed the continued flow of arms as well as the necessary food provisions for the population during the cease-fire months.

Residents of al-Battuf recall the error made by the mukhtar of Sakhnin, Ibrahim 'Abdullah Khalayle, who decided to surrender his village to the Israeli army on the eve of the cease-fire. The middle man in that deal was Jad Mustafa Dhiyab from Tamra, who was related to the mukhtar, and who convinced him to follow in his footsteps. Indeed, a delegation from Sakhnin and neighboring villages reached the occupied village of Mi'ar[97] on 18 July and signed a surrender agreement.[98] Then some Israeli soldiers entered Sakhnin, but withdrew later to Mi'ar because of the continuing skirmishes with the unit headed by Abu Is'af in the neighboring village of Sha'b. When a cease-fire was declared on the same day, the ARA command became aware of the case of the mukhtar of Sakhnin and his surrendering his village before the Israeli army had reached it. The mukhtar and some of the people close to him were arrested and subjected to insults. They were moved to the police station in Majd al-Krum, which was a stronghold of the ARA and a jail at the same time.[99] This situation, which many of the residents of central Galilee experienced, left them in a quandary between their desire to protect their villages from the vengeance of the Israeli army and their fear of punishment at the hands of the ARA.

The inhabitants of the Galilee were Muslim, Christian, or Druze and some villages were inhabited by two or three sects at different times. The fact that the Lebanese border remained open took the pressure off the siege imposed on the residents of the Galilee pocket on the remaining sides. The residents of this rural area used to work and shop in 'Akka, Haifa, Safad, Nazareth, and other cities, all of which fell under Israeli control. After that, the small traders, smugglers, and others went to south Lebanon and even to the capital Beirut to bring goods back to central Galilee; some preferred instead to go only as far as Kufr Yasif, Shafa 'Amr, 'Akka, and elsewhere. These movements by the residents were not unknown to the Israeli authorities, who took advantage of these trade routes for their own ends.[100] The open borders with Lebanon, and the transmission of information about the refugees, made the residents of central Galilee more cognizant of the options available to them. Testimonies of people from that period confirm that many who had migrated from their cities and villages at the beginning of the war and had reached Lebanon decided to return, and did so during the cease-fire period.

By way of example, Najib Susan was a seventeen-year-old boy when he was expelled from 'Akka along with others after the occupation of the city in May. After a period of homelessness and dislocation in Lebanon, he reached Beirut, and found help from the residents of the city. However, after about a month, he decided to return to his family in 'Akka. Susan relates the story of his return in his autobiography and speaks of the route he took from Rumaysh to upper Galilee. Crossing the border with a group of refugees and the help of a guide, he reached the village of al-Bi'na where, according to his account, he joined the Abu Is'af unit which was stationed in the Shaghur area.[101] When central Galilee fell, he joined the Arab Rescue Army and retreated with them to Lebanon. After a brief period he returned once again to the Galilee on his own, and then reached 'Akka where he rejoined members of his family.

We have another story of departure and return related by Elias Srouji, who left Nazareth in June to take his father, who was suffering from cancer, for treatment in a Beirut hospital. In the middle of October, he decided to take his family back to Nazareth. Srouji agreed with a Nazarene taxi driver (Fu'ad Nasrallah Zahr) to take the family in his car as far as the village of al-Rama. Indeed, they travelled from Beirut by car on 25 October and reached the house of a friend of the family, Yusif 'Awad (Abu Salim). After resting two days in al-Rama, the members of the family decided to hire two cars to take them to the village of Dayr Hanna, but the difficult road and the health of the poor father forced them to change the plan. Having gone as far as Dayr Hanna, 25 kilometers north of the occupied zone around Nazareth, they were forced to return to al-Rama, and reached the house of their friend Abu Salim in the evening. The new plan was for them to spend the night in al-Rama, and then to return back to Beirut the following day.

Barely an hour after arriving at al-Rama they heard the sounds of extraordinary explosions outside. Salim burst into the living room to announce that a plane was hovering over the village and bombing it. The damage of this air raid on al-Rama was not severe, as it became apparent later, but it was a signal that the operation to occupy the rest of the Galilee had begun with the aerial bombardment of several villages to terrorize the population. In this way the cease-fire, which had lasted a hundred days, ended and Operation Hiram began towards the end of October. The inhabitants of al-Rama, like others in the region, had experienced tension and anxiety since the renewal of fighting on the Egyptian front, and were expecting an Israeli attack to begin. When the attack did begin, all of central and upper Galilee were occupied quickly and easily, as we shall see in the next chapter.

Completing the Occupation of Galilee—Operation Hiram

The population of the Galilee had been 241,000 in November 1947 on the eve of the partition of Palestine. More than 200,000 were Arabs, a few thousand were Circassians and Armenians, and 31,790 were Jews. Muslims constituted the vast majority of the Arab population in the region, numbering 169,000, followed by 29,000 Christians and 10,700 Druze. The dominant understanding that the population of the Galilee escaped the Nakba is not accurate, since of the 220 cities and villages in the Galilee populated by Arabs, only 70 remained after the Nakba. Over two-thirds of the Palestinian towns and villages had been destroyed and their populations expelled; 100,000 Arabs or fewer escaped this fate, representing about half of those who were living in the Galilee until the end of 1947. It is true that more Palestinian residents remained in the Galilee than in any other area occupied by Israel in 1948; nevertheless, ethnic cleansing in some parts of the Galilee was almost total.

In the Safad area, the destruction of Arab cities and villages was thorough.[1] Under Operation Hiram, at the end of October 1948 the fate of Arab villages in eastern Galilee was worse than in the rest of the Galilee, as had been the case from the beginning of the war. In addition to eastern Galilee's proximity to the Lebanese border, the fact that Jewish settlements were fairly thick in that region played an important role in the expulsion of Palestinians. As for central and lower Galilee, which were in the area allocated to the Arab state under the partition resolution, Jewish settlement had been sparse before the Nakba. In many population centers, Druze lived alongside Christians and Muslims, which contributed to a larger number of residents remaining. As we have mentioned, the Druze received special treatment from the Jewish state, no harm befell them, and all of their villages remained intact.

After the summer of 1948 the Druze in the mountain region became aware of the agreement between the leadership of the Druze along the coast with the state of Israel. The Maʿdi family from Yarka, which was a party to this agreement, maintained good relations with both the Arab and Jewish sides, and some family members managed to play an important role in events during and after the war. Despite the fact that many Arab inhabitants of the Galilee were not pleased with this agreement between the Druze and the Jews, they still maintained good relations with them, which contributed toward many villages in the Galilee—Druze and some neighboring villages—being able to escape destruction.

Similar to the situation of the Druze, the ties between the inhabitants of central Galilee and the National Liberation League in Haifa and Nazareth played a role in enabling some residents to stay. Many activists and leaders of the league returned to Haifa from Lebanon by way of al-Biʿna, Kufr Yasif, and other villages in the region. Some league members from these villages had helped distribute a pamphlet signed by the league and fraternal parties in Arab states at the beginning of October 1948. According to one activist, Hanna Ibrahim, an officer in the Arab Rescue Army (ARA) in Majd al-Krum had approved of the content of that communist pamphlet.[2] Such verbal and published testimonies by contemporaries of these events affirm that the inhabitants of central Galilee were fully aware of the military balance of power, which encouraged them to find ways to save themselves from uprooting and destitution.

During October 1948 there were indications of the imminent resumption of fighting. On the southern front, the Israeli army carried out an attack on the Egyptian army; in the north, predictions by ARA officers that the Galilee would soon fall became more frequent.[3] News of the retreat of the Egyptian army in the face of the Israeli army and the proximity of an attack on what remained of the Galilee greatly concerned residents of the area, particularly those who had cooperated with the ARA. People followed the news on the few radio sets available in the villages, while others sought news from their neighbors on the Israeli side, or from *al-Yawm* and *al-Ittihad* newspapers. On the eve of the launch of Operation Hiram, some contemporaries spoke of a sense that a new chapter of the Nakba was about to unfold.[4]

By the end of October, Israel emerged victorious from the war and, with no Arab armies posing a threat, sought to expand into more territory at the expense of the Palestinians. The inhabitants of central Galilee, the so-called "Galilee pocket," were extremely alarmed when they saw the ARA withdrawing from their villages and region as the attacking Israeli army entered. Appeals by Israeli leaders to the Palestinian people to remain peaceful and be rewarded by a life of equality and dignity in the Jewish state were not respected. Sixty thousand people lived in central Galilee in fifty villages—between Majd al-Krum to the west, ʿIlabun to the east, al-Battuf to the south, and the Lebanese border to the north—which the Israeli army occupied in sixty hours.

Prior to the start of Operation Hiram, some Israeli cabinet ministers expressed reservations concerning completing the occupation of the Galilee, where there were tens of thousands of Arab inhabitants. Foreign Minister Moshe Sharett, for one, said it was better for Israel to forego occupying the Galilee because it was "full of Arabs," including refugees from western and eastern Galilee.[5] This statement came in the wake of a proposal by Ben-Gurion at the 26 September 1948 cabinet meeting to resume the fighting and to occupy what remained of the Galilee. The prime minister replied during the meeting that: "Assuming there is an outbreak of fighting, we will clean central Galilee in one stroke; to cleanse it, including the refugees . . . that will not be possible without war." He then sought to convince the ministers: "If war were to break out in the whole country, as far as the Galilee is concerned . . . and without a great effort . . . it will be cleansed."[6]

Despite Ben-Gurion's statements and reassurances, the majority of cabinet ministers voted against his proposal to initiate a renewal of the fighting with the Arab states and to expel the 100,000 residents of the Galilee. However, as Tom Segev writes, the expulsion of the population that the Israeli prime minister had proposed was merely postponed, not cancelled. A month after that meeting in which Ben-Gurion found himself in the minority, he commented on a statement by military intelligence operative Ezra Danin which irritated him: "There is only one task left for the Arabs in Israel: to run."[7] Thus the unambiguous statement about taking the opportunity of war to "cleanse Galilee," and the plans of the army command to occupy the region and expel its population, became an agenda that was executed with the renewal of hostilities. These plans from the top of the Israeli political and military pyramid near the end of 1948 are more evidence against the Zionist narrative about the dispersal of the Palestinians as an unplanned result of war.

Predictably, completing the occupation of the Galilee met with no serious resistance from the Arab side.[8] As noted earlier, Druze residents knew about the agreement between their leaders and Israel, and the communist activists in some villages (al-Bi'na, Tarshiha, al-Rama, and 'Ilabun) knew of the league branches in Haifa and Nazareth joining the Israeli Communist Party.[9] The vast majority of the population hoped that the fate of their villages after occupation would be like Nazareth and its district, which had escaped destruction and dispersal. To achieve that, they were prepared to surrender their villages without resistance to the Israeli army. Indeed, the Arab residents did not confront the Israeli forces, and there were no casualties in the Israeli army ranks, apart from a few random cases. In spite of that, the inhabitants paid a heavy price: hundreds were executed and thousands were forced to migrate during and after the occupation. These criminal acts took place at a late stage in the war, implementing Ben-Gurion's plan and his previous promises to ministers in his government.

During Operation Hiram, the Israeli army perpetrated a number of massacres,[10] when there was a government and organized state institutions in place, contrary to the first half of 1948. On the eve of the occupation of Nazareth

Ben-Gurion had issued strict orders to the army and its commanders not to attack the population and their holy places; as a result, tens of thousands of residents remained in their homes. However, a hundred days later he allowed the army to act in an entirely different way in Muslim and Christian villages, since Ben-Gurion wanted the upper Galilee totally void of its Arab inhabitants; the soldiers carried out actions to guarantee that result. The opening event of the occupation was the bombardment of several villages by aircraft, which spread fear and terror among the population. In the bombardment of Tarshiha, for example, dozens were killed and others were buried under the rubble of their homes.[11] Yet despite the terrorizing of defenseless residents, at least half of the population remained in their homes and villages. Why did they stay despite the occurrence of massacres and acts of expulsion?

THE WESTERN FRONT OF THE GALILEE POCKET

Majd al-Krum lies to the west of al-Shaghur region which separates upper from lower Galilee. Until 1948, the village land extended to the houses on the eastern side of al-Birwa village. The population of Majd al-Krum on the eve of its occupation was about 2,000, swelled by hundreds of refugees from neighboring villages, such as al-Birwa, Sha'b, al-Damun, and others. Between the second cease-fire and Operation Hiram, men from the village, along with youth from neighboring villages, helped the ARA to defend the region and prevent its occupation.[12] Despite advances and retreats during the summer months, which caused casualties on both sides, the front lines did not change. Due to the strategic position of the village and the collaboration between the villagers and the volunteers stationed there, they feared Israeli retaliation.

Members of the ARA had good relations with the people of Majd al-Krum; there were no reports of tensions or sensitivities between them, as was the case in some other villages in the Galilee. The local ARA command were headquartered in the former British police station on the east side of the village. Some residents (Muhammad 'Ali Sa'id Qaddah, Muhammad Kan'an, and others) said that the volunteers used to help the locals gather the harvest and plant their crops in the summer. In return, the villagers fed, housed, and even washed the clothes of the volunteers.[13] Khaled Dhiyab Farhat (who had graduated from high school before the Nakba) testified that he was the secretary of the local committee that ran the affairs of the village in cooperation with the commanders of the ARA. Nevertheless, these witnesses stressed that they were apprehensive about the future on the eve of the occupation. News about the the Arab world in general and the Palestinian front in particular did not bode well. They feared a fate similar to that of the villages of al-Birwa, al-Damun, and Sha'b, whose inhabitants were uprooted and forced to migrate.

There was some glimmer of hope that the fate of the village would be similar to that of some villages in western Galilee which had escaped destruction and dispersal. Among the nearby villages which had escaped were al-Makr, al-Jadida, Kufr Yasif, Abu Snan, Yarka, and Julis.[14] However, most coastal villages, such as al-Manshiyya, al-Samiriyya, Um al-Faraj, al-Nahr, al-Zib, al-Bassa, and others were destroyed and their residents were expelled. The question that preyed on the minds of residents of Majd al-Krum was: How could they ensure that they remain and not be expelled? It was not hard for the residents to learn that members of the Ma'di family of Yarka had played an important role in the survival of many villages in western Galilee through their ties with the Israeli side; so they made sure to maintain good neighborly relations, according to some of those whom I interviewed and who had witnessed the events of those days. Regardless, circumspection and watchfulness were the order of the day, particularly after news that fighting had resumed on the Egyptian front.

After sunset on Friday, 29 October 1948, the commander of the ARA unit asked the people of Majd al-Krum to go to al-'Ayn Square,[15] and when they gathered there, he informed them that he had received orders to withdraw to Lebanon immediately. This officer thanked the inhabitants for their kindness and hospitality, and he asked them not to leave their village so as not to lose it. He recommended that they get in touch with the Jewish side to conclude a surrender agreement that would protect the village from destruction and the expulsion of its residents.[16] The people of the village feared for what would become of the young men who had fought alongside the ARA in previous months, and the officer recommended that the youth seek refuge in the mountains and hide there until after the village surrendered. Indeed, the ARA withdrew from the village that same night, and dozens of young men and some families went with them towards the northeast. However, the vast majority of the inhabitants remained in their homes, according to the advice of the Iraqi officer.[17]

The advice from the officer in Majd al-Krum prior to the withdrawal of his unit was similar to that of his counterpart in the ARA in Nazareth on the eve of its fall. The behavior of the villagers was also similar to that of the leaders of the city. On the same night on which the ARA volunteers withdrew, a delegation from the village went to see acquaintances from the Ma'di family in neighboring Yarka.[18] From there Haim Orbach, the intelligence officer for western Galilee, was contacted, and together they arranged for a meeting with the army unit camped in al-Birwa village. In this meeting agreement was reached on a surrender document for Majd al-Krum and neighboring villages in al-Shaghur region.[19] On the basis of this document, soldiers from the 123rd company entered the village the following morning, accompanied by some residents. Muhammad Ziho (Abu 'Atif), who was a twelve-year-old child at the time, testified that he saw dozens of infantrymen enter from the western side and go in the direction of the center of the village.[20] The soldiers of this company respected the articles of the surrender agreement; they collected arms from the village, and did not engage in any acts of retribution. It is interesting that the testimonies of the villagers are in complete agreement with the narrative of Israeli military documents concerning the process of the village surrendering in an orderly fashion and without incident on 30 October.

Hanan Levi, the intelligence officer of the 123rd company, sent a report to army headquarters in Haifa concerning the surrender of Majd al-Krum in the presence of some notables from the village, and the signing of the surrender document.[21] The villagers turned in twenty rifles of various types with some ammunition to the army, and "after a bit of pressure" they handed over fifteen more rifles. In the afternoon (at 4:15 p.m.) the commanding officer of the 122nd company arrived in the village with his men and took charge, and the officer received the rifles and ammunition which the villagers had surrendered that same day.[22] He chose about a hundred villagers who then headed to al-Layyat area, west of the village, where they cleared the street of the rocks and stones which blocked traffic. On the same day, the villagers were informed that there would be a curfew at night, starting at six in the evening and ending at six in the morning of the following day. According to the military report, the villagers accepted the orders with understanding and the surrender of the village went peacefully.

Another document by Haifa intelligence officers dated 31 October 1948, classified "secret and urgent," relates the surrender of Majd al-Krum from the perspective of the army.[23] After the withdrawal of "enemy forces" from the region of al-Birwa–Majd al-Krum, a delegation of villagers from Majd al-Krum, al-Bi'na, and Dayr al-Asad arrived in al-Birwa and were met by the commander of the 123rd company. The following morning (30 October) troops entered the village, and the surrender was signed at 14:25.[24] The document adds that there were 2,000 original inhabitants plus some refugees from neighboring villages. Of the few inhabitants of the village who left, most were young men who were hiding in the mountains and would likely return to their homes in a few days. It mentions that many young men were present in the village, and that some were refugees from neighboring villages "who had surely taken part in the fighting."

We return once again to the sequence of events in Majd al-Krum on the day of its surrender, 30 October 1948. In the afternoon (after the signing of the surrender), the sound of gunfire and cannon fire were heard from the east. The soldiers of the 123rd company returned fire, and one or two were hit by the surprise attack.[25] The source of the firing from the east were the soldiers of the Golani Brigade who had entered the village of 'Ilabun that morning, and then headed northwest to Majd al-Krum. Once the mistake and misunderstanding became clear and firing from both sides stopped, the soldiers of the brigade were informed that the village had surrendered and given up its arms according to the agreement. In this way the day ended without any casualties among the villagers, and the local residents and the refugees could breathe easy, especially after hearing what the brigade had done in 'Ilabun and its threat to do even worse in Majd al-Krum.

What follows are the events of the surrender of the village according to the testimonies of a number of villagers, as told over a ten-year period. The story relayed by Dr. Khalid Dhiyab Farhat includes important details of what happened to his family. As we mentioned above, Khalid was secretary of the local committee that ran the affairs of the village. After the spread of the news that this "army" had withdrawn, his father and his grandfather asked him that same evening to accompany two of his unmarried sisters to a safe Arab region,[26] fear for the honor of the two young women being the motive for this family decision. Dhiyab added that dozens of young men from the village accompanied the ARA in its retreat to the northeast by way of al-Biʿna and Dayr al-Asad until they reached Rumaysh. A few days after their arrival in Lebanon, he, along with other refugees, heard about a massacre that had taken place in al-ʿAyn Square in the village, so he decided to remain in Lebanon with his sisters and not return to Majd al-Krum. Eventually, Dr. Dhiyab arrived in the United States (he died there in 2012), while his sisters returned to the village through the family reunification provision two years after migrating.[27]

Muhammad Kanʿan (Abu ʿAtif) said that his wife had delivered her first child two weeks before the surrender of Majd al-Krum, so he remained with her following the withdrawal of the ARA. However, he and some young men in his extended family decided late that night (29 October) to seek refuge with Druze friends in neighboring Sajur.[28] The Kanʿan family arrived at the house of their friends at dawn next day. At noon, there was a commotion in the small village, and he understood from his hosts that Sajur notables were to go to the entrance of the village to welcome Jewish soldiers who were to arrive soon from the east; the welcome festivities never took place because the soldiers were in a hurry on their way west, according to their hosts, to Majd al-Krum "to punish its residents as they had done in ʿIlabun."[29] This news spurred the young men from the Kanʿan family to return quickly to their houses and their families before the arrival of those soldiers.

Here we shall relate another testimony from a third party who lived through the events, and was an active participant. Farid Butrus Zurayq from ʿIlabun went with the soldiers from the Golani Brigade who raced from his village to Majd al-Krum. Farid had been a policeman in Jerusalem for several years, where he had learned Hebrew. When the brigade entered ʿIlabun he was chosen with four other youth to accompany the soldiers travelling from there in three military vehicles.[30] When they arrived at the eastern entrance to Majd al-Krum on the afternoon of 30 October, the soldiers began to bombard the village. After a brief exchange of fire, it became apparent that Israeli soldiers had entered a village that had surrendered. Israeli officers in Majd al-Krum conveyed this to the soldiers from the Golani Brigade and asked them to return from where they had come. Zurayq recalls that officer Orbach was the one who spoke to the soldiers from the Golani Brigade, and he asked twice, in a surprised tone: "Why have you come here from ʿIlabun?"

The day ended relatively peacefully under an orderly surrender, according to the testimonies of the villagers and the army records. The results were quite different when events moved to the nearby villages of al-Shaghur. On the following day, an army unit entered neighboring al-Biʿna and Dayr al-Asad near the pool which separates the two villages. The soldiers separated the men from the women and children. In accordance with the surrender agreement concluded by notables from al-Birwa with the army, the inhabitants of the two villages surrendered the weapons in their possession. Then the soldiers chose two young men from each village, and an officer told them to go fetch water for the soldiers. As the four youth walked a short distance away, the soldiers fired on them, killing them. Thus they were executed before the eyes of residents of the two villages who were horrified and panicked. The deceased were Subhi Muhammad Dhabbah (twenty-three years old) and Ahmad ʿIsa (twenty-seven years old) from Dayr al-Asad, and ʿAli Muhammad al-ʿAbid (seventeen years old) and Hanna Elias Farhud (twenty-five years old) from al-Biʿna.[31] Then the soldiers picked dozens of young men and took them to prison camps. The officer ordered the rest of the inhabitants to begin moving north in the direction of Lebanon, but he allowed them half an hour to go to their homes to gather some necessities and their valuables before leaving. The women's tears and the children's cries did not change the mind of the officer who then ordered his troops to fire in the air to speed up the operation.[32]

When the villagers realized that the expulsion order would be carried out, they began to leave their houses and head north towards Lebanon.[33] However, when they had traveled far from the soldiers they decided to head east. They reached an area north of the village of Nahaf, and learned from inhabitants they met in the mountains that the Israeli army had executed four of its residents also, and ordered the rest to leave to Lebanon. The Biʿna and Dayr al-Asad villagers continued east until they reached the Druze village of Sajur where they stopped close to the village. The villagers were of two minds: some thought they should go back to their homes instead of continuing their travels,[34] and so headed back to their homes in Biʿna and Dayr al-Asad, but others continued their journey, joining tens of thousands of refugees from the Galilee. As it turned out later, the return of some inhabitants played a big role in the two villages remaining and being saved from destruction.

The fate of the people of Nahaf was similar to that of their neighbors to the west. The soldiers of the unit that entered the village, ordered the inhabitants to assemble on one of the threshing floors, then chose two young men and shot them in front of the villagers. The officer in charge ordered the rest of the villagers to leave north to Lebanon. The execution of the two youths and the continued shooting in the air left the residents with no choice but to leave, so they began their way north. On the mountainous trek to Lebanon, they stopped near houses of neighboring Druze villages and were offered some food and water. The hospitality of their neighbors helped to ease their terror. The fact that they were far from the soldiers encouraged some of them to return to their villages, and they were later joined by others from the village. So the same scene repeated itself in Nahaf, as in al-Biʿna and Dayr al-Asad.

One eyewitness from the Qadiri family (Abu Shawkat) spoke of what he had seen from the cave where he and his family were hiding at the top of a mountain overlooking Nahaf.[35] He saw and heard the Israeli soldiers open fire on four men from among the residents of the village, and the expulsion of others with shots being fired in the air to speed them on their way. Abu Shawkat added that the mukhtar of the village, Hamad Ahmad 'Abdullah (Abu 'Awad), went to Yarka with the help of two residents from neighboring Julis village. This visit to the Ma'di family, according to this testimony and others stories told by villagers from Shaghur, played a significant role in the residents of the area remaining in their houses. The agreements signed with the army in al-Birwa through the facilitation of Haim Orbach and the Ma'di family, and the help that residents of Druze villages offered to their neighbors who were scattered in the mountains, contributed to the residents remaining and returning to their villages. In addition, the difficult mountain terrain and the fact that the soldiers did not accompany the expelled villagers encouraged them to risk returning to their homes quickly.

A ruling of the Supreme Court in Jerusalem in 1951 confirms the details of some of the events that occurred in al-Shaghur villages as related by eyewitnesses. On 30 October 1948, "the people of Nahaf surrendered to a unit of the Israeli army which approached the village from the west. The following day, another army unit approached from the east, collected the villagers in the threshing floor area, and fired on four men, killing them under circumstances which are not sufficiently clear to us."[36] Then the court decision states: "The rest of the villagers were ordered to leave their village and go north to Lebanon and refugees from Sha'b who had taken refuge in the village left with them. Some villagers reached neighboring villages, while others continued walking until they reached the Lebanese border, where they concentrated in the village of Rumaysh near the border. The village mukhtar, Hamad Ahmad 'Abdullah, contacted the army authorities who allowed the inhabitants of the village to return to their houses. This happened only two to three days after they had been expelled; the news quickly reached the villagers who were scattered across the Galilee mountains, and they returned to their village in small groups."[37]

A military unit entered the village of al-Rama, east of Nahaf, on Sunday 31 October. The soldiers gathered the men east of the village, near the houses of the Nakhla family. Shortly after the inhabitants had gathered an explosion was heard, and they saw a dense cloud of dust at the same location. It became clear later that this was the result of blowing up Elias Shukri's house. "There was a hot southerly wind blowing that day," wrote Elias Srouji in his memoirs. Srouji was from Nazareth, and he had arrived in the village from Lebanon the previous day with his sick father. It was noon when a soldier "with dark complexion," thought to be a Yemeni Jew,[38] addressed the villagers. He then approached the rows of young men sitting on the ground, and ordered some of them to stand up and wait on the side. The young men whom the officer had chosen were taken as "prisoners of war" by the army and were moved to Israeli prisons.

Sitting next to Dr. Srouji was his colleague Dr. 'Atallah Shayban, who had brought a stethoscope with him. When this soldier came close to him, he said: "You, doctor, stand up." The Latin priest, who feared for the lives of those young men, stepped forward and asked the officer to release the doctor "so that he could treat a woman who was delivering a baby at home." The officer agreed to the priest's request and set Dr. Shayban free.[39] According to Srouji, after 'Atallah's release from among the prisoners, he went to his friend Srouji "and said: 'Come, let us talk to the officer.' I agreed and we walked together in the direction of the command center. Dr. 'Atallah's request to remain in al-Rama was approved immediately. Then the officer asked me what I wanted, and I explained to him that I had arrived in Rama with my father who was suffering from cancer, and I asked that we be allowed to return to our homes in Nazareth." Srouji writes in his memoirs that his request was approved and members of his family were allowed to return from al-Rama to their city.[40]

The possibly Yemeni soldier then stood on an elevated patch of ground and said: "Our Druze friends were with us from the beginning of the road. Everyone else is our enemy. Under the orders of the Israeli government you have one hour to go back to your houses and fetch what you want; after that you will have to head north." This statement caused a commotion among those present, and some asked: "Where are you expelling us to? What about the promises of the army yesterday that no harm would come to us?" The same soldier answered: "We know nothing about any promises. We were not here yesterday."[41] The soldiers began to fire in the air to speed the departure of the gathered men in keeping with the expulsion order.

The al-Rama residents who were not expelled heard the shots being fired in the air, and saw with their own eyes the departure of the majority of the population northwards towards Lebanon. The Christian residents obeyed the orders and began their slow uphill climb towards Jarmaq Mountain north of their village. Others ran away and hid in caves and in the mountains. When the caravan of expellees reached al-Sahla region near Bayt Jan,[42] the Druze inhabitants of that village and of neighboring al-Buqay'a met them and proposed to help them to prevent their expulsion. Indeed, they contacted Shaykh Jabr al-Ma'di and other Druze notables whose intervention was largely responsible for the return of the inhabitants of al-Rama to their village.[43] In this way, the order to expel the Christians from al-Rama was reversed, and they were permitted to return to their homes. Subsequently, the inhabitants who returned sent messages to their families, who were near the southern Lebanese border, and the great majority returned to their homes in al-Rama.

There are many written and oral accounts concerning the reasons for the reversal of the order to expel Christians from al-Rama and the subsequent permission for them to return to their homes in the following few days.[44] However, all these accounts agree that only the Christians were expelled (and not the Druze), in an effort to uproot them and expel them to Lebanon. There is unanimity that the expellees returned to their homes after spending a day or two near the village of Bayt Jan.[45] We shall return later to the expulsion of residents from al-Rama and then the allowing of their return, which happened within the same time frame as the expulsion of residents of 'Ilabun, which stirred up controversy. The news of the expulsion of 'Ilabun villagers reached minister Bechor Shitrit, who went to see Minister of Defense and Prime Minister Ben-Gurion concerning this matter. Furthermore, the expulsion of Christians from the Galilee stirred up criticism and considerable correspondence from clergy in the country and in Lebanon and the Western world. Which factor played a bigger role in the decision to allow the residents of al-Rama to return: the reaction from the churches and fear of the repercussions, or the intervention of the Druze leaders in Yarka and elsewhere? There is no clear answer to this question in Israeli archives or historical literature on the subject. It would appear that both reasons combined to lead to the cancellation of the expulsion order and the permission to the residents of al-Rama and other villages to return to their homes.

In concluding this section of the chapter, it should be emphasized that attempts to expel Muslim and Christian residents of al-Shaghur villages failed to a large extent. The residents refused to bow down to the expulsion orders which were issued by officers of military units, and resisted the orders to expel them in various ways, including by efforts to gain time, peaceful resistance, asking their Druze neighbors for help, and other means. Verbal and written accounts confirm that the residents during this period of the war were aware that resistance through such means was far more preferable than acceptance of being uprooted from their country and their homes. Those residents, the majority of whom had not taken part in fighting the Israeli army following the withdrawal of units of the ARA, surrendered, and the soldiers who entered the area met no resistance from the residents. These facts made it difficult for Israel and its army to use an iron fist policy to expel the population. In addition, the demographic composition of the inhabitants of al-Shaghur villages, which consisted of Muslims, Christians, and Druze, was an important factor in the "hesitancy" of some military units to use excessive force or to harass those whom the state did not wish to expel. For these reasons, most of al-Shaghur villagers escaped destruction and expulsion, and the villages of al-Rama, Nahaf, Sajur, Dayr al-Asad, al-Bi'na, and Majd al-Krum are still populated to this day.

THE MASSACRE IN 'ILABUN AND THE EXPULSION
OF ITS RESIDENTS

'Ilabun was a peaceable village nestled in the southeastern section of the Galilee pocket before it was occupied in Operation Hiram. In this relatively small village lived hundreds of Catholics and Christian Orthodox residents,[46] most of whose ancestors came from neighboring villages in the mid-eighteenth century, and they continued to maintain familial and friendship ties with their ancestral villages.[47] Some 'Ilabun residents had relatives and friends in Lebanon, which was helpful when they were expelled from the village, as we shall see below. Until 1948, the very few residents who had finished high school went to work in Haifa, 'Akka, Jaffa, and other cities. Like other residents of the Galilee villages, the vast majority of the inhabitants of 'Ilabun worked in agriculture, from which they were able to secure what they needed to feed themselves and live a modest life.

'Ilabun's location on the front lines and the stationing of units of the ARA nearby caused the inhabitants to fear retribution from the Israeli army. Many felt that they were in a sensitive situation, and that they should be careful not to anger either party to the conflict.[48] The residents followed the news of the fighting on the radio and some newspapers which arrived from neighboring villages. The radio news was from the BBC, which they considered to be more accurate and truthful than other outlets, and the villagers passed the news to one another.[49] The villagers also received news from refugees passing by on the northward route about the fall of the villages of Hittin, Lubya, and al-Shajara, and their expulsion after occupation. The news was of the weakness of the Arab side and the defeats it suffered, and the lessons were about trusting the ARA, which had failed to save the cities and villages of the Galilee from falling into the hands of the Israeli army.

The tension and fear of the future caused dozens of the inhabitants of 'Ilabun to leave their houses and to live in the vineyards and caves near the village. Some families sent the women and children to stay with their relatives in the villages of Dayr Hanna, al-Maghar, and al-Rama, which were far from the battlefront. But when autumn came, many had to return to their houses despite their fear of what the days ahead might bring.[50] In the period preceding Operation Hiram, 'Ilabun's residents lost contact with the cities they used to visit and work in, which had fallen under Israeli occupation, such as Tiberias, Nazareth, Haifa, and 'Akka. The residents of these cities and the villages which escaped the depopulation of their districts lived under Israeli military rule. The road from central Galilee to south Lebanon remained open and relatively easy to travel on, but the clouds of renewed fighting began gathering in October 1948. When the inhabitants heard that fighting had renewed on the Egyptian front, tension and pressure increased, as a number of those whom I interviewed recounted.

Habib Zurayq resided in 'Ilabun through that period, and preserved many of its events in his memories. He joined the National Liberation League several years before the Nakba.[51] Like the majority of his comrades he supported the partition resolution and defended it in gatherings with relatives and friends. When at the beginning of October the League decided to distribute its anti-war pamphlet against the intervention of Arab armies in the war, he volunteered to complete the task in the Galilee pocket, in the villages of al-Rama and its neighborhood. Riding his donkey, he brought the pamphlets to his own village of 'Ilabun which he reached by way of Wadi Salama at night, leaving bundles of pamphlets in the village center before going to bed.[52]

The residents of 'Ilabun were the first to document the story of their village in detail, in books, films, and filmed testimonies. The following pages rely to a great extent on the publications of the "village historian" Elias Surur, whose testimony I heard before his sudden death.

According to Surur, "On the evening of 29 October, the 'Ilabun villagers climbed onto their roofs to sleep as they were accustomed to do on hot nights. But they did not hear the sounds usually made by the ARA to the southeast of their village." It became apparent later that the ARA had withdrawn from the region without allowing the young men from the village, who had been with them, to return to their families.[53] Some young men who had cooperated with the volunteers accompanied them to Lebanon, while others chose to hide in the mountains, to see what would happen to their village when the Israeli army entered it. The residents on the whole stayed in their homes, and many of them put up white flags on the roofs of their houses as a sign of surrender. Indeed, the soldiers of the Golani Brigade who entered the village the next morning met no resistance from the villagers; on the contrary, clergymen from the Catholic and Orthodox churches hailed the soldiers in welcome and peace.[54]

A large number of the residents of 'Ilabun had spent the night in the Catholic church and in the neighboring house of the priest, Murqus al-Mu'allim, and in the Orthodox church. After the entry of the soldiers of the Golani Brigade into the village, the officer asked all the inhabitants to gather in the village center, al-Hara, where the soldiers proceeded to separate the men from the women, as was their custom in occupied Arab villages. They shouted at anyone who delayed in leaving the churches, using gunfire to speed up the operation. As a result of the shooting, 'Azar Salim Maslam was killed, and two other youths, Yusif Ilyas Sulayh and Butrus Shukri Hanna, were wounded.[55] A short while after completing the ceremony of surrendering the village, a soldier stood up in front of the men and chose a number of them, asking them to stand aside. Seventeen young men were chosen, mostly in their twenties. Afterwards the soldiers ordered the rest of the residents to walk in the direction of al-Maghar. The priest begged the soldiers to take the men and leave the women and children in the village, but they refused.

After the residents of 'Ilabun had moved a few dozen meters from the houses in their village, the soldiers divided the young men who had been told to stand aside into five groups:

1. The first group consisted of Milad Sulayman, Fadl Fadlu 'Ilabuni, and Zaki Musa Nakhla. The soldiers accompanied them to Subhi Matar's vegetable garden, and shot them there.[56]
2. The second group consisted of Khalil Nakhla, Mikha'il Mitri Shami and Abdulla Sam'an Shufani. Other soldiers took them to the cemetery and killed them.
3. The third group consisted of Na'im Ghantus Zurayq, Hanna Ibrahim Khoury Ashqar, and Muhammad Khaled As'ad (a refugee from Hittin). The soldiers took them to Elias Hawwa's bakery and killed them.
4. The fourth group consisted of Badi' Jiryis Zurayq, Jiryis Shibli al-Hayik, and Fu'ad Nawfal Zurayq, whom the soldiers took to the south of the village center and killed.

5. The fifth group consisted of Faraj Hazima Zurayq, Farid Zurayq, Fadlu Ghantus Zurayq, Dhiyab Dawud Zurayq, and Habib Zurayq, who were placed in a
   military vehicle driven by Faraj Zurayq who was ordered to drive in front of
   the vehicles carrying the soldiers which headed north, behind the caravan
   of expelled villagers walking on foot.

The inhabitants of 'Ilabun migrated from their village not knowing the fate of the
youth whom the soldiers had killed. When they got to al-Maghar, they begged
the soldiers to let them go back home, but the soldiers told them to continue walking north in the direction of Lebanon. When the villagers left al-Maghar, one of
the old men yelled at the top of his voice: "People, 'Ilabun is dead!" and the crying
and lamentations of the women became louder.[57] When the caravan of refugees
reached the vicinity of Kufr 'Anan, the soldiers ordered everyone to sit down under
the great terebinth tree west of the main road. When people asked for something
to feed the children, the soldiers gave them some boiled potatoes, but they had
hardly begun to eat when the soldiers started firing, and Sam'an Jiryis Shufani was
killed in front of everyone.[58] Later in the evening, the forced migrants reached the
village of Farradiyya where they slept in and around the mosque.

The villagers have told the details of how they were uprooted from 'Ilabun
and the migration journey up to their arrival in Lebanon—and they have
documented it.[59] These villagers also are an example of the revival of the memory
of the Nakba in their village after their return to it. They erected a monument
for the martyrs of the massacre, and persist in reviving its memory and transmitting
the story from one generation to the next. We shall relate briefly the details of the
migration journey and the return; readers can find more copious details of the
events in 'Ilabun during the Nakba in books, testimonies, films, and other accessible documentation cited below.

On the morning of the following day, 31 October, soldiers picked thirty-four
young men from the inhabitants of 'Ilabun and took them to prisoner of war camps,
along with the five young men from the Zurayq family who had accompanied the
soldiers in the military vehicle as far as Majd al-Krum and who had returned the
same day.[60] When the prisoners reached the village of al-Maghar (where similar
groups from other Arab villages in the Galilee gathered) they learned some details
of the massacre of the young men from 'Ilabun whom the soldiers had detained
after the expulsion of its inhabitants.[61] News of what had happened in the village
travelled quickly throughout the Galilee, ramping up the fear and terror already
experienced by defenseless civilians. Nevertheless, most of the people of the Galilee tried to overcome their fears and to cling to their villages, cities, and land, so
that they would not suffer the same fate as the refugees whom Israel had uprooted
from their homes and then prohibited from returning.

After the caravan of refugees from 'Ilabun reached the Mirun crossroads the
soldiers accompanying them allowed the exhausted villagers to rest and search for
something to eat. The men went to the deserted houses of the depopulated Mirun
village and returned after a short while carrying sacks of flour and some legumes.[62]

The women kneaded the dough, then baked it on a fire using pots and pans they found in the abandoned houses. After everyone ate, some slept under the olive trees. During the night, the soldiers disappeared, and the villagers rejoiced; however, at midnight, army trucks arrived and the soldiers ordered the villagers to get on and transported them to the Lebanese border.[63] There they were put out of the army trucks and ordered to march north. When dawn broke, the villagers discovered that the soldiers and the trucks had disappeared.[64] When they saw Rumaysh, which was the closest town, they knew that they were in south Lebanon. There the 'Ilabun villagers met others from their village who had arrived a few days before them on their own.

Despite the harsh circumstances, the expelled villagers from 'Ilabun relaxed when they reached south Lebanon and saw some young men from their village who had arrived ahead of them. After a short rest, the villagers continued on their way to the village of 'Ayn Ibil, about eight kilometers northeast of Rumaysh, and headed to the church to camp there.[65] The news of the arrival of the forced refugees from 'Ilabun spread, and the mukhtar of 'Ilabun, Faraj Surur, came to see the people of the village, as did Abdullah Murqus al-Mu'allim, who had reached on his own to the town of Damur where he sought refuge. The people of 'Ilabun stayed for several days in the church of 'Ayn Ibil until they were transported to Miya Miya refugee camp east of Sidon.[66]

After more than a week of wandering along the paths of migration, the expelled villagers from 'Ilabun arrived at the refugee camp, and a new chapter of their lives began far from their village, but it did not last long. They were permitted to return to their homes at the end of December, as we shall see later. The 'Ilabun saga is one of the most well-known stories of expulsion and massacre perpetrated inside or outside the Galilee. However, the causes of this act of retribution—aberrant in its cruelty against a Christian village far from the border—presents a riddle to this day.[67] Who took the decision to carry out this cruel act of collective punishment in 'Ilabun, and why? This matter has still not been clarified despite all that has been said and written on the subject. Furthermore, the decision to allow the return of the refugees from Lebanon in a quasi-secretive fashion and through devious channels is another puzzle. In the absence of Israeli archival documentation, the story of 'Ilabun shows the importance of verbal testimonies by the residents, for, without their words, it would not be possible to document the massacre, expulsion, and subsequent return of the villagers to their homes.

Compared to the many Arab villages through which the displaced villagers passed on their way to Lebanon, the fate of 'Ilabun was better, relatively speaking, except for the village of al-Maghar. The villages of Kufr 'Inan and Farradiyya joined the list of depopulated and destroyed villages.[68] Similarly, the residents of Mirun, Safsaf, Sa'sa', Kufr Bir'im, and other villages along the Lebanese border were expelled. The residents of Jish were partially spared the ethnic cleansing in that area of the Galilee. It is clear that the large number of killings and expulsion of the residents of upper Galilee was a planned policy, with high-level orders. The fact that al-Maghar and 'Ilabun endured was also part of this general policy to allow Druze villages to remain untouched.[69]

KILLINGS AND EXPULSIONS IN OTHER VILLAGES

The residents of Kufr 'Inan and Farradiyya who had stayed in their homes did not remain there long after the expelled villagers from 'Ilabun passed by. A few weeks after the occupation of both villages, the Israeli army returned and expelled those who remained, either to the West Bank or to al-Rama and Majd al-Krum,[70] leaving no one. In the villages of upper Galilee closer to the Lebanese border, however, the war crimes and expulsions were more severe and cruel. The Israeli army carried out killings (including massacres), pillaged, and raped in a number of border villages, including Safsaf, Saliha, Jish, Hula, and Sa'sa', on the day the villages were occupied or shortly thereafter. The killings and expulsions were carried out in villages that had put up no resistance to the occupiers. The inhabitants of some villages (Saliha, for example) even resisted the presence of the ARA in their village, but this did not save them when the soldiers of the Israeli army entered their village.

The murders of the residents of the "friendly" village of Saliha evoked reactions of condemnation even among the Jews themselves. According to the report by Yisrael Galili at the political conference of the Mapam party, ninety-four people were killed in the massacre at Saliha. However, documentation published in 1985 based on verbal testimonies lists one hundred and five people killed, with their names and ages.[71] The massacre at Dayr Yasin holds a central symbolic position in the Palestinian memory of the Nakba, but few have heard of the Saliha massacre, carried out by regular Israeli soldiers at a late stage of the war as part of Operation Hiram, despite the enormity of the murders and expulsions in that village. As this chapter shows, they were neither unique nor exceptional in the context of the ethnic cleansing of Palestinians at that time, particularly in upper Galilee.

The events in 'Ilabun also affected the Arabs of al-Mawasi, who lived near that village and had good economic and social ties to it. Members of the tribe heard what the Israeli army soldiers had done in 'Ilabun, but they did not leave their dwellings, merely put up white flags. On Monday, 1 November, a unit of the Israeli army encountered sixteen-year-old Salih Irshayd as he was grazing his cattle, and shot and killed him; Salih Jaber, seventeen years old, was wounded but survived. On the same day soldiers met thirteen-year-old Salih Yusif al-Ramli with his cattle near the spring east of 'Ilabun, and shot and killed him.[72] The following day, army soldiers attacked whoever remained of al-Mawasi Arabs in al-Hinnawi district; they arrested twelve men and led them westwards to the eastern entrance of al-Battuf plain. There they killed them all, except for Sa'd Muhammad Dhib who was gravely wounded and escaped death by a miracle. Upon his recovery, he told his mother and relatives the details of what had happened.[73]

Husayn al-Shawahda was one of the first to hear about the massacre of al-Muwasi Arabs from Sa'd Dhib, and he in turn related what he had heard in the Um al-Thanaya region near the eastern al-Battuf plain. Sa'd testified that he was grazing his cattle when he saw someone hiding behind a tree. He asked what had happened, and the reply was that a massacre had taken place in which fourteen al-Mawasi Arabs had been killed. Sa'd added: "I and Mu'jal al-'Usba' were merely wounded. The soldiers sensed Mu'jal had not died, so they approached him and shot him in the head, killing him."[74] A woman, Zahiya al-Fawwaz, came along with her donkey. She put the wounded man (Sa'd) on her donkey and took him to a nearby cave to hide him. This woman continued to bring him food to the cave and to tend to his wounds. The soldiers found out that Sa'd Dhib was alive, so they searched for him in 'Ilabun but did not find him. A few days later Sa'd's mother found out he was alive and hiding in a cave, so she came to his hiding place and moved him to Syria, where he spent the rest of his life.

As to what became of the victims of the massacre of al-Mawasi Arabs, Husayn al-Shawahda testified that he went to the scene with his brother Muhammad and his son Isma'il, and they buried the martyrs in a cemetery near the 'Ayn al-Natiq cave. Husayn al-Shawahda said that he knew all of the martyrs, and he listed them by name, one by one.[75] After that massacre, the remaining al-Mawasi Arabs were expelled to Syria; only a few remained and took up residence in 'Ilabun. Several years later, when the Israeli Mekorot Water Company carried out excavations in the area, the martyrs' remains were moved to another cave, and years later they were moved to a cemetery in 'Ilabun where a monument for them was erected similar to the one for the 'Ilabun villagers themselves.

A terrible massacre carried out by soldiers of the Israeli army also occurred in Safsaf. This village near the Lebanese border was occupied on Saturday, 30 October. The soldiers gathered all those who remained in their homes and shot and killed twelve young men. Then they took dozens of men (some of whom had fought with the ARA) to a well where they executed them.[76] Not satisfied with killing the men in cold blood, the soldiers picked several women and asked them to fetch water to the village. After they had moved away some distance, the soldiers followed and raped them, killing two in the process. One old man could no longer control himself when he heard the cries of the victims of the rapes, and began yelling and rebuking the soldiers. As for the soldiers who were "guarding" the residents of the village, some attacked him by kicking and hitting him in the face and all over his body.[77] One of his female relatives testified that his face was still swollen from the soldiers' blows when she saw him a few days later. This old man had been carrying a letter in his pocket from a Jewish friend, called Balty, which he was to have used to protect himself. Later he joined the caravan of expellees who became refugees in Lebanon.[78]

Um Muhammad Hulayhal and other members of her family who saw with their own eyes or heard what happened in Safsaf, 'Ayn al-Zaytun, and other villages in the region of Safad, buried those memories for dozens of years, and did not tell anyone outside the family. There was special sensitivity concerning the rape of young women from the village by the soldiers, which was considered a dishonor to the family.[79] Another reason which contributed to the burial of such memories was that those who remained in their homeland, despite the great suffering they endured, considered themselves relatively fortunate. They saw with their own eyes how residents of many villages in the region were uprooted and forced to migrate to Syria and Lebanon, so they chose not to annoy the "new masters" with stories of what their soldiers had done in the year of the Nakba.

One of the women assaulted was 'Aziza Shrayda, a relative of Fatima Shrayda who gave birth to a daughter several years after the Nakba whom she named 'Aziza. The murders, rapes, and expulsion of residents of Safsaf had a shattering impact on the population of the area who feared the prospect of a repetition of those events in their villages. No one who knew or heard of 'Aziza Shrayda's story ever forgot its details. 'Aziza was a woman in her thirties. Soldiers entered her house and found her with members of her family. The soldiers decided to rape this woman in front of her oldest son (seventeen years old) and her husband and her small children, but she resisted. The soldiers threatened to kill her firstborn son if she did not do as they wished, and in fact they did kill him before her eyes.[80] Then they threatened to kill her husband if she did not take off her clothes, and she refused, so the soldiers opened fire on her husband, killing him. Then they killed her in front of her small children before they left her house. One of her relatives took it upon himself to bring up her children who were orphaned and joined the caravans of refugees.

News of what happened in Safsaf reached the ears of some leaders of the state who quickly condemned what had happened and asked that the perpetrators be put on trial.[81] Haim Laskov, head of the seventh army guidance division, carried out an investigation. The officers admitted that some residents had fled the village and were pursued by soldiers who killed them. They also admitted that after the occupation of the villages was complete there was "disorder and confusion," after which a number of prisoners were killed and some residents were severely mistreated.[82] Yet despite the investigation and the confessions no soldier was punished for what he had done. Ben-Gurion and army officers persisted in covering up the soldiers' crimes against civilians and prisoners, and the expulsion of tens of thousands of residents in Operation Hiram. This coverup proves that the acts of murder and severe maltreatment of the residents in the Galilee were part of a top-level policy in which the Israeli government and army command were complicit. The fact that the army perpetrated fifteen massacres during a single week after occupying the Galilee speaks to the presence of a formal policy.[83]

Most villages in Safad suffered the same fate as a result of uprooting and expulsion in 1948. Residents of ten other villages joined this caravan as part of Operation Hiram: Qadas, Fara, Saliha, Dayshum, 'Alma, 'Ammuqa, Dallata, Qadditha, Taytaba, and al-Malikiyya, in addition to Safsaf. To the west of the village of

Jish, which was fated to escape that painful destiny, were the villages of Sa'sa', Dayr al-Qasi, Suhmata, al-Nabi Rubin, Suruh, and Tarbikha, which suffered uprooting and expulsion as well. Later, before the end of the Nakba, the villages of Iqrit Kufr Bir'im, and al-Mansura joined the list. In all, the inhabitants of more than thirty Arab villages were forced to leave their homes and to migrate during the operation to complete the occupation of the Galilee. The policy of ethnic cleansing was largely implemented in that late phase of the war. However, despite the great efforts expended by the army to terrorize the population and expel them, dozens of villages endured and their residents remained in their homes after Operation Hiram.

The Israeli army not only perpetrated massacres and expelled residents in upper Galilee, but it also acted similarly in southern Lebanon border areas. After the occupation of the Shi'a village of al-Hula, where ninety-four people were murdered in one of the worst massacres in the year of the Nakba including thirty-four prisoners who were blown up in the house in which they were being detained, Dov Yermiyahu, the Deputy Battalion Commander in the Carmeli Brigade during Operation Hiram, insisted that First Lieutenant Shmuel Lahis, who was under his command and who was responsible for this incident, be put on trial.[84] On the insistence of this senior officer, Lahis was tried, and convicted of perpetrating the crime, but he did not spend one day of his short sentence in jail.[85] This incident also confirms that the policy of killing and terrorizing civilians was not a matter of decisions by individual officers, but a general policy which was covered up by both the military and civilian leaders.

The large number of cases of murder and expulsion of residents in the Safad district requires a comprehensive study to uncover its causes. Was it a matter of geography, that is, the proximity of these villages to the Syrian and Lebanese borders, which was the cause of this aggressive policy, or was the main consideration the fact that a large number of the Galilee villages were in the area allocated to the Jewish state? What was the role of Jewish settlers in this area who were greedy for depopulated land that they could use for expansion? Did the fact that most of these villages were inhabited by Muslims play a role? Finally, did the fact that this area was far from Haifa and other cities where journalists and representatives of international organizations, including the United Nations, were to be found, play an auxiliary role? These are important questions but require a separate study.

To the west of the Safad and Tiberias districts, a larger number of Palestinians stayed in their towns and villages despite the killings and expulsions. In al-Battuf plain, the villages of Sakhnin, 'Arraba, and Dayr Hanna remained standing.[86] To the north, all al-Shaghur villages remained, from al-Rama to Majd al-Krum. North of al-Shaghur the picture was more complicated. The closer villages were to the Lebanese border, the less chance they stood of surviving, and the same was true of the villages near the Mediterranean coast. In general, about half the villages Israel occupied in Operation Hiram escaped uprooting and destruction. Half of the thirty villages which survived were either Druze, or mixed villages with Christian,

Muslim, and Druze residents. As we saw earlier, it was clear that the army received instructions on how to deal with these villages and executed them in full.

The presence of tens of thousands of Arabs in the upper Galilee was an important element in the initial opposition of some Israeli ministers to its occupation. Ben-Gurion tried to calm the fears of his ministers who were opposed at the 26 September cabinet meeting, saying that in the event of a renewal of the fighting, the Galilee would be "clear of Arabs" or "clean." Ben-Gurion reiterated the point on 21 October when he said, "There is nothing left for the Arabs in Israel to do except for one thing—to flee." A significant number of politicians and army leaders shared this opinion. Yosef Weitz, the well-known supporter and advocate of the transfer plans, sent an urgent letter to Yigal Yadin on the day that Operation Hiram was launched, proposing that the army should expel the refugees from the villages it occupied.[87] The policy of transfer was apparently not as fully realized as advocates had hoped, since Ben-Gurion declared after a tour of the northern front, "There is no enemy [left] in the Galilee," then added with some disappointment, "but there are many Arabs [who are still] in the Galilee."[88]

On 31 October, Ben-Gurion recorded in his diary a summary of the report by Moshe Carmel on the results of Operation Hiram. Out of approximately 60,000 residents of the occupied area, about half remained, while the rest had migrated. Ben-Gurion commented: "Many will migrate later."[89] This last sentence was not a mere wish; there was a plan with Carmel to arrive at this result on the ground. Indeed, on the morning of 31 October, Carmel sent a telegram to all the commanders of military units containing the following order: "Do everything you can to achieve a quick and immediate purification of the occupied areas of all enemy elements, according to standing orders. It is imperative to help the residents leave the occupied regions."[90] That same day, he sent a report about the partial fulfilment of the mission, and that he hoped to complete it in coordination with the prime minister and minister of defense. The policy was clear from the top of the pyramid to the field officers, and the only open question was the method of implementation and reactions inside the country and abroad.

Army officer (later minister) Yitzhak Moda'i wrote a research paper on Operation Hiram and its results for the history department of the Israeli army at the end of the 1950s. His research was based on military documents unknown to the general public.[91] The research question was: why did a large number of Arab residents remain in the Galilee pocket compared to other places? Moda'i wrote the following: "Some may think that the residents of the Galilee were not compelled, as others were compelled in other places, to flee to save themselves from severe maltreatment. However, the testimonies of officers and soldiers and official reports . . . show that our forces did not stand idly by, and that their treatment of the population could not possibly have been the reason they stayed under any circumstances." To emphasize his conclusions, Moda'i quoted Carmel's order. He then wrote in the conclusion to his study: "Most of the Arab residents of the Galilee remained in their villages, but it was not because our forces did not try to expel them, quite often through means that were neither legal nor nice."[92]

The last sentence in Moda'i's report can be translated as "war crimes" and other many acts of maltreatment, whose oppressive details I have sometimes spared the reader. In this chapter, the emphasis has been on acts that were systematic and a matter of general policy, not exceptions. Some eyewitnesses have told stories about the amputation of fingers and other body organs to steal rings, gold, and jewels from those who were killed and mutilated. Some of these incidents reached the ears of Mapam party activists in the north, one of whom, Yosef Waschitz,[93] known for his research into Arab affairs in the country, wrote a report in which he discussed savage incidents in Safsaf and Saliha and other villages which were occupied in Operation Hiram.[94] However, Waschitz and Mapam leader Aharon Cohen and others who heard about those ugly deeds in the Galilee did nothing about them. Thus, those who knew about those crimes and kept silent became complicit in them in one way or the other. The same could be said of the army and other security agencies who concealed documents and information concerning murder and forced migration from researchers.

Officer Moda'i admitted in his research, which is based on army documents, that while a major effort was expended to get rid of the Arab population of the Galilee, those villagers resisted attempts to expel them, and some of them succeeded in foiling the policy of expulsion, with the residents of 'Ilabun being the best example.[95] In the final analysis, the massacre perpetrated by the army in that village and its criminal actions in Safsaf and other villages brought an end to the attempts to "help" the Arab population leave their villages and homes, even if it was for a limited period. But the killings, maltreatment, and terrorizing of the population did not stop altogether in the succeeding weeks. One example of that was the massacre that the army perpetrated in Majd al-Krum on 5 November, one week after the surrender of the village.

THE MAJD AL-KRUM MASSACRE
AND ITS REPERCUSSIONS

As noted above, a report by a Haifa district intelligence officer in November monitored the situation in Majd al-Krum after its occupation but before the massacre in the village.[96] It mentioned that the population of the village was 2,000, counting the original villagers and refugees from the region. It also mentions that the village was full of young men of draft age, and it appeared that at least some of them had participated in the fighting on the side of the ARA which was stationed in and around Majd al-Krum. The officer mentioned that many of the men in the village, particularly the youth, had hidden in the mountains, and would try to go back in the following days.[97] His recommendations for action to be taken resemble the orders given by Moshe Carmel in those days, amounting to: "There is a need for a speedy and serious combing operation, and a search for arms and collaborators with the ARA in the region." This recommendation was carried out a few days after the report was written.

On Friday, 5 November, an army unit arrived in Majd al-Krum, imposed a curfew on the village, and ordered the men to assemble in al-'Ayn Square.[98] Then the officer in charge went to the mukhtar, Hajj 'Abd Manna', and ordered that the villagers should surrender whatever arms were in their possession which they had not handed over a week earlier on the day the village surrendered.[99] Hajj 'Abd replied that there were no arms left in the hands of the residents as far as he knew; at any rate investigating this matter and conducting a search would take over an hour. Still, the officer insisted that his demand be carried out and threatened that in one hour a young man would be executed every half hour until the residents surrendered the "hidden arms." In the meantime, soldiers were sent into the houses to search for arms and for the men who were in hiding and had not assembled at al-'Ayn Square. All attempts by the mukhtar to convince the officer to retract his demand failed, as did the explanations they gave concerning the surrender document and the surrender of all arms and ammunition. The officer and his men appeared to be nervous and under pressure, which further alarmed the residents concerning what they might do when the deadline expired.

At the end of the hour, a number of young men were chosen to be executed according to the officer's warning. Those who were chosen and made to stand in the "execution line" were mostly refugees from the villages of Sha'b and al-Birwa, and a few from Majd al-Krum. Abu Ma'yuf (Muhammad al-Hajj) watched the soldiers blow up his house before his eyes were bound and he was shot in al-'Ayn Square in front of hundreds of men sitting on the ground. The officer continued carrying out his threat; he would issue orders to a six-man firing squad to execute a young man about every half hour, and in this way four more young men were killed, one after the other following Abu Ma'yuf.[100] To make certain they were dead, one soldier would approach each youth and shoot him in the head, in front of the residents, some of whom became frantic after this series of executions.

In addition to the five men executed in al-'Ayn Square, other soldiers killed two young men from the neighboring village of Sha'b who were visiting relatives. Soldiers who were monitoring the curfew in the southern sector of the village caught 'Ali As'ad and one of his relatives and tortured them before killing them in an olive orchard.[101] Still other soldiers fired on two women in the village while searching houses. In this way eight to nine people were killed.[102] This massacre was clearly premeditated, without any justification for killing, and happened one week after the village had surrendered. The deliberate and systematic execution of one person every half hour to terrify the village distinguishes this crime from similar ones in the Galilee villages during Operation Hiram.

Perhaps the calamity in Majd al-Krum would have been greater had it not been for the arrival of Shafiq Abu 'Abdu and Haim Orbach, the intelligence officer for western Galilee, in the village. Immediately upon his arrival and his discovery of the results of the executions in al-'Ayn Square, he spoke to the officer in charge and ordered a halt to the killings. Three men had already been chosen and told to stand aside awaiting their turn, the first of whom was the mukhtar, Hajj 'Abd Manna'.[103] For the residents who witnessed the execution of one man every half hour before their eyes, the arrival of Shafiq Abu 'Abdu and Haim Orbach was a miracle which saved the three men who were standing next in line to be shot. It is no wonder then that the names of these two individuals are well known and are on the tongues of the residents to this day. The villagers and the refugees who had gone to the square calmed themselves and thanked God that the disaster had not been worse. The remaining damages that day were limited to the theft of some valuable items from the houses and shops, and the seizure of hundreds of livestock which the soldiers drove before them on leaving the village headed east.[104]

When news of the massacre in Majd al-Krum spread, it reached the ears of United Nations observers whose ship had docked in Haifa, according to the villagers. When the observers inquired as to what had happened in the village, the army denied that it had carried out a massacre there, and accused the residents of spreading rumors. Colonel Baruch Baruch wrote a short confidential letter about this matter, complaining that "Majd al-Krum is neglected by our forces, and it has no military governor or officer in charge."[105] When the UN fact-finding mission visited the village, Baruch claimed that "the residents had gone too far with charges against us of committing atrocities, murder, and theft." He added in the same document that had there been a "suitable remedy" they would not have dared spread such rumors. Baruch also predicted "when the observers' reports reach Paris and are blown out of proportion, they will cause us a lot of harm."[106] He concluded his letter to those in charge in the command by stressing the need to pay attention to such matters, which needed to be dealt with in a suitable and speedy manner.

Yosef Schnurman (Shani), the Haganah liaison officer with the UN observers in Haifa, had tried, along with other army officers, to cover up the massacres perpetrated during Operation Hiram. In the case of Majd al-Krum, there was total denial (as was the case with 'Ilabun), but this did not work. Officers of the Ninth Brigade, some of whose soldiers carried out the massacre, denied that it ever happened, and stressed that "it was possible to visit the village and satisfy oneself that there is no proof we were involved." Like Colonel Baruch, Schnurman also complained of the lack of a military governor who could intimidate the villagers with his stature, adding: "This situation has allowed Arabs to engage in conduct unbecoming in testifying before UN observers."[107] As we shall see later, the army's threats did not deter the village residents and notables from testifying about the events in Majd al-Krum before the observers, and then in the halls of the High Court of Justice.

The UN observers who visited the village a few days after the massacre sent a report to the United Nations, which Benny Morris relied on in his writings.[108] Over several years I had heard about the massacre from my parents and relatives. Until I published an article in a newspaper in which I mentioned what had happened in the village, I had no archival document in my possession that could prove that those events had occurred. Some readers reacted harshly to my accusation that the army had killed some people in my village.[109] I quote below from a letter to *Haaretz* from a reader by the name of Ze'ev Yitzhaki who strongly denied what I said, adding: "I was the commander of the unit that received the surrender agreement by the village in the war of independence, but I affirm that there were neither thefts nor expulsions or executions."[110] Yitzhaki's testimony may be sincere, because it seems that he was the leader of the 122nd or 123rd Company, which came from the west and took charge of the village on 30 October. The massacre was perpetrated by other soldiers who came from the east a week later.

The new (or revisionist) Israeli historians have, since the end of the 1980s, uncovered a few of the atrocities perpetrated against Palestinians in the year of the Nakba. Although hundreds of villages were destroyed and their inhabitants expelled following massacres which were part of the ethnic cleansing policy to empty the country of its original inhabitants, little has been written about the atrocities—despite these having being witnessed by those who remained, whose testimonies no historian, including the revisionists, bothered to listen to. Even Morris writes: "But the army did not order the inhabitants to leave the village."[111] He was not aware of the massacre in Majd al-Krum until I had spoken to him in person. Once again, like Yitzhaki, he told a small part of the big picture. The unique type of massacre in Majd al-Krum, the theft of livestock, and the looting of some houses, convinced many that there was no safe place for the residents despite the surrender agreement, so dozens left the village. Morris himself gave me copies of military documents concerning the return of the army to the village in January 1949 and its expulsion of hundreds of residents; yet, he decided to overlook them when he defended the army and its actions.[112]

Finally, the name "Khawaja Ghazal" was mentioned by many residents of Majd al-Krum whose tales I had been hearing since my early years. They added that this *khawaja* (a term for a Westerner) spoke vernacular Arabic as we did. In the 1990s I had obtained some military documents from Israeli army archives concerning a massacre and expulsion of residents in Majd al-Krum. The name of the intelligence officer in the Haifa district, Tsvi Rabinovich, cropped up in those documents and reminded me of "Khawaja Ghazal" (his name meaning "gazelle" in Arabic), so I began looking for Rabinovich and tried to meet him. This was no easy task, and I did not succeed until 1998, which was before I published an article in Arabic on the occasion of the fiftieth anniversary of al-Nakba.[113] The intermediary who put me in touch with "Khawaja Ghazal" was Colonel Dov Yermiyahu from Nahariya who fought in the Galilee in 1948.

I had met Dov Yermiyahu following the Israeli invasion of Lebanon in 1982 when we participated in more than one demonstration against the war. When I asked him in early 1998 about Mr. Ghazal, he remembered him, added that he knew his brother Yonatan (Yunis), and gave me his home telephone number in a kibbutz near 'Akka. When I spoke to Yonatan I obtained his brother's telephone number in Haifa, and it turned out that he had changed his family name to Bah-rav. When I spoke to Rabinovitch (Mr. Ghazal) and told him I was a historian at Hebrew University, he quickly expressed his readiness to cooperate and to answer my questions. He did not deny the occurrence of the massacre in Majd al-Krum, but he claimed that it was the result of confusion and error. Later in the interview, he was eager to surprise me with a new and unknown bit of information about the visit by the United Nations team to the village after the massacre. He said: "Seeing as the army denied the occurrence of premeditated killing, the residents proposed to exhume the bodies of the martyrs which had been buried only a few days earlier.[114] The accompanying army officer agreed, so the villagers dug up one of the graves and brought out the body, which the UN observers photographed." Rabinovitch added that the officer stopped the exhumation of other bodies and told the observers that their mission was over, and that they had to return to their camps and their headquarters.[115]

Rabinovitch himself was not present in the village of Majd al-Krum that day; he was in the village of al-Rama, according to his testimony. He received an order to proceed to the western side of Majd al-Krum and set up a military roadblock to search the car of the United Nations team and to extract the film from the camera. Rabinovitch said he carried out his mission quickly and successfully, adding: "When the United Nations car arrived, we stopped it and asked all passengers to get out and stand to one side. After a quick search of the car we found the camera and took out the film despite the protests of the observers and their denunciations."[116]

When Rabinovitch noticed my agitation and surprise at his actions, he caught himself and said: "What? I hope you do not think that we have to allow those foreigners (goyim) to publish pictures of the atrocities for the world to see."[117] I was shocked and replied quickly: "Of course not." Nevertheless, I hurriedly concealed my anger and embarrassment and apologized that I had to cut the interview short, and promised to complete it at a later date. However, when I tried to resume the interview after several years I learned from Rabinovitch's wife that he had died, and I told her that I shared in her sorrow.[118] By sheer coincidence, I was later to meet the doctor who had treated "Mr. Ghazal" in his last years, Dr. Bashir Karkabi from Rambam Hospital in Haifa. The doctor was surprised by the stories of the Nakba that I had gathered and the role of his patient in the events at Majd al-Krum. He said that he had heard from Rabinovitch only about his Arab friends and how he helped them during and after the war in Shafa 'Amr and other villages and towns in the Galilee.[119]

The army continued to deny the massacre which it had perpetrated in Majd al-Krum and its expulsion of hundreds of villagers during 1948–49. Many who had fled from the massacre or whom the army expelled in January 1949 "infiltrated" back into the village and resorted to the courts in 1951, particularly the High Court of Justice in Jerusalem. In the proceedings of one case heard by the court, a contradiction between the testimonies of residents of Majd al-Krum and the allegations of the representatives the state and the military government became apparent. When the judges (Heishin, Zilberg, and Zohar) wrote their decision, they clearly stated, "The statements of Mukhtar Dhiyab Qasem Farhat . . . who told his story without fear or trepidation, are credible." But the testimony of the officer from the military government, Shmuel Pesitsky, "relies on unknown or dubious sources."[120]

THE FATE OF THE RESIDENTS OF THE BORDER STRIP VILLAGES

Israel completed the occupation of the Galilee through Operation Hiram, and expanded its territory to the international border with Lebanon and beyond. Following a meeting between Ben-Gurion and Moshe Carmel, commander of the northern front, the prime minister wrote in his diary that half of the residents of the Galilee had moved out of the region, "and many shall leave." On the same day, he submitted a report to his cabinet to the effect that "there is no enemy in the Galilee after Operation Hiram, but there are still many Arabs in the Galilee."[121] To attain their objective, after consulting with the general staff, Carmel decided to impose a curfew on all Arab villages in the 5–15 kilometer strip along the length of the border with Lebanon. He also issued orders to the soldiers to begin expelling the residents of those villages in order to create a border strip "clean" of Arab residents. Thus, the residents of al-Nabi Rubin, Tarbikha, Suruh, al-Mansura, Iqrit, Kufr Bir'im, and Jish were ordered to evacuate their villages.[122] The residents of Muslim villages were expelled to Lebanon, but the fate of the Christian villages was slightly different.

Most residents of Jish—Christian Maronites, along with a few Muslims—who received orders to migrate to Lebanon escaped expulsion and remained in their village. The Christian dignitaries went to see Mano (Emanuel) Friedman, the representative of the ministry of minorities in the Safad region, concerning their fate. Bechor Shitrit, who headed the ministry, contacted the leaders of the state, notably Yitzhak Ben-Tzvi, a leader in the ruling party, Mapai, and a specialist in Arab affairs. Shitrit and Ben-Tzvi together contacted army command in the area and managed to get the expulsion order changed. In this way, this border village escaped the fate of being uprooted which befell most border villages in eastern upper Galilee; the majority of Christians stayed in Jish, while most Muslims were uprooted, and joined the tens of thousands of refugees in Lebanon.

One of the villages which received the order to migrate was Iqrit, close to Fassuta. The Israeli soldiers had entered the village for the first time during Operation Hiram on 31 October without any incident of resistance. The villagers signed a surrender agreement, and handed over the arms and the ammunition they had in their possession. The residents of Iqrit had put up white flags as others had done, and the correspondent of *Davar* published an article with photos two days after the event. Barely a week had passed after the surrender of the village when Israeli soldiers returned (on 6 November) and asked the residents to leave their homes and go to al-Rama, thirty kilometers away. According to the testimony of the residents, the army officer who delivered the evacuation order, Ya'qub Qarra, promised that they could return to their houses after two weeks, and to take necessities and provisions to last them through that short period. That is what the villagers did, leaving a few men in the village to guard their houses and possessions.[123] That day 126 families, numbering 616 people, were evicted.

The fate of Kufr Bir'im was no different. After the decision was taken to evict its residents, they tried, like their neighbors, to have that unjust order lifted. People were busy with the olive harvest, and they contacted their Jewish friends to rescue them from their calamity. On 7 November, Mano Friedman arrived in the village accompanied by Raful, the director of the office of minorities in Safad, and they carried out a census of the population, which totaled 1,050 people. This step reassured the residents to some extent, giving them hope that their fate might be like that of the residents of Jish; however, these hopes were quickly dashed. Friedman came back on 13 November accompanied by four soldiers, and they told the residents to leave their homes and go to Lebanon within forty-eight hours.[124] In this case also, residents were promised that the expulsion would be temporary and was for security reasons, and that they could return to their homes after a few weeks.

The residents of Kufr Bir'im feared going too far from their homes, so some residents spent the days and nights in the olive orchards and the forests near the village. However, the bitter winter conditions in upper Galilee led to children falling ill and some dying. News spread that seven children had died from the cold and harsh living outdoor conditions. Therefore, on 19 November many of the villagers agreed to go to Jish and live in the abandoned houses there. Unfortunately there weren't enough houses so some moved to the village of Rumaysh in southern Lebanon with promises from Mano that their rights would be preserved. Notables from the village contacted Shitrit who came to visit and inspected their conditions in Jish on the following day with the military governor in Nazareth, Elisha Soltz.[125] The mukhtar of Kufr Bir'im, Qaysar Ibrahim, and the priest Yusif Susan met minister Shitrit and conveyed their grievances to him; they heard more promises from the minister that the displacement of the villagers from their homes was a temporary matter and that they would return to their village soon.

After a short while it became apparent that the promises of the Israeli army officers and politicians were mere deception. On 24 November the government took a decision to ratify the decision to expel the residents of Arab villages in the strip along the Lebanese border. Ben-Gurion explained his government's policy, saying: "Along the whole border and in each village, we shall take everything based on the requirements of settlement. As for the Arabs, we shall not bring them back."[126] Shitrit had forwarded the grievances of the residents of the evacuated villages—concerning the fact that the military government under General Elimelech Avnir had not halted expulsion operations—to the prime minister. Shitrit also complained that these operations were being conducted without his knowledge or even consultation with him.[127] Following the correspondence with Minister Shitrit, the government approved the return of the inhabitants of Kufr Bir'im from Rumaysh in Lebanon, not to their houses, but to live in Jish or elsewhere.

As the end of 1948 approached, the residents of most villages in the border strip had been expelled one way or the other; however, a few villages escaped this fate: Fassuta, Mi'lya, and Hurfaysh, as well as the Arab al-'Aramsha, in western Galilee. In eastern Galilee we have already seen that Jish remained, as did the Circassian village of al-Rihaniyya.[128] Despite Ben-Gurion's support for the army's demand that the border region be "clean" of Arab residents, the inhabitants of some villages managed to remain in their homes due to international and local pressures on the government in the final weeks of 1948. As happened in other areas in the Galilee, the residents of some villages took advantage of their connections and used procrastination and other means to remain in their villages, and they succeeded despite their proximity to the border, and despite the murders and massacres in Jish, Sa'sa', and Tarshiha.

Israel had tried to expel the inhabitants of Tarshiha, one of the largest villages in the area, but achieved only partial success. Tarshiha had over 4,000 inhabitants on the eve of the Nakba. During the occupation of the village as part of Operation Hiram, most of the residents were uprooted and forced to migrate, especially the Muslims who constituted the vast majority, so that only a few hundred residents remained, mainly Christians. The government wanted to settle some Jews from Romania in the abandoned houses, and the army put pressure on the residents to leave the village, but they did not submit to the pressure and contacted several parties asking for help, which led to their remaining in their homes.[129]

During the last few months of 1948, many of those who had been forced to migrate during or after Operation Hiram tried to return to their villages on their own; the army, on the other hand, was persistent in using various ways to prevent this from happening, particularly in those villages where most of the residents had been forced out. The army also conducted "combing" operations in the remaining villages to arrest "infiltrators" and expel them across the border once again. During the last months of the war, Israel and its army exerted a great effort to force out the largest possible number of residents of upper Galilee. However, the 'Ilabun villagers had managed to make their voice heard by the outside world, which compelled the government to allow those whom it had expelled from the village to begin quietly returning to their homes at the end of December 1948. It seems that their return, which took place gradually, was in fact one of the factors that helped some border villages to survive.

THOSE WHO REMAINED AT THE END OF 1948

Upon completing the occupation of the Galilee and the Naqab, and on the eve of the first elections in Israel in January 1949, the number of Arabs in the Jewish state stood at 125,000. The residents of Haifa and the Galilee, who numbered around 100,000, constituted the bulk of this population. The rest lived in mixed cities and some villages in the center of the country, in addition to the Bedouins in the Naqab.[130] Based on these numbers, it is clear that the official figure of 156,000 quoted by historians and researchers prior to the transfer of the villages of the Triangle to Israeli control is inaccurate.[131] A quick glance at the map of Palestine reveals that the majority of those who remained lived in those areas allocated to the Arab state under the partition resolution. Those who remained in the cities of Haifa, 'Akka, and Nazareth and the seventy villages in the Galilee constituted, then and still today, the nerve center of the Arab minority within the Jewish state, a state which created and imposed its own borders by force of arms and occupation.

How does one explain the success, to a considerable extent, of the Palestinians of the Galilee in foiling the expulsion plan? What is the secret of the reversal of Israeli policy which permitted the population of Nazareth and most of its villages to remain while violent efforts were made to expel the majority of the population of upper Galilee?

Under the partition resolution, the Arab state included three basic areas: the Galilee mountains in the north, the mountains of central Palestine (subsequently called the West Bank), and a coastal strip which extends from north of Isdud (Ashdod) to Rafah. The presence of the Egyptian army in the south explains why the Gaza Strip remained under Arab rule, and the presence of the Jordanian Arab Legion in the center, and the prior agreement between King Abdullah and the Zionist leadership, explains what became of the West Bank. The Galilee had no strong Arab army to protect it, nor was there an ambition on the part of states such as Lebanon to annex it either by force or through agreement. Therefore, when it became clear at the end of the war that Israel was in a position to annex the whole of the Galilee, the political and military leaderships of Israel wanted to expel the majority of the population, particularly those close to the border. It was the combined factors of geography, the demographic composition of the population, prior agreements with the Druze, and fear of an international reaction to the continuation of ethnic cleansing following the defeat of the Arab armies, that partially foiled the expulsion policy.

This chapter clearly demonstrates that the residents, and their resistance to expulsion, played an important role in their ability to remain. At the outset of the war, many Palestinians thought that leaving their homes would be temporary, and that they would return when the guns fell silent. Others believed that the Arab armies, which had entered the war in mid-May 1948, would protect them and return them to their homes. These armies had occupied regions of Palestine to which the expellees from the center and south of the country had migrated. The residents of the Galilee, whose lands Israel occupied at a late stage, had absorbed the lessons of the experience of those who were prohibited from returning. Furthermore, the contours of the Arab defeat and the Palestinian Nakba had become apparent by the summer of 1948, as had the bitter experience of refugees in Lebanon. All of these reasons made the residents of the Galilee cling hard to their homes and villages, to avoid falling prey to what had happened to their neighbors in villages which were destroyed and residents expelled.

The Palestinians in the Galilee pocket observed that the residents of Nazareth and most of its villages had remained, along with a number of villages in western Galilee as well, particularly the Druze villages. The Druze and their villages contributed by encouraging the Galilee residents to stay in their homes and villages, through indirect and direct support. These experiences convinced them that they too could endure in their villages and homes should they be occupied by the Israeli army. The mountainous terrain played another important role in enabling residents of some villages to return easily after their expulsion, as long as soldiers did not accompany them to the Lebanese border. In addition, some who did reach south Lebanon had no difficulty returning to the Galilee with the help of guides from the border villages. We can see then that a number of factors combined to contribute to a large number of Palestinians remaining even in areas that Israel wanted cleansed of Arabs, particularly in upper Galilee.

The discrepancy between the conduct of the Israeli army in the ten-day battles in July and in Operation Hiram in late October was considerable, and cannot be explained in terms of decisions by army commanders in the field. Without Ben-Gurion's written instructions and orders to the army, Nazareth and its residents would not have escaped unscathed; the same can be said about the dozens of villages in its district. On the other hand, Ben-Gurion's position was at variance in Operation Hiram, as he wanted to complete the occupation of the Galilee without its Arab population, as we explained above. Thus the top level decisions by Ben-Gurion, the prime minister and minister of defense, played the most important role in the conduct of the army in the Galilee, a region where it did not face a real threat, and which it occupied despite the fact that it was allocated to the Arab state. The justifications and explanations that Benny Morris and other Israeli historians put forward are not at all convincing.[132] The Galilee, whose occupation was completed by the army in the final months of the war, constitutes a good test case for research into many of the generalized historical narratives in the year of the Nakba.

In the Druze village of Yanuh a bloody battle took place in which the Israeli army lost a large number of soldiers; however, neither that village nor any of the neighboring villages were subjected to killings and maltreatment of its residents, due to specific top-level orders. Morris says that the Israeli army discriminated in its treatment of different sects: "Generally speaking, Christians and Druze were treated better than Muslims."[133] This statement conceals more than it reveals about the policy and conduct of the army instead of clarifying and exposing it fully. There were no repercussions against the Druze in their villages, even after the battle of Yanuh. Christians, on the other hand, were subjected to killings and expulsion, such as in 'Ilabun, Iqrit, Kufr Bir'im, and other villages. It is true that Christian villages received better treatment than Muslim ones, but to equate the treatment of the Druze with that of Christians is incorrect.

Morris's inaccuracy can also be detected in his conclusions about Muslims. On the heels of Operation Hiram, he wrote, for example: "Muslims had several villages left—Dayr Hanna, 'Arraba, Sakhnin, and Majd al-Krum—and their residents remained in place after the occupation and were not expelled."[134] The reader has the right to inquire, after what we learned earlier about the massacre in al-'Ayn Square in Majd al-Krum, and the expulsion of hundreds of residents from the village (detailed in the next chapter): How can the treatment of this village be similar to that of the villages of al-Battuf? Once more, it is clear that the army did all that it could to expel most of the population of upper Galilee north of the al-Shaghur villages. Its lack of success in doing so was due to the resistance of the inhabitants and local and international reactions to the massacres and acts of expulsion, as happened in 'Ilabun and other Christian villages.

Morris amended some of his conclusions concerning Operation Hiram in his book *Correcting a Mistake*. He wrote a sort of self-criticism, saying: "I have described a chaotic situation including the absence of instructions from the center or a fixed policy, a situation in which the numerous military units acted in a discrepant manner towards the Arabs whose villages were occupied."[135] After presenting this self-criticism concerning his conclusions regarding Operation Hiram, he ended with an important statement concerning the study of the 1948 war: "In the future, researchers should pay attention to a central issue concerning the 1948 war, which is the conduct of the Haganah—the Israeli army—and the ethics of war which has been described as 'the purity of arms.'" He then added that the researcher will have to wait until documents in the army archives, and other related archives, are declassified in their entirety. As we know, many years have passed since the beginning of this century, yet the documents relating to the massacres and mistreatment of the residents have remained classified.[136] The question is how long will historians wait before taking that step, and why do they not make use of testimonies of the victims and other written sources outside Israeli military archives?

In fact, the testimonies of residents of the Galilee villages which Israel occupied in Operation Hiram sheds substantial light on this foggy picture. Eyewitnesses who were present at the time of the massacres and expulsion operations cannot forget the psychological trauma and the harm that those events caused. We can detect what the army documents conceal from the writing of Yitzhak Moda'i, as quoted by Morris himself.[137] Those documents "admit" that the army did what it could to cause the inhabitants of central Galilee and upper Galilee to migrate. Moda'i's research provides some answers to the question posed in this book: why did a large number of Arab inhabitants remain in that region? Namely:

—resistance by ARA officers to the migration of Arab residents from their villages and towns;
—the topography of the Galilee mountains; and
—the presence of "friendly" villages whose residents were promised good treatment and non-interference in advance.

The reference in the last factor is first and foremost to Druze villages. As a result of this policy toward the Druze in the Galilee, all members of that sect, about 11,000 people, remained, as did the residents of two villages in Jabal al-Karmil: 'Isfiya and Daliyat al-Karmil. Until 1947, the Druze constituted only 1 percent of the population of Palestine. However, at the end of the war, they became a significant percentage of the 100,000 Palestinians who remained in the north of the country. Even after the inhabitants of the Triangle were placed under Israeli sovereignty (May 1949), the Druze came to constitute 8 percent of the entire Arab population of Israel. As we shall see in later chapters, the position of members of that sect was consolidated not only numerically but also qualitatively, due to the so-called "blood alliance" with Jewish Israelis.

The majority of villages which were destroyed and their residents uprooted and forced to migrate to neighboring Arab countries were Muslim villages. There were no Druze villages in the districts of Safad and Tiberias, and the number of Christians in the two cities and particularly in the villages in both districts was very small. As a result, we find that ethnic cleansing in both districts and in the district of Bisan as well was virtually total. After the expulsion of the majority of Muslims in the Galilee to neighboring Arab countries, the percentage of Christians among the remaining 100,000 Arabs in Haifa and the Galilee also rose, from 10 percent to 20 percent. The number of Christians remaining in the whole of the country was estimated at 30,000 in 1949. As opposed to the Druze and Muslims, the majority of Christians lived in the cities in the north: Haifa, 'Akka, Nazareth, and Shafa 'Amr. Even among the remaining population of the central cities, Jaffa, Lydda, and Ramla, the percentage of Christians, with a population of about 10,000, was quite high.

Whatever the circumstances and causes of the new demographic reality after the Nakba, the residents of Haifa and the Galilee held an important role in the history of the Palestinian minority in Israel. The residents of Nazareth and 'Akka and the villages in their districts maintained a high status, quantitatively and qualitatively, in the history of this minority. The fact that residents of those cities and a large number of nearby villages remained in place reinforced their self-confidence, despite their experience with the tragedies and horrors of the war. On the other hand, in the coastal region south of Haifa, and the mountainous region around Jerusalem, only small, isolated villages remained. The residents of those isolated villages, and the remaining Arab population of Lydda, Ramla, and Jaffa, lived in the village or city centers in constant fear and isolation due to their distance from the Arab demographic center of gravity. This new state of affairs after the Nakba left its psychological, social, and cultural imprint on those who remained, manifested in the mechanisms of the struggle for survival of the Palestinian minority in a Jewish state.

The Arab Communists

Between the Nakba and Independence

A general sentiment became pervasive among those who remained under Israeli rule after the Nakba—a sense of being like orphans who could only hope for scraps from the table. Only a small discordant minority was the exception to this, and not afflicted with this overwhelming sense of defeat and loss. Some individuals and groups in northern Palestine collaborated with the Jews and supported their war effort in 1948. Prominent among them were al-Hayb 'Arabs in eastern Galilee, the leader of the Zu'bi villages (Sayf al-Din al-Zu'bi) in Marj ibn 'Amr, and the Circassians and Druze in the villages of Mount Karmil and Shafa 'Amr.[1] Those and their like had cooperated with their Israeli settler neighbors and their institutions since the 1930s. When skirmishes began following the partition resolution, many of them chose to join the Jewish side instead of fighting it. In an early instance of this behavior, al-Hayb 'Arabs under the leadership of their shaykh, Abu Yusif, struck a deal with Yigal Alon to conscript some young men of the tribe from the villages of Tuba al-Zanghariyya to fight on the side of the Haganah on the eve of Operation Yiftah to occupy eastern Galilee. They continued enlisting for military service after the spring of 1948 and became an example to be emulated by others in the Bedouin villages in the north of the country.

Eastern Galilee was within the border of the Jewish state according to the partition resolution. When the Zionist leadership decided to launch their offensive military operation Plan Dalet, the weakness of the Palestinian people and their internal divisions became quite visible. The military superiority of the Jews was apparent in Haifa as it was in eastern Galilee, prompting some Druze leaders in Mount Karmil and Shafa 'Amr to strengthen their cooperation with Israel. After the fall of Haifa and the uprooting of the majority of its Arab population at the end of April 1948, some of those leaders enlisted their sons to fight alongside the Haganah. An agreement concluded between the Druze shaykhs and the Zionist side saved all members of that sect from being uprooted and exiled. However, the split in ranks, and tying the sect's destiny to that of Israel in the year of the Nakba contributed a great deal to tearing Druze youth away from their people and imposing the draft on them later. This prominent case of Arabs remaining by a clear decision of the Zionist and Druze leaders is familiar to researchers and readers. Certainly, there were similarities among collaborators with the Zionist side, but there were differences also which warrant an in-depth examination in a future study.

Arab communists were another group that did not consider the establishment of Israel a catastrophe for the Palestinian people, based on their class analysis of the conflict and their acceptance of the partition resolution. One can consider the Palestinian communists a special case of "pessoptimists" who thought the Arab region was on the verge of a bright future in the aftermath of the disaster. Expelling British colonialism from the Middle East and reinforcing Soviet influence were their guideposts in adopting a position on the events of 1948. Whereas most Palestinians felt overwhelming loss and despair on the eve of the creation of the state of Israel, the members of the National Liberation League emerged relatively quickly from the ruins and charted their own path, which went against the Arab nationalist current. Later, they joined the Israeli Communist Party (Maki) in October 1948 and became the first among the Arabs who remained to choose to integrate in the political organizations of the Jewish state.

The Arab communists in Israel later took pride in the realism of their political decision to accept the 1947 Palestine partition resolution. After the Nakba they reorganized quickly and led a daring struggle against the Israeli military government and its agents, and promoted the reconstruction of cultural life—giving birth to resistance poetry and literature which they published in their journal and celebrated in their clubs during that period. On the other hand, activists in national and religious movements accused the communists of collaborating with Israel and Zionism in the 1948 war and justifying the political and military support of the communist camp for Israel, instead of standing with their people at a time of adversity during the Nakba. These accusations, which generally were not based on comprehensive and balanced research, lost their edge by the mid-1970s but did not disappear altogether. This political polarization in evaluating the role of the communists during and after the Nakba should be deconstructed and studied with academic rigor based on existing sources, foremost among which are the literature and documents of the communists themselves.

Although the Israeli Communist Party (Maki) has no official archives, its press offers researchers an abundance of documentation on its positions and activities in 1948 and the years after. Reviewing the party literature in both Hebrew and Arabic is essential for forming a comprehensive picture. On sensitive and controversial matters, there is an obvious difference between party publications in the two languages. In addition to the party's output in Hebrew, prominently in *Kol HaAm*, important archival material can be found in *al-Ittihad* newspaper (which resumed publishing in its new headquarters in Haifa on 18 October 1948). In addition, there are a considerable number of party publications in Arabic, autobiographies of comrades, and dozens of interviews with the rank and file of the party covering the timeframe of this study, which constitute important sources for research. A large number of comrades, more than their contemporaries, published their memoirs, and gave oral testimonies to this author and other researchers.

Two organized entities in the Jewish state played an important role in the history of the Arabs who remained: governmental institutions and Maki. Despite the huge difference in roles and positions between these two, there was a secret or veiled partnership between them, particularly in 1948 and the early years of state formation, and each produced documents and sources that expressed its point of view. This material has been used by their researchers in the past, sometimes selectively, which obfuscated some facts—shedding light on aspects compatible with their propaganda but obscuring other aspects that they preferred to keep hidden. The historian, unlike the politician, aims to reveal facts in their historical context, to give the reader a comprehensive picture of past events. This duty creates challenges and difficulties for the academic researcher, particularly when examining known positions and actions which later became a source of embarrassment and accusations against them.

This chapter offers a new interpretation of the role of Palestinian communists in Haifa and the Galilee in the year of the Nakba. My thesis is that the decision taken by the majority of the League activists to join Maki and support its policies was a choice they made in order to remain, to which those in northern Palestine clung. This decision was later packaged and marketed as an independent ideological choice, but it was in essence the result of the change in the Soviet position from opposing Zionism to allying with it, if only temporarily. Most League activists chose to follow the communist camp and join Maki, whose Jewish members fought in the ranks of the Haganah. This act paved the way for staying in Israel alongside the victors. It also gave the communists the right to be active politically, having proved their loyalty to Israel and defended the right of the settler community to establish a Jewish state. The League members, among whom Emile Habibi was a prominent leader, represented a special model of the "pessoptimists" during the Nakba and the following lean years.

After most National Liberation League members joined Maki, they began to play the major role among Palestinians in Haifa and the Galilee in resisting the despotic policies of the military government. This resistance found fruition in the 1970s: Tawfiq Zayyad became mayor of Nazareth in 1975, Land Day was celebrated the following year, and over half of the Arab votes went to the Communist Party in the 1977 Knesset elections. These victories were the crowning achievement of resistance by the communists and of support by the Arab citizens of Israel for the party. Maki, renamed Hadash (the Hebrew acronym for the Democratic Front for Peace and Equality) after 1965, remained the sole political framework for political resistance by the Palestinian minority in Israel up to the 1980s, earning it the respect of researchers and activists who appreciated the sacrifices this entailed and their successes.

The picture would be more comprehensive if we include aspects of the party's history in the 1948 war that have been neglected in the past. We can see a clear dialectical relationship between the position of the communists during the war and the role they were permitted to play afterwards. The truce observed between their camp and leftist Labor Zionism—hegemonic in Israel at the time—is an important point in assessing their historical role. The permission by the Israeli government to create Maki during the war, thus enabling its activists, both Arabs and Jews, to participate in free organized political action in Israel, and the first parliamentary elections in January 1949, had wide-ranging significance. Most Arab historical literature on Maki neglects linking what the communists said with what they did and the role they played during the war and after. This approach would bring about a more genuine discussion between supporters and opponents of the party, from the dichotomy of either heroism or treason, and toward political and social reality in order to explain and analyze the issues, rather than prejudge on the basis of ideological positions and personal differences.

THE DRUZE: THE FIRST REMAINERS

The Druze have constituted a small minority among the Arabs of Palestine since they arrived from Lebanon to the north of Palestine in the days of Emir Fakhr al-Din al-Maʻni II in the early seventeenth century. Relations between the Muslim majority and the Maʻrufiyya sect (Bani Maʻruf)—the Druze—were occasionally marked by tensions and conflict, a bitter memory for the latter. Their relations with Christians in the Galilee were also characterized by tension and quarrels, particularly during the period of sectarian conflict in Mount Lebanon in the mid-nineteenth century. The situation in Palestine did not deteriorate into bloody conflicts such as occurred earlier in Syria and Lebanon. Nevertheless, the historical legacy of those events was likely instrumental in marginalizing the Druze role in the Palestinian national movement and minimizing their participation during the British Mandate; this, and a sense of self-preservation, constrained Druze participation in the 1936–39 revolt as well. Some members of the sect had taken the initiative in establishing cooperative relations with Abba Hushi in Haifa and other Zionist leaders, which contributed to the rift between them and the rebels.

Most of the Druze in Palestine lived in the mountains of upper Galilee, while a few lived in ʻIsfiya and Daliyat al-Karmil, and the town of Shafa ʻAmr, closer to the seacoast. The latter were the first to establish cooperative relations with the Jews and their institutions in Haifa. When the revolt broke out in 1936, some Druze continued cooperating with the Zionists, which led to the rebels accusing them of being Zionist agents. The accusation of collaboration cost a few their lives, and led to attacks on others and humiliation in their own homes and villages. But the sons of those who were attacked or assassinated by the rebels were undeterred; they remained on the same path and sought vengeance for their kinfolk.[2] This destructive internecine fighting weakened the Palestinian people at a time when they were in the greatest need of solidarity in the year of the Nakba.

When skirmishes between Arabs and Jews began following the adoption of the partition resolution, pressure was applied on the Druze to take part in the Arab war effort. Leaders of the sect in Palestine, after consultations with Druze leaders in Syria and Lebanon, decided to create a special battalion consisting of volunteers within the Arab Rescue Army (ARA). Most volunteers in the Jabal al-Arab battalion came from Syria and Lebanon, and the battalion leader was a retired Lebanese officer, Shakib Wahab. There were about five hundred combatants in this battalion, which deployed to Shafa ʿAmr and established a fortified position there in March 1948. The mountain Druze defended their villages in coordination with the ARA, as did the majority of their neighbors, but they chose a defensive strategy, like the Arab battalion, and they tried not to initiate clashes with the Jewish side.

In return, the Haganah intelligence unit (Shai) consolidated its ties with two Druze leaders: Labib Abu Rukn (1911–1989) from ʿIsfiya and Salih Khunayfis (1913–2002) from Shafa ʿAmr. Khunayfis succeeded in convincing Jabr Dahish Maʿdi (1919–2009) from Yarka to become a party to the cooperation with the Israeli side, and together they led a reversal of the sect's position towards the parties to the conflict.[3] The Druze remained neutral until the battle of Husha and al-Kasayir (16 April) in which the Arab battalion gave a good account of itself, suffering dozens of dead and wounded, while the Jewish side also lost a large number of men, the most prominent among them Zohar Dayan, the brother of Moshe Dayan. However, when Haifa fell a week later (22 April), it became obvious to all that the balance of force favored the Jews. At that point, Salih Khunayfis and Jabr Maʿdi convinced Shakib Wahhab, the battalion commander, to withdraw his men from the combat and tend to their own affairs. The withdrawal agreement was concluded in Khunayfis's house in Shafa ʿAmr on 9 May 1948.[4] The volunteers were given the choice of returning to their homes in Lebanon or Syria or joining the Haganah, and most chose to return. For the dozens who chose to stay and join the Israeli army in the war, it was agreed that they would be paid twenty-seven Palestine pounds monthly.[5]

According to the agreement, cooperation and coordination between the Druze along the coast and the Jewish side increased in early May 1948, and dozens of Druze participated in the occupation of ʿAkka and some western Galilee villages in mid-May. Ismaʿil Qablan, one of Shakib Wahhab's assistants, reportedly entered ʿAkka during the Haganah siege of the city, and then gave a detailed report to the Jews about its fortifications and the location of the fighters. As for Salih Khunayfis, he advised the besieging forces to cut off water and electricity to the city to speed up the surrender of the inhabitants. Others added that a number of Druze were

in the vanguard of those who entered 'Akka when it fell on 16 May and went from
street to street "ululating and exulting in the victory."[6] Thus news of the positions
of the Galilee Druze as of the spring of 1948 raised the level of ethnic tensions for a
while, but also opened an important door for sheltering and remaining.

After the withdrawal of Druze volunteers from Shafa 'Amr, ARA leader
Mahmud al-Saffuri entered the town at the head of a local force of about two hundred men, and he and his assistants went about arresting some alleged collaborators and interrogating them. Some of these interrogations reportedly involved
assault and humiliation, which raised the level of tension and lack of trust between
Muslims and Druze in Shafa 'Amr and the whole region in general.

The leaders of the Zionist movement took advantage of the special situation
of the Druze in northern Palestine by making them a generous offer that guaranteed a successful policy of divide and conquer. The agreement assured the survival
of all Druze villages and towns, and their inhabitants, in return for services by
their leaders in that critical phase of the war, on the eve of the entry of the Arab
armies. Most of the Galilee Druze tried to remain neutral until the spring of 1948,
but the survival instinct and an awareness of imminent danger propelled them to
accept the Israeli hand extended to them. The leaders of the Jewish state had their
own regional motivations which prompted them to exclude members of that sect
from the ethnic cleansing plan of the Nakba. In this way, the Druze in northern
Palestine became the first large group of residents who remained, and in a position
to help many of their Muslim and Christian neighbors to stay in their homes, as we
saw earlier.[7]

The cooperation agreement with the Druze was tested on the eve of the Israeli
attack on Shafa 'Amr, a town inhabited by members of all three sects. Through
negotiations with Salih Khunayfis via the mediation of Labib Abu Rukn and others, an agreement was reached that facilitated the entry of Israeli forces into the
town. In accordance with that agreement, Israeli forces under the command of
Ben Dunkelman entered the town from the Druze side on the evening of 14 July
without any actual fighting taking place, both sides firing in the air in a mock
battle. The Shafa 'Amr agreement was the launch of successful and open cooperation between the two sides, in which a Druze unit led by Sulayman Abu Rukn
joined the Israeli army in occupying the town.[8] The same unit later participated
in completing the occupation of the Galilee in Operation Hiram. This activity by
Druze in the 1948 war consolidated what is often referred to as the "blood pact"
(Brit Damim) in Zionist writings.

The story of the Druze in northern Palestine represented the first and most
important model for how a collectivity was able to resist displacement through
cooperation with the victorious side. The Druze were unique among the Arabs
of the region in their ability to maneuver and seize opportunities at an important
juncture in order to guarantee that the sect might continue to live in their villages.
Despite the problematic perspectives on that survival in place, it nevertheless

created an exception in the policy of ethnic cleansing which could be used in other occupied Arab areas—as the Druze in the Galilee contributed to the neighboring Muslims and Christians remaining as well. Arab researchers have bypassed this topic in large part because of the sensitivities it evokes for many parties. There have been attempts to broach the subject by collecting verbal testimonies,[9] but these are no substitute for historical research which relies on all available sources and documents in order to present a comprehensive and integrated account of this prickly issue.

THE COMMUNIST CAMP
AND THE PALESTINIAN NAKBA

Constantine Zurayk mentioned the role of "the Russians" along with the English and the Americans among the external factors leading to the Palestinian tragedy.[10] Musa al-'Alami, in his book *The Lesson of Palestine*, expanded the circle of those responsible to the great powers. In his opinion, the foremost party responsible was the English, who promised Palestine to the Jews, and then opened the doors of the country to them, turning a blind eye while they armed. He then added: "The Americans and the Russians share this [heavy responsibility]."[11] George Hanna (1893–1969), not content with such fleeting references to the role of the Russians, expanded on this with explanations and analysis: "Russia . . . is also responsible. Despite its hostility to Anglo-American policy . . . it endorsed the idea of partition, and the establishment of a Zionist state alongside an Arab state, hoping this would provide it with a gateway to the East."[12] These words by Hanna, who was a Lebanese socialist and a friend of the Soviet Union, have special significance, as they reinforce the Arab consensus at the time concerning the role of the Russians in establishing the state of Israel and in fomenting the Palestinian tragedy.

The role of the communist camp under the leadership of the Soviet Union in the Nakba of the Palestinian people and the establishment of Israel was subsequently expunged from Arab historical and political literature (along with the voices of those who remembered this role),[13] a phenomenon that reflects the ambiguities of the widespread narratives of the Nakba and the sensitivity of issues in the modern history of the Arabs, particularly those concerning Palestine. The National Liberation League's merger with the Maki party—joining the Israeli side—enabled Arab communists to play an important role in leading the Palestinian minority in the Jewish state. This was the price paid for Israel's permission to play this leadership role in a legal way.

Prior to the League's merger with Maki, they expressed their positions on the Palestine war in a publication signed with three Arab communist parties.[14] This document, dated early October 1948, contained an unsparing criticism of "English and American colonialist war projects and reactionary Arab regimes which are subservient to colonialism." Its authors agreed with the assessment of Zurayk in *The Meaning of al-Nakba* of the enormity of the disaster which befell "the Arabs of Palestine and resulted in their ruin and the expulsion of hundreds of thousands of Palestinians and the usurpation of new parts of their lands."[15] The communists primarily blamed colonialism and reactionary Arab parties, more than Israel, for the non-creation of a Palestinian state according to the UN partition resolution. The role of the Soviet Union in supporting the establishment and expansion of the Jewish state was completely absent from this publication. Since the communist intellectuals, unlike the nationalist intellectuals, did not return to the analysis of the causes of al-Nakba, the treatment of the role of the communist camp in the Palestinian Nakba remained for them "a frivolous campaign of obfuscation, lies and fabrications that maligned the great Soviet Union."[16]

By the time the position paper was released, the communists had gone a long way in cooperating with the activists of Mapam. The finger of accusation which they shyly pointed at Israel's policy and its criminal acts placed only some of the responsibility for the Nakba on "reactionary Zionist leaders." The Marxist Zionists who carried out several of the massacres and expulsions through the Palmach (the Haganah's strike forces), and subsequently joined the leading ranks of the army, were absent from the picture altogether. This obfuscation of the role of the Zionist left was also necessary to justify cooperating with it and lifting it to the rank of a class ally in contrast to the Arabs, who were portrayed as reactionary elements collaborating with colonialism. This analysis, which obscures the nationalist dimension of the struggle, remains the key to understanding the positions of the Communist Party even after the Zionist left allied itself with Ben-Gurion and launched the invasion of Egypt in 1956. A critical interpretation of the position of Maki and its leadership in that historic period of foundation has remained absent even after the passage of dozens of years.

Despite the distinctive role played by National League activists who joined Maki, they did not fully write their own history. Some members of the second generation made an effort to rectify this by documenting the experiences of first generation members in the 1948 war.[17] However, the testimonies of leaders and activists are no substitute for a written history of the party and, before that, a history of the role of Jewish and Arab communists after the Palestine partition resolution was adopted. But neither should autobiographies and personal testimonies be disregarded, particularly if they are truthful, rich in detail, and offer a penetrating perspective. The first and most prominent testimony in Ahmad Sa'd's book, *Roots of the Evergreen Tree*, is by Tawfiq Tubi. This communist leader did not publish an autobiography, so we shall rely instead on that testimony and his activities in the Israeli parliament. In addition to Tubi's statements, the book includes the testimonies of twenty-four living and committed members of the party; a few important individuals are missing from this group, such as Emile Habibi and Hanna Abu Hanna, whose writings are readily accessible.

Musa al-Budayri, a research specialist in the history of the Communist Party in Palestine, conducted more than twenty interviews with communist leaders in the mid-1970s, but did not publish them until forty years later.[18] Most of the communist leaders during the British Mandate with whom al-Budayri recorded interviews were not active in Maki, except for the two Emiles: Tuma and Habibi. Considering that they both became prolific writers, their publications constitute important material for the study of the history of this party after the Nakba. But interview statements by others, such as Radwan al-Hilu, shed light on aspects that the communists rarely talk about. Despite the passage of more than half a century since that historic period for the party, no one was "provoked" into chronicling the events, role, and positions of the communists during the 1948 war in a critical way. The available historic literature either uncritically praises the party or criticizes it in an imbalanced way without crediting its importance after the Nakba.

What is missing from the history of those who stayed, particularly the communists, is the connection between their actions in the year of the Nakba and their role in the following decade. The leadership role that the Jewish state allowed the communists (both Arabs and Jews) served the Zionist enterprise; it was also an expression of gratitude to the Soviet camp. The communist acceptance of formal stateless citizenship—without full and equal citizenship for the entire population—ensured there would be no objections to the identity of the Jewish state and its Zionist symbols.[19] This political position represented the full reversal of the communist position from opposing Zionism to accepting it, and then supporting the Zionist project to establish a Jewish state on the ruins of Palestine. In contrast to those who remained and accepted citizenship after the Nakba to ensure they could stay in their homeland and prevent expulsion, members of the League sought to make it ideologically palatable through an organized political decision to dissolve the League and be absorbed into the Israeli Communist Party (Maki) in October 1948.

Just as the Nakba that befell the Palestinian people is not a past event that ended, so the positions adopted by the members of the Liberation League who joined Maki define the positions of their descendants towards Zionism, and historical analysis and future solutions to the Palestinian problem. Until today, the communist activists in this trend have still not critically evaluated their political role and conduct during the Nakba and the legacy of these positions in subsequent decades. More surprising is that most Palestinian historians still distance themselves from this subject. In fact, a courageous and critical study of the past is the first step toward a deep understanding of the tragic present and prognosis of the future.

The communist camp, under the leadership of the Soviet Union, remained hostile to the Zionist movement and its project to establish a Jewish state in Palestine until World War II. Zionism was considered a settler movement in collaboration with British colonialism, one that was hostile to liberation movements in the Arab Orient. Based on this position, there were attempts to arabize the Communist Party in Palestine after the events of 1929. Considering that most members of the

Palestine Communist Party were Marxist Zionist immigrants, the party faced major challenges even after Radwan al-Hilu became its secretary general.[20] The contradiction of accepting equal rights for the Zionist immigrant settlers and the indigenous Palestinians was a major contradiction, disguised under the slogan of "Arab-Jewish brotherhood." When the Arab Revolt (1936–39) against Britain and Zionism broke out, the Palestinian communist camp supported the nationalist effort, increasing tensions and eventually open division among the ranks of communists in Palestine on the basis of national origins. When the split occurred in 1943, the National Liberation League was established in isolation from the Jewish communists. However, both Arab and Jewish communists maintained their negative position on the Zionist project, and demanded independence for Palestine, an end to colonialism, and support for one united and independent country. Despite the establishment of two communist organizations, the unequal relationship between the League and the party did not change much on the eve of the war in Palestine (1944–47), and the two sides continued to meet and coordinate. However, the activists in the League, who drew closer to the Palestinian national movement and its positions, faced a real dilemma when the socialist camp changed its position on Zionism in 1947, as part of its policy change toward liberation movements and the adoption of Cold War policies in the Middle East. Their support became public with Soviet acceptance of the partition resolution and the establishment of a Jewish state in 1947. The important turning point for the party in the year of the Nakba was obscured in the deluge caused by the shock of the war and its harsh consequences. When the Arab peoples awoke years later, the communist camp had returned to supporting liberation struggles, and the role of the Soviet Union in the Palestine war was forgotten.

THE POSITION OF THE LEAGUE ON ZIONISM AND THE PARTITION RESOLUTION

The communist bloc support, under the leadership of the Soviet Union, of the 1947 partition resolution and establishment of a Jewish state, created a political earthquake for the League.[21] While the Jewish communists welcomed this transformation and joined the Haganah to fight for the establishment of Israel, the League's leaders and activists were shocked and divided. Even after the communist position of support for partition became clear, *al-Ittihad* newspaper came out in October 1947 with a firm declaration stating that the position of the League had not changed and was "to demand a British withdrawal and an end to the Mandate, full independence, and the right of the Palestinians to self-determination."[22] This opposition to partition and hostility to the Zionist project remained a constant position until the eve of the adoption of the UN Partition Plan on 29 November, after which turmoil ensued for several weeks, ending in February 1948 with the declaration (in Nazareth) of support for partition.[23] This important chapter in the history of the League from the Nazareth conference to the absorption into Maki is still much obscured.

Days before the UN vote, *al-Ittihad* published a communique signed by the League's central committee describing partition as a "colonialist proposal which has been under preparation from the first day that [British] colonialism set foot on the land of Palestine." It warned the Jewish masses in Palestine of the danger of supporting the Zionist objective of partition and a Jewish state, that the policy of partition would not guarantee security and stability to the Jewish masses and would transfer a racist war from Europe to Palestine. The communique concluded by exhorting the Palestinian people to work "for a democratic and independent, undivided Palestine."[24]

Jewish communists readily accepted the new Soviet position on Zionism, and accommodated to the UN resolution permitting a state for the Jews in Palestine, as this change placed them in the heart of the Zionist consensus and opened up the opportunity for them play a future political role. The situation of the League comrades was starkly different: for them, accepting partition meant not just turning away from resisting Zionism, which they had been struggling against for decades. It also meant accepting the Zionist project, which was based on tearing apart the Palestinian people—a choice between standing with their people or aligning with the Soviet camp. It took months to make a final decision, which was reached not by consensus but by simple majority.

What was the explanation by the League for supporting partition and the establishment of a Jewish state at the expense of the Palestinian people? What were the ramifications of this support for their positions on the 1948 war in Palestine? And how did these positions during the war affect the Arab communists who stayed in Haifa and the Galilee after the Nakba? Whatever the reasons for the change in the Soviet position under Joseph Stalin regarding Zionism and its project to establish a state for the Jews in Palestine, all communist parties had to line up behind this position and support it. Jewish communists hastened to embrace the partition resolution and join the Zionist Jewish consensus.[25] The leaders and activists of the League, on the other hand, had to depart from the Arab national consensus, and disown their previous positions, and the fact of the tragic failure of the partition resolution for the Palestinian people. The League therefore underwent a sharp division between supporters and opponents of partition, despite the clarity of the Soviet position as of the summer of 1947. The camp of supporters of partition was led by Fu'ad Nassar, Tawfiq Tubi, and Emile Habibi who held their convention deliberately in Nazareth.[26] After that conference, Emile Habibi went to Belgrade to attend the conference of communist parties (Cominform).

Emile Tuma (1919–1986), the editor of *al-Ittihad* until early 1948, was the most prominent of the opponents of partition, and paid a huge price for his dissenting position. He continued to oppose it even after the partition resolution was adopted and the League conference was held in Nazareth, expressing his opinion of partition in the newspaper, saying: "Our friendship with the Soviet Union, in its capacity as a non-imperialistic state that supports the freedom of peoples, does not mean that we are bound to a Western foreign policy. We and all democrats adhere to an independent policy, not tied to the policy of the Soviet Union, or any other organization, because our policy aspires to freedom and justice for our people."[27] Emile Tuma stayed in Haifa until the city fell, then left for Lebanon where he was arrested because of his membership in a communist party and held in Baalbek prison for months. He remained in Lebanon after his release in September, until he was allowed to return to Haifa in April 1949. But he faced a period of exclusion which delayed his return to a leadership position in the Communist Party until the early 1960s.[28] The party did not readmit members who did not apologize for their opposition to partition, which Bulus Farah for one refused to do.

There is little available information concerning the League conference in Nazareth. Why was this city in particular chosen? What were the precise dates and venue of the meeting? How were invitations to the conference issued? How many attended and what percentage of members did they represent? I have sought answers from more than one veteran communist, but have been unsuccessful so far. Maki's publications rarely mention the event and give no details. Even after Bulus Farah raised doubts concerning the legitimacy of the meeting and the veracity of "a majority vote" in favor of accepting partition, the facts remain hidden with the leadership of the party.[29] Tawfiq Tubi and Emile Habibi led the League in northern Palestine on the path that took them to the Israeli Knesset. As was retroactively demonstrated, this path allowed the communists to play an important role in defense of the civil rights of those who stayed, but the fact that following the positions of the Soviet Union contributed to the Nakba of the Palestinian people is overlooked.

Accepting the partition resolution was not easy, but it was even more difficult for the Liberation League to continue opposing the position of the Soviet Union. However, after the Nazareth conference the position of members of the League moved onward from supporting the partition to allying with friends and partners on the Jewish side and harboring hostility to the Arab Palestinian consensus. The fighting among Jews and Arabs in northern Palestine caused a large number of casualties as well. This painful reality exacerbated the political and ethical dilemma for members of the League, some of whom fought alongside the Arab Rescue Army to protect the Galilee while their communist and Marxist friends (in Mapam) fought alongside the Haganah. Even though Haganah, along with the Palmach, committed a number of massacres in the villages of al-Khisas, Balad al-Shaykh, Sa'sa', and elsewhere in northern Palestine in late 1947 and early 1948, well before the Dayr Yasin massacre, the leaders of the League enhanced their coordination and cooperation with the Israeli side, as we shall show below.

THE TRANSITION OF THE LEAGUE FROM ACCEPTING
PARTITION TO SUPPORTING THE JEWISH STATE

'Awda al-'Ashhab (Abu 'Adnan) mentions in his memoir that Fu'ad Nassar asked him to secure a visa for Emile Habibi from the Yugoslav consulate prior to Habibi's departure to Belgrade. Al-'Ashhab adds that in the consulate he met comrade Wolf Erlich who was there for a similar reason, as a service to party secretary Shmuel Mikunis, and so he learned that Mikunis and Habibi would be travelling together to the conference in Belgrade.[30] At that time, Habibi had become the new spokesman for the League and was one of the most prominent Palestinian communists known for his cooperation with Labor Zionism in Israel. Tawfiq Tubi oversaw cooperation with Marxist comrades in the communist and Mapam parties. Fu'ad Nassar, the League secretary, played an important role in this coordination and in leading the organization at that difficult stage. This trio, Nassar, Tubi, and Habibi, became responsible for the new direction of the League which led to integration in Israeli political life as of October 1948.

Emile Habibi claimed, after taking part in the Belgrade conference, that Mikunis had invited him to accompany him to Prague, and that he had known nothing about the Czech arms deal. When *al-Sinnara* newspaper of Nazareth accused him of going to Prague with Mikunis in order to secure arms for Israel, he raised a libel suit against the paper in an Israeli court and won.[31] But despite the court ruling, the suspicions about Habibi's trip to Prague with Mikunis dogged him for several years. Is it credible that Habibi accepted Mikunis's invitation to travel to Prague with no knowledge of the trip's objectives, and without the approval of the League? Similarly, is it credible that the two representatives of communist parties in Palestine should go to Prague without the approval of, or at least coordination with, Moscow, which had been pressing for sending arms to the Jewish side quickly? These and similar questions concerning arms deals and sending volunteers from Prague and other states in the communist camp to Palestine were never posed and never answered, at least on the Arab side.[32]

The British authorities banned *al-Ittihad* newspaper from publishing at the beginning of 1948, while *Kol HaAm*, the organ of the Israeli Communist Party, continued to publish. At the beginning of March, the party was invited to join the interim government of the Jewish state, and Mikunis was chosen to represent it in the cabinet.[33] That same month, the U.S. State Department appeared to be pulling back from the partition resolution, and a search began within the UN for other possible alternative solutions. This U.S. position worried the Zionist leadership, but the Soviet Union fended off all of the proposed alternative solutions to secure a cease-fire and made sure none passed. Any international reversal of the partition resolution was tantamount to a gain for the Arabs and would have been a diplomatic setback for Zionist diplomacy at the time. The Jewish communists, under the leadership of Mikunis, expressed very strong opposition to proposed alternative solutions, and commended Moscow's support for the establishment of a Jewish state, without postponement or delay.

A reader of *Kol HaAm* in early 1948 and later would not have found a big difference between the newspaper's positions and those of the Labor Zionist discourse under the leadership of Ben-Gurion. When U.S. proposals were put forward to place Palestine under UN trusteeship for five or ten years, they were categorically rejected by the communists. Their newspaper criticized the American proposal and called it "a shameful betrayal by the American government." On the other hand, the paper was jubilant about Andrei Gromyko's statements "forcefully demanding that the partition resolution be implemented."[34] *Kol HaAm* dedicated its editorial that day to a discussion of "the American betrayal," in contrast to the continuing political and military support by the USSR for the establishment of the Jewish state. The communist camp became convinced that the Jewish state would provide the USSR with a foothold in the Middle East. The alliance between Moscow and Tel Aviv became clearer in March 1948, with the communist camp placing all of its political weight on the side of establishing the state of Israel without delay, and supporting that position with speeded-up Czech arms shipments.

Aharon Cohen, a prominent leader of Mapam, commented on the importance of the Czech arms: "In the wake of the arms embargo by the West, there developed a severe shortage of arms in March 1948.... This shortage was overcome through the arrival of the first Czech plane carrying munitions at one of the secret Jewish air-fields."[35] At the same time, a ship carrying thousands of rifles and hundreds of light artillery pieces arrived in the country. Important heavy arms arrived by aerial convoy on 20 May, and continued to arrive until 10 August 1948. These arms "played a decisive role in the war of independence," according to an Israeli army report.[36]

The role of Czech arms in the victories of the Jewish state is no longer disputed in the historical Zionist literature despite Zionism's differences with communism. Studies in Arabic which revealed the truth about the Czech arms deals emanated only from those who accused the communists of treason. Arab armies were not allowed to intervene to help the Palestinians at this point in time, so modern arms sent to the Jewish side were first used in fighting the Arab native population and expelling them from their homes and homeland. Jewish communists supported this war which the leaders of Israel launched to carry out their policy of ethnic cleansing in Palestine. The arrival of the weapons put the comrades in the League in a tight spot, and this became a sensitive topic they preferred not to delve into, especially in Arabic.

Simultaneously with the arrival of quality weapons from Prague, Ben-Gurion began implementing Plan Dalet which caused hundreds of casualties among the Palestinians. In the north of the country, activists in the League learned of the occupation of Tiberias and Haifa and dozens of villages in the proximity of the two cities, and the expulsion of their Arab residents. Earlier those same imported arms had been used in the battles of Bab al-Wad, including the famous battle of al-Qastal, and in the villages in the Galilee mountains. The devastating results of the Jewish war on the Palestinians should have sounded the alarm for the Arab communists, but the ethnic cleansing policy, which had entered a decisive phase in April, did not change the League's position from favoring the establishment of a Jewish state with the support of the communist camp. Instead, the members of the League increased their coordination with their Jewish comrades, and officially declared their opposition to the entry of Arab armies which came to the aid of the ill-fated Palestinians.

Apparently the League leaders who were supporting Soviet policy deluded themselves into thinking at the time that it was possible for them, through cooperation with the Jewish Marxists, to play a decisive historic role in the Palestinian question. Prominent among them was Fu'ad Nassar (1914–1976) who met with Aharon Cohen in Tawfiq Tubi's house in Haifa at the beginning of 1948 before he left Nazareth.[37] Nassar then traveled from the north of the country to Gaza, to take part in setting up an Arab government under the leadership of the communists and their friends. However, a few weeks after he arrived Egyptian forces entered Gaza, and he was forced to flee because he was wanted by the Egyptians. From Gaza, Nassar went to the West Bank, as the area became known later, disguised as a Bedouin shaykh. In his new location he continued his work and kept up his contacts with Aharon Cohen through messengers, including Midhat al-Sha'ar.[38] The cooperation between the League and representatives of Mapam led to actions by the communists in Gaza and Jabal al-Khalil against Egyptian soldiers, which we will explain later.

At the time that Emile Habibi went from Prague to Beirut to coordinate the positions of the League with Arab communist parties, and Nassar went to southern Palestine to lead the activities of the comrades against the Egyptian army, Tawfiq Tubi remained in Haifa to coordinate with Labor Zionists. Tubi mentions that after the fall of Haifa and the expulsion of the great majority of its population (including members of the League and their families), he could find only two comrades in the city, 'Isam al-'Abbasi and Muhammad 'Abdu.[39] The Czech arms were used by the Haganah in occupying Haifa and expelling its Arab population, including dozens of Arab communists and their families, which Tubi witnessed. In testimony published in the 1990s Tubi said that he and 'Isam al-'Abbasi wrote a handwritten leaflet on 2 May addressing the residents remaining in Haifa at the time.[40] This leaflet, which was distributed only ten days after the fall of the city, describes what occurred in the tragedy. Tubi gives a biting and strongly worded attack on British colonialism for what happened in Haifa and its district, saying: "The painful calamity that befell the existing Arab society in Haifa and its district is a catastrophe which colonialism wanted and worked for very diligently,"[41] by stoking "the fire of nationalist warfare" to safeguard its interests. Accusations are also made at the Palestinian leadership, and even more so at King Abdullah, "the agent of British imperialism." This leaflet was a bold voice which differed from the nationalist discourse, since it called for fighting colonialism, and for an end to the fighting between Jews and Arabs.[42] However, there is no mention of the criminal activities of the Zionist leaders headed by Ben-Gurion, who planned and implemented the occupation of Haifa, the terrorizing of the city's Palestinian inhabitants, and their expulsion, nor any condemnation or denunciation of them. Whoever examines this leaflet (which was not appended to the book of testimonies by the comrades) will not find any trace of the citations and statements that Tubi put forward in his later testimony.[43] It appears that this leaflet, which assigned responsibility for the Nakba of Haifa to others rather than its perpetrators, was the natural cost or result of the political position of the League and its following Moscow's line of support for Israel.

Consistent with its military and political support for the Zionist side, the Soviet Union recognized the state of Israel (without defining its borders) and its interim government immediately after the declaration of its creation. Minister Molotov expressed the hope that the establishment of "the independent state of the Jews will reinforce peace and stability" in the region, and stated the confidence of his government "in the development of amicable relations between the USSR and the state of Israel."[44] The editorial in the communist paper stressed that after this recognition, relations between Israel and the USSR must be based on friendship and cooperation and mutual assistance. Those days were the "honeymoon" which crowned Soviet support for Israel and formed a solid basis for the cooperation of the communists with Zionist labor parties.

The representative of the Israeli Communist Party in the cabinet of the interim government was a signatory to "the declaration of independence" of the state of the Jews.[45] The interim cabinet also included two ministers from the Mapam (Zionist Marxist) party, the ally of the communists. These developments appeared to be the realization of Moscow's dreams and the USSR intensified its support for the Jewish state after its formation. As for the activists in the League who supported the partition resolution and the establishment of a Jewish state in accordance with the Zionist project, they found that there could be no turning back and had nowhere to flee except forward on the same path. Consequently, we find them continuing to follow the Soviet position of supporting Israel and its policies and to place responsibility for the Nakba, the tragic aspects of which had begun to manifest themselves, solely on the shoulders of Arab leaders and colonialism. At this stage, leaders of the League intensified their negotiations with the activists in Mapam and the Jewish communists, in order to unify their capabilities and prepare for the political role they anticipated for themselves in the Jewish state.

PARTNERS IN SETTING UP THE JEWISH STATE?

Early in the summer of 1948, the competition between the supporters of the mufti, Hajj Amin al-Husayni, and King Abdullah broke out into open conflict over what was left of Palestine. At this stage, the leaders of the League decided to elevate their support for the Jewish state in preparation for their political role in that state. In June, the League escalated its verbal attack on reactionary Arab regimes and their armies which had entered Palestine, which the League described as "invaders" and "foreign." Members of the League distributed leaflets to Egyptian soldiers. The leaflet, which bore the title "An Appeal to the Soldiers," read: "Return to your homelands and aim your fire at the chests of the colonialists and their lackeys."[46] This leaflet, and the role of the comrades in the League in distributing it and in incitement against the soldiers of the Arab armies, are issues which have been largely hidden in the communist literature on the war.

The authors of the leaflet asked: "For whose sake did your governments send you to be killed in Palestine? Are the claims of these reactionary governments about their desire to liberate Palestine true?" The leaflet describes those governments as "treasonous, offering their nations and peoples for sale to the Anglo-American colonialists." It asks: "Aren't these treasonous governments, which claim to have sent you to liberate Palestine, the same governments who play the role of watchdog for colonial companies and interests?" The leaflet concludes: "Soldiers, our brethren, you are being slaughtered here and sent far from your homes and families for the sake of treasonous Arab feudalists who have sold their lands and fled Palestine."[47] This escalation in the communist rhetoric against Arab leaders in the summer of 1948 reflects the extent of the rapprochement between them and their new Zionist Marxist allies in Mapam.

It is not difficult to understand the positions of the communists on British colonialism and reactionary Arab regimes. What is perplexing about supporting the war that Israel launched with Czech arms was the silence concerning the massacres and expulsion of the Palestinian people. While their Jewish comrades were fighting on the side of the Haganah to expand the borders of Israel, activists in the League were objecting to the participation of Arab armies in the war. The war that Israel continued to wage since the summer of 1948 was to expand the territory of the Jewish state at the expense of the contemplated Arab state under the partition resolution. How can we explain the League's silence about the Zionist expansion and criminal actions at the very time that members of the League were opposing the Arab war effort? Would the withdrawal of Arab armies from Palestine, as the communists were demanding, have served the cause or harmed it? These are some of the questions that must be asked in any critical evaluation of the League at the time. The facts on the ground clearly showed that Israel expelled Arabs from all the cities and villages which it occupied in southern and central Palestine.

Fu'ad Nassar, the League's secretary, appears to be the person responsible for editing that leaflet and distributing it to Arab soldiers; on the first anniversary of his death (1976) his close friend Tawfiq Tubi revealed that Nassar had been responsible for distributing the leaflet during the war.[48] However, Tubi quoted a reworded version of the last sentence concerning Palestinian leaders, so that it was transformed into: "Soldiers, our brethren, you are the fuel on which this base conspiracy feeds and its innocent victims. Palestine shall gain its freedom only through a common understanding between the Arab and Jewish peoples against colonialism."[49] The distribution of this leaflet, which undermined the morale of the soldiers of the Arab armies, was particularly ill-timed. It coincided with the Israeli attack on Lydda and Ramla on 11–12 July 1948. The leaflet was greeted with scorn for the communists and led to their persecution on the Arab side, while it was well received by the Israeli side, which saw it as a real participation in the psychological warfare against the Arab armies.

After the distribution of this leaflet, there was an upsurge in the legal prosecution of communists on the Arab side so that some had to go into hiding and work in secret. Fu'ad Nassar himself was detained in Bethlehem and charged with distributing the leaflet, yet he managed to escape that same night and dropped out of sight. Other distributors of the leaflet were less fortunate, including 'Awda al-'Ashhab and Hasan Abu 'Isha, both of whom were arrested on 11 July in Hebron, and were taken to the Abu 'Ujayla prison in Sinai, where they spent months until the end of 1948. There they met some comrades from Gaza and elsewhere in southern Palestine, which was under the control of the Egyptian army.[50] Thus, the position of the comrades of the League gradually changed from accepting the partition of Palestine and the establishment of a state for the settlers, to supporting the establishment of that state, politically at least. Once again, that position was coherent with the support of the Soviet camp for Israel and its war on the Palestinian people.

Recently, some of the historical leaders of the Liberation League plucked up the courage to criticize the positions and activities of the communists in the year of the Nakba. They spoke out in criticism of the secretary of the League, Fu'ad Nassar, in particular. In Na'im al-'Ashhab's discussion of how the idea of a democratic state overwhelmed the leadership, he recently wrote that "Nassar overemphasized the idea of class struggle in the days of the war and neglected the nationalist aspect of the struggle in Palestine."[51] Concerning the position of the Soviet Union on the war in Palestine, he added: "Apparently there were more than a few delusions, even among Kremlin leaders including Stalin and those around him, concerning the speed with which [Israel] would convert into a socialist country." On the other hand, "the Kremlin viewed the Arab states as states governed by reactionary, quasi-feudal regimes. But within a few years only, it was shown that this assessment was superficial and wrong, even defeatist."[52] Al-'Ashhab, not content to level bold criticism at the Kremlin, also accused Nassar of responsibility for these wrong analyses, saying: "One of the characteristics of the leader of the League at that time was that if he was convinced of an idea he would be strongly driven by it, even recklessly at times."[53]

While about ten men were arrested for distributing the leaflet to "the soldiers of Egypt and the Arab countries" and led off to Abu 'Ujayla, League activists in Nazareth were arrested on the charge of treason and collaboration with the Jewish side. On 12 July, some League activists were arrested in Nazareth by the Arab Rescue Army in the city. However, city leaders from the al-Fahum family, in cooperation with the poet 'Abdul Rahim Mahmud, who was a respected officer in the ARA, intervened on behalf of the detainees and freed them quickly.[54] Nevertheless, the arrests of members of the League, with Saliba Khamis at the top of the list, turned into a legend and tales about the "heroism and sacrifice" of the communists in opposing the war as a whole and the ARA in particular. At the end of this chapter we shall provide examples of those tales which were created by the Arab communists to prove that the League played a role in supporting the establishment of the Jewish state.

The communists in Haifa and Nazareth constituted a special type of Palestinian survivor, as became apparent from their positions as of July 1948. On the heels of the fall of Nazareth that month, the minister of minorities, Bechor Shitrit, visited Nazareth and met with the mayor and notables in the city, including a delegation that represented the League, headed by Saliba Khamis. During the meeting with Shitrit, League members made clear their position of cooperating with Israel by saying: "There are elements who are prepared to cooperate with the Jews, just as they cooperated earlier with Britain and with the mufti and al-Qawuqji,"[55] and then added that the Jews should not rely on those, but on "the popular forces" like the League. Minister Shitrit listened to them and promised that there would be nothing to prevent the activities of the League and the "Workers' Conference" in Nazareth. Indeed, the activities of the communist organizations in Nazareth revived strongly after the occupation, in cooperation with the military governor, Elisha Soltz.

Members of the League saw themselves as ideological partners of the Israeli state and not as collaborators with an occupying state, as did some collaborators in Nazareth and elsewhere. Their conversation with Minister Shitrit was a genuine expression of their beliefs based on the priority of the class dimension of the struggle and reliance on the support of the communist camp for Israel. This viewpoint made their expectations from the state much higher than those of most Arabs who stayed in the north of the country. At that stage in the Palestine war, the communists thought they were capable of being in the vanguard of laying the foundations of a better future for both the Arabs and the Jews. But this "revolutionary" vision clashed at the end of the war with the reality of the policies of the Ben-Gurion government, which was prepared to accept cooperation with its interests from several Arab sources but did not see them as true partners. Still, the second part of 1948 witnessed the peak of dreams—or communist delusions—about the possibility of constructing an international partnership with Labor Zionism.

THE BEGINNING OF COMMUNIST LEADERSHIP OF THE ARAB MINORITY IN ISRAEL

The months of ceasefire in the wake of the occupation of Nazareth and lower Galilee (July to October) were the real beginning of the communist assumption of leadership of the Palestinian minority remaining in Haifa and the Galilee. After the meeting with Minister Shitrit and other representatives of the Israeli government, the League, under the leadership of Saliba Khamis, became active in organizing Arab workers to cultivate the fields and orchards of the refugees in cooperation with the military governor and the trustee of absentee property.[56] Unlike their competitors, such as Sayf al-Din al-Zuʿbi, the communists had wide experience in organizing labor and their success increased their political influence and expanded League membership in Nazareth and elsewhere. The communist growth in the City of Annunciation angered their rivals, particularly the sons of families who had been cooperating with the Jewish side for decades. These grievances reached the ears of Ben-Gurion's advisors and his inner circle, and they in turn forwarded these complaints to the leadership of the Mapam party.

When complaints about the communists multiplied, to the extent that people in the city began to believe that only the communists and those close to them could find work in Israel, activists in Mapam rose to defend their policy and their support for the Liberation League. Prominent among them was Eliezer Beʾeri Bauer who wrote, in an article titled "The Nazareth Scandal," that there were no casualties among the people of Nazareth during the occupation of the city and the occupation was not accompanied by pillaging and the expulsion of the residents.[57] He added that life in the city quickly returned to normal, and what is the harm in that? The author responded to the criticism directed at the activists in his party who supported the communists, saying: "The League has been active in Nazareth for many years, and it has acquired much influence in the city. However, this organization ceased to be active during the war because of Qawuqji's gangs." He concluded his defense of the communists by saying, "The IDF freed men of the League and the Workers' Conference from jail, and some are now working behind the front lines in Gaza and Beirut."

Beʾeri did not stop at this defense of the League; he also asked those close to Ben-Gurion to read what their party newspaper *Davar* had printed on 15 July 1948. The paper's editorial said that "words of gratitude and respect" were in order for the leaflets which members of the League had distributed to soldiers in the Egyptian and Jordanian armies. He asked: "Well, then, how do we treat our allies?" He clarified his defense of the communists by adding: "This is the first time in the history of Zionism, and during the days of war in particular, that an Arab organization which is popular with the masses supports a political project in Palestine (originally the Land of Israel), which is close to the official Jewish project."[58] The writer stressed, "We were not given friends like these so as to allow ourselves to spit in their faces." This article was not unique in the statements and writings of Mapam activists in that period. Aharon Cohen, mentioned earlier, also put forward a defiant defense of the need to continue giving special treatment to men of the League in Haifa and Nazareth and elsewhere. He stressed that this good treatment had borne abundant fruit which was important to Israel as it began to chart its path in 1948.[59]

I return to an important sentence at the end of the article by Eliezer Beʾeri concerning the activities of members of the League "behind the front lines in Gaza and Beirut," which served the interests of Israel in an attempt to explain it. Putting aside the activities of members of the League in Gaza for later, as far as Beirut is concerned, a number of League members reached the city after the fall of Haifa and the expulsion of its population at the end of April 1948. Emile Habibi's arrival in the Lebanese capital following his visit to Prague with Mikunis and his presence there for about six months remained a shrouded secret. While Emile Tuma was arrested upon his arrival in Lebanon, as we mentioned earlier, Emile Habibi, the supporter of partition and the League's spokesman, remained free. In the several months he spent in Beirut, Habibi met with representatives of Arab communist parties as well as his friends and acquaintances. Was this the activity that Eliezer Be'eri was referring to in his article mentioned above?

As compared to the leaders of Mapam who were eager to ally with the League, influential figures in Mapai were not so pleased with the way the communists in Nazareth were being pampered. They had received several complaints about the huge privileges which the communists had been granted, particularly in the area of organizing work and workers in the city at the time. Even Moshe Chertok (Sharett) became involved in the case, and wrote to Minister of Minorities Shitrit, saying: "While we should allow members of the National Liberation League to participate in the institutions we are setting up, we should do so according to what is suitable, as long as this does not exclude other elements which we care about . . . we should not set up League members as bosses over the Arab masses. In all arrangements for local self-government for the Arabs of the occupied areas, we should rely basi-cally on the circles and men who have cooperated with us from early on."[60]

Sharett was well versed on the Arab population of Nazareth and their circum-stances and had himself established relations with them from long ago. He did not object to allowing League members to participate in the institutions of govern-ment, but only placed some conditions on them. Some old collaborators, such as Sayf al-Din Zu'bi, had long cooperated with the Haganah and HaKeren HaKay-amet. After Shitrit received Sharett's letter, he followed his instructions and wrote Elisha Soltz, the military governor, saying: "The major families in Nazareth, the Fahum family and the Zu'bi family, whose members have cooperated with us for a long time, are complaining because it appears as though workers' affairs have been put in the hands of the communists. Such ideas should not take hold in the Arab public's mind since they do not like socialist ideas or find them palatable."[61] These positions on the part of prominent Israeli leaders make it abundantly clear that they appreciated the important role that the communists were playing at that vital juncture, reflected in their treatment of members of the League, but there is no doubt that this positive Zionist position was first and foremost a recognition to the debt owed to the socialist camp.

In addition to Nazareth, League members managed to reestablish their orga-nization in Haifa as well. Although the vast majority of League activists and its leaders migrated from the city when it fell and its Arab residents were expelled,

many communists returned to the city in coordination with Israeli political and
military leaders. Tawfiq Tubi was one of the few who did not leave the city (more
or less) and he played a central role in bringing his comrades back.[62] Emile Habibi,
who had returned from Beirut, joined him in Haifa, where they made preparations
to resume *al-Ittihad*. Due to these numerous activities by the leaders and activists
of the League in Haifa, some of their rivals made complaints to the authorities
concerning the freedom of movement and activity granted to the communists.
A report registered with city officials by one of the objectors states: "The Arab
who is not affiliated with their (the communists') organizations feels very unjustly
treated. There is a dominant belief among the Arabs that only communists can live
in freedom and dignity in Israel."[63] This belief, which was no secret in Haifa and
Nazareth, contributed a great deal to consolidating the role of the communists in
the leadership of the survivors.

At that stage, clearly some Israeli leaders were supporting the communists as
a thank you to the Soviet Union for its support of a Jewish state, and the communists acquired special privileges regarding their travel, movements, and approval
for many to return from Lebanon and elsewhere. Mapam leaders were the biggest
supporters of the policy favoring the communists. Zahi Karkabi testified that he
travelled from 'Akka to Beirut, but decided to return a few weeks later.[64] He arrived
in the village of al-Bi'na in central Galilee with two other comrades, Jamal Musa
and Matiya Nassar, at the end of June 1948. The three spent the night in the village,
then travelled on to al-Makr, which was under Israeli control at the time. There
they searched for members of Mapam, seeking their help, and traveled to 'Akka
aided by soldiers. They were detained there for a few days, then set free and went
to Haifa safely with help from a Mapam leader.[65] This story is repeated in various forms with other comrades who gave testimonies on how they returned from
Lebanon in 1948.

The story of Matiya Nassar, who returned with Karkabi, is unusual and quite
astonishing. Matiya was born in the village of al-Tayba in the Ramallah district in
1927. His father, who was married to a Spanish woman, migrated with his family to
Spain when Matiya was six months old. In 1938, the father decided to return with
his family to Palestine. Matiya, who could only speak Spanish, could not enroll
in the existing schools, so he worked from an early age in printing presses, where
he met some communists, including 'Awda al-'Ashhab.[66] When the family moved
to Haifa in 1941, Matiya also worked at a printing press. After the city fell, Matiya
found himself being swept along with dense crowds to the port and boarding a
ship which took him to the port of Marseilles in France. In that city he managed to
find the Sahyun house, belonging to an Arab family from Haifa, who helped him
get to Beirut.

In Beirut Matiya again found himself working at a printing press for a short
while. He met Emile Habibi, who informed him that the League intended to
resume publication of *al-Ittihad*, and convinced him to return to Haifa to work

at the paper. Matiya mentioned in his testimony that comrades in the Lebanese Communist Party helped him and his two companions to travel to Rumaysh, and from there they travelled to Tarshiha. On his way to Tarshiha he was captured by members of the Arab Liberation Army, who thought he was a spy because he could not speak Arabic well. However, Zahi Karkabi, whose father was well-known in Shafa 'Amr, saved him from that predicament. From Tarshiha he went to al-Bi'na and on to 'Akka and Haifa.[67]

The story of the three comrades on their way back from Lebanon is similar in many ways to those of other League members who returned to Haifa and the Galilee in 1948. Israel agreed in the summer and fall to the return of dozens of communists and members of their families, most of them by land. Lawyer Hanna Naqqara, however, returned by plane on 10 August 1948, via Nicosia.[68] Naqqara became one of the pillars of Maki's public activities, and played an important role in the defense of the rights of the Palestinian survivors in Haifa and the Galilee after the Nakba. With the inclusion of the returning comrades of the League, Tawfiq Tubi succeeded into turning the city of Karmil into a second stronghold of the League, alongside Nazareth. Despite the fact that the number of veteran and experienced comrades in both cities did not exceed one hundred (in the fall of 1948), they managed to play an important role in leading the Palestinian minority that remained in Israel.

The political position and role of the communists in Israel was formulated gradually during the year of the war, not after its end. The period from February to October 1948 witnessed a rapid shift in the position of the League leadership, from a timid endorsement of partition to integration into the Israeli political regime. This race to join Maki constituted an implicit renunciation of partition and of fighting for the establishment of a Palestinian state. Most members of the League came from Nazareth, 'Akka, Shafa 'Amr, and the Galilee villages in the area allocated for the Arab state under the UN resolution. Had it not been for this role of implicit legitimization for the annexation of the Galilee to Israel, it would have been difficult to imagine the Zionist "generosity" to the Arab communists. So, in addition to Israel's gratitude to the Soviet camp, the role played by the leaders and cadres of the League justified their acceptance as a subordinate partner of the Israeli political establishment.

FROM THE LIBERATION LEAGUE TO THE ISRAELI COMMUNIST PARTY

In the summer of 1948, the last shipments of heavy arms from Prague arrived, including dozens of fighter aircraft. As is well known, Zionist and Marxist Jews from the Mapam party in particular played an important role in concluding the Czech arms deal. The Israeli leadership's treatment of Arab communists was an acknowledgement of the receipt of those arms. Indeed, a security services document dated August 1948 provided an analysis of the activities of League members and indicated that no one should suspect them of posing any military danger to Israel. It added, "Our enemies are their enemies. In all their activities and actions, they demonstrate loyalty to our state. We therefore see in them (the League members) an important political factor and real ally of the state of Israel."[69] This kind of language largely explains the "generosity" of the Israeli government towards the comrades of the League who joined Maki in October 1948.

The Mapam activists continued to be most eager to support the members of the League in Nazareth and elsewhere. Eliezer Be'eri published his memoirs on that period in the party newspaper, and spoke with fervor about the grave dangers that the Arab communists courted in distributing leaflets to soldiers from Arab countries.[70] He mentioned that the leaflet distributors asked his help personally, as well as the help of IDF officers and the Haganah intelligence service (Shai) under his command.[71] In the following month, on the eve of the Israeli attack on the Egyptian army, Abba Kovner, who was in charge of cultural affairs in the army, wrote to Aharon Cohen asking him for a copy of the communist leaflet distributed to Arab soldiers so that he could use it in the Israeli psychological war against the Egyptian army on the southern front.[72]

In return for their services, League members asked for freedom of movement along the front lines, and for permission to publish a newspaper in Arabic. Some of their leaders asked for financial support from the government in return for their positions and services.[73] The Arab communists succeeded in the 1950s in concealing the statements and actions which would cause them embarrassment in the future. However, they made sure, with pride, that the references to the "secret movement" which they led and their acts of resistance to the soldiers of the "invading" Arab countries reached the ears of the Jews in late 1948 and early the following year. Such statements, examples of which we will look at later, contained much exaggeration—in my opinion—but they served the interests of the party in Israel during that period. Several years on, however, they came into conflict with the reversal of the position of the socialist camp and the party, and the bursting of illusions about the policy of the Jewish state; it then became necessary to keep these statements in secrecy and to attack anyone who tried to bring them to light.

Hanna Abu Hanna related in his memoirs a story that may seem peculiar to the reader in our day and age, but that illustrates the mentality of some League leaders at the time and the atmosphere of facilitating cooperation with leftist (mainly Mapam) Zionists. About two weeks after the fall of Nazareth, Tubi met Saliba Khamis in his office in the city. After Tubi left, Khamis called Abu Hanna and let him in on the substance of the secret meeting, which amounted to a proposal for the League to participate in the operation to oust the Arab Rescue Army from the Galilee, and asked him to prepare a list of young men who might be prepared to take part in this secret mission.[74] A few days later Abu Hanna gave Saliba Khamis a list containing the names of about thirty young men. A month later Abu

Hanna asked Saliba Khamis about that mission and when it might be carried out, but Khamis told him that the subject was closed. Abu Hanna adds in his memoirs that when he asked Tubi fifty years later (1998) what had happened to that ambitious plan, the latter simply told him the idea had not been practical.[75]

Whatever the circumstances that prevented the League's participation in expelling the ARA from the rest of the Galilee, the mere proposal indicates the confidence of the League members in believing that they could play a leading role in governing the Galilee and other areas in Palestine in cooperation with Israel. To play this role, they were actually prepared to cooperate with the army of occupation and Zionist political leaders, particularly the Mapam party. League members in Nazareth under the leadership of Saliba Khamis had no objection to cooperating with the military government and the other Israeli occupation authorities at the time. It would appear that the successes the League achieved as a result of this cooperation "intoxicated" the leaders of that organization in the summer and fall of 1948. At the personal level, it is well known that the Israeli authorities gave Saliba Khamis a pistol and a car for his sole use, privileges that were only granted at the time to the Israeli authorities and to major collaborators, such as Sayf al-Din Zu'bi. Incidentally, Saliba Khamis kept the pistol even after the war ended in 1949.[76]

The month of October 1948 was decisive in the military and political battles in southern and northern Palestine. At the beginning of that month, the mufti's men were trying to set up an All-Palestine government in Gaza. Meanwhile in Amman, King Abdullah was completing the process of annexing the "West Bank" to Jordan. In northern Palestine the League had completed its preparations for inclusion in Israel by way of merging with the Israeli Communist Party, Maki. The first step in that direction was distributing the famous leaflet, signed by three Arab communist parties in addition to the Liberation League. Emile Habibi, Tawfiq Tubi, and Fu'ad Nassar played a major role in coordinating efforts for the publication of the leaflet at the beginning of the month, a copy of which was smuggled from Beirut to Haifa by League comrades from al-Bi'na.[77] From there dozens of comrades distributed it in various parts of Palestine, particularly in the north of the country. The distribution of the leaflet in the Galilee villages was a source of pride for many comrades documented in their memoirs and testimonies concerning their activities in those difficult days.[78]

The communist leaflet was distributed in early October, at the same time that Zurayk was publishing the second edition of his book, *The Meaning of al-Nakba* . The term "al-Nakba" was used several times in the leaflet to describe the tragic circumstances in which the Palestinians found themselves,[79] but the burden of responsibility was put on the shoulders of colonialism and Arab reaction, with only a timid reference to "reactionary Zionist leaders." The contradiction in the positions of the communists was particularly apparent at that time when they continued to talk about partition and the "invading" Arab armies while maintaining silence about Israel's occupation of the Galilee and other areas allocated to the Palestinian state. In effect, the communists implicitly accepted Israel's occupation of the Galilee by joining Maki and rushing to take part in the Israeli elections at the end of 1948 without any reservations.

The story of Jibra'il Bishara and his brothers from Tarshiha may be the best example of the dangers which members of the League and the distributors of the leaflet in upper Galilee were courting. Jibra'il served as the secretary of the Maki branch in his village for decades, but before that had been a League activist in Haifa until 1948. He was arrested after he distributed the Communist Party's leaflet in Mi'lya, Fassuta, and other villages.[80] He and his three brothers were led off to the ARA's detention center in Bint Jubayl. Bishara referred to his arrest and trial before a Lebanese military judge, Sa'id Shihab, in his handwritten memoirs.[81] When news spread of the fall of upper Galilee to the Israeli army near the end of October, he was released. His three brothers had been released earlier and returned to their village, Tarshiha. One brother, Antoine, moved to Nazareth years later, where he raised his family.[82]

Along with criticizing Arab leaders, the communists also conducted self-criticism concerning the League's responsibility for dividing the ranks of the Palestine Communist Party along nationalist lines in 1943. These positions paved the way for the decision to merge the League with the Israeli Communist Party in October 1948. The record of events of the Conference of the Union of Arab and Jewish Communists in Haifa includes a request by the League on 1 October to join the Maki party, the same day on which the leaflet of the Arab communist parties was distributed.[83] Maki's central committee considered this request and approved it on 5 October, and the decision was officially issued the following day. At the same time, the League put forward its request to the Israeli authorities for permission to publish al-Ittihad newspaper in Haifa and the paper began publishing on 18 October. A few days later, on 22–23 October, the conference was held in the Mayo movie theatre in Haifa; it was not a union between two equal partners, but rather an acceptance of the conditions of the Jewish communists under the leadership of Mikunis.

The "unity" conference opened with speeches by the leaders of the party, Jews and Arabs, who enthusiastically repeated their blessings for the renewed "international unity."[84] Prominent among the speakers were Esther Vilenska, Tawfiq Tubi, Shmuel Mikunis, and Emile Habibi. Habibi gave a fiery speech in the name of the League and "the secret popular resistance movement against the armies of occupation in Jerusalem, Ramallah, Nablus, and Gaza,"[85] in which he said: "I speak in the name of a party which stands in the vanguard of the popular war to expel the armies of occupation from the Arab part of the land of Israel." Habibi claimed that the League "represents thousands of comrades who stand in the vanguard of popular resistance against the armies of occupation."[86] Of course, what Habibi meant were the Jordanian and Egyptian armies, not the Israeli army which had occupied Nazareth and other cities and villages in the Galilee, to which "army of occupation" was not applied. Instead it was considered a liberator of the people from the "Qawuqji gangs."

Habibi, Tubi, and the other League comrades—mostly from Haifa and the Galilee—who joined Maki were young men who were excited at the time about the triumph of socialism in Israel. This atmosphere reached its high point in the unity conference in Haifa. During the days of the conference itself it was no longer a secret that Israel, which had renewed its attack on the Egyptian army in the south, would soon occupy the rest of the Galilee. While comrades of the League in Gaza and the West Bank were being tracked down and arrested, its members in Israel were honored and well treated. Therefore, it was not strange that we did not hear any criticism of Israel's actions on their part, including for its expansion into the territory allocated to the Arab state under the partition resolution. *Al-Ittihad* newspaper, after it began appearing in Haifa, expressed the enthusiastic views of the League about the victories of the Jewish state, as we shall relate below. But the killings and the expulsion of the population which accompanied the finalization of the occupation of the Galilee and other areas did not earn a mention, much less condemnation, in the Maki party press at the end of 1948.[87]

The position of the members of the League, as with the armies of Arab states, was very hostile to the volunteers in the Rescue Army. They increased their incitement against the ARA in the Galilee. After the occupation of the Galilee was completed, the communists revealed their hostility towards Fawzi al-Qawuqji's army in a new attempt to prove their loyalty to Israel. In return, the comrades in Maki, both Jews and Arabs, took pride about their role in the war of "independence" and the sacrifices they made for the creation of the Jewish state. At the end of December an opportunity arose to shed light on those sacrifices when the plane carrying Eliyahu Gozansky, one of the most prominent leaders of the party at the time, crashed. The plane, carrying arms and volunteers, fell over Athens, and Gozansky and his companions were killed.[88] *Al-Ittihad* newspaper carried the news of the accident and the death of the party leader the following day, on the front page: "He lived as a warrior, he died as a warrior. . . . He died for the sake of duty. May his memory be a lantern that guides warriors."[89]

Gozansky's mission was mentioned only briefly and with some secrecy at the beginning, yet as the date of the parliamentary elections (25 January 1949) approached, the Maki press carried abundant details on the subject. The Hebrew-language party organ mentioned that in addition to Gozansky, twelve Jews had died in the accident, their bodies transported from Greece and buried in the Nahalat Yitzhak cemetery in Tel Aviv.[90] On the thirtieth-day anniversary of the death of the leader, party secretary Mikunis published a long article under the title: "Eliyahu Gozansky: the Man and His Deeds,"[91] in which he showed how proud Maki was of its hero on the eve of the first elections for the Israeli parliament. Thus the members of the League transferred their affiliation and activities from the

Palestinian national camp to the Israeli Communist Party. They adopted Maki's discourse and its positions, thinking that they would be partners in the leadership of the Jewish socialist state, the friend of the communist camp which supported Israel's establishment politically and militarily. These illusions were gradually dispelled after 1949, but at that time party leaders did not carry out a critical review of their positions and analyses.

"PARTNERS" IN ISRAEL'S VICTORY AND PROPAGANDA

During 1948, the Jewish communists expressed their pride in the victories which Israel scored against the Arabs. *Kol HaAm* newspaper was full of headlines and news which reflected its adoption of Zionist discourse to a large extent. The victims of the war on the Israeli side were heroes who fell either in a just war or in criminal massacres perpetrated by the Arab side, according to the paper. On the other hand, Arabs who were killed were, according to the paper, the victims of defensive retaliation against the "centers of gang activity." The news about the Czech arms with which the Israeli army fought was a cause for pride and esteem because these arms were the instrument through which the Jews scored their victories.[92] When the United States complained about the arrival of heavy arms to Israel during the period in which there was supposed to be a total embargo on the sale of arms to states in the region, the party organ carried the answer of the Czech foreign minister who said he could not have cared less about the American condemnation.[93]

Even after the conference of Jewish and Arab communists in Haifa, the Hebrew-language party paper did not alter its Israeli nationalist tone. By the end of October Israel had completed its occupation of the Galilee, and *Kol HaAm* carried the news with pride without any mention of the massacres and expulsions of the Arab population.[94] The Arabic-language party paper published not dissimilar articles about the renewal of the fighting. Concerning the refugee problem and the Nakba in general, analysis and commentary in the paper continued to assign responsibility to colonialism, Arab reactionary forces and the Higher Arab Committee. Israel's role was lopped off at the end of an abbreviated list of indictments, although there was mention of "certain circles" which dreamt of a purely Jewish state free of any Arab residents.[95] The communists (both Jews and Arabs) had no reservations concerning the expansion of the borders of Israel at the expense of the territory of the Arab state under the partition resolution. The concepts of "occupation" and "occupied territories" were reserved (in both the Hebrew and Arabic-language Maki newspapers) for Gaza and the West Bank. The Galilee was "occupied" when it was under the control of Arab Rescue Army, according to the discourse of the communists and their press; however, after it was occupied by the Jewish army, references to the term "occupation" disappeared from the party's papers.

The formation of Maki came as talk increased about holding elections in the Jewish state, the borders of which were not yet determined. The fact that members of the League joined the Israeli Communist Party held great significance in the opinion of Ben-Gurion and his colleagues in the Zionist leadership. Completing the occupation of the Galilee and its annexation to Israel met no opposition from Maki and its press. Even after news of the massacres and the expulsion of the residents of villages in upper Galilee leaked out at the end of the year, the major figures in Maki did not express criticism of these actions.[96] The communists in Nazareth and other cities and villages in the Galilee saw no dilemma in joining an Israeli party at the end of 1948 or regarding their infatuation with taking part in the Knesset elections at the beginning of the following year. In this way the Liberation League in the Galilee was integrated into the Jewish state at an important juncture in the year of the Nakba, while the majority of the Palestinians who remained in the Galilee were overwhelmed by a sense of tragedy and mourning.

The communist camp imagined that it would reap the fruits of its unconditional military and political support for the young Jewish state by way of the Marxists in parliament. At the time, the communists did not speak of "saving what could be saved" in the wake of the Nakba. The Soviet Union had participated in the Nakba of the Palestinian people, and the local communists (Jews and Arabs) contributed to the legitimization of the annexation of the Galilee to Israel. Members of the League had joined the Maki party late in 1948, as Israeli flags fluttered and the chant of "Hatikva" reverberated in the Mayo movie theater in Haifa. In the festive atmosphere of the "unity conference" there was no voice reminding of the Nakba of the Palestinian people and its suffering.

Like the USSR, the Maki press and its leaders recognized the borders of Israel, which had expanded at the cost of the Palestinians. They defended those borders when the party endorsed the position of the Israeli leaders who refused to withdraw from the territory they had occupied in the Arab region as it was defined by the partition resolution. When Israel came under pressure from the representatives of the UN and other international organizations, the party hastened to defend the expansionist Zionist position. For example, *Kol HaAm* supported the statements of Foreign Minister Sharett, who declared that Israel "would not relinquish the Negev and the Galilee."[97] What is worse, when it appeared as though Israel was prepared to make territorial "concessions" for peace near the end of 1948, the Mapam and Maki parties strongly opposed the idea. They even refused the concept that "territories from the land of Israel" remain "under the control of the invaders," a clear reference to the Gaza Strip and the West Bank.[98]

The communist bloc states opposed United Nations General Assembly Resolution 194 concerning the right of Palestinian refugees to return or receive compensation for their property. Arab countries also opposed this resolution, but for different reasons than the states of the communist bloc, whose opposition was based on unconditional support for Israel. The Maki press embraced this position when it opposed the proposal by Israeli foreign minister Sharett to accept the return of 100,000 Palestinian refugees to Israel, which Maki said was the result of American pressure.[99] At that time competition between the communist and capitalist camps over who was the stronger and more important supporter of the nascent Jewish state was at its height. The illusion that the Jewish state would stand by the socialist camp was still strong among communists. That is why they were not concerned about what consequences that support would have for the Arab peoples in general and the disaster-afflicted Palestinian people in particular.

The Palestinians who remained in the Galilee after it was occupied suffered from repression and repeated attempts at uprooting them, but the Maki press made no reference to this subject on its pages even after the electoral battle was over. The first criticism that *al-Ittihad* directed at Israeli policy after the occupation of the Galilee had to do with the hundreds of young men who were arrested in their villages and sent to prisoner of war camps,[100] which included dozens of comrades and friends among them. *Al-Ittihad* described them as being combatants "in the secret resistance movement against the armies of Arab states." They had even risked their lives—"Qawuqji had threatened to execute them, and the Egyptian army locked them up in prisons and detention centers"—so how could the Israeli authorities arrest them? The communists were reprimanding the authorities, speaking as partners in the establishment of Israel and its victories, in a tone that no one else in the Arab community was using at the time. The paper added, "Public opinion in Israel has heard much about the heroic acts of the men of the National Liberation League in upper Galilee against Qawuqji's troops. The popular resistance movement had in fact prevented the entry of Qawuqji's troops into several villages. The elements who conspired with Qawuqji's troops . . . have been allowed to go free. But the elements who risked their lives for peace . . . to evict the invaders from the homeland, and to implement the [UN] resolution of 29 November 1947, were thrown into the dark recesses of jail."[101] In this way, the Arab activists in Maki attempted to prove that they had played an effective role in the defense of the establishment of the Jewish state and its expansion, and the merger with Maki made them feel like partners in Israel's victory over "the reactionary Arab regimes."

When dozens of comrades continued to be detained in POW camps for months, the leaders of Maki raised this issue with their contacts in government and on the pages of newspapers. The decision by detained League comrades to go on a hunger strike brought renewed attention to this issue. *Al-Ittihad* reported on the reasons for the strike: "When the Israeli army entered the villages of upper Galilee the villagers expected this action would end the days of occupation, pressure, and slavery. But then we saw the military authorities arresting young men in the villages, the biggest share being Arab communists. They have arrested and ill-treated 75 communists,"[102] so they decided to go on a hunger strike. These admonitions were repeated on more than one occasion, and reflected the sense of partnership that the communists felt with the victors, as opposed to the feeling of defeat dominant among Arabs in the year of the Nakba. This tone of blaming the government on the one hand, and incitement against everyone who fights Israel on the other, continued for a long time.

By end of 1948 and early 1949, the Maki leaders were busy with the first parliamentary elections in Israel, and they needed their comrades who were detained. But those few dozen were a small minority of the thousands of civilian detainees whom Israel called prisoners of war, and kept in jail for a year or more.[103] The party fought the elections of January 1949 using a purely Israeli nationalist discourse, particularly in front of Jewish audiences. The principal role of Arab communists in these elections was to convince the residents of Haifa and the Galilee to participate and not boycott the elections. After the League comrades decided to become Israelis by merging with Maki, they felt no embarrassment in calling on the people of Nazareth, Shafa 'Amr, and villages in western Galilee to vote, that is, to legitimize the occupation and annexation of the Galilee to Israel. Their participation helped open the door for the leadership role played by communist Arabs of the Palestinian minority in the Jewish state.

Following the elections, which made Tawfiq Tubi a member of the Israeli Knesset, the statements and actions of the communists in support of Israel and its policies did not end. The political battles which they fought did not go far beyond civil rights for the Arabs as a minority in the state of the Jews. The leaders of Maki tried to outdo Ben-Gurion in their nationalism and protectiveness for Israel's interests. When the compulsory military service law (which exempted Arab youth) came before the Knesset, the leaders of the party, with Tawfiq Tubi at their head, demanded that Arabs be drafted like their Jewish comrades. In taking this position in 1949 Tubi was reflecting the position of his party. In 1954 Tubi once again supported military service in the Israeli army for young Arab men when the Sharett government favored that, but the government then retreated from that position. The Maki leaders also did not object to the law of return for Jews or to the ban on Palestinian refugees exercising their right to return to their homeland. Maki also supported the Zionist policy of settling Jews in the lands of Palestinian villages which had been denuded of their populations—including settlements established by Marxists from the Mapam party, allies of the communists, on land belonging to the villages of Kufr Bir'im and Sa'sa', as well as others.

In line with most "believers," they deluded themselves into thinking that the leaders of the communist camp in Moscow were, in their wisdom, leading the region to what would be best for its peoples, along the path of international socialism. The "believers" only had to hear and obey and accept the wisdom of the leadership, which often conceals its wisdom from the simple common people. The new Soviet position impelled the communists to undergo challenges pertaining to the line of policy supporting Israel in the year of the Nakba, not opposing the occupation of land allocated to the Palestinian state in the Galilee and elsewhere under the partition resolution, legitimizing this annexation by joining Maki, and then participating effectively in the first Israeli elections in January 1949.[104]

The call by the Maki party for the Palestinians remaining in Nazareth and western Galilee to participate in the elections represented an important step toward their "Israelification" at that early stage, when the fate of the Galilee had not yet been determined politically, and no one had acknowledged its annexation to the state of the Jews at that stage in the war (early 1949). Ben-Gurion quickly grasped the opportunity and allowed those remaining in Haifa and the Galilee to participate in the parliamentary elections. Consequently, these elections became the historic "initiation" of those who remained of their own free will, or at least the will and encouragement of the remaining communist leaders and collaborators, such as Sayf al-Din al-Zu'bi.[105] Those elections laid down the rules for political organization for the Palestinian "survivors" in Israel. There were only two choices: either Maki's or the Zionist parties' lists; there was no third choice. The independent and nationalist survivors were deprived of the blessing of organized political action, and found both of these choices equally unpalatable.

Until the mid-1950s, the communists remained hopeful that they could play an important role in the leadership of the Jewish state and its institutions; however, Ben-Gurion excluded them from his government and reinforced Israel's relations with the United States and the West in general, and was publicly hostile to the communist camp during the Cold War. He not only excluded the communists, but excluded the Mapam party as well in his first government. The leaders of Maki lost hope that they would have an important political role after the first elections (in 1949), and illusions about Israel becoming a socialist state and an ally of the USSR began to be gradually shed. The ramifications of this were clear in 1956 when the socialist camp stood by Abdel Nasser's Egypt and against Israel, the ally of Britain and France in the Tripartite Aggression Pact. At the beginning of the attack on Egypt, the well-known Kafr Qasim massacre took place, and Tawfiq Tubi helped in exposing the Ben-Gurion government's effort to conceal that massacre, as it had done with the massacres of 1948.

SUMMARY

This chapter dealt with three topics and research areas each of which has its specialized literature and historians: the establishment of the state of Israel, the Nakba of the Palestinian people, and the role of the communist camp from the UN partition resolution to the end of 1948. But the main point of the chapter was to uncover the ramifications of the Soviet support for Israel for the unification of Arab and Jewish communist ranks in the Maki party in 1948. It is no coincidence that the history of the Liberation League in that period is enveloped in mystery even decades after the events, and a quarter of a century after the fall of the USSR and the Soviet bloc in 1989. Party comrades and their friends prefer to remain silent about the events of that period and to jump to their undeniable role and the causes for which they fought following the end of the war with all of its tragedies. The enemies and rivals of the communists remind us of this "behind the scenes" or forgotten role, which they label "treasonous" at times. We tried to present here an unabridged first reading of the important developments in the positions of the League leaders in the year of the Nakba only.

Uncovering the role of the Soviet Union in the Palestinian Nakba and shedding light on the statements and activities of the communists in 1948 does not detract from their role in the struggle after that. No one could ignore their political capital as leaders since they played an important role in the survival of the Palestinian minority and in building the cultural and political institutions of the Arabs in Israel. Critiquing the performance of the leaders, as well as acknowledging the good they have done, places their role in a historical perspective which can be explained and analyzed to draw lessons from any errors that were made. Leaders are not infallible. Bringing leaders down from the level of symbols to that of human beings is essential for anyone who seeks to benefit from the legacy of the past and to build a better future. Acknowledging errors and explaining them in their historical context is far better than concocting or conniving to deceive oneself.

This chapter tried to present a new reading of the positions and actions of the communists in the year of the Nakba based on their statements and writings at the time of the events, in order to deconstruct the typical tales of heroism and treason which prioritize the political dimension over the criteria of academic research which is biased towards truth in historical context. Seven decades have passed since the Nakba and the many calamities which the Palestinian people suffered; it is time to hold oneself accountable instead of colluding to deceive oneself and others. The Soviet Union and the subservient communist regimes have collapsed, and researchers have uncovered the deeds of Stalin during his years in power. In light of all that, it is strange that some Arab comrades insist on stoning anyone who tries to lift the curtain to reveal what many in the world know about us and about them.

In that fateful year, the communists deviated from their previous analyses of the essence of the struggle in Palestine and joined the Zionist left. This alliance, which could not have come about were it not for the reversal in the Soviet position, enabled the communists to play a role of leadership for the Palestinian survivors in Israel, but it also tied them to a discourse and positions which held them until the fragility of their assumptions and limited nature of their vision became clear to everyone. Accepting the partition resolution and backing the Soviet camp in supporting the establishment of a Jewish state on the ruins of Palestine in 1948 were actions that continued to cast their shadow on the positions of the Israeli Communist Party for decades after. Despite the fact that the hopes (or delusions) which had been attached to labor Zionism when making the alliance with the Soviet camp in the 1950s were dashed, the leadership of Maki has not conducted a courageous and critical review of its positions in the year of the Nakba. In conclusion, it is useful, in light of the above, to summarize the many turning points for the League leaders in the year of the Nakba:

—The first turning point was the decision of the League majority in Nazareth to accept the partition resolution and to support it in practice, not just in words (in February 1948), then the trip by Habibi and Mikunis to the communist parties' conference in Belgrade, and from there to Prague. Mikunis, according to his own testimony, was coordinating his actions with Ben-Gurion on one side and with the USSR on the other, which proved to play an important role in speeding up the Czech arms supply deal at the end of March 1948. These facts about the position of the communists from the beginning of the war point to a special ideological perspective about staying in Palestine, unlike the rest of the Arabs who simply preferred living under the occupation and its humiliations to being expelled and losing both land and homeland.

—Secondly, the decision by the Liberation League to resist the presence of Arab armies on Palestinian soil as of May 1948. The communist bloc under the leadership of the USSR recognized Israel immediately after its establishment was declared and started supplying it with heavy arms, including aircraft, while the Israeli army was expanding the borders of the Jewish state at the expense of the territories allocated to the Arab state. That expansion included massacres and the intensive forcible expulsion of the population, as in Lydda, Ramla, the Galilee, and other towns and villages in the ethnic cleansing effort. None of this affected the continued Palestinian communist support for Israel.

—October 1948 was a third important turning point towards the communists' alignment with Israel and their alliance with Zionism, witnessing the distribution of the leaflets by the League and other Arab communist parties in early October, followed by the decision to join the Israeli Communist Party based on the acceptance of the state for the Jews. The merger was crowned by the convening of the so-called "unity" conference in Haifa and the resounding speeches by the Jewish leaders and Emile Habibi.[106] Maki's Hebrew-language newspaper celebrated the coming event by saying: "The union of Jewish and Arab communists in the framework of the Israeli Communist Party will reinforce the war for the independence of the state of Israel," without any reference to the ramifications for the Palestinian people even in the territory allocated to their state under the partition resolution.[107]

—Fourth, comrades in the League "forgot" the partition resolution after October and participated enthusiastically in elections for the Knesset on 25 January 1949. The significance of joining Maki, and participation in the elections in Nazareth and other occupied Palestinian areas, could be seen during the war. Thus, the annexation of the Galilee and other areas to Israel was legitimized before any international or Arab party knew where Israel's borders were. Following that, the communists adopted an Israeli form of discourse and participated in a crucial way in separating the remaining Palestinian minority in Israel from the rest of their people. Party gatherings, conferences, and demonstrations were held under the Israeli flag which was raised high with pride, following the singing of the Israeli anthem "Hatikva" on occasion. These positions were the price paid in advance for Israel allowing Maki to make demands for some civil rights for the Palestinians and to oppose the military government and its policies.

—Finally, one of the most prominent manifestations of the communists' adoption of Israeli nationalist discourse was the 1949 request by Tawfiq Tubi to draft Arab youth into the Israeli army. Tubi and his friends in the leadership of Maki at the time could not see the political and moral dilemma inherent in pushing the fate-struck Palestinian people to serve their executioners. It was the good fortune of the Palestinians who remained in Israel that Ben-Gurion and members of his government refused the request. When Moshe Sharett became prime minister and his defense minister proposed to call up Arab young men to register for compulsory military service in October 1954, the communists supported this idea enthusiastically. They also continued to celebrate Israel's "Independence Day" at international communist conferences until 1956. After illusions about the essence of the Jewish state and its (international and local) policies kept being dismissed, the discourse of the party changed at its 1957 conference, followed by clashes in Nazareth on 1 May 1958. But the party quickly retreated once again and fell into the trap of Soviet policy in the Middle East, as we shall see later.

4

Forced Migration Continues
After the Cannons Fall Silent

Shortly after the fighting between Egypt and Israel ended in early 1949, the two states began talks on an armistice and the drawing of borders between them. Israel's signing of an armistice agreement on 24 February 1949 with the biggest Arab state consolidated its military victory. Egypt was the first Arab state to sign an agreement, followed by Lebanon on 23 March, and Jordan on 3 April. According to the agreement with Jordan signed at Rhodes, the "little triangle" area, with a population of 31,000, was transferred to Israel. Syria was the last to sign an armistice agreement, on 20 July 1949, and the uncertain period between the end of military battles and the drawing of actual borders ended. Some historians regard these agreements as the real and official end of the 1948 war in Palestine.

Civilians anywhere who are caught in the middle of battlefields are often prey to being killed or expelled, or to suffer property destruction at the hands of soldiers. The 1948 war's end and the signing of armistice agreements with neighboring Arab countries should have relieved pressure on the Palestinians in Galilee, and raised their hopes concerning reconstruction, the return of refugees to their homes, and the resumption of normal life. Such were the expectations of the Palestinians based on logic and the experience of people of the area for hundreds of years, as well as the promises made by Israel since May 1948. In addition, the state of the Jews, which was established on the basis of a United Nations resolution, was in dire need of international support. It was therefore expected that Israel would heed the December 1948 declaration of the United Nations concerning human rights and Resolution 194 which gave the Palestinian refugees the right of return and compensation for the property they had lost. Yet events contradicted the expectations of the fate-stricken people inside and outside their homeland.

Israel opened its doors to the Jewish diaspora of the world so that they could "return" and live in Israel, but slammed them shut in the face of Palestinians who had been forced to migrate from their homes only yesterday. What is worse is what a number of Israel's leaders declared publicly after the signature of the armistice agreements: that the question of Arabs remaining in the Jewish state in the future had not been finalized, and that if Palestinian refugees were settled in neighboring states, that could become the model for ridding themselves of the Arab survivors in Israel. This was not just a matter of words; the words were accompanied by real acts of expulsion, as we shall see in the following. In addition to preventing the return of the forced migrants, thousands of Arabs were expelled from their homes after the end of the war under various pretexts. This situation of insecurity and fear of expulsion lasted for many years after the 1948 war, and intensified the sense of tragedy for those who remained.

In the summer of 1949, 160,000 Palestinian Arabs were estimated to be living in Israel under military rule.[1] This and other officially accepted figures in the first years of the Nakba and after conceal a complicated and painful story in the history of those who remained. Thousands of Palestinians from Galilee were expelled during that period from their cities and villages to the West Bank and other regions outside Israel's borders. Even after the "little triangle" was transferred to Israeli sovereignty, expulsion operations against the Galilee population to the Kingdom of Jordan continued. On the Lebanese front, thousands of Palestinians succeeded in returning to Galilee while Israel expelled thousands of others to Lebanon. Among the relatively well-known examples of late expulsions, carried out during the Sinai War in October 1956, was the forced migration of those who remained in the southern Hula villages. Before that, Israel had expelled a few thousand inhabitants of Majdal 'Asqalan in autumn 1950 to the Gaza Strip.

As we have seen, there was a consensus among decision makers in Israel on preventing hundreds of thousands of Palestinian refugees from returning to their homes and lands, and wide agreement that "too many Arabs" had remained in the state of Israel.[2] At a meeting of the ruling Mapai party secretariat, others expressed similar opinions and sentiments. For example, MK Eliahu Hacarmeli said: "I am not prepared to accept a single Arab, even a single non-Jew. I want Israel to be entirely Jewish." MK Zeev Oan, secretary of Mapai, acknowledged: "I am delighted that I do not see a single Arab on the road from Tel Aviv to Haifa during my trip."[3] Such views and sentiments were common among security agencies, settler movements, and other Zionist institutions, which put pressure on the government to expel more Arabs. However, satisfying all of those demands would have exposed the government to internal and external pressure and criticisms. To avoid this pressure, it acted carefully, resorting to subterfuge at times or giving "security" justifications for expelling the remaining Arabs.

Ideas and plans were proposed to reduce the number of Arabs and concentrate them in limited areas. These ideas were implemented in practice by expelling Palestinians from their homes to neighboring countries or, at other times, to places inside Israel. Just as Israel banned the return of refugees, it also banned the expellees, who were now categorized as the "present absentees," from returning to their towns and villages. Arab towns and villages became special border districts under military rule, which separated them into closed areas ruled by the 1945 emergency regulations. In this way those who remained were considered a security problem which made them subjected to the worst kind of daily humiliation and maltreatment, which undermined their most basic human rights of travel, work, and dignity, not to mention citizen's rights.

The question of Palestinian refugees has usually been discussed and studied at the level of international politics and Israel's relations with Arab countries. This study will approach the refugee issue from a different perspective—as a formative experience and phenomenon that became an integral part of the history of the Palestinians who remained in Israel and affected their relations with the state after the end of the war. Despite the massive effort expended by the army and police to halt the occurrence of refugees attempting to return to their homes, labeled "infiltrators" by Israel, Israel's success was only partial, since thousands returned to their homes and remain there. The historical literature has not dealt fully with their story, leaving much of it unknown despite its importance. Their issue is intertwined with the history of those who remained in the 1950s, as many of those who remained in the Galilee (and elsewhere) found themselves torn between their humanitarian and moral obligation to help their relatives who were returning, and their fear of punishment since Israel had criminalized the act of not informing the authorities of the presence of the "infiltrators." Many of those who remained found themselves in a haunting dilemma of handing over their children and siblings to the authorities or going to jail and paying exorbitant penalties.

Israel's leaders saw the departure of Palestinians from their homeland as a great achievement. Some expressed their opinion frankly, while others said they were looking for the means to rid Israel of the rest of the population in the Galilee Triangle and the Naqab.[4] The main argument on this subject took place inside the Zionist camp regarding the extent, practicality, and price which Israel might have to pay if it carried out collective expulsion operations after the end of the war. Moshe Sharett and other Israeli leaders were cognizant of the political circumstances behind pressure at the international and regional levels which placed limits on the forced migration of the remaining Palestinians to Lebanon and Jordan. Nevertheless, the proponents of the transfer argument continued to pressure in favor of wresting control of the largest possible extent of Arab land and leaving the smallest number of Palestinians in the country.[5] This is how the policy of ethnic cleansing continued for years after the 1948 war.

Ben-Gurion was the leading proponent of the policy of violent confrontation and the critical decision-maker regarding the return of Palestinians and treatment of the remaining Palestinians. Contrary to his foreign minister Sharett and the Mapam ministers, who were concerned about world public opinion, he took a firm and decisive stand about them. In 1950 in one cabinet meeting discussion on the issue of the Arabs in Israel and the refugee question, Ben-Gurion declared frankly: "Of course we should not allow 600,000 to return; not even 600." He then threatened: "If some wish to discuss the issue of allowing Arabs to return, they will have to do so in a different cabinet."[6] At another meeting, in 1951, the prime minister summarized the discussion by saying: "I think it is better for us and for the Arabs that they should be in an Arab state and we should be in a Jewish state, but this will not be brought about by force unless a war breaks out. . . . If they begin a war, I do not know what we shall do then. We shall deal with that when it happens."[7]

The reaction of the Arab population to the Israeli policy of oppression and persecution was split between submission combined with attempting to stay in the country, and limited attempts at resistance. The communists led the open and organized political resistance to the policy of repression and discrimination against Arab citizens. This sort of resistance has been studied and illuminated in the specialized literature on the history of Arabs in Israel, but other less organized and quieter forms of local steadfastness and resistance have not been discussed, invisible to the eyes of the researchers. Many Palestinians overcame the obstacles on the road of return and found "pragmatic" paths to return to their families and homes. In confronting the games played by the authorities, those who remained used to their advantage the gaps between the jurisdictions of the various authorities amid the chaos in the aftermath of the war. Israel was more careful in dealing with members of the Christian and Druze sects for reasons connected with its regional and international policies. This sensitivity was sometimes successfully exploited to allow the return of some migrants and to prevent new acts of forced migration.

SHUTTING THE DOOR TO RETURN
AND EXPELLING "INFILTRATORS"

The survival of some villages near the Lebanese border stymied the military authorities from their task of completely closing off the border strip and made it easier for groups of forced migrants to return without the approval or even knowledge of the authorities. The mukhtars of the villages and the collaborators sometimes found themselves caught under pressure from their families and fellow villagers. The fact that the "infiltrators" hid in Arab villages led to "combing" and expulsion operations which sometimes affected many relatives who had not left their homes during the war. Many of the new expellees were young men, so the authorities expected that the rest of their families, who were dependent on them for livelihood, would follow them. The expulsion of young men also weakened the remaining relatives under military rule and made them more liable to persecution and repression by the authorities.

Israel's security policies following the signing of the armistice agreements with neighboring Arab countries fell into three policy areas:

1. External: regarding the confrontation with the Arab states and their armies. This policy amounted to preparing the Israeli army for the possibility of a renewal of hostilities in a so-called "second round."
2. Between external and internal: concerning the attempt of migrants to return from Arab countries to their homes and lands, in most cases for economic and social reasons, rather than for attempts at revenge against the Jews. In spite of this, Israel considered them to be a threat to its security and fought them through all available means.
3. Internal security: involving how to deal with the Palestinians who remained, whom Israel considered to be a "fifth column." For the Jewish state, which was trying to prevent the return of refugees at any cost, the willingness of the Arabs who remained in Galilee to help their returning brethren and their children was a crime to be punished with an iron fist.

The return of thousands of Palestinians from Lebanon to Galilee did not lead to Israeli retaliation against Lebanese territory, in contrast to their reactions on the Jordanian and Egyptian fronts. About 100,000 Palestinians from Haifa and Galilee had sought refuge in Lebanon, and thousands of Palestinians continued to cross the border in both directions, as they had done in 1948. The fact that Israel completed the occupation of Galilee and signed armistice agreements did not lead to any significant change in the field along the border. The rugged mountainous terrain in upper Galilee, combined with the weak military monitoring of the border from both sides, did not make for a difficult crossing. The returnees at the beginning of 1949 were mostly expellees from the villages which Israel had occupied in Operation Hiram. After experiencing the harshness of life as refugees in Lebanon, many Palestinians tried to secure their return to their families, in towns and villages near the border. Consequently, those "infiltrators" did not engage in violent activities and, in any event, were not armed.[8] Essentially, violence was the tool of the Israeli army and police who tried to prevent the return to Galilee by force of arms.

The Arab press published the stories of some "infiltrators" and stressed the extreme importance of this subject in the life of those who remained in Israel in the 1950s. For example, the story of Muhammad 'Abd al-Qadir Nabulsi, first published by al-Yawm newspaper,[9] reported that Nabulsi had "infiltrated" more than once from Lebanon to Israel in the early 1950s, and was arrested and expelled more than once, sometimes to Jenin (in Jordan-controlled territory) and at other times to Lebanon. Nabulsi claimed to have lost the receipt proving he had been registered in the census, but the authorities rejected his claim and expelled him from the country time and again. The last time he was arrested, he was detained in Haifa in preparation for his deportation once again. According to the newspaper report, Nabulsi jumped from the roof of the police station to his death. However, al-Ittihad newspaper, which published a lengthy story, asked: "Are we talking about an attempted escape, or of suicide which reflects the extent of Nabulsi's despair and his decision to end his life as a result of repeated expulsion to a refugee existence?"[10]

The Israeli military government forces, who were acting on the basis of the defense (emergency) regulations of 1945, arrested many "infiltrators" either near the border or deep in the country and brought them to detention centers, from where military courts sentenced them to exorbitant fines and harsh jail terms. In November 1951, for instance, 195 "infiltrators" were in detention, and 148 others were indicted for crossing the border without a permit and entering closed-off military areas. In the same year, these two categories represented about 80 percent of detainees in prison.[11] Even two years later, at the end of May 1953, there were 341 infiltrators in jail who constituted about 30 percent of Arabs in prison at the time.[12] Israel did not set up special detention camps for those it described as infiltrators; they were jailed along with others in Shatta, al-Damun, and other prisons. Of course, many of the returnees managed to evade the grip of the various security agencies.

The line separating the Arab population who were registered in the census, including Arabs who had participated in the first Knesset elections in January 1949, and those whom the authorities defined as "infiltrators," was not clear. Many of the refugees who returned from Lebanon and who were pursued by the authorities were hard to identify once they reached populated villages. The military government agencies often declared curfews during which soldiers and police officers would conduct searches to find "infiltrators" and expel them beyond the borders. During these surprise searches of Arab villages, the authorities expelled many residents who had never been refugees at all. Even after the census of the population of Galilee in early 1949, the authorities did not distribute identity cards and registration receipts to everybody. Against this background, and given the attempt by the security agencies to score "successes" in their operations, citizens who had never left their homes and could not have infiltrated back were often expelled.[13]

General Elimelech Avnir, head of the military government in the administered areas, wrote a report on the surprise searches of Arab villages in Galilee and the number of those expelled in January 1949, which he sent to the minister of defense and the chief of staff: "Regarding our discussion on 4 January 1949, orders were given to conduct surprise searches and to check the identities of the population."[14] He added that the search operations were conducted in eleven villages during which 1,038 people were expelled beyond the borders. Strikingly, the number of expellees from Majd al-Krum (536 individuals) exceeded half of the total. The list of towns and villages from which people were expelled included those from the districts of 'Akka and Nazareth. Added to the numbers of those expelled, the report spoke of men "who had been arrested in order to continue investigating them and detainees who were moved to prisoner of war camps," as well as others "who had been expelled to other villages."[15]

The concise report did not explain why more than 1,000 people were expelled from their homes and villages in the Galilee. At the beginning of 1949, it was clear that the Israeli government and the prime minister were trying to expel the maximum possible number of Arabs from the northern villages during the interim period between the end of the war and the entry of armistice agreements into force. Some of these operations were conducted on the eve of the first elections and many were conducted afterwards. Some residents were expelled after the census, but before the registration receipts and identity cards were issued. There was no policy for the collective expulsion of Arabs from the villages of central and upper Galilee, but there was an attempt to reduce the numbers of residents, especially Muslims and some Christians. The army was the main driver of the expulsion operations and the principal agent of enforcement as the military establishment continued its war against Arab citizens in the Galilee, even after a ceasefire had entered into force. Military documents did not always explain to what region "beyond the borders" the expellees were sent, or what became of them after they were expelled from their homes.

General Avnir's report spoke of expulsion operations in the villages of al-Bi'na and Dayr al-Asad, but gave no precise dates and few details. According to the report fifty-nine people were expelled from al-Bi'na, while five others were taken to the prisoner of war camp. But in neighboring Dayr al-Asad only eight people were expelled and there was no mention of other prisoners or detainees. This report, like many other military documents from the Israeli Army and Security Forces Archives, is useful to us in that it provides numbers and dates, but it is empty of details, particularly the impact of those operations on the inhabitants. In such cases, the testimonies of the inhabitants themselves about events constitute a treasure of information concerning the point of view of the victims. The use of military archives combined with oral testimonies provides us with a moving composite picture that is more truthful than one without the other.

In a report by the intelligence officer of the military government in western Galilee to the military governor of the region, dated 1 June 1949, expanded reference was made to expulsion operations from these two villages. The operation in al-Bi'na took place on 6 January.[16] According to the report, "taking part were Tsvi Rabinovich, representing the Haifa command; Israeli police, military police and an intelligence unit; and a representative of the military government, Shlomo Pulman." The report adds: "The identities of 113 men were investigated, four of whom were expelled." This number is much smaller than the fifty-nine men mentioned earlier in General Avnir's report. The difference may be explained by the fact that Avnir's report was monthly whereas the report we are examining reports for a specific single operation on 6 January.

The same report by the intelligence officer refers to an operation in Dayr al-Asad on the same day. The same individuals and forces mentioned in the operation in neighboring al-Bi'na village also carried out this operation. About the Dayr al-Asad operation the report says: "The identities of 140 men were investigated, and sixteen were expelled along with their families, numbering sixty-two individuals."[17] This number is much larger than what is in Avnir's report above, and does not match the number fifty-nine from the neighboring village of al-Bi'na. The report estimates the number of infiltrators in al-Bi'na as forty, whereas the number of infiltrators in Dayr al-Asad is estimated as thirty-five. In the same document, the number of infiltrators in Majd al-Krum on 1 June 1949 is put at forty-two men. These figures clearly indicate that a "cat and mouse" game was being played between the returnees and the Israeli authorities which lasted through the entire first half of 1949 at least.

The document that the Haifa intelligence officer wrote as a summary of other operations conducted in the villages of Abu Snan, Um al-Faraj, al-Jdayde, Tamra, Kufr Yasif, al-Mazra'a, Mi'lya, al-Makr, 'Iblin, Fassuta, and Kabul, in addition to the Shaghur villages mentioned above, does not say where the expellees were sent in all cases, just in a few. In the Abu Snan (29 March 1949), Kabul (31 March), and al-Makr (11 April) operations, it was said that the inhabitants were expelled to al-Muthalath, the Triangle area. Some Druze villages were also subjected to search operations and surprise raids. Usually the objective in those cases was to go after smugglers and unlicensed arms merchants and "infiltrators" who had found refuge among their Druze neighbors. The report of the intelligence officer for western Galilee, for example, said eleven rifles were seized in the Yarka operation on 31 December 1948. In Julis a combing operation was conducted on 24 January 1949 which led to the "confiscation of ten weapons." The author of the report estimated that dozens of "infiltrators" were hiding in the houses of these last two villages.

Dozens of young Druze men enlisted in the Minorities Brigade in the Israeli army, while others worked as guides for returnees and as smugglers of commodities. The arms held by some members of the sect, and the relative immunity of their villages from surprise raids and retaliation by the security forces, enabled some Druze to pursue a career of smuggling and guiding returning refugees as a way of making a living. This complicated reality worried the military government authorities, and there were various views in the army and the government about how to deal with the Druze and the arms they possessed. Ben-Gurion settled the debate by saying that the friendship of the Druze inside and outside the country was important for Israel and ordered the security forces to be extremely cautious in dealing with members of the sect.[18]

Lastly, it is worth mentioning what happened to the villages of Kufr 'Inan and Farradiyya, which were still partially populated after they were occupied under Operation Hiram. The remaining villagers were pressured to move to other neighboring villages, but the authorities did not wait for villagers to leave their homes voluntarily. From the report of the commander of the military government 128 villagers (a large number) "were expelled to other villages" while 64 villagers were expelled beyond the borders.[19] 'Awad Hasan Mansur was one of those who had remained in Kufr 'Inan whom the army moved to Majd al-Krum in 1949. After a short stay in this village, which was crowded with hundreds of refugees from neighboring villages, he moved with his family to the nearby village of al-Rama, which was closer to his home village. Mansur testified that he had tried repeatedly, along with some fellow villagers, to return to Kufr 'Inan "but our repeated requests for permission to return to our lands were refused, so we remained as refugees in al-Rama."[20] The refugees from Kufr 'Inan lived in temporary shelters on top of a hill at the western entrance of al-Rama (called al-Dabba) where they lived for dozens of years, until they were permitted to build lasting and permanent homes for themselves.

WHOLESALE EXPULSION: MAJD AL-KRUM

The Israeli authorities conducted a census of the population of Majd al-Krum from 12 to 14 December 1948. Registration receipts were distributed to the population more than a month later, on 17–18 January 1949.[21] Before distributing those receipts, the Israeli security forces carried out two combing operations in the village, during which 536 individuals were expelled beyond Israel's borders, according to the report by General Avnir. The first operation was carried out on 9 January, the second on 14 January. Fortunately, a relatively large number of those included in the expulsions were still alive when I became interested in documenting and studying events in the village, so I was able to interview many of them. Their testimonies reveal many aspects of the history of the Arab minority in Israel which have been concealed and silenced in military documentation. A few also shed light on the many forms of resistance adopted by those who succeeded in returning to their homes despite the dangers.

The first large expulsion operation in Majd al-Krum was widely documented in the Army and Security Forces Archives.[22] A report on 9 January 1949 mentions that the objective of the operation was "arresting infiltrators and criminals in the village." The forces that carried out the operation included a detachment from the Minorities Unit and soldiers from the 123rd Battalion, ten military policemen including an officer, two soldiers, nine policemen and a ranking police officer, and representatives from military government agencies. "The village was surrounded at night and at 3 a.m. barriers were placed on all roads in and out of the village. After 7 a.m. orders were issued to the notables in the village to gather all the men over the age of twelve within half an hour. At 8 a.m. a curfew was announced, and four units began combing operations to catch anyone who was trying to hide. At the same time, men from intelligence and the police began interrogating the men."[23] Tsvi Rabinovich added in his report that the identities of 506 individuals were investigated, of whom 355 were deported. After the investigation and deportations "the mukhtar and notables were warned that they had to inform the authorities about the arrival of any infiltrator in the village."[24]

In Rabinovich's summary of the operation in Majd al-Krum, he expressed his satisfaction with "the good coordination among the forces, except for the following two incidents," complaining that "transportation did not arrive on time to transport those arrested, which prevented the transportation of 300 additional individuals." The second problem had to do with "two soldiers from the 123rd Battalion [who] took some merchandise from the shops. After a short investigation, most of the property was returned to its owners, and the above-mentioned [soldiers] will be tried." This document includes valuable and detailed information concerning the expulsions from Majd al-Krum from the perspective of the authorities and their representative Tsvi Rabinovich. However, like all the rest of the military documents, it is not concerned with news of the expellees after their expulsion "beyond the borders," or with the impact of the expulsions on those remaining. To examine the events from the point of view of the Majd al-Krum inhabitants, I interviewed many eyewitnesses of the expulsion operation. Those testimonies, some of which I had been hearing since childhood, relate the details of tribulations absent from the Israeli archives.

Before reviewing some of these testimonies, it is useful to read what the representative of the military government (Shlomo Pulman)—who accompanied the Israeli forces during the combing of the village and the investigation into the identities of villagers—wrote about the operation.[25] His evaluation complained about how the combing operation was carried out and about the interrogation of the inhabitants of Majd al-Krum, which differs from the Rabinovich document. This officer's letter to the military governor of the Western Galilee district included details of how the soldiers and policemen treated the inhabitants: "The treatment of the inhabitants by the soldiers was very violent."[26] "The operation was conducted with curses and acts of humiliation and the soldiers kicking the inhabitants, from the commander of the operation, Tsvi Rabinovich, down to the other participants in the investigation." After the investigation into the identity of one of the inhabitants ended, "when it was decided to expel him because he was a refugee in the village, he was driven out of the interrogation room, chased with curses and kicks."

The height of brutal behavior came when the soldiers reached the house of the mukhtar, Hajj 'Abd Salim Manna', who was sick that day, but nevertheless had gone to the square where the investigation into the men's identities was being conducted. He was released, and went back to his house accompanied by officer Shweili.[27] Afterwards, soldiers came to his house and, without hearing him out, hit him with their rifle butts and kicked him in the stomach. According to written testimony by one of the officers on the scene—which corresponds with what I had been told by the villagers about the physical and psychological violence to which they had been subjected—Hajj 'Abd Salim suffered "bruises, wounds, and internal bleeding in the stomach and liver, and he was taken to Nazareth Hospital, where he is still lying in critical condition."[28]

"Shlomo" also went into the issue of thefts, which showed another aspect of the treatment by the soldiers and their conduct. In his letter, "Shlomo" said that during the operation, soldiers from the 123rd Battalion broke into two shops and also stole from private homes; they took an alarm clock, clothes, and various small items "despite the repeated warnings by the unit's officer not to do such things and to keep their hands off private property." "Shlomo" added that after the operation had ended, "orders were issued to the military police to search the soldiers, and most of the stolen items were found and returned to their owners. But some stolen items are still missing, and complaints will be lodged by the affected parties."[29] "Shlomo" ended his letter with a clear recommendation: "In my opinion we should not keep silent about such conduct and put those responsible on trial." This letter shows that some army officers had not lost their humanity (or simply wanted to keep discipline among the troops); however, army command did not listen to the recommendation to put those responsible for disgraceful conduct on trial, according to the available documents.

After the massacre that took place in al-ʿAyn Square, dozens of young men fled to the mountains and caves out of fear of being ill-treated or killed. But many of them came back to their homes and were registered in the census of mid-December. By the beginning of 1949, hundreds of forced migrants from Shaʿb, al-Birwa, al-Damun, and other villages had sought refuge in Majd al-Krum and taken up residence there. These figures seem to explain the large number of people who were expelled from the village. A large number were, in fact, refugees the state wanted to be rid of so that they would not be able to demand to return to their villages. Others were considered infiltrators simply because they did not happen to be in the village when the census was conducted. In addition, a number of young men in their twenties were registered at the time of the census but the authorities decided to expel them from the country anyway. My father belonged to this group, so our family was expelled that day.

While my father (Husayn Salim Mannaʿ) was in the interrogation room with the other men, three soldiers arrived at our house, which was near the mosque. My grandmother Zahra al-Jaʿuniyya went around with the soldiers who searched the rooms in our house. When they were done, one soldier stopped in front of my mother Kawthar (who was twenty years old at the time) while she was hanging the laundry, and she did not know if the soldier was staring at her body or the gold bracelets she was wearing. At any rate, she was alarmed and called for help, and Zahra, who knew a few words of Hebrew from her childhood, yelled at the soldier, who quickly left the house with his companions.[30] Shortly thereafter my father arrived and asked my mother to prepare herself and her child for a long journey. My father said that married men who were to be expelled were ordered to bring their wives and children, if they had any, so that they could ride on the same military busses together. Consequently, 355 residents including men, women, and children were expelled on 9 January 1949 from Majd al-Krum.

Something resembling a miracle happened to "Abu Sa'id" who was to be expelled from the village. He had been a friend of Haim Orbach since they had worked together at the British army camp near 'Akka. After the soldiers led Abu Sa'id to the bus that was to transport the expellees, he insisted on talking to the officer in charge, whom he told confidently: "Haim Orbach is coming to visit me tomorrow, and he will be very upset if he does not find me in the village."[31] The officer was surprised by this statement, and he asked Abu Sa'id again: "Is what you say true?" When the officer became convinced of what he was saying and that he was a friend of Orbach, he let him and the members of his family off the bus and sent them home. This success encouraged others to try their luck with the same officer, but they were only yelled at and cursed instead of being set free. The vehicles carrying the expellees set off westward at sunset; the people remaining breathed more freely, since the tragedy could have been even worse, and returned to their homes and families in the village.

When the military vehicles reached al-Birwa crossroads (Ahyahud today) they turned south and continued moving until they reached the lands of the village of Khubbayza near Wadi 'Ara. There the soldiers made the expellees get out of the vehicles and fired their rifles in the air warning against any attempt to go back. Indeed no one tried to go back that night. They headed to nearby 'Ara, where they stayed at the mosque and other places. In the days following they walked in the direction of Nablus and the refugee camps which were set up nearby, while some chose to go on to Jenin and the area around it, and from there tried to return to Galilee. Among these was my uncle Husayn 'Ali Sa'id (sixteen years old at the time) who arrived in Nazareth on foot from Jenin, and in Nazareth found means of transportation back to Majd al-Krum.[32] But most expellees reached Nablus, including my small family, and remained in the Bayt 'Ayn al-Ma' camp for several months. At the beginning of spring, dozens chose to move to Transjordan; the caravan reached the city of Irbid, and from there busses took them through Syria to Lebanon.

The Israeli army and security agencies carried out a new expulsion operation on 14 January 1949, one week after the first one. This time most of the expellees were refugees from Sha'b, al-Birwa, al-Damun, and other villages, but few from Majd al-Krum. One of the expellees from the village, Muhammad 'Ali Sa'id Qaddah, described the expulsion operation in detail.[33] Qaddah recalled, "A curfew was imposed in the village, and after a close examination of the identities of the men, it was decided who would be expelled and the rest went back to their homes." He added, "It was decided that I would be expelled because I had come back from Lebanon after I had been a refugee there for about two months. I was married and had two small daughters. The vehicles took us west and they delivered us to the region of Wadi 'Ara, where the soldiers fired in the air and ordered us to go to the Arab side."[34]

Qaddah remembered that among the expellees was Muhammad Hasan Kan'an who was carrying a sack full of clothes. "One of the Druze soldiers who was accompanying us had his eye on it and wanted to get hold of it before we crossed over to the other side. He ordered Kan'an to drop it, and out of fear for his life Kan'an did so and marched with his wife and daughter into the diaspora [or exile]. We arrived in an area controlled by Iraqi soldiers who helped us to find the houses belonging to the village of 'Ara." Qaddah added: "We continued our journey the following day and arrived in Jenin and went from there to Nablus. At the 'Ayn Bayt al-Ma' camp large tents had been set up, each of which housed three families." UNRWA had begun operating and was helping refugees, so it accommodated hundreds, even thousands of them in the area. But the camp was severely overcrowded and health conditions were quite bad, so some started to look for ways to go back to Galilee; a number of expellees did go back on foot from Nablus and Jenin to their homes despite the difficulties and dangers of the way.

With the onset of spring 1949, many refugees, including hundreds of expellees from Majd al-Krum, made their way to Jordan and from there to Syria and Lebanon. The Jordanian authorities were encouraging the return of expellees from Galilee or their transport to Lebanon after signing the armistice agreement with Israel in Rhodes (23 April). The tens of thousands of refugees in the regions of Jenin and Nablus were a heavy economic burden on the kingdom, and a source of political disturbances. Some whom I interviewed said that the vehicles went from Nablus to Jerusalem and from there to Amman where they took buses belonging to al-'Alamayn Bus Company. Muhammad Qaddah (who had an excellent memory) testified that he "arrived with my family in Beirut on Thursday, 15 April 1949, on a rainy day." He added that a generous Lebanese man came to the 'Umari Mosque where we were staying and gave every refugee one Lebanese lira."[35] Qaddah's testimony was not the only one that referred to the generosity and kind treatment the refugees received in the Lebanese capital.

Most testimonies by the villagers of Majd al-Krum expelled in January 1949 tell of a similar route taken to the West Bank, and from there to Syria and Lebanon. Many recalled feeling lost dignity and humiliation from losing their land and homes and needing to live on the charity of others. Most who returned from Lebanon to their village later were overwhelmed by a sense of pride and self-respect because they had not submitted to the fate mapped out for them by Israel and its army. The majority of expellees were in their twenties, so they were able to endure the hardships of the road of return. After experiencing homelessness for the first time, their basic concern was for the future of their small children in the difficult conditions of life in refugee camps. The story of the return of hundreds, even thousands of those Israel had expelled from Galilee is largely missing from the history of the Palestinian Nakba. The survival of dozens of villages in Galilee played an important role in the determination of thousands of refugees to return to their homes by any means. Their determination grew in parallel with the efforts by Israeli security agencies to minimize the number of Palestinians remaining in Galilee.

When I heard the testimony of Tsvi Rabinovich who was in charge of expulsion operations in Majd al-Krum, I asked him how he chose those to be expelled. He claimed that the men had to prove that they were permanent residents and that they were not infiltrators by showing their registration receipt from the census. He added: "All those who did not have a receipt we considered to be illegal residents of Israel whose fate was expulsion." I asked again: What was the fate of an individual who was counted in the census but had lost his registration receipt? Tsvi had an answer ready: "He was expelled. It was his problem since he had not retained the receipt."[36] My questions did not arise from a vacuum: in January the authorities had not yet given all the inhabitants of the Shaghur area registration receipts. In fact, the census itself had not been completed on the eve of the January 1949 elections. Even in the villages where the census had been completed, it took at least several weeks before the receipts were distributed to the villagers.[37]

The expulsion of 536 individuals from Majd al-Krum in January 1949 emptied the village of most of its young men. Aside from the collective punishment meted out to the expelled residents, the expulsions strongly affected those who remained in the village and even the neighboring villages. Most who remained in Majd al-Krum were either elderly or children who were original residents of the village, alongside the refugees who came from neighboring villages.[38] We mentioned earlier that Israel used to expel the remaining residents in some villages which had been largely depopulated in order to gain control of the land belonging to the village. At the same time, they picked certain villages to absorb the refugees, Majd al-Krum being one of these. In this manner, the policy of minimizing the number of Palestinians in Galilee and taking over the land belonging to the expelled residents at the end of the war continued. Still, hundreds risked their lives and returned to their villages and homes. Below we shall present examples of dozens, even hundreds of Majd al-Krum residents who returned from Lebanon while the chase-arrest-exile operation continued.

ROUTES OF AGONY: EXPULSION AND RETURN

We mentioned earlier that among the hundreds expelled from Majd al-Krum at the beginning of 1949 were "infiltrators," "refugees," and residents of the village whose sin was that they were in their twenties. Their families saw how the Israeli authorities exiled their sons who had committed no offense. When the expellees reached Lebanon, most joined the tens of thousands of refugees from Haifa and Galilee and found shelter in Beirut and in the refugee camps in south Lebanon. The distance between the camps near Sidon and Tyre and northern Galilee was short and could be traversed in a few hours. Qaddah (born in 1928) testified that he had left one of his two daughters with his mother in the village in 1949. He said he had crossed the border and returned to the village at least four times over two years.[39] But crossing the border and reaching his relatives was not the end of the paths of sorrow associated with return.

Qaddah testified that he was extremely careful not to be seen by any of the collaborators with the military government who used to report the presence of "infiltrators." But simply being careful was not enough, since information kept reaching the desks of officers of the military government concerning the presence of dozens of young men who had returned from Lebanon. When the authorities increased the penalties for harboring "infiltrators," Qaddah built a shack out of olive tree branches in his family's small vegetable garden and slept there so that members of his family, who were old, would not be penalized. Informing the authorities would also subject their children to arrest, torture, and expulsion, which was not even considered by the families. In the early years that followed the 1948 war thousands of Galilee inhabitants lived torn between the hope that their children would return and the agony of seeing their children arrested and expelled once again to the other side of the border.

On 6 November 1949, ten months after the last mass expulsions, a strict curfew was imposed on Majd al-Krum while an aircraft hovered overhead in an attempt to capture "infiltrators" who had fled or were in hiding. At the same time, the military government spread a rumor through its informants that "the authorities plan to distribute identity cards to everyone who had been registered in the census but had not received an identity card to date." Qaddah testified that he had believed that rumor and had gone with good intentions to the place where the inhabitants gathered. That day, the authorities brought five vehicles which transported 250 to 260 individuals (men, women, and children) whom they exiled to the Jenin area.[40] Some of the expellees were not married, and they crossed the border once again from Jenin to the village of al-Marja. But Qaddah had his family (his wife and two daughters) with him, so he went on to Lebanon by way of Jordan and then Syria, and arrived in Beirut, where he remained until 1951. This large expulsion operation, which occurred one year after al-ʿAyn Square massacre, deepened the grief of the surviving residents that had beset them with the fall of the Galilee, and would last for a long time due to the continuing cascade of tragic events.

News of the mass expulsion of Majd al-Krum residents reached the ears of Maki leaders. Al-Yawm newspaper published an article about the expulsion of two hundred "infiltrators" from the village. Al-Ittihad, which quoted the news in its rival paper, went on to say that most of the expellees were not "infiltrators" but residents who had been expelled before they had received registration receipts, having gone back to the village to receive them.[41] The paper also relied on a news item published by Kol HaAm which "published the whole truth." The communist press pointed out that the number of expellees was three hundred, not just two hundred. It stressed that the only fault of those individuals was that they had not received registration receipts from the authorities. Al-Ittihad added that dozens were expelled from the villages of al-Biʿna, Dayr al-Asad, and Tarshiha in the same week.[42] Toward the end of 1949, it seemed as though Israeli security agencies had energetically gone back to work to reduce the Arab population of the Galilee. In return, Communist Party activists intensified their uncovering of expulsion operations and scaled up their resistance to them. Their backbones stiffened after the first parliamentary elections and their disappointment with the Ben-Gurion government's policies, the Arab communists escalated their opposition.

Qaddah monitored the news from Galilee during 1950–51, and crossed the border alone twice to visit his parents in the village. At the beginning of the summer of 1951, Hanna Naqqara brought a case on behalf of forty-eight residents of Majd al-Krum at the central court. His success in that case contributed greatly to the return of dozens of expellees from Lebanon. Qaddah testified that after he had heard news of these events, he quickly returned from Lebanon by land, and went to police headquarters in 'Akka to receive his identity card based on the precedent set by the court case. Then he went back to Lebanon to bring his wife and daughters from Shatila camp. He added in his testimony that he arrived in Beirut on their election day, and heard about the assassination of Riyad al-Sulh, the Lebanese prime minister, in Amman, on 16 July.[43] In Beirut, Qaddah met a refugee from the village of al-Zib (near Ra's al-Naqura) who was transporting refugees to Galilee by sea—easier and faster for children—so he struck a deal with the owner of the boats and returned that night with twelve people from the port of Tyre to Shavei Tzion, north of 'Akka.

Qaddah's testimony overlapped with what I had heard from my mother, Kawthar Manna', more than once about our return journey from the 'Ayn al-Hilwa camp: One day my father returned from Galilee and told my mother to be ready to return to Majd al-Krum that night. My mother could not believe what she was hearing; pointing to her belly she asked: "How can I walk for hours in the mountains at this advanced stage of pregnancy?" But my father calmed her fears, saying that she would not have to walk at all. She just had to not ask questions "and prepare to travel without letting the neighbors know" because if the news spread and reached the Lebanese authorities it could delay the plan. That night, we took a car from the refugee area in Sidon to Tyre, which is close to Ra's al-Naqura. Then fishing boats brought the returnees by night to their destination, and our family arrived with four others to safety near Shavei Tzion, north of 'Akka. The return trip by sea was expensive, but it spared the travelers the difficulty and danger of crossing borders on foot and risking death by being shot by border guards.

During my search for the timing of our return from Lebanon to Galilee, I was able to verify the date from multiple sources. My mother told the story—bitterly—more than once of how my father had hidden the news of her mother's death from her, which he had learned of on his last visit to the village. She added that she only discovered the tragic news after she returned to our house in Majd al-Krum. When I searched in the diaries of Muhammad Haydar (Abu Jamil) I found that he had recorded the news of the death of Mariam, the wife of 'Ali Sa'id Manna', on the main road in the village on 24 June 1951, and her burial the next day.[44] Thus I was able to determine that the date of our return from Lebanon was in mid-July, because my mother kept complaining that three weeks had passed since her mother's death without her knowledge. This date relied on Abu Jamil's diaries aligned with the iron memory of Muhammad Sa'id Qaddah, as a number of returnees remembered his arrival in the village from Lebanon on the eve of the Knesset elections, held on 30 July.

Abu Nahi was one of the hundreds of residents expelled from Majd al-Krum in January 1949. He arrived in Lebanon with a large group from the village and suffered refugee life for over two years. After Hanna Naqqara's court success and the return of dozens of refugees from Lebanon, Abu Nahi's relatives in the village sent him a message that he had to return quickly.[45] Abu Nahi, who was not married at the time, crossed the border by land without difficulty and returned to his family's home. He and other residents hired attorney Sharif al-Zu'bi from Nazareth to obtain their registration receipts days before the summer 1951 Knesset elections.[46] After the legal precedents set by the central court and the Supreme Court, dozens who had been expelled—before they had received their registration receipts and despite the fact that their names were recorded in the census—did not have to go to court a second time. In this way dozens of young men who had been expelled from the village with their families in January 1949 returned to their homes after more than two years living as refugees.

On the eve of the elections at the end of July 1951, Mapai's Arab lists were trying to win Arab votes, which made it possible for dozens to be allowed to return through the family reunification provision. Abu Nahi and others whom I interviewed mentioned the names of relatives who had returned just before the elections "through Haim Orbach," the intelligence officer who had been instrumental in the village's surrender and in enabling most residents to remain. Orbach was active then in attempts to win votes for the Mapai party and the Arab lists. These testimonies, which are corroborated by contemporary written sources, prove that the expellees and their relatives who remained took advantage of legal loopholes provided by the ruling Israeli establishment to bring their loved ones back to their homes. In return "the family" would promise to vote for the ruling party and its lists.

Luck did not favor all expellees from Majd al-Krum and other villages. Abu Jamil's diaries mention many cases where "infiltrators" in the villages were arrested and deported by the authorities to Lebanon during 1950–51. Others were less fortunate and paid with their lives for attempting to return to live in their homes or just to visit relatives. On 15 January 1950, for example, news reached Majd al-Krum that Husayn Khalil Qaddah had been killed near the border. On 31 October 1950, news spread in the village of the shooting death of Sa'id Rafi' and his brother Mustafa on the northern mountain above the village of Dayr al-Asad.[47] In another incident on 28 May 1951, a refugee from the village of Sha'b, who was a former resident of Marj al-Krum, was killed in a mine explosion near the Lebanese border, and two others from the same village, Ahmad Mustafa Taha and the wife of Khalid Sa'id Kiwan, were wounded. These individuals who were fired upon, killed or wounded, had not been armed, nor had they threatened state security, but the Israeli authorities were determined to prevent anyone from returning from Lebanon to Galilee.

Still, the risks did not dissuade many. The Israeli authorities had arrested Muhammad Hikma in Majd al-Krum and deported him to Lebanon on 11 May 1950, one year before his death along the border. Abu Jamil mentions in his diaries that the news of his death (he had been killed and two others wounded by a mine planted by the soldiers) on 28 May spread throughout the village. In another case, Muhammad As'ad Sghayyir and Husayn Sarhan were sentenced by a military court on 6 September 1951 to two and a half years in prison because of their multiple arrests for repeated attempts to return to the village.[48]

Collective punishment was a basic tool in the military government's arsenal for dealing with the Arab population. Despite that, attempts by Palestinians to return did not stop. Abu Jamil's diaries, which document events in the village, including army operations, mention the names of many of the men and women expelled that are absent from military documents. His diary reports a unique case in which the army imposed a curfew on Majd al-Krum for "seven consecutive days and nights, not allowing anyone to enter or leave the village,"[49] the objective being to apply pressure on the inhabitants to turn in their relatives to the authorities instead of hiding them.

Chapter 6 presents cases in which dozens of Palestinians from Majd al-Krum went to the Supreme Court to prevent their expulsion and ask to be allowed to live in their homeland. It is sufficient here to mention one of those court decisions concerning dozens of villagers whom the military government and police wanted to expel for a second time.[50] Those plaintiffs said that they had not received identity cards during the 1951–53 period either because they had been expelled the first time in January 1949 along with others, or because they had left the village after al-'Ayn Square massacre, which had occurred two months earlier. The Supreme Court judges found their testimonies credible and obliged the authorities to issue identity cards to those plaintiffs. In this and other cases the justices sometimes demonstrated an understanding of the grievances of the Arab residents, documented through their testimonies and histories, that the army had carried out massacres and expelled the population, in contrast to the Zionist narrative, which later denied those actions had taken place in whole or in part. The public had to wait for decades for the documents in military archives to be released, and for revisionist historians to expose the killings and abuses during the war and after.[51]

THE REMARKABLE STORY OF THE VILLAGE OF SHA'B

After Israel occupied Sha'b village in Operation Hiram, it expelled the villagers, who became refugees, but did not demolish the houses. Israeli state institutions then moved other Arabs into the vacant houses. The first to be allowed to live in that village was Shafiq Abu 'Abdu and some of his relatives from the Buqay'i family from Damun village in western Galilee.[52] One of the tasks assigned to Abu 'Abdu and his relatives was to prevent the original inhabitants from returning to their homes. Indeed, the authorities partly succeeded in their objective for some time.[53] The policies of settlement organizations concurred with the directives of the prime minister's advisor Yehushua Palmon that "under no circumstances should land in the village be leased to the local population or whoever originally came from that village." In the case of Sha'b there was an additional factor, which was to exact revenge on the villagers, who had demonstrated enthusiasm for fighting during the war. Hillel Cohen, who mentions these directives and assesses the role of Sha'b in the fighting, adds that "a combat unit led by a local hero whose *nom de guerre* was Abu Is'af . . . one of the best fighting units operating in Galilee," had been active in the village.[54]

Indeed, Abu Is'af was a local hero not just in the village of Sha'b but throughout the villages of Shaghur and elsewhere. His name crops up several times in the novel by Elias Khoury *Gate of the Sun*, which tells the story of this unit through its fictional heroes. In fact, two heroes who withdrew with their unit to the south of Lebanon became refugees and continued to strive to return to the Galilee for several years. Consequently, it is no surprise that Sha'b's villagers in Lebanon, who published a book several years ago documenting their village's history, reserved a special place in the book for Abu Is'af and his combat unit.[55] Who then is this Abu Is'af, whose zeal to fight was the justification the Israeli authorities used to prevent the return of the people of Sha'b to their village after the war ended and the guns fell silent?

Abu Is'af is Ibrahim 'Ali al-Shaykh Khalil (1908–2002) was one of the fighters who joined the organization of 'Izz al-Din al-Qassam and took part in the 1936–39 revolt. After the partition resolution was adopted, he became a supporter of Hajj Amin al-Husayni and tried to enlist combatants and procure arms in Galilee to defend Sha'b and the neighboring villages. He took part in several battles until all of Galilee was occupied in Operation Hiram. When the operation was launched, he was in Majd al-Krum, where many villagers from Sha'b had gone, along with most fighters in his unit. The unit withdrew along with the others in the Arab Rescue Army. When the ARA was broken up, he moved to Syria and then to other Arab countries. Sha'b villagers in Lebanon say that Abu Is'af continued his activities with Palestinian organizations for a long time. He spent his last years in Damascus, where he died in 2002.[56]

The other hero from Sha'b in this fighting unit was Sa'id Salih al-Asadi (1918–1997), whose story was memorialized in the book *Gate of the Sun*.[57] The story of "Abu Saleh," who is called Yunis in the novel, begins with how his life ended, in the al-Hamshari Hospital in Sidon where he lay in a coma from which he never awakened, on 28 January 1997. Like Abu Is'af, his companion in his adventures, Sa'id Salih, took part in the 1936 revolt and the 1948 war. After Israel completed the occupation of Galilee, he withdrew with his unit, and went to 'Ayn al-Hilwa camp where he spent the rest of his life. What is distinctive, even unique, about Sa'id

Salih's story is that he went back to Galilee dozens of times from 1948 to 1956, particularly to a cave near Dayr al-Asad which Elias Khoury named the "Gate of the Sun" in his novel. In this cave Saʿid Salih would meet his wife, called "Naheeleh" in the novel, who continued to live with her children next to the elderly parents of her husband.

Al-Asadi and Abu Isʿaf are two examples of the role played by the people of Shaʿb village in the struggle against the Haganah and the Israeli army until the fall of all Galilee. The villagers had later found refuge in the villages of al-Shaghur, Majd al-Krum, Biʾna, Dayr al-Asad, and Nahf. They were not present when the Israeli army entered Shaʿb after the fall of Miʿar on 18 July 1948. Within two days Abu Isʿaf had gathered the men of his unit, attacked the village, and regained control over it. His unit continued to fight the Israeli forces centered in Miʿar and caused casualties and deaths—including an officer named Segev, for whom an Israeli settlement in the area was later named. The cease-fire was not observed in the area between Miʿar and Shaʿb,[58] and Abu Isʿaf's unit suffered a large number of casualties, including dozens killed among the combatants from the village and the volunteers in the ARA.

A number of Supreme Court decisions supported the oral testimonies of the inhabitants of Shaʿb. One of these rulings stated: "Up to Operation Hiram at the end of October, the village lay for several months between the front lines of the IDF and the Rescue Army, so it was unpopulated except for some elderly people."[59] In the same ruling as well as other documents, it was mentioned that most of the inhabitants had become refugees in neighboring villages in al-Shaghur region, lying between Majd al-Krum to the west and Nahf to the east. Near the end of October these villages were occupied by Israeli forces, who tried to evict their original inhabitants as well as those who had taken refuge there. But most of those evicted from Shaʿb remained in the region and engaged in a constant struggle to return to their homes in their own village—until it was declared a closed military region in April 1951.[60]

After the Israeli authorities enlisted the help of Shafiq Abu ʿAbdu and his relatives to prevent the villagers from going home, some members of the Faʿur family, who were Abu ʿAbdu's in-laws from Shaʿb, were allowed to return to the village, despite this being inconsistent with the general policies of the authorities. The authorities devised a plan to relocate hundreds of residents of the villages of Krad al-Baqqara and Krad al-Ghannama (south of Hula) and house them in the empty houses in Shaʿb.[61] But once the door to return was opened to some Shaʿb villagers it became difficult for the state and its institutions to close it completely to others.

In one of the cases pleaded before Supreme Court justices Olshan, Rossmann, and Landau, Muhammad Nimr al-Hawwari represented eight villagers from Shaʿb, plaintiffs against the ʿAkka police inspector and others. The proceedings of 1953 continued a preliminary decision issued on 1 January of the same year.[62] The eight plaintiffs testified that they had identity cards in their possession, but that the military governor of the Galilee in Nazareth had ordered them to leave the village within fifteen days, and if they did not do so he would expel then by force and bring them before a military court. As we mentioned earlier, Sha'b was declared a closed military area (under article 125 of the emergency regulations of 1945) to prevent the population from returning. However, the eight pleaded that they were residents of the village from the days of the Mandate and had remained there until its occupation in October 1948. They admitted that they had left their homes for a few days and had hidden in the surrounding mountains, but had returned there before it was declared a closed military area in 1951.[63]

In the discussion of the case of the eight plaintiffs, it emerged that "after the village was occupied, a single Arab, Shafiq Abu 'Abdu, had been allowed to live there, and he was not from the village of Sha'b," and it also emerged that he had been granted the right to cultivate the lands of the village, and that the plaintiffs, at least some of them, had been working for him on those lands. The judges added that "there is a basis for saying that this person is well-connected with the authorities." It was also mentioned that his brother was the mukhtar of the village, and according to accusations by the residents, the two used to mistreat the villagers and take advantage of their connections with the military and civilian authorities, so that they became the ultimate decision makers in the village. The residents added in their charges that the above-mentioned Shafiq used to assault them and force them to work for him for very low wages, and when they objected, he would threaten them with dismissal. In view of this, they testified that the attempt to expel them should be seen as part of a conspiracy by their employer in which he accused them of returning to the village after 1 April 1951, when it was declared a closed military area.[64]

Those eight plaintiffs were not the only ones to have recourse to the Supreme Court from among the inhabitants of Sha'b.[65] The deliberations in this case shed light on an aspect of the use made by the authorities of the testimonies of mukhtars who collaborated with Israel in general and the military government in particular. One of those, as we said, was the brother of Shafiq Abu 'Abdu, who was one of the defendants. The judges said of Abu 'Abdu that he and his brother, the mukhtar, were "well-connected with the government"; the ARA had condemned Shafiq Abu 'Abdu to death, but he had been released from jail in Nazareth after the city fell to the Israeli army. The brothers admitted in their testimonies that they had a special relationship with the Israeli army authorities, and they had therefore been allowed to live in Sha'b and lease land there. These court testimonies from the early 1950s correspond to what the elderly villagers recalled about the activities of Abu 'Abdu and his men who were supported by the authorities.

Shafiq Abu 'Abdu admitted under investigation that he was present when the residents of Sha'b were being registered in mid-1949, and that registration had taken place in the house of his brother, the mukhtar. He added that "Not everyone who came to register had in fact been registered, only those who had received a prior permit to live in the village, based on lists in the possession of the military government." In commenting on Abu 'Abdu's statements, the judges noted that "he did not present such lists to the court during the investigation." They added: "We are not confident that the mukhtar and his brother did not play a role in the failure to register villagers whom they did not want to help."[66] These and other statements by the Supreme Court judges concerning the testimonies of mukhtars and representatives of the military government during the deliberations in courtrooms highlight some of the methods used by the military government to reward those who were closely connected to them and to punish those who were unwilling to cooperate with them.

The Sha'b villagers gave examples of how Abu 'Abdu and his brother exploited their strong connections to the authorities to extort money from them. In this connection the judges wrote in their decision that they would like to draw the attention of the legal councilor to the need to "examine what is below the surface in Sha'b and to enforce justice if it turns out that the above accusations are true."[67] Regarding the demand by the Sha'b villagers to be recognized as inhabitants of the village, the court agreed partially (five individuals out of the eight). In this way the villagers showed Abu 'Abdu and his brother the mukhtar that they were not the ultimate decision makers, despite their close connections with the authorities. Most of the people of Sha'b continued to live as refugees in Majd Krum and Dayr al-Asad and other villages in the area, but within a few years dozens had succeeded in returning to Sha'b and living in their own homes despite Abu 'Abdu and his brother the mukhtar.[68]

The story of another refugee from Sha'b exposes some of the methods used by the authorities in dealing with the people, and sheds light on the suffering of the inhabitants who were forced to live away from their village for years. Among the papers of attorney Hanna Naqqara was a letter to the military governor from Sa'id Husayn 'Abbas, who lived in Majd al-Krum.[69] 'Abbas wrote, explaining his case: "When the Israeli authorities occupied our village, Sha'b, I left the village and went to Wadi Sha'b near the Sawa'id Arabs. I had a flock of about 45 goats. About five days after the occupation, while I was wandering in the above-mentioned valley with the goats, Ibrahim, who was in charge of Sha'b and Fayyad Sulayman al-Heibi from Mi'ar village, who now lives in Kabul, came by and started shooting at me and the goatherds." Sa'id 'Abbas added: "The shooting resulted in my being hit in the leg . . . at which point I fell down, and they took the goats and went off in the direction of Sha'b village."

'Abbas also wrote that after he was wounded "Husayn Hamid al-Ayyub and Mahmud Abu Dalleh came and moved me to a cave near the above-mentioned Wadi Sha'b, where I remained for two and a half months, until I heard that there were some employees registering the inhabitants of the villages. I went to al-Bi'na and found them handing out receipts to the inhabitants. I asked them to register me, and they instructed me to go to Majd al-Krum and wait there for them to return from al-Bi'na. I went to Majd al-Krum and waited for five days but they did not come, so I went back to the cave and was left unregistered. Six months later I went to my uncle's wife's house in Majd al-Krum. That night curfew was declared, and I was arrested and exiled to a neighboring Arab state. I came back after just one day, and I alternated between staying in the mountains and going to villages from time to time. Later I was arrested, and they took me to the Lebanese border and left me at al-Mansura Bridge."[70]

'Abbas added in his letter to the military governor, "I was away just for one day and then I came back. I used to spend most of my time in the wilderness and sleep in the cave. While I was wandering in the wilderness, I found two rifles, one Ottoman and the other British. I handed them over to a police officer, Shweili, in 'Akka. The surrender of the weapons took place through Hamad 'Othman."[71] 'Abbas thought that this action on his part would help redeem him, but to no avail. He ended his letter by saying: "For more than a year and a half I have not left the country. So, I am appealing to Your Excellency to look into my case and issue a just ruling by granting me a permanent residence permit in the venerable state of Israel."[72]

This document—unique among the collected papers of attorney Naqqara in Haifa—was in a brown cardboard file, on the cover of which was written "Husayn Sa'id 'Abbas from the village of al-Bi'na v. the Ministry of the Interior," which indicates preparations were being made to bring a court case. My attempts to locate the rest of the papers related to the case failed, but the presence of the file might indicate that the military governor had not approved 'Abbas's request, and he sought out the attorney Naqqara so that he might plead the case in court. Without the rest of the papers from the 'Abbas case it is difficult for us to know what happened after that. Nevertheless, the content of this unique document sheds light on the difficult living circumstances of many inhabitants of Galilee, particularly those who were not registered. Time and again they tried all ways and means available to stay in their homeland and not to surrender to forced migration and expulsion.

Let us go back to the story of the Sha'b villagers who saw others settle in their homes and plant their fields, from which the authorities had expelled them. They did not accept that fate and tried to change it; occasionally their efforts bore fruit, and some were allowed to live in their village. Also some of the residents of the al-Hula villages who had been relocated by the authorities in Sha'b asked to be returned to their original villages.[73] Despite these partial successes, most of the villagers from Sha'b remained refugees in Lebanon and Syria, such as the officers in Abu Is'af's unit. The majority of expellees who had sought refuge in neighboring villages, thus becoming part of the "present absentees," did not succeed in returning to their homes in the 1950s. But some did return to Sha'b gradually after the cancellation of military rule, through the land swap agreements with the Land Office in Israel and other state institutions.

Like the hero of *Gate of the Sun*, Ahmad Mutlaq Hamid also joined Abu Is'af's unit. Following the retreat of the unit to South Lebanon and then Syria, Ahmad

Mutlaq first remained with his comrades in the diaspora, while his wife and his parents were in Majd al-Krum. He decided to return to the Galilee, and the authorities arrested him twelve times, according to his testimony.[74] They would sometimes expel him to the Jenin area, but most frequently to south Lebanon. The last time he was arrested and sentenced to two years in jail. After his release (in 1961) Majid al-Fahum of Nazareth helped him to obtain an identity card, and he returned to live with his parents in Majd al-Krum until September 1982, after which he returned to Sha'b with his family.

Finally, we shall tell the story of a villager from Sha'b, Salih Ibrahim Ghanim, who lived in Majd al-Krum and made great efforts to return to his home and village. One of the documents he submitted to the Supreme Court, in a case he brought against the military governor in 1956, showed that he had leased agricultural land in the villages of al-Birwa and Sha'b, and he occasionally received permits to travel outside Majd al-Krum to visit his lands there.[75] At a certain point, Ghanim decided to live once again with his family and his plentiful livestock on the land of Sha'b. According to his testimony, he lived in Majd al-Krum until 12 February 1954, long after Sha'b had been declared a closed military area. That was why his appeal to the military government for a permit to reside permanently on his property in Sha'b was rejected. At that point he appealed to the Supreme Court, which turned him down and fined him 75 liras to be paid to the defendant and in court costs.[76]

The story of Sha'b and its people is one of the most difficult among Galilee villages and the most egregious. In the final analysis, the village was not torn down and did not become one of the destroyed and depopulated villages, yet most of its population remain refugees in Israel and outside it to this day. Many who were allowed to return to live in Sha'b were considered refugees, and were forced to rent their lands from the state land office. In addition, Israel settled refugees from other villages in Sha'b, and the village became a refuge also for those expelled from their lands and homes from villages south of al-Hula.

This chapter's review of general and personal cases of the inhabitants of Sha'b is not a substitute for a serious academic study of the village's history. I hope that one day an Arab academic will carry out such a study.

EXPULSIONS CONTINUE IN THE NAME OF SECURITY AND COMBATTING "INFILTRATORS"

At the beginning of 1949, there were six Arab villages left near the Lebanese border, in spite of the army's plans to expel the inhabitants of all Palestinian villages along the border strip. Still the efforts to uproot those remaining villages and to settle Jews on their lands did not stop. Tarshiha had been emptied of most of its population (4,000), leaving a few hundred residents, the vast majority of them Christians.[77] Many families who feared retribution from the Israeli army found refuge in neighboring villages (mostly Druze). Indeed, many of the remaining Tarshiha residents were first registered in the villages of Kufr Smei', al-Buqay'a, and others. Those villagers kept in touch with the few remaining residents in the houses of Tarshiha following its occupation, and began to return gradually in November 1948.

The soldiers gathered the remaining inhabitants of Tarshiha in and around the church, imposed a curfew on the rest of the village, and proceeded to systematically rob the contents of the vacant houses. The soldiers entered the houses and emptied them of everything useful and of value, tossing broken furniture outside; the list of war loot included oil, olives, wheat, cotton, furniture, and dried tobacco.[78] Tarshiha was known for the volume and quality of its tobacco, and the dried leaves were ready for sale when the authorities snatched the harvest from the houses. The plunder of Tarshiha houses was similar to what took place in the neighboring Arab villages, even those which were partly populated during and after the war. This subject—the organized and unorganized looting of the surviving Arab villages—has not received the attention it deserves from researchers.

Yusif Nahhas from Tarshiha was a worker in the Dubek Cigarette Company and the company's representative for the purchase of tobacco from the villagers for over a decade before the Nakba. When the village was bombed and occupied, Yusif left his house and sought refuge in the neighboring village of al-Buqay'a. A man named Farraji and his son Elie, who used to trade with the people of Tarshiha for tobacco, searched for Yusif. They found him and asked him to return to his village so that he could resume working with them. On the same day, 1 November 1948, Farraji wrote a recommendation letter by hand in Hebrew stating that Mr. Nahhas was an old and faithful employee of the Dubek Company.[79] Farraji and his son, who were on good terms with the authorities, arranged for Yusif Nahhas to live in one of the beautiful vacant houses in Tarshiha, and it became his duty to collect tobacco from the abandoned houses for the company free of charge. Jamil, Yusif's son, testified later that he returned from Lebanon and helped his father in his work for the Dubek Cigarette Company. Thus economic/trade motives sometimes helped inhabitants of Galilee to stay or even to return to their homes and villages.[80]

There were a few soldiers in the streets of the village to prevent the return of expellees from Lebanon, but they were not totally successful in their mission, particularly late at night. Dozens of expellees from the village who had sought refuge in neighboring villages returned gradually and went back to living in their houses. Anis Bishara (Abu Salim) was one of them. He said in his interview that he happened to return on a Sunday, so he went directly to the church, intending to leave with the mass of worshippers and go home.[81] But at the entrance to the church he met Mr. Butrus, who was known for his collaboration with the army and for turning in "infiltrators." Except that this collaborator surprised Abu Salim by saying: "Don't be afraid, enter the church." And in fact he did enter and afterwards he went to his house as he had planned, and was counted in the census of the village and continued to live there until he died.

What happened to the Hawwari family in Tarshiha stands out as stirring and distinctive from all of the similar stories from the Nakba. Ten members of the family were killed during the aerial bombardment of houses in the village carried out by Abie Nathan—who later became a famous activist for peace between Arabs and Jews. Despite the tragedy that befell the family, the members who survived took refuge for several months in the neighboring village of Kufr Smei' and were registered there before they went back to their homes in September 1949. However, attempts by other members of the Hawwari family to return from Lebanon did not succeed and they were exiled once again beyond the borders.[82] Fatma Hawwari was grievously wounded during the aerial bombing of the family home, and she left Tarshiha to Sidon and then Beirut to receive treatment; at the end she returned home to her village through the Red Cross in 1950. She continued to receive treatment in Israeli hospitals after her return but her condition did not improve a great deal and she remained paralyzed for many years.[83] Fatma and other members of her family were determined to live in their homes and on their lands despite being expelled multiple times. Their stories serve as examples of the great price paid by many who remained in Galilee.

Jibra'il Bishara, imprisoned by the ARA for nearly three months, was released from jail on 6 December 1948. Jibra'il wrote in his memoirs that he left for Beirut where met his brother Hanna and found dozens of Tarshiha inhabitants who used to meet at a hotel near Martyrs' Square.[84] After a few days he decided to return to Tarshiha with some people from his village. This group crossed the border easily, went to Fassuta and from there to Tarshiha. Jibra'il did not mention encountering any problem on their return journey, even after they arrived at the village. When the Israeli authorities decided to record the names of the villagers, Jibra'il even became a volunteer census worker as did his brother, who had also returned from Lebanon.[85]

After the names of the villagers were recorded, expellees from Tarshiha continued to return from Lebanon and other places. The return of hundreds of villagers did not go unnoticed by the security forces, who decided to put a stop to this phenomenon and to expel the "infiltrators." A few days after the census was concluded, a curfew was imposed on the village and the residents were asked to come to the local council building, where three officers called out people's names according to lists they had and asked them to surrender the weapons in their possession. After the weapons were collected, those whom they considered to be "infiltrators" were taken to rooms on the side along with people whom the authorities accused of participating in the war against the Jews. These were expelled even if they were registered in the village census. Jibra'il Bishara recorded in his memoirs that the expellees were taken to the Jordanian border. Other sources confirm that about 130 people from Tarshiha were expelled on 16 January 1949.

The older residents of Tarshiha remember two expulsion operations affecting villagers. The first was the 16 January operation when the soldiers combed the village, searched houses, and arrested 33 heads of families along with 131 family members (the aged, women, and children).[86] In the same operation another 30 individuals were expelled from neighboring Ma'liya, including historian Elias Shoufani (who was sixteen at the time) who described the procession of the caravan of forced migrants in his memoirs.[87] The expellees were taken to Majjidu (Megiddo), near Wadi 'Ara, from where they went on foot to Nablus, and then travelled to Amman, where they received help from the Catholic Patriarch 'Assaf. Like many of those expelled from the Galilee, the Tarshiha residents also continued on from Amman to Syria and Lebanon. Shoufani wrote that he and a number of his friends returned to their homes in Mi'lya. About three months after his return he was able to obtain an identity card with the help of Melkite Bishop Hakim, who helped hundreds of members of his sect to settle anew in Haifa and Galilee.

A few days after the expulsion of "infiltrators" from Mi'lya and Tarshiha, on 21 January 1949, a governmental committee took up the question of transferring the inhabitants of Tarshiha from their village to somewhere else. Yosef Weitz proposed moving the farmers to neighboring Mi'lya, while the rest preferred 'Akka. General Avnir, the military governor, proposed moving everyone to Majd al-Krum. However, the majority of the members of the committee chose to transfer the inhabitants of Tarshiha to Haifa or 'Akka. In the field, intensive efforts were made to convince the inhabitants to move voluntarily. It appears that the authorities predicted at that time that transferring part of the population a week in advance, combined with the attractions of city life on the other, would produce the desired result. Weitz, for example, believed that the entire village had to be depopulated so as to enable 1,000 Jews to settle there.[88] However, the government feared the international reaction to forced removal of the population and continued efforts to convince the residents. But the majority of villagers, with the communists in the vanguard, refused all inducements and maintained their right to live in their village.

Even so, pressure continued to be applied on the inhabitants. Bishop Hakim tried to convince those left in Tarshiha, most of whom belonged to his denomination, to accept moving somewhere else. In early June 1949, Hakim came to the village to meet the inhabitants and promised that he would try to settle them in 'Akka or anywhere else they chose.[89] However, the Tarshiha villagers were neither tempted by Bishop Hakim's proposals nor convinced by his implied threats, and were adamant about remaining in their village. Indeed, hundreds of villagers remained in Tarshiha despite the continued planning and work by the security agencies to uproot them along with the other Arab villages on the border with Lebanon.[90]

Jibra'il Bishara met with Knesset member Tawfiq Tubi in February 1949 and explained the circumstances of the village to him. Tubi promised to follow up the case and to bring it up in the Knesset. Consequently, Tubi conveyed news of the attempts by the authorities to expel the villagers of Tarshiha to representatives of the United Nations in the region. Some UN personnel came to visit the village to check on the veracity of the news, but their military guide denied there was such a plan. Even Ben-Gurion, in his answer to Tubi's questions, denied any knowledge of orders being issued to expel the inhabitants of Tarshiha. In December 1949, there was talk of expelling the inhabitants of Tarshiha and the villagers of al-Jish, Hurfaysh, Fassuta, and Mi'lya as well, which Ben-Gurion and most ministers in his cabinet approved, but others opposed, mainly Moshe Sharett.[91] The final outcome was that Tarshiha and the other villages survived.

The introduction of "new arrivals" into the houses of an Arab village in the Galilee while some of the original villagers were still living there was a unique event. The remaining villagers in Tarshiha did not object to the presence of their new neighbors out of fear of the reaction of the state; in fact, some common interests and cooperation arose at times between the two sides, new good relations that alarmed the authorities,[92] as many of the remaining inhabitants of Tarshiha had the skills, such as construction, carpentry, and ironworking, needed by the new arrivals. The military governor exploited those with these skills to repair and reconstruct the houses in which Jews were settled. Some of those I interviewed in Tarshiha testified that the army did not remunerate them for this work, but they did not object, hoping that this would help them to prevent the expulsion of the Arab population. It seems that this actually contributed to allowing them to stay, but the more important factor was that hundreds of those who remained in Tarshiha were Christians.

To this day the people of Tarshiha remember the good neighborly relations that were established between the newcomers from Romania and the original inhabitants who remained in the village. The fundamental problem lay with the authorities, who confiscated houses and land for the sake of the settlers, some of whom behaved as the new masters of the country.[93] A few cases occasionally reached the Supreme Court; for example, Fahd Mikha'il Khalil complained that his name was registered in the village census, and he received registration receipt no. 93767. He added that he continued to live in his house which was registered in the name of his grandfather until May 1949,[94] when the military governor asked him to leave his house and move to another house in the village; so he surrendered his keys to the authorities. This action was a step in what the judges called "Reconciling the residence of Jews and Arabs in Tarshiha by the Military Government."

A Jew by the name of Zalmanovich lived in Fahd Khalil's house until 12 August 1953. On that day, as he recounted, "Zalmanovich evacuated the house and gave his friends the key to the house, and they sent them to the plaintiff." Once Fahd Khalil received the keys, and fearing for possible damage to his house, he moved in with his family on 14 August 1953. The next day the police came and forced him out with his furniture, but the plaintiff returned to live in his house once more, and the police forcibly removed him once again. Consequently, he went to court asking that the police stop forcing him out of his house. But the court refused and ruled that the house had become the property of the state, and that the police had acted legally.[95] This court decision is an example of decisions by the Supreme Court legitimizing the unjust laws enforced on the remaining Palestinians.

CONDEMNING AND RESISTING FORCED MIGRATION

The condemnation of forced migration by the communists increased, as did their resistance to it, following the first parliamentary elections. Maki's success in these elections in Haifa and Nazareth and the Galilee villages consolidated the position of the communists among those who remained and raised the ceiling of their expectation that the party's representatives would defend them. As we saw earlier, MK Tawfiq Tubi and the party press condemned and fought against the expulsions. The reaction of the communists and their press to the combing operations and the expulsion of hundreds of residents from Kufr Yasif on 1 March 1949 was strong.[96] It turned out later that most of the expellees from the village were refugees from 'Amqa and Kuwaykat, and only a few were original inhabitants.[97] The reason for the expulsion was that the expellees had not been registered in the census conducted in Kufr Yasif in November 1948. As we have seen repeatedly, all of those whose registration in the Galilee village census could not be proven were subject to expulsion and deportation.

The expellees from Kufr Yasif went to the village of Salim which was under the control of Iraqi forces, according to a UN observer who wrote in his report that "the Jews stole their jewels and the money they had with them."[98] The Israeli soldiers fired over the heads of the expellees so that they would panic and speed up their crossing to the Arab side. Charles Freeman, a Quaker relief activist, was a witness to the expulsion from Kufr Yasif. He had arrived at the village before the expulsion operation with a truckload of food supplies for distribution to the refugees. Freeman said in his testimony that 239 individuals were expelled from the village. The people of Kufr Yasif tried to prevent the expulsion but could only save a few, and hundreds were taken in truckloads and expelled from the country.

Al-Ittihad newspaper wrote about the expulsion operation in Kufr Yasif with anger and condemnation; the title of the article questioned whether there was a premeditated attempt to expel communists from the village. The paper condemned the expulsion of hundreds "despite their participation in the elections." The thing that provoked the ire and bewilderment of the paper more than anything else was the fact that "the authorities arrested a large number of members of the National Liberation League and put them in the cars."[99] Thus the event in Kufr Yasif elicited a powerful backlash. But as we saw in this chapter, it was not the first nor the last operation of its kind. The paper gave this subject considerable coverage because the communists feared that the event could be an indication of a change in the government's policy towards the communists after the elections.

The second time that Maki's press showed interest in such an incident was a similar combing and expulsion operation in Nazareth on 18 June 1949, although not a single communist in the city was affected. But *al-Ittihad* stressed that it had provoked a wave of condemnation and a strike declaration, and emphasized that popular gatherings had taken place in the city, with two leaders of the party, Saliba Khamis and Mun'im Jarjura, addressing the crowds.[100] In addition to the communists, the operation of expelling the inhabitants of the eastern quarter of Nazareth was condemned by the activists in Mapam. This position was echoed in '*Al Hamishmar* which mentioned that women and children were detained for eight hours under a blazing sun. Even Moshe Sharett objected to Ben-Gurion over this operation in Nazareth, and expressed fear of the repercussions of the events on the image of Israel in the world.[101] Sharett asked the prime minister and defense minister to conduct an investigation into what occurred in this operation and the harsh treatment of the population by the soldiers, with no discrimination between the common people and the notables. However, the army representatives denied the charges against them, and the deputy military governor of Nazareth only admitted that the detainees "had been left for several hours without water to drink."[102]

The communists also raised in the Knesset the question of forced migration. Near the end of 1949 Tawfiq Tubi placed the issue of "army searches in Arab villages" on the agenda.[103] In a strongly worded speech, he presented members of the Knesset with the details of the Arab expulsion operations. He began with a reference to the report in the press about the "expulsion of five hundred infiltrators," and he quoted some statements in the Hebrew press in praise of "the good conduct of the army." He commended that those statements were "untrue, false and shameful." He then moved on from generalities to the specifics of what had happened in Majd al-Krum, pointing out, "Among the expellees from this village are two hundred men and one hundred women and children who do not have registration receipts, but they are citizens who never left their country." He added: "They were registered in the village census, but the authorities delayed giving them registration receipts. The husbands of many of the expelled women have registration receipts and identity cards."[104]

Tubi continued his hard-hitting speech by saying that it was difficult to speak of humane treatment by the army units which carried out the expulsion: "Some cases I heard of during my visit to the village are simply a stain on the reputation of those responsible in the Israeli government." Tubi then went on to talk about the expulsion operations in Shafa 'Amr, Dayr al-Asad and al-Bi'na. He concluded by saying: "I propose that a parliamentary committee be formed to investigate these actions, which are condemned by most members of the Knesset." His speech caused a strong reaction from the prime minister and defense minister who asked to respond to the speech and the proposal to set up a parliamentary investigating committee.

To begin with, Ben-Gurion expressed his astonishment at the way the Knesset session was being conducted, which allowed Tubi's statement to be heard from the Knesset podium. In a defensive-aggressive speech, he accused Tubi of maligning the state of Israel and its army, thanks to which "members of minorities have the freedom to sit here on a footing of equality."[105] Then the prime minister went on the offensive, saying: "This is not the first time that Tubi engages in such defamation," adding: "This defamation is just the continuation of the incitement which his party has carried on for many years, in cooperation with the Mufti."[106] Then Ben-Gurion asked that "this defamation" be stricken from the Knesset record, and he asked the Knesset committee "to use all means possible to protect the dignity of the Knesset from this out-of-control behavior."[107] During the stormy debate, Ben-Gurion, who was seething with anger, attacked Tubi, saying: "Shut up. You are sitting here thanks to us."

The expulsion of the population from Galilee continued, and the communists were almost the only ones who resisted these actions, although occasionally some protesting voices from the Zionist left could be heard as well. Yosef Waschitz, mentioned earlier, wrote in his party's paper 'Al Hamishmar that the term "infiltrator" now corresponds in the Israeli dictionary to "killer and robber."[108] The security forces usually denied any accusations about their activities in the expulsion of Arabs from the country. Moshe Dayan's opinion concerning the presence of Arabs in the country was that they were a "fifth column." He said in a meeting of the ruling Mapai party:

> The policy of the party must make clear that we consider the fate of this population, which consists of 170,000 Arabs, in the country as still undecided. I hope that in the next few years there will be an opportunity to transfer those Arabs out of the land of Israel. As long as the shadow of this possibility remains open, we must do nothing that conflicts with it. It is probable that when we settle 700,000 refugees there will be an opportunity to repatriate those was well. It is possible that we may find an Arab country, or Arab countries, which may be willing, with international support, to settle the Arabs elsewhere. At that time there will be approval to transfer those residents.[109]

Nor was Dayan alone in supporting the expulsion of Arabs from Israel and settling them in Arab countries like the other refugees. The military governor Colonel Emmanuel Moore claimed in 1950 that "all the people who live in Zion . . . do not want Arabs for neighbors."[110] Chief of staff Yigael Yadin also supported the transfer of the Arabs from Israel that year. During a consultation with Ben-Gurion on 8 February 1950 he declared that "an Arab minority in our midst constitutes a danger in times of war as in times of peace."[111]

Since 1952 ideas had been put forward for expelling Arabs from Israel to Libya and Argentina.[112] Although the army had played the main role in expelling Arabs from the country by force during and after the war, the foreign ministry, HaKeren HaKayemet, and other civilian organizations shared in devising plans to expel the remaining Arabs. The objective of these plans was to encourage the emigration of educated urban Palestinian businessmen as well as villagers who had relatives outside the country. The ideas were not discussed in secret, but unashamedly in public and in the media. The Histadrut newspaper Al-Yawm encouraged the publication of articles and opinion pieces that promoted the emigration of Arabs whereas *al-Ittihad* replied to these voices with strong condemnations and accused the authors of treason and collaboration with the senseless policies of the government.

In the early 1950s, for example, the idea was discussed of the absorption of Palestinians in post-colonial Libya under the new monarchical rule established by King Idris in December 1951.[113] Moshe (son of Eliyahu) Sasson, who was a recognized expert in Arab affairs, announced a plan along these lines in a letter to Foreign Minister Sharett. The letter mentions Muhammad Nimr al-Hawwari as one of the Arab leaders who had expressed support for the idea and who was willing personally to immigrate to Libya.[114] Sasson also mentioned that Yehoshua Palmon, the prime minister's advisor on Arab affairs, supported this idea.[115] In addition to Sasson and the idea of immigrating to Libya, Yosef Weitz, Ezra Danin, and others had supported similar ideas for the migration of Arabs to a country in South America, Canada, or Australia.

Most of these ideas remained ink on paper, and few Arabs left the country. In a report by an intelligence agency in September 1951, reference was made to the number of Arabs who had left over the two previous years. Until July 1951 about 2,000 individuals had left the country voluntarily, most to neighboring Arab countries. The unnamed authors of the report said that the number of migrants would have been greater had the state allowed the sale of the property of emigrants.[116] Meanwhile, Yosef Weitz tried to encourage a plan for the inhabitants of Jish to move to Argentina, chosen because some relatives of Jish villagers had already immigrated there. This plan had a code name, Operation Yohanan, after Yohanan bin Levi from the village of Jish on the border with Lebanon. Weitz won the approval and blessings of the prime minister and the foreign minister for his plan. However, the plan failed, as most Jish residents continued to live on their lands and in their country.[117]

The communists took on the migration proposals and their supporters, whom they dubbed "The Expulsion Party."[118] This firm position by the communists made things difficult for some Arab supporters of the plans and caused them embarrassment. When Shaykh Tahir al-Tabari (1895–1959), the shari'a judge of Nazareth, plucked up the courage to send a letter to the prime minister supporting the migration of Arabs from the country, he was attacked even by his friends and allies in *al-Rabita* magazine.[119] In the letter to the head of state, al-Tabari had asked for compensation for the emigrants' property in order to facilitate their journey. This proposal and similar ideas by the judge about population exchanges brought strongly-worded objections, the communists foremost among his critics, but not the only ones. Some of his friends tried to explain that what he had said was a result of the repression of, and discrimination against, Arabs, but nearly everyone expressed objections towards his position, including Muhammad Nimr al-Hawwari, who published a withering critique in *al-Rabita* magazine.[120]

Five years after the Nakba and the creation of Israel, the remainers were even more determined in the face of attempts to make them leave their country. In addition to opposition in principle to the idea of emigration, led by the communists and nationalists, news spread of the difficult living conditions of Palestinians in the Arab countries, as well as the difficulties facing those who decide to leave the country. One rumor said that Arab countries would not issue passports or grant citizenship to those who sold their property and emigrated. Such information, true or not, caused concern among Israeli authorities who were trying to encourage emigration. Al-Yawm newspaper concluded, in an article titled "Various Rumors," that the opposite was true, saying it was well known that "many Arabs who sold their property in Israel and moved to Arab countries obtained Arab citizenship and enjoy equal rights with the rest of the citizens."[121]

CONCLUSION

At the end of 1948, estimates by the Israeli army indicated that 3,000 to 4,000 Palestinian refugees had succeeded in returning to the country to live once again in their towns and villages or in neighboring villages.[122] These estimates were not based on accurate data, which was difficult to obtain under the unstable circumstances, prior to the conclusion of the census in the villages of upper Galilee. Consequently, the foreign ministry and the military government put pressure on the interior ministry to conclude that task so that the security forces could identify the "infiltrators" and expel them. Ben-Gurion agreed. He wrote in his diary: "We should not expel any Arab if there is any doubt whether he is an infiltrator or an original resident. If it becomes clear that he is an infiltrator, then he should be expelled."[123] Indeed, since January 1949, the policy of expulsion intensified.

Not having conducted a census in upper Galilee enabled some returnees to claim they had not left the country. On 17 January, General Avnir sent a report to Ben-Gurion informing him that the census had been completed. Depending on that report, Ben-Gurion wrote in his diary (7 February 1949) that there were 102,000 Arabs living under Israeli rule, including 14,000 Druze.[124] The number of Druze was accurate and did not change much that year or in subsequent years. The numbers of Muslims and Christians were incomplete. The given number (102,000) did not include the Bedouins in al-Naqab (the Negev), who were estimated at 19,000,[125] nor did it include the inhabitants of south Majdal ('Asqalan). There were various estimates of the inhabitants of that town, ranging between 1,400 and 4,000. The real number may be closer to the estimate of the military government in al-Majdal, which was 2,600.[126] As is well known, these Palestinians were unable to continue living in their town after their expulsion in October 1950.

There is also the question of the thousands of prisoners of war who were in Israeli POW camps until early 1949. Of the 9,000 prisoners of war, Ben-Gurion said there were "about 5,000 local Arabs" who were arrested because they were

close to the age of conscription.[127] The thousands of prisoners constituted an economic and political burden, so Ben-Gurion decided that the locals should be sent
back to their places of residence, if their homes were still standing, and if they
were not facing other charges. For all these and other reasons, it is difficult to estimate the real number of the Arab residents of Israel on the eve of the first Knesset
elections. However, it is likely that the number 120,000 is more accurate than the
102,000 Ben-Gurion recorded in his diary.

In the expulsion operations Israel carried out against the Arab population
from the end of the war to the mid-1950s, at least 10,000 individuals among those
who remained were expelled. If we also add the Arabs who were expelled from
the Naqab, the number doubles.[128] These numbers shed light on one new and
important aspect of the reality of Arab life in the country during the first decade
after the Nakba. However, the other aspect, which is no less important, is the success of a similar number of Palestinians in returning to their homes and villages
and settling there for good. The stories of entire villages which did not give in
to the policy of forced migration, such as 'Ilabun and Majd al-Krum and others
among al-Shaghur villages, and along the Lebanese border, are living examples
of endurance. These stories of return are transmitted to grandchildren from their
parents and grandparents. They are known only locally. One result of the success
of those who returned, despite the Nakba which paralyzed so many, is that they
were able to achieve a new and permanent life for their families on their land and
in their homeland.

Five years after the Galilee was completely occupied, official Israeli sources estimated that about 20,500 "infiltrators" had succeeded in gaining citizenship and
thus the guarantee that they would spend their lives in the country.[129] In the same
period, Israel agreed to a family reunification program for about 3,000 people.
These numbers confirm that most returnees succeeded in returning through their
own capabilities, despite all the dangers and Israeli policies to stem that phenomenon. The returning "infiltrators" constituted about a quarter of the population of
the Galilee after the Nakba. However, if we remember that Israel expelled a similar
number of Arabs from the end of the war until 1956, it is difficult to accept the
conclusion that the number of those who remained in the country increased during that period by 15 percent due to so-called illegal return.[130]

The phenomenon of the "present absentees" remains one of the suspended
painful issues after the Nakba. "Security" issues were not behind the prevention
of a quick solution for this problem in the 1950s; rather this policy was driven by
Israel's desire to gain control over the largest possible share of Palestinian lands,
including the lands of those who remained and who had become Israel's permanent citizens. Israel planned and worked to expel the largest possible number of
those who remained in the country after the guns fell silent, but the fear of international, regional, and local repercussions prevented the full realization of those
blueprints. These factors compelled Israel to accept the return of all the inhabitants

of 'Ilabun from Lebanon to their homes after they had been expelled. The government was also compelled to accept the return of the inhabitants of 'Illut from Nazareth to their homes. So the inhabitants of Iqrit and Kufr Bir'im ask to this day: why do we have to accept the continued theft of our lands by the government, and to live as refugees in Jish near the Lebanese border? Those who were expelled to Nazareth from Saffuriyya and other villages also ask: why do we have to accept our banishment from their village, while the inhabitants of nearby 'Illut have been allowed to return to theirs?

5

Stories About Individuals and Villages

Previous chapters focused on the experiences of Palestinians who remained in Haifa and the Galilee. This chapter delves into the events in the Triangle villages and the city of Jaffa, as told by the original residents—later known as the "present absentees." By refusing those villagers permission to return to their depopulated villages, the state opened up opportunities to take control of their lands and to settle Jews in their place. Yet three villages escaped that fate: 'Ilabun, 'Illut, and Kufr Qari'. Their return to their homes is in contrast to the cruel fate of villagers of Iqrit and Kufr Bir'im and other depopulated villages, recounted in the previous chapter. This chapter also presents individuals' distinctive narratives about the events which overtook them, revealing very personal perspectives of the Nakba—rich material for an engrossing future film or novel. Too little attention has been given to the human lives affected by the Palestinian tragedy of 1948 and its aftermath; we and the world need to become more acquainted with it.

Most Palestinian stories have to do with their social ties (and at times their familial ties) being severed after the armistice agreement lines were drawn. These new borders, which often ruptured relations among members of the same family, were not immediately recognized, and for several years people would undertake great risks to cross them. Life under the control of the military government, which was responsible for imposing the new reality on the population, became a Kafkaesque theater in which the scripts of the plays were leavened with fear for those who were missing and joy at encountering loved ones. The stories of some inhabitants of border villages in the Triangle represented a new kind of human suffering—the ramifications of disrupted relations between relatives separated by the new border—recently exposed and documented by the researcher Honaida Ghanim.[1]

The stories of the Triangle residents represent a new stage in the struggle to survive inside Israel. Several small villages were destroyed and their inhabitants dispersed, and thousands of those who had sought refuge in those villages (such as

Baqa al-Gharbiyya) were also uprooted. At the end of the period of transition from Arab rule to Israeli control in the spring of 1949, villages in the area in close proximity to the Jordanian border endured a series of retaliatory operations by Israel in what became known as "the border war" in which thousands of Palestinians were wounded or killed. The conditions of constant tension left their imprint on the population: villages in the Triangle witnessed a steady series of acts of killing and maltreatment for seven years, which were to climax in the Kafr Qasim Massacre (29 October 1956).[2]

THE TRANSFER OF THE TRIANGLE
TO ISRAELI CONTROL

In early 1949, while Israel was preventing the return of refugees and expelling—under the pretext of "security needs"—thousands of those who had remained along its borders, it was also negotiating with Jordan on transferring the border villages of the Triangle to Israeli control. This contradiction in Israeli policy was never seriously discussed either by the government or in the press, even in opposition party organs. The Mapam party, for instance, continued to attack the government for accepting that the West Bank should remain under King Abdullah's control. As for the proposal that Israel accept 100,000 refugees to facilitate solving the refugee problem, the leftist opposition mounted fierce criticism against the government and accused it of bowing to American pressure. Maki's position on these issues was not much different from Mapam's at the time. After King Abdullah submitted to Israeli pressure and accepted the transfer of the Triangle to Israeli control, there was no criticism of the government nor was there any opposition from the leftist parties.

Much has been said and written about Jordan's transfer of the Triangle region to Israel. Abdullah al-Tal set aside a whole chapter in his memoirs to discuss "the tragedy of the Triangle."[3] Nevertheless, the facts surrounding the surrender of the villages of the Triangle to Israeli control remain shrouded in secrecy. The transfer was the best evidence of the rapaciousness of the victor and the limp determination of the Jordanian king. On the other hand, the Palestinians, being powerless, were the hapless victims in this equation. The fate of the Palestinians became a football in the hands of local and international powers and governments, with no consideration given to their opinion. Thus, the population of Wadi 'Ara and a border strip extending as far south as Kafr Qasim, were transferred to Israel and "peacefully" joined the remaining Arabs in northern and southern Israel.

'Arif al-'Arif, whose writings on the Nakba are distinguished by their substance and balance, abandoned his silence to write about the deception practiced by the Israeli side in the annexation of the Triangle to its territory.[4] His criticism, in which he goes as far as accusing all those from the Jordanian side who participated in the surrender of that region of treason, is surprising and audacious. Under the title "The Rhodes Agreement and the Tragedy of the Triangle," he wrote in detail about the types of maps used and how they were exploited by the Israeli side. The issue was discussed by the Jordanian parliament in 1953, and MPs representing West Bank cities placed the blame squarely on the ministers and the prime minister.[5] Despite this strong criticism no one was held accountable for the negotiating failure and the calamity which cost tens of thousands of dunums of land. (A dunum is 1,000 square meters). The documents related to the Triangle transfer agreement and its implementation on the ground are still not available to researchers, like many other sensitive issues related to Israel's relations with King Abdullah before and after the Nakba.

The armistice agreement between Jordan and Israel, which was signed on 3 April 1949, included a number of amendments to the cease-fire lines between the two sides, the most important of which was the transfer of the Triangle villages to Israeli control.[6] The Jordanians, the British, and other international parties feared that Israel might expel the population of the Triangle, as it had done with some of those who remained in the Galilee, so they repeatedly asked for written and verbal commitment that Israel would respect the rights of the inhabitants of the region. Consequently the signed agreement for the transfer of the Triangle included clear commitments that the villagers' rights to their land and property would not be violated.[7] While Israel respected most of these commitments, it interpreted them in a narrow way so that most of the original inhabitants of the Triangle (31,000) continued to live in their villages after they were transferred to Israeli sovereignty in May 1949, but thousands of refugees in Baqa al-Gharbiyya and other small villages were expelled in one way or the other.

The Triangle is a small strip of territory fifty kilometers long running from Kafr Qasim in the south to Megiddo in the north, and only five kilometers wide. The Triangle included twenty-seven villages, large and small, and a number of smaller hamlets (*khirab*). Israel considered this area, particularly the northern section, to be strategically important since it was the main transportation route connecting the coast with the northern and eastern parts of the Galilee. Jordan consented to Israel's demand to transfer the Triangle without consulting the population or even informing them beforehand. This was how the strip was added to Israeli territory after the end of hostilities, significantly increasing the number of Israel's Arab inhabitants in the middle of the country. This step demonstrated the contradictions in Israel's policy which made every effort to shrink the number of remaining Arabs at the same time it sought to annex a region inhabited by tens of thousands of Palestinians.

Some residents of the Triangle who wrote their memoirs about those days (April–May 1949) described a feeling of tension and foreboding about the transfer of their area to Israeli sovereignty.[8] It became evident quickly that their fears had not been misplaced, for the staff of the military government for the southern villages of the Triangle violated the terms of the armistice by confiscating and plundering thousands of dunums of land belonging to al-Tira and Qalansuwa villages and imposing a permanent nightly curfew on the inhabitants of the region. The soldiers and police were allowed to do what they liked, irrespective of the agreement. Most members of the police in the area were Circassians and Druze who had fought alongside Israel in 1948, and were later mobilized after the war. Their officer in the village of Qalansuwa was a Circassian called Idris Bakir, and he and his unit treated the inhabitants violently and contemptuously, according to the testimony of one of the villagers.[9]

The transfer of control over the villages of the southern Triangle began in early May 1949, according to the quasi-official *al-Yawm* newspaper, which exaggerated the happiness of the villagers on the occasion. The paper added that the inhabitants could have left their villages and moved to an area under Arab rule, but they chose to stay in their villages.[10] The villagers of Kafr Qasim were the first to be transferred to the Israeli side, on Friday, 6 May, "and the reception of the population for the Israeli army was great, beyond all expectations." The paper put out similar propaganda writing about the arrival of the military governor in al-Tira being celebrated by the villagers and the mukhtar with "great enthusiasm."[11] In Qalansuwa, which had about 2,000 inhabitants, the mukhtar, 'Abd al-Hamid Faris al-Natur, gave a speech in Hebrew expressing the relief of the residents at being liberated from the Iraqis and the Jordanians.[12] The paper reported similar signs of happiness and contentment at the entry of the Israeli government into the area of Wadi 'Ara, from Kufr Qari' to Umm al-Fahm.

The inhabitants of the Triangle feared for their future under Israeli rule, but like all people who come under occupation, they "rejoiced" over their new rulers. Defenseless citizens who come under the control of their enemies with a fearsome reputation often go too far in the effort to earn the satisfaction of the occupiers so as to protect their lives and their survival in place. That was natural, even though the agreement between Jordan and Israel included commitments to protect the citizens and their property, and mentioned the creation of an Arab police force to maintain law and order in the Arab villages.[13] Indeed, an Arab police unit was formed at the beginning, but the entire area was quickly placed under Israeli military rule, and there was no further mention of that unit. The inhabitants suffered from repression, maltreatment, curfews, and other forms of harassment because of the proximity of their villages to the Jordanian border. All in all, Israel annexed the population of the Triangle in an atmosphere dominated by fear and trepidation.

Israel's narrow interpretation of the articles of agreement concerning protecting the inhabitants and their rights excluded the territory west of the cease-fire line.[14] Most of those considered to be refugees were expelled during the first few months of coming under Israeli military rule. Estimates of those who were expelled and forced to migrate from the Triangle vary between 4,000 and 8,500 individuals.[15] In addition, the remaining inhabitants of smaller villages were uprooted, and the state took control over their lands. In that period, the massacres of the year of the

STORIES ABOUT INDIVIDUALS AND VILLAGES   167

Nakba were still weighing on people's minds, so the blows they received were tolerated, compared to the great fear which accompanied the transfer of the region to Israeli control. Those who most feared Israeli retaliation were villagers who had participated in battles with nearby settlements, such as al-Tira.

Israel began expulsion operations from the small *khirab* late in 1949. The military governor, Emmanuel Moore (Markovsky), informed officials that by March 1950 the remaining population of twenty small villages and farms had been forced to migrate.[16] The uprooting operations did not provoke much resistance or even wide condemnation among the population. The communists were at the forefront of the critics of the expulsions and forced migrations. In February 1951, *al-Ittihad* wrote about the expulsion of the inhabitants of the villages of al-Bayada, 'Ayn al-Sahla, 'Ayn al-Zaytuna, 'Ayn Jarrar, and others in Wadi 'Ara: "The army surrounded the villages at night, and forced women and children to move to Umm al-Fahm using force and violence."[17] Nearly one month after this news report, MK Tawfiq Tubi asked the defense minister a list of questions in the Knesset concerning those small villages, numbering thirteen, which had been subjected to expulsion.

As was the case with expulsion operations elsewhere in the Galilee, the population transfer in the Triangle took place in many cases without legal basis, even given the Israeli understanding of things. That is what happened to the inhabitants of the hamlet of al-Jalama who were expelled from their village in 1950. They hired attorney Muhammad Nimr al-Hawwari and went to court in January 1952, asking to be allowed to return to their homes. Attempts at a solution outside court failed, so the Supreme Court issued a final judgment ordering governmental institutions to "use all means at their disposal to return the situation to its prior status."[18] The proceedings of the Supreme Court revealed some details of the tragedy that befell this village: the residents testified that the authorities had forced them out of their homes and their village on 2 March 1950, expelled them from their lands, and settled them in the village of Jatt. All of these actions had been the result of directives from the military governor of the village of Baqa al-Gharbiyya.

The attorney for the defendants, Miriam Ben-Porat, said that "a kibbutz had been established on the lands of the plaintiffs and its residents are unwilling to move from the land voluntarily; and the authorities cannot force them to do that according to the law." The court replied to this claim in an unusually strongly worded statement: "The basic sense of justice rebels at hearing this claim, that the armed forces authorities cannot remove the kibbutz from the land on which it was set up." The court added in astonishment: "When the inhabitants were illegally expelled from their lands, the defendants did not trouble to check if the law allowed them to do what they did. And now that they have to repair the injustice done to the plaintiffs, they find the law has become an obstacle before them."[19]

On this basis, the Supreme Court decided, "We have no choice except to change the temporary order into a final and permanent one in its first section, i.e., concerning the defendants, who are required not to put any obstacles in the way of the return of the plaintiffs to their village and their lands." However, the members of kibbutz Lehavot Haviva, who had been living on the lands of the village since 1951, blew up the houses of al-Jalama with the help of the army on 11 August 1953, using force to prevent the carrying out of the decision by the Supreme Court. The members of that kibbutz came from Czechoslovakia and were members of the Zionist socialist Hashomer Hatzair. They conspired with the military authorities to steal the lands of the Palestinians, even in the rare case when the Supreme Court ruled in favor of others.[20]

The village of al-Jalama joined in the fate of its fellow villages, Iqrit and Kufr Bir'im, along the Lebanese border, where the army also blew up the houses and prevented the families from returning, despite court decisions to the contrary. The echoes of the al-Jalama tragedy reached the Arabic and Hebrew language press. The church-affiliated *al-Rabita* magazine carried the news of how the village houses were destroyed in spite of the Supreme Court ruling, and then added in its commentary: "The Rhodes agreement too should have protected the inhabitants of the village from this unjust action. . . . Where are the commitments? Where are the signed agreements?"[21] The mukhtar of the village, Muhammad Naddaf, who lost his house (and before that 4,500 olive trees had been uprooted from his land), sent a letter to the prime minister on 11 August 1953, in which he said: "The court ruled in our favor," but the authorities had supported the aggressors and criminals. "Is this a state or a gang?" he asked, and concluded his letter by saying: "Kill us. We are tired of life under your tyranny. I am now eighty years old, and I have not seen worse oppression and injustice than yours. Pay for my property or kill me so that I may have some rest. I [will] complain to God about you."[22]

THE RETURN OF THE INHABITANTS OF 'ILABUN, 'ILLUT, AND KUFR QARI'

Contrary to the case of the villagers of 'Illut and 'Ilabun, the Israeli army did not expel the inhabitants of the village of Kufr Qari' directly; they moved to a neighboring village in Wadi 'Ara following a bloody encounter in which their houses became a battlefront for eleven months. They returned to their village on the eve of the transfer of the Triangle to Israeli control, with the tacit approval of the authorities. In the case of 'Illut, the majority of its inhabitants were refugees in Nazareth for a year and a half (as of July 1948) but they returned to their village and homes at the beginning of 1950, unlike the inhabitants of most neighboring Galilee villages. We have already seen the first part of the story of 'Ilabun—the massacre, the expulsion of the population, and their travel to Lebanon. In this section, we present the second part concerning the return of the inhabitants to their village, which was depopulated during most of 1949.

There are similarities as well as differences among the cases of the three villages. The inhabitants of Kufr Qari' were the first to leave their homes in May 1948, and they returned later without the official approval of the Israeli authorities in April 1949. The residents of 'Illut, who experienced two massacres in which dozens of martyrs were killed in July 1948, were forced by the Israeli army to migrate and seek refuge. Some went to Nazareth where they found shelter in monasteries, but others went further and reached Syria and Lebanon. The story of the return of the people of 'Illut to their homes a year and a half later with the approval of the Israeli authorities is unique among similar villages of "present absentees." The same could be said of the villagers of 'Ilabun who were expelled by the Israeli army to Lebanon. Israel later approved their return (quietly, without much noise) near the end of 1948, so that by the summer of 1949 the vast majority had returned.

The Return of the Villagers of 'Ilabun

Some residents of 'Ilabun had left the village before the Israeli army entered it on 30 October 1948. Some young men who hid in the mountains tried to return to the village after the massacre and the expulsion of the population, and some of them found a place to hide in the house of the priest, Murqus Yuhanna al-Mu'allim, and in other houses.[23] The return of those young men was a huge gamble which only a few were willing to risk. However, the 'Ilabun villagers whom Israel expelled to Lebanon refused to accept that their fate was to live in the diaspora and were active at various levels to ensure their return to their homes. No doubt the main factor responsible for their return was the quick action taken by the clergymen in the village, who contacted several local and international parties to ensure the villagers' return. Those clergymen succeeded in gaining wide sympathy and support in dealing with the tragedy that had befallen the village, which greatly embarrassed the Israeli government at a time when it was in dire need of the support of Western states. Within Israel itself, minister Bechor Shitrit acted quickly, in cooperation with various Israeli parties, to guarantee a solution to the problem.[24]

On Saturday 20 November 1948, Mikha'il Damuni and Butrus Shukri Matta carried a letter from the priest Murqus to the 'Ilabun villagers in Lebanon telling them to return quickly to their village. Many villagers were afraid to return, as if the aftereffects of the shock and the tragedy they had endured just a few weeks earlier still had a hold on them, but some chose the risk, and the return journey to the village began on 22 November.[25]

The tragedy of the 'Ilabun villagers did not end with their return to their homes, as they found them stripped of all their contents.[26] The organized looting included the theft of hundreds of cows, goats, sheep, and donkeys which the army and the authorities took as war prizes, and also furniture, clothing, and stores of grain, oil, and olives. The villagers heard from the priest and some elderly people who had not been expelled that soldiers and civilians had searched the houses and loaded their contents on trucks. All attempts by the villagers to get back the looted items, or at least to be paid compensation, failed but they did receive help from the United Nations Relief and Works Agency (UNRWA) in the Middle East and from the residents of neighboring Arab villages. This assistance helped them to rebuild their lives in their village.[27] Next was the struggle over the land, which many Zionist organizations had wanted to loot as the property of "present absentees," but the villagers determinedly went back to planting their land as in the past. Thus, normal life gradually returned to the village, but the massacre and the expulsion of the population with unparalleled cruelty remained engraved in the memories of the villagers for many years.

The events of the Nakba in 'Ilabun, whether the massacre, the expulsion of the population, or the return of the inhabitants to the village, have received brief and not very accurate treatment in Israeli historical research literature. As with other war crimes committed by the army in 1948 and later, Israeli authorities imposed a blackout about the events and related documents. Although Minister Shitrit, as the representative of the Israeli government, reached a consensual agreement with the representatives of the villagers which secured their quiet and gradual return, the details of that agreement have remained secret, which is consistent with other attempts to bury embarrassing criminal operations. The consent of the authorities to the return of the inhabitants of 'Ilabun to their lands, and the fact that those lands were not expropriated in accordance with Israeli policy and law, constitutes a special and particular case. The attempt to quickly fix what the Israeli army had done took place essentially to relieve the pressure on the government and its institutions by local and international representatives of the church. Thus the 'Ilabun villagers benefited from the great embarrassment that their tragedy caused the authorities, by being allowed to return to their homes from the diaspora, including hundreds who had not been expelled by the army but had left on their own.

One of these returnees in December 1948 was Fawzi al-Zayna, who related what happened to him on his return journey with dozens of 'Ilabun villagers on Christmas Eve.[28] He said they were set upon by bandits near the Lebanese border, and split into two groups. In many cases, soldiers were lying in wait for the returnees from Lebanon near Sa'sa' and confronted them, but they permitted the 'Ilabun villagers to proceed on their way after checking their identity. The group that returned on Christmas Eve included Khalil Salim Matar, who said that three brigades had attacked his group of friends: "They made us sit on the muddy ground and ordered us to raise our hands above our heads." Matar also spoke of being interrogated by the soldiers and their attempts to intimidate the members of the group and to rob them before they left them and went on their way.[29] The group continued walking until they reached Hurfaysh. "One of the villagers accompanied us. He asked us for two lira, which we gave him, although had he asked for five lira we would not have begrudged him that. Then we continued on our way and reached 'Ilabun on 24 December 1948, Christmas Eve."[30]

Mu'in Salim Zurayq told the story of his return with his brother from Junya, north of Beirut, to 'Ilabun. After he heard about the return of many villagers, he decided in mid-February to join them. Mu'in returned with his brother Munir, their sister Nayfa, and her three children, who were accompanied by Rashid Ayyub al-Zayna. When they reached Rumaysh, Elias Samara from the village of al-Rama joined them. They hired the services of a guide from Dayr al-Qasi and began on their way in the evening. When they crossed the asphalt road running along the border, they fell into a trap set by the Israeli army. Some of the soldiers spoke Arabic. "They took us to Hurfaysh, then to 'Akka," he said. The following day members of the 'Ilabun group along with other detainees were taken to Haifa, from there to the Austrian hospital in Nazareth, then to 'Afula, and then the caravan headed in the direction of Umm al-Fahm. "Halfway between 'Afula and al-Lajjun they told us to get off and chased us in the direction of Jenin, firing in the air behind us so that we would not think of returning."[31]

Testimonies from Mu'in Zurayq and other 'Ilabun villagers concerning the difficulties they endured on the road to exile and back were collected by the village historian in his book *The Nakba in 'Ilabun*.[32] I heard some of these stories from the villagers when I visited 'Ilabun and met a number of eyewitnesses ten years after Elias Surur's book was published. But some of those whom Surur had interviewed had passed away by 2008. Thus, the book *Al-Nakba in 'Ilabun* and other similar books and documentary films saved the testimonies of many villagers for history.

The villagers of 'Ilabun continued their unorganized and gradual return over the spring of 1949. Some returned from Lebanon thanks to an agreement between Yehushua Palmon, the prime minister's advisor, and Bishop Hakim.[33] That agreement secured the return of hundreds of Christians from Lebanon to the villages of the Galilee in return for the bishop's cooperation with Israel and its policies. However, Benny Morris's statement that hundreds of 'Ilabun's inhabitants returned to their village following that agreement is not accurate, because the majority of the 'Ilabun villagers had returned by May 1949, that is, before the deal with the bishop. This is a certainty, well supported by the villagers' testimonies and written sources. Those who returned after the deal with the bishop were no more than several dozen. One of the last groups to return from Lebanon included Faris Salim Matar and his family at the beginning of January 1950.[34]

The events of the Nakba in 'Ilabun left an impact on the villagers for many years. Those who returned to that Galilee village went into mourning for over a year, during which weddings were not celebrated nor were the feasts and seasonal holidays.[35] After their return, the villagers (particularly the women) fell into the habit of visiting cemeteries and recalling the martyrs of the massacre before attending prayers in church. People in neighboring villages came to look on the 'Ilabun villagers as a symbol of resistance to injustice and forced migration at the hands of the Israeli army. Some young men from the village became famous for their political activity and for joining the Communist Party. The primary concern of the people of 'Ilabun turned to the struggle to free the dozens of prisoners in Israeli detention centers. When they were released in May 1949 the village held a special celebration for the occasion and the participants visited the graves of the martyrs who had been murdered by the soldiers of the Golani Brigade at the end of October 1948. Later, Habib Zurayq spoke to the villagers, memorializing the massacre and the suffering of the people of 'Ilabun over the previous six months.[36]

Despite their many tragedies, the 'Ilabun villagers were relatively fortunate in being allowed to return to their village. The theft of the property of the Arabs remaining in the Galilee has received little mention in published research. Many of the returnees and forced migrants told stories about Israeli soldiers stealing what little money or jewels they had had on them. State institutions themselves had organized the collection of "abandoned property" belonging to Palestinians in their cities and villages. The theft and plundering of property was total in cities and villages which were completely depopulated. 'Ilabun was a distinct case. Within weeks after their expulsion at the end of October 1948, they returned to find their houses totally empty of all contents. In addition to the testimonies of the returning villagers, the testimony of the clergy, one of whom chronicled the events in his diaries,[37] also bears witness.

The Departure and Return of the Kufr Qari' Villagers

The location of Kufr Qari' at the western entrance to Wadi 'Ara was of great strategic importance and made it a target of occupation. On 9 May 1948, soldiers of the Alexandroni Brigade attacked the village and managed to occupy part of it, expelling most of the villagers from their homes. Dozens of the inhabitants of Kufr Qari', armed with rifles and aided by temporary armed support from dozens of neighboring villages, managed to repulse the attack and caused a number of casualties on the other side, which is what prevented the fall of the entire village that day.[38] Sara Osetski-Lazar, who researched the events at Kufr Qari' and listened to testimonies of the villagers which complemented army documents, concluded that the attack on the village was halted with the help of ARA Iraqi volunteers, but the inhabitants subsequently decided to leave their homes to escape further danger.[39]

Following that assault, Kufr Qari' became a deserted village and a kind of no man's zone: the western side controlled by Israeli forces and the eastern side by Iraqi-Jordanian forces. Some villagers who had planted in winter tried to harvest them, but landmines placed by the Israelis and gunfire prevented them. When a rumor reached the expelled villagers of Kufr Qari' that the Jews were harvesting their crops, one villager said he went out to the fields with a friend to see if this was true, and "indeed, we saw harvesting machines at work in our fields, so we fired at them from afar, and they returned fire. When the other villagers heard the gunfire they joined us along with some residents of neighboring villages who came to our rescue, at which point the Jews fled to the Gil'ed settlement."[40] But the soldiers of the ARA, fearing that the situation would deteriorate into a major conflagration, calmed the villagers and took them from their houses in the village to Wadi 'Ara.

More than one researcher has listened to the testimonies of the Kufr Qari' villagers and documented those testimonies in their studies.[41] The narratives portray a clear picture of events, and show that the villagers were going back and forth to their houses and their fields to gather provisions or to plow and plant. For those *fellahin*, the act of going back was fraught with danger, and some were killed or wounded by gunfire or Israeli mines.[42] Despite the danger, the inhabitants kept alive their relations with the village, which in the end helped them to return to their homes. The villagers of Kufr Qari' had learned the lesson of dispossession from the experiences of other Palestinians who were uprooted and then lost contact with their homes: their houses were destroyed and all traces lost with time. Since Israeli soldiers had not occupied the entire village, the inhabitants were able to maintain connection with their village throughout their forced migration (eleven months) and took the courageous decision to return in April 1949, on the eve of the transfer of the Triangle region to Israeli control.

More than one source indicates that Hasan 'Isa 'Athamna played an important role in the return of the villagers. He led a delegation of notables from the village to the nearby kibbutz Kfar Glickson to secure a ceasefire agreement between the two sides, after which the inhabitants of Kufr Qari' returned to their village and their homes in April 1949.[43] When it was time for the villages of Wadi 'Ara to be transferred to Israeli control, the villagers had already returned under their own power. That timely and unusual initiative saved Kufr Qari' from destruction. Days later, the correspondent of *al-Yawm* reported the transfer of the villages of Wadi 'Ara to the Israeli side and the ceremony of raising the Israeli flag over the main traffic circle at the entrance of Umm al-Fahm.[44]

Were local initiatives and good neighborly relations the secret of the return of the Kufr Qari' villagers? Did the Israeli government and army turn a blind eye and allow Arab and Jewish neighbors to reach an agreement so as not to compromise the major agreement with Jordan? There are no clear answers yet to these and similar questions provided in documents from Israeli archives or other official sources. The testimonies which authenticate what happened in the field come mainly from the Arab side, most notably from the Kufr Qari' villagers who relayed their stories to researchers. The story of this village—well known to its inhabitants and their neighbors in Wadi 'Ara—is absent from the collective memory in other areas of Palestine. It has been relatively fortunate in garnering the attention of researchers, and is mentioned here in order to place it in the general framework of events of the year of the Nakba.

The Expulsion and Return of the Villagers of 'Illut

'Illut and other villages in the Nazareth district were occupied during the ten-day battles in July 1948. We mentioned earlier that Nazareth and most villages in its district were not subjected to massacres and expulsions by the Israeli army. However, 'Illut was among the exceptions, one of four villages where inhabitants were forced to migrate and join the thousands of forced migrants or refugees who became known as the "present absentees." The other three villages in the district which were depopulated were Saffuriyya, al-Mujaydil and Ma'lul in Marj ibn 'Amir. Most of 'Illut's expelled residents found refuge and a place to live in the city of the Annunciation at the Salesian monastery. Other refugees also lived in that monastery, next to the monks who had great difficulty taking in hundreds of refugees. Luckily for them, the Israeli authorities allowed the residents of 'Illut to return to their village in the end.

The story of the uprooting of the inhabitants of 'Illut began on 16 July 1948, when soldiers from the Golani Brigade attacked the village from the west and the south. The soldiers ordered all the inhabitants to gather in the courtyard near the mosque, men on one side, women on the other. The soldiers found arms in some houses, whereupon they blew them up. Such was the fate of the house of mukhtar Hasan Muhammad al-Ahmad and three other houses in 'Illut.[45] An officer by the name of Nassim led a group of young men to an olive grove and "he made them stand in a single line, then the machinegun on the officer's car mowed them down within minutes." The sixteen martyrs of this massacre were Sa'id Abu Ras, Taha Abu Ayyash, Muhammad 'Awdatallah, Sa'id al-Fallah, Muhammad Mustafa al-'Isa, Muhammad Ibrahim, Nimr al-Dabburi, Muhammad al-Fayiz, Ahmad Muhammad Abu Ras, Salih Muhammad, Nayif al-Salti, Hasan Muhammad al-Darwish, Mahmud Salim al-'Ali, Mir'i Husayn Mahmud, Mustafa Salim Abu Tanha, and Muhammad Salim Shehada. Two others were wounded but recovered later: Muhammad Mustafa al-Ma'mur and Khadr 'Ali Yusif Abu Ras.[46]

Soldiers of the Golani Brigade who had perpetrated the massacre continued on their way to 'Ayn al-Bayda, where a number of villagers were hiding. Their fate was similar to the others who were executed in cold blood; ten 'Illut villagers were killed near the spring. Some villagers who heard the gunfire arrived at the scene, collected the bodies, and buried them near the mosque. After the perpetration of these two massacres of dozens of men, two weeks later the soldiers returned and imposed a curfew on the village; they proceeded to loot the houses and the school, stealing furniture, horses, beehives, and dozens of heads of cattle. After that operation the majority of the population went to Nazareth,[47] leaving no one in the village except for a few elderly people.

As in other Palestinian cities and villages, the Israeli authorities managed to suppress the news of the massacre and expulsion of the population. The villagers of 'Illut acquiesced to this conspiracy of silence out of fear of retribution by the government and the army, particularly as they were allowed to return to their homes after a year and a half. Most historians and researchers have shown no interest in 'Illut's experiences and most Israeli historical literature has been silent on the topic, including the new revisionist historians. Benny Morris, for example, referred to the fact that 'Illut became an abandoned village, but he did not explain to his readers the circumstances that led to the migration of the villagers.[48] Ilan Pappé, in his book *The Ethnic Cleansing of Palestine*, also fails to mention the two massacres and the expulsion of the villagers from their homes.[49] Those historians could have learned about the massacre in 'Illut from 'Arif al-'Arif's book which came out in the 1950s, as well as the testimonies of the inhabitants who returned to the village.[50]

Army authorities had given permission to Bedouin families living near 'Illut– from the tribes of al-Hayb, al-Jawamis, al-Ghrayfat, al-'Iyadat, and al-Mazarib– to stay in the houses of the village during the winter months. The army appointed a mukhtar over them by the name of Muhammad al-Hayb (Abu Falah). The army even allowed a number of villagers from Saffuriyya who had originally remained in their village but later abandoned it to move to 'Illut. However, a year and a half after it had uprooted the population, the Israeli authorities consented to the return of the expellees from 'Illut from the Salesian monastery to their village. About half of the expellees from the village returned to their homes, while the other half remained refugees in Jordan and Syria. The military governor appointed a new mukhtar, Dhib Abu Ras, from among the villagers, and normal life returned to the village.

The historian Mustafa 'Abbasi, who studied events in 'Illut and Nazareth, argues that the pressure brought to bear by senior figures at the Salesian monastery and the French consul in Haifa was the most important factor leading to the decision to allow the 'Illut villagers to return.[51] He mentions that on 3 January, an official representative of the government came to the head of the monastery and delivered a copy of the order by the government permitting the return. The villagers were told to be ready to return to their homes the following day. Indeed, on 4 January, the villagers, led by the monk Dubrovsky, walked to their homes.[52] The villagers had to struggle for many more years to regain their lands; in the end they regained part of their lands while the rest was expropriated and given to neighboring Jewish settlements.

The villagers who returned to 'Illut did not forget what had happened to them, but fear prevented them from commemorating those events for dozens of years. On 8 May 2008, the villagers dared to commemorate the martyrs of the village in the presence of hundreds of participants. Three survivors of the bloody events in the village recounted the killings and expulsion to Nazareth and life at the monastery until their return in early 1950. The head of the local council, Ibrahim Abu Ras, spoke about the lands of the village prior to the year of the Nakba, which had extended to 27,000 dunums. Large sections of the land were expropriated as deserted property or the lands of refugees who could not return to their homes, or confiscated for other reasons, so that in 2008 only 3,330 dunums were left. On the same occasion, some 'Illut villagers in Syria and elsewhere published their memoirs on social media and in press interviews.[53]

The Israeli authorities considered the villagers of 'Illut to be "present absentees" and confiscated their lands after they left the village in July 1948. The inhabitants of neighboring Jewish settlements coveted those lands and asked the government to annex a part of the land to their settlements. For example, the residents of the *moshav* Nahalal asked the authorities to annex about 700 dunums of the deserted land of 'Illut; on 8 August 1948 they wrote: "It seems to us that the time is ripe to transfer these lands to permanent Jewish ownership."[54] Nor were they alone in seeking to loot the property of refugees and to ask the annexation of their land. The villagers of 'Illut who returned to their homes lost a major part of their property, yet they considered themselves to be relatively fortunate because their period of exile was somewhat short, and they could eventually return to their village and to a part of their lands.

THE "PRESENT ABSENTEES" AS REFUGEES IN THEIR OWN COUNTRY

After the end of the war, about twenty thousand Palestinians who remained in the Galilee found themselves living a short distance from their homes but unable to return to them. Nazareth had a large share of those forced to migrate, as there were about five thousand migrants in the city at the end of 1948. About half of them were expellees from Haifa, Tiberias, Bisan, 'Akka, and Shafa 'Amr.[55] Sami Juraysi prepared a detailed report on "refugees" in Nazareth and their living conditions in the city.[56] The report showed that the circumstances of the villagers among them were particularly harsh. At the Salesian orphanage there were about six hundred refugees from 'Illut, al-Mujaydil, and Um Qubi. The halls of the monastery were crowded with those individuals, and "there was nothing to separate families except for a string or a rope or a piece of wood."[57] Despite that, the circumstances of those refugees in Nazareth were much better than those of their brethren who ended up in refugee camps in Lebanon where they would spend the rest of their lives.

As we saw earlier, many residents of Haifa, Shafa 'Amr, and 'Akka were allowed to return to their cities, and the expellees from 'Illut to return to their village. However, all attempts by the villagers of Saffuriyya to return were met with very stiff resistance. Hundreds of those who had remained in their villages and dozens of those who had returned to their villages time and again were expelled. The forced migrants from Saffuriyya, al-Mujaydil, and Ma'lul remained the largest portion of refugees in Nazareth. The "present absentees" who still remained in Nazareth in the 1950s were half the original number. The consent of the Israeli authorities for the return of the residents of cities to Haifa, Shafa 'Amr, and 'Akka, was relatively cost-free. But the return of expellees to their villages was another matter, because settlers were greedy for the land; thus, the Israeli government continued to reject requests by expelled villagers to be allowed to return to their homes. Apart from Nazareth, Shafa 'Amr and Tamra in western Galilee absorbed thousands of refugees from that area,[58] while others went to villages in the Galilee pocket in upper and central Galilee and lived there until those villages were occupied in October 1948.

The stories of Iqrit and Kufr Bir'im, whose inhabitants were evacuated with false promises of returning within weeks, are well known. Those villagers discovered months later that Israel and its army had no intention of living up to their promises. They therefore decided not to keep quiet and to fight to return. In addition to direct contacts with the authorities, the villagers of Kufr Bir'im sent a delegation to meet with Maronite Archbishop Mubarak in Lebanon, requesting his help and intervention.[59] In February 1949 the Kufr Bir'im villagers carried out repairs and maintenance work on their houses to waterproof them for winter, but the army came and arrested sixty-five individuals, including the elderly and women, and transported them by truck to the Jordanian border near Jenin. But those exiles, like other forced migrants from the Galilee villages, did not remain in the West Bank; they went to the East Bank and from there to Syria and Lebanon. Shortly after they arrived in south Lebanon, they crossed the border and returned to their homes in the village of Jish.[60]

This incident aroused the fears of the residents, who understood from the conduct of the army towards them that there was no real intention to allow them back in Kufr Bir'im. Those fears were exacerbated when they saw the men of HaKeren HaKayemet working their lands, which was followed by the establishment of the nucleus of a settlement by the Hashomer Hatzair youth movement on their land on 5 June 1949. Days later the settlers, supported by the police, kicked out the Palestinian young men who had spent months guarding the houses of the village and their contents. The settlers lived for about two years in the deserted houses of the village until they moved in the summer of 1951 into their new and permanent kibbutz Bar'am.[61] During this period, the villagers continued their correspondence with the government and its representatives and met with officials in the hope that they would be returned to their village. However, their continued expulsion from Kufr Bir'im forced them to conclude that the authorities would never allow them to return.

In May 1951, after the Iqrit villagers had also despaired that the promises of return would be fulfilled, the residents of the two villages decided to go to the Supreme Court, and chose attorney Muhammad Nimr al-Hawwari to represent their cause. In the end the court did not come to the aid of the villagers and did not deliver the hoped-for justice, and subsequently the army and the settlers tore down the houses and uprooted most of the olive trees in 1953. Still, the inhabitants of the two villages did not give up hope, and became a symbol of the struggle by the "present absentees" to return. The cause of Kufr Bir'im and Iqrit gained fame locally and internationally but attempts to arrive at a compromise solution between the villagers and the government never gained traction.

The inhabitants of other villages in the Galilee also suffered as a result of experiences similar to Kufr Bir'im and Iqrit. The villagers of al-Ghabisiyya, located north of 'Akka, returned to their village at the end of 1948 after fighting in the area had ended. They had moved away from their houses following an attack on their village in May 1948 and found temporary refuge in neighboring Arab villages. However, their return did not last long, as the army forced them to leave their homes and move to al-Mazra'a and Shaykh Danun at the end of January 1950. When the authorities prevented all their attempts to return, they sought relief from the Supreme Court, which ruled on 30 November 1951 that the villagers had a right to return to their houses in al-Ghabisiyya.[62] Following this ruling the residents of al-Ghabisiyya went back to their homes the following month, but the army turned them out of their houses once again under the pretext that the village had been declared a closed military area. It became clear once again that the court ruling was merely formal and symbolic, and the army had overcome it through the use of the 1945 emergency regulations. As in Iqrit and Kufr Bir'im, the Israeli authorities tore down the houses of al-Ghabisiyya in order to put an end, once and for all, to the hopes of the villagers to return. Indeed, the only building left standing was the mosque, and in this way the authorities closed the file on returning to the village, a typical experience with many villages of the "present absentees."[63]

The story of the villagers of Qadditha, close to Safad, is no less provoking and peculiar. Most of the villagers moved away from their homes after the fall of Safad, because they had been terrorized by the massacre perpetrated in neighboring 'Ayn al-Zaytun. Furthermore, the soldiers stationed at 'Ayn al-Zaytun used to direct sniper fire at the houses of Qadditha from time to time. This situation continued until October 1948 when Israel completed the occupation of the Galilee. 'Ali Hulayhel (Abu Husayn) recounts that, at the time, he had rented a house in the nearby village of Jish and in the summer months managed to harvest what he had planted on his land in Qadditha. After the occupation of the area in Operation Hiram, he migrated along with others and went to south Lebanon. Most of the villagers ended up in refugee camps, but the extended Hulayhel family managed to return to the Galilee because of its ties to Mano Friedman.[64]

The villagers of Qadditha, which neighbors the villages of Jish and Safsaf, panicked after the killings by the Israeli army and decided to travel to South Lebanon. Mano Friedman was on good terms with several members of the Hulayhel clan with whom he had had commercial and agricultural dealings, and he sent an envoy to Khaled Hulayhel, who used to plow his land in Rosh Pinna, advising him to return to the Galilee at once. But Khaled said he would only come back with his entire clan, not by himself. Friedman agreed to that, so the members of the Hulayhel clan returned in December 1948, and were allowed to live in houses in the depopulated village of al-Ja'una, where they spent the winter.[65] Those expellees requested that they be allowed to return to their homes in Qadditha but all their requests were turned down, and it was suggested that they live in one of the depopulated villages. This was a general Israeli policy to prevent those who had been allowed to return from going back to their lands, leaving the land in the hands of the state and the returnees as "present absentees."

After repeated rejections of requests by the Hulayhel clan to return to their village Qadditha, the authorities had them move from al-Ja'una to the village of 'Akbara south of the city of Safad, which was accomplished by force and contrary to the wishes of the clan, in July 1949. Abu Husayn testified that the Hulayhel clan at the time numbered between 110 and 120. This forced removal of the Arab inhabitants from al-Ja'una was denounced, echoes of which reached the Knesset. There MK Eliezer Bray from Mapam raised questions about the matter and provided extensive details of the transfer operation which he called "an assault" by the army and police on the inhabitants of Arab villages in eastern Galilee.[66] Ben-Gurion as usual supported the security forces and justified what they had done until he had quieted the critics. The Hulayhel clan was isolated from the majority of the remaining Galilee population, so they were forced to accept their fate, which they preferred to living as refugees in south Lebanon.

MK Sayf al-Din al-Zu'bi wrote in his memoirs that he went to visit 'Akbara to see the conditions of the forced migrants first-hand and to try to help them. Zu'bi arrived at the village with the military governor Elisha Soltz and Mano Friedman. The Knesset member described the difficult circumstances of the refugees in 'Akbara, which was so isolated that it could only be reached on horseback. Al-Zu'bi added that in coordination with the military governor and kibbutz Kokhav HaShahar it was possible to solve the problem by building a road and extending water to the village. According to Zu'bi, that alleviated the problems of those forced migrants and improved their conditions, but he admitted that he "did not go back to visit the village" after that.[67] Those who did visit the village up to the mid-1970s found that the inhabitants were still living under conditions unfit for human habitation. The road linking the village was a dirt road full of potholes, and the houses were threatened with collapse because of the lack of permission to do maintenance work.

Abu Husayn still remembered to the end of his days that Mano Friedman and the members of HaKeren HaKayemet who worked with members of his family in the forests used to come to visit him at home and enjoyed his hospitality. On those occasions they would renew their promises to help the Hulayhel clan who were living in dilapidated houses and shanties in the depopulated village of 'Akbara, but those promises were just "tranquilizers." A year or more after the Hulayhel clan was moved to 'Akbara, the authorities blew up the houses of Qadditha, as in several other villages whose residents were expelled.[68] In the 1970s, some Jewish settlers decided individually and without planning or a permit from the government to build houses near the destroyed houses of the village. Despite warnings from the government, those new settlers expanded their settlement on the lands of Qadditha without fear of the reaction of the authorities.

We conclude this section on "present absentees" with the unique tale of the survivors among the villagers of al-Khisas. Following a punitive Palmach operation in

December 1947, the inhabitants of this village, which lies to the north of Lake Hula, migrated, and most became refugees in Syria. However, Shaykh 'Atiya and dozens of members of his extended family thought they would be protected because of their good relations with their Jewish neighbors.[69] A number of members of that family volunteered to fight in the ranks of the Haganah and subsequently in the Israeli army during the 1948 war. At the end of that year, the army asked members of Shaykh 'Atiya's family to vacate that border region temporarily, and they did so. After several weeks Shaykh 'Atiya and a number of his children who had served in the army returned to their homes and started planting their fields anew, but soldiers and policemen came to the village on 5 June 1949 and asked them, without prior notice, "to vacate the premises immediately."[70] The security forces transported dozens of al-Khisas inhabitants who had remained to the foot of Kan'an Mountain and left them there without food or shelter.

Jewish friends of Shaykh 'Atiya tried to dissuade the authorities from this action to no avail. The regional council for upper Galilee, along with members of HaKeren HaKayemet, with Yosef Nahmani at their head, sent letters, also to no avail. On 1 August 1948, the minister of defense was asked at the beginning of a Knesset meeting to submit an answer regarding the expulsion of the inhabitants of al-Khisas. Ben-Gurion provided an answer two weeks later to the effect that "the transport operation was carried out at the request of the commander of the northern region for military reasons and it was carried out by the military government of East Galilee." The government acknowledged the loyalty of the inhabitants of al-Khisas, but it decided for security reasons to prevent those Arabs from living along the border. When winter was near, they were moved to Wadi al-Hamam.[71]

After two years of mediation efforts, with the encouragement of his friends, Shaykh 'Atiya raised a case in the Supreme Court.[72] Two of the best Arab lawyers at the time, Hanna Naqqara and Elias Kusa, volunteered to take on the case, and the court accepted the claim that expelling Shaykh 'Atiya and his family from their homes and taking them to the foot of Kan'an Mountain, and from there to Wadi Hamam in 1949, was illegal. But the army repaired the "technical" error it had committed by issuing an order (expulsion) to each of the expellees (the plaintiffs) on 7 July 1952 in accordance with the defense (emergency) regulations of 1949 (security regions—no. 2). Following that step, the Supreme Court turned down the request by the plaintiffs and cancelled the provisional order it had issued earlier. The court added in its decision: "Seeing as the expulsion orders were issued after the provisional order, we hold the defendants responsible for court costs in the amount of 75 liras." The court also recommended that a solution be found for those people "who cooperated with the Jews of the country for a long time, some of whom even fought on the side of Israel in its war of independence." The court concluded its recommendations to the authorities concerned, asking that they "do what they can to find a suitable arrangement which is consistent with the requirements of security and allows the plaintiffs to return to their village."[73] But the recommendations were not acted on, and Shaykh 'Atiya and his sons still live in Wadi Hamam.

THE STORY OF "THE PRISONER" 'AWDA AL-'ASHHAB AND HIS FRIENDS

At the end of December 1948, Israeli soldiers reached Abu 'Ujayla in Sinai and found a number of communists in the detention camp who had been arrested after distributing leaflets attacking the intervention of the armies of Arab states in the Palestine war.[74] Among the detainees were Salim al-Qasim, Hasan Abu 'Isha, As'ad Makki, 'Ali 'Ashur, Muhammad Khas, and 'Awda al-'Ashhab. Instead of being given medals for their fight in favor of partition and against the intervention of Arab armies in the Palestine war, those comrades were moved to jails in Israel. From Abu 'Ujayla the prisoners were taken to Bir Sab'a (Beersheba) and from there to a POW camp in Ijlil (Glilot today).[75] Members of Maki, with the help of Mapam members, tried to obtain the release of their friends but failed, at which point MK Meir Vilner, a signatory of Israel's declaration of independence, decided to bring up the case for debate in the Knesset.

In a strongly-worded and aggressive speech, Vilner told the story of "the liberation of the warriors of the secret Arab resistance who fought against the Egyptians" from the Abu 'Ujayla jail. Out of all the comrades, he mentioned Salim al-Qasim, who was the general secretary of the organizations of Arab workers in the country and a friend of "an Israeli minister: Zalman Shazar." Then Vilner addressed the minister directly, inquiring: "Is it civilized that your friend should be imprisoned for months in a detention camp?" He replied to this question with a decisive demand that the matter be listed on the Knesset agenda. He added: "We must demand that the government free those warriors for freedom immediately." He concluded his speech by saying: "Those men do not deserve this treatment, while the supporters of the fascists (sic [in original]), such as Khaiyat of Haifa, have won the status of respected personalities in the official circles of the Israeli government."[76]

Despite the complaints about the conditions under which the members of the League were being held, the detainees themselves admitted, in their typed and oral testimonies, that they were being well treated compared to the rest of the Arab prisoners. The good treatment began even before they arrived in the detention camps and continued after they got there. 'Awda al-'Ashhab mentions an unusual event in his memoir: an army officer had heard him shout that they were Palestinian communists, not Egyptian soldiers, so the officer immediately asked: "If you are really communists, tell me: Which Palestinian communist is married to a Jewish woman?" Al-'Ashhab adds that his comrade, Hasan Abu 'Isha, who lived and worked in Jaffa, went up to where the officer was standing and said to him: "I know. It is our comrade Jabra Nicola and his wife, comrade Eliza." The officer answered: "That is right, and Eliza is my sister." From that moment on, the way the officers treated us changed, because we were all communists."[77]

Early in 1949, the communist press began demanding that the party comrades be released. *Al-Ittihad* published a news item on its front page about the prisoners Salim al-Qasim, Hasan Abu 'Isha, As'ad Makki and others, demanding that they be set free immediately.[78] Both Arab and Jewish communists continued raising the issue of the twelve detainees and demanding their release without delay. MK Vilner declared: "All the Hebrew press has published the news of their deeds and their struggle on the side of the state of Israel and its army." He asked: "Does it make sense that people who fought on our side should be imprisoned after we freed them from the Egyptian detention camp?"[79]

Most of the communists whom Vilner described as "warriors of the secret Arab resistance movement" were from Jerusalem, Hebron, and Gaza, which Israel had not occupied, and which were outside Israel's borders. In spite of that, the leaders of Maki insisted on the need to allow them to live in the state of the Jews on an equal footing. Most members of this group were not married, and after they were released and won approval to live in Israel, they became involved in party activities and institutions, and added new blood to the party alongside their Arab comrades. However, some were married, and submitted applications for family reunification, with a number of these applications approved on an extraordinary basis. This special treatment granted to the communist prisoners supports what was said in previous chapters concerning "bringing back many members of the League" from Lebanon to Haifa and Nazareth and other places.

At the beginning of 1949, prisoner of war camps in Israel held over 9,000 Arabs. Many of those came from the Galilee, and had been arrested and imprisoned after the end of the fighting because they were of recruitment age. A number of them were arrested in western Galilee and lower Galilee in the wake of the ten-day battles in July 1948. The majority had been arrested following the occupation of the Galilee under Operation Hiram. Hundreds of prisoners spent over a year in POW camps in servitude, working without pay instead of being with their families and supporting them. This subject has not received attention from Palestinian researchers and historians until recently, but a new study published in 2013 has shed light on many aspects of the lives of those prisoners and their experiences in Israeli detention centers.[80]

At the end of June, the twelve comrades were set free as a group and went to Nazareth. Activists in the league, led by Saliba Khamis, welcomed them like heroes and courageous warriors. After five days in Nazareth, 'Awda al-'Ashhab decided to visit Jerusalem without an official permit from the military government. When he got to the city to see his house in the German Colony, he found it deserted amidst signs of looting, like the rest of the Arab houses in West Jerusalem.[81] Al-'Ashhab found some solace in the reception he received from party comrades in Jerusalem and Tel Aviv, who organized a number of lectures for him on his experiences under detention.[82] When he returned to Nazareth, party leaders saw to it that he would have a place to live and employment (along with two of his comrades, 'Ali 'Ashur and Muhammad Khas) in the party newspaper in Haifa, and they obtained verbal permission from the military administration for him to travel freely after July 1949.

Once al-'Ashhab settled into his job in Haifa, he submitted a family reunification application to have his wife, Mariam, and his only daughter (who had remained in Hebron), join him, but the authorities did not approve the application, rejecting it multiple times. Party leaders went to work to arrange a family reunification deal for him through political means, using their connections with decision-makers in the government and the Knesset. MK Tawfiq Tubi submitted a list of questions for Minister of Police Shitrit on 11 December 1950 inquiring why the police were opposed to the reunification of the al-'Ashhab family. Minister Shitrit's reply in the Knesset on 1 January 1951 was that family reunification was the remit of the minister of migration.[83] But MK Tubi was not satisfied with this answer and added that the ministry in question had rejected the application on the basis of a letter dated 18 October 1950 from officer Shalush of the Tel Aviv police. The minister replied simply that he had no knowledge of this letter, but that he would look into the matter.

Two weeks later, Immigration Minister Haim Moshe Shapira replied to the question from MK Tubi concerning the case of al-'Ashhab family.[84] First, Shapira acknowledged the accuracy of Shitrit's response, and said that his ministry, not the police, was responsible for issuing "return permits" or rejecting the applications. As for the application in question, he explained the reasons for rejecting it, saying: "The return of al-'Ashhab and members of his family would be from their place of residence, Hebron, which is outside the borders of Israel." He added: "What is requested of us is to bring in this family, not allow it to return, since its members were never part of the permanent residents of a region that is now part of the state of Israel. Such a request is for something we unfortunately cannot do." However, MK Tubi was not convinced by the answer. He said: "But you approved family reunification for a friend of al-'Ashhab and his family who are from Jerusalem. Why then discriminate against the return of al-'Ashhab?" Minister Shapira replied: "I am prepared to study the case. Perhaps that was a special (humanitarian) case which was dealt with outside the scope of the law."[85] The minister concluded his remarks by saying that such a case could be approved, but the approval would not be obligatory.

The give and take in the Knesset were taking place in tandem with a changing situation on the ground. The al-'Ashhab family had in fact been united while Knesset members were listening to Tubi's questions and the minister's answers. 'Awda al-'Ashhab was a man steeped in political action and labor struggles in the field. He could no longer wait for his party leaders to convince the Israeli authorities to approve family reunification in his case, so he paid a man from the village of

Sandala, which neighbors Jenin, to smuggle in his wife and child. Thus, the family's hope of reuniting was realized after more than a year of separation.[86] Mariam and her young daughter lived in hiding in the houses of friends and party comrades for months. Meanwhile, *al-Ittihad* was highlighting the trials and tribulations of the family which the Israeli authorities were denying reunification "under the pretext of security risks."[87] When the authorities discovered that his wife and daughter had "infiltrated" into the country, they were furious and went looking for them day and night. At that time, the al-'Ashhab family were living in the houses of Jewish comrades, including the house of a member of the Knesset.[88]

The circumstances of the family, who lived constantly in hiding and on the move, deteriorated after Mariam al-'Ashhab became pregnant and gave birth "in secret" in August 1952. When she was close to giving birth, his party comrades came to help the family. Dr. Lieberman was working in the maternity ward at Rambam Hospital (in Haifa) and al-'Ashhab's wife was admitted to the ward, although she had no papers, and gave birth to baby daughter Shadya on 20 August 1952.[89] Mother and daughter were discharged three days later without a birth certificate or registration. When the police discovered this they concentrated on tracking down the family to arrest them, so Mariam al-'Ashhab was moved with her two children to the house of an Arab family in Jaffa. Ibrahim Sha'ath, who was originally from Gaza and was living in al-'Ajami quarter, hosted the family in spite of the risks. Soon, however, intelligence operatives found out where the family was hiding in Jaffa, so the comrades moved her to the house of MK Moshe Sneh in Tel Aviv.[90]

It was not easy for the al-'Ashhab family to continue living in hiding and to keep moving out of fear of the police. In addition to living apart from her husband, Mariam al-'Ashhab suffered from social and cultural isolation because it was difficult to socialize with her Jewish hosts in Tel Aviv and Haifa. This went on for about five years, until 1954, when Maki leaders and Knesset members decided on an extraordinary step and brought 'Awda al-'Ashhab and his wife and small daughter Shadya to the Knesset. The family had prepared a detailed account of its story in both Hebrew and Arabic along with a banner about a sit-in strike. Prime Minister Moshe Sharett called Minister of Police Shitrit and asked him to resolve the family reunification issue immediately. The office of Haifa Mayor Abba Hushi got in touch with the al-'Ashhab family and the issue was settled quickly after years of lobbying government offices and the Knesset and appealing to the courts.[91]

THE ATYPICAL RETURN OF THE ATTORNEY KHALIL TUMA 'ABBUD

We have seen what some Israeli institutions did to encourage the Arabs who remained in Israel to emigrate to far away countries, such as Argentina, Libya, and other elsewhere. *Al-Ittihad* published a news item in early 1952 exposing one such secret plan by the foreign ministry.[92] In tandem with the work by the Israeli authorities to have Jews from Libya immigrate to Israel, some employees of those authorities sought to convince Arab residents of Jaffa and other cities to emigrate from Israel to Libya. Many details of the immigration of the remaining Jews in the Arab states (including Libya) in which the intelligence agencies of many states were involved—such as the United States, Britain, and others—are still being kept secret from researchers.[93] Israel was successful in bringing Jews from Libya to Israel in the early 1950s, but it failed to convince the Palestinians who remained to leave their country.

Amidst these plans to encourage the immigration of Jews from Libya, the details of the story of the return of one Palestinian (a new arrival) could be woven into a literary work or film, with the hero being Khalil Tuma 'Abbud, who had been studying law in Britain before the war and the onset of the Nakba. He ended up in Tripoli, Libya, after a long journey and from there returned to Haifa in 1952. The story of his return along with hundreds of Libyan Jews on board a ship to Haifa is remarkable.

Khalil 'Abbud was born in 1926 in the village of al-Rama. After his father, Tuma, died when Khalil was nine years old, he lived alone with his widowed mother—her only son. After he completed secondary school, he travelled to London in 1945 to study law. He and his mother planned that he should return to Palestine on completion of his studies and that he would become a respectable lawyer in mandatory Palestine. The scholarship he won from the mandatory British government was sufficient to cover the cost of his studies at University College London (UCL) up to 1948. When war broke out, he had one more year to complete his studies. It did not occur to Khalil at the time that it might be wise to stop his studies and return to the Galilee. He said, "I did not think at the time that there would be problem concerning my return to the country after I completed my studies."[94]

Khalil 'Abbud was one of hundreds of Palestinians who had travelled to continue their studies in Beirut, Cairo, or in European countries before the Nakba. There were also dozens of businessmen and merchants outside Palestine when the war broke out. Many students and businessmen and others who were travelling for other reasons did not return to Palestine in 1948 and waited for the guns to fall silent. In earlier chapters we read the stories of some who returned to Haifa and the Galilee from Lebanon and other neighboring countries, but the Israeli authorities banned the return of hundreds of Palestinian students, although they were innocent of any wrongdoing. Palestine had disappeared from the map of the world, and many Palestinians found that their passports had become worthless after the end of the Mandate and the establishment of the state of Israel on the ruins of Palestine. The story of the student Khalil 'Abbud is typical of the situation of hundreds of others who, at the end of their studies, were cut off from their families and found themselves strangers in what was, out of necessity, a land of refuge.

In the summer of 1949, at the end of his studies, Khalil 'Abbud understood that his Palestinian passport would not enable him to visit his family in the Galilee. He therefore registered to continue his studies to obtain a master's degree. But after several months he decided to stop, and looked for a solution to his passport problem. It was then that he heard that Jordan was issuing passports at its London embassy, and granting citizenship to Palestinians. So he went to the embassy, and on 5 January 1950, he was issued a Jordanian passport (no. 033001). Then, he was faced with a dilemma: Where should he travel on that passport? Since five of his maternal uncles were living in Brazil he decided to go there, where he spent an enjoyable time with his relatives and found work in Sao Paulo as an English language teacher. At the end of the school year he decided to return to Europe and from there to Jordan, where he was now a citizen.

The ship on which Khalil 'Abbud was travelling took him from Brazil to Portugal and from there to Italy. From Italy he took another ship to Beirut, which stopped for a few hours in Alexandria. Since Khalil did not have an entry visa, he obtained a 24-hour transit permit for passage to Syria. When he reached Damascus, he met a number of his friends, and after spending a month there he travelled to Amman where he hoped to find work. He was not able to practice law in Jordan, so he took a temporary job teaching English. Libya was encouraging Palestinian professionals to come to work for the new government, so 'Abbud signed up to go work there, and a few months later he received a telegram informing him he had been accepted. He traveled via Cairo to Tripoli, where he was employed as a legal consultant at a government office.

In Tripoli, Khalil 'Abbud became acquainted with several Palestinians who, like himself, had come to work there, including Shawqi Bey al-Sa'd from Haifa.[95] Shawqi Bey had come to Tripoli with some of the British who had withdrawn from Haifa in 1948. These two Palestinians found many topics of conversation of mutual interest. The Sa'd family owned much land in the villages of Shajur and Kufr 'Inan which were close to al-Rama. Khalil's father was a large landowner in his village and was in the habit of selling land to cover his living expenses and to spend on his large house. Such topics and memories of Palestine and family before the Nakba stirred a yearning in Khalil 'Abbud for his village, his mother, and other relatives. One day Shawqi Bey surprised his guest Khalil with a direct question: whether he cared to go back to the Galilee. Naturally the answer was yes, but the more important question was how? Shawqi Bey said: "You will hear the answer to that right away."

Shawqi Bey al-Sa'd (according to Khalil 'Abbud's testimony) was head of the general security branch in Tripoli, which is similar to the British Criminal Investigation Department. Shawqi Bey picked up the telephone and spoke to Meir Shelon.[96] Khalil 'Abbud heard his host ask Shelon for help for a "dear friend by the name of Khalil 'Abbud," who wanted to return to Haifa and the Galilee. At the end of the conversation, Khalil asked who this Shelon was, and how could he help him in his journey? Shawqi Bey replied that Shelon was Israel's representative in Tripoli, with the rank of consul, and that his principal responsibility was to arrange for the remaining Jews in Libya to go to Israel on ships that sailed from Tripoli to Malta and Napoli and from there to Haifa. From that conversation it became clear that Shawqi Bey (the Palestinian refugee from Haifa) was the security official in charge of extending the residence visa of Shelon (the Israeli consul) in Tripoli. That is why Shelon said at the end of the conversation that he would investigate the available possibilities with the authorities and do what he could to help.

Just a few days later, Shelon invited Khalil 'Abbud to meet him, and he asked him to bring his passport so he could arrange a permit for him to enter Israel. Indeed, an entrance visa (no. 41227) was issued and opened the door for Khalil to return with the Jews who were emigrating from Libya to Israel. It is the remaining documentary proof of what happened to this Palestinian refugee. So, Khalil 'Abbud boarded the ship *Artsa*, which sailed to Haifa by way of Naples. His relatives were waiting for him at the port of Karmil and within hours had him back at his family's home. Thus Khalil 'Abbud was back in the Galilee after three years of moving from one country to the other in the Palestinian diaspora. The astonishing point in this story is that he achieved this as a "new immigrant" ["oleh hadash" in Zionist terms], based on an entrance visa printed on his Jordanian passport dated August 1952. On the first page of the passport was written in Hebrew: "Mr. 'Abbud Khalil relinquished his Jordanian citizenship in order to obtain Israeli citizenship."[97]

This is the story of a young Palestinian man whose Palestinian citizenship "evaporated" with the onset of the Nakba, and is an example of the consequences of the disaster of 1948. But the happy ending allowed Khalil 'Abbud to return to the Galilee and to become a lawyer and a teacher, and then a judge in Israel. Many like him who were studying outside Palestine were unable to return to their homeland as he did. One of those was Subhi Farah Khuri who began as a pharmacy student at the American University of Beirut in 1944. Subhi used to return to his family in Nazareth during summer break each year. He spent his last summer vacation there in 1947 and returned to Beirut in September by way of Ra's al-Naqura to complete his studies. When he graduated in 1951, his mother submitted an official application for his return to Nazareth, but the application was rejected despite the many recommendations that were submitted. His mother appealed to the Supreme Court for justice in seeking the return of her son,[98] but this court too rejected the mother's plea, leaving the family with no choice but to accept being divided from each other.

BETWEEN ROUTINE REPRESSION
AND TERRIFYING EVENTS

The agreement to transfer the Triangle to Israeli control included a clause according to which any citizen who decided to emigrate from his town or village had the right to take all his belongings from his house with him and to receive full compensation for the property and land he left behind. Israel brought pressure to bear on the residents of Wadi 'Ara to emigrate and leave the region. When the pressures and the temptations did not work, the authorities resorted to force to compel the residents of small villages to leave their homes and lands. Most of the forced migrants were moved to the village of Umm al-Fahm, Baqa al-Gharbiya, and several other villages. Thus, dozens of families were uprooted from the villages of Bayada, 'Ayn al-Sahla, 'Ayn al-Zaytuna, 'Ayn Jarar, and other hamlets.[99]

At the same time that the state was encouraging the inhabitants of the villages of the Triangle to migrate to the Arab side of the border, it intensified measures to prevent movement from there to the Israeli side. Several residents of the area paid with their lives for what Israel considered to be violations of its borders and laws. But the inhabitants, who had become accustomed for generations to move freely between the villages and cities of the area, did not stop altogether from crossing the border in both directions, despite the grave dangers. Thus, life for the population of the Triangle continued under repression and routine danger, on the one hand, and news about the killing of "infiltrators" and smugglers, on the other. The Israeli police and army would conduct searches of the houses and villages from time to time under the guise of security considerations. At times, the security forces themselves encouraged Palestinians whom they had recruited for the collection of intelligence to go back and forth, and even to assassinate people on the Jordanian side of the border.[100] Against this background, the line between ordinary and permitted movement and "infiltration" which cost people their lives remained hazy.

'Ara: Dead and Wounded in June 1952

The incident in 'Ara in which two were killed and five others wounded in the summer of 1952 at the hands of Israeli soldiers created a large political and media stir. The villagers had come close to the border on the Israeli side to meet their relatives on the Jordanian side on Eid al-Fitr (the feast ending the Ramadan fast), as had become customary each year. Such behavior was not unusual on feast days and special occasions and was permitted by the Israeli authorities and security forces. It is true that the killing of "infiltrators" or smugglers was routine in the early 1950s, but firing on unarmed civilians on a feast day when none of them had crossed the border or constituted a danger to anyone caused a disturbance in the press, the Knesset, and the government. The circumstances of this incident was replicated on a larger scale by the Kafr Qasim massacre of 1956. On both occasions, the narrative was of innocent citizens being fired on by soldiers in cold blood because they considered them to be "lawbreakers" with no prior notice being given of the application of a new policy that day.

On 21 June that year, the first day of Eid al-Fitr, the people of Wadi 'Ara prepared to meet their relatives from the Jordanian side near 'Ayn al-Sahla as usual each year.[101] The next day the army posted an observer force which prevented the villagers from coming near the border. However, those soldiers left the area at noon, and the villagers once again came close to the border so that they could see their relatives on the other side. On the morning of 23 June, the soldiers returned, and set a trap near the border. At 8:30 when dozens of villagers (men, women, and children) drew close to 'Ayn al-Sahla, the soldiers opened fire on them without warning. Two were killed and five others wounded, including an elderly man and two children eleven years of age.[102]

This painful incident made the population very angry, prompting denunciation by opposition parties and demands that the criminals be punished. MK Hanan Rubin of Mapam demanded that the officer responsible for giving the order to fire on innocent citizens be put on trial to remove the blot on the army's honor.[103] Other members of the Knesset went so far as to blame Prime Minister Ben-Gurion himself because he had not decided to have the accused tried. MKs Rustum Bastuni and Mordechai Bentov visited the village to offer their condolences, which soldiers in the village tried unsuccessfully to prevent.[104] An investigating committee was eventually formed which collected statements from all sides and submitted a report to the ministries of foreign affairs and security. Ben-Gurion announced the results of the investigation and said that the soldiers were not guilty of a criminal offense, just an unpremeditated error.[105]

Ben-Gurion chose to speak at length about the challenges that faced the army, the problem of "infiltration" in the region, and the difficult tasks with which the soldiers were burdened. Attorney Elias Kusa of Haifa replied to the speech by the prime minister and minister of defense in a letter rebutting the explanation of killing as combatting "infiltrators." In the case of 'Ara villagers there were no "infiltrators, just citizens who came close to the border from the Israeli side so that they could see their relatives."[106] But Ben-Gurion and the security establishment supported the soldiers and claimed that the problem lay in the error of the decision to shoot. Thus, this tragic incident was wrapped up and became part of a long sequence of ordinary events in which Arab citizens were killed by the police and army under the pretext of combatting infiltration. Due to the large number of such incidents in the villages of the Triangle, some villages created special cemeteries for "infiltrators."[107] In addition to hundreds killed along the borders and inside the West Bank, each year dozens of citizens of the Triangle were killed in their villages during combing and search operations for "infiltrators."

The Day of the Airplane: The Search Operation in al-Tira Village

The villagers of al-Tira faced major difficulties with their Jewish neighbors, who tried to occupy the village during the 1948 battles. The residents participated in the defense of their village alongside Iraqi volunteers under the command of Madlul 'Abbas. When the residents heard that the villages of the Triangle would soon be transferred to Israeli control, they became very fearful of retaliation from their neighbors. However, the first few years after the transfer (1949–52) passed relatively peacefully without any unusual incidents. In fact, the military government chose al-Tira in 1952 as the venue for celebrations of Israel's Independence Day for the entire Arab population of the south Triangle. The villagers, particularly the educated ones, exerted great efforts on that occasion to please the military government.

One al-Tira resident who was present at the time described those festivities in great detail, which included sports competitions, speeches, and the like.[108]

However, this relatively peaceful atmosphere changed abruptly following the allegation that gunfire from the village had been directed at an Israeli airplane; suddenly the al-Tira villagers felt the iron fist of the security forces. Some villagers feared that the army would carry out a massacre or expel the population as a belated reaction to their role during the war.[109] Suwaylih Mansur, the head of al-Tira's council, said that a curfew was imposed on the village on 31 July 1953. At 3:30 in the morning the search of the houses began, and continued throughout the day until 8:30 p.m. The army informed the village notables that an officer had been wounded the night before and that the accused was hiding in one of the houses of the village, which was why the military government was carrying out a combing operation.[110] At the end of the operation it became apparent that a great deal of damage had been done to the houses and their contents. In addition to the material damages, this incident had a psychological impact on the children who witnessed the soldiers insulting their relatives who had done nothing wrong.

MK Faris Hamdan visited al-Tira and held a press conference with Suwayla Mansur to expose the extent of the damages suffered by the villagers as a result of the breaking of furniture and the theft of valuable items by the soldiers.[111] A pregnant woman had suffered a miscarriage on the same day, and children had been terrorized by the violent conduct of the soldiers. MK Emil Habibi came to the village to express his support for the villagers and to examine the damages caused by the army operation in the village. The incident gave rise to critical reactions and condemnation by Arabs and Jews, who asked the government to investigate and to punish those responsible for the assaults on the al-Tira residents.[112] However, the acting defense minister, Pinhas Lavon, poured fuel on the fire in his satirical response in the Knesset, in the course of which he spoke arrogantly about the "excursion" by the soldiers and "the delicate pianos and aristocratic furniture" in the houses of al-Tira.[113]

The Story of the Conversion of the al-Subayh Arabs to Christianity

The story of the al-Subayh Arabs who settled near Mount Tabur is extraordinary and reflects a reality that challenges the imagination concerning the experiences of those who remained in Israel in the 1950s. Most of the clan of al-Subayh Arabs were forced to migrate during the Nakba and became refugees either in Jordan or Syria after the area was occupied and the Israeli army perpetrated a massacre in June 1948. Relations between al-Subayh Arabs and their Jewish neighbors had been generally good prior to the outbreak of the war. However, an incident in nearby kibbutz Keshet on 16 March 1948, in which seven Jewish young men were killed, including Eli Ben Tzvi, the son of a Zionist leader who became the second president of Israel, totally derailed good neighborly relations. Following that incident, voices were raised in the Knesset and outside it demanding immediate retribution; Yigal Alon, the head of the Palmach, calmed the atmosphere and urged postponing retaliation.

The time for vengeance came on 8 June 1948, to be exacted on the family of the head of the clan, 'Ali Nimr al-'Agla. That day most members of the al-Subayh clan were not at home, and dozens of the men who were there fled when they saw hundreds of Israeli troops heading towards their campsite. Only two blind men and two sisters of the head of the clan and their children remained. They were all killed and their bodies dismembered with axes and knives. Body parts were hidden in large oil containers so that the sight of the victims was blood chilling and terrifying. When the relatives returned, they buried the bodies in a collective grave in a cave near al-Mansur spring.[114]

This massacre had a tremendous impact on members of the clan, who tried to hide in Wadi Salama, the village of 'Ayn Mallaha, and elsewhere. Eventually, most of the clan left the area and became refugees in Jordan and Syria. A few dozen families who decided to stay found refuge among their relatives, al-Shibli Arabs. Some members of the al-Subayh clan who lost all their lands in the year of the Nakba became smugglers and would routinely cross the borders. The events of the 1948 war and the attending loss of land led to turbulent relations between the remaining clan members and the neighboring Jews. But in 1954 there was a unique event, due to the theft of some rifles from the Shadmot Dvora settlement.

Towards the end of 1954, rifles were stolen from the arsenal of the settlement near Mount Tabur in lower Galilee, and the settlers and police accused the al-Subayh clan of the theft with no evidence to substantiate their claim. The military government imposed a permanent curfew on the whole clan, which prevented them from making a living or maintaining contact with the neighboring Arab villages. The authorities also issued expulsion orders against some of those accused of the theft, who were exiled to Shafa 'Amr, Majd al-Krum, and Tarshiha.[115] This collective punishment and exile went on for six months, as did the curfew on the al-Subayh Arabs. In an effort to alleviate their misfortune, some clan notables climbed to the monastery on Mount Tabur and asked to convert to Christianity. The monks contacted the churches in Nazareth and the Vatican, while members of the clan started taking lessons on the Christian faith from the monks. This novel plan succeeded in lifting the siege imposed on them, and the press took up the story.

When the military government learned that the story of al-Subayh Arabs and the monastery had spread widely, they decided to end the embarrassing issue quietly. Some members of the clan (at the request of Giyura Zayed) agreed to go to Jordan to investigate the matter of the rifles and to acquire them.[116] Two of the rifles stolen from the settlement were brought back. The Israeli authorities came to believe that the theft had been motivated by commercial gain, not security considerations. That, along with the conversion of the clan to Christianity, contributed to the lifting of the curfew and the return to normal life. This story demonstrates the wide discretion of the military government in imposing collective punishment on the Arab population. On the other hand, the "craftiness" of the clan members and how they chose to press their grievances had proved useful; others who remained after the Nakba learned the sensitivities of the authorities and their weak points and exploited them for their own interests to counter the whims of the military governors.

The Events of Kufr Manda in 1954

In December 1954 the final touches were put on a plan to build a water catchment on the lands of Kufr Manda, between Shafa 'Amr and Nazareth. Attempts by the government to convince the villagers to sell their lands or to relinquish them for this purpose failed. When workers began to to build the catchment the villagers gathered to prevent further work on their lands in order to protect them from being confiscated. At one point, a clash broke out between the villagers and the police on the scene. The police responded to stone-throwing with violence and chased the villagers back to their homes, arresting dozens of them. On that day (13 December) the police led dozens of handcuffed detainees on foot from Kufr Manda to the Dhahir al-'Umar fort in Shafa 'Amr and locked them up in a stable for horses and other livestock. Some of the detainees were released after two or three days, but thirty-seven others were kept under detention and brought before a military court on the charge of assaulting police officers and obstructing their work and the work of employees of the water company.[117]

Hanna Abu Hanna visited the village a few days after the event, and recorded his impressions of the atmosphere in the village on "Uri's day," named after the officer responsible for the arrests.[118] The villagers told Abu Hanna and another Maki party activist about the clashes and arrests: Following the clash in the early hours of the morning, the police sent a large force of reinforcements that chased the inhabitants back to their houses. Many young men fled to the mountains while others hid in the mosque. The villagers said that dozens were arrested at the mosque and in their homes and were made to march a distance of twelve kilometers on foot to Shafa 'Amr. Abu Hanna heard the complaints of the villagers about the insults and the torture of the prisoners. That event, near the end of 1954, constituted the first mass protest action in defense of what was left of Arab land in the face of the policy of continuous expropriations since 1948.

The Communist Party, which played an important role in the struggle to protect what remained of Arab lands, attempted to organize protests and condemnation of what happened in Kufr Manda. In Nazareth, party representatives in the municipality demanded that an extraordinary session of the municipal council be convened, which the head of the council at the time refused. However, Khalil Khuri took advantage of the first ordinary session to declare that "the danger that the government may implement its project to steal the lands of al-Battuf and to expel over 15,000 Arab farmers there threatens all the masses of the Arab minority and not just the residents of al-Battuf."[119] After Nazareth, it was the turn of party activists in 'Ilabun, who signed a petition in the name of dozens of villagers which was sent to the prime minister, expressing their condemnation of the police attack on the Kufr Manda villagers and the arrest of dozens, including those injured, and forcing them to march on foot to Shafa 'Amr. The signatories ended their protest letter by saying: "The attack on the residents of Kufr Manda is an attack on all Arab citizens of Israel."[120]

A few days later another petition was submitted to the government concerning picking olives in 'Arraba and Dayr Hanna.[121] The text of these two petitions was similar to the text of the 'Ilabun petition. It was very clear that the Communist Party had organized this action of solidarity with the Kufr Manda villagers in protest against the violent assault in order to confront the daily policy of repression and the expropriation of land. To counter the military government policy of imposed isolation on the population, in the 1950s a movement of coordination and solidarity among the remaining Palestinians in their various locations was born. The activists of the Communist Party in Haifa and the Galilee, who had stood up to the military government policy since 1949, had acquired experience. They were therefore the natural candidates to lead the struggle in the villages of the Galilee. When news of the Kafr Qasim massacre spread two years later, Tawfiq Tubi and other Maki leaders were the first to break the silence which the Israeli government tried to impose on the event.

THE 1956 KAFR QASIM MASSACRE: A TURNING POINT

On 29 October 1956, just hours after Israel launched its aggression against Egypt, Border Guards perpetrated a massacre in which almost fifty people from the village of Kafr Qasim lost their lives. The villagers who became the victims did not know that the army had imposed a curfew on villages in the Triangle beginning one hour earlier than usual, at 5:00 p.m. instead of 6:00 p.m. When some of the villagers (men, women, and children) reached the village entrance, Border Guard troops stopped them at a barricade they had earlier erected, and opened fire on groups and on individuals, killing forty-nine people in cold blood.[122] Several others were killed that evening in other villages in the southern Triangle. This criminal act was the culmination of an Israeli policy of repression and discrimination, which saw the Palestinians remaining after the Nakba as a "fifth column" that was best eliminated. The massacre can also be seen as the result of statements by Israeli politicians who had been waiting for a second round of war with the Arabs in order to uproot and expel the remaining Palestinians. The aggression against Egypt and the massacre at the end of October 1956 represented a turning point in relations between Israel and its Arab citizens, reminding them that the Nakba had not ended with the war of 1948.

Some historians see the Sinai war and the massacre at Kafr Qasim as the result of the Israeli policy of collective punishment in the 1950s. For example, Benny

Morris wrote: "During that period, Israel implemented a policy along its entire border of shooting at infiltrators to kill. The soldiers, policemen, and border guards fired on everything that moved, particularly at night."[123] As is well known in Israeli historical literature, none of those killers was ever put on trial, neither members of the military nor civilian Jews who killed Arabs on both sides of the border. Morris added in *Israel's Border Wars* that "between 2,700 and 5,000 Arab infiltrators were killed. All indicators point to the fact that the vast majority of those killed were unarmed."[124]

Information about the massacre of the forty-nine victims from Kafr Qasim is well known and documented by the eyewitness testimonies of the survivors. There is also unanimity concerning the circumstances as well as the background of the event, which was the start of the Israeli invasion of Egypt as part of the Sinai War, along with France and Britain. The direct causes of the Kafr Qasim massacre and its details are documented in the court's judgment in the trial of the Border Guards. The few pages here merely attempt to place this massacre within the chain of painful events which began with the Nakba, to reveal to new generations the difficult times endured by the first generations of Palestinians who remained in Israel in the 1950s. There are still open questions for which the historical literature provides no definitive answers or consensus regarding the responsibilities of the Israeli political and military leaders at the time. Was the Kafr Qasim massacre part of a plan to terrorize the population of the southern Triangle to induce them to migrate, as had happened to hundreds of thousands of Palestinians in 1948?

As is well known, the Israeli government was obliged to put the officers and soldiers who carried out the massacre on trial. A great deal has been written in Israel concerning the fallout from this event inside the army, but few studies have investigated its consequences for relations between the state and its Arab citizens. To investigate the responsibility of the political and military Israeli leadership or the long-term objectives of what happened would require a special study and documents which are still unavailable to researchers. Here, the Kafr Qasim massacre is seen within the framework of the routine policy of Israeli repression since the end of the 1948 war, with its incidents of killing and terrorizing the Arab population.

The relationship between the Nakba in 1948 and the Kafr Qasim massacre became clear from the testimonies of some of those accused of participating in that crime. There is also a clear relationship between the killing of so-called infiltrators by the dozens, or hundreds, each year by soldiers with "itchy trigger fingers" and the killing of the Kafr Qasim villagers. Israeli soldiers in general and the Border Guards in particular had become used to killing Palestinians on both sides of the border without anyone being held accountable or punished for those crimes. This same policy had been implemented from time to time inside Arab villages in the Triangle and the Galilee. Consequently, the Border Guards in 1956 found nothing unusual in killing civilians who were returning to their homes in Kafr Qasim, nor did they think it illegal, particularly since they had received orders from their commanders to do so.

Among the series of retaliatory Israeli actions against targets in the West Bank, the operation in Qalqilya on the night of 10 October 1956 holds a special place because of its proximity to Kafr Qasim in location and time, two weeks prior.[125] 'Arif al-'Arif allocated special importance to the struggle of the inhabitants of that border city and their role in the 1948 war, and he devoted much space to the discussion of the bloody Israeli retaliatory act in October 1956 as a chapter in the struggle to hold onto the land.[126] Some Israeli leaders were apparently convinced that it was possible to cause the population of the southern Triangle to migrate under the smokescreen of the war in Sinai. Indeed, after the Qalqilya operation—which proved very costly to the Israeli side—its preparations for a war in the region increased.

Conditions in the Kingdom of Jordan under the young King Hussein were unstable. The parliamentary opposition, led by Sulayman al-Nabulsi, had won a majority. The government terminated the services of Glubb Pasha (Chief of Staff General John Bagot Glubb) and began coordinating with other Arab countries to safeguard its borders. With the beginning of summer 1956, the drums of war began to beat on the Israeli side, particularly after the costly Qalqilya operation, and a clash between the two sides seemed likely soon. The villages of the Triangle sensed that atmosphere and feared the results. When war broke out on the Egyptian front, far from the region, the tension and expectations of battles on the Jordanian front as well gave rise to the massacre in Kafr Qasim.

Operation Mole ("hafarperet" in Hebrew) was devised, according to which the army was supposed to expel the Arab population in the southern Triangle from their homes if war were to break out near the end of 1956. The researcher Ruvik Rosenthal uncovered some details of this plan, for which the army conducted exercises, and he believes that it was a cause of and the backdrop for the mindset which made the soldiers kill innocent civilians as though it was something ordinary.[127] According to this plan, the soldiers were to move the Arab inhabitants from their villages near the border in the southern Triangle to detention camps.[128] The available information on the planned operation reveals that the army looked on the Arabs as enemies who could be shoved into the camps. If we add to that the mood that was dominant in the ranks of the army, particularly the Border Guards, we can explain why they did not hesitate to fire on ordinary citizens returning from their fields to their homes. Those soldiers had become accustomed over the years to killing Arabs along the border, and they had no compunction against expelling them from their homes (according to Operation Mole) or opening fire on them and killing them when ordered to.

The Kafr Qasim massacre was the most shocking murder of Arab citizens after the 1948 war. Contrary to retaliation operations against Palestinian villages in the West Bank (Qibya, for example), the Kafr Qasim villagers were unarmed citizens of Israel who had not been charged with anything, and their basic transgression was to return home after the start of a curfew which they knew nothing about. This massacre, which was carried out by soldiers in the uniforms of

Israeli security forces, gave rise to condemnations which the government could not ignore. The Arab residents of Israel, who had become inured to the killing of those accused of infiltration, saw this massacre as crossing all red lines. The killing of dozens of innocents evoked memories of Dayr Yasin and the other massacres of 1948. Others saw it as worse and uglier because it was carried out by members of the Border Guards in official uniform under military orders from their superiors. The Kafr Qasim massacre was a lamentable event in the memory of residents of the Triangle, particularly those who remained in Israel after the Nakba.

CONCLUSION

The stories of individuals and villages presented in this chapter reflect the conditions of the difficult daily life of those who remained, and the bloody events which they endured. Even after the end of the war, Israeli policy sought for many years to reduce the number of Arab citizens and to expropriate the largest possible amount of their lands. This policy did not always achieve its goals because those who remained did not surrender to what the government and its institutions had planned for them. In many cases they proved that they could challenge that policy and defeat it. The stories of the residents of three Arab villages who returned to their homes ('Ilabun, 'Illut, and Kufr Qari') are examples of challenge and success in overcoming that general policy. Despite the weakness of the Arab residents and their isolation, they succeeded in enduring on their lands until the voices of the governments demanding their expulsion fell silent. In this context, the Kafr Qasim massacre occupies an important place in the drama of challenge and endurance. Despite the horrific nature of the massacre, the residents of Kafr Qasim and neighboring villages did not think of leaving their homes and migrating.

Those who remained in Israel under the shadow of a general policy occasionally found a narrow margin of possibility to overcome that policy. The way in which those who remained took advantage of those opportunities breaks the static black-and-white mold employed in most studies of the 1948 war and of Israel's war on so-called infiltrators in the 1950s. The stories of people and of villages represent a living example of local history—placing the Palestinians as human beings at the center of attention, rather than a symbol of lost cause and usurped collective rights. It also sheds light on the other side of Israeli historical literature, which basically recounts the victors' heroism without looking at the other side's tragedy; it speaks of the success of Palestinian villages and individuals in triumphing over policies of repression and expulsion. The Palestinians were not just powerless and hapless victims; often they were successful in defining their own destiny, in refusing to surrender to what others had planned for them.

The struggle and endurance of those to remain in their homes and their estranged homeland continued up to 1956, at least. Even the residents of villages which were not depopulated or severely damaged during the war found themselves in its aftermath fighting to keep their lands in al-Battuf plain, al-Shaghur villages, and elsewhere. Having gotten hold of the lands of refugees and those it had forcibly expelled, Israel and its settler institutions focused on expropriating the lands of those who remained—under the pretext of security and development. In this respect, there was little difference between the villagers of the Triangle or the Galilee or other regions; the villagers of the Triangle suffered because of their proximity to the Jordanian border due to a policy of repression and expulsion which reached its climax in the 1956 Kafr Qasim massacre. But the seeds of that horrific crime were embodied in the villages of the "border strip" between Wadi 'Ara and Kafr Qasim years before the event itself.

The Struggle to Remain

Between Politics and the Judiciary

UNDER "DEMOCRATIC" MILITARY RULE

Israel was established as a state for the Jews, not as a state for all of its citizens who have lived there since 1948. The tension, if not the outright contradiction, between its claim to democracy and this raison d'être is inseparable from its nature, its self-definition, and the general interest of Zionism. The fact that Israel never adopted a constitution, not even a human and citizens' rights document, makes the remaining Palestinians totally dependent on the good behavior of the Jewish majority. While it is true that the Declaration of Independence[1] (which affirms the Jewish character of the state) contains promises of civil equality and suitable representation for the Arab residents if they choose to live peacefully with the Jews, these promises were never translated into action, in 1948 or later. As we saw in previous chapters, the army and other Israeli institutions did what was in their power to reduce the number of Palestinians in Israel as far as possible. Even the surviving Palestinians did not escape acts of maltreatment and repression or the expropriation of their lands and property, which is inconsistent with the promises in the Declaration of Independence.

Several parties played a role in controlling the lives of the Palestinians remaining in Israel. Prime Minister and Defense Minister Ben-Gurion and his advisors were the most prominent among those parties. Others on both the left and right tried to influence the policies and decisions concerning the Palestinians. The two Mapam ministers in the interim government (which conducted the war) and some Mapam party activists in the office of minority affairs minister Bechor Shitrit supported a moderate and fair policy. In Nazareth and elsewhere they tried to back the position and activities of members of the National Liberation League. When the leaders of the ruling Mapai party fought against this alignment, Shitrit coordinated with Moshe Sharett, the second in line in the party after Ben-Gurion.

Despite this coordination, tensions mounted between the office of the minister in charge of minority affairs and those working for the military government in the final months of the war, until this tension manifested itself in open confrontations and contributed to the cancellation of the ministry of minority affairs and the transfer of its responsibilities to the military government and other parts of the government.

Minister Shitrit (b. 1895) was in charge of two ministries that were important for the Arab residents: police and minorities. This minister believed he was a more qualified expert on Arab affairs than anyone else in the government. Not only did he speak Arabic, he had grown up in a family that had come from Morocco to Tiberias in the mid-nineteenth century.[2] These qualifications made him the man to go to with complaints about the actions of the army and the military government. Shitrit usually took these complaints to Ben-Gurion, who was responsible for the army and its conduct, but instead of looking into them Ben-Gurion supported the army and covered up its actions, which weakened the minister's influence. Shitrit defended a lenient policy that took the interests of Arab residents into account, contrary to most leaders of the army and the ruling party who saw the Arabs as a fifth column. Previously, we saw examples of Shitrit's actions regarding the residents of the Galilee in 1948 which contributed to some of them being able to remain.

Shitrit's policy and his willingness to help the Arab residents who came to him annoyed those responsible in HaKeren HaKayemet and other Zionist organizations which were trying to wrest away control of Arab lands. Following the first elections and the formation of the Ben-Gurion government early in 1949 without Herut or Maki and even without Mapam, Mapai acquired a central role in deciding the fate of the Arabs and state policy towards them. Earlier, Shitrit had on more than one occasion opposed the entry of the army into Arab villages and the maltreatment of the residents and arbitrary arrests and expulsions. He also opposed the policy of tearing down houses and the illegal expropriation of land.[3] These positions were not in harmony with Ben-Gurion's policy and the position of his advisors from the Mapai party. So Shitrit's complaints became a burden on the ruling establishment, particularly the military government. The closing down of the ministry of minority affairs in June 1949 was one of the first indications of an iron-fist policy and the growing role of members of the Mapai party who encouraged agents and collaborators with the government and its institutions.[4]

Isolating the Arabs from the rest of the citizens of Israel and imposing military rule over them had abrogated their political rights. The military government resorted to the 1945 defense (emergency) regulations to legitimize the policy of repression, theft, and the expulsion of thousands of those who remained in the Galilee and elsewhere. The government's policy made Arab residents accused of being perpetual violators of those unjust laws. The imposition of permanent curfews at night, limiting the mobility of citizens, and the system of permits which were granted to those with close connections and denied to the rest, deprived people of a dignified life and basic rights. Even within Arab towns and villages the army declared large tracts of land "military zones" which the owners of the land were prohibited from entering or cultivating. In this way the system of military rule strangled the economy of Arab citizens and prohibited the development of their towns and villages so as to make it easier to control them. Ian Lustick well described and analyzed Israeli policy towards the Palestinian minority, which relied on control through a system of isolation under tight military rule.[5]

The policy of persecuting the remaining Arabs focused on three basic areas: controlling the economy and politics, controlling the movement of the population, and controlling their time. Despite this suffocating policy, those who remained sometimes managed to exploit the multiplicity of institutions that dealt with their issues to their own advantage. For example, they used the desire of several political parties to gain their votes in order to break down the isolation barriers and end their full dependence on the military government system. Some Zionist organizations, such as the labor organization Histadrut, allowed Arab activists room to breathe. Some Palestinians had recourse to Israeli courts in their search for justice and fairness, particularly the Supreme Court. This chapter will provide real-life examples of Arab citizens making use of the opportunities provided by civil organizations, particularly the courts, to overcome some of the actions and policies of the military government.

Against this background, noteworthy is the spirit of refusing to surrender to the policy of repression and rising to the challenge through peaceful means, such as making use of the court system. *Al-Yawm* mentioned in early 1949 that ten Arab lawyers had been permitted to bring cases in Israeli courts.[6] The most prominent and active of these were Hanna Naqqara and Elias Kusa from Haifa and two members of the Zu'bi family from Nazareth. Later a number of those whom Israel permitted to return, as we saw in previous chapters, joined them, but some of the ten original lawyers left the country and moved to neighboring Arab states. Consequently, up to the mid-1950s, there were still fewer than a dozen Arab lawyers in Haifa and the Galilee, and most of the lawyers were not fluent in Hebrew, which made it difficult for them to represent their clients in Israeli courts and other institutions. However, their mastery of the English language and the experience they had gained in the days of the Mandate allowed them to play an important role in the legal profession and in the area of extra-parliamentary public policy.

STORIES FROM JAFFA

The disappearance of this Palestinian city and the expulsion of its Arab population led to significant shrinkage in the number of political and cultural elites among those who remained. Apart from Nazareth, a few thousand in 'Akka and Haifa escaped displacement in northern Palestine. Outside Haifa and the Galilee, the number of Arabs remaining in the cities occupied by Israel in 1948 was limited indeed. The few thousand Palestinians remaining in Jaffa and Lydda and al-Ramla found themselves isolated and tied to the military government's repressive policy. However, in what came to be known as the "mixed cities" in the early 1950s, the military government was cancelled, but not before the agencies of the military government and state institutions completed their mission to loot the contents of Arab houses. Those remaining in these cities were isolated in a quarter fenced off with barbed wire. This policy of persecution affected rich and poor and no one escaped, not even prominent leaders.

Unlike the case of Haifa, some of whose residents found refuge in Nazareth and other places in upper Galilee and returned to the city later, Jaffa's displaced residents who had sought refuge in Lydda and al-Ramla were expelled, along with tens of thousands of the native population of those two cities. Whereas the Arab population of Haifa increased, the 3,000 who remained in Jaffa did not increase by much after the end of the war; only a few hundred Jaffa residents returned to their homes after the Nakba, while hundreds of others were forced to leave the city. Haifa's Arab population continued to absorb refugees from the Galilee cities and villages, but all of the villages in the region of Jaffa, Lydda, and al-Ramla were destroyed and had their residents expelled. Thus, those who remained in Jaffa found themselves living in a ghetto surrounded by old and new Israeli settlements.[7] Jaffa became the backyard of Tel Aviv, which developed and grew at Jaffa's expense. The following pages provide examples of the experiences of some leaders who tried to challenge and resist these Israeli policies.

Only a few thousand residents remained in the "Bride of the Sea" (Jaffa), which had had a population of seventy thousand Palestinians before the war. The bloody clashes that erupted between the Jews of Tel Aviv and the Arabs of al-Manshiyya and other neighborhoods in Jaffa did not leave many choices besides surrender or migration. Indeed, most details of the story of those who stayed in Jaffa after May 1948 are still unclear and require historical research and documentation. Most of what has been written about the city represents the point of view of the victors and omits the stories of the vanquished and their bitter experiences. However, a number of books published recently in Hebrew and Arabic shed light on the history of this city and its own special Nakba. These books, in addition to the documents and decisions of the Supreme Court and the testimonies of those who remained, enable us to glean a partial picture of the events of the Nakba in Jaffa in 1948 and of the fate of those who survived and continued to live there after the war.

After the fall of Haifa and the expulsion of its Arab population at the end of April 1948, the British feared a repetition of scenes from Haifa and the accusation of conniving with the Jews against the Palestinians. At the end of that month, attacks by the Irgun against al-Manshiyya quarter intensified and terrorizing news about the fate of its inhabitants began to spread. At that point, the British applied pressure on Ben-Gurion and the mayor of Tel Aviv to halt the Irgun attacks on Jaffa, and they followed this up by sending forces to the area and threatening to bomb Tel Aviv if the attacks on Jaffa did not stop. These measures led to a cease-fire and a respite from the constant bombardment of Jaffa but they did not save the city from falling nor did they prevent the expulsion of the majority of its population. During the truce in early May, Yusif Haykal, the mayor of the city, and some of its other leaders left. However, at least four remained, and under the leadership of Hajj Ahmad Abu-Laban, signed a surrender agreement on 13 May with the leader of the Haganah in Tel Aviv. The following day, 15 May, the British pulled out of Jaffa and the Jews entered in celebratory processions, waving flags and attacking the Palestinians who had remained in their homes.

Israel, which was officially established as a state one day after the surrender agreement was signed between the Jaffa leaders and the Haganah, did not honor the terms of the agreement or commitments it had made. Search operations conducted by the Haganah "were not gentle or polite, much property and furniture was stolen or destroyed by the soldiers and the civilians."[8] Complaints by the residents about ill treatment, theft, and damage of property were futile. One official wrote a report to the minister of minorities and police on 25 May 1948, saying: "I saw soldiers, civilians and policemen as well as military police themselves committing theft and robbery."[9] The savage maltreatment of the remaining Arabs included the rape of a twelve-year-old girl by soldiers and other attempted rapes, and the murder of fifteen Arabs whose bodies were found near the port, apparently at the hands of Haganah troops and its intelligence branch (Shai).[10]

The Jaffa leaders who had signed the surrender agreement, the Emergency Committee, appealed to the Israeli authorities on several occasions to protect citizens and their property, and to allow some residents who had become refugees in Lydda and al-Ramla to return, as specified in the 13 May agreement, quoting the relevant articles.[11] Yitzhak Chizik (subsequently Horfi), the first military governor of Jaffa, passed on the letter and the complaints to Minister Shitrit. The correspondence irritated members of the cabinet and the prime minister, and this was discussed by the ministers.[12] Finally, the cabinet adopted a decision on 16 June not to allow the refugees to return to their homes. The continuing complaints by the signatories of the surrender agreement concerning the refugees and rights of the remaining residents of Jaffa became an irritant for the Israeli side which was dealt with by shrouding it in silence using all means available.

While the Jaffa leaders were trying to defend the remaining Arab residents of the city, Israeli military and political leaders were exchanging ideas on how to expel the remaining Arabs in 'Akka. About four thousand Palestinians, either original residents or refugees from Haifa and other places, were left in the city. In early July, the Northern Command decided to expel the Arabs that remained in 'Akka to either somewhere beyond Israel's borders or to Jaffa. This was resisted by several parties. Yaakov Shimoni, the foreign ministry official who had heard about the army's plans, sent letters to Foreign Minister Sharett and Minister of Minorities Shitrit inquiring about their reactions. The latter hastened to express his opposition to expelling the residents, and made reference to the decision by the

General Staff that "residents should not be expelled from their location without a written order from the minister of defense." Shitrit added in his response of 19 July that as long as "the minister of defense has not adopted a clear position and issued a written order, the northern army command is prohibited from expelling the population of an entire city and maltreating women, old men, and children."[13]

The plan to expel the remaining population of 'Akka was likely indeed foiled due to the opposition of Minister Shitrit and his referencing the need for a written order from Ben-Gurion. It is well known that the latter was careful not to issue written orders to expel the population. The expulsion of forty thousand residents of Lydda and al-Ramla in the same period had caused a commotion which had not yet quieted down at the time. As a reminder, the day after the occupation of Nazareth on 16 July, the Northern Command tried to expel the population, but the insistence of the officer Ben Dunkelman on a written order from Ben-Gurion was a major factor in the ability of the residents of the city to remain in their homes. Those days in mid-July were rife with attempts to uproot Palestinians from the cities occupied by Israel, but some of these plans were never realized. The Palestinian survivors in 'Akka remained in their city, but Jews were allowed to enter the city to live in some quarters, so it became a "mixed city."

The military governor of the city of Jaffa, Yitzhak Chizik, tried in vain to respond to the complaints of the residents and their leaders to halt the maltreatment of residents and the abuse of their property. His correspondence with the prime minister and the government achieved nothing, which drove him to submit his resignation (on 25 July 1948) shortly after his appointment. Ben-Gurion appointed the attorney Meir Laniado as his successor, who, a few days after assuming the office of military governor, had all the remaining Arabs moved to al-'Ajami quarter, which became known as the ghetto. This step caused angry reactions from the Arab residents and their leaders, but the entry of Jewish soldiers and civilians into Arab homes and the eviction of the residents by force was not prevented. This situation of maltreatment of the remaining Palestinians in Jaffa continued for weeks and months without anyone stopping those repeated attacks.

THE KAFKAESQUE STORY OF HAJJ AHMAD ABU-LABAN

Ahmad Abu-Laban was born in Jaffa in 1910 and became one of the most prominent political activists in the city during the British Mandate. His family was well-to-do, and sent him to continue his education at the American University of Beirut. Later Hajj Abu-Laban became a successful businessman and a member of the Jaffa municipal council. During 1947–48 he became a leading member of the Arab party led by Hajj Amin al-Husayni and the treasurer of the National Committee in Jaffa.[14] After attacks on the city intensified in late April 1948, an Emergency Committee was established on 3 May to safeguard the lives and property of the remaining Palestinians in Jaffa. This committee had six members, with Abu-Laban at the head. Abu-Laban received the keys to the public institutions in the city, including the offices in the municipality, from the mayor, Yusif Haykal.[15] As recounted earlier, Abu-Laban and his colleagues, the members of the Emergency Committee, signed a document with the Haganah leader in Tel Aviv, Michael Ben-Gal, concerning the surrender of Jaffa.

The surrender document included promises to respect the civil rights of the residents of the city, and the orders issued by the Haganah commander on the day the document was signed were consistent with the spirit and letter of the agreement. The document also provided that no one in the city would be arrested or imprisoned, even if they had taken part in the fighting against the Jews,[16] and that those who had been expelled from Jaffa could return to their homes. However, those commitments evaporated in the days that followed. The assaults on the Palestinians turned their lives into a hell, as dozens were killed or wounded due to arbitrary shootings and hundreds were expelled from their homes. Figures on the number of Arab martyrs in Jaffa vary, with some estimates of up to 700 killed, of which 450 were residents of the city.[17] But the details of what happened in the city after its occupation are still scattered and obscure.

Members of the Emergency Committee who signed the surrender agreement of the city, under the leadership of Ahmad Abu-Laban, tried to stop the attacks on the inhabitants who remained, but to no avail. As a result of the large number of complaints Abu-Laban himself became a target of repression and assaults. At first he received letters at the municipality containing implicit threats warning him to "to keep quiet" and to tend to his own affairs.[18] When he continued to complain, the police arrested him, initially putting him under house arrest at his home in Jaffa near the end of July 1948, but then subsequently arresting him on the charge of illegal possession of arms. The police asked the magistrate court to extend his arrest by ten days until 16 August, which the court agreed to do, at the central prison in Jaffa. After ten days, the police asked to extend his detention, and the court agreed to an additional eight days.[19]

After the second extension, the judge said the defendant should be allowed to see his lawyer. This recommendation contributed to the release of Abu-Laban without an indictment at the end of the eight days. But the relief of Abu-Laban and his family was short-lived, as the authorities decided to teach him a lesson in a more effective way. The tale of Abu-Laban's detention and imprisonment went on in a manner reminiscent of Kafka's stories. File no. 1860/1950-76 in the Israeli Army and Security Forces Archives in Tel Aviv relates some of the details of the "disappearance" of Hajj Ahmad Abu-Laban. The message of the Abu-Laban affair to the remaining residents of Jaffa was unmistakable, with no ambiguity attached: if the leader of Jaffa was not immune to Israeli repression and maltreatment, the common people among Jaffa's Arabs were all the more at risk. The fact that Abu-Laban was the leader who signed the agreement with the Haganah and that he had inherited leadership of the city did not aid him when he tried to stand in the way of the displacement of the surviving Arab population of the Bride of the Sea.

On 12 September 1948, Hajj Abu-Laban was arrested again. When his lawyer, Yitzhak Benyamini, asked to see his client at the central prison in Jaffa, he was told that "the detainee is in the military section so he should see the military police."[20] The lawyer went to the military government offices and returned with a permit to see the detainee. When he presented this document at the military prison in Jaffa, the man in charge told him that the detainee Abu-Laban was not there and added that the order of the military governor was not compulsory. At that point attorney Benyamini sent several letters to Minister of Police Shitrit, who replied that the civil police were not in charge of this detainee. The lawyer did not receive an answer to his letters to the army's judicial counsellor and the military governor.

When the attorney Benyamini found all doors closed to him, he went to the Supreme Court, which issued a writ to the minister of defense asking him to show why Ahmad Abu-Laban had not been released. Attorney Haim Cohen (who later became a famous Supreme Court judge) replied in the name of the ministry of defense acknowledging all the facts and information which had been presented by Benyamini to the court. The long proceedings in the Abu-Laban case before the Supreme Court continued from 1 November to 3 January 1949 when a ruling was issued. It was clear from the first session that Abu-Laban was an administrative detainee under article 111 of the 1945 defense (emergency) regulations. In summary, the Supreme Court ruled that the detention had not been carried out in accordance with the legally required administrative procedures, and ordered that Abu-Laban be released.[21]

Even then, the ruling by the Supreme Court did not lead to the immediate release of Hajj Ahmad Abu-Laban. File no. 298/5 in the Israeli Central State Archives in Jerusalem contains several documents from the office of the minister of minorities dealing with the necessity of releasing him. Several Hebrew newspapers published the court decision and the fact that he had not been released several days later despite the court ruling.[22] When over ten days had passed after the court order and he had still not been released from prison, the people of Jaffa prepared a petition with 1,500 signatures which they sent to the Minister of Police and Minorities Shitrit asking him personally to act quickly to secure the implementation of the order. The minister sent a copy of the petition dated 15 January 1949 to the head of the military government a week later.[23] Another week passed without the minister receiving an answer to his letter, so he sent a second letter directly to the prime minister and defense minister asking him for an answer so that he could reply to the petition and letters from the people of Jaffa.[24]

In the end Hajj Abu-Laban was released several weeks after the court order was issued, but his life, and that of his family, was not easy even when he was outside of prison. The authorities found new ways to exact revenge, and to give people like him a lesson within the limits of "democracy" in Israel. Threats against his life continued, and there were physical assaults, apparently by men working with the authorities and collaborators.[25] Hajj Abu-Laban understood that his life and the future of his family was in danger, so he decided to emigrate to Jordan shortly after he was released. Information about his migration and the circumstances under which it took place is scanty. *Haaretz* commented at the time that the case would constitute a dangerous precedent if it turned out that "the tension between the rule of law and the administrative authority does not lead to the victory of the law."[26]

Hajj Abu-Laban and many members of his family joined the tens of thousands of refugees from Jaffa in the Arab countries. Many of those close to him among the remaining Arab population in the city learned a lesson from the calamity that struck their leader. Abu-Laban was not alone in the bitter experience of repression and the silencing of voices raised against Israel seizing most of the property of the residents of Jaffa. Indeed, many of the leaders and well-educated people in Jaffa who remained in 1948 found they could not live in their city because of this persecution, among them merchants, businessmen, and professionals, such as doctors with well-known names.[27] As a result of this Israeli policy of repression in Jaffa (as compared to Haifa), only a very small number of the city's elite remained.

Salah Ibrahim al-Nadhir was a member of the Emergency Committee that signed the Jaffa surrender agreement on 13 May 1948. Born in Hebron in 1910 and a graduate of Terra Sancta College and then the Arab College in Jerusalem in 1931, he was the director of the Riyadh Construction Company in Jaffa, a building contractor. His story of the fall of the city and the aftermath in Jaffa was published in Amman recently.[28] From his account, he left the city on 14 May 1948, with the last of the withdrawing British forces. He reached al-Ramla and tried in vain to contact his friends, the other members of the Emergency Committee, by telephone. Finally, he joined the many caravans of refugees and went to Amman, and lived there until his death in 1992.[29]

Amin Andrawus, another signatory of the Jaffa surrender agreement, was a merchant and a dealer in imported cars, well known to Arabs and Jews in the city up to 1948. Despite his diverse connections, he decided to send his daughters to a safe place in Jordan before the fall of Jaffa. One of his daughters, Widad, testified that her father refused to leave his house and move to al-'Ajami quarter in compliance with the order from the Israeli authorities. Members of the Emergency Committee submitted a letter on 20 August complaining about "concentrating all Arab inhabitants in one region."[30] Andrawus was able to keep his house due to his bargaining skills and talent in balancing the military government's policy and his personal interests. He scored another success when he brought his children back from Jordan in early 1950 through the family reunification plan. The semi-official paper *Al Yawm* published an item about the return of 117 Arab Jaffa residents to their homes, followed by an item listing the names of the returnees, which included Andrawus's three daughters, Laila, Widad, and Su'ad, and their 14-year-old brother, Salim.[31] Andrawus succeeded in securing the return of his children, but he lost much of the land he owned to state expropriation. He and his family remained in Jaffa after the Nakba and he lived there until his death in 1972.

In the first phase of the history of the Jewish state, the Palestinians who remained had to prove their loyalty to the state, or at least their non-opposition to the policies of the government and its settlement institutions, in order for them to continue to live in peace. Even the basic rights of Arab individuals in Israel were conditional and were granted as an act of charity. Those who believed they could resist the policy of repression and the theft of Arab land and property found themselves in many cases in a similar situation as Hajj Ahmad Abu-Laban.

Ahmad Abd al-Rahim, also a member of the Emergency Committee who signed the 13 May document, was one of Jaffa's well-known wealthy residents. His family, had moved to the city in the early nineteenth century and were owners of citrus orchards and prominent exporters of oranges. Abd al-Rahim built one of the most beautiful houses in the city in al-'Ajami quarter (1 Toulouse Street). The Tel Aviv architect Yitzhak Rappaport had designed the house and oversaw its construction in the mid-1930s.[32] Shortly after the fall of Jaffa, Abd al-Rahim decided to emigrate, but before he did so, he rented the house to the French consul through Rappaport, and later sold the house to the consulate. In this way a wealthy man from Jaffa managed to protect some of his property from being expropriated or stolen, and he went to live in Beirut.

THE RETURN OF FAKHRI JADAY

Fakhri Jaday had big dreams when he finished high school at the Collège des Frères in 1943 and travelled to Beirut to study pharmacology at St. Joseph University.[33] His studies at the French university went well despite the tragedies of World War II. Even when the skirmishes began in Palestine, and residents of Jaffa were descending on Beirut in the thousands, he did not think that he ought to stop studying and return to the "Bride of the Sea." Ahmad 'Abd al-Rahim, whose story was just described, was one of the Jaffa residents who came to Beirut.[34] He informed Fakhri and other refugees from Jaffa about conditions in the city. But generally speaking, there were conflicting news reports, including news about his parents. His father said in a letter to Fakhri that he had thought of coming to Beirut, but his mother, who was ill, and his sister strongly objected to the idea. The father asked his son to prepare to return to Jaffa, awaiting approval by the Israeli authorities of a request for family reunification. Indeed, the approval came and Fakhri was able to return to his family and city in 1950.

Fakhri Jaday returned from Beirut on 15 October 1950 by way of Ra's al-Naqura in a Red Cross car. The joy of the family at being reunited eclipsed the bitter reality through which the remaining Palestinians in Jaffa were living. But Fakhri, who had grown accustomed to the fast pace of life in Beirut, found it hard to adapt and became bored and depressed by what he saw each day on his way from the family home to the pharmacy in al-'Ajami. A year after his return, he decided to go to Paris to continue his studies and earn a PhD, but his family, who had been over-joyed by the return of their son from Beirut, did not consent to lose him again so that he could continue his studies abroad. The family's second son, Tony, who had gone to Los Angeles to continue his studies, had married an American and had begun a family in the United States. After pleading from his sick mother and his elderly father, Fakhri changed his mind about traveling abroad. Later, he inherited the family pharmacy from his father, where he worked for ten years after his return at the end of 1950.[35]

Despite Fakhri Jaday's decision to stay in Jaffa, he continued to find it extremely difficult to accept the city's new reality, and renewed attempts to convince his parents to accept his idea to continue his studies abroad. But his mother, who "wanted him by her side," remained adamantly opposed. As the years passed Fakhri grew more bitter whenever he compared his own circumstances in al-'Ajami quar-ter with the successful life of his brothers, emigrants to London and the United States.[36] His brothers had not been the only ones to leave Jaffa just before or after the Nakba. Most of the sons of the elite who had remained after 1948 left for one reason or the other in the early 1950s. One example was Hasan Barakat, another member of the Emergency Committee. Fakhri mentioned in his testimony that "Barakat owned plantations which he sold, and emigrated because he found great difficulty in staying and participating in rebuilding Jaffa." He added that of the one thousand Armenians who lived in Jaffa up to 1950, all but a very few had departed the city.[37] Fakhri Jaday's testimony is like a eulogy for the Bride of the Sea, which had been one of the most developed Palestinian cities, but which became a hinter-land for Tel Aviv. The Jewish city, built in the early twentieth century, "swallowed" its Palestinian neighbor, much as Israel did to Palestine after 1948.

The Jaday family was relatively successful in being able to keep their home and pharmacy in al-'Ajami quarter, unlike the experience most of the middle class and the wealthy in the city, such as Bassam al-Ayyubi. Bassam was the only son of the well-known merchant Harbi al-Ayyubi, one of the leaders of the Palestinian national movement in mandatory Jaffa. When Fakhri Jaday returned from Beirut he could not find his classmate Bassam and the rest of his family; they had left Jaffa in the spring of 1950. Fakhri heard from his father that the Ayyubi family could not continue living in the city after it fell under Israeli control, like many members of the elite. We know very little about the circumstances of the migration of Bas-sam and his family. However, the story of his uncle, the attorney Subhi al-Ayyubi, is well known and documented because he took his case to the Supreme Court, as we shall relay in the following pages.

As we saw previously, *al-Ittihad* newspaper persisted in exposing the injustices of military rule in Haifa and the Galilee. Since the beginning of the 1950s, it had uncovered many Israeli plans to expel the remaining Palestinians and force them to emigrate. In one news article, the paper exposed the policy of forcing Arabs to immigrate to Libya. It mentioned that Muhammad Nimr 'Awda, the former British agent, was a party to this policy, and that 'Awda was living in Libya and encouraging the absorption of Palestinians to work there.[38] The paper gave as an example of the success of this policy the case of the attorney Subhi al-Ayyubi of Jaffa. According to the news item, Subhi al-Ayyubi "recently sold all his belongings in the country and immigrated to Libya." The paper concluded its report by asking who was behind the emigration of Arabs from Israel to Libya.

So, then: who was Muhammad Nimr 'Awda, whom al-Ittihad accused of being an Israeli collaborator, and who encouraged Palestinians in the country to immigrate to Libya? And what are the circumstances that led the attorney Subhi al-Ayyubi to leave Jaffa?

Muhammad Nimr 'Awda was a prominent communist activist during the British Mandate. Because of his good relations with the Palestinian nationalist movement, the leaders of the Palestine Communist Party delegated him to gather information on the movement and pass it on to them. But this activity actually brought him closer to the nationalist movement and he apparently began to convey information about the Communist Party to the leaders of the nationalist movement.[39] Furthermore, some of 'Awda's independent initiatives and his nationalist positions caused friction between him and the leaders of the Communist Party, which led to a rupture in relations between them. 'Awda was accused of being an informant to the Arab Higher Committee, and he was thrown out of the leadership of the Communist Party in 1940 under the charge of "nationalist deviation."[40] 'Awda went to Iraq in 1941, where he participated in Rashid 'Ali al-Kaylani's revolt against the British and the Hashemite regime in Iraq. In this connection, Fu'ad Nassar, who became general secretary of the Liberation League, had also gone to Iraq like 'Awda and participated in the al-Kaylani revolt.[41]

The available information on the life and activities of 'Awda following his return from Iraq to Palestine is scarce. It would appear that his participation in the Arab Revolt (1936–39) against Britain and his close relations with the mufti Amin al-Husayni and his followers caused the leaders of the party, particularly the Jews among them, to distance themselves from him. Musa al-Budayri, who studied the history of the Communist Party under the British Mandate, published a book recently that includes interviews he conducted with leaders of the party.[42] One of those interviews was with Nimr 'Awda, in Beirut on 15 March 1974, revolving around his political activities in the 1940s, but without explaining much about the charges levelled against him of being a former collaborator with Britain. At the end of the interview, however, there is specific reference to his dispute with the Communist Party. 'Awda was answering a question about the communists' suspicions concerning his political position and the charge of "nationalist deviation." He mentioned that after his return from Iraq he did not join the Liberation League, whose activists joined the Israeli Communist Party (Maki) in 1948, as we mentioned earlier.[43]

THE TRAGIC AFFAIR OF THE ATTORNEY SUBHI
AL-AYYUBI AND HIS DEPARTURE FROM JAFFA

Subhi al-Ayyubi was a prominent name in Jaffa on the list of city leaders from the 1920s as an activist in the Islamic-Christian Society.[44] After the establishment of Israel, his name was not included on the list of ten Arab lawyers who were licensed to plead cases in the courts of Jewish state, because he was a resident of the Triangle at the time it was transferred to Israel after the Rhodes Agreement in the spring of 1949. At the end of the year, *al-Yawm* newspaper published a news item about the attorney Subhi al-Ayyubi pleading a case in court "on behalf of his client Muhammad al-Faqir who is accused of killing a wealthy merchant from Jaffa, Michel Fi'ani."[45] The paper which carried this news report was apparently unaware of the big drama unfolding at the Supreme Court in Jerusalem, the center of which was the attorney al-Ayyubi. The decision by the court was among the most important decisions by Judge Shimon Agranat and his colleagues to this day. Below is a summary of the drama, in fact the tragedy, which befell al-Ayyubi.

Al-Ayyubi had brought a case to the Supreme Court, submitted on 30 March 1950, to rescind the order of the military governor of the Jaljuliyya region in the Triangle that he should leave Jaffa and return to live on his plantation in Habla near Jaljuliyya. In the proceedings Judge Agranat wrote, as part of the decision, the facts of this case were simple and clear, but also unique and unusual.[46] The facts are a very important example of the wide authority given to military government officials, and the proceedings constitute an important historical document concerning the circumstances which drove al-Ayyubi in the end to immigrate to Libya.

The information presented to the Supreme Court in Jerusalem indicated that in August 1949 Subhi al-Ayyubi was living on his plantation near the village of Jaljuliyya, 150 meters from the Jordanian border.[47] Al-Ayyubi was an elderly man who had been suffering from asthma for fifteen years and from urologic problems for four years. Near the end of that month, thieves attacked him, hitting him and stealing money and jewelry from his house. After that incident, al-Ayyubi's health deteriorated, and he decided to travel to Jaffa for treatment. To do so he obtained the needed exit permit from the military governor to leave the Triangle according to article 125 of the defense (emergency) regulations of 1945, since the area where he resided had been declared "a closed military area."[48]

Subhi al-Ayyubi went to Jaffa and was treated at the French Hospital in the city. At the beginning of October 1949, he left the hospital after his recovery and decided to stay at his brother's house instead of returning to his plantation. The Supreme Court ruling mentioned that the plaintiff lived in Jaffa "on the basis of permits issued to him from time to time by the military governor general of the administered areas." On 31 October the last permit expired. Al-Ayyubi wanted to continue living at his brother's house, but the military governor objected and on 2 March 1950 (under the authority given to him by article 110 of the defense (emergency) regulations of 1945), he issued an order compelling him to leave Jaffa and to return to live at his plantation near Jaljuliyya. However, the risks to al-Ayyubi's life represented by his illnesses, and the fears he had that thieves would attack him again should he return to his plantation, induced him to appeal through his lawyer to the Supreme Court to rescind the military governor's order.

The judges concluded their decision by saying that they do not delve into examinations of the security justifications given by the military governors and that their legal role was limited to examining the extent to which the official administrative application of defense (emergency) regulations was correct. Contrary to the case of Abu-Laban discussed above, the Supreme Court said they found no technical administrative error, so they decided to reject al-Ayyubi's request, ruling on 26 May 1950.[49] The case attracted a great deal of attention because of the humanitarian issues involved. MK Moshe Aram from Mapam submitted the following questions to the minister of defense:

1. Why did the military government issue an unjust order to expel a patient who needs treatment according to his doctors?
2. What right does the military government have to issue such a decision on the pretext that Subhi al-Ayyubi exploited his presence in Jaffa to secure a permit to practice law? Is it forbidden "under the law" for a patient to deal with his papers? On what did the military governor base his decision that Subhi al-Ayyubi had violated the law when he brought a case in the central court? Is he forbidden from accepting an invitation to come before a governmental institution?
3. Why does the military governor consider Subhi al-Ayyubi a criminal for accepting membership in the Islamic Council of Jaffa, considering that the prime minister's advisor on Arab affairs did not object to this matter?
4. Can the prime minister and minister of defense rescind the unjust order and end this injustice?

The answers to MK Moshe Aram's questions came on 29 May 1950, three days after the Supreme Court issued its decision. The answer was succinct and official. Ben-Gurion said that al-Ayyubi appealed to the Supreme Court to issue a preventative order, therefore the matter must be left to the judiciary.[50] However, MK Aram's questions exposed the real reasons and circumstances which led to the retaliatory steps taken by the military government. The Israeli authorities did what they could to get rid of the Arab leaders who remained in the city after the majority of the Palestinian population had been expelled. Al-Ayyubi's attempt to rejoin the Islamic Council and to practice law once again became a disturbance to government policies, hence the order of the military government and the security ministry. He achieved nothing by resorting to the Supreme Court in Jerusalem for justice and fairness. The question for which we have no clear answer is: Did the authorities propose to Subhi al-Ayyubi that he should sell his property and immi-grate to Libya after he found all doors closed in his face?

The available sources do not give a clear answer about the circumstances that had a direct bearing on the emigration of al-Ayyubi, or who actually played a role in this matter. However, those sources do indicate that the overwhelming major-ity of those who chose to immigrate to Libya were educated urban residents. The world of this well-to-do urban community, in cities which became mixed, such as Lydda, al-Ramla, and Jaffa, changed and disappeared altogether in 1948 and later.[51] Those cities in which the elite lived a boisterous, culturally and politically rich life became almost deserted, and were gradually repopulated by Jews who became rulers and masters. From this perspective, the tragedy of the Palestinians who remained in those "mixed cities" was greater than of those who remained in Arab villages in the Triangle and the Galilee. On top of the national and collec-tive Nakba, those urban dwellers felt an alienation in their cities which grew more extreme and bitter with the passage of years. It was no surprise that many pro-fessionals such as medical doctors, engineers, and lawyers decided to leave their homes and cities after the Nakba. Their story is worthy of further specialized study and research.[52]

THE ATTORNEY ELIAS KUSA:
A ONE-MAN INSTITUTION

In the wake of the forced migration of members of the Palestinian urban elite in 1948 and afterward, the few attorneys remaining in the homeland who practiced their profession in Israel played an important role in defending the rights of those who remained. As we mentioned above, prominent among the ten pioneering lawyers who practiced their profession after the Nakba were two from Haifa: Hanna Naqqara and Elias Kusa. The first was not a communist until 1948, when he joined Maki and worked in coordination with the leadership of that party upon his return to Haifa.[53] Elias Kusa was always a "lone wolf" and a one-man institution, as he was described by many of his contemporaries who knew him in the 1950s. This lawyer from Haifa is considered to be a representative of members of the elite who endured and who resisted the policy of repressing the remaining Palestinians in Israel, despite the dangers this entailed. However, researchers into the history of the Arab minority in Israel rarely showed interest in his role.

Elias Kusa (1896–1971) was of Lebanese origin and ended up in Haifa through a tortuous path, but he spent most of his life there, as did many other Lebanese who migrated to "the Bride of Karmil." Kusa grew up in Tripoli in Lebanon and studied at the American University of Beirut. At the end of 1914 he left teaching and moved from Beirut to Egypt out of fear of being conscripted into the Ottoman army. In Cairo, he made contact with the British and activists of the Arab Revolt under the leadership of Sharif Husayn and his sons. In December 1917 he arrived in Jerusalem with the British forces under the command of General Edmund Allenby, who had just occupied the Sinai and southern Palestine.

Elias Kusa's legal education and his mastery of the English language enabled him to work in the justice department for over ten years. But he resigned from his job in 1928 at the time of the "disturbances" between Arabs and Jews concerning the Wailing Wall. In the same year, he left Jerusalem and moved to Haifa to work, specializing in civil and criminal cases, and he quickly became engaged in national political activities in the city, becoming one of the prominent activists in national committees and organizations.[54] Kusa remained in Haifa after it fell in late April 1948. But his life was turned upside down and fundamentally changed because of what happened to most of the city's Arab population. Despite the numerous difficulties, he decided to remain in his house in Haifa and not to leave. Only a few months into the Nakba, this home had become a much sought-after destination for the grievances of the population that remained, particularly since Kusa had seen with his own eyes the pillaging of Arab property by the state and its institutions.

Elias Kusa married Emily Khayyat in 1930. When skirmishes between Arabs and Jews intensified in Haifa and its district at the beginning of 1948, Emily left the city with her only son while her husband remained at the family residence.[55] Kusa saw how the Haganah imposed its authority on the Arab quarters in the city after 22 April 1948. Once it gained control over the city, state institutions began to transfer the property and possessions of Arabs in a systematic way to official storage facilities, in spite of the complaints and condemnation of the Arab Emergency Committee, of which Kusa was a member. In early July 1948, the government began selling the furniture and clothing which had been stacked up in storage depots to the incoming Jews at very cheap prices. By the end of the year, the possessions of the Palestinians of Haifa who had become refugees had been sold.[56] This systematic pillaging by the government of absentee property and possessions provoked Kusa's resentment and condemnation.

The Israeli Central State Archives contain much correspondence among employees of governmental offices concerning letters of protest from the attorney Kusa to David Cohen, the Knesset member representing Haifa, and other politicians and cabinet ministers. In one letter Kusa asks what the law had to say about a refugee whom the government had allowed to return and his property which he had not owned prior to his departure. Justice Minister Pinhas Rosen's opinion was that a refugee does not cease to be a refugee unless they obtain a certificate reclassifying their status. As long as they are an absentee (or refugee), then all of their property comes under the Custodian of Absentee Property, regardless of when and how it came into their possession.[57] However, Minister Shitrit disagreed with the minister of justice on this issue. Indeed, after this issue was discussed by the cabinet, the law was changed to enable "present absentees" to own new real estate which they did not have before. But Kusa was not satisfied with this amendment, and he continued to attack the government control of confiscated Arab land and property. He was particularly scornful of the law for the expropriation of the lands of "present absentees" on the basis of the law of absentee property, issued by the Knesset in March 1950.

Elias Kusa was an uncommon and distinctive personality by any measure. His correspondence and his independent and very daring political positions reflected that personality. He was not afraid to subject the government's policies toward the Arabs who remained to biting and uncompromising criticism. This lawyer did not have political backing on which he could rely or a newspaper to publish his actions and activities. He sent letters in Arabic and English not only to ministers in the Israeli government but also to international organizations, such as the United Nations. He published many articles in English in the dissident *Nir* biweekly magazine. The fact that Kusa chose a daring independent and critical position although he was not a member of Maki made him a very unusual phenomenon. Kusa was convinced that the monopoly the communists had on representation of the issues and grievances of Arab citizens was harmful to their interests, and he therefore found himself often in a difficult position. Despite this, he did not modify his critical positions, and became prominent in the 1950s as a strong defender of Arab rights and interests.

The basic rights of Arab citizens, such as the right of free speech and movement, and the right to possess land and other property which the government was expropriating, topped the list of Kusa's priorities. He wrote: "In theory, the Arabs in Israel have equal rights with the Jews, but in fact they are persecuted in almost all areas."[58] The most striking examples were the military government, the policy of permits, the discrimination in various budgets and appropriations and subsidies, and similar policies. What was worse, according to Kusa, was that the Arabs in Israel lived in a huge prison. Apart from some Christians who were permitted to travel to Rome and to Arab (East) Jerusalem (then under Jordanian control), Arabs did not have the right of movement and travel. Some of Elias Kusa's articles were published in the international press.[59] This lawyer from Haifa continued his multifaceted activities throughout the 1950s in the press and in attempting to establish an independent political organization for those who remained in Haifa and the Galilee.

Kusa's activities and articles angered the authorities and its agents, and also, on the other side, his rivals in the Communist party. The latter group was content to attack him—and others like him among the independent political activists— verbally and to accuse him of serving the policies of the government. However, the members of the intelligence services who monitored his activities began thinking of harsher ways to silence him. This able and experienced lawyer who lived outside the scope of the military government presented a "problem," so they went about looking for a charge that might put him in prison. In view of the difficulty of concocting a charge that could be used for "repression through legal means," they started talking about a plan "to break his bones." An anonymous letter (apparently written by an intelligence agent) containing this proposal was sent to Zalman Aran

(Ziama). It was kept in a file in the office of the prime minister's advisor on Arab affairs, and was discussed seriously. The handwritten letter is dated 21 August, and the text asks: "What shall we do with this scoundrel? Give your opinion. I am prepared to cooperate! Why don't we break all his bones one night?"[60]

The threats received by Elias Kusa were known to his friends and his family. One night when no one was at home the family home was broken into and the library ransacked, but only a few files and papers were stolen.[61] Despite the shock and apprehension that something worse might happen, Kusa did not stop his activities or let up on his criticism of government policy. His only son, Nicola, could not put up with the atmosphere and immigrated to Canada. He relates that the family was in constant fear of retaliation by the authorities. Even in the telephone interview I conducted with him in Canada, the effects of that period were apparent from his speech and his hesitation to answer some questions. Nor were the threats against the life of Kusa and members of his family unusual; in fact they were a gentler form of the repression and imprisonment which other political activists who opposed government policy and military rule endured.

One way of applying pressure on the Arab elite who lived in "mixed cities" was to refrain from issuing them passports except for those who wanted to leave and not come back. This form of collective punishment was harmful to businessmen, big merchants and others who had family outside the country. Those individuals found themselves prevented from travelling because they did not have the requisite permits from the ministries concerned.[62] The case of Hanna Naqqara, who tried repeatedly to obtain a passport without success, is one example of that policy. Elias Kusa also suffered the tribulations of being denied permission to travel. This attorney with multifaceted connections told his story (and that of all Arabs in Israel) in English in *Nir* magazine, published by the small radical leftist group, Ihud, which supported a binational state. Kusa revealed in that article the varieties of discrimination from which Arab citizens of Israel suffered. One issue Kusa brought up was the ban on their travel outside the country.[63]

The borders of Israel with the Arab world were closed to legal crossings except for rare and special cases. The few allowed to travel freely across those borders were Christian clergymen; very small numbers of others received permission to cross through Ra's al-Naqura and through the Mandelbaum Gate between the two halves of Jerusalem. Even the travel of Arab citizens inside the country depended on permits from the military government. This was not limited to residents of areas under military rule, but also applied to residents of coastal cities who were prohibited from entering the closed Arab areas. Thus, most of those who remained during the 1950s were under constant siege. Israel facilitated movement, however, for "one-way" travel—those who wanted to emigrate from the Jewish state to Arab or other countries.[64]

Elias Kusa detailed the issue of Arabs being prevented from travelling for an extended period in an article in *Nir*. He noted that even in neighboring Arab countries, such as Lebanon and Egypt, there was no such prohibition for members of the minority Jewish community; Iraq was the only Arab country to have adopted a policy similar to Israel's at the time. But he added that even there "the limitation applied only to those who wanted to travel to Israel, not for those who wanted to travel for educational or health or other reasons."[65] After the authorities repeatedly rejected the applications for a passport from Kusa himself and his colleague attorney Hanna Naqqara, Naqqara decided to bring a case to the Supreme Court.

On 19 November 1952, Naqqara had submitted an official passport application under article three of the 1952 Citizenship law. This application was rejected on the grounds of the circumstances of his entry to Israel in August 1948. But Naqqara claimed that his name was documented on the list of residents of the country "when he was a detainee on 8 November 1948. On 16 January 1949 he received a civil identity card." Furthermore, he participated in the first elections that month, running as a candidate in the Haifa municipal elections in November 1950. However, when the voter list for the second Knesset was published in June 1951 his name was omitted with the justification that he had entered the country illegally. Naqqara successfully appealed this decision at the central court in Haifa. Subsequently he voted in the second Knesset elections, and was later a candidate on the Maki list.[66] The Supreme Court accepted Naqqara's election on 16 October 1953, on the basis of the decision by the central court.[67]

Unlike Naqqara, whose passport application had been denied due to the claim that he had entered the country illegally, Elias Kusa had never left Haifa at all, and the authorities did not offer a justification for the rejection of his application. Following the rejection, Kusa wrote to the prime minister on 9 May 1957, asking him to intervene in the case. He said in the letter that he applied for a passport in Haifa in March 1957, and he applied two days later for an exit visa and paid 15 liras in fees, but his application was ignored. Seventy days after he had submitted his application, he had not received a reply despite his visits to government offices and his correspondence with officials in Jerusalem. Kusa wrote in conclusion that this treatment was no doubt due to the fact that he was an Arab.[68] Kusa's conjecture concerning this point was true, as documents in the prime minister's office confirm.[69] Not issuing a passport was one of the means employed by the authorities to apply pressure and exact retribution from opponents of its policies.

LAW IN THE SERVICE OF THE POLICY OF REPRESSION

In David Kretzmer's valuable book titled *The Legal Status of the Arabs in Israel*, the author exposes the gap between the objectivity and universality of the law in theory and its exploitation in the service of the policy of discrimination and the inequality between Jews and Arabs.[70] This study essentially deals with the existing situation in Israel near the end of the twentieth century and very little about the experience of Arabs with Israeli law in the 1950s. But the legal status of the remaining Palestinians after the Nakba was determined to a large extent in that period, and became rooted in a number of the laws promulgated at that time. One example of an unjust law is Israel's "citizenship law," which is one of the most important laws in any state.

In July 1950, the proposed "citizenship law," which stirred up controversy and strong opposition from leftist parties, began to be discussed. The discussion continued through the period of the first Knesset, and then after the elections to the second Knesset in 1951. The text of the law was finalized in 1952, as one of the most prominent indicators that Israel was a Jewish state. This law established several paths to citizenship, including: one path for Jews according to the law of return, and another path for non-Jews under article 3 which lays down conditions for non-Jews to prove that they are entitled to citizenship (nationality by residence in Israel). Three conditions need to be satisfied:

1. That [the person in question] was registered on 1 March 1952 as an inhabitant under The Registration of Inhabitants Ordinance of 1949, and
2. The person was an inhabitant of Israel on the day of the coming into force of this law, and
3. The person was in Israel, or in an area that became Israeli territory after the establishment of the state, from the day of the establishment of the state to the day of the coming into force of this law, or entered Israel legally during that period.[71]

This law, in its three conditions combined, excluded a large number of the remaining Palestinians from eligibility for Israeli citizenship. Many of them went to court, and some reached the Supreme Court, seeking to acquire an identity card that would end their classification as infiltrators. The struggle to acquire an identity card and citizenship was part of the struggle to remain. The identity card or Israeli citizenship for Palestinians did not protect those who remained from discrimination or repression under military rule, but it did protect them from being uprooted and expelled, in theory at least. Without an identity card, those who remained were constantly subject to the threat of expulsion.

During the period when the Knesset promulgated the 1950 Law of Return and the 1952 Citizenship Law, it also acted to legitimize the control of the state over the property of refugees and the expropriation of a large portion of the lands of those who remained. This issue of the pillaging of Palestinian lands has been dealt with in a number of studies. This issue remains an open wound, particularly in the case of the "present absentees" who were recognized as citizens but who lost their rights to their lands and property in the village from which they were forced to migrate. The use by the military government of the 1945 defense (emergency) regulations and new Israeli legislation played an important role in shrinking the area of land left to Arab citizens.

The scope of this study does not extend to a comprehensive research of cases of discriminatory laws and the legitimization of the activities of Zionist institutions in Israel which since 1948 served Jews only and contributed to expanding the gaps between them and Arab citizens. The only area which guaranteed equality between all citizens was that of parliamentary elections which Arabs participated in as of 1949. But even in this area, as we will see in the next chapter, equality was only theoretical under military rule and the policy of repressing independent Arab parties. Against this backdrop, Arab citizens occasionally had recourse to the Supreme Court in the quest for justice, and to prevent illegal policies being implemented by the government and its principal arm (military rule) in Arab cities and villages.[72]

One important work of research on the relationship between the law and the judicial system in Israel and Arab citizens was Alina Korn's doctoral dissertation at Hebrew University which showed clearly how the law and the judicial system were activated by state institutions to serve the system of monitoring and control over Palestinians in Israel.[73] Certain types of breaches of the law were tailor made so that they applied exclusively to Palestinians, and fell under the general category of violation of state security. The author of the study identified three groups of laws of this sort:

1. Controlling the entry of Arabs into the territory of the state under the 1952 law of entry into Israel.
2. The law to combat infiltration, violations, and the judiciary of 1954.
3. The laws for the control and monitoring of Arabs under the 1945 defense (emergency) regulations.[74]

The military government applied these laws to Arab citizens in a way that forcibly transformed them into violators of the law. In the name of security, thousands of Palestinians were expelled from their villages and exiled beyond the borders of the state even after the end of the war, and thousands of others were uprooted and forced to migrate from their lands to other towns and villages inside Israel. The pillaging of Palestinian lands and property was carried out through the implementation of unjust laws, including the 1950 law on "absentee property." Along with this, any attempt by the Palestinians to return to their homes and lands without the approval of the authorities was considered a crime punishable under the law. Thus, the law worked in the service of Zionist policy, and forcibly made most Palestinians who remained in Israel violators of the law in the first years after the Nakba.

Korn found in her study that in the 1950s at least half of the violators of the law were members of the Palestinian minority in the period 1950–52.[75] This situation continued under most years of military government which, as a matter of policy, made members of the Arab minority violators of the law. This was not a true reflection of the behavior of the inhabitants. Most Arab prisoners were "infiltrators" because of the delay—which sometimes went on for years—in listing their names in population records. The policy of using permits, which were handed out only to people who were in the good graces of the authorities, compelled many to violate the law and take risks in order to earn a living. Those who did not have permits were arrested and put on trial in military courts which automatically imposed prison terms and exorbitant fines. In this manner, judicial agencies drained the energies of the Arab inhabitants and participated in the system of monitoring and control.

Opposition parties criticized the military government and its excessive use of emergency laws for political control and repression. Those categorized as "infiltrators" were pursued for years because of the failure to list them in population records, a practice that infuriated the communists. In 1949 al-Ittihad published a large number of news reports on comb-and-search operations by the police and army in Arab villages. MK Tubi brought up this issue and the arrests and expulsion of those who had been accused of infiltration.[76] For several months, the paper listed the names of people who had lost their registration coupons along with the numbers of some of them in a bid to return them to their owners if found.

The military government divided up the Galilee into fifty-four closed regions which one could not enter without a permit. Most of those permits were issued for the purposes of work.[77] The refusal to issue a permit of this kind to a person was tantamount to sentencing that person to unemployment and poverty. Thus, permits became carrots which were given to the well-connected and collaborators, as well as a stick used against protestors and those who were out of favor. The sentiment of injustice and the authoritarian rule of the military governor system led some people to compare Israel unfavorably to government under the Ottomans, that rule by Israel was "worse than the days of the Turks."[78] Such statements were an expression of the sense of constant persecution and injustice in which all government institutions were complicit. When the Palestinians who remained despaired of getting justice, they would repeat the popular saying: "If your ruler is your oppressor, to whom do you complain?"

Some of those who failed to obtain a permit would travel without one in order to work or to some other reasons. For example, communist activist Philip Shehada went from the village of al-Maghar to Haifa without a permit from the military government.[79] The police arrested him, and he was brought before a military court which sentenced him to three months in jail or a fine of 50 liras. This incident is an example of the life of many whom the authorities drove into breaking the unjust law on a daily basis. Any resistance to the military government was suppressed with an iron fist even if the issue had nothing to do with security. For example, four residents of 'Arabat al-Battuf village found themselves under administrative detention for an entire month because of their opposition to the imposition of an education tax on the people.[80]

Many of those who remained in Israel were compelled to break the laws and evade the barriers imposed on them in order to earn a living and to try to lead a normal life in their surroundings. The 1945 defense (emergency) regulations were applied to them alone. On the rare occasions when those laws were applied to Jewish citizens, there was an uproar and sharp criticism about their illegitimacy.

In May 1951, for example, a number of people belonging to a terrorist cell were arrested and charged with creating an organization that was hostile to the state and possessing explosives with the intention of attacking the Knesset. Dozens of extremist Jews were imprisoned on the basis of article 111 of the defense (emergency) regulations. Those arrests created a wide media and political storm, which was echoed in the Knesset, the body responsible for extending the applicability of those regulations.

During the discussion about the relevant emergency regulations, Moshe Sharett, the acting prime minister, said that "a law is a law" in the course of his reply to MK Menachem Begin, the leader of the opposition. But Begin protested: "That is not true. There are tyrannical laws, there are immoral laws, there are even Nazi laws." He added in response to people who interrupted him: "Don't ask me who decides what is a Nazi law or what is an immoral law. The law you have applied is a Nazi law, it is tyrannical and immoral. An immoral law is an illegal law. Therefore, these arrests are illegal and the order you issued is tyrannical."[81] Begin concluded his speech by repeating his opposition to the use of the defense (emergency) regulations of 1945: "The existence of these emergency laws is a shame and their application is a crime. Therefore, I propose abrogating these laws and proposing a replacement for them within a week."[82]

However, those laws were not abrogated, and they continued to be used against Arab citizens during the period of military rule. They enabled agents of the military government to conduct administrative arrests without the use of courts and to expel political activists from place to place. For example, Nadim Musa was expelled from his place of residence in al-Bi'na to the village of Tuba, which is inhabited by al-Hayb Arabs.[83] This punishment was considered to be a deterrent as it led to social alienation, the loss of a workplace, and separation from family. Most communist activists were young, unmarried men, and this contributed to their ability to endure exile and prison. The party also lent support to their families. Often the outcome of exile was the opposite of the goal of the punishment, because those exiled spread the party's ideology and slogans in new and faraway places. That is what happened with Nadim Musa, who spent four months as the guest of the shaykh of the al-Hayb Arabs; he had all the time in the world to talk to the guests of the shaykh and to convey his views during evening chats and on special occasions.[84]

The goal of the military government in punishing communists and their like was to deter Arabs from supporting the party's policies or voting for the communists. Indeed, many Arabs who were in need of help and support were afraid to go to the communists and preferred to seek help from those connected to the regime. Bishop Hakim and members of the Knesset from lists connected to the ruling party offered their good offices to solve people's problems with the government, and were sometimes successful. Supporting the competition to the communists was an important factor in constructing the edifice of control based on the use of "the carrot and the stick." Permits, appointments in government jobs, and other rewards were granted to those with connections to the regime or to those who offered *wasta* (middleman) services and were not given to those whom the authorities considered to have "negative attitudes." Indeed, the numerous arrests and fear of punishment contributed a great deal to the intimidation of people, most of whom were struggling for survival not confrontation.

For example, the people of Iqrit and Kufr Bir'im chose for years to work through the government bureaucracy and avoided cooperating with the communists and supporting their struggle. When they decided two years later to appeal to the Supreme Court they hired attorney Muhammad Nimr al-Hawwari. The Supreme Court's ruling in the Kufr Bir'im case is famous.[85] However, the temporary success of the villagers did not alter their destiny. The priest Yusif Istfan Susan (1907–87) published the details of the unending struggle of the villagers to return to their homes, and included a number of documents and correspondence with governmental institutions as an attachment to his memoirs.[86] After decades, those expelled from the village learned a lesson from their steadfastness: that the many promises they had received from Israeli leaders were only efforts to procrastinate and gain time to establish alternative facts on the ground.

THE SUPREME COURT: ANOTHER BATTLEGROUND FOR THOSE WHO STAYED

The attorney Muhammad Nimr al-Hawwari left the political arena soon after his return in 1949, and moved to the judicial sphere to practice his profession. He became an effective lawyer and activist in cases before the Supreme Court. While Hanna Naqqara represented comrades and people close to the Communist Party, Hawwari argued cases for Palestinians who remained but were in fear of linking their names to the communists. As we said earlier, Naqqara and his colleague Elias Kusa did not hesitate to criticize the authorities and to resist them in court, which was for them an additional realm for fighting for the rights of those who remained. Hawwari had a more conciliatory approach than the two lawyers from Haifa. With fewer than a dozen Arab attorneys in the 1950s, the three divided the burden of pleading cases before the courts.

The Communist Party (Maki) had intensified its critique of population expulsion operations from villages in the Galilee after the first Knesset elections in 1949. MK Tubi raised questions in the Knesset in March 1949 about combing and expulsion operations "which were happening every week."[87] Due to the large number of complaints about the illegal expulsion of Arab inhabitants, Ben-Gurion announced in the Knesset on 8 April 1949: "We have issued orders to all the authorities concerned not to expel anyone who bears a legal registration coupon. If such a person who has an identity card is expelled, he has the right to return. He can do that himself or through an agent from the military government authorities."[88] As we mentioned earlier, Naqqara was a pioneer in resorting to the Supreme Court of Justice with such cases. The publication in *al-Ittihad* newspaper of news of his successes in important cases encouraged others to choose a judicial path to prevent expulsions and obtain permanent identity cards and permanent resident status.

In 1951, thousands of Palestinians in the Galilee were still without identity cards; some had only had papers or coupons showing registration during the census of inhabitants. The military government tried to distribute red temporary residence cards to the inhabitants of the village of al-Biʿna, but the villagers, under the leadership of communist activists, resisted that attempt, and insisted on receiving the normal blue identity cards only. Hanna Naqqara represented dozens of people from that village and neighboring villages in central Galilee before the Supreme Court. He asked on behalf of his clients that the court compel the ministry of interior to distribute blue citizenship identity cards.[89] In November 1950, Naqqara initiated the first such case on behalf of seventy plaintiffs from al-Biʿna. The Supreme Court issued a provisional order compelling the ministry of interior within fifteen days to submit "reasons why it had not delivered identity cards to all those who had been registered in the population survey."[90] This case was followed by similar appeals in 1951, during which the second Knesset elections were to be held. Naqqara's success in a number of these cases encouraged those who had remained in the Galilee to go to court to prove their existence and to acquire citizenship cards.[91]

Al-Yawm also published news of the authorities issuing identity cards to people who had "infiltrated" the country on the eve of the second Knesset elections. In one report from Majd al-Krum, for example, it was reported that the census registration employee "came to the village and exchanged permanent citizenship ID cards for red temporary cards." Dozens of people who had resorted to the Supreme Court requesting citizenship cards were told that they could go to the offices of the military government to obtain their cards.[92] Two months after that news item, the same paper published a report that twenty-two villagers from Majd al-Krum, al-Biʿna, and Dayr al-Asad had won cases in the Supreme Court after their expulsion and return to the country earlier.[93] Below are examples of similar court cases which were reported in the press, alongside other cases which had different outcomes which did not secure the plaintiffs' residence in the country.

Al-Hawwari pleaded a case on behalf of twenty-three people from Majd al-Krum against the minister of interior and the military governor of the Galilee and others at the Supreme Court with the judges Heishin, Zilberg, and Zohar presiding. The judges issued an order to the defendants "to explain the reasons for not delivering identity cards to the plaintiffs." After some proceedings the appeal was accepted and the temporary order was changed to a final and permanent decision.[94] So this group from Majd al-Krum joined the others for whom attorney Naqqara had obtained identity cards in 1951. However, another case which Hawwari pleaded on behalf of Muhammad ʿAli al-Husayn and nine others from the same village shortly after the previous case led to different results.[95] The statements in the decision created a surprising legitimization of the policy of expulsion and refusal to issue identity cards to forced migrants who had succeeded in returning to their homes and had gone to court seeking justice—but did not find it.

The case of Muhammad 'Ali al-Husayn and his nine companions was very similar to previous cases in which the judges decided that the authorities must issue identity cards to the plaintiffs. Due to the special importance of this case as a historical precedent, we shall quote directly from the proceedings. The request submitted to the judges of the Supreme Court was the following:

> The plaintiffs are inhabitants of the village of Majd al-Krum, in the Governorate of 'Akka, and all are Palestinian citizens [meaning, at the time of the British Mandate]. On 30 October1948, Israeli forces occupied the village, and the inhabitants, including the plaintiffs, surrendered to them. On 25 November 1948, a military unit came to the village and arrested the plaintiffs and some other individuals and expelled them to Lebanon. On 5 December 1948, the authorities began registering the inhabitants [of the village] under the defense (emergency) regulations of 1948 (registering the inhabitants.) Although the registration went on for three days in a row, the names of the plaintiffs were not listed on the register of inhabitants because they were absent from the village. They returned to their homes on 25 December 1948. However, in two subsequent expulsion operations, the first on 9 January 1949 and the second on 14 January 1949, a large number of young men from the village were expelled outside the borders of the state, including the plaintiffs in the second operation.[96]

This important court document goes on to relate other events in the village of Majd al-Krum after the end of the war, which reaffirmed the accuracy of verbal accounts of events by the inhabitants.

> On 17 January 1949, registration receipts were distributed to the inhabitants of the village who were previously registered. Also, some individuals who had not been registered were registered that day (17 January 1949). However, the plaintiffs were not registered this time either, because they had been expelled, as was mentioned above. Since that expulsion, the authorities have made it impossible for the plaintiffs to live in peace. They return to the country without an entry permit, they are arrested, and expelled beyond the borders. But they return to the village again, and they are arrested and expelled once again. They live in fear that these actions will be repeated with no limit and no end.[97]

The defendants, including representatives of the interior ministry, the military government, and the police denied the account by the plaintiffs. They claimed that the plaintiffs had fought against Israel before and after the establishment of the state, and then "infiltrated" back into the village after the occupation of the Galilee and the end of the war. Hence, their staying in Israel was not legal and they did not deserve to have identity cards.[98] Officer Shmuel Pisetsky tried to convince the court that the narrative by the authorities was the true account, and that the plaintiffs had not been in the village either at the time of its occupation or the days of registering the inhabitants. This testimony revealed that a teacher by the name of Hasan Yusif Sa'd from the village of al-Birwa was the one who recorded the names of the inhabitants, and that the list of inhabitants included names of persons "who had returned to the country a long time after the battles had ended, and that they had been expelled in the end."[99] This account by the officer from the military government did not convince the judges; they in fact refused to accept the account by the army's representatives and they believed the account of the inhabitants, particularly the account of the mukhtar of the village.

The plaintiffs gave sworn testimony before the judges and submitted the testimonies of two mukhtars of the village: Hajj 'Abd Salim Manna' and Dhiyab Qasim Farhat. The judges commented on the testimony of the second mukhtar, who spoke "without fear" despite the fact that he knew that the first mukhtar, Hajj 'Abd Salim Manna', had been arrested by the police because of what he said in court and testified in this case. Among the things he said which the court thought credible was:

> Leaflets were dropped over our village on 28 October 1948 from an Israeli plane. On 30 October the village was occupied. We brought out white flags and walked (westward) to greet the army. We were not afraid because there was confidence and security.[100] The first plaintiff was in the village the day it was occupied; he gave us a rifle which we in turn handed in to the army. So it went with plaintiffs number two to number five. They are inhabitants of Majd al-Krum and they were present when the village was occupied. Plaintiffs number six to number ten are from the village of Sha'b and they were in Majd al-Krum the day it was occupied.[101]

Despite the fact that the judges believed the accounts and testimonies of the plaintiffs and preferred them to the story told by the army, the court case did not help them a great deal in achieving their objective.

The judges referred more than once to the testimony of a representative of the authorities, Officer Pisetsky, expressing doubts about its credibility and accuracy. The court did not accept the army's account of what happened in the village, and the judges stressed that the statements by the inhabitants and the mukhtars were true and acceptable. The two mukhtars added in their testimonies that shortly after the occupation of the village (8 November 1948) a unit of the Israeli army came to the village, and after gathering the inhabitants in al-'Ayn Square, "it tore down some houses and then fired on a number of inhabitants and killed them."[102] The court affirmed more than once that it found credible the testimonies of the two mukhtars who were not intimidated by the threats of the military government, so they told the details of the military operation which the army conducted in the village at the beginning of the month. The judges added that this was no ordinary comb-and-search operation for two "infiltrators" ["two" according to the original text]. They described the operation by the Israeli army unit in the village as "an ordinary military retaliatory operation."[103]

The determination by the judges that the Israeli army unit had carried out a retaliatory operation in November 1948 is an important historical statement, particularly in the context of the continued and insistent denial by representatives of the authorities. The judges added: "After that operation the army unit left the village, and that operation had nothing to do with expelling the inhabitants."[104] This judicial document is very provocative seeing as it speaks of expelling the inhabitants and killing defenseless civilians a week or more after the occupation of the village, and describes it as "a customary military retaliatory operation," regardless of the fact that it is in violation of the international law of warfare and the Hague Treaty. What is worse is that Judge Heishin said in the decision he issued that he would not give the plaintiffs identity cards although "that would prevent the army from assaulting them."[105]

Despite the above statements, the court levelled very harshly worded criticism at the government and state institutions, and pointed out the inaccurate nature of the testimonies and documents they submitted in support of their position. Clearly, the methods of obfuscation and not telling the truth which the army and the other security agencies had become accustomed to had made their way to the Supreme Court. Those forces, notably the military government apparatus, did not hesitate to use methods of intimidation and retaliation against court witnesses, as the police did with the mukhtar they arrested.[106] The judges added their critique of a document signed by one of the mukhtars of the village: "This document is written and signed by the third mukhtar, Hasan Sarhan. The strange thing is that this mukhtar, who testified that the army had not surrounded the village from the day it was occupied, on 30 October 1948 to 8 January 1949, himself infiltrated and returned to the country in December 1948. Despite the fact that he was not in the village the day it was occupied, the "infiltrator" mukhtar's name is listed in the record of inhabitants of the village who were there when it was occupied."[107]

The judges came to the determination that the plaintiffs had left the village "with good will and without pressure or coercion," in the aftermath of "the customary military retaliation operation" by the army, then they crossed the border and "fled—that is, they were not expelled—to Lebanon." They concluded: "In those stormy days the plaintiffs left the country and moved to the enemy camp. They later returned, claiming they were citizens loyal to the country and demanding equal rights with the rest of the citizens. Not only that, they have come to the Supreme Court of Justice while trying to conceal the truth from the court. Nevertheless, they are asking for justice."[108]

The Supreme Court judges in Jerusalem simplified matters to a great extent when they set up the alternative categories of "forcible expulsion" against "leaving the country voluntarily." In cases where the army expelled inhabitants from Majd al-Krum in January 1949, the court agreed to their request to receive identity cards. But those [the plaintiffs] who left their homes in fear for their lives after the massacre which the court described a "customary military retaliation operation," were labeled as having left the country voluntarily. These classifications ignore the danger and how civilians behave under such circumstances, placing the responsibility on the victim rather than the executioner who has done his best to strike fear in the hearts of the inhabitants, as we saw in previous chapters. These black and white classifications conceal the wide grey area in between which compelled many inhabitants to leave. Such classifications and analysis by the judges of the Supreme Court enabled them to reject the appeal of Muhammad 'Ali al-Husayn and his nine companions and sentenced them to permanent exile and life in refugee camps. This ruling by the Supreme Court established an informal precedent on which the authorities relied in continuing the policy of expelling thousands of Palestinians who were classified as infiltrators.[109]

Needless to say, the position of the judges of the Supreme Court of Justice and their categories were unacceptable to the Palestinians who had been forced to migrate, and to those who remained after the Nakba. To them, crossing the international borders in 1949 was not "entering Israel," rather it was returning to their homes which they had been forced to leave for various reasons. Since most areas in the Galilee had been allocated to the Palestinian state under the UN partition resolution, Israel's occupation was an illegitimate and illegal act. The borders of Israel which were agreed to in the armistice agreements with Arab states had either not yet been drawn or were signed in early 1949. In this period Israel had not completed a census of the population in the villages of upper Galilee. The decisions of the Supreme Court, a few of which were referred to in this study, lent legitimacy to the government's policy retroactively, based on justifications which contradict international law and the norms of justice sought by the inhabitants when they went to court. In any case, this study relied on court decisions as historical documents, but the topic needs dedicated research by scholars in law, politics, philosophy, and other disciplines to take part.

The inhabitants of Majd al-Krum scored a relative victory in not submitting to the policy of expulsion and resisting it in all ways possible, including going to court. A large number among the hundreds who had been expelled from the village in January 1949 returned to their homes in 1951 and others fought for years after to return. Inhabitants who were pursued by the authorities were labelled "smugglers." Those who obtained residence permits and then citizenship had guaranteed that they would not be expelled again and were secure. However, some were unable to defeat the policy of forced migration, and found no relief through decisions of the Supreme Court. Some looked for other ways to secure their return, for example, bartering the votes of their families to the ruling party and its Arab lists in return for identity cards for an "infiltrator." Some inhabitants of Majd al-Krum continued to return until the mid-1950s, when the 1955 elections provided another opportunity for political barter.[110]

While some sought new ways to secure the return of their children, others continued to resort to the Supreme Court of Justice. In 1953, attorneys Naqqara and Waxman raised a case on behalf of Salam Ahmad Kiwan of Majd al-Krum, appealing for the overturn of an expulsion order against him. The proceedings in this case took place after the citizenship or nationality law of 1952 was passed. Like the rest of the villagers, Kiwan had been registered as a resident in the village according to the 1948 register of inhabitants, and he was expelled in January 1949 with hundreds of other inhabitants. The proceedings revolved around the place of residence of the plaintiff between the establishment of the state and the date on which the 1952 law came into force, which was 14 July 1952, and whether he had entered legally. Since the plaintiff had admitted that he had lived for a short time outside the country after his expulsion, the focus turned to "whether the plaintiff had been expelled illegally." The drawing of a distinction between those whom the army had expelled illegally and other expellees became a central issue in determining the fate of many seekers after justice.[111]

It became clear from the court proceedings that Kiwan had been expelled from the country more than once despite his name being on the register of inhabitants and his acquisition of an identity card in the past. When the authorities tried to expel him yet another time, he went to the Supreme Court in 1952.[112] As we saw earlier, this same court had accepted the account of the inhabitants of Majd al-Krum about the expulsion of hundreds of them (including Kiwan) in January 1949. Consequently, at the end of the proceedings the court accepted the plaintiff's request and the court issued its decision on 29 July 1953.[113] Thus, another person from Majd al-Krum managed to consolidate his residence and to acquire a new identity card with the help of attorney Hanna Naqqara.

The military government did not stop trying to arrest those it called "infiltrators" so as to expel them from the country. On 24 August 1952, for example, a combing operation took place in Majd al-Krum and Dayr al-Asad by units of the army and the police.[114] However, the frequency of these operations decreased after 1952. The number of those who attempted to return to the Galilee also decreased after that date. Still, the army intensified its monitoring of the borders and attempted to close the window through which Palestinians had crossed during their return to their homes and villages in the Galilee and other places. Up to the mid-1950s, the policy of trying to catch and expel the inhabitants, on the one hand, and the return of some men to their families, on the other, became a part of life for those who remained.

THE LOYALTY TEST: THE ATTEMPT TO RECRUIT INTO THE ARMY THOSE WHO REMAINED

Beginning in the early 1950s, that remaining Palestinians did not serve in the Israeli army was exploited as an indication that they were not loyal to the state, and was used to discriminate against them in work, housing, and other basic areas. Although most Israeli governments never attempted to recruit Arab citizens into the army, that issue continued to be used against them, the argument being that whoever demands equality of rights should not forget equality of responsibilities.

Most Arabs and Jews were agreed that it was neither logical nor humane to demand that members of the minority serve in an army that was fighting their people. Nevertheless, the Israeli government did try to recruit Arab youth into the army in 1954. The first step was to ask young men of recruitment age to register at offices which were opened specifically for that purpose. The strange thing is that most leaders of the Arab minority, with communists in the lead, supported this move. What was even more strange was that since 1949 the leaders of Maki (both Arabs and Jews) had been the first to demand, in the Knesset and on the pages of their Arabic and Hebrew language newspapers, that the Palestinians who remained be recruited. Hanna Abu Hanna recounted the recruitment of young men from the Liberation League, and its result, in his memoir *The Owl's Dowry*.[115]

The report about the readiness of the leaders of the League to participate in expelling the Arab Rescue Army from upper Galilee could explain the eagerness of Tawfiq Tubi, after he became a member of the Knesset, to ask Ben-Gurion to recruit Arabs in the Israeli army.[116] Ben-Gurion's reply to the proposals of the leaders of Maki in general, and Tubi in particular, was that their position did not represent the opinion of Israeli Arabs.[117] It is puzzling how the leaders of Maki could propose recruiting the remaining Palestinians to serve in the army that was responsible for the Nakba of their people and the destruction of their homeland. Nor should one forget, as we saw in previous chapters, that this army was still busy expelling Palestinians and preventing the return of refugees.

I tried to raise this subject during my interview with Tawfiq Tubi in his last years, but it was difficult to conduct a dialogue with him due to his deteriorating health.[118] Still, the positions of Tubi and his colleagues in the leadership of Maki were not so surprising, if one remembers their extreme eagerness for the establishment of the Jewish state. When it was established, they had faith in total civil equality and Jewish-Arab fraternity. Therefore, they had no objection to Arabs serving in the Israeli army despite all it did to the Palestinians. This class-based position, which prioritized patriotic loyalty to Israel over the [Arab] nationalist view of the conflict, had guided the communists during the war and afterwards. In view of these positions and reasons, it was not strange that the communists should demand the assimilation of the remaining Arabs into the state in 1949, including compulsory military service in the Israeli army.[119]

The question of the remaining Palestinians serving in the army was brought up seriously for the second and last time in 1954. This time the initiative came from the government and the ministry of defense, which issued an order to register all Arab young men as a prelude to their conscription. The official explanation was that this was a step toward "equality in rights and responsibilities for members of all sects in the country," in order to liberate all Arab inhabitants "from the sense of discrimination against them."[120] The conscription order for all Arab youth was published on 9 July 1954, and actual registration began on 25 July. The conscription order and the beginning of registration gave rise to a sharp debate between fathers

and sons and between the political leaders of all parties across the political spectrum. Few expressed their opposition to this step by the government publicly, but
some expressed doubts about the wisdom of this new policy and its timing. The
supporters of the plan thought that conscription would lead to equality of rights
and status for the Arabs in relation to the Jews, and they hoped that service in the
army would put an end to the attitude among Jews that the Arabs constituted a
fifth column.

As we said above, the leaders of Maki, particularly the Jews among them,
supported the conscription of young Arab men and women, without discrimination, with great enthusiasm. This position on the part of the communists did
not leave an opportunity for one-upmanship to their rivals who were cooperating
with the government. Al-Rabita magazine, for instance, devoted several pages to
a discussion of the conscription issue.[121] It reported on the registration of young
men between the ages of eighteen and twenty, and the debate on the subject in the
Hebrew and Arabic language press. The magazine reported on the opinion of
the Arab "man in the street," saying that many looked on this step with trepidation
and even fear of the consequences. It added that "some of those who are afraid and
worried thought of smuggling their children who are of conscription age out of the
country."[122] The magazine also published an unsigned opinion piece clearly opposing the conscription of Arab youth in the army.

The author of that article, who was likely the attorney Elias Kusa, maintained
that "People are conscripted in the armies of their countries after they gain independence, as happened recently in the Arab countries and in the Jewish state. Service in the army is for the defense of the independent nation and the homeland
against its enemies. However, colonial regimes do not conscript the sons of the
peoples they have occupied with their armies."[123] The author then asked a question: "The situation of Arabs in Israel since 1948 is special and distinctive because
of the policy of discrimination against them. In the past Israel has not recruited
Arabs because they are considered not to be loyal to the state. What has changed
now after a few years?" He added that their situation today is no better than in the
past. Does it make sense, for example, that the state should ask the people of Iqrit
and Kufr Bir'im or the village of Sha'b to safeguard its borders? Could the state
possibly give arms to young Arab men to protect it while it does not trust them to
move freely within the country and imposes a military government on them? He
concluded this daring article with a clear deduction in which there was no ambiguity: "Conscription should be rejected because the time is not suitable for it."[124]

After registering thousands of Arab young men, the authorities changed their
position and stopped conscripting them without giving a reason. So, what were
the government's real reasons for adopting this surprising step of trying to impose
conscription on Arab citizens in 1954? Also, what is the secret behind the sudden
change and the cancellation of the decision to conscript after several thousand
had gone to registration offices and enrolled their names? Amnon Lin, a Mapai

activist in Haifa, offered an explanation several years later. He said that the attempt at conscription was a test of the extent of the loyalty of Arab citizens and their willingness to assimilate into state institutions and agencies.[125] However, the prime minister's advisor on Arab affairs, Yehushua Palmon. said that he expected the effort to conscript young Arab men would cause them to leave the country.[126] At any rate, if the government's intention was to cause Arab citizens to fail a "loyalty test" then the plan failed. If, on the other hand, Palmon's view really reflects a hope on the part of the government that masses of young men of conscription age would leave the country, then those hopes would also have been disappointed.

In the end the government decided in 1956 to conscript members of the Druze sect only.[127] This step encountered partial opposition, but most Druze accepted it eventually and enrolled in military service. In addition to opposition from members of the community itself, the attorney Muhammad Nimr al-Hawwari sided with the opposition and sent a letter to that effect in the name of a number of young men from Shafa 'Amr. But the relatively small number of members of the Druze community and the fact that some of them had been performing voluntary military service in the Israeli army since 1948 made it possible to separate them from the rest of the Arab population. Indeed, the fact that members of this sect serve in the Israeli army contributed to the widening of the rift between them and the Palestinian people. In this way the policy of divide and conquer scored a very important victory since the 1950s.[128]

No Israeli government after 1954 repeated the attempt to conscript Arab youth into the army. However, the fact that they did not serve continued to be used against them to justify discrimination in governmental budgets and services, and other individual and collective civil rights. The pioneering pessoptimists managed in the early 1950s to transcend the calamity of their conscription in the army. However, this issue has two sides: the views that dominated in Israeli leadership circles on one side, and the perspective of the Palestinians who remained on the other. The blatant contradiction between imposing military rule on the Arab population and attempting to conscript Arabs into the army is a perplexing issue needing study in depth. The same could be said of the enthusiasm of the Communist Party, with Tawfiq Tubi at the top, to conscript the Arabs into the Israeli army after 1949.

The Palestinians who remained overcame the ordeal of conscription into the Israeli army, first and foremost because the government and the army command backtracked in 1954. The conscription of thousands of young Arab men would have created a major dilemma for the military government and its policies. Therefore, the government of Moshe Sharett and Pinhas Lavon went back on its decision. However, the readiness of thousands in theory to serve in the military in 1954 reflects the weakness of the minority and its leaders who did not dare oppose that attempt publicly. Members of that minority which was still suffering from the shock of the Nakba and its aftereffects were not in a position to challenge and engage in a clash. The main thing to which the remaining Palestinians aspired was to remain in the Arab villages and cities and prevent forced migration. This weakened minority managed to achieve its objective, and so today it is a strong community that is capable of defending itself and participating in the struggle of the Palestinian people for freedom and independence.

The Parliamentary Elections and Political Behavior

BETWEEN MILITARY AND ELECTORAL BATTLES

Israel was not concerned about the difficulties of the Arabs who remained in Israel and did nothing to enable their return to their lands within its borders. There were exceptions to this rule, such as with those whose return served Israel's interests, or those who had cooperated with the state, even if for a short time. Israel had consented both to the return of communists and to that of their rivals. MK Sayf al-Din al-Zu'bi wrote in his memoirs that at the beginning of his political career he took advantage of the return of a number of leaders of the Liberation League from Lebanon (including Emile Tuma) to demand the return of members of his own family and close friends.[1] In Israel, communists were considered allies because of the support of the Soviet Union for the establishment of a Jewish state, and due to their position against the intervention of Arab armies in the 1948 war. However, many Zionist leaders in power viewed most Arabs who remained in Israel, including some who had cooperated with the Jews in the past, as a demographic problem and a security threat. The Arabs in Haifa and the Galilee in particular were seen as an obstacle to Israel's control of the largest possible amount of Palestinian land.

The Israeli government, under the leadership of the ruling Mapai party, continued its confused and stumbling approach to the inclusion of the Arabs in the first elections, even after the election date was announced. Aside from the communists, no one among the remaining Arabs would have objected to being excluded from the Knesset elections. To facilitate a decision, the prime minister convened a meeting in mid-December 1948 to hear the opinions of party experts on this issue.[2] The majority of participants in the meeting did not support including Arabs in the elections, with some opposing the idea vehemently. But Ben-Gurion's opinion was decisive in swaying the outcome of the discussion in favor of including Arabs. His opinion was based on Israel's interests and domestic as well as international considerations. After taking that definitive decision, Mapai and other Zionist parties began to prepare for capturing a large share of the Arab vote, in part because they did not want to leave the field uncontested to the communists and Mapam activists, who enthusiastically supported including the Arabs in the elections.[3]

Mapai activists set up two Arab lists to compete for Arab votes. Mapai leaders chose suitable candidates for the two lists, to have a large measure of control over them. By controlling their representatives, and with the policy of collective social and political isolation of Arab citizens, the leaders of the ruling party voided the meaning of free elections. The lists associated with Mapai were not genuine parties, only organizational arrangements setup on the eve of the elections. These lists were headed by known collaborators with Zionist institutions prior to and during the Nakba. Their job was to compete with the Maki party in the electoral battle, molding Arab policy in Israel in the last weeks of the war: Maki against the Mapai lists. By not allowing Arabs to organize in independent Arab parties, the right to vote granted to Arab citizens had no meaning.

The enthusiastic participation of Arab communists in the January 1949 elections has been largely ignored by researchers. Most studies deal with the activities of the Arabs who remained after the mid-1950s, giving little significance to the Arab participation in Israeli elections during the war. The Israeli leadership that chose to organize those elections during the final days of fighting was comfortable with the merger of the Liberation League with Maki, and its participation in political life. At the international level, that participation had a favorable effect on consolidating the close relationship with the Soviet Union, which provided important political and military support for Israel. Furthermore, the existence of an Israeli Communist Party including Arabs and Jews served the aims of Israeli propaganda and the image of Israel as a democratic state when it was trying to be accepted as a member of the United Nations. Even at the level of local and regional politics, the communist positions of opposition to the intervention of Arab armies and to the nationalist movement headed by Amin al-Husayni made them a useful ally in that critical stage of the struggle.

This chapter will attempt to complete what was begun in chapter 3 and to verify the assertion that the leaders of Maki remained, for the most part, comfortable partners to Israel and its policies until at least 1955. The communists contributed to obscuring the Palestinian identity of the remaining Arabs and promoted in its place the government's line about "the Arab minority," "the Arabs in Israel," or even "the Israeli Arabs." As a consequence, they monopolized the political representation of the rights of the Palestinians who stayed, and confined their activities to civil struggles against discrimination among citizens. Consequently, the nationalist aspect of the struggle and resistance to Zionism, which was the official ideology of the state and its policies, was absent. This was comfortable and useful to Israel. The leaders of Maki did not resist either the Law of Return, or the settlement of Zionists on the lands of destroyed and depopulated Arab villages, or the flag, or the national anthem, or other symbols of the Jewish nature of the state. In this respect, the communists accepted the Zionist version of the Palestine partition resolution of 1947. Other remaining Arabs who dared to express nationalist positions contrary to the positions of Maki were severely attacked and accused of being nationalism-mongers.

The communists and the government collaborators who assumed the leadership of political action among the remaining Arabs in Haifa and the Galilee were only a small minority in early 1949. Studies which highlight the rivalry between these two trends fail to capture the full picture of the political behavior of Arab citizens after the Nakba. Support by Arab citizens for either of these two trends was due to the fight to stay and should not be read as a manifestation of either conviction or assimilation. After the tragedies of the Nakba, preservation of the family and the ability to stay in the homeland topped the list of priorities of the remaining Arabs, followed by holding onto their homes and lands. In order to secure these goals, people were prepared to temporarily sacrifice their dignity and human rights and the rights of citizenship. The expectations of the Palestinians who stayed in the Jewish state were not high; they believed that their situation was temporary and would end soon through liberation from the outside, despite everything that had happened to them in the year of the Nakba. Consequently, all they had to do was endure and remain in their homes until the "coming of the saviors."

The men of the ruling party who understood Arab society were optimistic that they would capture most of the minority's votes. Eliyahu Sasson estimated that 80 percent of the Arabs would vote for Mapai and its affiliated list, headed by Minister Bechor Shitrit. He also predicted that only 20 percent would vote for the Zionist leftist Mapam party and the non-Zionist Maki party.[4] Not all observers agreed with Sasson's estimate, but they were convinced that the ruling party would win the majority of Arab votes. When the election date drew near in January 1949, friction increased between party activists and the military government. Even Mapai activists in the north of the country (like Abba Hoshi) complained at the time about the conduct of the army in the areas under military rule. Ben-Gurion intervened and promised party members that he would issue the appropriate orders to the army.[5]

THE FIRST ISRAELI ELECTIONS AND THEIR RESULTS

Israel's census of November 1948 determined that there were 782,000 people living in the country, of which 713,000 were Jews and only 69,000 were Arabs (or non-Jewish minorities). We mentioned earlier that these figures on the Arab population did not reflect the true demographic facts concerning those who remained under Israeli rule. Many Arabs in northern Galilee were not included in the first census despite the fact that Israel had occupied this area in Operation Hiram; also the Arabs of the Naqab were not registered in the census for several reasons.[6] What is more important is that the borders of the state had not been clearly and officially defined. The census included the residents of Nazareth and the villages in its district, but ignored the fact that thousands of others were located in several other regions. The final result of this partial census of the Arab population was to undercount the number of remaining Arabs with voting rights.[7]

Those eighteen years of age and older were given the right to vote. Photo identity cards with details of family status and the names of children under the age of eighteen were distributed to those with the right to vote—personally handed out in exchange for a registration receipt.[8] Those who did not bring along pictures of themselves at the requisite time did not receive an ID card and lost the right to vote. For this procedural reason, in addition to many other reasons, the number of those with voting rights shrank a great deal from those listed in the population register. The total number of those with voting rights for the first election was 507,000, while the number of Arabs with voting rights was only about 30,000.[9] Some officials feared that many would not exercise their right to vote. Those fears dissipated when it became clear that about 25,000 Arabs, or more than 83 percent of registered Arabs, exercised their right to vote, not much lower than the percentage of Jews who did so.[10]

Most Arab voters in Israel's first elections in 1949 were residents of Nazareth and villages in its district, as well as Arabs who remained in Shafa 'Amr, 'Akka, Haifa, and villages in western Galilee. The areas of Nazareth and western Galilee had been allocated to the Arab state under the 1947 partition resolution. Ben-Gurion understood the importance of the participation of the residents of these Arab territories, named "administered territories" in the elections, as a step towards consolidating Israeli control and rule over them. What is interesting but less clear is how the Arab activists in Maki explained their participation in lending legitimacy to that step, which amounted to the annexation of regions of the Galilee to Israel, before the conclusion of armistice agreements with Arab countries. Communist sources do not raise this issue as being a matter that worried party leaders. In this respect, Maki's conduct was not different from that of Zionist leaders who accepted the partition resolution in principle and yet accepted the enlargement of the territory of Israel at the expense of the Palestinians.

Twenty-one lists competed in the election, of which twelve surpassed the required minimum threshold for inclusion in the 120-member Knesset. After the results were announced, parliamentary seats were distributed among the lists as follows: Mapai, under the leadership of Ben-Gurion, the largest number (forty-six), which established its position as the ruling party; Mapam in second place with only nineteen seats, although it gained a seat in August 1949 after one communist MK joined its ranks;[11] the bloc of Jewish religious parties (sixteen); the right-wing Herut party (fourteen); General Zionists (seven); Progressives (five); Maki (four); and the Nazareth Democratic list, headed by Sayf al-Din al-Zu'bi (two). Among these, the Arabs were represented by a total of three seats in the first Knesset: Sayf al-Din al-Zu'bi and Amin Jarjura from the Nazareth Democratic list, and Tawfiq Tubi from Maki. Three seats out of 120 was a weak and inadequate representation of the Arabs who had been counted in the census and granted the right to vote. What was the reason for this weak representation of the Arab population in the first Knesset?

The Arabs faced several difficulties along the path to the elections which led to this small number of representatives. As previously mentioned, not all Arabs living under Israeli rule were registered. Among the 69,000 who were, not all gained the right to vote. Arab voters were about 5.5 percent of the total. These elections were a new and strange experience for Arab voters under the prevailing circumstances at the end of the war. Concerns were raised about how many of the remaining Arabs would be able to get to the ballot boxes in view of the blatant discrimination, as efforts to uproot them continued, alongside attempts also to assimilate them. When Arab voters arrived to vote, they were not faced with many real worthwhile choices. Going to the polls, like obtaining identity cards before that, was a means to an end and a talisman to protect them against being uprooted and expelled.

The ruling Mapai party created two Arab lists, only one of which passed the threshold for inclusion in the Knesset; consequently thousands of votes were wasted. Even in Maki, Arabs were under-represented in the names at the top of the Communist Party list: among the top five only one Arab name was present, that of Tawfiq Tubi. The Liberation League had joined Maki at the end of 1948 from a clear position of weakness. Shmuel Mikunis and his Jewish comrades in the leadership of the party were more experienced and had better ties to the Soviet Union as well as to Israeli leaders. Also, the number of veterans, tried-and-tested members of the Liberation League who remained in Israel or who returned to it after the Nakba was quite small, no more than a few dozen. Consequently, naming one of them to be among the top five names on the list did not elicit objections from the Arab comrades at the time. However, this imbalance of forces inside the leadership of Maki began to give rise to tensions and conflicts in a later phase of the party's history.

After the official election results were released, Maki leaders had hopes that Ben-Gurion would include the party in the governing coalition and they let this be clearly known in *al-Ittihad*.[12] However the leader of the ruling party never considered including the non-Zionist Maki party in running the affairs of the state. He went further by coining his famous phrase, "neither Maki nor Herut," thereby delegitimizing the two parties on the far left and the far right. By doing this, Ben-Gurion laid the cornerstone for rendering Arab citizens' right to vote to be an inconsequential act in Israeli politics, while still lending the process a democratic hue. Arabs, and their representatives in the Knesset, were excluded from any real influence in Israeli politics from 1949 onwards; they had the right to vote but no influence on decision-making or implementation.

The situation of the two Knesset members from the Nazareth list associated with Mapai was no different, despite their connection to the ruling party. Sayf al-Din al-Zuʻbi (b. 1913) entertained no ambitions beyond leadership at the local level of Nazareth and its region. He was chosen to be at the head of the list because of his long cooperation with Zionist institutions, which he served without reservation.[13] Al-Zuʻbi was content with his status as a faithful follower, and his demands on the ruling party were limited to mediation for some of his close friends and relatives in return for serving the policy of the state. Sayf al-Din was an example of "the good Arab" whom the authorities helped in the service of their own interests and in an attempt to domesticate the Palestinians who remained under the control of the military government. The majority of Arab voters in that period only saw the elections as a means to consolidating their ability to stay. Therefore, many saw no problem with voting on election day for Sayf al-Din and his sort.

The three Arab members of the first Israeli Knesset were urbanites from the north of the country, which reflected the demographic and social center of gravity. At that time, the remaining Arabs in Haifa and the Galilee were the vast majority of voters, so it was therefore natural that their representatives in the Knesset should be from Haifa and Nazareth. Those two cities continued to represent the center of gravity for the remaining Arabs even after the addition of the Triangle to Israel and the participation of its inhabitants in elections after 1951. Two of the three Arab members of the Knesset were Christians, which reflected the consolidation of the political status of members of that community in Israel after the Nakba and following the loss of the urban city and the Palestinian elite in 1948. The Arab activists in Maki were mostly Orthodox Christians, which also reflected the cultural and historical relationship between that sect and Russia since the end of the Ottoman era. The inclusion of Muslims and some Druze in the Communist Party, particularly in its leadership, did not happen until the 1970s.[14]

The historical literature is full of inaccurate generalizations about the Arab Knesset members from lists associated with the Mapai party, describing them as agents of the governing authorities in Israel. This generalization is unjust to one of them and does not present an accurate picture of the positions and actions of this parliamentarian. The second on the Nazareth list, Amin Jarjura (1886–1975), proved more than once that he had independent positions and critical views which he expressed inside and outside the Knesset. In his first speech in February 1949, he chose to stress that the values of justice and equality should be the basis for government and for the state's treatment of Arab citizens.[15] Amin Jarjura was a lawyer from a well-known Nazarene family whose autobiography does not match what we know about the other Knesset members from lists associated with the ruling party in the 1950s. Jarjura's audacity and his independent positions at times embarrassed the leadership of Mapai in the Knesset. In a debate in June 1949 about the problem of refugees and their right to return, this parliamentarian told the Knesset: "These are people who have been driven from their quarters and their lands and their homeland under conditions of fear and terrorism and the disproportionate use of direct and indirect violence. People's attachment to their homeland is well-known and clear and in no need of investigation and proof." Jarjura added: "If the Jewish people have retained their right in Palestine, including the right to live there, for two thousand years, why do the Arab refugees not have the right to return to their lands and cities and villages? They were forced to leave only a few months ago, under coercion as is well known."[16]

MK Jarjura was not satisfied with making those brave statements concerning the circumstances of the uprooting of Palestinians refugees from their homeland. He also debated the claim of foreign minister Moshe Sharett that their expulsion was the result of the attack by Arab armies, saying: "It is very well known that the expulsion of the Arabs from Haifa, Jaffa, Tiberias, 'Akka, Bisan, and other places took place prior to 15 May 1948 and the withdrawal of British mandatory forces, and before their own eyes." Jarjura concluded: "There is no relationship between the expulsion of the refugees and the entry of Arab armies in Palestine, so that has nothing to do with our subject."[17] These frank words from the podium of the Knesset in response to the foreign minister who was one of the prominent leaders of the ruling Mapai party in June 1949 are nothing to make light of.

Let us look at another example of Jarjura's courageous statements. In a debate about a permit for the Galilee Bus Company to operate in Nazareth, he said: "The Galilee company in Nazareth is the only one that continued to operate after the Israeli occupation."[18] The assertion, on the eve of the second parliamentary elections in June 1951, that Israel had "occupied" Nazareth was a bold and dissonant note amidst the dominant political discourse of that period. It should be pointed out that such statements were unheard of even from the leaders of Maki, be they Arabs or Jews. MK Jarjura, despite his election as no. 2 on the Nazareth slate alongside Sayf al-Din al-Zu'bi, gave voice to quite distinct political positions. The lawyer/parliamentarian demonstrated a measure of self-confidence and independence that did not suit what the leaders of Mapai expected. Consequently, his days in the Knesset were numbered, and his name was not placed high on the slate which al-Zu'bi headed in 1951, ensuring his non-election.[19]

Jarjura was well educated by the standards of those days following the Nakba. He was replaced in his capacity as "representative of the Christians" in the second and third Knessets by Mas'ad Qassis from Mi'lya, who we will discuss later. Although Mapai chose for its associated lists people who would advance the government's policies and interests, some occasionally behaved in a manner that was not entirely consistent with the party's expectations. From this perspective, one can see the significant difference between the conduct of Sayf al-Din al-Zu'bi and Jarjura, his partner on the Nazareth Democratic list. Amin Jarjura remained active in politics after 1951, and was elected mayor of Nazareth in 1954, remaining in that position until 1959. He set a noble example for the survivors, reminiscent of the

Palestinian elite that had existed before the Nakba. He was quite different from Sayf al-Din and his sort who willingly served the Israeli authorities.

Returning to the results of the elections and the distribution of Arab votes, we see that the choice available to Arab voters was between Mapai and its lists and the Communist Party. It is difficult to determine the distribution of Arab votes with sufficient accuracy because of the absence of information from ballot boxes in "mixed cities." Still, it is estimated that 10,600 Arab votes were given to the two lists associated with Mapai.[20] Maki received about 6,000 votes from Arabs, representing about one quarter of Arab voters in those elections. Other Zionist parties had also tried to attract Arab votes, such as Mapam and the General Zionists. Mapam created an Arab list named the Popular Arab Bloc, but it received a mere 2,812 votes, below the threshold for the Knesset. Thousands of Arab votes went to other Zionist parties which had no Arab representatives at all. Thus, the biggest winners from Arab participation in the 1949 elections were Maki on one side and the Nazareth list headed by Sayf al-Din al-Zu'bi on the other.

At first glance these results look like what one would have expected, involving no surprises. However, a more in-depth analysis of the distribution of Arab votes would indicate some surprising victories for the Communist Party in Arab cities, where it received one quarter of the Arab vote, according to official data.[21] Maki won a decisive victory in Nazareth, receiving over half of the votes of the only Arab city to escape destruction, which had great significance. The semi-official *al-Yawm* newspaper, which highlighted the large Arab turnout in the election, tried to belittle the significance of the victory of the Communist Party by attributing it to the importing of over 170 Arab laborers from Ramla to vote in Nazareth.[22] However, the real reason behind the victory of Maki in the city of the Annunciation was that there had been ten months of persistent and organized work before the elections. The activists of the Liberation League in the city, under the leadership of Saliba Khamis, managed to attract a number of supporters beginning in summer of 1948. During those days, relations between activists of the League and Mapam's civilian and military activists were consolidated. Relations with governmental offices led by Mapam ministers contributed to the flow of workers to the ranks of the League.[23] Therefore, it came as no surprise at the time of the elections that the activists of Maki should have been better prepared than any other party to enter and win the contest, particularly in Nazareth.

The victory of the communists in Nazareth was their most prominent and important, but it was not an isolated triumph. According to official party data, Maki won about 52 percent of the Arab vote in Nazareth, almost 28 percent of the vote in 'Iblin and Kafr Yusif, and 25 percent in Shafa 'Amr and 'Akka. Overall, Maki won 28 percent of the votes of Arabs in Israel.[24] Despite the fact that some of these figures are a bit higher than the final official figures, there is no doubt that it was a big victory for the communists. Official results estimated that only 22 percent of Arab votes went to the party, although it was admitted that Maki gained over half the votes in Nazareth. These results were an important victory in themselves, a success rate that the party was unable to duplicate in electoral battles over the next two decades.[25]

The results were all the more significant since many Arab residents of the Galilee and other areas did not participate in the elections because they were not allowed to vote. Some Mapai leaders also objected to the remaining Arabs voting, and claimed that many Arab voters would refrain from doing so.[26] The Palestinians in Haifa and the Galilee were for the most part still traumatized by the consequences of the war. One may ask: how is this consistent with the strong showing for the opposition Communist Party in January 1949? This party was opposed to Zionism. It was the only party that opened its ranks to Arab citizens, and it also represented the interests of the minority people. For these reasons the authorities began to pursue communist activists and their supporters. So how do we explain the success of the Communists in their electoral battle and in overcoming the military government? Why did the authorities not succeed in terrorizing the Arab citizens against voting for Maki? And how do we explain the remarkable success of the Communists in Nazareth, where they obtained more than half of the vote?

In addition to the organizational abilities of the Liberation League and its political experience, particularly with workers, in contrast to its rivals among Arab slates, other factors existed which researchers into the history of the Communist Party have not mentioned. For instance, the Arab-Jewish partnership in Maki served to dispel some fears of retaliation by the authorities, as did the fact that the communists were close to activists in Mapam, the second biggest Zionist party. We saw earlier how civil servants in Israeli ministries belonging to Mapam supported the activities of the Liberation League before it merged with Maki. Also, the communists supported the partition resolution and the establishment of a Jewish state. These reasons—and the role of the Soviet Union –all contributed to the communists' ability to consolidate their position among the remaining Palestinians many months before the elections.

Even after the Liberation League decided to merge with Maki, the Zionist left under the leadership of Mapam saw the Arab communists as an important ally.[27] The first Knesset elections took place then at a time when the communists were not considered a bitter enemy of Zionism, as happened later in the 1950s. If we add to all this the fact that the viable alternatives before Arab voters were not attractive, we can understand why the success of Maki exceeded the expectations of the advisors of the ruling Mapai party regarding Arab society. Perhaps the hesitancy of Mapam to create an Arab list played a role in the success of the communists as well. The failure of the Mapam-associated list to exceed the minimum threshold for representation in the Knesset led to recriminations against Ben-Gurion's policies and self-criticism on the part of activists in the Marxist-Zionist Hashomer Hatzair.[28]

The activists in the Arab department in Mapam found reasons to justify their lack of success in attracting Arab voters to their list, but they later admitted their failure and frankly accepted responsibility for it. Aharon Cohen, for example, was outspoken in a letter he sent to the political committee on 15 May 1949. In the course of his self-criticism of the party, he said: "We cannot do what Mapai does and copy its methods. The Arabs who chose to go with us will leave us and go to Maki if we do not accept them as equals. Therefore, it is up to Mapam to decide if it wants to remain a Jewish party and leave the Arabs of Israel to the others, or if it wants to be the party of all workers in Israel."[29] Rustum Bastuni made similarly bold statements at the 14 June 1949 meeting of the party secretariat in which he attacked the establishment of an Arab list. He added: "We are convinced that this method of setting up a separate slate for the Arabs was not democratic, and that it did not aspire to full equality free of discrimination." He warned that if Mapam did not open its doors to the Arabs "then that would mean the party was treating us like the British treat the people of the African continent."[30]

Indeed, the exclusion of Arabs from membership in all Zionist parties, including Mapam, was a factor in making the slates associated with them unattractive, which in turn strengthened the position of Maki. If we add that Israel did not permit the establishment of independent Arab parties throughout the period of military rule, it is not hard to see what was distinctive about the Communist Party and why it succeeded. Maki spoke frankly and unequivocally about discrimination against Arab citizens and demanded full equality for them. In those early days after the Nakba, when the wounds were still open, those who remained in Haifa and the Galilee were looking for a savior from expulsion and a life of exile, and Maki was a lifeboat for them. For those with political awareness, the party, with its Jewish/Arab leadership and its anti-Zionist positions, was the most attractive among the alternatives.

On the other hand, Maki never changed its position on leftist Zionism under the leadership of Mapam, and continued to seek cooperation with it. On many occasions these two parties voted together against the government of Ben-Gurion. For example, both parties voted against the armistice agreement between Israel and Jordan on 3 April 1949. Maki also stuck by its position of supporting unrestricted Jewish immigration to the country, and used the Zionist term *aliyah* (ascent) for it.[31] When rivals of the communists questioned this position, party leaders responded sharply. MK Meir Vilner, for example, conveyed Maki's clear position to members of the Knesset in a special session, stating: "We see aliya as a vital need for the state of Israel." He reminded them that "during the difficult days of the war, Mikunis organized a collective fighting aliya. At the time, the leadership of Maki not only supported aliya, it also supported settlement."[32] Indeed, Maki did not object even to leftist Zionist settlement and the establishment of kibbutzim on the ruins of Arab villages such as Kufr Bir'im, Sa'sa', and others.

THE RETURN AND POLITICS: THE RETURN
OF TWO RIVALS AND ENEMIES OF COMMUNISM

MK Sayf al-Din al-Zuʻbi wrote in his memoirs that after the return of Emile Tuma from Lebanon in the spring of 1949, he went to the authorities and asked that his brother-in-law (Ahmad Tawfiq al-Fahum) be allowed to return.[33] Tuma was one of the last of the communists whose return to Haifa by way of Nazareth had been approved by Israel. Before him, a large number of activists in the League and their families had returned from Lebanon and other countries. After the elections, the authorities agreed to most of al-Zuʻbi's demands for the return of his relatives and close friends, including Hanna Abu ʻAsal, the father of the Anglican priest (later bishop) Riyah from Nazareth, a number of fishermen from ʻAkka, and Hanna Daklush from Haifa, among others.[34] Thus, the mechanism of family reunification was exploited for political reasons in the service of Mapai and its collaborators in the Arab slates.

Mapai activists and consultants on Arab affairs exploited all means available to them after the first elections to weaken the communists. One avenue was to bring back leading figures who were anticommunist, or at least rivals to the communists. While Israel needed the support of communists and the Soviet Union during the 1948 war, and rewarded local communists for that, Mapai leaders were surprised by the extent of Maki's success at the ballot box, and tried to reduce its influence on the Arabs. The ruling party was not looking for Arab partners, but for collaborators with its policies. As for Maki's Arab leaders (with Tawfiq Tubi at their head), they created illusions of Arab-Jewish fraternity, a partnership of worker's parties, and the establishment of a socialist regime allied with the Soviet Union. Maki's leaders became greatly disappointed with Ben-Gurion and his international policies, and with the governing coalition he put together, in which not even Mapam was included.

Ben-Gurion's advisors began work from spring of 1949 on limiting the influence of the communists on the Arabs. Bishop Hakim was the first to benefit from this policy. He had been the leader of the Melkite Catholic community and a well-connected figure with considerable influence, well-known for his hostility to communism. This is why he was selected on his return to the country to become, by dint of his personality and his office, a strong rival to the communists. In this way the return of Bishop Hakim contributed to weakening the influence of Maki, on the one hand, and to furthering the policy of divide and rule among Palestinian Christians, on the other, since most communist leaders came from the Orthodox sect. His return also served Israel's international interests due to his multifaceted relationship with the Vatican concerning Palestinian refugees, which helped the government fend off pressure for their return.

Bishop Hakim's return to the country on a permanent basis was preceded by a series of talks and dealings with the Israeli government. Hakim first returned to

Haifa after its fall as a visitor at the end of June 1948. During that visit he explored the possibility of the return of members of his Catholic sect. At that stage Israel did not agree to all of his demands, but it left the door open for further talks. Hakim left and began a tour of neighboring Arab countries.[35] In December 1948, Israel came under international pressure to accept the return of Palestinian refugees, particularly in light of the adoption of United Nations Resolution 194. At that stage, a number of those working in the Israeli foreign ministry assessed that the return of Bishop Hakim to Haifa would be useful for Israeli propaganda and foreign relations, and in fact his return was approved in early 1949 and implemented very soon thereafter.[36]

Al-Yawm reported the return of Bishop Hakim to Haifa by plane on 18 February 1949.[37] In contrast to the paper welcoming his return in the name of the authorities, the communists directed strong criticism at this event, and accused him of serving the interests of the Mapai party. Maki activists rightly estimated that the return of the Bishop was part of government efforts to weaken their influence among the Arab population. Indeed, Hakim was openly prepared to offer his services in this regard. In his application for a license for his printing press, he wrote that he was seeking to "purify the air that was full of communist poison and to publish the truth and correct principles in Arab circles."[38] In return, the authorities encouraged him "to establish a moderate Arab party" so as to distance a large section of his religious community from the influence of the communists.

Bishop Hakim obtained a permit to resume publishing *al-Rabita* magazine which had stopped in 1948; it quickly became a pulpit for attacks on the communists and their leadership. He also used his clerical authority to impose a ban by the church on communists and their supporters among members of his denomination.[39] The magazine, which spoke in the name of the church, published sharp rebuttals of the statements and propaganda by the communists. One article dealt with the issue of the persecution of Catholics in eastern Europe under communist regimes.[40] The magazine reported on the celebration of the return of dozens of children from Lebanon to Haifa on 13 October 1949. The bishop and his supporters went even further when they asked the Israeli authorities to close down *al-Ittihad* newspaper after its "vilification" of the bishop, who was the supreme local spiritual authority of the denomination.[41]

Maki leaders redoubled their accusations that Bishop Hakim was working with the Israeli authorities and serving their interests.[42] MK Tubi commented on Israel's granting him permission to return to Haifa "despite the fact that he had agitated against the UN partition resolution and had known connections to imperialism."[43] The leaders of Maki and their allies in Mapam understood the clear motives of Mapai for allowing the bishop to return to the country. The statements of Tubi and other Maki leaders after the Nakba indicate that they considered the granting of permission to Palestinians to return to the country at that time to be a political reward for their positions on partition and the establishment of the Jewish state rather than a basic right of the expellees. The written and verbal statements by Maki activists included criticisms of the government for allowing the opponents of partition, supporters of the mufti, and those who had cooperated with the Rescue Army to return to live in the country. The pages of *al-Ittihad* in 1949 were full of examples of these strange statements.

In the years following the return of Bishop Hakim and hundreds of members of his sect in 1949, he was helpful to dozens more people. Members of the Srouji family of Nazareth who had been studying in Beirut and were stranded there after the Nakba were able to return to their city in 1951 thanks to the help of the bishop. For example, Dr. 'Aziz Srouji had graduated with a degree in medicine from the American University of Beirut in 1947 and arrived to visit his family. He returned to Lebanon to work in the university hospital and then worked for two years (1949–50) with the Red Cross in Palestinian refugee camps. On 1 January 1951, he learned that the health of his father, who was suffering from cancer, had deteriorated, so he decided to return to the country with the help of smugglers.[44] He was arrested near Fassuta and detained in 'Akka for two days before his brother, Dr. Elias Srouji, managed to arrange his release with the help of Hakim and the Nazareth police chief Wanderman. Initially he obtained a residence permit in Nazareth for a month, which was renewed several times. In the end, he acquired an identity card and citizenship, and remained in Nazareth where he worked as a doctor.

'Anis Srouji (b. 1928) went to Beirut in 1945 to study engineering and completed his studies in June 1950. He found work in Tartus, Syria, and resided there for ten months.[45] From Tartus he went to Aleppo to work with an infrastructure company run by a Palestinian, Sa'id Saffuri, from Kafr Kana, on Aleppo's water system. In the summer of 1951, he found his name on a list of those approved for family reunification. He arrived at the border with his brother 'Afif, crossed to the Israeli side through Ra's al-Naqura, and returned to Nazareth. Several months later he opened a civil engineering office and over the years became a well-known architect in Nazareth. Bishop Hakim contributed to the success of 'Anis Srouji's office as he chose him to manage all of his building projects inside and outside the city. Thus, the Srouji brothers succeeded in returning to their homes and became an important part of the social and political elite of Nazareth.[46]

Bishop Hakim's assistance to the Srouji family and others in his denomination yielded political benefits, too. In 1954, in the first elections for the Nazareth municipal council held since the Nakba, 'Anis Srouji became one of the pillars of the "Home Bloc" (al-Kutla al-Ahliya), which was close to the bishop, and he remained active in municipal affairs for twenty-six years. During my interview with him, 'Anis expressed pride in the role that MK Mas'ad Qassis (who was also close to the bishop) was playing. Thus, the government's plan to promote rivals to the Communist Party, preeminently the bishop, had succeeded. The return of a number of academics of the Catholic faith (such as the Srouji family) played an important role in that success.

Following the initial successes of Bishop Hakim, he established a scout move-ment to compete with the Maki youth. The bishop's scouts spearheaded the rivalry with the Communist Party in Arab cities and villages, and sometimes initiated vio-lent confrontations with the Communist Party activists. The competition between the two sides intensified and worsened at times into bloody clashes, especially with marches organized by the church scout movement during holidays and other occasions, leading to tragic events in 'Iblin and 'Ilabun.[47] Towns and cities inhab-ited by Orthodox and Catholics became arenas for the struggle between the two sides. The government had helped consolidate the bishop's position and his role by restoring church property which had been appropriated and paying compensation for property not returned. In this way the strong economic base of the bishop and his supporters grew, which contributed to the expansion of their political activities and the capture of new supporters, and drove others away from Maki.[48]

On 14 April 1952 (Easter), the bishop's scouts from Haifa, Shafa 'Amr, and a few other Galilee villages came to Nazareth to demonstrate a clear show of force.[49] Hundreds of young scouts gathered and then marched in the streets of the city, which fed rising tensions and exploded in a clash in the eastern quarter with young men on both sides injured. Ni'mat al-Qasim was seriously wounded and died two days later, which provoked fevered emotions in the city, and threatened a wider explosion between Muslims and Catholics. At this point, the military government declared a curfew in Nazareth for a month, and a residents' committee worked quickly to calm things and arrange a truce between the two sides.[50]

Despite the predicament that the death of al-Qasim caused the camp of the bishop and his scouts, it did not stop their attempts to challenge the activities of the communists in the Galilee. Another tragic event occurred between the two camps in October 1952 in 'Ilabun. The 'Ilabun villagers were still suffering from the events of the Nakba at the end of 1948 when they were surprised by a fire which broke out in the Communist Party club, which claimed the life of young Suhayl Zurayq. Hillel Cohen reported on the events in 'Ilabun, giving the view of the arsonist, who frankly declared his blind hatred of communists.[51] The events in 'Ilabun led to counter-intuitive results: they consolidated the position of the party in the vil-lage, and added to the condemnation of the activities of the bishop's scouts and his supporters. The killing of Suhayl Zurayq became a symbol of the bloody actions of the authorities, in an oft-repeated slogan, "those who worked with them worked against those fighting for the rights of the Arabs in Israel." Hanna Abu Hanna, the young poet in charge of the communist youth at the time, composed a poem dedicated to "the soul of the martyr Suhayl Zurayq" titled "Smoke in 'Ilabun."[52]

Aside from Bishop Hakim, the Israeli government permitted the return of another leader who was a communist rival, the attorney Muhammad Nimr al-Hawwari, in December 1949. Al-Hawwari's return was part of the government's policy to encourage rivals of Maki among the Arabs who remained in the Galilee.[53] Al-Hawwari was born in Nazareth in 1908 and grew up there. After completing his studies in Nazareth, he worked as a teacher for ten years in Jerusalem, then studied law and became a trial lawyer. In 1945 he took over leadership of the youth organization al-Najjada in Jaffa. Initially, he was close to the mufti, who became the leader of the Palestinian nationalist movement. But the internal divisions and the rivalry for jobs made him drift away from Hajj Amin and his supporters. In 1947 he established relations with the Haganah in Tel Aviv. His opponents said that he was one of the first to run away from Jaffa when military skirmishes began following the partition resolution.[54]

The man who took the initiative in bringing al-Hawwari back to the country was the prime minister's advisor on Arab affairs, Yehushua Palmon. When he was criticized for this undertaking, he hastened to announce that Hawwari "has worked with us since 1945." Palmon, who represented and implemented the policies of the authorities towards the Arabs who remained, maintained personal relations with al-Hawwari for years after al-Hawwari quit politics and went back to working as a lawyer, then a judge.[55] After al-Hawwari returned to the country, he set up residence in Haifa, where he found a number of supporters, but also much enmity. This was instigated by the communists who were concerned about the role that this able lawyer might play, given that the authorities had allowed his return as part of their divide and rule policy. The activists of Maki and the party's press launched strongly worded attacks on al-Hawwari and accused him of "serving Israel and its policies."[56] The communist press also referred to his old ties to the mufti and his role in organizing al-Najjada, and raised questions about his role as a representative of the refugees at the Rhodes talks with Israeli representatives and his subsequent surprising arrival in the country with his family only.

The communists had heard reports of al-Hawwari's possible return to the country a month before it happened. Al-Ittihad reported in November 1949 about a rumor circulating that al-Hawwari might be brought back to Nazareth, the purpose being to create an Arab party sympathetic to the Mapai party and Ben-Gurion's policies.[57] Contrary to Bishop Hakim, however, al-Hawwari did not have strong reliable backing and became an easy target for communist arrows. The communists feared an alliance of al-Hawwari, Hakim, and others who were opposed to Maki and supported by the government and its institutions. Indeed, the hostile reception that the communists organized for al-Hawwari's return was a clear statement of those fears that followed their successes in the Knesset elections that same year. Compared to the leaders of Arab slates connected to the ruling party, Bishop Hakim and al-Hawwari were considered heavyweight, experienced leaders.

After al-Hawwari settled in 'Akka, the communists organized demonstrations and verbal attacks against him which at times extended to the rest of his family. In one demonstration, the participants screamed, "Al-Hawwari to the gallows." The party organ which reported this news added that the authorities "are bringing back al-Hawwari while they hunt down infiltrators in Haifa" and imposed curfews and arrested people in Wadi al-Nisnas.[58] But this communist harassment did not deter al-Hawwari from continuing his hostile political activities against them, at least for a while. Al-Hawwari moved from 'Akka to Nazareth, where he consulted with several known figures about establishing an anticommunist Arab party. After he published his memoirs and political opinions in *al-Yawm*, the communists intensified their attacks on him and his activities.[59] Compared to 'Akka, al-Hawwari found greater support in Nazareth from his extended family and other rivals of the communists who were pleased that he joined their camp.

Al-Hawwari's return took more than two years, during which time he and his family moved from one country to another. He was considered a leader of the Palestinian national movement, yet we do not find in his memoir *The Secret of al-Nakba* any self-criticism or deep analysis of the causes of the tragedy. Instead, in his preface to the book he directed his barbs at the communists who had accused him of being an agent and traitor, even a war criminal.[60] The party activists accused al-Hawwari of being one of the mufti's men who contributed to igniting the war between Arabs and Jews. He, on the other hand, claimed that in December 1947 he had done all he could to preserve peace and tranquility between the Arab inhabitants of Jaffa and their neighbors in Tel Aviv. He added that his activism for the sake of peace between neighbors was what forced him to leave at the end of that month.[61] Al-Hawwari went beyond defending himself against the communists' accusations; he turned those accusations on their head, claiming that it was the communists who were responsible for the actions in question.

Al-Hawwari's return did indeed seem unusual against the backdrop of his activities and the role he played in Jaffa before 1948, followed by his defense of the Palestinian cause and right of return. The communists speculated, correctly, that his return with the authorities' blessings was part of a divide and rule policy, so they never let up in their attacks. When he cooperated with Bishop Hakim to establish an Arab party before the 1951 elections, their attacks resumed in force. However, in contrast to the enmity between the bishop and the communists which continued throughout the 1950s, al-Hawwari chose to renounce politics fairly quickly. As of 1950, he left the political arena and—belonging to no church or party or large family which could protect and support him—devoted most of his time to the judicial system, working as a lawyer and later a judge, providing support for his extended family.[62]

THE SECOND KNESSET ELECTIONS OF 1951 AND THEIR OUTCOME

The second parliamentary elections in Israel took place under relatively comfortable circumstances for the Arabs remaining in the Galilee and other areas. The shock which had unsettled the Arabs who had escaped the uprooting and expulsion measures metamorphosed into gradual acclimatization to the new political reality. The number of Arabs with voting rights doubled,[63] and when election day came, a greater number exercised the right to vote; the rate of voters reached 86 percent of those eligible, higher than the general average.[64] As a result, the number of Arabs elected to the Knesset in 1951 increased from three to eight. Tawfiq Tubi and Emile Habibi from Maki were elected, and five others were elected from Arab slates associated with the ruling party; Rustum Bastuni from Mapam was also elected. While the ratio of Arab members of the Knesset was smaller than their demographic ratio to the general population, it was nonetheless a significant jump which represented a measure of stability.

The number of Arabs with voting rights increased to about 70,000 in 1951, but still constituted only 40 percent of the Arab population, which totaled 160,000 at the end of 1949. One obvious reason for this low rate was the large average size of Arab families, such that many were below voting age. Another reason was the continuing practice of denying Israeli citizenship to many of the Arabs who remained, who only had temporary registration cards and red identity cards. The available information on this category of the population in 1951 is scant. Even the official numbers which have been adopted by some researchers about those elections and the Arabs who participated in them is not very clear.[65] The election results indicate that the number of actual Arab voters that year was less than 60,000.

The relatively large number of Arabs who had the right to vote did attract the attention of parties that competed for their votes. The elections also gave the remaining Arabs an opportunity to exploit their right to vote in the service of personal, familial, or sectarian interests. Some had learned from the first elections the value of votes as an in-demand commodity that could be profitable. Some took to bargaining with the votes of their families or their clans to secure personal or group demands from the government. The competition by Zionist parties for Arab votes played a role in relaxing the iron grip of the military government and securing promises from the government to improve their living conditions. Thus, the Arabs who remained had acquired something they could trade, particularly considering that they did not consider the elections game as anything serious.

The 1951 elections reflected the increase in the importance of the votes of the remaining Arabs, demonstrated by eight Arab Knesset members being elected. Mapai was the biggest winner of Arab representation in the Knesset, with five seats for slates associated with the party.[66] Two of Maki's five seats went to Arab candidates. Mapam did not form a separate Arab slate this time, but included a number of Arabs in the list of its own candidates, which was how Rustum Bastuni was elected to the Knesset. If we focus on the sectarian breakdown of the Arabs elected in 1951, we find it quite different from the previous elections. Two members of the Druze sect, Salih Khunayfis from Shafa 'Amr and Jabr Ma'di from Yarka, were elected. Residents of the Triangle, who took part in the elections for the first time, succeeded in electing a member of the Knesset to represent them from Baqa al-Gharbiyya.[67]

The composition of the eight Arab candidates elected to the Knesset in 1951 shows that the ruling Mapai party succeeded in pushing through and consolidating its policies in this electoral battle. Mapai was careful to choose people to head their Arab slates who had proven their loyalty to Israel and the Zionist movement, and people who represented group, sectarian, and tribal interests which were compatible with the policy of divide and rule. Most of those nominated to their slates and elected perceived this to be a reward from the regime for services rendered, so they did not try to express individual political positions. Most of the parliamentarians on those slates were, for the most part, lacking the educational and cultural background which would have enabled them to play a free and independent political role. Their knowledge of Hebrew was minimal or nonexistent, which made it easy for the representatives of the ruling party to gain control over them. The representatives of leftist parties, on the other hand—Rustum Bastuni, Tawfiq Tubi, and Emile Habibi—were educated young men and holders of clear political positions. The clear difference between members of Mapai-affiliated slates and leftist opposition parties remained unchanged during the years of military rule, with some exceptions which will be discussed later.

The increase in number of Arab parliamentarians to eight resulted in better representation for the Palestinians who remained, reflecting their different inclinations and social and sectarian affiliations. As we mentioned above, two members of the Druze sect were elected in 1951, which came at the expense of the Muslims, who also had two representatives (Sayf al-Din al-Zu'bi, the head of the list, and Faris Hamdan) out of five Knesset members from the Mapai slates. Catholic supporters of Bishop Hakim were represented by Mas'ad Qassis from Mi'lya, who succeeded 'Amin Jarjura in that capacity. The two Arab parliamentarians from the Maki list were also Christians from Haifa, and Maki's Arab representatives were consistently urban Christians for a long period, a fact which their rivals used against them.[68] But Maki did not change its leaders, and did not try to include Muslims in the party leadership until the 1970s.

Of the two men allowed to return with the authorities' blessings to challenge the communists, one (al-Hawwari) abandoned politics, but Bishop Hakim continued to fight them, and succeeded in bringing Mas'ad Qassis back from Lebanon to make him a member of the Knesset in 1951.[69] Although the election results showed that the strength of the communists shrank that year, Maki remained one of the important winners, receiving 31,000 votes, of which 10,000 were from Arabs, constituting 16.3 percent of the total number of Arab votes. Communist propaganda emphasized that this was in spite of "terrorism, pressures, and deceptions."[70] Indeed, the government and its institutions had mobilized in 1951 to weaken the influence of the communists among the remaining Arabs, and used the politics of the "carrot" to that end. It was widely believed in Arab villages that the authorities allowed a number of "infiltrators" to remain in order to ensure their families would vote for the Arab lists affiliated with Mapai; the rumored price of an identity card for an infiltrator was 200 votes.[71]

The authorities did all they could to obstruct the communists and their supporters, and included some leaders of Maki. A file found among the papers of lawyer Hanna Naqqara included a court appeal by Emile Habibi in June 1951 against a decision eliminating his name among eligible voters in Haifa. This appeal was discussed in central court before Judge Ya'ir Azulai. The ministry of the interior claimed that Habibi had entered the country illegally, which while technically accurate, was a case of the government "playing dumb," because Habibi, like his "Pessoptimist" character, had returned with the blessings and full knowledge of the authorities in the autumn of 1948. Habibi and his lawyer Naqqara challenged this claim, and showed their papers to the court, including an identity card (no. 46386) which the plaintiff had obtained on the eve of the first elections on 16 January 1949.[72] The court of appeals accepted this, and Emile Habibi became a member of the Knesset in 1951.

Activist supporters of Maki were the main target of repression and legal prosecutions by the authorities on the eve of the elections. However, Arab citizens who supported Mapam were also targeted by this repressive policy, including some party activists who complained of legal prosecutions by the military government. Mapam received only 3,300, or about 5.6 percent, of total Arab votes.[73] However, some activists in Mapam were convinced that their limited success was the result of other factors besides the authorities' pressure and techniques of deception. For instance, Eliezer Be'eri (Bauer) argued that rather than pressure from Mapai being responsible for the relative failure of the party to win Arab votes, even greater pressures from the authorities were brought against Maki, but the party had nevertheless been successful in winning 10,000 Arab votes. Of his several other reasons for the failure of Mapam, he placed pressure from Mapai and its propaganda as third on the list.[74]

A close look at the 1951 election results shows some relative success by the communists; the party received about 4 percent of the total number of votes cast, compared to 3.5 percent in 1949, but this slight increase came primarily from Jewish voters. At the beginning of the 1950s a large number of communists from Eastern Europe and Iraq had immigrated to Israel, which strengthened Maki's support, but at the same time support for the party in Arab cities and villages had shrunk. The most prominent decrease was in Nazareth, where only 3,146 votes were cast for Maki in 1951, less than half the votes the party received in 1949.[75] Despite that, the fact that it received about 10,000 votes from Arab citizens overall was considered a success, although those votes constituted only 16.3 percent of Arab votes, compared to the 22.2 percent it received in 1949.

How does one explain this communist retreat in the second elections? Was the result due to the pressures applied by the authorities and their legal prosecutions?

Let us first focus on the changes which affected the social and cultural backgrounds of the Arab voters in the Naqab, despite inadequate information on the Bedouin Arabs in the Naqab who were counted in the census and voted in the second elections. What is known is that this segment of the Arabs who remained lived in greater fear than the northern Arabs. The Bedouins were under constant threat of expulsion until the end of the 1950s. Considering the known custom of this group of following the lead of the shaykh of the tribe and voting in a bloc, the chances that Maki would attract the votes of the Naqab Arabs were meager indeed, particularly since the communists did not make a real effort to reach those voters during the entire period of military rule. Even the Arab slates affiliated with the ruling party did not put much effort into this, and did not place the names of Bedouin residents on the early lists of candidates during that period.[76]

The other large group that voted for the first time in 1951 was the population of the Triangle, who lived in more than twenty villages, big and small, similar to most residents of the Galilee. But they differed in that these villagers were all Muslim, among whom it was rare to find a Marxist. The Communist Party and its Arab leaders did not have much influence in this conservative society. For these reasons, it came as no surprise that the success of Maki in the Triangle was modest.[77] The nomination of Faris Hamdan from the Triangle village of Baqa al-Gharbiyya for one of the Mapai-affiliated lists attracted many voters in the region away from the communists.

The third large group of Arabs who voted for the first time in 1951 were the inhabitants of upper Galilee. Many were mountain Druze who were socially conservative, and close to the leaders of the sect who had tied their destiny to the state. Furthermore, the listing of Druze candidates Salih Khunayfis from Shafa 'Amr on the Progress and Work slate, and Jabr Ma'di from Yarka on Sayf al-Din al-Zu'bi's slate, significantly reduced the likelihood of the communists attracting any Druze votes. The Ma'di clan in general, and Jabr Ma'di in particular, were quite instrumental in attracting Arab votes from the villages of al-Shaghur and other places to this slate, because of the help Jabr had given to the inhabitants to stay in their villages in 1948. Consequently, Sayf al-Din al-Zu'bi's list won three seats, which consolidated its position and influence in that period.[78]

These factors, which emerge from breaking down the majority of the new Arab voters in 1951 into categories, constitute "objective" causes for the decline in Maki's strength. With the old voters from Haifa and the Galilee, the communists were largely able to hang on to their influence and margin of success. This was complemented by inhabitants in some Galilee villages who voted for the first time in the second elections and contributed in no small measure to the relative success of Maki.[79] Nevertheless, the headlines in the communist press which indicated an increase in the strength and influence of the party were not accurate. Support for Maki shrank in Nazareth, Shafa 'Amr, Kufr Yasif, and other villages. Alongside this decline, the slates affiliated with the regime scored significant success, and three of them were able to cross the entry threshold into the Knesset, capturing 32,288 votes, about 55 percent of total Arab votes.[80]

Pressure from the military government and other government agencies partly explain the results of the 1951 elections. So why did these factors not deter the Arabs who remained in 1949?

Let us look at the Israeli political map leading up to each of the elections. After the first elections, the ministry of minorities under the leadership of Bechor Shitrit, which employed a number of Mapam activists, was abolished[81] after members of the ruling party complained of the support the communists were receiving from Mapam and its activists. But the government did not seek at the time to end support for the communists in Haifa, Nazareth, and other cities for reasons related to Israel's foreign and domestic policies. However, after the results of the first elections became known, government agencies did what they could to promote the influence of communist rivals. Also, Mapai, under the leadership of Ben-Gurion (who was also the minister of defense) fired the military governors who were members of Mapam and replaced them with members of the ruling party. Thus, government agencies acted in many ways to sap the influence of the communists and to win votes for the ruling party and electoral slates affiliated with it.[82]

For all of these reasons, the ruling party managed to win the majority of Arab votes in 1951. Most of the Arabs who remained were still engaged with the struggle to survive, and needed all means they could muster to protect themselves from repression and expulsion. Some of those who voted for the communists in 1949 thought at the time that Maki was close to the government and in its good graces. This impression was plainly challenged in the summer of that year, when the authorities began firing dozens of teachers and aggressively following a number of Arab Maki activists while supporting their rivals.[83] This domestic policy reflected the change in Israel's foreign policy; the government had distanced itself from the USSR and the eastern bloc and drawn closer to the West. These new rules for Israel's foreign and domestic policies changed the situation and continued to influence political strategies and Arab voters' conduct under military government.

The authorities' use of the carrot and stick policy was successful in the early 1950s, demonstrated by the increase in the number of Arab voters and the consolidation of Mapai's influence and that of its affiliated slates. In spite of that, Maki managed to situate itself and its leadership as the true representative of the interests of the Arab public. The communists continued to oppose the government's policy of discrimination and repression, and especially the system of military government. The Arab Knesset members affiliated with the ruling party, on the other hand, did not dare criticize those policies, nor did they have any influence over them. Normally, they were able to go only as far as to offer their good offices to people who were close to them to help secure permits from the government and to solve some individual problems at government offices. Governmental representatives sometimes displayed a measure of magnanimity on the eve of the electoral battle by visiting Arab villages and promising to carry out development projects in the areas of water distribution, building roads, improving the electric network, and other services. As a result, electoral seasons came to be known in Arab folklore as "the year of *marhaba* (greetings!)."[84]

BETWEEN A ROCK AND A HARD PLACE: THE
INDEPENDENTS AMONG THE REMAINING ARABS

At the beginning of 1951, *Haaretz* published a report by Amos Elon on the passage of thirty months since the imposition of Israeli rule over Nazareth.[85] The gist of the report was that the Arabs were disappointed with promises of equality and the possibility of achieving a form of Israeli citizenship that would unite Jews and Arabs in the state. Months later, Elon went back to the Galilee and then published a new article on his impressions of the general climate of opinion among eligible voters. Elon quoted one of the teachers he met, who said: "I shall not vote, just as prisoners do not vote. Israel has pushed us all into a giant prison."[86] Elon commented that the Arabs could elect ten or eleven members of the Knesset "if they were to establish an independent national Arab organization," but not a single independent Arab representative would be elected. He continued: "We know that there is not a single independent Arab slate among the 20 slates of candidates." Still, he expected that Arab citizens would vote, and that most of their votes would go to Mapai and Maki. Those who were afraid, or who believed the promises of the regime, would vote for Mapai and its Arab slates; those who were not afraid would vote for the communists. At any rate, the Arabs would not vote for independent candidates because there was no such slate.

Elon's article included frank criticism of the ruling party, and the order of fear which it imposed on the Arab population. Preventing the creation of an independent party or even an electoral slate served the policy of monitoring and control, leaving only two options open to Arab voters: either Maki or the Arab lists associated with Mapai. The option of not voting was considered the most dangerous, and was not viable since it was interpreted as non-recognition of the state and disloyalty to its legitimate institutions. Although what Elon said was true in general, it did not give a complete picture of political reality at the time. Not all of those voting for the slates associated with the government were doing so solely out of fear, while the prospects of success for an independent Arab slate, even if one had been established at the beginning of the 1950s, were dim, falling between a rock and a hard place. The remaining Arabs were a vulnerable group that had lost its urban elite, and it was difficult for them to establish an independent national organization that could achieve a brilliant victory in the elections so soon after the shock of the Nakba.

There were a few attempts to establish an independent Arab party in the 1950s. One study of the political behavior of the Arabs remaining in Israel claimed that the first to think of establishing an independent Arab political party was the wealthy leader, Hajj Ahmad Abu-Laban, of Jaffa.[87] It described Abu-Laban's efforts to defend the survivors among the Jaffa population, his subsequent jailing, and his appeal to the Supreme Court, but it is doubtful that he would have tried at that time to establish an independent Arab party in Israel. Nevertheless, the story of

Abu-Laban and his difficulties with the Israeli authorities is an example of what any Arab would encounter who tried to preserve his dignity and his rights. The attorney Elias Kusa encountered similar problems in Haifa.

On the eve of elections in the summer of 1951, propaganda from the Mapai party tried to highlight the progress made by Arab society in education, health, and agriculture. Foreign Minister Moshe Sharett took part in this effort in a speech broadcast in Arabic on 28 July 1951. The attorney Elias Kusa responded to this speech, saying: "It contains nothing new; it merely repeats the usual propaganda of government representatives."[88] He added that Israel's Declaration of Independence had included promises of equal civil rights for all without discrimination on the basis of gender or religion, rights that were not limited to voting or to running in elections, but involved "full equality in civil rights." Kusa reminded his readers of the existing areas of discrimination against Arabs in Israel, stressing in particular the right of Arabs to their confiscated lands, freedom of movement and work, which were "much more important than the right to elect members of the Knesset. . . . It is true that Arabs have the right to vote, but it is doubtful that the Arabs, who are under military rule, will be allowed to use this right freely."[89] As for Sharett's statement that Arabs had the right to establish political parties, Kusa pointed out that this had not been applied in actuality. He referred to the experience of a group of Arabs who wanted to establish an Arab slate but could not get a license to do so, just as they were about to meet with their likely voters. As for the three slates affiliated with Mapai, he said: "Mr. Sharett knows very well the circumstances under which those lists are created . . . and that their candidates were not elected by Arabs or any Arab party."[90] Kusa concluded his reply by saying that he agreed with Minister Sharett on one point only, that "there is no discrimination in Israeli courts on the basis of gender or religion," which might be why those courts enjoyed the confidence of the Arabs. But he made a point to add: "The judges are bound at times by the laws that the Knesset passes which restrict their role."[91]

The number of university-educated activist Arab intellectuals, such as the attorney Kusa, was very small in Haifa and the Galilee after the Nakba. Apart from a few dozen university graduates in Haifa, Jaffa, and Nazareth, few were left from the ranks of the Palestinian elite who had vanished along with those urban centers. The attorney Wadi' al-Bustani, who had also stayed in Haifa, was famous for his activities in the Palestinian national movement during the days of the British Mandate, like Kusa. Kusa and al-Bustani differed from the activists of the Liberation League who merged with Maki due both to their long experience and their advanced age. Both had immigrated to Palestine from Lebanon and made Haifa their home. While many like them left Haifa and other coastal cities after the Nakba, Kusa and al-Bustani chose to remain in the city.

Wadi' al-Bustani (1888–1954) was a well-known figure in the Arab world by 1948. He graduated from the American University of Beirut and became a famous author, poet, and translator, fluent in English and French as well as Arabic. He arrived in Haifa in 1917, where he soon became a member of the prominent political and cultural elite in the city. His nationalistic activities led him to the study of law at a late age and, after receiving his license in 1930, he defended many farmers whose lands were threatened with appropriation or sale.[92] al-Bustani became disillusioned with the British policy of supporting Zionism and its project to establish a Jewish state in Palestine without regard for the native population.

Although he remained in Haifa after the Nakba, al-Bustani experienced great difficulty adapting to the new reality under Israeli rule where the Arabs were treated as an undesirable minority.[93] He found it unbearable to be cut off from the Arab world in general, but especially from his family and friends in Lebanon. He tried to continue his literary and juridical activities but the many difficulties prompted him to leave Haifa in 1953 to return to his village of Dibya in Lebanon, where he died the following year.[94] The only way for the remaining Palestinians to visit the Arab world was to renounce Israeli citizenship, as Elias Kusa wrote. In fact, dozens of members of the educated elite of Jaffa, Haifa, Nazareth, and other cities and villages made that choice—renouncing their citizenship and moving to other Arab countries in the early 1950s.

In addition to Elias Kusa, there remained some individuals in Haifa and Nazareth, and other cities and villages in the Galilee, who had adopted independent positions and saw *al-Rabita* magazine as a pulpit for these independent ideas and positions. This group included: Jabbur Jabbur, the mayor of Shafa 'Amr; Mas'ad Qassis from Mi'lya; Shaykh Tahir al-Tabari, the shari'a judge of Nazareth; and others. This group, which tried to organize politically on an independent basis, was later joined by Tahir al-Fahum, Shukri al-Khazin, Hanna Shumar, and others. This coalition of individuals, some with close ties to members of the regime, tried more than once (in 1953 and then 1955) to establish an independent political organization. In the spring of 1955, it appeared that this group might succeed in entering the electoral fray, under the name of the Arab-Israeli Bloc, and the attorney Kusa obtained a letter of approval for registration of the bloc from a Haifa district official, Jacob Bergman.[95]

The communists, who had a monopoly on the representation of the interests of Arab citizens, were not pleased with the close relations between this group and Bishop Hakim. Kusa and his friends were attacked in *al-Ittihad* newspaper, by innuendo at times and openly at other times. In 1953, when the talk of starting a new Arab party to include independents with well-known names became serious, the communists intensified their attacks on the initiative, just as every other attempt to establish an independent Arab organization had met with intense opposition from both the authorities and the communists. *Al-Ittihad* published a strongly worded attack on "Hakim, al-Hawwari, Kusa, and others" who were trying to set up "the Deportation Party."[96] The paper tied the names of the three to the American and British consuls "who were behind this initiative."

In contrast to the image that the communists were trying to build for themselves as the heroes of the struggle for the rights of the remaining Arabs, Kusa had an altogether different understanding of the situation. A joint letter[97] to Arab citizens by Kusa and Tahir al-Fahum in November 1954 contained blistering criticism of the work of the Arab parliamentarians. After reviewing the situation of Arabs in Israel, the two spoke of the need for an independent Arab political organization. The letter said that the eight Knesset members had failed in their mission to relieve the existing oppression and persecution and to improve the situation. Special criticism was levelled at the communists, "who claim to be the spokesmen for the Arab public and the real fighters for its interests." The two concluded their letter by saying that an independent and democratic organization is the way to work seriously and honestly to relieve oppression and stop the confiscation of land, to return the refugees to their villages, and to ensure equality in rights and responsibilities for all citizens.

Elias Kusa wrote a lengthy reply in *al-Rabita* to the attack on the Arab bloc initiative, speaking of his astonishment at the "lies and slanders" of *al-Ittihad*. He pointed out, "I recited the objectives of the Arab bloc for the correspondent of *al-Ittihad* and Mr. Hanna Naqqara to hear." Kusa explained that those objectives included defending the rights of the Arabs, and then shared his own experience in cooperating with Maki: "In the past a committee was established for the defense of the rights of Arabs which included members of the Communist Party, but they exploited the situation to advance the interests of their party. That is why I left the committee and placed a condition for my return, that the committee not be exploited for narrow party objectives."[98]

Kusa then went on to attack the Communist Party: "*Al-Ittihad* claims that the Communist Party serves the interests of the Arab minority, but it has not provided one bit of evidence that the party has done anything tangible." He resumed in a sharp satirical tone: "All of the beating of drums and the sounding of horns and holding general meetings and raucous demonstrations and failed conferences organized by the communists achieved nothing except to repel Jewish public opinion and hurt the interests of the Arabs." In Kusa's opinion, the speeches by communist members of the Knesset achieved nothing except to convince noncommunist members that what the communist MKs said was recommended by Russian colonial sources.[99] Kusa concluded his criticism by writing: "I challenge the MKs belonging to the Communist Party, both Arabs and Jews, to mention one single Arab problem which they managed to solve in the interests of the Arabs, whether inside the Knesset or outside it."

After levelling biting criticism at Arab parliamentarians, particularly the communists, Kusa referred to his own personal efforts in the service of Arab citizens, performed "without drumming or honking." He listed the areas where he had put his efforts and the achievements he had scored, such as amending the Absentees Law, convincing the government to print bank and other official payment checks or receipts in Arabic, and his lengthy memoranda to the Knesset concerning the Nationality Law, the Land Acquisition Law, and other subjects. He concluded this testimony about his activities (without modesty) by saying that he had done all of that quietly: "If an Arab can do these productive things on his own, without the support of a party . . . there can be no doubt that an organized Arab party which represents the Arabs and speaks in their name and gives expression to their hopes and sufferings can easily outdo these individual achievements in the service of its people."[100]

Kusa and his colleagues who had organized and made the necessary measures to establish an independent Arab organization ended up withdrawing before the 1955 elections. The positions adopted by Kusa and some of his independent colleagues, which were published in "the bishop's magazine," had stirred up opposition on the part of "moderate Christians." One complained that *al-Rabita* had recently turned into a propaganda pulpit for the Arab bloc under the leadership of Tahir al-Fahum and Elias Kusa, in contrast to recent years. Kusa did not keep quiet in the face of the criticism directed at him, and replied in a strongly worded article in *al-Rabita* titled "Who Is the Deceiver?" He began by saying: "There are people who read and understand what they are reading and there are those who read but do not understand what they are reading. Then there are those who read and do not understand, but claim that they understand, and these people are like a curse on people." Kusa then clarified what he had written earlier, by saying: "There is no deception in saying that Israel has a democratic system, but it discriminates against and oppresses the Arab minority."[101]

THE THIRD ELECTIONS (1955) AND THEIR RESULTS

The third Knesset elections were the first to take place without Ben-Gurion in the role of prime minister or as the sole leader of the ruling Mapai party. But the Arabs did not feel much change in the government's policy toward them under Moshe Sharett. As we saw earlier, the short-lived Sharett government tried to conscript the Arabs into the Israeli army in 1954 and, in the same year, elections were held for Arab municipal councils, following Maki's repeated demands. In these local elections, first in Kufr Yasif and then in Nazareth, the authorities used all means to limit the influence of the communists; however, the party scored a victory that could not be easily dismissed, which embarrassed the government at the local level.

This study has not taken up the issue of local government so far, but the local elections that took place in 1954 attained a symbolic importance and had particular repercussions for the general parliamentary elections the following year. In January 1954, in the elections held in Kufr Yasif, Yani Yani was elected to head the council for a second term with the support of two communist members of the council. Military governor Ya'cov Muhriz and his men tried unsuccessfully to prevent the formation of this coalition with members of the Maki party.[102]

This failure by the governmental authorities set off alarms in the ministry of the interior and the military government, and officials feared similar results in the Nazareth elections set for 12 April 1954. The emergence of non-submissive local authorities would present a dilemma for the imposition of governmental policies on Arab citizens.

When it came time for the elections in Nazareth, a clear confrontation arose between the slates with connections to the authorities and Maki's local slate. However, despite the pressure applied by the government and its agencies, many voters supported the communist slate. When it became obvious that those collaborating with the government were unable to form a coalition in the municipal council without Maki's six members, the authorities procrastinated and used threats, even physical violence from supporters of Sayf al-Din al-Zu'bi. In the end, a former Knesset member, Amin Jarjura, was elected mayor in July 1954.[103] However, the Nazareth elections and the struggle over the formation of the coalition led to increased tensions in the city. Geremy Forman, who examined those elections in detail, nevertheless wrote that he saw no direct connection between what happened in the municipal elections and the government's decision to build a new Jewish city next to Nazareth by the name of Nazareth Elit (Upper Nazareth) that same year.[104]

The third Knesset elections took place on 26 July 1955. Of the one million eligible voters, there were 86,723 Arabs, of whom 77,750 actually voted, a 90 percent participation rate.[105] Eight Arab Knesset members were elected this time too, and almost all were incumbents, except for Mapam's Arab representative, whom we will discuss later. The very high participation rate among Arabs who remained demonstrated the consolidation of voting patterns which had emerged in previous elections. The political competition for the Arab street was essentially between Mapai's agencies and its slates on one side and Maki and its supporters on the other. These two camps held on to their relative power share among Arab voters, and together they received the majority of votes.

In the 1955 Knesset elections, Mapai and its affiliated slates won over 62 percent of Arab votes. Although the Democratic slate headed by Sayf al-Din al-Zu'bi took first place among the three, their 15,475 votes were sufficient to elect only two Knesset members, not three as in the past. Some votes had gone directly to the Mapai party, and others to the affiliated Progress and Work list, which won two seats. A problem arose in the Democratic list when Jabr Ma'di did not make it into the Knesset, and his relationship with Sayf al-Din al-Zu'bi deteriorated. Al-Zu'bi was pressured to give up his seat in favor of Jabr Ma'di in March 1956.[106] Mas'ad Qassis, who was supposed to be the third seat, refused to step down, and did not have to do so because of the support he had from Bishop Hakim. This problem within the slate and the way it was solved clearly showed that the influence of the bishop on the Democratic list was strong and enduring.

Maki increased its strength among Jewish voters in 1955, which allowed it to acquire six seats, but it did not have the same support with Arab voters.[107] In fact, the strength of the communists declined, and they received just over 15 percent of Arab votes, one percent less than in the previous election. The party held on to its strength in large Arab cities and villages, but its efforts to expand its share of votes in small villages and among the Bedouins of the Naqab were not successful. These conservative segments of the population were ruled by shaykhs and notables, many of whom cooperated with the authorities either out of fear or due to narrow factional interests. Thus, the ruling party managed to consolidate the policy of monitoring and control on Arab population centers far away from the cities and large villages which were known for their support of the communists.

MK Rustum Bastuni (1923–1994), who had been elected to the second Knesset, lost his seat in the 1955 elections. Bastuni was born in Tirat Haifa, and had the distinction of being one of the first Arabs to study at the institute of engineering (the Technion) in 1947. This promising young man left his house and city in the spring of 1949, like tens of thousands of Arabs, and became a refugee in Lebanon and Syria. But his older brother Muhammad, who remained in Haifa, encouraged him to return to the city, and paved the way for his return through his Jewish acquaintances.[108] After his return to Haifa, Bastuni became one of the most prominent Arab activists of Mapam. Although he was elected to the second Knesset, the success of his party with Arab voters was weak, as we saw above. In September 1951 the party issued a magazine called *al-Mirsad* which criticized the Mapai and Maki parties. Most of those who wrote in this weekly were Jews, except for Bastuni and a few of his Arab comrades.

Mapam was a severe critic of the government's policy and was opposed to the military government, but it did not succeed in broadening its base among Arab citizens. The Zionist positions of the party, particularly regarding the confiscation of Arab land for Jewish settlement, were confounding for Arab citizens. Similarly, the party fought discrimination against Arab citizens on the one hand, but did not accept them as equal members in its Zionist agencies and institutions on the other. Mapam activists spoke a great deal about the need for economic equality, even while the party was establishing kibbutzim on the lands of depopulated Arab villages, including Kufr Bir'im, Sa'sa' and others, at the same time. Nevertheless, Bastuni managed, after his election to the Knesset and the publication of *al-Mirsad*, to attract Arab youth to the ranks of Mapam. The party proudly announced after the third election that it had received about 6,000 Arab votes, double the number it had received in the earlier elections.[109]

But Bastuni was not renominated, and Yusif Khamis took his place on the slate. Bastuni had become involved in the whirlpool of contradictions which beset the socialist Zionist doctrine of Mapam—such as the calls for Jewish-Arab equality while supporting Jewish settlement on Arab lands—and he was openly critical of these contradictory positions towards Arab residents. This Knesset member from Haifa, an able orator with few equals among the remaining Palestinians in the 1950s, first criticized his party for not opening up membership to Arab citizens: "We cannot show the generations the equality of peoples unless we serve as examples of that."[110] He also had great difficulty remaining quiet about self-deception.

Radical leftists in Mapam found it problematic to accept these critical positions, leading to Bastuni being replaced with Khamis.

In 1955 Mapam joined the governing coalition at a time when it was clear that Israel was headed toward war with Egypt.[111] During that war, Mapam and Maki, which had been on the same path since 1948, went their separate ways. Mapam had found itself a partner in a government which initiated the war on Egypt in a conspiracy with colonial France and Britain. The main objectives of France and Britain in this war were, respectively, to prevent Algeria from gaining its independence and to maintain control over the Suez Canal. Maki, like the Soviet Union, took the side of Egypt under Abdel Nasser, who had concluded an arms deal with Czechoslovakia. Mapam, on the other hand, adopted the policy of the Ben-Gurion government which was hostile to Egypt, and continued its fierce attacks on Abdel Nasser's regime. So Mapam and Maki separated into two different camps during the 1956 war and afterwards.

On the eve of the Sinai War outbreak, Maki made its second reversal in less than ten years in its political positions regarding the Jewish state.[112] Up to the Knesset elections in 1955 the activists in the party expressed moderate opposition to Israeli foreign policy toward Arab states. Nevertheless, Maki retained an Israeli nationalist position regarding the state's important interests. But as Israel continued to distance itself from the USSR, at the same time that Abdel Nasser was drawing closer to the socialist camp, Maki's positions changed swiftly. When Ben-Gurion spoke during the war about establishing a "third Israeli kingdom," Maki leaders launched a sharp attack on the policy of not withdrawing from Gaza and large sections of occupied Sinai. Contrary to the case in the 1948 war, the party found itself in 1956 standing (with the Soviet Union) on the side of Egypt, "which is defending itself against a colonialist-Israeli plot."

During the 1956 Sinai War Maki's Arab and Jewish activists found themselves leading the camp opposed to the aggression against Egypt and condemning the massacre perpetrated by Israeli security forces in the village of Kafr Qasim. At the beginning of the withdrawal of British and French forces from the cities on the Suez Canal, the party's press quoted Radio Moscow regarding "the need for immediate withdrawal" by the Israeli army as well.[113] Three days later, that press published news of preparations for a day of mourning and a strike on 6 January 1957 in condemnation of the massacre in Kafr Qasim. Indeed, a general strike was held on the announced date, described by al-Ittihad in a published report as "the unity of the Arab masses in their struggle against national oppression."[114] Thus, once again, Soviet foreign policy combined with local events to bring about a revolution in the position of the communists.

On the domestic political scene, Maki's leaders intensified their criticism of the government's decision to reserve for Jews—exclusively—the first neighborhood (shikun) of the new Upper Nazareth (Nazareth Elit), under construction next door to Nazareth. The Judaization of the Galilee, or construction for Jews only on confiscated Arab lands, led many to compare Israel with South Africa. *Al-Ittihad* wrote: "Nazareth will not become South Africa."[115] The significance of the start of construction on Upper Nazareth was not lost on the residents of the city, particularly not the communists among them. The Judaization of the Galilee began with an effort to stifle the development of the only Palestinian city that had escaped destruction in the year of the Nakba. This position completed the circle of the gradual reversal in the positions of the Communist Party towards Israel's foreign and domestic policies. Just as most members of the Liberation League followed the path outlined by the Soviet Union in 1948, the comrades in the political party found themselves supporting Egypt under Abdel Nasser during the Sinai War, along with the socialist camp.

Moving away from the general picture, we will now look more closely at the life story of a leader in the party, the author of *The Pessoptimist*, Emile Habibi, who returned from Lebanon to Haifa to become one of the most prominent leaders of Maki. He decided eventually to move his family from the mixed city of Haifa to Nazareth in 1956. His mother, who had also moved to Haifa in 1948, had nine sons and daughters, most of whom became refugees after the war; only two were left near her, Emile and his sister Nada. Emile noticed that his mother was yearning to see her children, particularly the youngest, Na'im. In 1954, his mother decided to leave Haifa to spend the rest of her life next to her refugee children, after despairing of the possibility of their return to live next to her. She surrendered her Israeli nationality, and left the country by way of the Mandelbaum gate to Jerusalem. Emile Habibi accompanied her and later wrote a short story titled "The Mandelbaum Gate."[116] It was after the Kafr Qasim massacre that Habibi himself decided to move his residence from Haifa to Nazareth.[117]

Not long after Habibi's move to Nazareth, the Shabak (or Shin Bet, the Israeli Security Agency), accused him of calling for a rebellion against Israel, similar to the Algerian rebellion, during an evening gathering with his friends. The intelligence agency, which was monitoring the changes in the position of communist leaders after the Sinai War, was looking for ways to repress Arab communist leaders. The agents were particularly wary of cooperation and coordination between the communists and some activist nationalists and independents in that period, since such a rapprochement would undermine Israel's policy of divide and rule and could lead to political organization for the Arab minority in Israel. Indeed Maki's discourse in 1957 drew closer to nationalist thought, which was evident in the resolutions of the party's thirteenth congress.[118] What had been said at the congress—that the Arabs in Israel were an inseparable part of the Palestinian people, and an affirmation of this people's "right to self-determination, even separation"—had crossed a red line in the view of Israeli intelligence, and represented a revolution in the positions the party had adopted since 1948.

TENTH ANNIVERSARY AND TURNING
THE TABLES (1948–58)

We saw that Maki retreated from its positions of support for Israel after the elections of the summer of 1955, and that by May 1957 the party's discourse at its thirteenth congress moved closer to Arab nationalist positions. One Israeli researching this rapprochement concluded that the years 1955–57 were the "golden age" of the party for the Arab in the street, with a perfect alignment in that period between Marxist theory and Nasserist Arab nationalism supported by the Soviet Union.[119] Another Israeli researcher, however, criticized this hasty generalization, and showed in his study that the Maki leaders were never, at any point in their history, torn between their loyalty to communism and their solidarity with Nasserist Arab nationalism.[120] This is true since Maki did not embrace Zionism in 1948–49, nor did it adopt Arab nationalism earlier in the mid-1950s when it followed Moscow's line.

A more accurate reading of the reversal in Maki's Arab nationalist positions (1955–58) points to a temporary honeymoon linked to the position of the USSR on Abdel Nasser. Even during that period of rapprochement, differences in points of view did not disappear altogether, and were manifest after the coup in Iraq when the USSR took the side of Abd al-Karim Qasim against Abdel Nasser. The change in Moscow's and then in Maki's positions on Arab nationalism was a tactic connected to the superpower's policy during the Cold War. At the local level, the rapprochement between the positions of Maki and the Arab nationalists supporting Abdel Nasser and the alignment of their political discourses was indeed temporary, and was influenced by the Sinai War against Egypt and the shock created by the Kafr Qasim massacre. But before we elaborate on the reversal in the positions of the communists in 1957–58, let us return to the analysis of Maki's position in 1948–49.

In previous chapters we saw that the Communist Party stood by Israel without reservation in its war against the Palestinian people and neighboring Arab countries; it called for participation in the celebration of the anniversary of Israel's independence as of 1949. Its leaders, including Tawfiq Tubi, supported the conscription of Arab youth in the Israeli army to defend Israel's borders and its independence. Al-Ittihad newspaper was full of Israeli nationalist discourse, which the party's leaders used at every occasion since its reemergence in Haifa near the end of 1948. This continued into the 1950s, including the annual call to participate in the festivities of Independence Day.[121] The paper's editorial board explained the reasons for their call by saying: "The establishment of Israel was the proclamation of an essential development in the struggle of the peoples of the Middle East." Even more cunning was their statement that: "The rise of Israel marked the beginning of serious development in the struggles of the Middle East peoples. The creation of Israel laid down the foundations for a solution to the Palestine issue," and for "constructing the edifice of real fraternity between the masses of the Jewish and Arab peoples."[122]

Even after the Soviet Union became disillusioned by Israel's foreign policy, the party's position toward Israel did not change significantly. Maki, which Ben-Gurion had kept away from joining his government coalitions, continued its Israeli nationalist discourse for a while. This spilled over onto the pages of al-Ittihad, but was much more prominent in the party's Hebrew-language press and publications. The proceedings and resolutions of the twelfth party congress, near the end of May 1952, contain clear expressions of these Israeli nationalist positions.[123] In the report of party secretary Mikunis to the congress, disappointment is expressed in Ben-Gurion's policy in the Cold War, and in the government's domestic policy. But there is no deviation of support for Zionist positions and the Zionist view of history, nor in slogans about defending Israel against the colonialist camp and aggressive Arab states.[124] There is no mention of Palestinians or of those who remained –that is, those classified as an Arab minority in Israel—at that congress or, as one might have expected, at least in the summary of conference proceedings and resolutions. This communist discourse to a large extent aligned with the Zionist discourse on events, and ignored the Palestinian people and their legitimate rights.

In the 1950s, Maki leaders continued their policies supportive of the establishment of a Jewish state, even after the death of Stalin. An enduring expression of that was each year's invitation on the front page of al-Ittihad to participate in the celebration of Israel's Independence Day, which they called the national day for all Israelis, both Arabs and Jews.[125] At the same time, the party's position on Abdel Nasser, who along with his fellow officers had overthrown Egypt's monarchy, remained negative and very critical, and accused Nasser of collaborating with Britain and colonialism.[126] Well worth remembering here are the activists of the Liberation League who distributed leaflets in the summer of 1948 to Egyptian army soldiers and officers fighting in southern Palestine, exhorting them to leave and return to Egypt to overthrow the reactionary monarchical regime there. The coups that took place in a number of Arab countries, including Egypt, did not alter the position of Maki on the regime of Abdel Nasser until the mid-1950s.

The Israeli Communist press's attacks on Abdel Nasser ceased only after the Czech arms deal in late 1955. The conclusion of that deal, and the rapprochement between Abdel Nasser and the socialist camp under the leadership of the USSR, were clearly reflected in a change in the position of Maki and its press towards Abdel Nasser. Political developments in Egypt were felt throughout the Arab world and affected even the Arabs remaining in Israel. The anti-British atmosphere had an impact in Jordan, leading King Hussein to dismiss the British commander of the Jordanian army, John Bagot Glubb (known as Glubb Pasha). That bold step increased the popularity of the young king among the ranks of the opposition, who saw Glubb as responsible for carrying out plots against the Palestinians since 1948. Syria too was affected by the optimistic nationalist spirit which spread through the people of the region. The Soviet Union calculated that the new atmosphere was full of opportunities to extend its influence in the Middle East. Emile Habibi gave expression to this revolutionary optimism in a speech he delivered in Kafr Kana, near Nazareth: "The dismissal of Glubb Pasha, then the nationalization of the Suez Canal, and then the settlement of the Israeli-Arab conflict, are links in the chain of getting rid of colonial domination."[127]

Indeed, the period 1955–57 witnessed an important transformation in the position of Maki on the heels of the increase in rapprochement and cooperation between Abdel Nasser and the socialist camp. This change was apparent in the discourse of the party leaders and in its press, and reached its zenith at the thirteenth party congress at the end of May 1957, which bridged the gap between them and the nationalist activists.[128] In addition to the overwhelming support for Abdel Nasser, the points of view of the two sides also drew closer on domestic issues relating to Palestinian identity, the symbols of political struggle, and other issues.[129] All of these events paved the way to the events of 1 May 1958 in Nazareth. The attempt by the government to impose the celebration of the tenth anniversary of the creation of Israel created a tense atmosphere and a willingness for the first time since the Nakba for a confrontation. In the ensuing confrontation, the independent nationalist forces united with the leadership of the Communist Party in together reframing Israel's Independence Day as the Nakba Day for the Palestinian people.

Between the Sinai War in October 1956 and the end of 1959, there were several reversals in the positions of the communists which led to withdrawal of support for Abdel Nasser, then a clash with him against the background of support for the rival regime of 'Abd al-Karim Qasim in Iraq. In July 1958, Qasim led a military coup against the pro-British monarchy, similar to what Abdel Nasser had done in Egypt. At the beginning, the two ambitious leaders found common ground permitting cooperation between the two revolutionary regimes, but they had disputes, and Qasim in Baghdad turned against the Arab nationalists with support from the Iraqi communists. Differences between Abdel Nasser and Qasim came to a head concerning the leadership of the Arab world. The Soviet Union stood with Qasim against Abdel Nasser, who had entered into a union with Syria in early 1958. The leaders of Maki and its press quickly joined Moscow's caravan, and attacked the Egyptian regime using various accusations. But the Palestinians in general, including those remaining in Israel, maintained their support for Abdel Nasser, which created a split with the communists. The rivals and enemies of Maki fully capitalized on this dispute and the open confrontation between the two camps in the elections of 1959.[130]

The reversal in the position of Maki on Abdel Nasser, which ran against the general trend among Arab voters, resulted in voters punishing the party in 1959. Maki won only three seats, down from the six seats it had previously, receiving only 11 percent of the Arab vote, a major reversal from the outcomes of previous elections.[131] Mapam won a big share of the votes of those who distanced themselves from Maki, successfully capitalizing on the fluctuations in Maki's positions since 1948 and its clash with Abdel Nasser in its electoral propaganda against the communists. The most prominent of Mapam activists was the poet and journalist Rashid Husain, who wrote the now famous article "When History Grows Hungry."[132] This anticommunist propaganda fell on receptive ears and Mapam jumped to second place after Mapai and its Arab slates, while Maki took third place for the first time since the elections of 1948.

In addition to the communists' clash with Abdel Nasser, some nationalist activists could not forget Maki's unconditional support for Israel in the war of 1948, nor did they accept the party's ideology and its propaganda over the previous decade that the struggle between Jews and Arabs was a class struggle, not a nationalist one. Maki was fated to flip its positions whenever the positions of the Soviet Union changed, which cost the party its credibility and the independence of its ideology during the Cold War. Moscow's international interests and its positions were the primary determinant of the positions of the other communist parties circulating in the USSR's orbit. Initially, this reversal enabled members of the Liberation League to merge with Maki and to play an important leadership role for the Arabs who remained in Haifa and the Galilee. But closeness to Moscow had a price, as was evident in 1959, when the party won less than half of the Arab votes it had won in the first election in 1949.

Epilogue

"THE SECOND ROUND" AS A TURNING POINT

Both the United States and the Soviet Union supported the establishment of a Jewish state at the expense of the Palestinian people. The two superpowers competed with each other in 1948 over who would provide greater political and military support for the Zionist movement, so that it might succeed in establishing a state, and even in expanding its borders. Not surprisingly, neither the Western nor the Eastern bloc was shaken by the Nakba, which afflicted the Palestinian people in particular, but also the whole of the Arab nation. Neither of the two camps tried to apply pressure on Israel to participate in finding a solution to the refugee problem and permitting the exiles' return to their lands in accordance with UN Resolution 194. These states had a strong sense of guilt concerning a prior catastrophe that had befallen millions of Jews on the European continent. Thus, for several years Israel did what it pleased with the Palestinians without being held accountable or punished. All of its actions against the Arabs and the Palestinians in particular were considered self-defense, at least until 1956.

Near the end of 1956, Israel found itself in an unfamiliar position, in fact the opposite of its position since its establishment in 1948. Both superpowers opposed Israel launching a colonial war on Egypt with Britain and France. In the postcolonial era after the Second World War, this event was seen as a political adventure. Despite the fact that the Israeli army had no difficulty in occupying the Gaza Strip and the Sinai Peninsula, the political outcome was at variance with the military one. For a few months Israel was absorbed by the exuberance of military victory, but this time it faced a decisively negative judgment from the United States and the USSR, which compelled it to withdraw its forces from all of the territories it had occupied during the confrontation. On the other side, Egypt's political victory in its defensive war boosted Abdel Nasser's standing and his popularity in the Arab world, making him a nationalist hero. He lifted Arab morale and boosted Arab self-confidence less than a decade after the Nakba. His popularity extended among the Palestinians as well, including those who remained in Israel.

Arab communists in Israel aligned their position with their people in 1956 and afterwards. Whereas they had broken ranks in 1948—and some had been imprisoned for their opposition to the entry of Arab armies in the war—in the Sinai War they were thrown into Israeli jails for their opposition to the collusion by Israel, Britain, and France against Egypt. The administrative detention of dozens of Maki activists deepened the split between the communists and their previous partner Mapam. *Al-Ittihad* newspaper waged a campaign against the government and its policy, and demanded "a halt to the aggression and occupation and massacres and arrests."[1] The same issue carried a news item about a visit by MK Meir Vilner and MK Tawfiq Tubi to Kafr Qasim, and reported that popular gatherings were held in solidarity with its inhabitants in 'Ilabun and Jerusalem. The demonstrators denounced the massacre and demanded that those responsible be put on trial.[2]

The perpetrators of the massacre in Kafr Qasim were in fact eventually brought before the courts. This was the first time that Israeli security personnel were put on trial and punished for killing Palestinians since 1948. Despite the criticism of the short sentences imposed on the criminals, and the subsequent pardons which aroused strong revulsion, the trials and sentences in themselves were a new and important event in the history of the Arabs who remained in Israel. The army and the government had tried to conceal the crime, evade responsibility, and avoid putting the killers on trial. But the pressure of both Arab and Jewish public opinion forced the government for the first time to change its usual modus operandi. Between the war of 1948 and the massacre of Kafr Qasim, Israeli security forces had killed an estimated three to five thousand Palestinians along the border and in Arab villages, with no one being held to account. But in the Kafr Qasim case, it was considered that the decision to kill innocent civilians during the Sinai war, under orders of army officers, was a crime for which the perpetrators had to be held accountable. Although this precedent concerned the values and conduct of soldiers, not senior officers or politicians, it remains a landmark event.[3]

The Kafr Qasim massacre evoked the memory of the Nakba, and the killings and massacres in Dayr Yasin and in many Galilee villages, in the minds of the Arabs who remained. The inhabitants of Kafr Qasim and the villages of the Triangle had no connection to the war that broke out between Israel and Egypt in Sinai. The slaughter of forty-nine innocent villagers in cold blood, only because they were returning home after their workday spent tending their fields and were unaware of a sudden curfew, was a traumatic shock. MK Tawfiq Tubi and MK Latif Dory, a Mapam activist, snuck into the village to interview some villagers and published the news of the massacre, which the government had been trying to keep under wraps.[4] When the details of the event and its atrocious nature became known, the communists intensified their attacks on the government and its bloody policy. Before all the details of the massacre were known, *al-Ittihad* took the position on its front page that it was necessary "to stop the national persecution and aggression on peaceful Arab inhabitants."[5]

At the end of 1956, the Arabs who remained after the Nakba, and who were steadfast in facing the policy of uprooting and repression, escaped the plans for a "second round" of war. As of the early 1950s, those Israelis who believed in ideas of "transfer" despaired of expelling the Palestinians who remained in the Jewish state unless it would be under "the fog of war." When the Sinai War came along, this group thought it was a suitable opportunity to evict the Arabs, at least from the villages of the southern Triangle. There, along the Jordanian front, several bloody clashes occurred on the eve of the Sinai War. Despite the terrible nature of the Kafr Qasim massacre, the inhabitants of that village and neighboring villages (Kufr Bara, Jaljuliyya, al-Tira, and others) did not contemplate leaving their homes. The Palestinians in general, and especially those who remained in the country, had learned the lessons of the Nakba and its consequences: that to die in their homes and on their lands was preferable to leaving and leading the humiliating life of refugees.

The stoic reaction of villages in the southern Triangle and Arab villages in Israel in general served as a bulwark against the policy of scaremongering and terrorizing the population. The Palestinians who remained kept their composure so as not to provide those in charge of security with any excuse to expel them or move them away from the border region. Despite the many statements by Mapai leaders, it became evident that the remaining Arabs were not behaving like a fifth column. Thus, the days of the Sinai War passed without offering the opportunity to get rid of the Arabs that many of the security-obsessed in Israel had been hoping for. At least in this respect, the 1956 war was a turning point for the remaining Arabs, who firmly established themselves in their homes and villages, particularly in the villages of the Triangle, where Israel had not been successful in expelling the population during 1948–49.

Contrary to the days after the Nakba, the period which followed the Sinai War began with positive developments and optimism throughout the Arab world. Abdel Nasser, whom the three aggressors had hoped to humble, emerged from the war as a national hero who had challenged Israel and the colonial powers and defeated them, politically at least. France and Britain were forced to withdraw their forces from the Suez Canal without scoring any gains worth mentioning, and Israel, under the leadership of Ben-Gurion, had to yield to American and Soviet pressures and threats and to withdraw Israeli forces from the Sinai and Gaza Strip in March 1957. The Soviet Union's clear stand on the side of Egypt was in marked contrast to that superpower's position in the 1948 war. This reversal in Soviet policy made an impression on the Arab population, particularly the communists and activist nationalists among them, who found themselves on the same front against Israel and the colonial powers.

As a result of the swift Israeli withdrawal and the increase in popularity of Abdel Nasser, the remaining Arabs felt proud and their morale improved after years of disappointment and despair in the wake of the Nakba and its consequences. They also grew more confident that the period of threats, uprooting, and expulsions had ended and would not return. The solidarity with the inhabitants of Kafr Qasim and the role played by Tawfiq Tubi and other Maki leaders led to an increase in the influence of the party and had a positive impact on the villages of the Triangle. One could say that the 1956 war contributed to launching a new political era in which the remaining Arabs transitioned from the struggle for survival to the phase of rebuilding a collective identity. One initiative in this direction was the increased activism of Arab students at Hebrew University, which represented a new challenge to Israeli repression and persecution by the second generation. A decade after the Nakba, one began to hear voices challenging the reality created by the 1948 war which had become the established order from the Naqab to the Galilee.

Most of the published studies and research on Arabs in Israel center on the policies of the government and its institutions towards the Arab minority. Considering that the Yohanan Ratner committee, appointed by Ben-Gurion to study the military government system, recommended not eliminating the system, researchers did not see a significant impact from the 1956 war on the remaining Arabs. However, if we focus on the conduct rather than the policies of the government towards the remaining Arabs, the picture is different. The 1956 war, on the one hand, and the Kafr Qasim massacre on the other, significantly influenced the organization and behavior of the Arabs who remained, which had not happened before. The anger stirred up by the massacre, and the hopes awakened by Abdel Nasser's success, created a political spirit which overcame the fear of repression, even if just for a short while. Consequently, political actions and organizational initiatives emerged which defied the governmental repression and control which had been operative since the Nakba. In 1957 political winds blew which hastened rapid rapprochement between the communists and independent nationalist activists. This rapprochement, followed by organized cooperation, laid down the basis for a confrontation which played itself out in the famous events of Nazareth on 1 May 1958.

AWARENESS AND IDENTITY FORMATION

Israel had not only plundered the majority of Palestinian lands, including the lands of the remaining Arabs; it had also waged war on their national consciousness and identity. The authorities and their agents promoted a distorted identity for the "Arabs of Israel," which became an inseparable part of the process of making Palestinians disappear from geography and history. As we saw earlier, the authorities reinforced sectarian, tribal, and ethnic identities as part of their policy of divide and conquer. This policy was successful in the Druze community, most of whose members enlisted in military service and gradually split off from the rest of the Palestinian citizens. After conscripting the Druze into military service, Israel consolidated their sectarian identity and tried to turn it into a separate national identity. The previous chapter, which dealt with elections and political behavior, did not delve into the distribution of Arab votes along sectarian lines. However, a look at the voting pattern in Druze villages reveals clearly that there is an essential difference between them and the rest of the Arab citizens.[6]

One mechanism that the authorities used to try to reengineer the national consciousness of Arabs in Israel was to make them participate in the Independence Day festivities. Since the spring of 1949, it had attempted to induce them (including the inhabitants of the Triangle) to participate in the first celebrations. Many inhabitants of Triangle villages who had trepidations about being subjected to Israeli rule and sovereignty participated in that bit of theater, like their brethren in the Galilee.[7] The Israeli media played up news about the residents' participation in festivities which had been organized by the military government.[8] Many political adversaries, Arab and Jewish, communists and agents of the regime, also agreed to participate. As for the daring nationalist activists, they were afraid to give voice to their opposition to "Independence Day," so they decided on the "wisdom of silence," without rushing to either participate or calling for a boycott of the celebrations.

The military government employed the carrot and stick policy on this occasion in particular in order to encourage Arabs to take part in the celebrations. The policy of repression and intimidation, for example, was used on the eve of Independence Day to ensure widespread participation by government schools. But the authorities, concerned with ensuring the participation of the general public, permitted Palestinians to move freely on that day and through any means of transport without the need for a permit, while the police—to imbue the occasion with unaccustomed joy—permitted travelers to use tractors, trucks, and other vehicles. Indeed, many villagers who were denied freedom of movement and travel throughout the year seized on this opportunity for family trips, recreational visits, and other social activities. They also facilitated the travel of young Arab men to the "mixed cities" and other Jewish cities and towns where celebrations were held until very late at night.[9]

The Communist Party did its part in encouraging people to celebrate Independence Day, as we mentioned earlier, as an expression of its Israeli nationalist posture. Communist discourse did not change until the mid-1950s, despite the contradiction between granting legitimacy to the Jewish state (within the armistice lines), and the fate of the Palestinian people in general and the repression and persecution of the remaining Palestinians. Despite that, Emile Habibi, who became a member of the Knesset in the summer of 1951, gave expression in his own way to the gap between what ought to be and what exists. In 1952 in an article on the front page of *al-Ittihad*, Habibi wrote: "On Independence Day the people affirm their determination to achieve the independence which they sold and to end their subordination to American imperialism."[10] However, Maki's discourse and the position of its activists changed very significantly after the Sinai War, and a discourse of challenge and rebellion developed which led in the end to the confrontation in Nazareth in 1958.

Worth remembering is that in 1956 the government began implementing a policy of Judaizing the Galilee by establishing the city of Upper Nazareth. After plundering the land of the refugees and the forced migrants inside the city, it began to confiscate what was left of Arab lands within the Galilee in order to sever the geographic connections among Arab villages by planting Jewish settlements between them. In addition to beginning to build a Jewish city near Nazareth, the government decreed 200,000 dunums of Arab lands between al-Shaghur and al-Battuf a closed area, in the first step towards expropriating the land to build the city of Karmiel. Thus, the Jewish state and its governmental institutions became an essential partner in Zionist settlement after the Nakba. This settlement drive poured fuel on the flames of anger ignited by the Kafr Qasim massacre in 1956. The communists found themselves quickly drawn to the positions of activist nationalists during 1957–58.

The Israeli government's reaction to this transformation was to consider the possibility of declaring Maki an illegal organization. Discussions regarding this matter were conducted with the other parties at the end of January 1958 to solicit their support.[11] In order to legitimize such a radical step, the intelligence services were asked to monitor the Arab leaders of the party and to try to incriminate them. Yair Bäuml has concluded that the charge against Emile Habibi and some of his comrades in Nazareth of planning a rebellion was without foundation and had been fabricated for political reasons.[12] What really caused concern for the Israeli authorities was the rapprochement between Arab Maki leaders and the Arab nationalist movement after the Sinai War. As we said earlier, the positions of the party at its thirteenth conference clearly reflected this major transformation in the policy of the communists, who had taken Israel's side since 1948. These new political positions rattled the government, so it tried to put a stop to them.

After 1957 the positions of the party became more radical and less in the service of Israeli domestic and foreign policy. In March 1958, the first objections were being heard to participation in celebrations of the tenth anniversary of the establishment of the state of Israel.[13] Consequently, Maki escalated its opposition to Israeli policies, and *al-Ittihad* wrote that all "the artificial celebration programs on Independence Day will not end our attachment to our national and daily rights."[14] The nationalist discourse worked its way into the slogans of the Arab communists in Israel, and this transformation reached its height on the eve of the celebrations when the communists declared frankly: "We will celebrate when we regain our nationalist rights."[15] The focus moved to Nazareth on 1 May where the authorities tried to ban the traditional communist march on the occasion of International Labor Day, which in fact turned into a historic day as the city became the scene of unprecedented confrontations between demonstrators and police. Dozens on both sides were wounded, and the police arrested hundreds of demonstrators that day and in the days that followed. The date, 1 May 1958, became symbolic of open confrontation and challenge by the remaining Arabs to the policy of repression and persecution.

After Labor Day, al-Ittihad published news reports of the arrests following the demonstrations and confrontations in Nazareth and Umm Fahm. Those detained, who were tried by military courts, were described as victims of terrorism in the name of the state. As a reaction to the authorities' tactics of repression, discussions began in July for the formation of an Arab front which would include the leaders of Maki and nationalist activists headed by Yani Yani, the head of the Kufr Yasif local council.[16] The military government and other government agencies acted quickly to prevent the establishment of the front which was considered tantamount to an act of rebellion and an unprecedented challenge in the political conduct of the Arabs who remained in the country. The government placed dozens of activists under administrative detention and others under house arrest. Despite all these measures, meetings were held in 'Akka and Nazareth on 6 July 1958 and the establishment of the Arab Front was announced.[17]

Many of the leading figures in the Arab Front were independent activists who had tried in the past to set up a political organization as an alternative to the Communist Party and the Arab slates affiliated with Mapai. The attorney Elias Kusa was among those who joined the front along with the communists and, in a published interview, he was one of the first to predict that it would not last long, days after the declaration of its creation.[18] Indeed, Kusa withdrew from the front, claiming that "it had become a pliable instrument in the hands of the communists," and predicted, "All Arabs who are not members of the party who fell into Maki's trap will withdraw their names from the declaration of the establishment of the front and will resign from its membership soon."[19] His expectations came true. In January 1959, less than six months after it was founded, and shortly after it had opened branches in many Arab cities and villages, its non-communist leaders resigned, including Tahir al-Fahum, Yani Yani, Jabbur Jabbur, Mansur Kardush, and others. This trial followed by the resignations was the first step towards the creation of the al-'Ard (The Land) movement by those nationalist activists.

FROM STRUGGLING TO SURVIVE TO FIGHTING TO BUILD A FUTURE

One can view the establishment of the Arab Front in 1958 in the wake of the confrontations in Nazareth as a symbolic political event in the history of the Palestinians who remained after the Nakba. In Karl Mannheim's political terminology, such important events represent a transformation that is the harbinger of the rise of a new political generation. From the war of 1956 and its ramifications arose an opportunity for the remaining Arabs to crystalize common political experiences and meaning as a minority suffering from repression and persecution. The Kafr Qasim massacre entailed a unique experience compared to all the killings and repression carried out by the Israeli authorities previously. This massacre aroused a spontaneous feeling of solidarity in the Galilee and the Triangle with the inhabitants of the village and laid out new bases for collective social action. Thus, the political developments in the Arab world and their consequences combined with local events to unify the ranks of the remaining Arabs, even if only temporarily.

On 27 December 1956, Elias Kusa issued invitations for a meeting at his house, which was attended by dozens of political activists of different persuasions.[20] The attendees discussed the Kafr Qasim massacre, and the need to establish a suitable organization for Arabs in response. They signed a declaration addressed to Arab citizens to inform them of the details of what had happened, and to expose the responsibility of the government for that massacre which it had tried to conceal. The signatories affirmed their decision to send letters of protest to the prime minister and to the speaker of the Knesset. At the head of the list of those who signed the letters of protest were Judge Musa al-Tabari, three Christian clergymen from Haifa and the Galilee, the mayor of Shafa ʿAmr Jabbur Jabbur, and the head of the Kafr Yasif local council Yani Yani.[21] The list of signatories also included teachers and merchants, some of whom later became activists in al-ʾArd (Habib Qahwaji and Mansur Kardush), and also leaders of the Israeli Arab Party such as Tahir al-Fahum and Elias Kusa and known activists in the Communist Party.[22]

It appears that the political events in the Arab region reinforced the determination of Kusa and his activist nationalist friends. On 11 January 1957, the Haifa lawyer sent a letter to fifty-six leading Arab figures, urging them to establish a political organization which his own previous efforts had not succeeded in creating. The intelligence agencies that were monitoring these activities tried to foil the move by increasing pressure on the activists to divert them from cooperating with the initiative. In a handwritten note to the office of Uri Lubrani, signed "Carmel," the sender said that he had gone to Bishop Hakim to tell him to warn Kusa to keep quiet.[23] The letter adds that despite Hakim's promises Kusa had again contacted the leaders of Maki. Although pressures from the authorities increased, the rapprochement between the communists and activist nationalists continued until the establishment of the front in 1958.

Discussion of what happened in 1959 and later would take us beyond the scope of this study, but it is nevertheless worth adding some important although concealed information about Elias Kusa and his activities, despite the intense pressure on him from the authorities. Kusa was one of the prominent figures who helped to establish al-ʾArd after the failure of the common front with the communists in 1958. This lawyer came to prominence once again due to his courage in publishing his own frank and penetrating observations. In 1960 he issued a booklet which included harsh criticism of the Ben-Gurion government and its collaborators, Bishop Hakim being the most notable among them. The publication of the booklet, with its harshly critical content, made him the talk of the town, according to the testimonies of some of his contemporaries whom I interviewed. The author became the subject of hostile campaigns of incitement in sections of the Hebrew and Arabic language press which worked hand-in-hand with the authorities.

Kusa did not keep quiet as a result of the attacks and incitement against him. He sent replies to the papers that had attacked him, which they refused to publish. Nevertheless, that did not sap his determination. He published another 40-page booklet, printed by al-Ittihad press in Haifa, in which he attacked his adversaries in his own way.[24] Kusa dedicated his book "to every Arab who is proud of his Arabism and who cherishes his human dignity, who resists persecution and tyranny, who fights to gain his rights as a citizen . . . and to every lofty-minded Arab wherever they may be, who wishes to know the conditions of the Arab minority in Israel."[25] This nationalistic call showed the failure of the Israeli authorities to silence the Arabs who remained, regardless of all the years of repression and persecution.

Kusa was an example of the generation of fathers and Palestinian nationalist leaders who disappeared from the scene after Israel destroyed the Arab cities and expelled the Palestinian Arab elites from the country. Despite his advanced age and the fact that he did not have a party organization to support him, he remained a model to be emulated by the new generation of Arabs who remained and who did not submit to the policy of oppression. Kusa and his friends did not succeed in the 1950s in establishing the independent political organization which they had sought to create time and again. Nevertheless, the efforts of the select few like him laid the foundation for the establishment of al-'Ard, and for the engagement of a new generation of literary and political activists in the 1960s. One of these was the lawyer Sabri Jiryis, who became a nationalist activist in that movement and in various other organizations and institutions.

The Palestinians who remained in Haifa and the Galilee broke the barrier of fear and trauma which had constrained them since the Nakba. Although the authorities managed to suppress the demonstrations and confrontations of contentious politics in Nazareth, those events were the beginning of a new consciousness and hope in a promising future under the leadership of nationalist leaders like Abdel Nasser. It is true that the Israeli government retreated from the idea of declaring Maki an illegal organization, yet it laid down new red lines which caused the Communist Party to retreat to the positions it had occupied in the decade of the 1950s. Nevertheless, the readiness to challenge and engage in confrontation became an important aspect of the experience of the Arabs who remained. The next time that the communists decided to organize a broad Arab front and to challenge the policy of the authorities was on "Land Day" in 1976. The children of the 1970s had learned from the wisdom of their fathers' generation, and they developed the tools of struggle which have made them an important stream of the Palestinian national movement.

Appendix 1[1]

Secret—Urgent

Northern District Command/Intelligence Battalion 123/Intelligence
Battalion 131, 122, 121/Intelligence
31 October 1948
Information report from 10/30 (8:00 hours)—to 10/31 (8:00 hours)

Enemy status: The enemy withdrew from the al-Birwa and Majd al-Krum region on the evening of 10/29.

Orders for the operation: in keeping with the standing orders for Operation Hiram following the surrender of Majd al-Krum.

Actions taken by our forces: Following the arrival of a delegation of the residents of Majd al-Krum, al-Bi'na, Dayr al-Asad, and Nahaf at the barricade around our forces in the Birwa area on 10/29, the battalion commander arrived with a platoon from the first company and a platoon from the second company and a platoon from the third company. On the morning of 10/30 al-Jamal position was secured to guarantee the safety of the platoons that had advanced beyond the barricade. Following a cautious advance accompanied by Arab guides we reached the road and entered Majd al-Krum.

After we entered, our forces observed a column of armored vehicles on the road coming from the direction of al-Rama—which appeared to be French-made—and which fired on Majd al-Krum. Our forces returned fire, and withdrew to points to the west of Majd al-Krum. After the armored column entered Majd al-Krum it became clear it was a detachment from Battalion 12 which had received orders while in al-Rama (11:00 hours) to advance quickly from there to Majd al-Krum.

At 12:30 the notable of the village of Majd al-Krum accepted the conditions for a cease-fire and at 14:25 they signed the agreement in front of the battalion officer.

Our casualties: One wounded from the first company who was wounded in the exchange of fire with Battalion 12 near Majd al-Krum.

Our plan: To transfer control over the Majd al-Krum area to the forces belonging to Company 122.

Status of enemy forces: Nothing worth mentioning.

Miscellaneous items: Majd al-Krum has about 1,800 residents according to a first estimate. During the withdrawal [of the Arab Liberation army] a number of women and children fled to the neighboring Christian village of al-Bi'na. A number of men also fled to the neighboring mountains, as we were informed at the time of surrender. There is a large number of men of military service age in the village, as well as refugees from areas which had been occupied previously.

In accordance with the surrender terms of Majd al-Krum, we gave them until the morning of 10/31 (8:00 hours) to gradually turn in their weapons.

Signed by:

Hanan Levi

Intelligence Officer/Battalion 123

Appendix 2[1]

Secret—Urgent

Haifa District/Intelligence Battalion 123
Battalion 131, 121, 122/Intelligence
31 October 1948
Daily report from 10/30 (8:00 hours) to 10/31 (8:00 hours)

Assessment of our forces: Majd al-Krum region

Our forces left Majd al-Krum today. A detachment of 3rd Company left at 11:00 and re-joined the company in Acre. The remainder left . . . after the arrival of Battalion 122 and its commander at 16:15.

Actions by our forces: An overnight curfew was imposed on Majd al-Krum. By 8 o'clock in the morning the Arabs had not surrendered their weapons, as they were asked to do. We gave them until 12:00, and they turned in twenty rifles, most of them German-made and some others French and British-made, along with their ammunition. After pressure was applied and threats made, they turned in another fifteen rifles with their ammunition.

At 16:15 the commander of Battalion 122 and his men arrived to relieve us. They took con-trol of the situation and immediately chose 1,000 Arab laborers to repair the road leading to Acre. At 17:00 the road had been repaired and cars passed through. Sappers also dis-armed mines on the road to Birwa, and ditches were filled in.

Miscellaneous:

It appeared, on the basis of the interrogation of inhabitants of the village, that the Arab [Liberation] Army had withdrawn from the village on Friday evening. The village sur-rendered the following day. The village has about 2,000 inhabitants. Some gang members remained, including Hajj ʿAbid, who is one of the mufti's men, who was in charge of weap-ons. The other important gang members were: Husni, who is the deputy of the aforemen-tioned individual, and mayor [mukhtar] of the village, and Muhyi al-Din, and Hasan bin

'Ali Mahmud Isma'il and his brother, and Muhammad 'Abd al-Rahman. The last person mentioned has two sons who are gang members, one of whom remained in the village, and the other fled with the army. Hajj 'Abid was insolent and arrogant when he handed in arms. . . . Some villagers fled to the mountains, and will try to return in the coming days. Also, some weapons were hidden in the forests and orchards in the region.

Signed by

Intelligence Officer

[Name illegible]

Appendix 3[1]

Operations Officer 1 Haifa District Intelligence Officer
District 9 Operations Officer Operation /29/
Northern Front/Intelligence 1 November 1948
Subject: Intelligence

Below are excerpts from reports by battalion intelligence officers:

Battalion 122

There are young Arab men of military service age throughout the occupied area. It seems that when the Liberation Army withdrew quickly it left large quantities of weapons with the inhabitants. It appears that many Arabs who belonged to the Liberation Army were unable to withdraw and changed clothes at the last moment. Consequently, there is a pressing need to carry out a swift and precise combing operation and to investigate and search for arms and for members of the Liberation Army.

Battalion 123

According to what was discovered in the interrogation of inhabitants of Majd al-Krum, the Arab [Liberation] Army withdrew from the village on the evening of 29 October, and the village surrendered the next day. The village has about 2,000 inhabitants. Some gang members remained, including the mayor [mukhtar] Hajj 'Abid, who is one of the Mufti's men, who is the leader of the gangs and is in charge of weapons. The other important gang members are: Husni, who is the deputy of the aforementioned individual and is hiding in the village, and Muhyi al-Din and Hasan Abu 'Ali Mahmud Isma'il and his brother, and Muhammad 'Abd al-Rahman who has two sons, one of whom remained in the village, and the other fled with the army. Hajj 'Abid and his deputy are also in charge of a munitions depot containing explosives and bombs and they know where they are hidden. Hajj 'Abid was insolent and arrogant when he handed in arms. . . . Some villagers, particularly the young men, fled to the mountains, and will try to return in the coming days. Also, most of the weapons were hidden in nearby forests and orchards.

We came across a letter dated 10/27 written by an Arab intelligence officer from the Yarmuk Brigade which belongs to the Liberation Army [sic] addressed to a member of the general staff asking him to dispatch explosives for the battle. This could be interpreted to mean that the Arabs had intended to launch an attack on that date. We also found a report written in the Latin alphabet listing the arms available on 10/10 which indicates there were 56 German, 22 French, and 16 British rifles.

Haifa District Intelligence Officer

Appendix 4[1]

Secret

Occupied Territories Administration Command General Staff Command/Baruch
Northern Front
18 November 1948
Lieutenant Colonel Schnurman No. 179

Subject: Majd al-Krum

1. It appears this locale has been neglected by your men. There is no military governor, not even an officer, there. During the visit by [United Nations] observers to the locale on 10 November, the residents made many accusations that we had committed atrocities of plunder and murder. No doubt, if a proper remedy had been applied, I would not have heard of these accusations. These reports will cause a lot of damage when they are transmitted to Paris, where they will be exaggerated.

2. We would like to draw your attention to the situation, which requires a speedy remedy.

Col. Baruch

Chief Liaison Officer with the United Nations

Appendix 5[1]

Minister of Defense Military Government of the Administered Areas
Chief of Staff
10 February 1949

Subject: The Adoption of Measures Against the Infiltrators

1. Pursuant to our conversation of 4 January 1949, orders were issued for the conduct of combing operations and ascertaining the identities of the residents from time to time.

2. During January combing operations were conducted in eleven villages, resulting in:
   1,038 individuals being exiled beyond the borders;
   20 individuals being transferred to a prisoner of war camp;
   69 individuals being arrested so that they could continue to be interrogated; and
   128 individuals being moved to other villages.

3. Combing operations were carried out in the villages shown below:

Location	Results of Operation			
	Expelled	Moved to POW camp	Arrested to continue interrogation	Moved to another village
Shafa 'Amr	42	5		
'Iblin	15	6	67	
Kabul	128	1	1	
Majd al-Krum	536			
Al-Bi'na	59	5		

(Continued)

(Continued)

Location	Results of Operation			
	Expelled	Moved to POW camp	Arrested to continue interrogation	Moved to another village
Dayr al-Asad	8			
Mi'lya	28			
Tarshiha	90	3		
Saffuriyya	14			
Farradiyya & Kufr 'Inan	54			
al-Mujaydil	64		1	128
Total	**1038**	**20**	**69**	**128**

4. Regarding the reorganization of army forces in the north, operations were suspended and then resumed on 4 February 1949.

(signed by)

Gen. Elimelech Avnir

Commander of military government in the administered areas.

Appendix 6[1]

Haifa District Command
10 January 1949

Report on Combing Operation in Majd al-Krum

Date of Combing Operation: 9 January 1949
Objective: To arrest infiltrators and criminals in the village.

Participating forces:

A company from the Minorities Division, a platoon from Battalion 123, ten military police, a sergeant, two female soldiers, nine policemen, a police officer, and two representatives of the military government.

The village was surrounded by the company from the Minorities Division. After 3:00 all entrances and exits to and from the villages were blocked.

At 7:00 forces from the Israeli police and military police and a platoon from Battalion 123 arrived.

Village notables were ordered to gather all men twelve years of age and older within half an hour. At 8:00 a curfew was declared, and five combing operation patrols were sent to look for men who were hiding. Each patrol consisted of a policeman, a military policeman and two soldiers. Then intelligence agents and policemen began interrogating the men. The identities of 506 men were checked.

After ascertaining their identities, 355 men were expelled outside the borders.

Summary:

Coordination among forces was good, except in the two following cases:

1. The transport vehicles did not arrive on [the desired] time, consequently an additional 300 individuals were not transported.
2. Two soldiers from the platoon belonging to Battalion 123 took several objects from one of the shops.

After a brief investigation the objects taken were returned to their owners. The above-mentioned soldiers will be tried.

Haifa District Intelligence Officer

Tsvi Rabinovich

Appendix 7[1]

12 January 1949
Military Government of Western Galilee

Subject: Report On the Combing Operation in the Village of Majd Al-Krum On 9 January 1949

Regarding my letter no. 25 of 10 January 1949 concerning the matter above, I would like to draw your attention to the following issues:

1. The conduct of the soldiers towards the inhabitants was extremely boorish. The entire operation was accompanied by curses, insults, and physical abuse on the part of the soldiers, beginning with the officer in charge of the operation, Tsvi Rabinovitch. After checking the identity of each inhabitant, if it was decided that someone was to be expelled, even if merely for being a refugee, he was brought out of the interrogation room with blows and kicks.

   The boorishness of the soldiers was at its worst in dealing with the mayor (mukhtar) of the village, Hajj 'Abd al-Salim. Despite the fact that the above-mentioned person was sick that day, he came to the square to be interrogated. The police officer, Mr. Shuwaili, released him. While he was at home, soldiers entered the house and without listening to what he had to say or to his entreaties they fell on him, hitting him with the butts of their rifles and they kicked him in the stomach. As a result of that he suffered an inflammation in his stomach membrane and from a blow to his liver, which necessitated taking him to the hospital in Nazareth where he now lies in a critical condition.

2. During the operation, soldiers from the platoon belonging to Battalion 123 broke into two shops and robbed them. Private homes were also looted, including an alarm clock, clothes and a variety of small items, despite repeated warnings to officer Shlomo not to harm the furniture and the contents of the houses.

Following the operation, I ordered the military police to search the soldiers, and we found most of the stolen items, which were returned to their owners. However, there are still some items missing, and complaints regarding this will be sent to those concerned.

In my opinion we should not keep quiet about this behavior and those responsible should be brought to trial.

Please refer to my letters no. 34 and 44 dated January 10.

(Signed)

Shlomo [No surname]

PREFACE

1. Adel Manna', "Mekhtav el yadid Yesraeli" [Letter to an Israeli Friend], *Haaretz*, June 1984, 9.

2. The festivities of the tenth anniversary were an important event in Israel's relations with its Arab citizens and it tried to compel them to participate in these celebrations. Many were opposed to this, including the leaders of the Communist Party, which led to demonstrations and clashes in Nazareth on 1 May 1958.

3. The term *istihlal* was commonly used in colloquial language to mean occupation—rather than *ihtilal* – so at school we began using the expression "Occupation of My Country Day" as a means of expressing dissatisfaction with these celebrations.

4. The arrival of Palestinian refugees by sea to a place with such a name is reminiscent of Israeli tales of the success of Zionist immigrants in reaching Palestine during the British Mandate despite the British authorities' opposition and attempts to prevent the arrival of immigrants, particularly after 1939.

5. The Wadi 'Ara region was under the control of Arab (Iraqi and Jordanian) armies until April 1949. This is why Israel evicted inhabitants of the Galilee to this region as I detail later.

6. For further details of my grandmother's life, see my article "Hikayat Zahra al-Ja'uniyya," *Annals of Jerusalem* 6 (Winter/Spring 2008): 67–81. English readers will prefer "From Seferberlik to the Nakba: A Personal Account of the Life of Zahra al-Ja'uniyya," *Jerusalem Quarterly* (Spring 2007): 59–76.

7. Later it was found out that Haim Orbach had worked in the Haganah intelligence service, and that he had made friends with the Arabs to gain information about their villages. He was also on good terms with the Ma'di family in Yarka, including Shaykh Jabr Ma'di. They tried to convince the residents of villages in the Galilee to surrender and not to fight the Jews in return for ensuring their security and safeguarding their property.

8. The role of Shafiq Abu 'Abdu, from the village of al-Damun which was destroyed, will be discussed in detail later. The authorities allowed him and some of his relatives to settle in the village of Sha'b.

9. Adel Manna', "Majd al-Krum 1948: 'Amaliyyat tamshit 'adiyya' " [Majd al-Krum 1948: "Ordinary Combing Operations"], al-Karmel 55–56 (Spring-Summer 1998): 184–200.

10. Danny Rabinowitz and Khawla Abu Baker, Hadur ha-Zakuf [The Stand-Tall Generation: The Palestinian Citizens of Israel Today] (Jerusalem: Keter, 2002).

11. Rabinowitz and Abu Baker, Hadur ha-Zakuf, 36.

12. Indeed, my mother, who passed away in January 2019, had been happy to see the book published in Arabic and in Hebrew.

INTRODUCTION

1. Those villages were described in the military orders for the operation as "communications bases" and not enemy positions, as was usually the case in relation to Arab villages. See Benny Morris, 1948: Toldut ha-melhama ha-'Arvit ha-Yesraelit ha-rishona [1948: A History of the First Arab-Israeli War] (Tel Aviv: 'Am Ovid, 2010), 307.

2. Israeli researchers, with Morris at their head, estimate that the number of Arabs who were killed in the "border wars" and labeled as "infiltrators" was between three and five thousand individuals. This study demonstrates that tens, if not hundreds, of them were "Israeli Arabs."

3. This is the case of most studies on the Arab-Israeli conflict. Morris, who devoted serious study to the Israeli war on "infiltration" by Palestinian refugees, treated it as a fight to protect Israel's borders from the neighboring Arab countries, without devoting much attention to its repercussions and daily impact on the lives of Arabs in Israel.

4. See the article by Hassan Jabareen, in which he stresses the "Hobbesian moment" relating to the January 1951 elections: "Hobbesian Citizenship: How the Palestinians Became a Minority in Israel," in Multiculturalism and Minority Rights in the Arab World, ed. Will Kymlicka and Eva Pföstl (London: Oxford University Press, 2014), 189–218.

5. Constantine Zurayk, Ma'na al-Nakba [Meaning of the Catastrophe] (Beirut: Dar al-'Ilm l-il-malayin, 1948).

6. Yitzhak Rabin, Penkas sherut [Service Identity Card] (Tel Aviv: Maariv Bookstore, 1979), 1:97.

7. Rabin, Penkas sherut.

8. For more on the Kafr Qasim massacre, see Rubik Rosenthal, ed., Kfar Qasim: iru'im ve-metus [Kafr Qasim: Events and a Legend] (Tel Aviv: United Kibbutz, 2000).

9. Uzi Benziman and 'Atallah Mansour, Dayyari meshne: 'Arveyyi Yesrael, mamadam ve-hamdenyut klapeihim [Sub-Tenants: The Arabs of Israel, Their Status and the Policies Toward Them] (Jerusalem: Keter, 1992), 54–59.

10. Many of those who remained were accused of naiveté and of not putting up a sufficient defense of the country and the homeland. As in the case of other peoples who suffered tragedies and defeats, the sons failed to appreciate the conditions in which their fathers found themselves during the days of the catastrophe.

11. Subhi Abu-Ghosh, "The Politics of an Arab Village in Israel" (PhD diss., Princeton University, 1965).

12. Sabri Jiryis, *Al-'Arab fi 'Isra'il* [The Arabs in Israel] (Haifa: al-Ittihad Press, 1966).

13. "Anqidhuna min hadha al-hub al-qasi" [Save Us from This Cruel Love] was first published in *al-Jadid* 6 (1969) in Haifa, which Darwish edited, before being widely published and circulated in the Arab world.

14. The fame of Habibi's *Pessoptimist* spread internationally; it was translated into several languages, including into Hebrew by Mefras publishers in Haifa in 1985. In English, it has been translated by Salma Khadra Jayyusi and Trevor Le Gassick as *The Secret Life of Saeed: The Pessoptimist* (London: Zed Books, 1985).

15. Ghassan Kanafani, *'Awd ila Hayfa* [Returning to Haifa] (Beirut: Dar al-'Awda, 1969).

16. Emile Habibi, "Al-Hiwar al-akhir" [The Last Interview], *Masharif* 9, June 1996, 19.

17. Ian Lustick, *Arabs in the Jewish State* (Austin: University of Texas Press, 1980).

18. Tom Segev, *1949: Hayestaelim hareshonim* [1949: The First Israelis] (Jerusalem: Domino, 1984), 20–104.

19. Benziman and Mansour, *Dayyari meshne*.

20. Ilan Pappé's book was translated from the original English (Oxford: One World, 2006) into Arabic (and very well received) under the title *Al-tathir al-'arqi fi Filastin* [The Ethnic Cleansing of Palestine] (Beirut: Institute for Palestine Studies, 2007).

21. Such positions represent the Zionist second line of defense after the fall of the first line, which denied that the massacres had occurred and blamed Arab leaders for the refugee problem because of the orders they issued.

22. Ari Shavit, "Mehake la-barbarim, Benny Morris" [Waiting for the Barbarians: An Interview with Benny Morris]," *Haaretz*, 6 January 2004.

23. Morris's statements in this interview constituted an important turning point for him, and resulted in a storm of debate inside Israel and outside it.

24. Nur Masalha, ed., *Catastrophe Remembered: Palestine, Israel and the Internal Refugees* (London: Zed Books, 2005); Ahmad Sa'di and Lila Abu-Lughod, eds. *Nakba: Palestine, 1948, and the Claims of Memory* (New York: Columbia University Press, 2007).

25. For a collection of his articles in English, see Mustafa Abbasi, *The Cities of Galilee During the 1948 War: Four Cities and Four Stories* (Germany: Lambert Academic Publishing, 2014).

26. Cohen's study was translated into Arabic and published in Jerusalem and then Beirut; Hillel Cohen, *Al-gha'bun al-hadrun: al-laj'un al-Filastiniyun fi 'Isra'il min 1948* [The Present Absentees: Palestinian Refugees in Israel since 1948] (Jerusalem: Center for the Study of Arab Society, 2002; Beirut: Institute for Palestine Studies, 2003).

27. Hillel Cohen, *Arvim tuvim:ha-mudi'een ha-Yisra'eli ve-Harvim be-Yesra'el* [The Good Arabs: Israeli Intelligence and the Arabs in Israel] (Jerusalem: Keter, 2006).

28. For the published version of her dissertation, see Shira Robinson, *Citizen Strangers: Palestinians and the Birth of Israel's Liberal Settler State* (Stanford, CA: Stanford University Press, 2013).

29. The daily newspaper *Al-Yawm* began to publish in September 1948, and was followed a month later by the weekly *Al-Ittihad*.

30. Sometimes referred to as the Arab Salvation Army or the Arab Liberation Army.

31. These villages differ in terms of the circumstances under which the residents were expelled and then allowed to return to their homes; they have in common the fact that the inhabitants did return, the villages were spared from destruction, and their population

saved from dispersal, contrary to what happened to hundreds of other Palestinian villages.

32. Published originally in Arabic as Elias Khoury, *Bab al-shams* (Beirut: Dar al-Adab, 1998); English translation by Humphrey Davies, *Gate of the Sun* (London: Vintage, 2006).

33. Tom Segev, "Roman 'Arvi" ["An Arab Story"], *Haaretz*, 1 March 2002.

34. Segev, "An Arab Story."

35. S. Yizhar [Smilansky], *Khirbet Khiz'eh* (Jerusalem: Ibis Editions, 2008); published originally in 1949 in Hebrew as *Khirbet Hiz'eh*.

36. Tom Segev, "Ha-Sodut ha-reshonim" [The First Secrets], *Haaretz*, 2 March 1995.

37. Benny Morris, *Tekkun ta'ut* [Correcting a Mistake: Jews and Arabs in Palestine/Israel 1936–56] (Tel Aviv: Am Ovid, 2000).

38. Morris, *Tekkun ta'ut*, 146.

39. See the website of this organization, www.zochrot.org (accessed 30 March 2020), for publications and testimonies about the Nakba in Hebrew, Arabic, and English collected by activists. They also publish booklets concerning villages that were demolished.

40. Examples are *Nir* and *Ha-Olam Hazeh* newspapers in Hebrew, and the Catholic church's magazine, *al-Rabita*, all of which contain important material and critical points of view towards government policy.

1. AL-NAKBA AND ITS MANY MEANINGS IN 1948

1. Constantine Zurayk, *Ma'na al-Nakba* [The Meaning of the Catastrophe] (Beirut: Dar al-'Ilm l-il-malayin, 1948).

2. Zurayk, *Ma'na al-Nakba*, 7. Walid al-Khalidi collected four books which dealt with the Nakba and republished them in one volume, performing a great service to readers and researchers. Along with Constantine Zurayk's book, works by Musa al-'Alami, George Hanna, and Qadri Hafiz Tuqan were published under the title *Nakbat 1948: asbabiha wa subul 'ilajiha* [Nakba 1948: Its Causes and Its Solutions] (Beirut: Institute for Palestine Studies, 2009), introduction by Walid al-Khalidi. The use of the term "al-Nakba" spread after Zurayk's book; it was used by Arab communists in a leaflet distributed at the end of September 1948 and in the titles of many books published on the 1948 war and its tragic consequences, including the works of Muhammad Nimr al-Khatib, Muhammad Nimr al-Hawwari, and 'Arif al-'Arif, among others.

3. The five other notions were: defeat (*hazima*), setback (*naksa*), evil (*shar*), tribulation (*mihna*), and elsewhere in the book, disaster (*karitha*).

4. For Zurayk, his life and achievements, see Aziz al-'Azma, '*Arabi lil-qarn al-'ishrin* [Constantine Zurayk: A Twentieth Century Arab] (Beirut: Institute for Palestine Studies, 2003). See also a commemoration of Zurayk from the American University of Beirut at online-exhibit.aub.edu.lb/exhibits/show/constantine-zurayk (accessed 27 December 2019).

5. Zurayk et al., *Nakbat 1948*, 5.

6. Zurayk et al., *Nakbat 1948*, 7.

7. Near the end of 1948, the dispute between King Abdullah of Transjordan and Mufti Hajj 'Amin al-Husayni, in particular, intensified and Arab countries supported one side against the other.

8. For the "cold war" among Arab states in the 1950s, see Malcolm Kerr, *The Arab Cold War 1958–67: A Study of Ideology in Politics* (London: Oxford University Press, 1967).

9. George Hanna, *Tariq al-khalas: tahlil wad'i li mihnat Filastin wa al-qadaya al-'Arabiyya* [The Path to Deliverance: A Situational Analysis of Palestine's Affliction and Arab Issues] (Beirut: Dar al-Ahad, 1948); republished in Zurayk et al., *Nakbat 1948*. Worth noting is that the author chose the term "affliction" rather than "Nakba" to describe the defeat in Palestine.

10. For more on the author and his other publications, see Zurayk et al., *Nakbat 1948*, xiii-xiv.

11. George Hanna, a socialist, does not ignore the role of the Soviet Union in the Palestinian Nakba, and also talks about Russia and the Russians.

12. Hanna, *Tariq al-khalas*, 61.

13. Hanna, *Tariq al-khalas*, 77.

14. Hanna, *Tariq al-khalas*, 58.

15. Musa al-'Alami, *'Ibrat Filastin* [The Lesson of Palestine] (Beirut: Dar al-Kashaf, 1949); reprinted in Zurayk et al., *Nakbat 1948*.

16. Al-'Alami studied law in Britain. When he finished his studies in 1923, he returned to Jerusalem and worked for several years as a public attorney.

17. Al-'Alami assigns the responsibility for what happened in Palestine to Britain first of all, then secondly to the Americans and the Russians. See al-'Alami, *Ibrat Filastin*, 144.

18. Some researchers, particularly on the Israeli side, describe the events of the war in its first months as a "civil war." This description is inaccurate and controversial; it is preferable to divide the war into two stages without describing the first stage as a civil war.

19. Muhammad Nimr al-Hawwari, *Sirr al-Nakba* [The Secret of the Nakba] (Nazareth: Hakim Press, 1955). The content of the introduction and the book indicate that al-Hawwari had finished writing his book in 1950, but its publication was delayed.

20. Hawwari, *Sirr al-Nakba*, 107, 196, 200.

21. Hawwari, *Sirr al-Nakba*, 315.

22. 'Arif al-'Arif gives detailed accounts of the events of the Nakba, its causes and remedies, and the price Palestinians paid in terms of lives and property in *Al-Nakba: Nakba Bayt al-Maqdis wal-firdaws al-mafqud,1947–49* [The Nakba: The Nakba of Jerusalem and the Lost Paradise 1947–49]. The first of these volumes was published in Sidon in 1956, and the last in 1961.

23. Following the Jerusalem turmoil during the Nabi Musa festival in the spring of 1920, 'Arif al-'Arif and Hajj Amin al-Husayni fled and were pursued by the British authorities, but the two returned the following year. Al-'Arif occupied many posts in the British Mandate administration, including that of *qa'immaqam* (governor) of the Bir Sab'a district. Following the Nakba and the annexation of the West Bank to Jordan, he worked in the Jordanian administration, and served as mayor of the Jerusalem municipality during 1950–55.

24. For further information on this, see Rashid Khalidi, *The Iron Cage: The Story of the Palestinian Struggle for Statehood* (Boston: Beacon Press, 2006).

25. In the last few decades new historical and critical readings of the Arab revolt of the 1930s and its negative ramifications have appeared. It is sufficient here to note that there was a focus on the negative results of the revolt, going beyond the discussion of heroic acts, sacrifices, and achievements.

26. Perhaps the outbreak of World War II and the absence of a large number of Palestinian leaders from the political scene because of imprisonment or exile played a role in this.

27. We do not intend here to explain and analyze the effect of this partition into two states, one Arab and the other Jewish, and its ramifications for the Palestinian people and its right to self-determination on the soil of the entirety of its homeland.

28. The UN resolution did not include the establishment of an international body to oversee the implementation of the plan, but it was sufficient, as far as the Zionist movement was concerned, to legitimate the establishment of a Jewish state in Palestine.

29. David Ben-Gurion, *Yawmiyyat al-harb, 1947–49* [War Diaries, 1947–49], ed. Gershon Rivlin and Elhanan Orren, trans. Samir Jabbur (Beirut: Institute for Palestine Studies, 1993), 99.

30. Ben-Gurion, *Yawmiyyat al-harb*, 101.

31. Rashid al-Hajj Ibrahim, *Al-difa' an Hayfa waqadiyyat Filatin: Mudhakirat Rashid al-hajj Ibrahim, 1891–1953* [The Defense of Haifa and the Palestinian Cause: The Memoirs of Rashid al-Hajj Ibrahim, 1891–1953] (Beirut: The Institute for Palestine Studies, 2005), 190.

32. The Arab press in Palestine voiced this faulty understanding of the battle for destiny towards the end of 1947, as did the testimonies of dozens of people who lived through those events, whose *ad hoc* testimonies I have heard. Arab sources called the participants in the strike "rebels," and the discussion was about "the revolt" and not "the war"; the events were compared to the events of the 1936–39 revolt.

33. Khalil al-Sakakini, *Yawmiyat Khalil al-Sakakini: yawmayat, rasayl,t'amulat,al-kitab al-thamn:al-khuruj min al-qatamun, 1942–52* [The Diaries of Khalil al-Sakakini: Diaries, Letters, Insights, Book Eight: Leaving al-Qatamun, 1942–52] (Ramallah: Khalil al-Sakakini Cultural Center and the Jerusalem Studies Institute, 2010), 238.

34. al-Sakakini, *Yawmiyat*.

35. Twelve residents of Khisas village were killed in the Palmach operation, including a woman and four children, some of whom were found under the rubble of houses that had been blown up.

36. Yoav Gelber, *Komimyut ve-Nakba: Yesrael, ha-Falastinimu-medinut 'Arav, 1948* [Independence and Nakba: Israel, the Palestinians and the Arab States in 1948] (Tel Aviv, Zamora Beitan, 2004), 65, 139; Benny Morris, *Lidata shel ba'yat ha-Plitim ha-Falastinim, 1947–49* [The Birth of the Palestinian Refugee Problem 1947–49] (Tel Aviv: 'Am 'Ovid, 1991), 56; Adel Manna' and Motti Golani, *Two Faces of the Coin: Independence and Nakba, Two Narratives of the 1948 War and Its Consequences* (Holland: The Historical Justice and Reconciliation Institute, 2011), 65, 139.

37. Attempts by residents of the village to return to their homes, and their subsequent recourse to the Supreme Court in Jerusalem, will be discussed in later chapters of this book.

38. Some sources say that two of the perpetrators were wounded in the operation.

39. Some of those who returned to their villages were young men who were working for the mandatory government, some in the police.

40. These acts of collective punishment enjoyed the support of the [Jewish] leadership without reservation. In one session convened by Ben-Gurion, Gad Machnes said: "We must strike without mercy, including women and children" and added: "There is no need to differentiate . . . between the innocent and the guilty" (Ben-Gurion, *Yawmiyyat al-harb*, 99).

41. According to estimates, up to the end of 1947 about 450,000 Palestinians lived in the area allocated for the Jewish state under the partition resolution; 95 percent of them became refugees, and only about 5 percent remained in Israel and became citizens.

42. Nadim Musa, *Dhikrayat shuyu'i mukhadram* [Memories of a Veteran Communist] (Acre: Abu Rahmun Press, 2008), 32.

43. Musa, *Dhikrayat.* Those comrades who were members of the League and their role in villages of mid-Galilee will be discussed in the next chapter.

44. There are many works of Palestinian and Israeli historical literature on the Arab Rescue Army in the Galilee.

45. A very interesting question concerning this subject is: what if the United Nations had in fact gone back on the partition resolution and accepted the State Department's proposal for a Trusteeship?

46. Ben-Gurion, *Yawmiyyat al-harb*, 135.

47. Walid al-Khalidi stirred up controversy when he became the first to write about this plan beginning in 1959: "Why Did the Palestinians Leave," *Middle East Forum* 34, no. 6 (July 1959): 21–24, 25; republished in *Journal of Palestine Studies* 34, no. 2 (2005): 42–54. Also see "The Fall of Haifa," *Middle East Forum* 35, no. 10 (December 1959), republished in *Journal of Palestine Studies* 37, no. 3 (Spring 2008): 30–58; and "Plan Dalet, the Zionist Blueprint for the Conquest of Palestine," *Middle East Forum* 37, no. 9 (November 1961): 22–38. In 2007, Ilan Pappé published his study, *The Ethnic Cleansing of Palestine* (London: One World), which supports the Palestinian position expressed by Khalidi.

48. Al-'Arif, *Al-Nakba*, 223–25.

49. Al-'Arif, *Al-Nakba*, 225. Al-'Arif refers to the change in the position of the Druze and the move by some of them to the side of the Jews in the fighting, basing his information on the testimony of one of the well-known fighters in Nazareth, 'Abd al-Latif al-Fahum.

50. 'Abd al-Qadir al-Husayni (1908–48) was one of the prominent leaders of the 1936–39 revolt, and Mufti Hajj Amin's choice to command the Jihad Muqaddas (Holy War), the most important Palestinian military organization in the 1948 war.

51. For several years Haganah sources were relied on, which the British and others adopted, and which indicated that over 250 people were killed in the Dayr Yasin massacre. However, recent Palestinian research indicates that the number of those killed was 104, less than half the original Haganah estimate.

52. Ben-Gurion, *Yawmiyyat al-harb*, 284.

53. Ben-Gurion, *Yawmiyyat al-harb*.

54. Ben-Gurion, *Yawmiyyat al-harb*, 284–85. In the latter chapters of the book, there are further details on this committee and the role played by Elias Kusa in defending the rights of Arab citizens in Israel in general and Haifa in particular.

55. Bulus Farah, *Min al-'uthmaniyya ila al-dawla al-'ibriyya* [From the Ottoman Empire to the Jewish State] (Haifa: al-Sawt, 1985), 196.

56. Farah, *Min al-'uthmaniyya*, 196–97. Farah mentions in his memoirs that the only communists he met in Haifa at the time were 'Isam al-'Abbasi and Yusif 'Abdu.

57. Motti Golani, *Yamim Ahrunim: Hamemshal hamandaturi-pennuy ve-melhama* [The Last Days: The Mandate Government, Withdrawal and the War] (Jerusalem: Zalman Shazar Center, 2009), 82–83.

58. Abraham Sela, "Tzva ha-Hahatzla ba-Galil be-melemet 1948" [The Arab Liberation Army in the Galilee in the 1948 War], in *Melhemet Ha'atzma'ut: 1947–49, Diyyun Mehuddash* [War of Independence 1947–49, Renewed Discussion], ed. Elon Kadish (Tel Aviv: Ministry of Security, 2004), 207–68.

59. The most prominent among them is Benny Morris's *Lidata shel ba'yat ha-plitim ha-Falastinim*, which documents many acts of murder and expulsion, but then arrives at the conclusion that there was no blueprint for the expulsion of the Palestinians.

60. That became clear during the occupation of central and upper Galilee in Operation Hiram.

61. The most prominent examples of that at the collective level were the Druze and communists in the north of the country.

62. The absence of regular armies as existed in the center and the south of the country gave the people a wider opportunity to adopt different positions in the interest of staying on the land and preventing massacres and uprooting.

63. Elias Khoury, *Bab al-shams* (Beirut: Dar al-Adab, 1998), 73; translated by Humphrey Davies as *Gate of the Sun* (London: Vintage, 2006).

64. The number of Arab residents of Israel, according to the official census before the renewal of fighting in October 1948, was 69,000.

65. Hillel Cohen, *Army of Shadows: Palestinian Collaboration with Zionism, 1917–1948*, trans. Haim Watzman (Berkeley: University of California Press, 2008), 252.

66. Cohen, *Army of Shadows*, 258. Testimonies by refugee and expelled individuals who were trying to return from Lebanon also spoke about these experiences in late 1948 and later.

67. Kais Firro, *The Druzes in the Jewish State: A Brief History* (Leiden: Brill, 1999), 51.

68. Nimr Murqus, *Aqwa min al-nisyan: Risala ila ibnati* [More Powerful than Forgetfulness: A Letter to My Daughter (1)] (Tarshiha: Makhul and Hazbun, 2000), 89; Nimr Murqus, ed., *Yani Qustandi Yani* (Kafr Yasif: al-Majlis al-Mahalli, 1987). Also author interview with Murqus at his home, 28 June 2008.

69. Eliezer Bray, "Ha'umnam transfer?" [Was it really a Transfer], *'Al Hamishmar*, 13 November 1948.

70. Most prominent among them in the leadership of the League was its secretary Fu'ad Nassar, Tawfiq Tuba, and Emile Habibi, who spearheaded the acceptance of the partition and the rejection of war.

71. Laila Parsons, *The Druze Between Palestine and Israel, 1947–49* (New York: St. Martin's Press, 2000), 69–70.

72. Just as the Dayr Yasin massacre is the most famous operation in the killings of defenseless Palestinian civilians, the expulsion of tens of thousands of the inhabitants of Lydda and Ramla became the most famous ethnic cleansing operation carried out by the Israeli army with orders from the top leadership.

73. Only a few hundred of the inhabitants of Lydda and Ramla were allowed to stay in their homes, and isolated in a quarter which became known as "the ghetto."

74. Gelber, *Komimyut ve-Nakba*, 230.

75. Sa'd al-Din al-'Alami, *Watha'iq al-Hay'a al-Islamiyya al-'Ulya*, 1 [Documents of the Higher Islamic Committee: Jerusalem, 1967–1984] (Amman: Dar al-Karmil, 1986), 10.

76. Al-'Alami, *Watha'iq*, 10–11. Al-'Alami, the shari'a judge of Nazareth in 1948, was renting the Jisr family house, where the surrender agreement was signed.

77. The document for the surrender of Nazareth was published in Hebrew and Arabic in several books. 'Atif al-Fahum kept an original copy of the document signed on 16 July 1948.

78. Morris, *Lidata shel ba'yat ha-plitim ha-Falastinim*, 270.

79. Such as the refugees from Shafa 'Amr, Kafr Kanna, and 'Illut. As for the refugees from al-Mujaydil, Ma'lul, and Saffuriyya, they received different treatment, as they

were prevented from returning to their villages which remained deserted, and were later destroyed.

80. This contradicts Benny Morris's conclusions. Morris attaches greater weight to the conduct of army officers in the field. The orders issued in Lydda and Ramla on the one hand, and Nazareth and the Druze on the other, led to the desired results.

81. Nafidh Abu Hasna, ed., *Khalid al-Fahum yatadhakar* [Khaled Fahum Remembers] (Beirut: al-Ruwad Printers and Publishers, 1999), 43.

82. Peretz Kidron participated in the writing of those memoirs in Toronto, Canada, then published that story which he had heard in "Truth Whereby Nations Live," in *Blaming the Victims: Spurious Scholarship and the Palestinian Question*, ed. Edward W. Said and Christopher Hitchens (London: Verso Books, 1988), 87.

83. Morris, *Lidata shel ba'yat ha-plitim ha-Falastinim*, 153–54.

84. There are memoirs or autobiographies by Hanna Abu Hanna, Mansur Kardush, and other residents of Nazareth who lived through these events in 1948.

85. Eliezer Bray, "Ha'umnam transfer" [Transfer, Really?], *'Al Hamishmar*, 19 November 1948.

86. Eliezer Bray, untitled article, *'Al Hamishmar*, 23 November 1948.

87. Bray, untitled, 23 November 1948.

88. Bray, untitled, 23 November 1948.

89. Morris, *Lidata shel ba'yat ha-plitim ha-Falastinim*, 272.

90. Hillel Cohen, *'Arvim Tuvim: ha-mudi'een ha-Yisra'eli ve-Harvim be-Yesra'el* [Good Arabs: Israeli Intelligence and the Arabs in Israel] (Jerusalem: Keter, 2006), 35–36.

91. Cohen, *'Arvim Tuvim*, 36. There is more than one reference to Sayf al-Din al-Zu'bi's cooperation with the Israeli authorities on the eve of the 1948 war and after.

92. Bernadotte's proposals reinforced the feeling among some observers that the Galilee would end up as part of Israel, either by agreement or by force.

93. Muhammad Khaled al-Az'ar, *Hukumat 'umum Filastin fi dhikraha al-khamsin* [The All-Palestine Government on its Fiftieth Anniversary] (Beirut: Dar al-Shuruq, 1998).

94. Hanna Abu Hanna, *Khamirat al-ramad* [Yeast of Ashes] (Haifa: Maktabat Kul Shay, 2004), 130–31; Sayf al-Din al-Zu'bi, *Shahid 'iyan: muthakarat Sayf al-Din al-Zu'bi* [Eyewitness: The Memoirs of Sayf al-Din Zu'bi] (Shafa 'Amr: Dar al-Mashriq, 1987), 26–27.

95. Abu Hasna, *Khalid al-Fahum yatadhakar*, 44.

96. They called the ARA the "galloping army."

97. The name of this village is written as Mi'ar in local books and newspapers.

98. Mas'ud Ghanayim published a series of articles in *al-Mithaq* newspaper, organ of the Islamic movement, in May 2000, in which he defended the reputation of the ARA as he tried to justify and explain the conduct of the mukhtar of Sakhnin.

99. Mas'ud Ghanayim, *Makalat akhira* [Last Article], *Al-Mithaq*, 19 May 2000, 9.

100. Gelber, *Komimyut ve-Nakba*, 290.

101. Najib Susan, *Sada al-'ayam* [Echo of the Days] (Haifa: self-published, 2001), 32–35.

2. COMPLETING THE OCCUPATION OF GALILEE—OPERATION HIRAM

1. Three villages which the Jews considered to be "friendly" escaped destruction and their populations were not expelled: Tuba al-Zanghariyya which was inhabited by 'Arab al-Hayb, the Circassian village of al-Rihaniyya, and the village of Jish, whose remaining population after 1948 were mostly Maronite.

2. Hanna Ibrahim, *Shajarat al-ma'rifa: dhikrayat shab lam yatagharrab* [Tree of Knowledge: Memories of a Youth Who Did Not Emigrate] (Acre: al-Aswar, 1996), 81–82.

3. Ibrahim, *Shajarat al-ma'rifa*, 85.

4. Ghattas Ghattas, *Al-Bustan al-'amir wa al-rawd al-zahir* [The Resplendent Garden and the Flowering Meadow] (al-Ramah: self-published, 2001), 546; and interview with Mr. Ghattas at his home.

5. *Provisional Government Records*, 26 September 1948.

6. Tom Segev, "Asun ha-plitim nedha lzman mah" [The Refugee Crisis Has Been Postponed for a While], *Haaretz*, 15 March 2015.

7. Benny Morris, *Lidata shel ba'yat ha-plitim ha-Falastinim, 1947–49* [The Birth of the Palestinian Refugee Problem, 1947–49] (Tel Aviv, Am Oved, 1991), 291.

8. Mordechai Maklef, commander of operations on the northern front, told Ben-Gurion in September that occupying the Galilee pocket would take no more than two to three days. Reuven Erlich, *Besvakh ha-Levanon, 1918–58* [Lebanon's Predicament, 1918–58] (Tel Aviv: Security Ministry, 2006), 210.

9. Maggie Karkabi testified that her brother Tawfiq Tubi met her mother, who had come from Lebanon, in the village of al-Rama during the summer of 1948. See Husayn Aghbariyya, ed., *Yahkun Haifa: hikayat min dhakirat ahliha* [They Speak of Haifa: Stories from the Memories of Its Inhabitants] (Haifa: Social Development Society, 2010), 113.

10. The massacres of Operation Hiram constitute about half of the major known massacres of the entire war, indicating a policy at the highest level, particularly as Ben-Gurion protected the identities of the perpetrators who were never brought to justice.

11. Benny Morris, *1948 and After: Israel and the Palestinians* (New York: Oxford University Press, 1994), 371.

12. Ibrahim, *Shajarat al-ma'rifa*, 74–75, and many talks and interviews with eyewitnesses from Majd al-Krum.

13. Interview with Muhammad 'Ali Sa'id Qaddah in his house in Majd al-Krum, 23 November 2007.

14. Notables from the Ma'di clan of Yarka played an important role in extending their protection to residents of neighboring villages.

15. Dozens of interviews were conducted with residents who witnessed this event. Some said the name of the officer was Jasim al-'Iraqi, while others said it was Salah Turk.

16. Indeed, a delegation consisting of 'Ali al-Mansur, Tawfiq al-Jabir, and Muhammad Haydar (the author of a diary) went to Yarka, contacted Haim Orbach, and went with him to the army command in al-Birwa.

17. This account contradicts what Nafez Nazzal wrote in his book about the Galilee, on the basis of the testimony of a refugee from the village. Nazzal claimed that most inhabitants of Majd al-Krum migrated to Lebanon and only a few elders and those who feared exile remained. In *Lidata shel ba'yat ha-plitim ha-Falastinim* (304), Morris reported this account by Nazzal without close examination, despite the facts on the ground and the documents to which we shall refer below. Nafez Nazzal, *The Palestinian Exodus from Galilee, 1948* (Beirut: Institute for Palestine Studies, 1978).

18. Muhammad Haydar, a member of the delegation, said that in Yarka they met with Marzuq, and 'Ali and Milhem Ma'di who got in touch with Haim Orbach in Nahariyya. (Interview with Haydar in his house, 30 June 1984, less than a week after the publication of my article, in which there is a brief account of the events in the village.)

19. The testimonies of inhabitants of al-Shaghur villages on this issue are supported and confirmed by telegrams and documents of the army.

20. For his testimony, see Shukri 'Arraf, *Lamasat al-wal'* [Touches of Loyalty] (Mi'lya: Center for Village Studies, 2007), 505.

21. Levi, intelligence officer of the 123rd company, wrote: "At 13:30 the notables of Majd al-Krum received the terms for the surrender of their village; at 14:26 they signed them in the presence of the officers from the company." A copy of this document, with its addenda, is in my possession.

22. Two days after the publication of my article in *Haaretz*, 24 June 1984, Ze'ev Yitzhaki wrote: "I was the officer of the force to which the villagers surrendered in the war of independence."

23. An English translation of this military document, no. 616/13, from the Israeli Army and Security Forces Archives, is included in appendix 3.

24. Villagers whom I met said that the signing of the surrender document took place at the 'Izzat Café on the corner of al-'Ayn square.

25. Documents in the Israeli military archives agree with the testimonies of the villagers. The commander of the company (Ze'ev Yitzhaki) to whom Majd al-Krum surrendered also confirmed the details of the incident.

26. Interview with Khalid Dhiyab Farhat in Florida on 27 January 2007. I met him several times after that in Jerusalem and Majd al-Krum.

27. Interview with Khalid Dhiyab Farhat.

28. Interview with Muhammad Kan'an (Abu 'Atif) in his home in the village, early August 2008.

29. Muhammad Kan'an's statements corroborate the testimony of Farid Zurayq (b. 1915), which I heard at his house, 8 August 2008.

30. Interview with Muhammad Kan'an, and with Habib Zurayq at his house on the same day.

31. Ibrahim, *Shajarat al-ma'rifa*, 89; Morris, *Lidata shel ba'yat ha-plitim ha-Falastinim*, 303.

32. See Ibrahim, *Shajarat al-ma'rifa*; Morris, *Lidata shel ba'yat ha-plitim ha-Falastinim*. A Supreme Court decision affirmed the expulsion operation; one judge wrote: "According to the credible testimony of Shukri Najib al-Khazen and the statements by officer Shmuel Pesitsky, the residents of al-Bi'na were expelled from their village at the time of its occupation" (no. 157/51).

33. Events in the villages of Shaghur demonstrate the existence of a pattern that was repeated elsewhere. The soldiers would gather the inhabitants, execute a number of youth, then order the residents of the village to go to Lebanon. The killing of a number of young men was intended to create fear and strike terror in the hearts of the villagers so that they would not delay in carrying out the expulsion order by officers of units of the Israeli army.

34. Ibrahim, *Shajarat al-ma'rifa*, 92–94; the testimony of one of the refugees from the village of Sha'b, who witnessed the killing of two residents of Bi'na, before Nafez Nazzal, quoted also in Morris, *Lidata shel ba'yat ha-plitim ha-Falastinim*, 303.

35. Interview with Abu Shawkat in Nahaf, on Saturday, 23 February 2013.

36. Supreme Court ruling no. 236/51, 'Abdul Ghani Hasan Muhammad Qays vs. the minister of the interior and two other representatives of the Israeli authorities.

37. Supreme Court ruling no. 236/51; also interview with Abu Shawkat.

38. Elias S. Srouji, *Cyclamens from Galilee: Memoirs of a Physician from Nazareth* (New York: iUniverse, 2003), 159.

39. Srouji, *Cyclamens from Galilee*; Ghattas, *Al-Bustan al-'amir*, 545–47. About forty young men from the Christian inhabitants of al-Rama were arrested, and sent to prisoner of war camps.

40. Srouji, *Cyclamens from Galilee*; Elias Srouji, "The Fall of a Galilean Village during the 1948 Palestinian War: An Eyewitness Account," *Journal of Palestine Studies* 33, no. 2 (Winter 2004): 71–80.

41. Elias Srouji relates that they found refuge in one of the village churches with clergymen whom the army did not expel, and returned to Nazareth a few days later.

42. Several eyewitnesses (from the Ghattas and al-Qasim families) related the details of this story during my interviews.

43. Interview with the poet Samih al-Qasim at his house in al-Rama, 7 August 2008, who confirmed in his testimony the role played by Jabr al-Ma'di in the abrogation of the expulsion order.

44. *Haaretz* newspaper recently published an interview with the historian Yehuda Bauer conducted by Dalia Karpel in which he mentions meeting with residents of Bayt Jan, and the orders of officer Tabinkin who returned the expelled Christians to their village, al-Rama. Karpel, "Prof. Yehuda Bauer Explains Why the Jewish People is Impudent," [Hebrew] *Haaretz*, 13 February 2013.

45. Morris, *Lidata shel ba'yat ha-plitim ha-Falastinim*, 302.

46. Morris mentions erroneously in *Lidata*, 305, that "most of the residents of 'Ilabun were Maronites."

47. Elias Saliba Surur, *'Ilabun: tarikh wa dhikrayyat* ['Ilabun: History and Memories] (Nazareth: al-Hakim Press, 1997), 31–51.

48. Volunteers in the ARA took up fortified positions in a line of defense outside the houses of the village; however, the residents offered them food and other assistance from time to time.

49. Interview with Habib Zurayq in his house in 'Ilabun, 9 May 2008.

50. Elias Saliba Surur, *Al-Nakba fii 'Ilabun* [Al-Nakba in 'Ilabun] ('Ilabun: Local Council, 1998), 11.

51. Interview with Habib Zurayq in his house in 'Ilabun, 9 May 2008.

52. Habib Zurayq could not remember the date he distributed the pamphlets in his village at the beginning of October, but he did remember that he encountered refugees in Wadi Salama eating green olives from the trees out of sheer hunger.

53. Surur, *Al-Nakba*, 4–15.

54. From the diaries of the priest Murqus Mu'allim, in Surur, *'Ilabun*, 116.

55. Surur, *Al-Nakba*, 14–15.

56. All the names and events mentioned are taken from Surur's book, *Al-Nakba*. Surur is considered the local village historian. In addition to the testimonies of villagers, he relied on the diaries of his grandfather, Murqus al-Mu'allim.

57. Surur, *Al-Nakba*, 28–29.

58. Surur, *Al-Nakba*, 29–31. There are also testimonies by men and women from 'Ilabun about the expulsion of the residents and their subsequent return in a documentary film; see Hisham Zurayq, *Abna' 'Ilabun* [The People of 'Ilabun] (2007), 24 minutes.

59. Surur, *Al Nakba*, 31. These details corroborate the testimonies of villagers from the Zurayq family and others whom I interviewed (including Elias Surur) in 2007–8.

60. As we mentioned earlier, Elias Saliba Surur benefited from the diaries of his grandfather in addition to the testimonies of villagers which he complied and documented.

61. Surur, *Al Nakba*, 32–33; my interviews with Habib Zurayq and Farid Zurayq in May 2008.

62. Yisrael Galili, the author of "Israel Report" on which Yoav Gelber draws, met the residents of 'Ilabun at the Mirun crossroads. He mentions in the report that the migrants left there without any food or drink. See Yoav Gelber, *Komimyut ve-Nakba: Yesrael, ha-Falastinimu-medinut 'Arav, 1948* [Independence and Nakba: Israel, the Palestinians and the Arab States in 1948] (Tel Aviv: Zamora Beitan, 2004), 352.

63. Surur, *Al-Nakba*, 36–37; Gelber, *Komimyut ve-Nakba*, 351.

64. Surur, *Al-Nakba*, 38.

65. Surur, *Al-Nakba*, 38. Rumaysh was the first stop, and a central one in south Lebanon, for refugees expelled from the Galilee, as is evident from the testimonies of people expelled from several villages in 1948.

66. Surur, *Al-Nakba*, 39.

67. The attempts at justification by the army related by Morris are not convincing. The villagers, at least some that I interviewed, believe that the main reason was to expel the population in order to gain control over the land.

68. The 'Ilabun villagers, on their way to Lebanon, saw hundreds of inhabitants of Kufr 'Inan and Farradiyya in the villages, but the army returned in 1948 and expelled them from their homes.

69. The army unit that entered the village of al-Maghar tried to separate the Druze from the Christians and Muslims and to expel the others, but the Druze village notables rejected that and told the officers: "Either you kick us all out, or we shall remain together in our homes and country."

70. Morris, *Lidata*, 321–22.

71. Fayez Hasan al-Rayyis, *Al-qura al-junubiyya al-saba': dirasa watha'qiya shamila* [The Seven Southern Villages: A Comprehensive Documentary Study] (Beirut: al-Wafa Publishing, 1985).

72. Surur, *Al-Nakba*, 22.

73. Surur, *Al-Nakba*.

74. Interview with Khalil Husayn al-Shawahda in early October 2010 in 'Ilabun.

75. Interview with Khalil Husayn al-Shawahda.

76. Morris, *Lidata*, 307, 517–18.

77. Testimonies of relatives of the old man; they prefer to remain unidentified.

78. Interview with (Mrs.) Um Muhammad Hulayhel, who saw the bruises on the face of her relative from the soldiers' blows before he joined one of the caravans of refugees and left for Lebanon.

79. It seems likely that cases of rape during and after the 1948 war were underreported in the historical literature. With time, it becomes more difficult to investigate those events.

80. Interview with (Mrs.) Um Muhammad Hulayhel.

81. Morris, *Lidata*, 517–18. Yisrael Galili reported the news of the massacres, particularly the murders and rapes in Safsaf, to Ben-Gurion on 11 September 1948 and asked that the soldiers guilty of murder and rape be put on trial, but Ben-Gurion disregarded that request.

82. Gelber, *Komimyut ve-Nakba*, 353.

83. The Israeli army carried out massacres in 'Ilabun, against al-Mawasi Arabs, in Kufr 'Inan, Farradiyya, Majd al-Krum, al-Bi'na, Dayr al-Asad, Nahaf, Tarshiha, Safsaf, Jish, Sa'sa',

Hula, and Saliha. In the massacres of upper Galilee alone hundreds of defenseless civilians and prisoners were executed by the soldiers.

84. The news about the Hula massacre spread later, and an expanded report on the incident was published under the title "Khirbet Lamis" [in Hebrew] in *Ha-Olam Hazeh* (1 March 1978).

85. "Khirbet Lamis"; Morris, *Lidata*, 307.

86. These three villages were treated differently from the rest of the villages that were occupied in Operation Hiram; the army did not maltreat the population or expel them. Morris documented thoroughly the massacres of "Hiram Operation" in his book *Tekkun ta'ut* [Correcting a Mistake: Jews and Arabs in Palestine/Israel 1936–1956] (Tel Aviv: Am Oved, 2000), 146.

87. Morris, *Tekkun ta'ut*, 290–91.

88. Gelber, *Komimyut ve-Nakba*, 351.

89. David Ben-Gurion, *Yawmiyyat al-Harb, 1947–49* [War Diaries, 1947–1949], ed. Gershon Rivlin and Elhanan Orren, trans. Samir Jabbour (Beirut: Institute for Palestine studies, 1998), 3:604.

90. Telegram no. 597, from Moshe Carmel to the brigade commanders in the north, marked "urgent."

91. Morris, *Tekkun ta'ut*, 143.

92. Morris, *Tekkun ta'ut*, 144. Few historians have examined this study or the documents on which Morris based his attempt to analyze the events and consequences of Operation Hiram.

93. Waschitz published a book titled *Ha-'Aravim be-Erez Yisrael* [The Arabs in Palestine: Economics, Society, Culture and Politics] (Ha-kibuz ha-arzi, 1947).

94. Document in the file of Yosef [Joseph] Waschitz, Ya'ri archive in Giv'at Haviva.

95. The army tried to deny that it had perpetrated a massacre and attempted to expel the residents of 'Ilabun. However, news of what had happened in that village had spread quickly, as indicated by a letter from Elisha Soltz, the military governor of Nazareth, to the northern army command on 30 October 1948.

96. An English translation of this military document, no. 616/13, from the Israeli Army and Security Forces Archives, is included in appendix 3.

97. The army document speaks of those young men as though they had been regular soldiers, which is not true.

98. The testimonies of residents of Majd al-Krum, told to me since the 1980s, are consistent with their testimonies before the High Court of Justice in Jerusalem in 1951.

99. Interview with Muhammad Haydar (Abu Jamil) at his house in Majd al-Krum, 30 June 1984. Hajj 'Abd Manna' was one of the witnesses before the High Court of Justice in 1951.

100. One of the soldiers refused to take part with his comrades in the massacre in al-'Ayn square, and was sent to search the houses, which is a more dangerous task, as the officer told him.

101. My Aunt Sa'da was a witness to the torture and killing from the window of her kitchen, and told me the details of this event more than once in my interviews with her.

102. Morris, *Lidata*, 304. For his brief description of the massacre, Morris relied on a report by United Nations observers who visited the village and wrote a report on 13 November 1948.

103. The other two were Ahmad Dhiyab and Mustafa Najm.

104. Morris, *Lidata*, 304; several interviews with the villagers.

105. The date of this document is 18 November, a few days after the visit by the UN team.

106. A copy of the same document addressed to the "Occupied Areas Government Command" for the northern front, officer Schnurrmann, is included in the appendices.

107. Gelber also mentioned this. It appears that the temerity of the villagers to tell the truth to the observers and implicate the Israeli army is what is meant by "conduct unbecoming." See Gelber, *Komimyut ve-Nakba*, 354.

108. Morris, *Lidata*, 304, 516n29.

109. Among readers' responses that did not express anger were those from Ya'cov Shim'uni, vice director of the Middle East Department in the Israeli Foreign Ministry, as well as Eliezer Be'eri, an activist in Mapam. They both had connections and contacts with the battles in the north during the war.

110. "Letters from Readers," *Haaretz*, 26 June 1984.

111. Morris, *Lidata*, 304.

112. See chapter 3 concerning the question of the expulsion of hundreds of residents of Majd al-Krum in January 1949.

113. Adel Manna', "Majdal al-Krum 1948: 'amaliyat tamshit 'adeyya'" [Majdal al-Krum 1948: Ordinary Combing Operations]," *Al-Karmel* 55–56 (Spring–Summer 1998): 184–200.

114. I had heard about this from the villagers, and Mr. Gazelle confirmed what I had already heard.

115. After a telephone conversation with Tsvi Rabinovich (Bahrav), I conducted the interview with him in Haifa on 16 May 1998.

116. Interview with Rabinovitch, 16 May 1998.

117. I realized then that Tsvi had not known up to that point that I was an Arab, and that my fluency in Hebrew made him speak with me more freely as a lecturer at Hebrew University.

118. I regretted that I was too late, but I had been able to hear from Tsvi his nearly comprehensive testimony prior to his death in December 2002.

119. Dr. Bashir Karkabi is the son of Zahi and Maggie Karkabi (nee Tubi), whom I met more than once in their house.

120. High Court of Justice ruling no. 125/51, Muhammad 'Ali Husayn and Nine Others v. The Minister of the Interior, the Military Governor of the Galilee, and the Chief of Police of 'Akka.

121. Quoted by Gelber in *Komimyut ve-Nakba*, 351.

122. Morris, *Lidata*, 316–17.

123. Sarah Osatski-Lazar, *Iqrit ve-Bir'm: ha-Sippur ha-Male* [Iqrit and Bir'im: The Whole Story] (Givat Haviva: Institute for Arab Studies/Institute for Peace Studies, 1993), 8.

124. Osatski-Lazar, *Iqrit ve-Bir'm*, 24; Najib Susan, *Sada al-ayyam* [Echo of the Days] (Haifa: Self-published, 2001), 14.

125. Morris, *Lidata*, 317; Susan, *Sada al-ayyam*, 14.

126. Quoted from Morris, *Lidata*, 317.

127. Osatski-Lazar, *Iqrit ve-Bir'm*, 10.

128. Morris, *Lidata*, 318.

129. Morris, *Lidata*, 336.

130. Official Israeli estimates place the number of Arabs who remained in the Naqab at only 13,000, indicating that these figures need greater examination.

131. Most researchers use this figure from official Israeli statistics without scrutiny or reference to the fact that it may be inaccurate.

132. In a famous interview conducted by Ari Shavit in *Haaretz* on 9 January 2004, Benny Morris admitted that Ben-Gurion had carried out a programmed and methodical expulsion of the residents of the Galilee, which he defended, even criticizing Ben-Gurion for not finishing the job.

133. Morris, *Lidata*, 392.

134. Morris, *Lidata*, 392. The villages of Sakhnin and 'Arraba were not on an important transportation route for the Jews, unlike the villages of al-Shaghur.

135. Morris, *Tekkun ta'ut*, 141.

136. These facts, which are known to Morris, did not prevent him in his book on the 1948 war—particularly in the pages relating to the massacres of Operation Hiram—from returning to the defense of the army and blaming the victims in a manner that is coherent with his political positions, particularly since 2000. See Benny Morris, *1948: Toldut ha-melhama ha-'Arvit ha-Yesraelit ha-rishona* [1948: History of the First Arab-Israeli War] (Tel Aviv: Am Oved, 2010), 367–78.

137. As quoted by Morris in *Tekkun ta'ut*, 143–44.

3. THE ARAB COMMUNISTS: BETWEEN AL-NAKBA AND INDEPENDENCE

1. For further details on the matter of collaborators with the Zionist movement and its settler and intelligence agencies, see Hillel Cohen, *Army of Shadows: Palestinian Collaboration with Zionism, 1917–1948* (Berkeley: University of California Press, 2008), 252; Hillel Cohen, *Good Arabs: The Israeli Security Agencies and the Israeli Arabs, 1948–1967* (Berkeley: University of California Press, 2010), 35–36.

2. Cohen, *Army of Shadows*, 169; Laila Parsons, *The Druze between Palestine and Israel, 1947–49* (New York: St. Martin's Press, 2000), 56.

3. Cohen, *Army of Shadows*, 236, 254; Yoav Gelber, *Komimyut ve-Nakba* [Independence and Nakba] (Tel Aviv: Zmora Beitan, 2004), 115.

4. Gelber, *Komimyut ve-Nakba*, 123–25; Parsons, *The Druze*, 69–75.

5. The historian Kais Firro, relying on the papers of Khalil Quntar, said that the salaries of Druze officers and soldiers were paid in Kiryat 'Amal. See Kais Firro, *The Druzes in the Jewish State* (Leiden: Brill, 1999), 50–51.

6. 'Arif al-'Arif, *Al-Nakba: Nakbat Bayt al-Maqdis wa l-firdaws al-mafqud 1947–49* [The Catastrophe: The Catastrophe of Jerusalem and the Lost Paradise 1947–49] (Sidon: al-Maktaba al-'Asriya, 1956), 1:424.

7. See Mansur Khudur Ma'di, *Rajul al-karamat: al-Shaykh Jabr Dahesh M'adi* [The Man Through Whom God Worked Miracles, His Excellency Shaykh Jabr Dahesh M'adi: Positions, Challenges and Achievements] (Yarka: published by family, 2014).

8. Parsons, *The Druze*, 80–82. This account is supported by several researchers, including Kais Firro. For further details on how the agreement was concluded and the entry into Shafa 'Amr, see Ben Dunkelman, *N'manut kfula* [Dual Loyalty: An Autobiography] (Jerusalem, Tel Aviv: Shoken, 1975), 165.

9. See Shukri 'Arraf, *Lamsat wafa'* . . . *wa* . . . [Touches of Loyalty . . . and . . .] (Mi'lya: Center for Village Studies, 2007). 'Arraf gives prominence to this one aspect of the picture.

10. Constantine Zurayk, *Ma'na al-Nakba* [The Meaning of the Catastrophe] (Beirut: Dar al-'Ilm li al-Malayin, 1948).

11. Musa al-'Alami, *'Abira Filastin* [The Lesson of Palestine] (Beirut: Dar al-Kashaf, 1949).

12. George Hanna, *Tariq al-khalas* [The Path to Deliverance: A Situational Analysis of the Palestine's Affliction and Arab Issues] (Beirut: Dar al-'Ahad, 1948); Constantine Zurayk, Musa al-'Alami, George Hanna, and Qadri Hafiz Tuqan, *Nakba 1948: Asbabha wa halulha* [Nakba 1948: Its Causes and Its Solutions], introduction by Walid al-Khalidi (Beirut: Institute for Palestine Studies, 2009).

13. Communist Arabs had a monopoly on institutionally and legally permitted national action in Israel up to the 1980s. They managed to market their narrative of heroism and to silence the majority of voices that mentioned some of what was known about their role in 1948 and their support for conscripting Arabs in the Israeli army and other matters.

14. These parties were the Iraqi Communist Party, the Syrian Communist Party and the Lebanese Communist Party.

15. Ahmad Sa'd, *Judhur al-shajara dai'mat al-khudra* [Roots of the Evergreen Tree] (Haifa: Ma'had Emile Tuma, 1996), 232.

16. Sa'd, *Judhur al-shajara*.

17. "We do not mean that this book should write the history of the Communist Party in our country—we hope that this book will spur communist authors to write their history in a scientific and objective way" (Sa'd, *Judhur al-shajara*, 7).

18. Musa al-Budayri, *Shuyu'iyyun fi Filastin: shadhaya tarikh mansi* [Communists in Palestine: Fragments of a Forgotten History] (Ramallah: Muwatin, The Palestinian Institute for the Study of Democracy, 2013).

19. There is a rich literature in this field in the form of political and social theories critical of the diminished form of citizenship for Arabs in Israel. It is sufficient to mention Nimr Sultani, ed., *Muwatinun bila muwatana: Isra'il wa al-aqaliyya al-Filastiniyya: taqrir Mada al-sanawi li al-rasd al-siyasi, 2000–2002* [Citizens Without Citizenship: Israel and the Palestinian Minorities, Mada's Annual Political Monitoring Report 2000–2002] (Haifa: Mada al-Karmil, Arab Center for Applied Social Studies, 2003). Several studies were subsequently published, including Shourideh Molavi, *Stateless Citizenship: The Palestinian-Arab Citizens of Israel* (Leiden: Brill, 2013).

20. For more on this topic, see the interview with Radwan al-Hilu in al-Budayri, *Shuyu'iyyun fi Filastin*, 55–80.

21. Tawfiq al-Tubi writes, as a witness to the events of the period: "The period when the partition resolution was issued . . . up to the point when we arrived at a clear position in support of a solution based on the establishment of two states, was one of the most difficult times we went through." Cited in Sa'd, *Judhur al-shajara*, 16.

22. *Al-Ittihad* (organ of the National Liberation League), 5 October 1947.

23. Tawfiq Tubi's testimony, in Sa'd, *Judhur al-shajara*, 16; Bulus Farah, *Min al-'Uthmaniyya ila al-dawla al-'Abriyya* [*From the Ottoman Empire to the Hebrew State*] (Haifa: al-Sawt, 1985), 172–73. The circumstances of the convening of this conference remain shrouded in mystery, as well as the time and place in which it was held in Nazareth.

24. *Al-Ittihad*, 25 November 1947.

25. For more on this subject, see Joel Beinin, *Was the Red Flag Flying There? Marxist Politics and the Arab-Israeli Conflict in Egypt and Israel, 1948–65* (Berkeley: University of Californian Press, 1990).

26. Prominent among the ranks of the opponents were Emile Tuma and Bulus Farah from Haifa, and others among the leaders of the League in Jerusalem, Jaffa, the Galilee, and elsewhere.

27. *Al-Ittihad*, 25 October 1947.

28. Emile Tuma was obliged, after his return to Haifa, to write a letter of apology for his position against partition and admit the error of his ways in order to be reaccepted as a member of Maki.

29. Farah, *Min al-'Uthmaniyya*, 172–88.

30. 'Awda al-'Ashhab, *Tadhakurat 'Awdah al-'Ashhab: sira dhatiyya* [The Remembrances of 'Awda al-'Ashhab: An Autobiography] (Birzeit: Birzeit University, 1999), 120–21.

31. Lutfi Mash'ur v. Emile Habibi, Civil Appeals Court, case no. 809/89.

32. On the Israeli side, however, a great deal was said and written on the subject. For example, see Arieh Dayan, "Hakuministim asher hitzulu et hamdinah" [The Communists Who Saved the State], *Haaretz*, 5 September 2006.

33. *Kol HaAm*, 5 March 1948.

34. *Kol HaAm*, 21 March 1948.

35. Aharon Cohen, *Yisrael ve-ha'ulam Ha'rbi* [Israel and the Arab World] (Tel Aviv: Workers' Bookshop, 1964), 382.

36. Cohen, *Yisrael ve-ha'ulam Ha'rbi*, 407. Also see statements in 'Arif al-'Arif, *Nakbat Bayt al-Maqdis*, 3:563–64, in which he confirms the decisive role that Czech arms played in the battles of June 1948 and later.

37. Na'im al-'Ashhab, *Durub al-alam . . . Durub al-amal* [Paths of Pain . . . Paths of Hope] (Ramallah: Dar al-Tanwir, 2009), 48.

38. Al-'Ashhab, *Tadhakurat*, 174–75.

39. Tawfiq Tubi's testimony in Sa'd, *Judhur al-shajara*, 18.

40. Tawfiq Tubi's testimony in Sa'd, *Judhur al-shajara*.

41. Thanks to Dr. Musa al-Budayri who provided me with this and other documents from the National Liberation League. Dr. Budayri later published a book containing some of those documents, in addition to interviews he had conducted with some leaders of the League in the 1970s; see al-Budayri, *Shuyu'iyyun fi Filastin*.

42. Al-Budayri, *Shuyu'iyyun fi Filastin*.

43. Al-Budayri, *Shuyu'iyyun fi Filastin*.

44. *Kol HaAm*, 18 May 1948.

45. Meir Vilner signed the document of the establishment of Israel as a state for the Jews, and became a member of the interim cabinet which was created in May 1948.

46. Al-Budayri, *Shuyu'iyyun fi Filastin*.

47. This is a clear reference to, and an attack on, the aristocratic Palestinian leadership led by Hajj Amin al-Husayni and others who were labeled feudalists.

48. Bashir Sharif al-Barghuthi, *Fu'ad Nassar: al-rajul wa al-qadiyya* [Fu'ad Nassar, the Man and the Cause] (Jerusalem: Dar Salah al-Din, 1977), 55.

49. Al-Barghuthi, *Fu'ad Nassar*. The final paragraph was altered, and was not part of the original document.

50. Al-'Ashhab, *Tadhakurat*, 131–32.

51. Al-'Ashhab, *Durub al-alam*, 49.

52. Al-'Ashhab, *Durub al-alam*, 50–51.

53. Al-'Ashhab, *Durub al-alam*, 51.

54. Sa'd, *Judhur al-Shajara*, 111; Hanna Abu Hanna, *Mahr al-buma* [The Owl's Dowry] (Haifa: Maktabat kul shai, 2004), part three of the autobiography, 98–99.

55. "Bnazrat Haya Gam Kivush Halvavut" [In Nazareth, There Was an Occupation of the Hearts as Well], *'Al Hamishmar*, 23 July 1948.

56. 'Isa Habib said in his testimony that the League organized about a thousand workers from Nazareth who travelled to Lydda and Ramla and other places to work the land there. See Sa'd, *Judhur al-Shajara*, 209.

57. Eliezer Be'eri (Bauer), "Sha'ruriyat Nazret" [The Nazareth Scandal], *'Al Hamishmar*, 18 August 1949.

58. Bauer, "Sha'ruriyat Nazret."

59. Aharon Cohen, "Dvarim brurim" [Clear Issues], *'Al Hamishmar*, 22 August 1948.

60. Bechor Shitrit received Moshe Shertok's (later Sharett's) letter on 8 August 1948; see Gelber, *Komimyut ve-Nakba*, 417.

61. Bechor Shitrit's letter to Elisha Shultz on 12 August 1948, in Gelber, *Komimyut ve-Nakba*.

62. Maggie Karkabi (Tubi) related in her testimony that all members of her family (apart from her brother Tawfiq Tubi) went to Brummana near Beirut. The mother yearned for her son and insisted that he come from Haifa to visit her, so he came to Beirut for a brief period, and then insisted on bringing them all back to Haifa. Interview with Maggie Karkabi in her home, 26 September 2008.

63. Report dated 23 September 1948 in Gelber, *Komimyut ve-Nakba*, 418.

64. Interview with Zahi Karkabi in his house in Haifa, 26 September 2008.

65. Karkabi mentions the name of Eliezer Bray. After their arrival in Haifa, the three played an important role in the activities of the League, and in Maki later.

66. Interview with Matiya Nassar at his home in Jerusalem, 1 April 2009.

67. Interview with Matiya Nassar. The interview with Karkabi confirms most of what was said in the interview with Nassar and vice-versa.

68. Hanna Ibrahim, ed., *Hanna Naqqara: Muhami al-ard wa-sha'b* [Hanna Naqqara: Lawyer of the Land and the People] (Acre: al-Aswar, 1985), 177–78.

69. Cohen, *'Arvim Tuvim*, 59.

70. The reference is to the pamphlet mentioned above in n41, which was distributed on 11 July 1948 in the cities and villages of southern Palestine, particularly in Gaza and Hebron.

71. *'Al Hamishmar*, 14 September 1948, as quoted by Yossi Amitay in *Akhvat 'amim ba-mivhan: Mapam 1948–1954* [The Brotherhood of Peoples Tested: Mapam 1948–1954] (Tel Aviv: Tcherikover, 1988), 35.

72. Amitay, *Akhvat 'amim bamivhan*.

73. Gelber, *Komimyut ve-Nakba*, 417.

74. Abu Hanna, *Mahr al-buma*, 132.

75. Abu Hanna, *Mahr al-buma*.

76. This was confirmed by Hanna Abu Hanna who knew Saliba Khamis well because of their familial links. 'Awda al-'Ashhab referred to it frankly in al-'Ashhab, *Tadhakurat*, 149.

77. There is a consensus among a majority of League members in the Galilee, particularly those who had written memoirs (Hanna Ibrahim, Nimr Murqus, Nadim Musa, and others) that Ramzi Khuri from al-Bi'na was the one who brought the pamphlet from Lebanon.

78. In addition to the above-mentioned memoirs, the testimonies of a number of League veterans are available in Sa'd, *Judhur al-shajara*.

79. The term "Nakba" in the singular and its plural were used more than once in that pamphlet as an introduction to the ramifications of the war for the "Arabs of Palestine and all Arab peoples."

80. The testimony of Su'ad Bishara, the widow of Jibra'il Bishara, in an interview in her house, July 2008. Subsequently one of his sons gave me his father's handwritten diaries, sections of which were included in a book that was published a year after his death.

81. *Jibra'il Butrus Bishara: 1925–2005* (Tarshiha: published by the family, 2006), 33–40.

82. Among them was Dr. Rawda Bishara who died at the end of 2013, and Dr. 'Azmi Bishara, a prominent Arab intellectual, who grew up in the Israeli Communist Party, and later founded the National Democratic Assembly (Balad).

83. *Kenis ha'hadut shel hakuministim hayihudim ve-ha'rvim beMaki* [The Conference of the Union of Jewish and Arab Communists in the Framework of the Israel Communist Party] (Haifa, 22–23 October 1948), 15.

84. *Kenis ha'hadut*, 14–15; *Kol HaAm*, 24 October 1948.

85. *Kenis ha'hadut*, 21.

86. *Kenis ha'hadut*, 21–26. These exaggerated numbers of the comrades in the League and the secret resistance movement were meant to legitimize joining Maki in the eyes of the Jewish public.

87. Some believe that the strict censorship at the time may explain the silence concerning those criminal actions carried out by the Israeli army. However, what the communists said and wrote in Hebrew leave no doubt that it was due to the adoption of Zionist discourse, which laid the blame for the Nakba on the Palestinians.

88. *Kol HaAm*, 2 January 1949.

89. *Al-Ittihad*, 3 January 1949. The article also contained information about his life and struggle.

90. *Kol Ha'Am*, 21 January 1949.

91. Shmuel Mikunis, "Eliahu Gozansky: the Man and His Deeds," *Kol HaAm*, 21 January 1949.

92. *Kol HaAm*, 19 July 1948.

93. *Kol HaAm*, 6 September 1948.

94. *Kol HaAm*, 1 November 1948.

95. *Al-Ittihad*, 25 October 1948. This accusation from the Arabic-language Israeli Communist Party (Maki) paper levelled at Arab leaders helped Israel evade responsibility for the birth of the refugee problem and enabled its rejection of the right of return endorsed by the United Nations towards the end of 1948.

96. The murder and expulsion of defenseless civilians involved the residents of the villages of 'Ilabun, al-Mawasi Arabs, Kufr 'Inan, Majd al-Krum, al-Bi'na, Dayr al-Asad, Nahf, Sha'b, Mirun, Jish, al-Safsaf, Sa'sa', Tarshiha, Salha, Hula, and others.

97. *Kol HaAm*, 16 November 1948.

98. *Kol HaAm.*

99. *Kol HaAm,* 20, 22 and 30 June 1949. At the same time that the paper expressed its opposition to the return of the Palestinians it wrote that Jewish migration to Israel (*aliyah*) was a vital necessity for Israel.

100. *Al-Ittihad,* 8 November 1948.

101. *Al-Ittihad,* 8 November 1948.

102. *Al-Ittihad,* 1 January 1948.

103. For more on this subject, see Mustafa Kabha and Wadiʿ ʿAwawda, *Asra bila hrab: al-muʿtaqlun al-Filistinyun wal-muʿtaqlat al-Israʾiliyya al-ula* [Prisoners with No Spears: Palestinian Detainees and the First Israeli Detention Centers, 1948–49] (Beirut: Institute for Palestine Studies, 2013).

104. Hassan Jabareen recently published an important article on the meaning and significance of participation in the first Israeli elections, "Hobbesian Citizenship: How the Palestinians Became a Minority in Israel," in *Multiculturalism and Minority Rights in the Arab World,* ed. Will Kymlicka and Eva Pfostl (London: Oxford University Press, 2014), 189–218.

105. For further detail on the historical significance of participation in the first Israeli elections, see Jabareen's article ("Hobbesian Citizenship"), which was also published in Hebrew in the journal *Theory and Criticism* (Jerusalem: Van Leer Institute).

106. All of the communist literature published by Maki appeared in both Hebrew and Arabic except for two important books: *Kenis haʾahdut* [Unity and the Establishment of Maki] (Tel Aviv: ICP Central Committee, 1948); and *Ben-Gurion v. Kol HaAm* (Tel Aviv: ICP Central Committee, 1951).

107. *Kol HaAm,* 14 October 1948. *Al-Ittihad,* which reappeared that same month, adopted the same political discourse which made the Arabs responsible for the tragedies and calamities that befell them in the Galilee and other Palestinian areas.

4. FORCED MIGRATION CONTINUES AFTER THE CANNONS FALL SILENT

1. *Israeli Annual Census Book* [in Hebrew] (Jerusalem: Central Statistical Bureau, 1951), 2:4. Ben-Gurion gives different (not final) figures on the number of Arabs remaining in Israel near the end of 1948, after the occupation of Galilee and the Naqab was completed. See David Ben-Gurion, *Yawmiyyat al-harb, 1947–1949* [War Diaries, 1947–1949], ed. Gershon Rivlin and Elhanan Oren, trans. Samir Jabbour (Beirut: Institute for Palestine Studies, 1993), 633, 640–41.

2. Said by Yitzhak Tzvi at a Mapai party meeting, as reported by Tom Segev in *1949: Hayesraelim hareshonim* [1949: The First Israelis] (Jerusalem: Domino, 1984), 46.

3. Segev, *1949: Hayestaelim hareshonim.*

4. Nur al-Din Masalha dealt with Israel's transfer policy extensively in *Ard akthar wa ʿArab aql: Siyasat al-transfir al-Israʾiliyya fi al-tatbiq, 1949–96,* 2nd ed. [Maximum Land and Minimum Arabs: The Israeli Transfer Policy in Action, 1949–96] (Beirut: Institute for Palestine Studies, 2002), 17–55.

5. Masalha, *Ard akthar wa ʿArab aql.*

6. Minutes of Israeli cabinet meeting on 12 July 1950 as reported in Yoav Gelber, *Komimyut ve-Nakba: Yesrael, ha-Falastinimu-medinut ʿArav* [Independence and Nakba: Israel, the Palestinians and the Arab States in 1948] (Tel Aviv: Zemora Beitan, 2004), 428.

7. Minutes of the meeting of the Foreign Relations and Security Committee on 3 December 1951; Gelber, *Komimyut ve-Nakba*.

8. From April 1951 to March 1952 Israeli sources speak of thirty-seven cases of violent infiltration, only one of which was along the Lebanese border. In the following year, forty-four cases of violent infiltration were reported on all fronts, not a single one across the Lebanese border. See Reuven Erlich, *Besvakh ha-Levanon, 1918–58* [The Predicament of Lebanon, 1918–58] (Tel Aviv: Security Ministry, 2006), 398.

9. *Al-Yawm*, 29 February 1952.

10. *Al-Ittihad*, 8 March 1952.

11. Alina Korn, "*Psha', Status politi ve-akhifat khuk: ha-mi'ut ha-'Arvi be-Yisrael betkufat hamemshal hatzva'I (1948–66)* [Criminal Activities, Political Status and Implementation of the Law: The Arab Minority in Israel under Military Rule (1948–1966)] (PhD diss., College of Law, Hebrew University, 1997), 113–14.

12. Korn, "*Psha*."

13. Ben-Gurion mentioned in his diary that the phenomenon of "infiltration" had increased and reached 3,000 to 4,000 people. Ben-Gurion, *Yawmiyyat al-harb, 1947–49*, vol. 3, 692–93.

14. "Elimelech Avnir to the Defense Minister and the Chief of Staff," 10 February 1949, Israeli Army and Security Forces Archives, no. 1/3/2/35. A translation of the document can be found in appendix 5 in this book.

15. "Elimelech Avir to Defense Minister."

16. Israeli Army and Security Forces Archives, no. 841/72/721. My thanks to Hillel Cohen for helping me obtain a copy of this document.

17. Israeli Army and Security Forces Archives, no. 841/72/721.

18. Moshe Carmel, governor of the northern district, supported "collecting all the arms of the Druze," but Ben-Gurion decided that the government should not ask the Druze to surrender their weapons. See Ben-Gurion, *Yawmiyyat al-harb, 1947–49*, 3:630–31.

19. Segev, *1949: Hayestaelim hareshonim*, 67.

20. Interview with 'Awad Mansur at his home on 7 August 2001. The refugees from Kufr 'Anan were resettled on an infertile mountainous hilltop at the western entrance to the village, in barracks until the 1960s, away from the houses of al-Rama and close to our secondary school where I was a student.

21. Handwritten diaries of Muhammad Haydar, Abu Jamil. The information from his memoirs is corroborated by testimonies in Supreme Court cases raised by the people of Majd al-Krum, discussed more expansively in chapter 6.

22. *Army and Security Forces Archives*, Haifa District Command, no. 580/6, titled: "Combing Operation in Majd al-Krum," signed by Tsvi Rabinovich. A translation of the document can be found in appendix 6.

23. *Army and Security Forces Archives*, no. 580/6.Those who were interrogated and chased that day testified that the soldiers and policemen assaulted the men verbally and with their hands and legs.

24. *Army and Security Forces Archives*, no. 580/6. On that day, my family was expelled from the village.

25. *Army and Security Forces Archives*, Shlomo [Pulman] to the military governor—Western Galilee, 12 January 1949, no. 436. This document, unlike the previous one, is handwritten and signed with the first name only. A copy can be found in appendix 7.

26. *Army and Security Forces Archives*, 12 January 1949, no. 436.

27. Shweili from Nahalal, who was nicknamed Abu Khadr, maintained good relations with many villagers in Majd al-Krum and villages of western Galilee in general.

28. I had heard the stories told by relatives about the blows which mukhtar Hajj ʿAbd Salim Mannaʿ had received and how he escaped death several years before I became a student of history.

29. *Army and Security Forces Archives*, 12 January 1949, no. 436. The villagers in many cases chose to remain silent and not to submit complaints out of fear of retaliation by the soldiers.

30. I heard this story many times from my mother and aunts as an example of the courage of Zahra al-Jaʿuniyya.

31. I first heard this story in my father's house. In 1984 I conducted several interviews, one with Muhyi al-Din Saʿid Mannaʿ (Abu al-Saʿid), who told me the story of Orbach in detail.

32. Interview with Uncle Husayn ʿAli Mannaʿ at his home in Majd al-Krum, 23 November 2007.

33. Interview with Muhammad ʿAli Saʿid Qaddah at his home in Majd al-Krum, 23 February 2003.

34. Interview with Muhammad ʿAli Saʿid Qaddah.

35. Muhammad Qaddah had an excellent memory for numbers and details. He mentioned, for example, that one Palestinian lira was worth about 12 Lebanese liras at the time.

36. Interview with Tsvi Rabinovitch in his home in Haifa, 16 May 1998.

37. The registration of the population of Majd al-Krum, as we said earlier, took place during 12–14 December 1948, but the receipts were not distributed until five weeks later, on 17 January 1949.

38. The testimonies of residents of Majd al-Krum clearly indicate that the authorities decided to expel the majority of young men of military service age, even though some had been registered in the census. However, many of them came back to the village, went to court in Israel, and obtained permanent identity cards and citizenship.

39. Interview with Muhammad ʿAli Saʿid Qaddah.

40. Interview with Muhammad ʿAli Saʿid Qaddah. See also Charles Kamen, "Akhre ha-ʾAson: ha-ʿArvim be-mdinat Yesrael, 1948–51" [After the Catastrophe: Arabs in the State of Israel, 1948–51] in *Mahbarut le-mekhkar ve-bekkuret* [Notebooks for Study and Critique] 10 (1984), 35.

41. *Al-Ittihad*, 13 November 1949, 4.

42. *Al-Ittihad*, 13 November 1949. The paper mentioned that three hundred individuals had been expelled from Tarshiha, while sixty-three others were expelled from al-Biʿna and Dayr al-Asad.

43. Riyad al-Solh had been accused of conducting negotiations with Israel to reach a peace agreement.

44. I found this important information in the diaries of Muhammad Haydar (Abu Jamil) who was in the habit of recording deaths, births, and weddings in the village as well as other local news and some general news.

45. Interview with Dhib Asʿad Mannaʿ (Abu Nahi) at his home in Majd al-Krum, 6 August 2008.

46. Interview with Dhib Asʿad Mannaʿ. As we mentioned earlier, dozens if not hundreds of expellees from Majd al-Krum and other villages returned to their homes in the summer of 1951 on the eve of the second Knesset elections.

47. Diaries of Muhammad Haydar (Abu Jamil), who was one of the few educated people who remained in the village. He became the local news correspondent of the quasi-official daily *al-Yawm*.

48. Diaries of Muhammad Haydar (Abu Jamil).

49. This operation began on 31 August 1950 according to Abu Jamil's diary.

50. Supreme Court Decision no. 1951/155. We shall take up this case and other cases before the Supreme Court more expansively in chapter 6.

51. Benny Morris, *Melhamut ha-gvul shel Yesrael, 1949–56* [Israel's Border Wars, 1949–56] (Tel Aviv: Am Oved, 1996), 165–98.

52. Hillel Cohen, *'Arvim tuvim: ha-mudi'een ha-Yisra'eli ve-Harvim be-Yesra'el* (Jerusalem: Keter, 2006), 125–26; translated as *The Good Arabs: The Israeli Security Agencies and the Israeli Arabs, 1948–1967* (Berkeley: University of California Press, 2010).

53. Cohen mentions that up to 1950, about two hundred of Sha'b's original inhabitants managed to return to their homes and lived there.

54. Cohen, *'Arvim tuvim*, 125.

55. Yasir Ahmad 'Ali et al., *Sha'b wahamiyatuha: qaryat sha'b al-jaliliyya wal-difa'a 'anha* [Sha'b and Its Garrison: The Galilee Village of Sha'b and Its Defense] (Beirut: Thabet, al-Munadhdhama al-Filastiniyya li Haqq al-'Awda, 2007).

56. 'Ali et al., *Sha'b wahamiyatuha*, 97–100.

57. Elias Khoury, *Bab al-shams* (Beirut: Dar al-Adab, 1998); in English as *Gate of the Sun*, trans. by Humphrey Davies (London: Vintage, 2006).

58. 'Ali, *Sha'b wahamiyatuha*. This source gives details of the battles and martyrs among the Sha'b villagers during that stage of the war.

59. Supreme Court Decision no. 51/236, *'Abdul Ghani Qays et al. v. the Minister of the Interior et al.*

60. 'Ali, *Sha'b wahamiyatuha*, 51–52. Also Sulayman Khwalidi has studied the question of the relocation of the inhabitants of Krad al-Baqqara and Krad al-Ghanama in "History of the Beduin villages of Krad al-Baqqara and Krad al-Ghanname" (PhD diss., University of Erlangen, Germany, 1992).

61. Cohen, *'Arvim tuvim*, 126–127.

62. Supreme Court Decision no. 52/303, 724. Dahir Husayn Fa'ur v. the Inspector of the Police of 'Akka et al.

63. Supreme Court Decision no. 52/303, 724; Volume 7 (1953), 725. These decisions were published in several volumes.

64. Supreme Court Decision no. 52/303, 724.

65. Supreme Court Decision no. 52/263.

66. Supreme Court Decision no. 52/263.

67. Supreme court Decision no. 52/303.

68. Some of the Sha'b villagers who lived in Majd al-Krum maintained cooperative relations with Shafiq Abu 'Abdu until the day he died, and a number of them, including Muhammad Haydar (Abu Jamil) attended his funeral in Sha'b in November 1969, as Abu Jamil reported in his diary.

69. The letter is in the archives of the attorney Hanna Naqqara, dated 13 March 1952. My thanks to Na'ila Naqqara, the daughter of Hanna and wife of my colleague, historian Butrus Abu-Manneh, for allowing me access to her father's papers at her home in Haifa.

70. Letter, archives of Hanna Naqqara, dated 13 March 1952.

71. Letter, archives of Hanna Naqqara, dated 13 March 1952. Hamad ʿOthman and his son Nur were on good terms with the policeman, Shweili. The father had been a policeman and his son was appointed for a period to serve in the police force, according to the testimonies of village residents.

72. The letter is written with beautiful penmanship and in the language of an educated man. Saʿid Husayn ʿAbbas signed it with his thumbprint, indicating that he could neither read nor write, like many of his generation.

73. Cohen, ʿArvim tuvim, 127–30.

74. Shukri ʿArraf, Lamsat waf... wa... [Touches of Loyalty] (Miʿlya: Markaz al-Dirasat al-Qurawiyya), 308.

75. Supreme Court Decision no. 56/157.

76. The Supreme Court ruling was issued on 27 November 1956.

77. Benny Morris, Lidata shel baʿyat ha-plitim ha-Falastinim, 1947–49 [The Birth of the Palestinian Refugee Problem, 1947–49] (Tel Aviv: ʿAm Oved, 1991), 319.

78. Interview with Suʿad Bishara in her home in Tarshiha, 8 July 2008.

79. ʿArraf, Lamsat waf... wa..., 144.

80. ʿArraf, Lamsat waf... wa..., 145.

81. Interview with Anis Bishara in his home in Tarshiha, 8 July 2008.

82. ʿArraf, Lamsat waf... wa..., 130–35.

83. Interview with Fatma Hawwari in her home in Tarshiha, 7 August 2008. She made a point during the interview of referring to Abie Nathan who, she said, visited her in her house in 1995 and asked for her forgiveness for what he had done in his youth when he bombed the village and caused a tragedy for her and her family.

84. Jibraʾil Butrus Bishara, Jibraʾil Butros Bishara: 1925–2005 [in Arabic] (Tarshiha: published by the family, 2006), 42.

85. According to the census, there were 720 people living in the village. See Jibraʾil Butros Bishara, 42–43.

86. Morris, Lidata, 320.

87. Elias Shoufani, Rihla fi al-rahil: fusul min al-dhakira . . . lam taktamel [A Journey in Departure: Chapters of Memory . . . not completed] (Beirut, Dar al-Kunuz al-Adabiyya, 1994, 51; Segev, 1949: Hayestaelim hareshonim.

88. Morris, Lidata, 320.

89. Interview with Anis Bishara (Abu Salim), 8 July 2008.

90. Morris, Lidata, 323. More than one person I interviewed in Tarshiha indicated that the bishop later helped people from the village to obtain permanent identity and residence cards.

91. Hillel Cohen, Al-Ghaʾibun al-hadirun: al-lajiʿun al-Filastiniyyun fi Israʾil mundhu sanat 1948 [The Present Absentees: Palestinian Refugees in Israel Since 1948] (Beirut: Institute for Palestine Studies, 2003), 75.

92. The authorities later moved the newcomers from Romania to the cooperative settlement Maʿunah, which is located today between Tarshiha and Miʿlya.

93. These good relations found literary expression in a collection of stories by the attorney Tawfiq Muʿamar, particularly in "Al-Kamin (The Trap)" in Al-Mutasallil wa qisas ukhra [The Infiltrator and Other Stories] (Nazareth: al-Hakim Press, 1957), 73–89.

94. Supreme Court Decision no. 53/185, Fahd Mikha'il Khalil v. the police and military government in Tarshiha.

95. Supreme Court Decision no. 53/185. The court issued its decision on 26 January 1953.

96. *Al-Ittihad*, 14 March 1949.

97. Nimr Murqus, who participated in the attempt to resist the expulsion, testified that the number of original inhabitants of Kufr Yasif who were involved was thirty-five, including three comrades, Nicola Dawud, Raja Sa'd, and Ahmad Shehada. Interview with Nimr Murqus in his home in Kufr Yasif, 28 June 2008.

98. Morris, *Lidata*, 168.

99. *Al-Ittihad*, 14 March 1949.

100. *Al-Ittihad*, 19 June 1949; 26 June 1949.

101. Morris, *Lidata*, 173.

102. Morris, *Lidata*, 174.

103. *Minutes of Knesset Sessions*, vol. 3, 1949/1950, 71.

104. *Minutes of Knesset Sessions*, vol. 3, 1949/1950, 71.

105. Ben-Gurion's statements here in his reply to Tawfiq Tubi reflect Israel's propaganda and the arrogance of the prime minister and defense minister who was known for his anti-Arab positions, even at the personal level, towards Arab Knesset members in general and the communists in particular.

106. What Ben-Gurion was referring to was Tubi's party during the days of the mandate, the National Liberation League, which had a hostile attitude towards Zionism until 1947, as we mentioned earlier.

107. *Minutes of Knesset Sessions*, vol. 3, 1949/1950, 72.

108. *Al-Ittihad*, 12 June 1949, quoting *'Al Hamishmar*.

109. Benny Morris, *Melhamut ha-gvul shel Yesrael, 1949–56* [Israel's Border Wars, 1949–56] (Tel Aviv: 'Am Oved, 1996); originally published in English, Oxford University Press, 1994, 533 n212.

110. Benny Morris, *Melhamut ha-gvul*, 190.

111. Meeting of the Mapai party on 18 June 1950, as cited in Morris, *Israel's Border Wars*, 190.

112. There is a lengthy review of such ideas in Uzi Benziman and 'Atallah Mansur, *'Ar-veyyi Yesrael, mamadam ve-hamdenyut klapeihim* [Sub-Tenants: The Israeli Arabs: Their Status and Policies Toward Them] (Jerusalem, Keter, 1992), 54–60.

113. Masalha, *Ard akthar wa 'Arab aql*, 36–37.

114. Hawwari had been permitted to return to Israel near the end of 1949, and led a policy that was hostile to the communists, but he had reservations about ideas for the migration of Arabs to Arab countries. In fact he opposed them, contrary to what Sasson said.

115. Masalha, *Ard akthar wa 'Arab aql*, 38.

116. From a report of the secret services, as cited in Benziman and Mansur, 58.

117. *Minutes of Knesset*, as cited in Benziman and Mansur, 58; Mustafa 'Abbasi, *al-Jishsh: tarikh qarya Jaliliyya* [Al-Jishsh: The History of a Galilee Village] (Al-Jishsh: al-Majlis al-Mahhali], 2010), 169–76.

118. *Al-Ittihad*, 17 July and 7 August 1953.

119. Tahir al-Tabari's letter to the head of state sent via the military governor of Nazareth was published in *al-Rabita* 8, July 1953, 13–15.

120. *al-Rabita* 9–10, August–September 1953.

121. *Al-Yawm*, 25 April 1954.

122. Benny Morris, *Melhamut ha-gvul*, 165; Ben-Gurion, *Yawmiyyat al-harb, 1947–1949*, 3:692.

123. Ben-Gurion, *Yawmiyyat al-harb, 1947–1949*, 693.

124. Ben-Gurion, *Yawmiyyat al-harb, 1947–1949*, 3:726.

125. Ben-Gurion, *Yawmiyyat al-harb, 1947–1949*, 640.

126. Ben-Gurion, *Yawmiyyat al-harb, 1947–1949*, 673.

127. Orna Cohen, *'Arveyyi Majdal (Ashkelon) Tmurot be-matzavam memelhemet 1948 ve-'Ad le-penuyyam memdinat Yesra'il* [The Arabs of Majdal: Transformations in Their Circumstances from the 1948 war Until Their Exile from Israel], MA thesis, Hebrew University, September 1999, 32; Ben-Gurion, *Yawmiyyat al-harb, 1947–49*, 3: 726.

128. Morris, *Lidata*, 338.

129. Cohen, *'Arvim tuvim*, 119.

130. Cohen, *'Arvim tuvim*.

5. STORIES ABOUT INDIVIDUALS AND VILLAGES

1. Hunaida Ghanim, "Al-Hudud wa al-hayat al-sirriyya li al-muqawama al-yawmiyya: qaryat al-Marja al-Filastiniyya, 1949–1967" [The Borders and The Secret Life of Daily Resistance: The Palestinian Village of Marja, 1949–1967], *Journal of Palestine Studies* 102 (Spring 2015): 121–43.

2. The conditions of transfer of control over those villages and the proximity of Triangle villages to the border (and witnessing bloody clashes) contributed to the atmosphere of constant tension and the occurrence of extraordinary incidents.

3. Abdallah al-Tal, *Karethat Filastin: mudhakirat 'Abdullah al-Tal qa'id ma'rakat al-Quds* [The Tragedy of Palestine: The Memoirs of Abdullah al-Tal, Commander of the Battle for Jerusalem], 2nd ed. (Kufr Qari': Dar al-Huda, 1990), 487–544; originally published in Cairo, Dar al-qalam, in 1959.

4. 'Arif al-'Arif, *Al-Nakba: Nakbat Bayt al-Maqdis wal-firdaws al-mafqud 1947–1949* [The Catastrophe: The Castrophe of Jerusalem and the Lost Paradise, 1947–1949] (Sidon: al-Maktaba al-'Asriya, 1956–1961), 4:897–99.

5. These critical remarks were published prior to similar accusations by Abdullah al-Tal in *Karethat Filastin*, first published in 1959.

6. *Al-Yawm* published the details of the agreement the day after it was signed, and mentioned that Reuven Shiloach and Moshe Dayan signed for the Israeli side.

7. Al-'Arif, *Al-Nakba*, 5:1032–41.

8. 'Abd al-Rahim 'Iraqi, *La takhaf: dhikrayat 'ala sa'id al-khawf* [Don't be Afraid: Memories about Fear], (Yafat al-Nasira: al-Tali'a, 1996), 315–18; Abdul al-Raziq Abu Ras, *Qalansuwa: Ma'alim wa-ahdath* [Qalansuwa: Landmarks and Events] (Tulkarm: al-Matba'a al-Ahiliya, 1999), 143–44.

9. Abu Ras, *Qalansuwa*, 149–50.

10. Contrary to what *al-Yawm* newspaper tried to convey, the villagers remained not out of love for Israel but so that they could continue to live in their homes and on their land instead of living as refugees in the West Bank.

11. *Al-Yawm*, 8 May 1949.

12. *Al-Yawm*, 9 May 1949.

13. 'Arif al-'Arif discusses the article in the armistice agreement which protects the rights of the inhabitants after their transfer to Israeli control. See *Al-Nakba*, 4: 897–99.

14. Hillel Cohen, *Al-Gha'bun al-hadrun: al-laj'un al-filastiniyun fi 'isra'il min 1948* [The Present Absentees: The Palestinian Refugees in Israel after 1948] (Beirut: Institute for Palestine Studies, 2003), 67.

15. Cohen, *Al-Gha'bun al-hadrun*, 46. After the expulsion of the vast majority of the refugees, a few hundred were left in the Triangle area who lived in Baqa al-Gharbiyya.

16. Cohen, *Al-Gha'bun al-hadrun*, 72.

17. *Al-Ittihad*, 15 March 1951.

18. Cohen, *Al-Gha'bun al-hadrun*, 166. Cohen mentions that the Supreme Court decision was issued on 30 June; in fact it was issued one month later, on 28 July 1952. Supreme Court Decision 52/36, Nadaf and seven others v. the Minister of Defense and the Military Governor.

19. Supreme Court Decision no. 52/36.

20. Cohen, *Al-Gha'bun al-hadrun*, 166–67.

21. *Al-Rabita* 12, November 1953, 32.

22. *Al-Rabita* 12, November 1953, 32.

23. Elias Saliba Surur, *Al-Nakba fii 'Ilabun* [Al-Nakba in 'Ilabun] ('Ilabun: al-Majlis al-Mahhalli, 1998), 44–45.

24. Benny Morris, *Lidata shel ba'yat ha-plitim ha-Falastinim, 1947–49* [The Birth of the Palestinian Refugee Problem, 1947–49] (Tel Aviv: Am Oved, 1991), 306. What Morris has to say about what happened in 'Ilabun, including the date of the return of the villagers (summer of 1949) contains many errors.

25. Surur, *Al-Nakba*, 44–45.

26. Morris, *Lidata*, 305. The priest Murqus Yuhanna al-Mu'allim, who recorded the events in 'Ilabun in his diaries, wrote that at the beginning of November the army entered the houses of 'Ilabun and looted them in a methodical way over several days, leaving nothing of the contents; they also stole the cows, goats, sheep, and horses.

27. Elias Saliba Surur, *'Ilabun: tarikh wa dhikrayat* ['Ilabun: History and Memories] (Nazareth: al-Hakim Press, 1997), 114–15.

28. Surur, *Al-Nakba*, 61.

29. Surur, *Al-Nakba*, 63–64.

30. Surur, *Al-Nakba*, 64.

31. Surur, *Al-Nakba*, 65–66.

32. Surur, *Al-Nakba*, 66–67. That group returned to Juniya in Lebanon; they set off from there and crossed the border to the Galilee returning once again to 'Ilabun.

33. Morris, *Lidata*, 306.

34. Surur, *Al-Nakba*, 68.

35. Interviews with Elias Surur and several members of the Zurayq family in the summer of 2008.

36. *Al-Ittihad*, 25 May 1949. Bishop Hakim also held a special prayer for the martyrs on the occasion of the passage of a year since the 'Ilabun massacre. See Surur, *Al-Nakba*, 79.

37. The village historian Elias Surur wrote, based on the diaries of Murqus al-Mu'allim, that the army planned to blow up all of the houses of the village after expelling the

population; see *Al-Nakba*, 81. On 25 November 1948, it had taken measurements and placed markings on twenty houses in preparation for their demolition.

38. Sarah Osetski-Lazar, "Kufr Qari', 1948–49: Ha'ziva vi-hashiva" [Kufr Qari', 1948–49: Migration and Return], unpublished paper presented at a conference on the 1948 war, Jerusalem: Van Leer Institute, 2010.

39. Osetski-Lazar, "Kufr Qari'," 14–15.

40. Osetski-Lazar, "Kufr Qari'"; Muhammad 'Aql, al-*Mufassal fi tarikh wadi 'Ara* [A Detailed History of Wadi 'Ara] (Jerusalem: al-Sharq Arabic Press, 1999), 284.

41. In addition to Sarah Osetski-Lazar and Muhammad 'Aql, another historian of the events of Kufr Qari' and the region as a whole, Mustafa Kabha, merits attention. See Mustafa Kabha and Nimr Sarhan, *Bilad al-rawha fi fatrat al-intidab al-Baritani* [The Land of the Evening Journey During the British Mandate] (Ramallah, Dar al-Shuruq, 2004).

42. Osetski-Lazar, "Kufr Qari'," 16–17.

43. Osetski-Lazar, "Kufr Qari'," 20–22.

44. According to *al-Yawm*, the villages of Wadi 'Ara were transferred to Israeli sovereignty on 20 May 1949. Two days later, the paper reported about the raising of the Israeli flag in the Wadi 'Ara region.

45. Muhammad 'Amin Beshr-Saffuri, *'Illut abr al-tarikh* ['Illut through History] (Nazareth: Maktab al-Nuris, 2002), 97.

46. Beshr-Saffuri, *'Illut abr al-tarikh*, 99. The author included a photo with the description of the scene of the massacre, as well as photos of the victims of that massacre in the olive grove.

47. See Beshr-Saffuri, *'Illut abr al-tarikh*, the testimony of Sabri 'Ali Abu Ras in an interview with Wadi' 'Awawde in May 2004. The author thanks Mr. 'Awawde for providing a copy of the interview.

48. In his book *Lidata* (The Birth of the Palestinian Refugee Problem), Morris does not mention the killings in 'Illut. In his later book *Border Wars* he notes the massacre in a footnote; see Benny Morris, *Melhamut ha-gvul shel Yesrael, 1949–56* [Israel's Border Wars, 1949–56] (Tel Aviv, Am Oved, 1996), 563.

49. Ilan Pappé mentions 'Illut in his book only once by mistake as he places this village next to other villages in northern Galilee, such as Fassuta and Tarbikha, as targets of raids. Ilan Pappé, *Al-Tathir al-'irqi fi filastin* [The Ethnic Cleansing of Palestine] (Beirut: Institute for Palestine Studies, 2007), 85.

50. Al-'Arif, *Al-Nakba: Nakbat Bayt al-Maqdis*, 3:631.

51. Mustafa Abbasi, "Nazareth after the War, 1948–1949: Refugees and Demographic Changes," in *The Cities of Galilee During the 1948 War: Four Cities and Four Stories* (Germany: Lambert Academic Publishing, 2014), 189.

52. Father Dubrovsky (1913–52) was of Czech origin. He arrived in Nazareth in 1933, and died young in a road accident during his return to Nazareth from Haifa in 1952.

53. Ahmad al-Bash, "Majzarat qaryat 'Illut" [The Massacre in 'Illut Village], *Al-'Awda* (August 2008): 3–4.

54. Morris, *Lidata*, 237.

55. Abbasi, "Nazareth after the War," 173.

56. Cohen, *Al-Gha'bun al-hadrun*, 51–52. In addition to the refugees in Nazareth, there were another 1,600 expellees in the villages of the district.

57. Cohen, *Al-Gha'bun al-hadrun*, 52. Abbasi mentions that the top clerics at the monastery said there were about 2,000 expelled villagers who had taken refuge there.

58. Cohen, *Al-Gha'bun al-hadrun*, 53.

59. Sarah Osetski-Lazar, *Iqrit ve-Bir'm: ha-Sippur ha-Male* [Iqrit and Kufr Bir'im: The Whole Story] (Giv'at Haviva: Institute for Arab Studies/Institute for Peace Studies, 1993), 13.

60. Yusif Susan, *Shahadati: yawmiyyat Bir'imiyya, 1948–68* [My Testimony: Bir'im Diaries] (D.M.: self-published, 1986), 17–18. Also, the testimony of 'Afif Ibrahim in Osetski-Lazar, *Iqrit and Kufr Bir'im*, 16.

61. Susan, *Shahadati*.

62. Supreme Court ruling no. 51/220 in al-Ghabisiyya case.

63. Dawud Badr, *al-Ghabisiyya: baqiya abadan fi al-qalb wa al-dhakira* [Al-Ghabisiyya Will Live Forever in Our Hearts and Memory] (D.M.: self-published, 2002).

64. Interview with Ahmad Hulayhel (born 1916), 10 January 2001 in his house in the village of Jish.

65. Interview with Sa'id Hulayhel, son of Khaled Khalil Hulayhel, and Mariam Hulayhel, at her home in Jish.

66. Morris, *Lidata*, 322; Cohen, *Al-Gha'bun al-hadrun*, 152.

67. Sayf al-Din al-Zu'bi, *Shahid 'ayan: mudhakkarat Sayf al-Din al-Zu'bi* [Eyewitness: the Memoirs of Sayf al-Din al-Zu'bi] (Shafa 'Amr: Dar al-Mashreq, 1987), 37.

68. 'Ali Hulayhel died in the summer of 2001, six months after I interviewed him. People remarked that even in his last days he had expressed a sense of bitterness and injustice over the treatment he and his extended family had received from state institutions that barred their return to Qadditha.

69. In the wake of the operation, about 240 people migrated from al-Khisas, while about sixty from the family of Shaykh 'Atiya stayed.

70. Aharon Duleb, "Ma irei' be-Khisas?" [What Happened in al-Khisas?] *Nir* 4, no. 3 (December 1952), 12.

71. Duleb, "What Happened in al-Khisas?," 13.

72. The Supreme Court issued a provisional order on 12 June 1952; Supreme Court Decision, *Shaykh 'Atiya v. the Ministry of Defense*, no. 52/132.

73. Supreme Court Decision, *Shaykh 'Atiya v. the Ministry of Defense*, no. 52/132.

74. The pamphlets were distributed on 11 July 1948.

75. 'Awda al-'Ashhab, *Tadhakurat 'Awda al-'Ashhab: sirat dhatiya* [The Memoirs of 'Awda al-'Ashhab: An Autobiography] (Birzeit: Birzeit University, 1999), 162–74.

76. *Minutes of the Knesset*, vol. 1, 1949, 532.

77. Al-'Ashhab, *Tadhakurat*, 162.

78. *Al-Ittihad*, 17 January 1949.

79. *Minutes of the Knesset*, vol. 1, 1949, 532.

80. Mustafa Kabha and Wadi' 'Awawde, *'Asra bila harb: al-mu'taqalun al-Filastiniyyun wa al-mu'taqalat al-Isra'iliyya al-ula, 1948–1949* [Prisoners Without War: Palestinian Detainees and the First Israeli Detention Centers, 1948–1949] (Beirut: Institute for Palestine Studies, 2013).

81. Al-'Ashhab, *Tadhakurat*, 191–94.

82. Al-'Ashhab, *Tadhakurat*, 191–94.

83. *Minutes of the Knesset*, vol.7 (a), 1950–1951, 618–19.

84. *Minutes of the Knesset*, vol. 8, 1951, 784.

85. What Tubi was referring to was the case of Hasan Abu 'Isha and his family.

86. Al-'Ashhab, *Tadhakurat*, 207–9.

87. *Al-Ittihad*, 15 December 1950.

88. Al-'Ashhab, *Tadhakurat*, 213. The reference is to the house of MK Moshe Sneh, as told to me by Abu 'Adnan over several sessions at his house in Shu'fat.

89. Al-'Ashhab, *Tadhakurat*, 216.

90. Al-'Ashhab, *Tadhakurat*, 217–19.

91. A solution to the problem of Mariam al-'Ashhab was quickly found in 1955, to the extent that she participated in the Knesset elections that year, according to the testimony and recollections of Abu 'Adnan.

92. *Al-Ittihad*, 16 February 1952. The paper reported the immigration of the attorney Subhi al-Ayubi to Libya which, it asked, raised an open question: "Who is behind the plan to encourage the immigration of Arabs to Libya?"

93. In 1951 a government was formed that united the various parts of Libya and declared Libya's independence in December of the same year, after which Muhammad Idris al-Sanusi was crowned king of Libya.

94. Author interview with the retired judge Khalil 'Abbud at his house in Nazareth, at the beginning of June, 2009.

95. Farid al-Sa'd, a wealthy and prominent activist in the national movement, was mentioned in ch. 1. This family is originally from Umm al-Fahm.

96. Meir Shelon arrived in Tripoli, Libya in September 1951 as the replacement to the previous consul, Meir Wardi, and remained there until December 1952. During that period, he worked to arrange for the emigration of Libyan Jews to Israel by way of Italy. For further details, see "The Heritage of Libyan Jews," particularly the topic "The Big Migration from Libya," online at livluv.org.il (accessed 7 April 2020).

97. According to his testimony, Khalil 'Abbud worked as an English language teacher in al-Rama high school then, after passing the bar exam in December 1955, practiced law. In 1982 he was made a judge and remained on the bench until his retirement in 1996.

98. *Decisions of the Supreme Court*, Decision no. 52/24, Nu'aima Nasr Hakim v. Minister of the Interior, 631–39.

99. *Al-Ittihad* newspaper reported that thirteen small villages in the Wadi 'Ara region had their inhabitants uprooted and their lands confiscated. *Al-Ittihad*, 10 February 1951.

100. Cohen gives three examples of that in his book, *'Arvim tuvim:ha-mudi'een ha-Yisra'eli ve-Harvim be-Yesra'el* [Good Arabs: Israeli Intelligence and the Arabs in Israel] (Jerusalem: Keter, 2006), 100–9.

101. The account of this event is taken from an article titled "Parashat Kfar 'Ara" [The Case of 'Ara village] in *Nir* 4, no. 1 (October 1952), 8.

102. "Parashat Kfar 'Ara, 8.

103. *Haaretz*, 29 August 1952; *'Al Hamishmar*, 29 August 1952.

104. *'Al Hamishmar*, 14 July 1952.

105. Sarah Osetski-Lazar, "Ha-Memshal ha-tsva'i ke-mangnon le-shlita ba-ezrahim ha-'aravim: ha'asor ha-rishon, 1948–58" [The Military Government as a System of Control over Arab Citizens: The First Decade, 1948–1958], *Hamezrah Hahadash* 43 (2002): 103–32.

106. Osetski-Lazar, "Ha-Memshal ha-tsva'i ke-mangnon."

107. 'Iraqi, *La takhaf*, 367.

108. 'Iraqi, *La takhaf*, 355–65.

109. 'Abd al-Rahim 'Iraqi devoted several pages of his memoirs to talk about this inci-dent in al-Tira; the people feared that the army may carry out a massacre during the search, which struck terror in the hearts of the children. The source of these fears was the villagers' recollections primarily of what had happened in 1948, and followed by the killings along the border, and the Israeli retaliation against West Bank villages. See 'Iraqi, *La takhaf*, 290.

110. News item [in Hebrew], *Nir* 4, 12, (August 1953), 16.

111. A local committee of villagers estimated the damages suffered by the residents to be in the region of ten thousand liras.

112. *Nir* 4, no. 12 (August 1953), 15–16. The magazine published expanded reports of the incident and the reactions of condemnation by Arabs and Jews, including an English-language letter from the attorney Elias Kusa, 28–31.

113. *Minutes of the Knesset*, vol. 14 (5 August 1953), 2147–49.

114. Testimony of Fatima Qasem 'Eid, quoted in 'Isa Muhammad Dhiyab 'Awna, *'Arab al-Subayh: Tarikh wa Riwaya* [Al-Subayh Arabs: A History and a Tale] (Kufr Kana: Dar al-Hikma Press, 2006), 106.

115. Testimony of 'Abed Hasan Turki, in 'Awna, *'Arab al-Subayh*, 119.

116. Testimony of Ghayura Zayed, in 'Awna, *'Arab al-Subayh*.

117. *Al-Ittihad*, 17 December 1954.

118. Hanna Abu Hanna, *Khamirat al-ramad* [The Yeast of Ashes] Part 2, *al-Sira al-dhati-yyah* [Autobiography] (Haifa: Maktabat Kul Shay', 2004), 16–19.

119. Abu Hanna, *Khamirat al-ramad*, 20.

120. Nadir Zu'bi, *Ha-Tefruset ha-merhavit shel tuf'at hameha'h bekerev hayeshuvim Ha'arvim, 1949–66* [The Geography of Protest in the Villages of the Galilee under Military Rule, 1949–66]. PhD diss., Haifa University, 2007, part 2, 187.

121. Zu'bi, *Ha-tefruset ha-merhavit*, 189. Both petitions are dated December 1954.

122. Rubik Rosenthal, ed., *Kfar Qasim: iru'im ve-metus* [Kafr Qasim: Events and a Leg-end] (Tel Aviv: United Kibbutz, 2000).

123. Morris, *Melhamut ha-gvul*, 444.

124. Morris, *Melhamut ha-gvul*, 445.

125. Morris, *Melhamut ha-gvul*, 424–25. Between seventy and ninety Arabs were killed in the Qalqilya operation, while dozens of Israeli soldiers were killed or wounded.

126. Al-'Arif, *Al-Nakba: Nakbat Bayt al-Maqdis*, 5:904–5.

127. Rosenthal revealed "Operation Mole" for the first time in a newspaper article pub-lished in *Hadashot*, 25 October 1991.

128. Rosenthal, *Kfar Qasim: iru'im ve-metus*, 14–15.

6. THE STRUGGLE TO REMAIN: BETWEEN POLITICS AND THE JUDICIARY

1. Formally, the Declaration of the Establishment of the State of Israel, available at mfa.gov.il/mfa/aboutisrael/israelat50/pages/the%20declaration%20of%20the%20establish-ment%20of%20the%20state.aspx (accessed 8 March 2020).

2. The personality of Minister Shitrit, and his achievements in 1948 and after, were singular among all other ministers in the Ben-Gurion government. This deserves more at-tention from researchers.

3. Uzi Benziman and 'Atallah Mansur, *Dayyari meshne: 'Arveyyi Yesrael, mamadam ve-hamdenyut klapeihim* [Sub-Tenants: The Israeli Arabs: Their Status and Policies Toward Them] (Jerusalem: Keter, 1992), 63.

4. For more on this subject see Hillel Cohen, *'Arvim tuvim:ha-mudi'een ha-Yisra'eli ve-Harvim be-Yesra'el* (Jerusalem: Keter, 2006); published in English as *Good Arabs: The Israeli Security Agencies and the Israeli Arabs, 1948–1967* (Berkeley: University of California Press, 2010).

5. Ian Lustick, *Arabs in the Jewish State: Israel's Control of a National Minority* (Austin: University of Texas Press, 1980).

6. *Al-Yawm*, 14 February 1949.

7. See the recently released Haim Hazan and Daniel Monterescu, *'Ir been 'Arbayem: le'umiyyut mezdakenet be-Yafo* [A City at Sunset: Aging Nationalism in Jaffa] (Jerusalem: Van Leer Institute and the United Kibbutz, 2011).

8. Benny Morris, *1948: The History of the First Arab-Israeli War* (Yale University Press, 2008), 177; published in Hebrew as *1948: Toldut ha-melhama ha-'Arvit ha-Yesraelit ha-rishona* (Tel Aviv: 'Am Ovid, 2010), 307.

9. Morris, *1948: The History of the First Arab-Israeli War.*

10. Morris, *1948: The History of the First Arab-Israeli War.*

11. Letter from the Emergency Committee in Jaffa to the command of the Haganah in Tel Aviv, dated 26 June 1948. Israeli Central State Archives in Jerusalem, File No. 2566/15.

12. Benny Morris, *Lidata shel ba'yat ha-plitim ha-Falastinim, 1947–49* [The Birth of the Palestinian Refugee Problem, 1947–49] (Tel Aviv: Am Oved, 1991), 199–200.

13. Shitrit's answer to Yaakov Shimoni, dated 19 July 1948, quoted from Morris, *Lidata*, 154.

14. *Lexicon ha-ishim shel eretz yesrael* [Dictionary of Prominent People in Palestine, 1799–1948] (Tel Aviv: Am Oved, 1983), 11.

15. 'Arif al-'Arif, *Al-Nakba: Nakbat Bayt al-Maqdis wa l-firdaws al-mafqud 1947–49* [The Catastrophe: The Catastrophe of Jerusalem and the Lost Paradise 1947–49] (Sidon: Al-Maktaba al-'Asria, 1956), 1:264. Al-'Arif adds that the role of Abu-Laban grew in importance and his status was elevated after the departure of Yusif Haykal from the city.

16. Arif al-'Arif, *Al-Nakba: Nakbat Bayt al-Maqdis*, 265–66.

17. Arif al-'Arif, *Al-Nakba: Nakbat Bayt al-Maqdis*, 268.

18. Interview with a Jaffa resident who lived through these events but did not want his name mentioned.

19. These facts emerged in the Supreme Court hearings, and were mentioned in the court's decision no. 48/7, Ahmad Shawqi al-Kharbuti v the minister of defense et al.

20. Supreme Court decision no. 48/7, 7.

21. Supreme Court decision no. 48/7, 16. It should be pointed out that the authorities also arrested 'Abdul Razzaq Abu-Laban, as the Hebrew-language papers, *Hamoked* for example, reported on 11 November 1948.

22. Several Hebrew newspapers carried news of the court proceedings, the issuing of an order for his release, and the fact that he had not been released several days later. See *Haaretz*, 5 and 7 January 1949.

23. Shitrit sent a translation of the petition to Ben-Gurion on 23 January 1949. The original document and translation are in the Israeli Central State Archives in Jerusalem, file no. 298/5 (Ministry of Minorities).

24. Letter from Shitrit to Ben-Gurion, dated 23 January 1949, Israeli Central State Archives in Jerusalem, file no. 298/5 (Ministry of Minorities).

25. Interview with anonymous Jaffa resident.

26. *Haaretz*, 13 January 1949.

27. Interview with anonymous Jaffa resident. The stories of some of them are related in this chapter, particularly those who signed the surrender agreement along with Hajj Abu-Laban.

28. Nasir al-Din al-Nashashibi, *Yafa lil'abd: kama'ayshha Nasir al-Din al-Nashashibi wa Salah Ibrahim al-nathirwa Muhamad Sa'id 'Ishkantna* [Jaffa Forever, as Experienced by Naser al-Din al-Nashashibi and Salah Ibrahim al-Nather and Muhammad Sa'id Ishkantna] (Beirut/ Amman: Arab Institute for Studies and Publication, 2013), 41–63.

29. Nashashibi, *Yafa lil'abd*, 63.

30. Hazan and Monterescu, *'Iir been 'Arbayem*, 119.

31. *Al-Yawm*, 10 January 1950, 4. The list included the names of a large number of Armenians.

32. Ahmad Mashhuwari, "When They Travelled in Cadillacs in Jaffa," *Maariv*, 16 August 2001.

33. His father Yusif Jaday owned a pharmacy in al-'Ajami quarter, and that influenced his choice to study pharmacy, as he told me when I interviewed him for the first time in September 2011.

34. Mashhuwari, "When They Travelled in Cadillacs in Jaffa."

35. Fakhri Jaday continued to work part-time in the family pharmacy to the end of his days, with his son Yusif administering the pharmacy. In my interviews with Fakhri Jaday he expressed extreme bitterness and frustration about the conditions of life in Jaffa.

36. Hazan and Monterescu, *'Iir been 'Arbayem*, 54–55.

37. Hazan and Monterescu, *'Iir been 'Arbayem*.

38. *Al-Ittihad*, 16 February 1952.

39. Interview with 'Odeh al-'Ashhab (Abu 'Adnan) at his home in Haifa, 3 September 2011.

40. Samuel Dotan, *Adumim: hameflaga ha-kumunistit be-Eretz Yesrael* [The Reds: The Communist Party in the Land of Israel] (Kafr Saba: Shibna Hatsofer, 1991), 438.

41. Dotan, *Adumim*. The participation of Nassar in Rashid 'Ali al-Kaylani's revolt is mentioned in the book which the Communist Party published one year after his death. See Bashir al-Barghuthi, *Fu'ad Nassar: al-rajul wa al-qadiyya* [Fu'ad Nassar: The Man and the Cause] (Jerusalem: Dar Salah al-Din, 1977), 16–17.

42. Musa al-Budayri, *Shuyu'iyyun fi filastin: shadhaya tarikh mansi* [Communists in Palestine: Fragments of a Forgotten History] (Ramallah: Muwatin, the Palestinian Institute for the Study of Democracy, 2013).

43. Budayri, *Shuyu'iyyun fi Filastin*, 153–56.

44. Report by Nuwaihed al-Hut, *Al-Qiyadat wa al-mu'assasat al-siyasiyya fi Filastin, 1917–1948* [Leaders and Political Institutions in Palestine, 1917–1948] (Beirut: Institute for Palestine Studies, 3rd ed., 1986), 860.

45. *Al-Yawm*, 2 November 1949.

46. Supreme Court Decisions, no. 50/46, dated 26 May 1950, 222–232.

47. Supreme Court Decisions, no. 50/46, 223.

48. Supreme Court Decisions, no. 50/46.

49. Supreme Court Decisions, no. 50/46232. The judges took care to mention at the end of their decision: "We recommend to the military authorities that they rethink where the plaintiff's residence should be (under police supervision), and that they take his claims concerning his illness and his fear for his life from probable surprise acts of violence [at his plantation] into consideration."

50. Minutes of the Knesset, vol. 3 (1949/50), 1501.

51. In this chapter we provided examples of the lives of those who remained and those who were forced to leave. However, the question of the fate of those Palestinian cities in the middle of the country which were marginalized (such as Lydda, Ramla, and Jaffa) still await specialized studies that will chronicle and document what happened to them after the Nakba of 1948.

52. An example of the late emigration of some elites from the Palestinian coastal cities after the Nakba are the cases of Dr. Hasan Far'un, who moved from Jaffa to Amman, and the departure of Albert al-Sa'd and Wadi' al-Bustani from Haifa.

53. Hanna Naqqara received public appreciation and attention from researchers for his role in defending the usurped rights of the remaining Palestinians. See *Hanna Naqqara: Muhami al-ard wa-sha'b* [Hanna Naqara: Lawyer for the Land and the People], ed. Hanna Ibrahim (Acre: al-Aswar, 1985). A revised and expanded edition, *Mudhakkarat muhami Filastini: Hanna Dib Naqqara, muhami al-ard wa Sha'b* (Remembering the Palestinian Lawyer: Hanna Dib Naqqara, the People's and Land Lawyer), was issued in 2011 by the Institute for Palestine Studies in Beirut, 2011, edited by 'Atallah Sa'id Qubti.

54. Al-Hut, *Al-Qiyadat*, 629–630; Rashid al-Hajj Ibrahim, *al-Difa' 'an Haifa wa qadiyyat Filastin: Mudhakkarat Rashid al-Haj Ibrahim, 1891–1953* [The Defense of Haifa and the Palestinian Cause: The Memoirs of Rashid al-Hajj Ibrahim, 1891–1953] (Beirut: Institute for Palestine Studies, 2005), 104, 106, 108.

55. Telephone interview with the son, Nicola Kusa (b. 1939), 13 May 2009. Elias Kusa's personal archives had been deposited by Hanna Abu Hanna with a charitable organization in Haifa concerned with Arab rights in Israel. Unfortunately all of my attempts, with the assistance of Hanna Abu Hanna, to locate Kusa's papers there were in vain.

56. Tom Segev, *1949: Hayesraelim hareshonim* [1949: The First Israelis] (Jerusalem: Domino, 1984), 90–92.

57. As in Segev, *1949: Hayesraelim hareshonim*, 26–28.

58. Elias Kusa, *Nir* 13 July 1951, 26–28.

59. Such as *Jewish Observer*, which published an article by him on 12 September 1952, in which he analyzed the situation of the Arabs in Israel. His article elicited many reactions inside Israel and abroad.

60. Israeli Central State Archives in Jerusalem, prime minister's advisor on Arab affairs, file on Elias Kusa, no. 17043. I would like to thank Nabih Bashir who photographed that document along with others and made them available to me.

61. Telephone interview with Nicola Kusa, 13 May 2009.

62. Albert Sa'd from Haifa, for instance, tried for two years to obtain a passport and a travel permit. When his dealings with government offices bore no fruit, he went to the Supreme Court; Decision no. 51/3 against the ministry of the interior.

63. Kusa, *Nir*, 13 July 1951, 26–28.

64. Christian clergymen were excluded from this rule, as were members of the Communist Party who travelled freely to the socialist countries and participated in conferences and tours which were organized for them from there.

65. Kusa, *Nir*, 13 July 1951, 26–28.

66. Supreme Court decision no. 53/112.

67. The decision was that the Ministry of Interior should pay Naqqara the sum of 30 liras to cover court costs.

68. Elias Kusa, "Tshuva le-Moshe Sharrett" [Letter to the Prime Minister], *Nir*, 5 May 1957.

69. Document dated 11 April 1957, no. 1546/41014, file of the prime minister's advisor on Arab affairs, Israeli Central State Archives in Jerusalem.

70. David Kretzmer, *Al-Makana al-qanuniya lil-'Arab fi 'Isra'il* [The Legal Status of the Arabs in Israel] (Jerusalem: Center for the Study of Arab Society, 2002). This is a revised and expanded Arabic-language version of the book released in 1995 and includes an introduction by the author.

71. Kretzmer, *Al-Makana al-qanuniya*, 50–51.

72. The case of Hajj Ahmad Abu-Laban discussed above (Supreme Court decision 48/7) was one of the first important cases that garnered wide attention from the press and public opinion in Israel.

73. Alina Korn, *Pshe'a, status politi ve-akhifat khuk: ha-mi'ut ha-'Arvi be-Yisrael betkufat hamemshal hatzva'I (1948–66)* [Criminal Activities, Political Status and Implementation of the Law: The Arab Minority in Israel under Military Rule (1948–66)] (PhD diss., Hebrew University School of Law, Jerusalem, 1997).

74. Korn, *Pshe'a*, 8.

75. Korn, *Pshe'a*, 112.

76. *Al-Ittihad*, 4 September 1949, and 13 November 1949, 4. The paper wrote about the expulsion of the inhabitants of Majd al-Krum, Dayr al-Asad, al-Bi'na, and Tarshiha.

77. Korn points out that 80 percent of the permits were for work outside the village (*Pshe'a*, 70).

78. *Al-Ittihad*, 4 September 1950, quoting villagers from 'Iblin following the arrest of seven residents and their exile to the Naqab as a punishment.

79. *Al-Ittihad*, 14 January 1951.

80. Habib Qahwaji, *al-'Arab fi zil al-ihtilal al-'Isra'ilimundh1948* [Arabs under The Shadow of Israeli Occupation Since 1948] (Beirut: Palestine Liberation Organization, Research Center, 1972), 152.

81. *Minutes of the Knesset*, vol. 9 (1951), 1807.

82. *Minutes of the Knesset*, vol. 9 (1951), 1807.

83. *Al-Ittihad*, 1 October 1950.

84. Nadim Musa, *Mudhakarat shiu'iyi mukhadram* [Memories of a Veteran Communist] (Acre, Abu-Rahmun Press, 2008), 79–80; *al-Ittihad*, 3 February 1951.

85. This case is famous in the historical literature, as is the Supreme Court ruling, no. 195/1951.

86. Yusif Susan, *Shahadati: yawmiyyat Bir'imiyya, 1948–68* [My Testament: Bir'imite Diaries, 1948–1968] (self-published, 1986).

87. Minutes of the Knesset, vol. 1 (1949), 239.

88. Minutes of the Knesset, vol. 2 (1949), 1637.

89. Hanna Ibrahim, *Shajaraal-maʿarifa: dhikarat shab lam yatagharab* [The Tree of Knowledge: Memories of a Young Man Who Did Not Emigrate] (Acre: al-Aswar, 1996), 133–36; *al-Ittihad*, 19 May 1951.

90. *Kol HaAm*, 3 December 1950. We shall see more detailed accounts of this and similar cases of Hanna Naqqara before the Supreme Court later.

91. Sabri Jiryis worked in the office of Hanna Naqqara (1964–65) in Haifa after his graduation from Hebrew University. Based on the files he found in the office, he said in his book that 865 persons had obtained their identity cards from the Ministry of Interior after appealing in the courts during 1950–52. For more on this see Sabri Jiryis, *The Arabs in Israel* (New York: Monthly Review Press, 1976), 258n31.

92. *Al-Yawm*, 30 May 1951.

93. *Al-Yawm*, 9 August 1951.

94. Supreme Court Decision no. 51/108, Muhammad Asʿad Izghayer and twenty-two others v. the minister of interior and the military governor of the Galilee, et al.

95. Supreme Court Decision no. 51/125, Muhammad ʿAli al-Husayn and nine others v. the minister of the interior and the military governor.

96. Supreme Court Decision no. 51/125.

97. Supreme Court Decision no. 51/125, 1387–88.

98. Supreme Court Decision no. 51/125, 1388; interview with Fahd ʿAli al-Husayn at his house in Majd al-Krum, near the end of June 2008.

99. Supreme Court Decision no. 51/125, 1389.

100. There is a large degree of agreement between these testimonies in the Supreme Court of Justice that I read only two years ago and the testimonies I heard from eyewitnesses I have met in the village since my research interest in the subject began in 1984.

101. Supreme Court of Justice decision no. 51/125, 1390.

102. Supreme Court of Justice decision no. 51/125. This testimony in the Supreme Court confirms the truth of information on the massacre in Majd al-Krum, mentioned in documents and in the testimonies of the inhabitants.

103. That this was the typology used by the judges for the act of the random killing of civilians and the tearing down of houses, without any reservation or criticism on their part, is astonishing.

104. The massacre in al-ʿAyn Square in Majd al-Krum occurred a week after the surrender of the village (5 November 1948).

105. Supreme Court of Justice Decision no. 51/125, 1392.

106. Supreme Court of Justice Decision no. 51/125, 1391; interview with Fahd ʿAli al-Husayn.

107. Supreme Court of Justice Decision no. 51/125. Once again it is worth noting that the judges were using terms that are more reflective of reality, such as "occupation," in relation to Majd al-Krum and central Galilee.

108. Supreme Court of Justice Decision no. 51/125. See the study by Oren Bracha on "infiltrators" titled "Confusion about Whether They Are Helpless or Dangerous: The Infiltrators, the Law and the Supreme Court of Justice, 1948–1954," *ʿIyyuni mishpat* 21, no. 2 (April 1998): 333–85.

109. In addition to the study by Bracha mentioned above, the researcher Leora Bilsky devoted an important section to the analysis of the case of Muhammad ʿAli al-Husayn

before the Supreme Court. See Leora Bilsky, *Transformative Justice: Israeli Identity on Trial* (Ann Arbor: University of Michigan Press, 2004), 174–77.

110. The connection between voting for the ruling party (Mapai) and its Arab lists and the approval of the authorities of the reunification for some families will be dealt with in chapter seven.

111. Supreme Court Decision no. 53/155, Salam Ahmad Kiwan v. the minister of defense et al.

112. Supreme Court Decision no. 52/81.

113. The final Supreme Court ruling on the case of Salam Ahmad Kiwan was issued on 9 March 1954.

114. Israeli Archives of the Army and Security Forces, file no. 54/7. This includes the reports of military governors for August 1952.

115. Hanna Abu Hanna, *Mhir bawma* [The Owl's Dowry] (Haifa: Maktabat kulshai', 2004), 132.

116. Minutes of the Knesset, September 1949, 1530, vol. 3 (Session of 16 January 19500, 534–35.

117. It appears that this "ambitious idea" of some leaders of the Liberation League and Mapam activists did not meet with Ben-Gurion's approval, so he closed the file on it.

118. I tried on several occasions to conduct an interview with Tawfiq Tubi during his final years (2009–2010) without success due to his ill health. When I finally did succeed (in March 2011) it was difficult to carry on a conversation with him even through the intermediation of his son, Dr. Elias, who attended the interview in his father's house.

119. *Al-Ittihad* on 29 May 1949 commented on the "special" project for military conscription for Arab citizens, saying: "Good luck to this special project, God willing. Are Arabs to be class B citizens even in defending the independence of the country?"

120. Special report no. 18/2402, Ministry of Foreign Affairs, file, Israeli Central State Archives in Jerusalem, 1October 1954.

121. *Al-Rabita* 15, October 1954, 12.

122. *Al-Rabita* 15, October 1954. Reports and articles expressed unease towards conscription in general.

123. *Al-Rabita* 15, October 1954, 14–17.

124. *Al-Rabita* 15, October 1954, 17.

125. Benziman and Mansur, *Dayyari meshne*, 118.

126. Benziman and Mansur, *Dayyari meshne*, 118.

127. Shim'on Avivi, *Tas nihoshet: hamdinyut ha-yesra'ilit klapi ha-'ida ha-Druzit, 1948–67* [Copper Tray: The Israeli Policy Towards the Druze Community, 1948–67], 84–85.

128. Avivi, *Tas nihoshet*, 86–95.

7. THE PARLIAMENTARY ELECTIONS AND POLITICAL BEHAVIOR

1. Sayf al-Din al-Zu'bi, *Shahid 'ayan: mudhakkarat Sayf al-Din al-Zu'bi* [Eyewitness: The Memoirs of Sayf al-Din al-Zu'bi] (Shafa 'Amr: Dar al-Mashreq, 1987), 40–42.

2. David Ben-Gurion, *Yawmiyyat al-harb, 1947–49* [War Diaries, 1947–49], ed. Gershon Rivlin and Elhahan Oren, trans. Samir Jabbur (Beirut: Institute for Palestine Studies, 2nd edition, 1998), 661–64.

3. Ben-Gurion, *Yawmiyyat al-harb;* Shim'on 'Avivi, *Tas nihoshet: hamdinyut ha-yesra'ilit klapi ha-'ida ha-Druzit, 1948–67* [Copper Tray: The Israeli Policy towards the Druze Community, 1948–67] (Jerusalem: Yitzhak Ben-Tzvi Center, 2007), 329–31.

4. Yoav Gelber, *Komimyut ve-Nakba: Yesrael, ha-Falastinimu-medinut 'Arav, 1948* [Independence and Nakba: Israel, the Palestinians and the Arab States in 1948] (Tel Aviv: Zamora Petan, 2004), 420.

5. Gelber, *Komimyut ve-Nakba,* 419; Ben-Gurion, *Yawmiyyat al-harb,* 661–64.

6. Roberto Beki, *'Arikhat reshum ha-tushavim be 8 be-November 1948* [The Population Census: Counting on 8 November 1948] Jerusalem: Central Census Bureau, Special Publications series, no. 26, 1949), 13–14.

7. There is confusion surrounding the given facts of the first census of the Arab population. It is not clear who was counted, and the reasons why others were not included.

8. Beki, *'Arikhat reshum,* 12.

9. Beki, *'Arikhat reshum.* Yoav Gelber claims that the number of Arabs with voting rights came to 37,000. See Gelber, *Komimyut ve-Nakba,* 420.

10. Melekh Noy (Neustadt), *Bereshit ve-b'asur ha-rishon le-mdinat Yesraeil* [At the Beginning and in the First Decade of the State of Israel] (Tel Aviv: Newman Press, 1958), 174.

11. Noy, *Bereshit,* 175.

12. *Al-Ittihad,* 21, 28 February 1949; *Kol HaAm,* 24 February 1949.

13. Al-Zu'bi was granted a medal in recognition of his services alongside combatants for the state.

14. The first among them was Tawfiq Ziyad who began his political activities at the local government level in February 1949.

15. Minutes of the Knesset, vol. 1, 1949, 23. Jarjura's speech in the second session, 15 March 1949.

16. Minutes of the Knesset, vol. 1, 1949, 753.

17. Minutes of the Knesset, vol. 1, 1949.

18. Minutes of the Knesset, vol. 9, 1951.

19. The name of this parliamentarian and his political activities do not crop up often in studies, particularly those that portray the duality of political action by the remaining Arabs in black and white, whether they be communists or their adversaries, the collaborators.

20. One of the lists, the Worker's Bloc, did not get enough votes to cross the threshold and qualify, so the votes cast for it were wasted.

21. Ya'cov Landau, *Ha-'Arvim be-Yesrael: 'iyyunim polityyim* [The Arabs in Israel: Political Analysis] (Tel Aviv: Security Ministry, 1971), 167.

22. *Al-Yawm,* 4 February 1949, 2.

23. See 'Isa Habib's testimony in Ahmad Sa'd, *Judhur al-shajara dai'mat al-khudra* [Roots of the Evergreen Tree] (Haifa: Emile Tuma Academy, 1996), 209.

24. *Al-Ittihad,* 31 January 1949. These figures, which were published a few days after the elections, were not exact. Furthermore, the boast that 90 percent of those with the right to vote actually voted was not true. Official figures published later place the total at 80 percent or less.

25. Ra'nan Cohen, *Besvakh ha-ne'manyyut: hevra ve-politica ba-megzar ha-'Arvi* [Battle of Loyalties: Society and Politics in the Arab Minority] (Tel Aviv: Am Oved, 1986), 134.

26. Ben-Gurion, *Yawmiyyat al-harb,* 661.

27. Yossi Amitay, *Achvat 'Amim bamivhan: Mapam 1948–54* [The Brotherhood of Peoples Tested: Mapam 1948–54] (Tel Aviv: Tcherikover, 1988), 135–37.

28. Amitay, *Achvat 'amim bamivhan*, 138–39.

29. Amitay, *Achvat 'amim bamivhan*, 139.

30. Amitay, *Achvat 'amim bamivhan*, 138.

31. Maki viewed Sharett's assertion that the party opposed the immigration of Jews from the Eastern socialist camp as a "base slander." See *Kol HaAm*, June 1949, 22, 30.

32. Joel Beinin, *Was the Red Flag Flying There? Marxist Politics and the Arab Israeli Conflict in Egypt and Israel, 1948–1965* (Berkeley: University of California Press, 1990), 124.

33. Al-Zu'bi, *Shahid 'ayan*, 41–42.

34. Al-Zu'bi, *Shahid 'ayan*, 36, 41–42.

35. Gelber, *Komimyut ve-Nakba*, 286.

36. Gelber, *Komimyut ve-Nakba*, 309–10.

37. *Al-Yawm*, 20 February 1949; 1 March 1949.

38. Hillel Cohen, *'Arvim tuvim: ha-mudi'een ha-Yisra'eli ve-Harvim be-Yesra'el* (Jerusalem: Keter, 2006), 65; in English, *The Good Arabs: The Israeli Security Agencies and the Israeli Arabs, 1948–1967* (Berkeley: University of California Press, 2010).

39. *Al-Rabita* 8, November 1949, 1–5.

40. *Al-Rabita* 8, November 1949, 5; *Al-Rabita* 7, October 1949, 1.

41. *Al-Rabita* 7, October 1949, 20.

42. *Al-Ittihad*, 31 July 1949.

43. Minutes of the Knesset, vol. II, 1949, 1514.

44. Interview with 'Aziz Srouji at his home in Nazareth, 24 May 2009.

45. Interview with 'Anis Srouji (Abu 'Isam) at his home in Nazareth, 6 March 2009.

46. The family included five brothers and three sisters, some of whom immigrated to the United States, where they spent the rest of their lives. Immigration was notably more widespread among the Christian middle class compared to the Muslim, which contributed to the decrease in their demographic ratio.

47. H. Cohen, *'Arvim tuvim*, 64–69; Landau, *Ha-'Arvim be-Yesrael*, 146–48.

48. Landau, *Ha-'Arvim be-Yesrael*, 147–48.

49. "Ahdath al-Nasara" [The Nazareth Incidents], *al-Rabita* 5, May 1952, 1–2.

50. A truce was in fact concluded between the two sides ("Ahdath al-Nasara," 3–7).

51. Cohen, *'Arvim tuvim*, 66–69.

52. "Dukhan fi 'Ilabun" [Smoke in 'Ilabun], *al-Ittihad*, 14 November 1952.

53. Muhammad Nimr al-Hawwari, *Sirr al-Nakba* [The Secret of al-Nakba] (Nazareth: Al-Hakim Press, 1955), 394; Cohen, *'Arvim tuvim*, 72.

54. In his book, *Sirr al-Nakba*, al-Hawwari talks about those accusations in greater detail, but he denies them altogether.

55. Gelber, *Komimyut ve-Nakba*, 425; also interviews with a number of family members who preferred to remain anonymous.

56. Cohen, *'Arvim tuvim*, 72–73.

57. *Al-Ittihad*, 13 November 1949.

58. *Al-Ittihad*, 22 January 1950.

59. Cohen, *'Arvim Tuvim*, 74–75; *al-Ittihad*, 14 May 1950.

60. Al-Hawwari, *Sirr al-Nakba*, 4–15.

61. Al-Hawwari, *Sirr al-Nakba*, 5. The well-known historian Bayan Nuwayhed al-Hut wrote a scathing criticism of Hawwari's book, *Sirr al-Nakba*, accusing him of being untruthful and levelling charges in every direction without facts; see Bayan Nuwayhed al-Hut, *Al-Qiyadat wa al-Mu'assasat al-Siyasiyya fi Filastin, 1917–1948* [Leaders and Political Institutions in Palestine, 1917–1948] 3rd ed., (Beirut: Institute for Palestine Studies, 1986), 509.

62. Al-Hawwari had to support a family of eighteen people, which included two wives and their children.

63. Ra'nan Cohen says that the number of Arab votes cast in 1951 reached 58,984 as compared to 26,332 votes in 1949 (*Besvakh ha-ne'manyyut*, 134).

64. Cohen, *Besvakh ha-ne'manyyut*, 135.

65. Landau, *Ha-'Arvim be-Yesrael*, 170. Landau says that the number of Arab voters reached 70,000, then two pages later he says the number was 80,000 out of 924,885 voters in the 1951 elections.

66. Three seats went to the Democratic list headed by Sayf al-Din al-Zu'bi, and one seat each to the other two slates.

67. Despite the election of Faris Hamdan, the Triangle remained underrepresented. The Arabs of al-Naqab (the Negev) did not manage to elect a representative.

68. Haifa was the Arab municipality with the highest number of representatives (three) while Nazareth had only one.

69. Mas'ad Qassis managed to get listed as number two on the list headed by Sayf al-Din al-Zu'bi in place of Amin Jarjura.

70. *Al-Ittihad*, 4 August 1951.

71. *Al-Ittihad*, 4 August 1951.

72. As previously mentioned, Emile Habibi returned from Lebanon to Nazareth and then Haifa with the consent of the Israeli authorities, like other Arab communist party activists.

73. The Arab Popular Bloc affiliated with Mapam had received 2,812 Arab votes in 1949, which constituted 11.6 percent of total Arab votes in those elections.

74. Amitay, *Achvat 'amim bamivhan*, 140.

75. *Al-Yawm*, 1 August 1951. The paper published detailed data on the results of the elections compared to the results of the first elections at the country level as well as the local level in Nazareth, Haifa, al-Ramla, and elsewhere.

76. Indeed, the Arab residents of the Naqab were not represented in the Knesset until the early 1970s. Hammad Abu Rabi'a was the first Arab elected from the region, and that was in the eighth round of elections.

77. The large village of al-Tayba was the exception to the other villages in the Triangle, giving Maki 35 percent of the total votes from the village.

78. Landau, *Ha-'Arvim be-Yesrael*, 168–72.

79. People talk about villages that are known for their support for the communists such as al-Bi'na, al-Rama, 'Ilabun, al-Buqay'a, and Tarshiha. Al-Bi'na in particular gained fame for its communist activists, becoming known as "Red al-Bi'na."

80. Landau, *Ha-'Arvim be-Yesrael*, 172.

81. Uzi Benziman and 'Atallah Mansur, *Dayyari meshne: 'Arveyyi Yesrael, mamadam ve-hamdenyut klapeihim* [Sub-Tenants: The Israeli Arabs: Their Status and Policies Toward Them] (Jerusalem: Keter, 1992), 198.

82. Among the activists of Mapam in the 1951 elections were Haim Orbach from Na-hariya, Baruch Noy from the 'Akka military government, and Moshe Raz from the west Galilee military government. Avivi, *Tas nihoshet*, 324.

83. For more detail on the prosecution and firing of communist teachers, see Cohen, *'Arvim tuvim*, 181–84.

84. An expression meaning that government officials and representatives only remembered Arab citizens and visit their villages on the eve of elections.

85. *Haaretz*, 5 January 1951.

86. The Hebrew language *Nir* published excerpts from Elon's article on 13 July 1951.

87. Landau, *Ha-'Arvim be-Yesrael*, 92.

88. Elias Kusa, "Tshuva le-Moshe Sharrett" [Reply to Foreign Minister Moshe Sharett], *Nir*, 31 August 1951, 20.

89. Kusa, "Tshuva le-Moshe Sharrett."

90. Kusa, "Tshuva le-Moshe Sharrett," 21.

91. Kusa, "Tshuva le-Moshe Sharrett." In his articles, Kusa had taken up the issue of such unjust laws affecting confiscated lands and property belonging to expellees in the articles.

92. Ya'qub al-'Awdat, *Major Intellectuals and Literary Figures in Palestine* (Jerusalem: Dar al-Isra', 3rd ed., 1992), 46; and Palestinian Encyclopedia Committee, *Al-Mawsu'a al-Filastiniyya. Al-qism al-'am* [The Palestinian Encyclopedia. General Studies Part] (Beirut: Hay'at al-Mawsu'a al-Filastiniyya, 1984), 4: 569.

93. What saddened al-Bustani and made remaining in Haifa particularly difficult was the fact that he and his wife were cut off from their four children who had left the city, along with most Palestinian inhabitants.

94. According to news items in the local Haifa papers, he died in Beirut on 19 January 1954.

95. *Al-Rabita* 5, May 1955, 33.

96. *Al-Ittihad*, 7 August 1953.

97. The letter is dated 11 November 1954. Yoni Mendel found the document in the file of the prime minister's advisor on Arab affairs and provided me with a copy (16/4 L), Israeli Central State Archives in Jerusalem.

98. Elias Kusa, "An Arab Bloc," *al-Rabita* 16, November 1954, 19–20.

99. Kusa, "An Arab Bloc," 21.

100. Kusa, "An Arab Bloc."

101. Elias Kusa, "Man huwa al-mudallal?" [Who Is the Deceiver?], *al-Rabita* 8–9, September/October 1955, 25–28.

102. For the local elections in Kafr Yasif see Ahmad Sa'di, "Control and Resistance at Local Level Institutions: A Study of Kafr Yasif's Local Council under the Military Government," *Arab Studies Quarterly* 23, 3 (Summer 2001): 31–47.

103. Geremy Forman, "Military Rule, Manipulation and Jewish Settlement: Israeli Mechanisms for Controlling Nazareth in the 1950s," *Journal of Israeli History* 25, no. 2 (September 2006): 335–59.

104. Forman, "Military Rule, Manipulation and Jewish Settlement."

105. Landau reports these numbers and says the participation rate was over 91 percent in *Ha-'Arvim be-Yesrael*, 177. However, a simple calculation using the given data shows that the rate barely reached 90 percent; Ori Stendal, *'Arveyyi Yesrael bein hapatish la-sadan*

[Arabs of Israel between Mortar and Pestle] (Jerusalem, Academon, 1992), 290; R. Cohen, *Besvakh ha-ne'manyyut*, 135.

106. Sayf al-Din al-Zu'bi, *Shahid 'ayan*, 103–6; Landau, *Ha-'Arvim be-Yesrael*, 117.

107. One reason for Maki's success with Jewish voters had to do with Moshe Sneh splitting with Mapam and moving over to Maki.

108. Interview with Rustum Bastuni's nephew, Hassan Bastuni, attorney, at his office in Haifa.

109. *Al-Mirsad* 148, 4 August 1955.

110. Amitay, *Achvat 'Amim Bamivhan*, 158.

111. There are many historical studies on Israel which indicate that; see Motti Golani, *Tehyye melhama ba-kayetz, 1955–56* [There Will Be a War This Summer: Israel on the Road to the Sinai War, 1955–1956] (Tel Aviv: Ma'rakhot, 1997).

112. The first revolution was in 1947–48.

113. *Al-Ittihad*, 22 March 1957.

114. *Al-Ittihad* published reports on the parties and solidarity in the regions of 'Akka, the Triangle, and Kafr Qasim itself in particular.

115. *Al-Ittihad*, 22 March 1957.

116. Emile Habibi, "Bawwabat Mandelbaum" [The Mandelbaum Gate], *al-Jadid* 5 (March 1954).

117. He spent most of his remaining years in Nazareth, but he wrote in his will that he wanted to be buried in Haifa.

118. *Al-Mu'tamar al-thalith 'ashr li al-hizb al-shuyu'i al-Isra'ili: 29 May–1 June 1957* [The Thirteenth Congress of the Israeli Communist Party] (Tel Aviv: United Kibbutz, 1993), 30.

119. Eli Rechess, *Ha-Me'ut ha-'Arvi be-Yesrael: bein kumunizim le-le'umiyyut 'Arvit, 1965–91*[The Arab Minority in Israel between Communism and Arab Nationalism, 1965–91 (Tel Aviv: United Kibbutz, 1993), 30.

120. Ya'ir Bäuml, *Tzel kakhul lavan: mdenyyut hamemsad hayesraeli u-pu'ulutav bkerev ha-'Arvim be-Yesrael-hashanin ha-mi'atzvut, 1958–68* [A Blue and White Shadow: The Israeli Establishment Policy and Actions Among Its Arab Citizens: The Formative Years, 1958–68] (Haifa: Pardis, 2007), 265–66.

121. "We Celebrate Israel's Independence Day" was the main headline on the front page of *al-Ittihad*, 16 April 1950.

122. *Al-Ittihad*, 16 April 1950. Maki's continued use of this discourse despite the dispelling of illusions concerning the essence and policy of Israel provides us with another model of believers whose faith is not shaken by facts or reality.

123. Shmuel Mikunis, "Al-nidal min 'ajl al-salam was 'istiqlal is'rail" [The Struggle for Peace and Israel's Independence], Central Bureau's political report submitted to the Israeli Communist Party's Twelfth Congress, 29 May—1 June 1953 (Haifa, al-Ittihad, n.d.).

124. Mikunis, "Al-nidal min 'ajl al-salam."

125. *Al-Ittihad*, 17 April 1956.

126. *Al-Ittihad*, 21 October 1954 described the treaty for the withdrawal of British forces from the Suez Canal region as "the deed of treason and submission," and in the following week (29 October 1954) it attacked the regime of the Free Officers, and asked it to halt the policy of terrorism against its enemies.

127. *Al-Ittihad*, 3 September 1956, 3.

128. Thirteenth Congress of the Israeli Communist Party.

129. Thirteenth Congress of the Israeli Communist Party, 39–41, 45, 47.

130. Hanna Ibrahim described the anticommunist atmosphere on the eve of those elections in great detail, and spoke also of the tensions within the party when the results of those elections became known; see *Shajarat al-ma'rifa: dhikrayyat shab lam yaghtarib* [Tree of Knowledge: Memories of a Young Man Who Did Not Emigrate]. 'Akka: al-Aswar, 1996), 205–11.

131. The party won 22 percent of the Arab vote in 1949. There was a major reversal in 1959 even compared to the results of the 1955 elections.

132. Rashid Husain, "Hina yaju' al-tarikh" [When History Grows Hungry], *al-Fajr*, 12 November 1959.

EPILOGUE

1. *Al-Ittihad*, 23 November 1956, 1.

2. *Al-Ittihad*, 23 November 1956, 3.

3. The trial of those accused of the Kafr Qasim massacre began on 15 January 1957 before a military tribunal in Jerusalem.

4. Tawfiq Tubi, *Kafr Qasim: al-majzara wa al-'ibra* [Kafr Qasim: The Massacre and the Lesson] (Tel Aviv: Central Committee of the Communist Party, 1996), 33.

5. *Al-Ittihad*, 20 November 1956, 1.

6. Avivi makes it clear that the Maki party did not succeed in getting a foothold in Druze villages in the 1950s and did not win any votes there. See Shim'on Avivi, *Tas nihoshet: hamdinyut ha-yesra'ilit klapi ha-'ida ha-Druzit, 1948–67* [Copper Tray: The Israeli Policy towards the Druze Community, 1948–67] (Jerusalem: Yitzhak Ben-Tzvi, 2007), 347–48.

7. 'Abdel Rahim 'Iraqi gives an expansive description of those festivities which the military government organized in al-Tira. See: 'Abdel Rahim 'Iraqi, *La takhaf: mudhakarat 'ala sa'id al-khawf* [Don't Be Afraid: Memories About Fear] (Yafat al-Nasira: al-Tali'a, 1996), 355–64.

8. On 3 and 5 May 1949, *al-Yawm* published detailed reports on the participation of Arabs in Independence Day celebrations in Jaffa and 'Akka.

9. Arab villages in the Galilee and the Negev were under nightly curfew and their inhabitants were not allowed to spend an evening out in nearby Arab cities like 'Akka, Haifa, or Jaffa.

10. *Al-Ittihad*, 26 April 1952.

11. Yair Bäuml, *Tzel kakhul lavan: mdenyyut hamemsad hayesraeli u-pu'ulutav bkerev ha-'Arvim be-Yesrael-hashanin ha-mi'atzvut, 1958–68* [A Blue and White Shadow: the Israeli Establishment Policy and Actions Among Its Arab Citizens: The Formative Years, 1958–68] (Haifa: Pardis, 2007), 261–63.

12. Bäuml, *Tzel kakhul lavan*.

13. *Al-Ittihad*, 14 March 1958.

14. *Al-Ittihad*, 15 April 1958.

15. *Al-Ittihad*, 25 April 1958.

16. In addition to Yani Yani, Jabbur Jabbur, the mayor of Shafa 'Amr, Tahir al-Fahum, and Shukri al-Khazen were named as leaders of that front.

17. Bäuml, *Tzel Kakhul Lavan*, 278; *al-Ittihad*, 8 July 1958.

18. *Ma'ariv*, 11 July 1958, interviewed by Raphael Bashan, as quoted in Bäuml, *Blue and White Shadow*, 278.

19. As quoted in Bäuml, *Tzel Kakhul Lavan*, 278.

20. My thanks to Dr. Yoni Mandel who provided me with this document. This letter is among the collection of documents concerning Elias Kusa which were found in the Israel State Archives in Jerusalem.

21. In addition to the individuals named, there were also municipal council members from 'Akka, Nazareth, and Shafa 'Amr.

22. Among them were Ramzi Khuri and the attorney Hanna Naqqara. Missing from the list of signatories were members of the Knesset and well-known politicians from Maki and the Arab slates.

23. Among documents in the files of the prime minister's advisor on Arab affairs at the Israeli Central State Archives in Jerusalem.

24. Elias Kusa, *Quddat madaji'ihum* [The Sleepless] (Haifa: *al-Ittihad* Press, 1960).

25. Kusa, *Quddat madaji'ihum*, 1.

APPENDIX 1

1. Israeli Army and Security Forces Archives, Tel Aviv.

APPENDIX 2

1. Israeli Army and Security Forces Archives, Tel Aviv, file no. 632 [hand-written].

APPENDIX 3

1. Israeli Army and Security Forces Archives, Tel Aviv, document no. 616/13.

APPENDIX 4

1. Israeli Army and Security Forces Archives, Tel Aviv.

APPENDIX 5

1. Israeli Army and Security Forces Archives, Tel Aviv, file no. 107 [hand-written].

APPENDIX 6

1. Israeli Army and Security Forces Archives, Tel Aviv, file no. 580 [hand-written].

APPENDIX 7

1. Israeli Army and Security Forces Archives, Tel Aviv, file no. 43/1 [hand-written].

BIBLIOGRAPHY

ARCHIVES AND MANUSCRIPTS

Israeli Army and Security Forces Archives, Tel Aviv.

Labor Party Archives, Beit Berl.

Israeli State Archives, West Jerusalem.

Archives and manuscripts of Hashomer Hatzair, Giv'at Haviva.

Diverse papers and documents relating to the 1948 war, and to the events of the early 1950s pertaining to individuals I interviewed in their homes, who gave me copies of documents in their possession, for which I am grateful. Special thanks go to: Anis Srouji, Abu 'Isam (Nazareth); Elias Saliba Surur and Farid Zurayq ('Ilabun); the historian Butrus Abu-Manneh and his wife Na'ila, daughter of attorney Hanna Naqqara (Haifa); Muhammad Haydar, Abu Jamil (Majd al-Krum); Su'ad Bishara and her children (Tarshiha).

ORAL TESTIMONIES

I conducted personally over 120 interviews, and additionally some interviews in Nazareth were conducted by Ahmad Mruwwat, for which I am grateful. I began conducting those interviews in 1984. However, the vast majority were conducted between 2008 and 2011. Most interviews were in the Galilee villages Kufr Yasif, Majd al-Krum, al-Bi'na, Dayr al-Asad, Nahaf, Sha'b, al-Rama, 'Ilabun, Jish, Tarshiha, and Yarka. I also conducted a number of interviews in Haifa and Jerusalem and in various other villages in the Galilee and the Triangle.

I also conducted three official interviews with Jewish Israelis who were active eyewitnesses in the events of the 1948 war and in what was written about it: Benyamin Ghonin, a veteran communist in Haifa who fought for the establishment of Israel, and participated, wearing his military uniform, in the unity conference of the Maki party in Haifa; Tsvi

Rabinovich (Bahrav), known as "Khawaja Ghazal," an intelligence officer for the Haifa district in 1948 in Majd al-Krum and other Galilee villages; and Peretz Kidron, whom I interviewed in his home in Jerusalem (in 'Ayn Karim). Kidron revealed some details of the attempt to expel the people of Nazareth following its occupation which Ben Dunkelman decided not to publish in his autobiography.

OFFICIAL ISRAELI DOCUMENTS

Decisions of the Israeli Supreme Court of Justice.
Minutes of the Interim Government (1948–49).
Minutes of the Knesset (1949–56).

FILMS

Druri, Gideon, dir. *Al-Mutasha'il* [The Pessoptimist], Israeli television film series.
Hasan, Nizar, dir. *Istiqlal* [Independence]. Tel Aviv: Keshet, 1994.
Karpel, Dalia, dir. *Emile Habibi: Staying in Haifa*, film biography. Tel Aviv, 1997.
———. *Yomane Yosef Nahmani*. Tel Aviv, 2005.
Zurayq, Hisham, dir. *Abna' 'Ilabun* [The People of 'Ilabun], 2007.

NEWSPAPERS AND PERIODICALS

Adala. Periodical of the Legal Center for the Defense of the Arab Minority in Israel.
Haaretz. Hebrew daily (Tel Aviv).
'Al Hamishmar. Newspaper of the Mapam party (1943–95).
Al-Ittihad. Newspaper of the 'Usbat al-Tahrir al-Watani [National Liberation League] (Jaffa, 1947).
Al-Ittihad. Communist Party-Maki party newspaper (Haifa, 1948–58).
Al-Jadid. Monthly periodical published by the Communist Party (Haifa, 1954–56).
Kol Ha'am. Newspaper of the Israeli Communist Party, Maki (1937–75).
Ma'ariv. Hebrew daily (1948–).
Masharif. Monthly periodical (Jerusalem and Haifa), esp. nos. 9 and 16 (1996–97), concerned with the life of Emile Habibi and his death.
Nir. Monthly periodical of Ihud, followers of Judah Magnes and others in the early 1950s.
Ha-Olam Hazeh. (*Hadha al-'Alam*). Weekly of the activist politician Uri Avneri (1937–93).
Al-Rabita. Monthly magazine of the Catholic Church (Haifa, 1949–56).
Sedeq. Magazine of al-Nakba al-Qa'ima (Tel Aviv, Zochrot, 2007–12).
Al-Yawm. Arabic newspaper of Hisdatrut (Jaffa, 1948–58).

BOOKS AND ARTICLES

Arabic

'Abassi, Mustafa. *Al-Jishsh: tarikh qarya Jaliliyya* [Al-Jishsh: The History of a Galilee Village]. Al-Jishsh: al-Majlis al-Mahalli, 2010.
'Abd al-Jawad, Salih. "Limadha la nastati' kitabat tarikhina al-mu'asir duna istikhdam al-masadir al-shafawiyya?" In *Nahwa siyaghat riwaya tarikhiyya li al-Nakba: Ishkaliyyat wa*

tahadiyyat [Toward Recounting the Nakba: Forms and Challenges], edited by Mustafa Kabha. Haifa: Mada al-Karmil, 2006.

Abu Hanna, Hanna. *Dhill al-ghayma: sira dhatiyya* [The Cloud's Shadow: Autobiography]. Nazareth: Dar al-Thaqafa, 1997.

———. *Khamirat al-ramad, al-Sira al-dhatiyyah*, Part 2 [The Yeast of Ashes: Autobiography]. Haifa: Maktabat Kul Shay', 2004.

———. *Mahr al-buma al-Sira al-dhatiyyah*, Part 3 [The Owl's Dowry: Autobiography]. Haifa: Maktabat Kul Shay', 2004.

Abu Hasna, Nafidh, ed. *Khalid al-Fahum Yatadhakkar* [Khalid Fahum Remembers]. Beirut: al-Ruwwadl lil-Tiba'a wa al-Nashr, 1999.

Abu Ras, 'Abd al-Raziq. *Qalansuwa: ma'alim wa ahdath* [Qalansuwa: Landmarks and Events]. Tulkarm: al-Matba'a al-Ahliyya, 1999.

Al-'Adhma, 'Aziz. *Constantine Zurayk: 'Arabi li al-qarn al-'ishrin* [Constantine Zurayk: A Twentieth Century Arab]. Beirut: Institute for Palestine Studies, 2003.

Aghbariyya, Husayn, ed. *Yahkun Haifa: hikayat min dhakirat ahliha* [They Speak of Haifa: Stories from the Memories of Its Inhabitants]. Haifa: Jam'iyat al-Tatwir al-Ijtima'i, 2010.

Al-'Alami, Musa. *'Ibrat Filastin* [The Lesson of Palestine]. Beirut: Dar al-Kashaf, 1949. Republished in *Nakbat 1948: asbabiha wa subul 'ilajiha* [The Nakba 1948: Its Reasons and the Means of Solution], edited by Walid al-Khalidi. Beirut: Institute for Palestine Studies, 2009.

Al-'Alami, Sa'd al-Din. *Watha'iq al-Hay'a al-Islamiyya al-'Ulya* [Documents of the Higher Islamic Committee: Jerusalem, 1967–1984]. Amman: Dar al-Karmil, 1986.

'Ali, Yasir Ahmad, et al. *Sha'b wa hamiyatiha: qaryat Sha'b al-Jaliliyya wa al-difa' 'anha* [Sha'b and its Garrison: The Galilee Village of Sha'b and Its Defense]. Beirut: Thabit, al-Munadhdhama al-Filastiniyya li Haqq al-'Awda, 2007.

'Aql, Muhammad. *Al-Mufassal fi tarikh Wadi 'Ara* [A Detailed History of Wadi 'Ara]. Jerusalem: Matba'at al-Sharq al-Arabiyya, 1999.

Al-'Arif, 'Arif. *Al-Nakba: Nakbat Bayt al-Maqdis wa l-firdaws al-mafqud 1947–49* [The Catastrophe: The Catastrophe of Jerusalem and the Lost Paradise 1947–49]. Sidon: al-Maktaba al-'Asriyya, 1956–61. Vol. 7. Republished in 3 vols.: Beirut: Institute for Palestine Studies, 2012, 2013.

'Arraf, Shukri. *Lamsat waf . . . wa . . .* [Touches of Loyalty . . . wa]. Mi'lya: Markaz al-Dirasat al-Qurawiyya, 2007.

Al-'Ashhab, 'Awda. *Tadhakkurat 'Awda al-'Ashhab: sira dhatiyya* [The Memories of 'Awda al-'Ashhab: An Autobiography]. Birzeit: Birzeit University, 1999.

Al-'Ashhab, Na'im. *Durub al-alam . . . durub al-amal* [Paths of Pain . . . Paths of Hope]. Ramallah: Dar al-Tanwir, 2009.

Al-'Awdat, Ya'qub. *Min a'lam al-fikr wa al-adab fi Filastin* [Major Intellectuals and Literary Figures in Palestine]. Jerusalem: Dar al-Isra', 1992.

'Awna, 'Isa Muhammad Dhiyab. *'Arab al-Subayh: tarikh wa riwaya* [Al-Subayh Arabs: A History and a Tale]. Kufr Kana: Matba'at Dar al-Hikma, 2006.

Al-Az'ar, Muhammad Khalid. *Hukumat 'umum Filastin fi dhikraha al-khamsin* [The All-Palestine Government on its Fiftieth Anniversary]. Beirut: Dar al-Shuruq, 1998.

Badr, Dawud. *al-Ghabisiyya: baqiya abadan fi al-qalb wa al-dhakira* [Al-Ghabisiyya Will Live Forever in Our Hearts and Memory]. Self-published, 2002.

Al-Barghuthi, Bashir Sharif. *Fu'ad Nassar: al-rajul wa al-qadiyya* [Fu'ad Nassar: The Man and the Cause]. Jerusalem: Dar Salah al-Din, 1977.

Al-Bash, Ahmad. "Majzarat qaryat 'Illut" [The Massacre in 'Illut Village]. *Al-'Awda* (August 2008).

Ben-Gurion, David. *Yawmiyyat al-harb, 1947–49* [War Diaries, 1947–49]. Edited by Gershon Rivlin and Elhanan Oren. Translated by Samir Jabbur. Beirut: Institute for Palestine Studies, 1993; 1998.

Beshr-Saffuri, Muhammad Amin. *Saffuriyya: tarikh, hadara wa turath* [Saffuriyya: History, Existence, and Heritage]. 2 vols. Nazareth, Maktab al-Nuris li al-Inma' al-Tarbawi, 2000.

———. *'Illut 'abr al-tarikh* ['Illut through History]. Nazareth: Maktab al-Nuris, 2002.

Bishara, Jibra'il Butrus. *Jibra'il Butrus Bishara: 1925–2005*. Tarshiha: family-published, 2006.

Al-Budayri, Musa. *Shuyu'iyyun fi filastin: shadhaya tarikh mansi* [Communists in Palestine: Fragments of a Forgotten History]. Ramallah: Muwatin, al-Mu'assasa al-filastiniyya li dirasat al-dimuqratiyya, 2013.

Bulus, Habib, ed. *Sami Juraysi, 1922–1999: Bayn 'azimat al-shabab wa hikmat al-shuyukh, sirat al-'ata* [Sami Juraysi, 1922–1999: Between the Greatness of Youth and the Wisdom of Old Age: a Biography of Giving]. Nazareth: Venus, 2000.

Cohen, Hillel. *Al-Gha'ibun al-hadirun: al-laji'un al-Filastiniyyun fi Isra'il mundhu sanat 1948* [The Present Absentees: Palestinian Refugees in Israel Since 1948]. Jerusalem: Markaz Dirasat al-Mujtama' al-Arabi, 2002; Beirut: Institute for Palestine Studies, 2003. In Hebrew, Jerusalem: Van Leer Press, 2000.

Fallah, Ghazi. *Al-Jalil wa mukhattatat al-tahwid* [The Galilee and the Judaization Plans]. Translated by Mahmud Zayid. Beirut: Institute for Palestine Studies, 1993.

Farah, Bulus. *Min al-'Uthmaniyya ila al-dawla al-'Ibriyya* [From the Ottoman Empire to the Hebrew State]. Haifa: al-Sawt, 1985.

Ghanim, Hunaida, "Al-Hudud wa al-hayat al-sirriyya li al-muqawama al-yawmiyya: qaryat al-Marja al-Filastiniyya, 1949–1967" [The Borders and The Secret Life of Daily Resistance: The Palestinian Village of Marja, 1949–1967]. *Journal of Palestine Studies* 102 (Spring 2015): 121–43.

Ghattas, Ghattas. *Al-Bustan al-'amir wa al-rawd al-zahir* [The Resplendent Garden and the Flowering Meadow]. Al-Rama: self-published, 2001.

Habibi, Emile. "Bawwabat Mandelbaum" [Mandelbaum Gate]. *Al-Jadid*, 5 March 1954.

———. *al-Waqa'i' al-ghariba fi ikhtifa' Sa'id Abi al-Nahs al-Mutasha'il* [The Strange Circumstances Surrounding the Disappearance of Sa'id Abu al-Nahs, the Pessoptimist]. Haifa: Al-Ittihad Press, 1974. 3rd ed., Jerusalem: Dar Salah al-Din, 1977.

———. "Al-Hiwar al-akhir" [The Last Interview]. *Masharif*, 9 June 1996.

———. "Emile Habibi: Hiwar qabl 'ishrin 'aman" [An Interview Twenty Years Ago]. Interview by Mahmud Shurayh, edited by Saqr Abu Fakhr. *Journal of Palestine Studies* 96 (Autumn 2013): 172–90.

Al-Haj Ibrahim, Rashid. *al-Difa' 'an Haifa wa qadiyyat Filastin: Mudhakkarat Rashid al-Haj Ibrahim, 1891–1953* [The Defense of Haifa and the Palestinian Cause: The Memoirs of Rashid al-Hajj Ibrahim, 1891–1953]. Introduction by Walid al-Khalidi. Beirut: Institute for Palestine Studies, 2005.

Halabi, Usama. *Al-Durue fi Isra'il: min ta'ifa ila sha'b?* [The Druze in Israel: From a Sect to a People?] Golan, Syria: Association of University Students in the Golan, 1989.

Hanna, George. *Tariq al-khalas: tahlil wad'i li mihnat Filastin wa al-qadaya al-Arabiyya* [The Path to Deliverance: A Situational Analysis of Palestine's Affliction and Arab Issues].

Beirut: Dar al-Ahad, 1948. Republished in *Nakbat 1948: asbabiha wa subul 'ilajiha* [The Nakba 1948: Its Reasons and the Means of Solution], edited by Walid al-Khalidi. Beirut: Institute for Palestine Studies, 2009.

Al-Hawwari, Muhammad Nimr. *Sirr al-Nakba* [The Secret of the Nakba]. Nazareth: Matba'at al-Hakim, 1955.

Husayn, Rashid. "Heena yaju' al-tarikh" [When History Grows Hungry]. *Al-Fajr* 12 (November 1959).

Al-Hut, Bayan Nuwaihid. *Al-Qiyadat wa al-mu'assasat al-siyasiyya fi Filastin, 1917–1948* [The Leaders and Political Institutions in Palestine, 1917–48]. 3rd ed. Beirut: Institute for Palestine Studies, 1986.

Ibrahim, Hanna. "Al-Mutasallilun" [The Infiltrators]. *Al-Jadid* 6, April 1954.

———, ed. *Hanna Naqqara: Muhami al-ard wa-sha'b* [Hanna Naqqara: Lawyer for the Land and the People]. 'Akka: al-Aswar, 1985.

———. *Shajarat al-ma'rifa: dhikrayyat shab lam yaghtarib* [Tree of Knowledge: Memories of a Young Man Who Did Not Emigrate]. 'Akka: 'Al-Aswar, 1996.

'Iraqi, 'Abd al-Rahim. *La takhaf: dhikrayyat 'ala sa'id al-khawf* [Don't Be Afraid: Memories About Fear]. Yaffat al-Nasira: al-Tala'i', 1996.

Jiryis, Sabri. *Al-Arab fi Isra'il* [The Arabs in Israel]. Haifa: al-Ittihad Press, 1966.

Kabha, Mustafa, ed. *Nahwa siyaghat riwaya tarikhiyya li al-Nakba: ishkaliyyat wa tahadiyyat* [Toward Recounting the Nakba: Forms and Challenges]. Haifa: Mada Karmil, 2006.

Kabha, Mustafa, and Nimr Sirhan. *Bilad al-rawha fi fatrat al-intidab al-Baritani* [The Land of the Evening Journey During the British Mandate]. Ramallah: Dar al-Shuruq, 2004.

Kabha, Mustafa, and Wadi' 'Awawda. *'Asra bila hirab: al-mu'taqalun al-Filastiniyyun wa al-mu'taqalat al-Isra'iliyya al-ula, 1948–49* [Prisoners with No Spears: Palestinian Detainees and the First Israeli Detention Centers, 1948–49]. Beirut: Institute for Palestine Studies, 2013.

Kanafani, Ghassan. *'Awd ila Haifa* [Returning to Haifa]. Beirut: Dar al-'Awda, 1969.

———. *Quddat madaji'ihum* [The Sleepless]. Haifa: Matba'at al-Ittihad, 1960.

Al-Khalidi, Walid. *Dayr Yasin: al-jum'a 9 April 1948* [Dayr Yasin: Friday, 9 April 1948]. Beirut: Institute for Palestine Studies, 1999.

———. "Walid al-Khalidi: Tahiyya" [Walid al-Khalidi: Greetings]. *Majallat al-Dirasat al-Filastiniyya* no. 96 (Autumn 2013): 279–447.

———, ed. *Nakba 1948: asbabiha wa subul 'ilajiha* [The Nakba 1948: Its Causes and the Means of Solutions]. Beirut: Institute for Palestine Studies, 2009.

Khoury, Elias. *Bab al-shams*. Beirut: Dar al-Adab, 1998. Translated by Humphrey Davies as *Gate of the Sun* (London: Vintage, 2006).

Kretzmer, David. *Al-Makana al-qanuniyya li al-'Arab fi Isra'il* [The Legal Status of Arabs in Israel]. Jerusalem: Markaz Dirasat al-Mujtama' al-'Arabi, 2002; revised and expanded translation of David Kreztmer, *The Legal Status of Arabs in Israel*. Boulder, CO: Westview Press, 1990.

Kusa, Elias. "Man huwa al-mudallal?" [Who Is the Deceiver?]. al-Rabita 8–9, September/October 1955, 25–28.

Ma'di, Mansur Khudur. *Rajul al-karamat, 'utufat al-maghfur lahu al-Shaykh Jabr Dahish Ma'di: mawaqif, tahaddiyat wa injazat* [The Man Through Whom God Worked Miracles, His Excellency Shaykh Jabr Dahesh M'adi: Positions, Challenges and Achievements]. Yarka: family-published, 2014.

Manna', Adel. "Majd al-Krum 1948: 'Amaliyyat tamshit 'adiyya" [Majd al-Krum 1948: Ordinary Combing Operations]. *Al-Karmel* 55–56 (Spring/Summer 1998): 184–200.

———. "Hikayat Zahra al-Ja'uniyya" [The Story of Zahra al-Ja'uniyya]. *Hawliyyat al-Quds* 6 (Winter-Spring 2008): 67–81.

Manna', Adel, and Motti Golani. *Wajha al-'imla: al-istiqlal wa al-Nakba, sardiyyatan hawla harb 1948 wa nat'ijaha [Two Faces of a Coin: Independence and Nakba, Two Accounts of the 1948 War and Its Results].* English and Arabic. Holland: Institute for Historical Justice and Reconciliation Institute, Republic of Letters, 2011.

Masalha, Nur al-Din. *Ard akthar wa 'Arab aqall* [Maximum Land, Minimum Arabs: The Israeli Transfer Policy in Action]. Beirut: Institute for Palestine Studies, 2002.

Mua'mar, Tawfiq. *Al-Mutasallil wa qisas ukhra* [The Infiltrator and Other Stories]. Nazareth: Matba'at al-Hakim, 1957.

Murqus, Nimr, ed. *Yani Qustandi Yani, 1895–1962*. Kufr Yasif: al-Majlis al-Mahalli, 1987.

———. *Aqwa min al-nisyan: Risala ila ibnati* (1) [More Powerful than Forgetfulness: A Letter to My Daughter (1)]. Tarshiha: Makhkhul wa Hazbun, 2000.

Musa, Nadim. *Dhikrayyat shuyu'i mukhadram* [Memories of a Veteran Communist]. 'Akka: Matba'at Abu Rahmun, 2008.

Al-Mu'tamar al-thalith 'ashr li al-hizb al-shuyu'i al-Isra'ili: 29 May–1 June 1957 [The 13th Conference of the Israeli Communist Party]. Haifa: Issued by the Central Committee, 1957.

Al-Nashashibi, Nasir al-Din, Salah Ibrahim al-Nather and Muhammad Sa'id Ishkantna. *Yaffa li al-abad, kama 'ayashaha Nasir al-Din al-Nashashibi wa Salah Ibrahim al-Nadhir wa Muhammad Sa'id Ishkantana.* [Jaffa Forever, as Experienced by Naser al-Din al-Nashashibi and Salah Ibrahim al-Nather and Muhammad Sa'id Ishkantna]. Introduction by 'Ali Mas'ud al-Darhali. Beirut: al-Mu'assasa al-'Arabiyya li al-Dirasat wa al-Nashr, 2013.

Pappé, Ilan. *Al-Tathir al-'irqi fi filastin* [The Ethnic Cleansing of Palestine]. Beirut: Institute for Palestine Studies, 2007.

Palestinian Encyclopedia Committee [Hay'at al-Mawsu'a al-Filastiniyya]. *Al-Mawsu'a al-Filastiniyya, Al-qism al-'am* [The Palestinian Encyclopedia: The General Studies Part]. Vol. 4. Beirut: Hay'at al-Mawsu'a al-Filastiniyya, 1984.

Qubti, 'Atallah Sa'ad, ed. *Mudhakkarat muhami Filastini: Hanna Dib Naqqara, muhami al-ard wa sha'b* [Memories of the Palestinian Lawyer: Hanna Dib Naqqara, the People's and Land Lawyer]. Beirut: Institute for Palestine Studies, 2011.

Qahwaji, Habib. *Al-'Arab fi dhill al-ihtilal al-Isra'ili mundhu 1948* [Arabs under the Shadow of Israeli Occupation Since 1948]. Beirut: Palestine Liberation Organization, Research Center, 1972.

Al-Rayyis, Fayiz Hasan. *Al-Qura al-junubiyya al-sabi': Dirasa watha'iqiyya shamila* [The Seven Southern Villages: A Comprehensive Documentary Study]. Beirut: Mu'assasat al-Wafa', 1985.

Sa'd, Ahmad. *Judhur al-shajara dai'mat al-Khudra* [The Roots of the Evergreen Tree]. Haifa: Ma'had Emile Tuma, 1996.

Al-Sakakini, Khalil. *Yawmiyyat Khalil al-Sakakini: yawmiyyat. rasa'il, ta'ammulat, al-kitab al-thamin: al-khuruj min al-Qatamun, 1942–1952* [The Diaries of Khalil al-Sakakini: Diaries, Letters, Insights, Book Eight: Leaving al-Qatamun, 1942–52]. Edited by Akram Muslim. Ramallah: Markaz Khalil al-Sakakini al-Thaqafi wa Mu'assasat al-Dirasat al-Maqdisiyya, 2010.

Susan, Najib. *Sada al-ayyam* [Echo of the Days]. Haifa: Self-published, 2001.

Susan, Yusif. *Shahadati: Yawmiyyat Bir'imiyya, 1948–68* [My Testimony: Bir'im Diaries] N.P.: self-published, 1986.

Sultani, Nimr, ed. *Muwatinun bila muwatana: Isra'il wa al-aqaliyya al-Filastiniyya, taqrir Mada al-sanawi li al-rasd al-siyasi, 2000–2002* [Citizens Without Citizenship: Israel and the Palestinian Minority, Mada's Annual Political Monitoring Report], Haifa: Mada al-Karmil, al-Markaz al-Arabi li al-Dirasat al-Ijtima'iyya al-Tatbiqiyya, 2003.

Surur, Elias Saliba. *'Ilabun: Tarikh wa dhikrayyat* ['Ilabun: History and Memories]. Nazareth: Matba'at al-Hakim, 1997.

———. *Al-Nakba fii 'Ilabun*. [The Nakba in 'Ilabun]. 'Ilabun: al-Majlis al-Mahalli, 1998.

Shoufani, Elias. *Rihla fi al-rahil: fusul min al-dhakira . . . lam taktamel* [A Journey in Departure: Chapters of Memory . . . not completed]. Beirut: Dar al-Kunuz al-Adabiyya, 1994.

Al-Tal, 'Abdullah. *Karithat filastin: mudhakkarat 'Abdullah al-Tal, Qa'id ma'rakat al-Quds* [The Tragedy of Palestine: The Memoirs of Abdullah al-Tal, Commander of the Battle for Jerusalem]. Cairo: Dar al-Qalam, 1959; Kufr Qari': Dar al-Huda, 1990.

Tubi, Tawfiq. *Kufr Qasim: al-majzara wa al-'ibra* [Kafr Qasim: The Massacre and the Lesson]. Tel Aviv: Central Committee of the Communist Party, 1996.

Al-Zu'bi, Sayf al-Din. *Shahid 'ayan: Mudhakkarat Sayf al-Din al-Zu'bi* [Eyewitness: The Memoirs of Sayf-al-Din al-Zu'bi]. Shafa 'Amr: Dar al-Mashriq, 1987.

Zurayk, Constantine. *Ma'na al-nakba* [Meaning of the Catastrophe]. Beirut: Dar al-'Ilm li al-Malayin, 1948. Republished in *Nakba 1948: asbabiha wa subul 'ilajiha* [The Nakba 1948: Its Causes and the Means of Solutions], edited by Walid al-Khalidi. Beirut: Institute for Palestine Studies, 2009.

Hebrew

Avivi, Shim'on. *Tas Nihoshet: hamdinyut ha-yesra'ilit klapi ha-'ida ha-Druzit, 1948–67.* [Copper Tray: The Israeli Policy Towards the Druze Community, 1948–67]. Jerusalem: Yitzhak Ben-Tzvi Center, 2007.

Amitay, Yossi. *Achvat 'Amim Bamivhan: Mapam 1948–54* [The Brotherhood of Peoples Tested: Mapam 1948–54]. Tel Aviv: Tcherikover, 1988.

Beki, Roberto. *'Arikhat reshum ha-tushavim be 8 be-November 1948* [The Population Census: Counting on 8 November 1948]. Jerusalem: Central Bureau of Statistics, 1949.

Bäuml, Ya'ir. *Tzel kakhul lavan: mdenyyut hamemsad ha-Yesraeli u-pu'ulutav bkerev ha-'Arvim be-Yesrael-hashanin ha-bi'atzvut, 1958–68* [A Blue and White Shadow: The Israeli Establishment Policy and Actions Among Its Arab Citizens: The Formative Years, 1958–68]. Haifa: Pardis, 2007.

Be'eri (Bauer), Eliezer. "Sha'ruriyat Nazret" [Nazareth Scandal]. *'Al Hamishmar*, 18 August 1949.

Benziman, 'Uzi, and 'Atallah Mansur. *Dayyari meshne: 'Arveyyi Yesrael, ma'madam ve-hamdenyut klapeihim* [Sub-Tenants: The Israeli Arabs: Their Status and Policies Toward Them]. Jerusalem: Keter, 1992.

Cohen, 'Aharon. *Yisrael ve-ha'ulam ha'rbi* [Israel and the Arab World]. Tel Aviv: The Workers' Library, 1964.

Cohen, Orna. "'Arveyyi Majdal (Ashkelon) tmurut be-matzavam memelhemet 1948 ve-'ad le-penuyyam memdinat Yesra'il" [Al-Majdal Arabs: Status Transformations Between the War of 1948 Until Their Exile from Israel]. MA thesis, Hebrew University, September 1999.

Cohen, Ra'nan. *Besvakh ha-ne'manyyut: hevra ve-politica ba-megzar ha-'Arvi* [Battle of Loyalties: Society and Politics in the Arab Minority]. Tel Aviv: 'Am Oved, 1986.

Cohen, Hillel. *'Arvim tuvim: ha-mudi'een ha-Yisra'eli ve-Harvim be-Yesra'el* [The Good Arabs: Israeli Intelligence and the Arabs in Israel]. Jerusalem: Keter, 2006.

Dotan, Shamu'el. *Adumim: hameflaga ha-kumunistit be-Eretz Yesrael* [The Reds: The Communist Party in the Land of Israel]. Kafr Saba: Shibna Hasovir, 1991.

Dunkelman, Ben. *N'manut kfula* [Dual Loyalty: A Personal Journey]. Jerusalem and Tel Aviv: Shukin, 1975.

Erlich, Reuven. *Besvakh ha-Levanon, 1918–58* [The Predicament of Lebanon, 1918–58]. Tel Aviv: Security Ministry, 2006.

Gelber, Yoav. *Komimyut ve-Nakba: Yesrael, ha-Falastinimu-medinut 'arav, 1948* [Independence and Nakba: Israel, the Palestinians and the Arab States in 1948]. Tel Aviv: Zamora Beitan, 2004.

Golani, Motti. *Tehyye melhama ba-kayetz, 1955–56* [There Will be a War This Summer: Israel on the Road to the Sinai War, 1955–56]. Tel Aviv: Ma'rakhot, 1997.

———. *Yamim ahrunim: hamemshal hamandaturi-pennuy ve-melhama* [The Last Days: The Mandate Government, Withdrawal and the War]. Jerusalem: Zalman Shazar Center, 2009.

Hashnatun ha-statsti ha-Yesra'ili [Israeli Annual Census (book)]. Vol. 2. Jerusalem: Central Bureau of Statistics, 1951.

Hazan, Haim, and Daniel Monterescu. *'Ir been 'Arbayem: Le'umiyyut mezdakenet be-Yafo* [A City at Sunset: An Aging Nationalism in Jaffa]. Jerusalem: Van Leer Academy and Unified Kibbutz, 2011.

Jabareen, Hassan. "Ha-Nakba, Hameshbat ve Haneman'ut: Harega' Habosiani shel haFalastinem be Yesrael." [The Nakba, the Law and the Loyality: The Hobbesian Moment of the Palestinians in Israel]. *Teorya ve Beqoret* 42 (Spring 2014): 13–46.

Kadish, Elon, ed. *Melhemet ha-'atzma'ut, 1947–1949: diyyun mehuddash* [War of Independence 1947–49: Renewed Discussion]. 2 vols. Ministry of Security, 2004.

Kamen, Charles. "Akhre ha-'ason: ha-'Arvim be-mdinat Yesrael, 1948–51" [After the Nakba: The Arabs in the State of Israel, 1948–51]. *Mahbarut le-mekhkar ve-bekkuret* [Notebooks for Study and Critique] 10 (1984).

Karmel, Moshe. *Ma'rakhut ha-tzafun* [The Battles of the North]. Tel Aviv: The Army and Unified Kibbutz, 1949.

Kenis ha'hadut shel hakuministim hayihudim ve-ha'rvim be Maki [Conference of the Union of Jewish and Arab Communists under the Auspices of the Israeli Communist Party]. Haifa, 22–23 October 1948.

Korn, Alina. "Psha', status politi ve-akhifat khuk: ha-mi'ut ha-'Arvi be-Yisrael betkufat hamemshal hatzva'I (1948–66)" [Criminal Activities, Political Status and Implementation of the Law: The Arab Minority in Israel under Military Rule (1948–66)]. PhD diss., Hebrew University School of Law, Jerusalem, 1997.

Kusa, Elias. "Tshuva le-Moshe Sharrett" [Response to Prime Minister Moshe Sharrett]. *Nir*, 31 August 1951.

Landau, Ya'cov. *Ha-'Arvim be-Yesrael: 'iyyunim polityyim* [The Arabs in Israel: Political Analysis]. Tel Aviv: Ministry of Security, 1971.

Lexicon ha-ishim beeretz Yesrael [Dictionary of Palestinian Personalities, 1799–1948]. Tel Aviv: 'Am Oved, 1983.

Lustick, Ian. *'Aravim bamdina hayehudit* [Arabs in the Jewish State]. Haifa: Mifras Publishing House, 1985.

Morris, Benny. *Lidata shel ba'yat ha-plitim ha-Falastinim, 1947–49* [The Birth of the Palestinian Refugee Problem, 1947–49]. Tel Aviv: 'Am Oved, 1991.

———. *1948: Toldut ha-melhama ha-'Arvit ha-Yesraelit ha-rishona* [1948: A History of the First Arab-Israeli War]. Tel Aviv: 'Am Ovid, 2010.

———. *Melhamut ha-gvul shel Yesrael, 1949–56* [Israel's Border Wars, 1949–56]. Tel Aviv: 'Am Oved, 1996.

———. *Tekkun ta'ut* [Correcting a Mistake: Jews and Arabs in Palestine/Israel 1936–1956]. Tel Aviv: Am Oved, 2000.

Noy [Neustadt], Melekh. *Bereshit ve-b'asur ha-rishon le-mdinat Yesraeil* [The Beginning and the First Decade of the State of Israel]. Tel Aviv: Newman Press, 1958.

Osetski-Lazar, Sarah. *Iqrit ve-Bir'm: ha-sippur ha-male* [Iqrit and Bir'im: The Whole Story]. Givat Haviva: Institute for Arab Studies/Institute for Peace Studies, 1993).

———. "Ha-Memshal ha-tsva'i ke-mangnon le-shlita ba-ezrahim ha-'aravim: ha'asor ha-rishon, 1948–58" [The Military Government as a Control Mechanism over Arab Citizens: The First Decade, 1948–1956]. *Hamezrah Hahadash* 43 (2002): 103–32.

———. "Kfar Qari', 1948–49: ha'ziva vi-hashiva" [Kufr Qari', 1948–49: Migration and Return]. Unpublished paper presented at a conference on the 1948 war, Jerusalem: Van Leer Institute, 2010.

Rabin, Yitzhak. *Penkas sherut* [Service Identity Card]. Vol. 1. Tel Aviv: Ma'ariv Bookstore, 1979.

Rabinowitz, Danny, and Khawla Abu-Bakr. *Hadur ha-zakuf* [The Stand-Tall Generation: The Palestinian Citizens of Israel Today]. Jerusalem: Keter, 2002.

Rechess, Eli. *Ha-Me'ut ha-'Arvi be-Yesrael: bein kumunizim le-le'umiyyut 'Arvit, 1965–91* [The Arab Minority in Israel Between Communism and Arab Nationalism]. Tel Aviv: Unified Kibbutz, 1993.

Rosenthal, Ruvik, ed. *Kfar Qasim: iru'im ve-metus* [Kafr Qasim: Events and Legend]. Tel Aviv: United Kibbutz, 2000.

Segev, Tom. *1949: Hayestaelim hareshonim* [1949: The First Israelis]. Jerusalem: Domino, 1984.

———. "ha-Sodut ha-reshonim" [The First Secrets]. *Haaretz*, 3 February 1995.

———. "Asun ha-plitim nedha lzman mah" [The Refugee Crisis Has Been Postponed for Awhile]. *Haaretz*, 15 March 2015.

Sela, Abraham. "Tzva ha-hatzla ba-Galil be-melemet 1948" [The Arab Liberation Army in the Galilee in the 1948 War]. In *Melhemet Ha'atzma'ut: 1947–49, Diyyun Mehuddash* [War of Independence 1947–49, Renewed Discussion], edited by Elon Kadish, 1: 207–68. Tel Aviv: Ministry of Security, 2004.

Shavit, Ari. "Mehake la-Barbarim, Benny Morris" [Waiting for the Barbarians: An Interview with Benny Morris]. *Haaretz*, 6 January 2004.

Stendahl, Uri. *'Arveyyi Yesrael bein hapatish la-sadan* [Arabs of Israel Between the Mortar and Pestle]. Jerusalem: Academon, 1992.

[Smilansky], S. Yizhar. *Khirbet Khiz'eh.* Jerusalem: Ibis Editions, 2008 (1949).

Zu'bi, Nadir. "Ha-Tefruset ha-merhavit shel tuf'at hameha'h bekerev hayeshuvim ha-'Arvim, 1949–66" [The Geography of Protest in the Villages of Galilee under Military Rule, 1949–66]. PhD diss., Haifa University, 2007.

English

Abbasi, Mustafa. "The Battle for Safad in the War of 1948: A Revised Study." *International Journal of Middle East Studies* 36, no. 1 (February 2004): 21–47.

———. "The End of Arab Tiberias: The 1948 Battle for the City." *Journal of Palestine Studies* 37, no. 3 (Spring 2008): 6–29.

———. "The Fall of Acre in the 1948 Palestine War." *Journal of Palestine Studies* 39, no. 4 (Summer 2010): 6–27.

———. *The Cities of Galilee During the 1948 War: Four Cities and Four Stories*. Germany: Lambert Academic Publishing, 2014.

Abdel-Jawad, Saleh. "The Arab and Palestinian Narratives of the 1948 War." In *Israeli and Palestinian Narratives of the Conflict*, edited by Robert I. Rotberg, 72–114. Bloomington: Indiana University Press, 2006.

———. "Zionist Massacres: The Creation of the Palestinian Refugee Problem in the 1948 War." In *Israel and the Palestinian Refugees*, edited by Eyal Benvenisti, Haim Ganz, and Sari Hanafi, 59–127. Berlin: Springer, 2007.

Abu-Ghosh, Subhi. "The Politics of an Arab Village in Israel." PhD diss., Princeton University, 1965.

El-Asmar, Fouzi. *To Be an Arab in Israel*. Beirut: Institute for Palestine Studies, 1978.

Baransi, Salih. "The Story of a Palestinian under Occupation." *Journal of Palestine Studies* 11, no.1 (Autumn 1981): 3–30.

Bashir, Bashir, and Amos Goldberg, eds. *The Holocaust and the Nakba: A New Grammar of Trauma and History*. New York: Columbia University Press, 2018.

Beinin, Joel. *Was the Red Flag Flying There? Marxist Politics and the Arab Israeli Conflict in Egypt and Israel, 1948–1965*. Berkeley: University of California Press, 1990.

———. "Forgetfulness for Memory: The Limits of the New Israeli History." *Journal of Palestine Studies* 39, no. 2 (Winter 2005): 6–23.

Ben-Ze'ev, Efrat. *Remembering Palestine in 1948: Beyond National Narratives*. New York: Cambridge University Press, 2011.

Benvenisti, Meron. *Sacred Landscape: The Buried History of the Holy Land Since 1948*. Berkeley: University of California Press, 2000.

Bilsky, Leora. *Transformative Justice: Israeli Identity on Trial*. Ann Arbor: University of Michigan Press, 2004.

Bracha, Oren. "Confusion about Whether They Are Helpless or Dangerous: The Infiltrators, the Law and the Supreme Court of Justice, 1948–1954." *'Iyyuni mishpat* 21, no. 2 (April 1998): 333–85.

Budayri, Musa. *The Palestine Communist Party, 1919–1948: Arab and Jew in the Struggle for Internationalism*. London: Ithaca Press, 1979.

Caplan, Neil. *The Israel–Palestine Conflict: Contested History*. Chichester, UK: Wiley–Blackwell, 2010.

Cohen, Hillel. *Army of Shadows: Palestinian Collaboration with Zionism, 1917–1948*. Translated by Haim Watzman. Berkeley: University of California Press, 2008.

———. *Good Arabs: The Israeli Security Agencies and the Israeli Arabs, 1948–1967*. Berkeley: University of California Press, 2010.

Cohen, Stanley. *Crime, Justice and Social Control in the Israeli Arab Population*. Tel Aviv: International Center for Peace in the Middle East, 1989.

Dallasheh, Leena. "Nazarenes in the Turbulent Tide of Citizenship: Nazareth from 1940 to 1966." PhD diss., New York University, 2012.

Elkins, Caroline, and Susan Pedersen, eds. *Settler Colonialism in the Twentieth Century: Projects, Practices, Legacies*. New York: Routledge, 2005.

Firro, Kais. *The Druzes in the Jewish State: A Brief History*. Leiden: Brill, 1999.

Forman, Geremy. "Military Rule, Manipulation and Jewish Settlement: Israeli Mechanisms for Controlling Nazareth in the 1950s." *Journal of Israeli History* 25, no. 2 (September 2006): 335–59.

Gelber, Yoav. "Druze and Jews in the War of 1948." *Middle Eastern Studies* 31, no. 2 (April 1995): 229–52.

Habibi, Emile. *The Secret Life of Saeed: The Pessoptimist*. Translated by Salma Khadra Jayyusi and Trevor Le Gassick. London: Zed, 1985.

Jabareen, Hassan. "Hobbesian Citizenship: How the Palestinians became a Minority in Israel." In *Multiculturalism and Minority Rights in the Arab World*, edited by Will Kymlicka and Eva Pföstl, 189–218. London: Oxford University Press, 2014.

Jiryis, Sabri. *The Arabs in Israel*. New York: Monthly Review Press, 1976.

Kamen, Charles. "After the Catastrophe 1: The Arabs in Israel, 1948–1951." *Middle Eastern Studies* 23, no. 4 (1987): 453–95.

Kanaana, Sharif. "Survival Strategies of Arabs in Israel." *MERIP Reports* 41 (October 1975): 3–18.

Kerr, Malcolm. *The Arab Cold War, 1958–1967: A Study of Ideology in Politics*. London: Oxford University Press, 1967.

Khalaf, Issa. *Politics in Palestine: Arab Factionalism and Social Disintegration, 1939–1948*. Albany, New York: Sunny, 1991.

Khalidi, Rashid. *The Iron Cage: The Story of the Palestinian Struggle for Statehood*. Boston: Beacon Press, 2006.

Khalidi, Walid. "Why Did the Palestinians Leave?" *Middle East Forum* 35, no. 7 (July 1959): 21–35.

———. "The Fall of Haifa," *Middle East Forum* 35, 10 (December 1959); republished in *Journal of Palestine Studies* 37, no. 3 (Spring 2008): 30–58.

———. "Plan Dalet: Master Plan for the Conquest of Palestine." *Journal of Palestine Studies* 18, no. 1 (Autumn 1988): 4–33.

Khwalidi, Sulayman. "History of the Beduin villages of Krad al-Baqqara and Krad al-Ghanname." PhD diss., University of Erlangen, Germany, 1992.

Kidron, Peretz. "Truth Whereby Nations Live." In *Blaming the Victims: Spurious Scholarship and the Palestinian Question*, edited by Edward Said and Christopher Hitchens, 85–96. London: Verso Books, 1988,

Lahav, Pnina. "The Supreme Court of Israel: Formative Years, 1948–1955." *Studies in Zionism* 11, no. 1 (1990): 45–66.

Lustick, Ian. *Arabs in the Jewish State: Israel's Control of a National Minority*. Austin: University of Texas Press, 1980.

Manna', Adel. "From Seferberlik to the Nakba: A Personal Account of the Life of Zahra al-Ja'uniyya." *Jerusalem Quarterly* (Spring 2007): 59–76.

Manna', 'Adel, and Motti Golani. *Two Sides of the Coin: Independence and Nakba* (*Wajha al-'imla: al-istiqlal wa al-Nakba, sardiyyatan hawla harb 1948 wa nat'ijaha*). English and

Arabic. Netherlands: Institute for Historical Justice and Reconciliation, Republic of Letters, 2011.

Masalha, Nur al-Din. *Expulsion of the Palestinians: The Concept of 'Transfer' in the Zionist Political Thought, 1882–1948.* Washington, DC: Institute for Palestine Studies, 1992.

——, ed. *Catastrophe Remembered: Palestine, Israel and the Internal Refugees.* London: Zed Books, 2005.

——. *The Palestine Nakba: Decolonising History, Narrating the Subaltern, Reclaiming Memory.* London: Zed Books, 2012.

Molavi, Shourideh. *Stateless Citizenship: The Palestinian-Arab Citizens of Israel.* Leiden: Brill, 2013.

Morris, Benny. "Yosef Weitz and the Transfer Committees, 1948–1949." *Middle Eastern Studies* 22, no. 4 (1986): 522–61.

——. *1948 and After: Israel and the Palestinians.* New York: Oxford University Press, 1994.

——. *Israel's Border Wars, 1949–1956.* New York: Oxford University Press, 1994.

——. *1948: The History of the First Arab-Israeli War.* New Haven, CT: Yale University Press, 2008.

——. *The Birth of the Palestinian Refugee Problem Revisited.* Cambridge, UK: Cambridge University Press, 2004.

Nazzal, Nafez. *The Palestinian Exodus from Galilee, 1948.* Beirut: Institute for Palestine Studies, 1978.

Pappé, Ilan. *Britain and the Arab–Israeli Conflict, 1948–1951.* London: Macmillan, 1988.

——. *The Ethnic Cleansing of Palestine.* Oxford: Oneworld, 2006.

Parsons, Laila. *The Druze Between Palestine and Israel, 1947–1949.* New York: St. Martin's Press, 2000.

Peretz, Don. *Israel and the Palestine Arabs.* Washington, DC: Middle East Institute, 1958.

Robinson, Shira. "Local Struggle, National Struggle: Palestinian Responses to the Qafr Qasim Massacre and its Aftermath, 1956–1966." *International Journal of Middle East Studies* 35, no. 3 (August 2003): 393–416.

——. *Citizen Strangers: Palestinians and the Birth of Israel's Liberal Settler State.* Stanford, CA: Stanford University Press, 2013.

Rogan, Eugene, and Avi Shlaim, eds. *The War for Palestine: Rewriting the History of 1948.* Cambridge, UK: Cambridge University Press, 2001.

Rotberg, Robert I., ed. *Israeli and Palestinian Narratives of Conflict: History's Double Helix.* Bloomington: Indiana University Press, 2006.

Sa'di, Ahmad. "Control and Resistance at Local Level Institutions: A Study on Kafr Yasif's Local Council under the Military Government." *Arab Studies Quarterly* 23, no. 3 (2001): 31–47.

Sa'di, Ahmad, and Lila Abu-Lughod, eds. *Nakba: Palestine, 1948, and the Claims of Memory.* New York: Columbia University Press, 2007.

Said, Edward. *The Question of Palestine.* New York: Times Books, 1979.

Said, Edward, and Christopher Hitchens, eds. *Blaming the Victims: Spurious Scholarship and the Palestinian Question.* London: Verso Books, 1988.

Sayigh, Rosemary. *Palestinians: From Peasants to Revolutionaries.* London: Zed Books, 1979.

Shlaim, Avi. "The Rise and Fall of All-Palestine Government in Gaza." *Journal of Palestine Studies* 20, no. 1 (Autumn 1990): 37–53.

——. *The Iron Wall: Israel and the Arab World.* New York: W.W. Norton & Company, 2001.

——. "Israel Between East and West, 1948–1956." *International Journal of Middle East Studies* 36, no. 4 (November 2004): 657–73.

Shoufani, Elias. "The Fall of a Village." *Journal of Palestine Studies* 1, no. 4 (Summer 1972): 109–21.

Smooha, Sammy. *Arabs and Jews in Israel.* Boulder, CO: Westview Press, 1989.

Srouji, Elias S. *Cyclamens from Galilee: Memoirs of a Physician from Nazareth.* New York: iUniverse, 2003.

——. "The Fall of a Galilean Village during the 1948 Palestinian War: An Eyewitness Account." *Journal of Palestine Studies* 33, no. 2 (Winter 2004): 71–80.

Suleiman, Yasir. *Arabic, Self and Identity: A Study in Conflict and Displacement.* New York: Oxford University Press, 2011.

Troen, Selwyn Ilan, and Noah Lucas, eds. *Israel: The First Decade of Independence.* Albany, NY: State University of New York Press, 1995.

White, Hayden. *The Content of the Form: Narrative Discourse and Historical Representation.* Baltimore, MD: John Hopkins University Press, 1987.

Wolfe, Patrick. "Settler Colonialism and the Elimination of the Native." *Journal of Genocide Research* 8, no. 4 (December 2006): 387–409.

Zureik, Elia. *The Palestinians in Israel: A Study of Internal Colonialism.* London: Routledge and Kegan Paul, 1979.

INDEX

Founded in 1893,
UNIVERSITY OF CALIFORNIA PRESS
publishes bold, progressive books and journals
on topics in the arts, humanities, social sciences,
and natural sciences—with a focus on social
justice issues—that inspire thought and action
among readers worldwide.

The UC PRESS FOUNDATION
raises funds to uphold the press's vital role
as an independent, nonprofit publisher, and
receives philanthropic support from a wide
range of individuals and institutions—and from
committed readers like you. To learn more, visit
ucpress.edu/supportus.

Printed in the USA
CPSIA information can be obtained
at www.ICGtesting.com
LVHW042145291023
762505LV00028B/266